A History of French Literature

For Olive

A History of French Literature
From *Chanson de geste* to Cinema

DAVID COWARD

Blackwell
Publishing

350 Main Street, Malden, MA 02148-5020, USA
108 Cowley Road, Oxford OX4 1JF, UK
550 Swanston Street, Carlton, Victoria 3053, Australia

First published 2002
First published in paperback 2004 by Blackwell Publishing Ltd

Library of Congress Cataloging-in-Publication Data

Coward, David.
   A history of French literature / David Coward.
      p. cm.
   Includes bibliographical references and index.
      ISBN 0–631–16758–7 (hardback); ISBN 1–4051–1736–2 (paperback)
      1. French literature—History and criticism.   I. Title.
   PQ103.C67 2002
   840.9—dc21

                                          2001004353

A catalogue record for this title is available from the British Library.

Set in 10/13¹/₂pt Meridian
by Graphicraft Ltd, Hong Kong
Printed and bound in the United Kingdom
by TJ International Ltd, Padstow, Cornwall

For further information on
Blackwell Publishing, visit our website:
http://www.blackwellpublishing.com

Contents

Preface

The end of the second millennium seems as appropriate a moment as any for a survey of a thousand years of French literature. But the task of the historian is made more, not less difficult by the present conjuncture. It is not simply that there is now more French literature to account for than ever before, but that there is no common agreement about what qualifies as 'literature'.

Of course, beyond its basic etymological connection with writing, the word has never had a fixed meaning. In the thirteenth century, *Le Roman de la Rose* (line 18,839) asserted that *clercs* were more likely to be 'gentiz, cortois et sages' than kings and princes 'qui ne sevent de letreüre'. In the sixteenth, literature was still equated with learning, a body of civilized and civilizing erudition, and the term continued to be used in this sense a hundred years later. But after 1700, *littérature* became an occupation, even a preoccupation. 'Les gens de lettres', normally a pejorative term, were authors who did not restrict themselves to imaginative writing but were concerned with a range of theological, philosophical, historical and scientific matters too. By about 1750, when the word was also current for 'the bibliography of a subject', it also began to mean written texts having primarily aesthetic qualities: in 1764, Voltaire consciously excluded technical writing from his definition of it. Even so, Fréron's periodical *L'Année littéraire*, despite its title, continued to reflect the wider scientific and intellectual concerns of the Enlightenment. Gattel's *Dictionnaire portatif* (1797) still defined literature as 'Science des Belles-Lettres; doctrine; érudition' and La Harpe's *Cours de littérature* (1799) took it to mean the knowledge and judgement of writers and their works. It was the Romantics, by writing subjectively about themselves and not, as hitherto, objectively about the world, who changed the focus of literature which in the 1820s and 1830s acquired a new spiritual, moral and social vocation. As part of the 'Religion of Art', it was considered to be the highest expression of human thought and culture. But from about 1840 onwards, when it became a product for popular consumption, literature acquired a new recreational role. By 1870, a rift had appeared between 'low' literature aimed at a non-cultured readership and the 'high' art intended for the educated elite, and thereafter the gap continued to widen between writings which were accessible to a wide audience and those which were 'difficult'. In the twentieth century, literature once more became part of the movement of ideas, as it had been during the Enlightenment, though since 1945 in particular its remit has been broadened by the demo-cratization of culture and, most recently, its systematic appropriation by the entertainment industry.

For the Renaissance, literature was an assertion of modernity. To Louis XIV, it was a jewel in the crown of the most sophisticated monarchy in Europe. For the Enlightenment, it was a powerful agent of intellectual and social change. It is only since the time of the Romantics that 'Literature' has consistently denoted a body of spe-cifically imaginative writing deemed to have qualities of permanence. Yet the word has also retained many of its old meanings. It is still a body of scholarly knowledge, a bibliography (the 'literature' of a subject), a system of aesthetic principles and ethical values, and a tool for the dissemination of ideas. The Lansonian belief that a nation is to be judged by its literature has not entirely disappeared, nor has the liberal, humanist tradition. But at the end of the twentieth century, 'Literature' is a word fiercely contested by the latest manifestation of the *querelle des anciens et des modernes* which no generation escapes. For devout traditionalists, living authors are not to be granted liter-ary status by definition. For the progressively minded, books are texts and to apply 'literary' standards indiscriminately is not only to adopt a retrospective standard based on outdated principles but to impose the authority of élitist taste upon all. What is still officially considered to be 'Literature' is a product of criticism, which claims to define its properties, of institutions which distribute honours and prizes, of publishers who tread a difficult path between art and com-merce, and, more insidiously, of education. Roland Barthes argued that literature is 'ce qui s'enseigne', with teachers devising examinable courses and, in the process, naming its 'best' and 'most significant' works.

There are now more voices engaged in telling us what literature is than ever before, and for the most part they generate more heat than light. At one extreme, the current Ancients remain wedded to the notion of the 'classics', a canon of Great Authors who have met the Darwinian challenge of survival. At the other, the Moderns maintain that literature is simply one of many forms of linguistic expression and that the production of texts is no longer to be linked to a moral vocation and the old aesthetic norms which were, in any case, fervently contested. The 'literary' qualities of a text are less important than its significance as a social document, a window onto the secret personality of the author, the embodiment of an intellectual idea or the encapsulation of the archetypal myths which inhabit the collective psyche. The proposition that Literature is 'the knowledge of Man' has become difficult to sustain, for its traditional function (to explain the world to readers and readers to themselves) has been usurped by newer disciplines which account for the human condition in analytical, scientific, quantifiable and, in a word, altogether more reliable terms. Psychiatry, biology, politics and economics constitute the new theology and their processes are less instinctive than technical, impersonal rather than subjective. It is not a new phenomenon. Just as the legislators of Classicism bowed to the authority of ancient writers, so the twentieth century looked to Marx, Freud and other system-builders for guidance and validation. Both periods devalued the imagination, the first as the dangerous path to disorder, and the second as an escape mechanism which sanitizes the reality which writers fear to confront directly, or as an inferior source of inspiration: why make up stories which merely imitate life when reality is so much more immediate?

Currently, the personal and spiritual anguish of mankind (what Maupassant called 'l'humanité saignante') is accorded a lower priority than shared points of view, group insights and collective concerns. There is no agreement that Literature is dead, merely a widespread assumption that the old standards which once defined it are now too narrow and exclusive. The Postmodernist age prefers to speak of Writing, for whatever is written is a valid cultural statement – a more sharply angled version of Bonald's 200-year-old dictum that Literature is the 'expression of society'. Scholars who, only a generation ago, laboured hard in learned exegesis (sources, influences, genre, etc.) now turn their expertise to crime fiction or television soaps. For many, Literature, which in this context may be said to have ended with Proust, has become a suburb of sociology or a branch of culture.

Literature is as much an Ideal Form as any of those which are concealed by the shadows thrown on the rocky wall of Plato's cave. We may know it when we see it, but we never quite see it in all its fullness in any single work. But of what does this 'fullness' consist? The good, the true and the beautiful, no doubt, though the modern world has difficulty in giving such grandiose concepts a content. We cannot be sure which aesthetic values rule: beauty is defined by the beholder who, however, is more vulnerable to changing taste and fashion than is generally acknowledged. Shall we call Literature the books that remain after the rest have been forgotten? Yet Ronsard was forgotten for three centuries and it is only in the last generation that Laclos' *Les Liaisons dangereuses* has overtaken Rousseau's *La Nouvelle Héloïse* as the finest of eighteenth-century novels. Authors and books wither and die while others are constantly rediscovered; and if whole genres (tragedy for instance) disappear, new ones (cinema, most obviously) emerge to take their place. It may well be that the only helpful characteristic of Literature is the ability of some plays, poems and novels to stir a vital reaction, irrespective of when they were written. They create an impression of truth by reaching out, sometimes across the span of centuries, to touch our imagination and engage with our pre-occupations. The 'truth' we detect may not be the truth which the author intended, but that scarcely matters. It is now a truism that as readers we rewrite what we read, making it our own in ways too multifarious and too mysterious to explain in general terms. Crime fiction or romantic novelettes, which say little to minds shaped by Racine and Proust, may provide for others a transposition of experience or opportunities for self-examination and reflection which go beyond the escapist label which is hung around their necks. Perhaps the ultimate test of what literature is derives from the capacity of a text to surprise us by communicating a sense of a unique, personal vision which we somehow recognize as authentic. Or as Ezra Pound neatly put it: 'Literature is news that stays news.'

But if there are, in this sense, as many books as there are readers, there are also different readerships, distinct by age, class, background, location and, not least, century. It might be more useful, therefore, to speak not of 'Literature' at all, but of 'Literatures'. A literature of priests and magicians, which was followed by a literature of the hero and gradually turned into a literature of the military and later the intellectual aristocracy. An oral literature which turned into written literature which, when art left the court and the noble house, became a recognized economic activity, developed into a bourgeois literature and, in due course, the literature of popular culture. A literature of patronage which only in the last two hundred years has become a literature of professionals. . . . There is every reason to believe that the IT revolution will generate new forms of interactive, consumer-led, transnational, virtual literatures at present impossible to imagine. But the holdings of great libraries furnish ample evidence that while literatures with different agendas and priorities may overlap and interact, they form a broad succession and, in a word, have a history. To some, literary historians are embalmers and literary history a museum, a cemetery for dead authors, a hospital for geriatric books kept artificially alive on twin life-support systems of the curriculum and institutionalized culture. Yet at the start of a new millennium when the electronic revolution promises change as far-reaching as that which followed the introduction of printing, it is salutary to be reminded of how we got this far. To forget the past is to jettison knowledge, and the knowledge offered by literature, however it is defined, is the sharing and understanding of experience. Carlyle defined history as the biography of great men. Literary history is the biography of the human imagination.

In immediate terms, however, it is the history of books. The circumstances in which books are produced have always helped to determine their nature and their audience. Yet a history merely of the book trade would miss the creative centre. A chronicle of authors popular in their own time (in which Eugène Sue and Sully Prudhomme loomed larger than Stendhal and Baudelaire) would provide a history of reading, while an account of how readers read would require a history of mentalities. To account for all the ingredients of Literature would call for a History of French Civilisation.

Choices had therefore to be made. The landscape of French literature has been extensively cultivated and its historical geography permanently drawn. There seemed no good reason to abandon the convenient division by ages and centuries, for despite the artificiality

of the proceeding, each period has its own priorities and distinctive character. Nor has the conventional 'canon' of great authors
been overturned: whatever their reasons, most readers still prefer
the tragedy of Phèdre to be told by Racine rather than Quinault.
On the other hand, the concept of literature now includes forms
of expression which until recently, because they did not wear a
tie, were denied entry to polite literary society: regional writing,
crime fiction, best-sellers, *bande dessinée* and, above all, cinema – a
French invention and the twentieth century's major innovation in
form. While 'high' literature and *beau langage* continue to command
greater respect in France than in the Anglo-Saxon world, the French
have also given a friendlier welcome to popular forms such as
graphic fiction and film. But if what was until recently described as
'paraliterature' is to be admitted, then it would seem logical to give
its earlier manifestations – the *bibliothèque bleue* of the ancien regime,
the libertine novel of the eighteenth century and the melodrama and
roman feuilleton of the nineteenth – a prominence lacking in previous
surveys.

This volume aims therefore to be an inclusive (though not all-
inclusive) history of literatures as is required by the very wide definition now given to the concept of Literature. It covers the old and the
new and has the form of an inverted pyramid, which means that it is
top-heavy with the concerns which have emerged strongly in the
last hundred years. Writers and writing are set in their historical and
social context and paths are laid which afford what are intended to
be the clearest views of both. It may be read vertically (from start to
finish) but also horizontally, by moving sequentially through the
sections devoted to the major genres (theatre, poetry, fiction) and
themes such as the status of authors or the development of French as
a literary language.

But at all times, the verdicts pronounced are partial and provi-
sional. I have come to appreciate the truth of the observation made
by George Saintsbury in the preface to his *Short History of French
Literature* (1882): 'Some familiarity with the subject has convinced
me that nowhere are opinions of doubtful accuracy more frequently
adopted and handed on without enquiry than in the history of literature.' I would add that this stricture now applies even more surely to
literary journalism. Yet I plead extenuating circumstances. Even the
devoutest bookworm would need several lifetimes to read the whole

of French Literature, and borrowed opinions are unavoidable. But second-hand does not mean second-rate and I freely declare my enormous debts to the published work of specialists in many disciplines on whose knowledge I have relied to supplement my own. I also acknowledge the generous help of friends and colleagues who have answered my queries, made helpful suggestions and even read portions of the typescript. Particular thanks are due to Ros Brown-Grant, Jim Dolamore, Jim Dryhurst, Howard Evans, Michael Freeman, Jim House, Michael Kelly, Lynette Muir, John Rothenberg, Max Silverman, Kamal Salhi, Pierre Testud, the late Philip Thody and Christopher Todd. I hasten to add that any remaining errors and intemperate judgements are mine alone.

D.C.

1

The Middle Ages

Introduction

The Middle Ages lasted a thousand years, from the break-up of the Roman Empire in the fifth century to the end of the fifteenth, when there was an awareness that a 'dark time' (Rabelais dismissively called it 'gothic') separated the present from the classical world. During this *medium aevum* or 'Middle Age', situated between classical antiquity and modern times, the centre of the world moved north as the civilization of the Mediterranean joined forces with the vigorous culture of temperate Europe.

Rather than an Age, however, it is more appropriate to speak of Ages, for surges of decay and renewal over ten centuries redrew the political, social and cultural map of Europe, by war, marriage and treaty. By the sixth century, Christianity was replacing older gods and the organized fabric of the Roman Empire had been eroded and trading patterns disrupted. Although the Church kept administrative structures and learning alive, barbarian encroachments from the north and Saracen invasions from the south posed a continuing threat. The work of undoing the fragmentation of Rome's imperial domain was undertaken by Charlemagne (742–814), who created a Holy Roman Empire, and subsequently by his successors over many centuries who, in bursts of military and administrative activity, bought, earned or coerced the loyalty of the rulers of the many duchies and *comtés* which formed the patchwork of feudal territories that was France. This process of centralization proceeded at variable speeds. After the break-up of Charlemagne's empire at the end of the tenth century, 'France' was a kingdom which occupied the region now known as the Île de France. Under the Capetian monarchs (987–1328) and the Valois kings (1329–1589), the power and influence of the crown grew, as did the authority of the French language.

Language

If the geographical boundaries of 'France' fluctuated, its language too evolved and changed shape. From the time of Constantine onwards, devotional literature was produced in Latin in Roman Gaul. Until the eleventh century it was unchallenged as the language of learned discourse and thereafter Latin remained the vehicle of intellectual expression, retaining its prestige into the eighteenth century. France had no equivalent of Old High German or Old English language and culture. Rome's legionaries and traders had not spoken the classical Latin of Caesar or Cicero but a 'vulgar' tongue which, remaining in use over a long span of time and incorporating local influences, served as the basis of all the Romance vernaculars. In France, the progress of Gallo-Roman (fifth to ninth centuries) is first attested by the instruction given to clerics in 813, at the Council of Tours, to preach their sermons not in the Latin of the Vulgate, judged incomprehensible to congregations, but 'in rusticam romanam linguam'. An oath, sworn at Strasbourg in 842 by one of the two grandsons of Charlemagne, is the first written trace of this modified Latin. Thereafter, the development of the language is broadly classified as Early Old French (about 950–1100), Old French (twelfth and thirteenth centuries) and Middle French (fourteenth and fifteenth centuries).

Progress was, however, far from uniform. Languages related, sometimes very distantly, to 'French' were established in provinces surrounding the royal domain but also served as the *lingua franca* of the south, from Catalonia to Northern Italy, and in the Holy Land. Distinctive varieties were spoken in England after the Conquest (Norman French) and in Languedoc, home of the first lyric poets. Change was gradual. After the Albigensian crusade against the Cathar heretics (1209–44), the *langue d'oc* lost ground to the tongues of the more powerful north, specifically to *francien*, which was spoken in Paris and the Île de France, geographically the heart of the *langue d'oïl* area.

Literature

Throughout the period, literature was shaped by specific historical traditions and a firmly circumscribed code of priorities, ecclesiastical and secular. The dominance of the Church ensured that literary expression was informed by a strong didactic spirit, while feudalism provided a common, if loose, framework of values until it was challenged in the thirteenth century by the growth of towns and a less courtly and more bourgeois public.

Just as the modern labels 'France' and 'French' are unhelpful when applied to the Middle Ages, so the word 'literature' needs considerable qualification. The earliest vernacular texts were clearly marked by a strong oral tradition. But by the twelfth century most works were intended to be read and by the thirteenth century literacy rates had risen further with the emergence of a new middle class of merchants, lawyers and civil servants. Though the existence of a tripartite social hierarchy (clergy, aristocracy and the rest) might suggest separate literary constituencies, the notion of a 'public' for literature is difficult to define. About 40 per cent of *chansons de geste* begin with variants of 'Oiez, seignor', which seems to imply a noble audience, yet they often proceed to explain basic chivalric rules as if for the benefit and instruction of less exalted listeners. After 1200, romances in verse and prose were read rather than heard and the *fabliaux* appealed not only to the bourgeois and popular milieus in which they were set, but also to higher social ranks. Lyric poetry, at first associated with the aristocratic courts of Languedoc, acquired a more bourgeois following when it was taken up in the thirteenth century by northern *confréries* and towns which organized poetry competitions and staged plays. Theatre outgrew its liturgical beginnings and, in addition to the miracle and passion plays performed by the Confrérie de la Passion, offered secular morality plays, farces and *soties* to a wide social mix.

Its diffusion

In the pre-book age, the written word was preserved by scribes and *clercs* inside and outside the monastic establishments where most had trained. Manuscript production and distribution grew into an organized trade which for a time competed successfully with the printed books which began appearing after 1470. Some manuscripts, richly ornamented, were specially commissioned. Regarded as valuable objects, they were owned by men and women of the aristocratic courts, by the bourgeoisie and the clergy, and many found homes in ecclesiastical libraries. Most surviving manuscripts are less ornate. Some are short (perhaps performers' texts, sometimes with musical notation) while others contain a single work or constitute miscellaneous or themed anthologies. The survival of multiple copies of a work is a useful indicator of its popularity. The identical copy is rare, however, for performers and scribes routinely altered the texts for a variety of reasons – simple errors of transcription, a wish to update or generally 'improve' the material – and not until the fourteenth century is there evidence that authors supervised copyists in any systematic way.

Authors

Not that it is appropriate to speak of 'authors' until late in the period when the term still meant scholars writing in Latin. 'Escrire' defined the role of the copyist, while narrators used 'faire', 'imaginer', 'trouver' to indicate a measure of creative input now difficult to assess. Though *La Chanson de Roland* ends: 'Ci falt la geste que Turoldus declinet', the meaning of 'declinet' is unclear and might indicate that Turoldus was author, translator, adapter, copyist or reciter. The works performed by the itinerant *jongleurs* were not normally their own creations but revisions of old materials drawn from sources as different as the Bible, Greek and Roman authors and oral traditions which were constantly reworked. In the twelfth and thirteenth centuries, author and performer could be the same person – most troubadours wrote the poems they performed – though no text was sacrosanct, a finished creation, but an exploitable resource. Any work could be continued, augmented and even buried beneath the weight of new accretions. *Le Roman de la Rose* was begun by Guillaume Lorris, but became the work of Jean de Meun, who expanded it beyond recognition.

By projecting the vision of the rose garden as his own dream, Lorris set an early example of how a narrator might be identified with an author. In the same way, the first person *dits* which emerged in the late thirteenth century helped launch the idea of an individual personality and individual experience. Yet writings were not routinely associated with an author. Compilations were based not on the output of a named writer but on genre, and the first extant collected works (of Adam de la Halle and Rutebeuf) did not appear until the thirteenth century. Even in the single-author codex of the fourteenth, an 'author' was less a person than a persona: the expression of a general point of view rather than of an individual mind or sensibility. Though some creators were by this time identified by name, they remain shadowy figures for the most part. Relatively little is known even about the greatest of them, François Villon.

Nevertheless, the production, reception and diffusion of literary texts indicate that authors were a significant link in a cultural and economic system. Between 1100 and 1300 many troubadours of Languedoc (which covered Poitou and Aquitaine, the Limousin and the Auvergne) had names and some were celebrated in *vidas*, brief, formulaic and unreliable biographies (the first surviving manuscripts date from the thirteenth century) which were used to introduce performances of their lyrics. Occitan poets included kings and nobles, but some, less well-born, were employed in royal and aristocratic households where they had the status of servants. Few were women (the *trobairitz*). The northern *trouvères* who followed them show a similar mix of social origins. For the high-born, poetry was a social accomplishment. *Clercs* who wrote did so with the security of a settled livelihood in the Church. Those less fortunate, the *jongleurs*, earned a living not so much from writing as by performing, always in the hope of finding patronage. Normally this meant being hired as *ménéstrels*: money payments were rare until late in the period. The rewards of writing were therefore dependent on ecclesiastical, royal or aristocratic patrons. By the fifteenth century, the court of Burgundy financed the production of manuscripts, commissioned histories and encouraged lyric poetry. By this time, Paris too had long been a centre for writers of all types.

Medieval literature embraced writing of many kinds and on a wide range of subjects. At a time when there were no critics to steer its growth (the learned commentary was the nearest approximation to literary theory), it drew eclectically on multiple sources: antiquity, ecclesiastical writing and a range of oral traditions. The concept of imaginative literature was fluid and non-compartmentalized and the taste of the age was capable of accommodating both the crude and the highly sophisticated. Contemporary sensibilities were accustomed to coping with rapid changes from tragic to comic, noble to ignoble, and even exponents of courtly love mixed high idealism with frank obscenity.

The Middle Ages spanned ten centuries. Medieval literature, however, covers a much shorter period: the 400 years which run from *La Vie de Saint Alexis* (*c*.1040), the first significant literary text to survive, to the age of Villon, about the same time in fact that Modern French literature has taken to advance from Montaigne to Postmodernism. From its beginnings, it was sophisticated in its forms, which proved sufficiently flexible to lend themselves to new imperatives and changing social attitudes.

Hagiography

Though few vernacular texts are extant before about 1100, earlier developments are discernible in works of piety aimed at the unlettered faithful. That the *clercs* who originated them worked within the twin traditions of ecclesiastical and contemporary Latin culture is demonstrated by a homily, in Latin and northern French, based on the book of Jonah (*c*.950). By then, the vernacular had a modest role in the liturgy. The 29-line *Séquence de Sainte Eulalie* (*c*.881–2) was inserted into the church service on the saint's day and was sung, as were, in the late tenth and early eleventh centuries, the *Vie de Saint Léger* and a version of Christ's Passion. One of the earliest surviving Provençal texts, the *Chanson de Sainte-Foy*, composed later in the eleventh century, was sung not in church but outside it, during the saint's procession.

From these liturgical and para-liturgical beginnings grew 200 or so lives of saints, the first of which were composed and sung by *clerici vagrantes* (wandering scholars) who had trained in the Church but could obtain no settled employment. They found their subjects in the Bible and Latin *vitae* of early martyrs of Eastern and Western Christendom and in time developed a formal narrative model: they tell of the birth and education of their subject who, when confronted by an obstacle to piety, rejects worldly success, faces the consequences (exile or death) and converts many by example. Some texts were written for the use and edification of pilgrims while others were commissioned by churches or abbeys to honour and publicize their patron. Some saints had strong regional followings (Saint Nicholas was popular in the north) or appealed to specific groups who believed in their powers of intercession: Saint Margaret, patron saint of pregnant women, Saint Gilles, healer of the sick, or Saint Marie l'Égyptienne, the penitent prostitute who lived out her days as a hermit. While most surviving texts revived martyrs long dead (Alexis died in the fifth century and Gilles in the seventh), the corpus includes biographies of contemporary holy men, notably the 6,000-line *Vie de Saint Thomas*, written by Guernes de Pont-Sainte-Maxence within five years of the murder of Thomas à Beckett in 1170. While accounts of Biblical saints remained close to Holy Writ and others claimed factual accuracy (Guernes spoke to eye-witnesses), legend became part of the tradition from an early date. The *Vie de Saint Brendan* (*c*.1106) recounts not the life of the sixth-century abbot of Clonfert but his fantastic voyage, which has both elements of Celtic myth and echoes of the Arabian Nights. But if Brendan at least has roots in history, later hagiographers borrowed from epic and romance to glorify purely fictitious martyrs, as in the case of Godefroi de Bouillon, King of Jerusalem. Yet in a sense, such developments grew out of the limitations of the genre. Stories about good people are usually duller than tales of the wicked and authors had always generated excitement by stressing miracles and the trials of martyrs: Saint Laurent toasted on his griddle or Saint Margaret emerging unscathed from the belly of the dragon.

The earliest surviving example, the *Vie de Saint Alexis* teaches renunciation of the world and shows a life dedicated to God. If the message is predictable, it is conveyed with unexpected pathos. More intriguing still is the sophistication of its 625 assonanced lines, where rhythm derives not from the feet of Latin verse but from an entirely different principle: the syllable, which would remain the building-block of French prosody. Is the life of Saint Alexis, then, merely the first surviving vernacular link in a much older Latin tradition which has left few traces? Or is it the work of an individual who, in artistic terms, invented the wheel?

The *chanson de geste*

The truth lies somewhere between the 'traditionalist' and 'individualist' sides of the argument, whether it applies to saints' lives or the *chansons de geste*. Three centuries separate the battle of Roncevalles (15 August 778) from the *Chanson de Roland* (*c*.1080) which tells how Roland, commanding the rearguard of Charlemagne's army, and his companion Olivier died as the result of the treachery of Ganelon. Though early Latin and Arab texts record the event, there is no written trace of a vernacular tradition of oral transmission before the

1060s when, according to William of Malmesbury, a *jongleur* named Taillefer sang the heroic exploits of Roland to Norman soldiers before the battle of Hastings. On the other hand, the times were favourable to a great leap forward and there is good reason to speak of a 'twelfth-century renaissance'. By 1200, both language and poetic form were capable of sustaining sophisticated expression, while the conflicts within feudalism posed problems which could be personalized in the warrior, a figure of greater literary potential than the passive saint. If feudalism fragmented France, the Capetian kings extended their rule through the allegiance of their barons; if it fragmented the West, the papacy sought to unify Christendom by launching the first (1095) of the eight main crusades (to 1270) which were intended to retake Jerusalem from the Saracens. The *chanson de geste* fused secular and ecclesiastical concerns. It showed the chain of feudal obligation reaching up to the throne; by upgrading local wars between feudal overlords into an international, holy war, it championed the true faith. Harnessed by loyalty to a lord and the office he represented, and pressed into the defence of Christendom, chivalry, a code of honour and military valour, was redefined in terms of the Christian ethic. The feudal, crusader epic expressed an alliance of politics and religion and promoted a new collective ideal of service.

About a hundred *chansons de geste* (from Latin *gesta*, feats, exploits) survive from the end of the eleventh century to the fourteenth. They are grouped (by content, not date) into the *Cycle du Roi* (which centres on Charlemagne), the cycle of Doon de Mayence, ancestor of the rebel barons of the Narbonne clan (who include Raoul de Cambrai, Ogier le Danois and Girart de Roussillon), and the cycle of Garin de Monglane, also known as the cycle of Guillaume d'Orange, its recurring hero. The earliest examples are decasyllabic, use assonanced strophes (called *laisses*) of unequal length and were designed to be sung to an accompaniment of viols.

La Chanson de Roland, which belongs to the first group, is one of the finest examples of the genre. The style is plain, images are rare, and if the slaughter is conveyed in repetitive, conventional terms, a third of the text is made up of dialogue which, in performance, added to the drama. If the manner is unadorned, the values are as stern as in any saint's life. Chivalry here is not courtly dalliance but the defence of the faith by epic heroes who are sharply individualized.

They behave according to the logic of their character and, while the victory of Christianity over Islam is never in doubt, the drama is presented in human terms. Although Olivier begs him to blow the oliphant to summon Charlemagne, Roland refuses out of pride and many – including his friend – are killed through his fault. Olivier is judged to be wise but Roland, though he dies in Christ, is judged to be impetuous and lacking in *mesure*: he already expresses something of the taste for *gloire* and *grandeur* which would remain a part of the French tradition of heroism.

Although the *chanson de geste* was born of a commitment to show the contest between Christians and Saracens, the genre soon turned its attention to other conflicts: quarrels between emperor and subject, lord and liegeman, one family and another. *Raoul de Cambrai*, the blackest and most brutal of all these epics, pursues a vendetta begun by the injustice of Charlemagne to his vassal. *Le Couronnement de Louis* (*c*.1131–50) sets Charlemagne against Louis, his son and appointed successor, while in *Le Charroi de Nîmes* (*c*.1150–70) Guillaume's adventures grow out of his quarrel with Louis. The genre mutated as it proliferated. In formal terms, assonance was replaced by rhyme, verse gave way to prose, and later examples were intended more to be read than sung. But there was also a degree of cross-referencing between cycles. Once a hero was established, new *chansons* gave him a genealogy and a future: they looked back to his father and grandfather and forward to his old age and, occasionally, to his glorious descendants.

The 24 *chansons* of the Guillaume cycle, the most unified of the three, run through a variety of tones. If the first part of *La Chanson de Guillaume* has been admired almost as much as *Roland*, the second introduced Rainouart, a giant, whose buffoonery contrasts violently with its noble, other-worldly idealism. *La Prise d'Orange*, a continuation of Guillaume's adventures, introduces melodrama and even more robust comic elements to which the initial sense of mission is made subservient. By the late twelfth and thirteenth centuries, the Christian purpose had already been overlaid by elements of folk tale and legend. The *Pèlerinage de Charlemagne* to Jerusalem is strong not on the Christian marvellous but on oriental fantasy, while *Huon de Bordeaux* features Auberon, son of Julius Caesar and Morgan le Fay, who went on to be developed in other contexts, not least as Shakespeare's Oberon.

The epic hero in his purest form was an ascetic figure close to the saints of the hagiographers. Beginning as the servant of a greater good, he came in time to reflect the popular view of the Baron and Knight, a rebel and a warrior who, like Raoul de Cambrai or Renaut de Montauban, rejected the ideal of subordination to higher authority and looked instead to pride and prickly personal honour. The *chanson de geste* began as an effective literature of propaganda but, via legend and romance, became a literature of adventure, fantasy and individualism. It was also, from the start, a warrior literature in which priests, peasants and town-dwellers have walk-on parts and women rarely occupy a central role. Its values were those of militant Christianity and it accorded no place to a new development which began in Languedoc in the early twelfth century: *fin'amor*.

Lyric poetry to Rutebeuf

From their first recorded beginnings in the mid-twelfth century, Occitan lyric poets used an astonishing variety of fixed forms which were defined by stanza length, rhythm, rhyme scheme and the presence or absence of a refrain. The *alba* (in which two lovers separate at dawn), the *pastorela* (where a knight converses with a shepherdess), the *sirvente* (which raised topical matters), the didactic *ensenhamen*, the *reverdie*, or spring song, and others besides, would evolve when lyrical poetry passed to the *trouvères* after the middle of the thirteenth century.

The poetry of the troubadours (from *trobar*, to find or invent) was largely written by men and from a male point of view, though a handful of female *trobairitz* reacted against misogyny and the imprisoning tenets of courtly love. They were musicians as well as poets (a tenth of extant lyrics survive with musical notation) and though they were based at the courts of Languedoc, they came from a variety of social backgrounds. The first, Guillaume IX (1071–1126), Comte de Poitiers and Duke of Aquitaine, was both poet and patron. Among his Occitan successors were Jaufré Raudel, Prince de Blaye, and nobles like Arnaut Daniel, *seigneur* de Riberac, but also commoners like Marcabru, a Gascon *jongleur*, Cercamon, and Bernart de Ventadorn (said to be the son of servants).

About half of the 2,500 works attributed to some 350 poets dealt with love, sometimes in the crudest terms. They elaborated a concept of *fin'amor* (the metaphor was taken from the refining of metals) which was less a doctrine than a form of sensibility that projected a social and ethical code which existed only in the poetry which expressed it. The image of the lover implied a nobility of heart which was not the preserve of the well-born, though real-life lovers were bound by the strict social hierarchy. The code, more clearly defined in the casuistic *jeu parti* than in the *cansos* which illustrated it, required selflessness from the lover. Though skilled in social and military arts, he deferred to his Lady who, though not inaccessible, was difficult of access, generally the wife of another, sometimes a *belle dame sans merci*, whose heart and mind were won by proofs of courtly conduct and the avoidance of what was *vilain*. The condition of the languishing poet is *joi*, a mix of anguish and fierce jubilation, and is expressed in verse whose intricacy – virtuoso variations of metre and rhyme – was itself the measure of his devotion.

After the Albigensian crusade, when the Languedoc was effectively annexed to the kingdom of France and its court structure slowly dismantled, the tone of Occitan poets grew nostalgic and, with Peire Cardenal (*c*.1170–*c*.1278), acquired a political and satirical edge. But by then, their lyricism had migrated north. In 1137, Aliénor d'Aquitaine (1122–1204) married Louis VII of France and she attracted poets like Bernart de Ventadorn (*fl*. 1147–70) to the royal court. Later, as queen of Henry II of England, whom she married in 1152, she continued to promote Languedoc culture as did her children, Richard Coeur-de-Lion, a noted poet, and her daughter, Marie de Champagne, who gave patronage to Chrétien de Troyes and Andréas Capellanus, author of *De Amore* (*c*.1185). Capellanus analysed 'pure' (or platonic) love and 'mixed' (sensual) love before rounding on carnal love in Christian and misogynistic terms.

By the 1170s a new generation of northern poets, the *trouvères*, had adopted the code and manner of the southern tradition, though they were less flamboyant and sensual and their style less inventive and intricate. Among the 275 known *trouvères* who flourished between the mid-twelfth and fourteenth centuries were nobles like Conon de Béthune (d. 1220) and Gace Brulé, a leavening of churchmen and larger numbers of professional and semi-professional poets who frequented the courts of Lorraine and Champagne. Yet by 1200 or so, poetic activity was increasingly part of the literary life of the growing towns of northern France which challenged the monopoly of the courts and helped diversify the lyric tradition. About half the lyric poetry of the thirteenth century originated from Arras where, from about 1200 onwards, the *confréries* organized competitions (*puys*) which attracted poets who were less well-born and continued the courtly vein before adding comic vulgarity and more substantial narratives to the *trouvère* repertoire. The *dit* emerged from various strains of Christian, moral and satirical denunciation of human vices. Recited not sung, it used a first-person voice to express individual experience and a wider range of emotion.

One of the last lyric poets, the versatile Adam de la Halle (d. *c.*1285–9), added a note of psychological realism to his presentation of love. Jean Bodel (d. 1210), who contributed to a *chanson de geste*, wrote *fabliaux* and left the earliest surviving miracle play, was the author of the first non-courtly *congé* in which he reviews his life as death approaches. A newer spirit of irony and *joie de vivre* is visible in the lyrics of Colin Muset (b. *c.*1210) but the Paris-based Rutebeuf (*fl. c.*1249–1277) used the *dit* to speak directly of his poverty, his companions in debauchery, and his physical decline. It may be that he drew on the Latin poetry of the Goliards (*clercs* who failed to find employment at court or in the Church) who complained of the wretchedness of their life and were concerned less with love than with the relationship of man to man, rich to poor, noble to bourgeois. Yet in Rutebeuf's 'personal' poetry is the first expression of a poetic *moi* which goes beyond a literary persona and expresses not collective values but a distinctive individual consciousness. Rutebeuf already prefigures a new autobiographical strain which would be developed by Machaut and emerge triumphantly with Villon in the fifteenth century.

Romance

Just as hagiography had been diverted into the crusader *chanson de geste*, so the epic was modified after the middle of the twelfth century by the mutation of *fin'amor* into *amour courtois* and by the rise of feudal ideals and customs. By 1100, heraldic devices and the code of chivalry were established in tournaments which grew more numerous after 1170. The first steps in the new direction were signalled by the appearance of a number of verse adaptations (called *romans* because they were written in 'romance' vernacular) rooted in Greek history and mythology, not taken directly from Homer but from the Latin of Virgil and particularly Ovid. There were three romances devoted to Alexander the Great (1130–90) while other *romans d'antiquité* told the stories of Thebes (1150), Aeneas (1160) and Troy (1165). This *matière de Rome* was the work of *clercs* who demoted Greek myth in favour of modern forms of magic and appealed to courtly taste by giving a new role to the dawning and ruses of love.

But they also purported to be history. The *Chronique des ducs de Normandie* (c.1175) of Benoît de Saint-Maure, author of the *Roman de Troie*, was a vast fresco which connected the world of antiquity to the Anglo-Norman kings: if Charlemagne is a descendant of Francus of Troy, so the Plantagenet family tree is traced to Aeneas. A much more significant dynasty was established by Wace who, in the *Roman de Brut* (1155), tells how Aeneas fled from Troy to Latium and how Brut, his great grandson, left Latium and came to Britain. Wace's major source was the *Historia regum britanniae* (1135) by Geoffrey of Monmouth who, after establishing Brut as the first king of the Britons, devoted a fifth of his History to Arthur's resistance to the Saxons in the sixth century. If Geoffroy mentions Uther Pendragon and Merlin, it was Wace who first spoke of the Round Table and in so doing provided a mythical counterpart to the *matière de France* which had centred on Charlemagne, also a ruler of a court and first among twelve peers.

This new *matière de Bretagne* was exploited through other traditions. The twelve *Lais* (1160–78), or miniature verse romances, of Marie de France are distinctive. These pointed, psychologically subtle and richly symbolic tales deal less with Love as a code than with the human experience of lovers who confront social convention or encounter marvels and magic. Instead of following custom and translating Latin texts, she drew on an oral tradition: the tales of love and adventure sung by Bretons which originated in ancient Celtic sources. Some of Marie's lays, like 'Lanval', are related to the Arthur story while 'Chèvrefoil' is part of the legend of Tristan and Iseut which evolved out of earlier Irish and Welsh tales. A story of tragic love which transgresses social and moral conventions, it was first told in non-courtly terms by Béroul (c.1160–70?) and then in a subtler version by an Anglo-Norman poet, Thomas, in the 1170s.

By this time, the new romance was in vogue, though not all romances derived from the *matière de Bretagne*. A tradition of Anglo-Norman adventure romances, some set in the Orient, grew up largely free of Celtic influence. In France, *Floire et Blanchefleur* (mid-twelfth century) unfolds in the East, *Partonopeu de Blois* (*c.*1182–5) places the ethic of chivalry in a Byzantine setting and the early thirteenth-century *Aucassin et Nicolette*, a lighter-toned and lastingly popular tale of young love, ranges through the Midi, Spain and North Africa. Unlike the decasyllabic, assonanced epic, the romance was intended to be read aloud, not sung, and its standard form reflects this change. The strophe is abandoned and with it tune-based structures, like the refrain, and the octosyllabic couplet is combined with a less declamatory style more suited to story-telling.

But it was Chrétien de Troyes who, between 1170 and 1190, divested Arthurian legend of its role as history and made it the vehicle for chivalric values and courtly love. Unlike Wace, who had dealt with generations and reigns, Chrétien's five romances each deal with the trials of a hero or a couple. *Erec et Énide* (*c.*1170), *Cligès* (*c.*1176), *Le Chevalier de la charrette*, *Yvain* (both 1171–81?) and *Perceval, ou le Conte du Graal* (*c.*1180–92?) reflect knightly ideals (social graces, valour, prowess) and a generally more positive view of conjugal love than the Tristan legend, which made love and marriage incompatible. Chrétien's sharper focus allows closer exploration of psychology and motive and he mixes well-observed reality with Celtic enchantments. Arthur is never a protagonist but a figure of authority who presides over the settled world of his court which is located not in real time but in a time of myth. When Erec or Yvain leave Arthur's court at Logres and enter the mysterious forest, they seek their destiny by facing dangers and, by overcoming them, achieve self-knowledge and find love. Here the narrative is structured around a dramatic crisis – a clash of personalities, a heroic adventure – which is resolved and marks a return to order.

Chrétien's unfinished *Conte du Graal* was continued in verse by other hands. But the most significant continuation was made by Robert de Boron who, in the first years of the thirteenth century, invested the grail with a new religious significance. In his prose *Roman de l'estoire dou Graal*, the grail becomes a Christian relic and is entrusted to Bron, the Fisher King of Celtic legend. Between about 1200 and 1210, monks at Glastonbury produced a courtly, chivalric version, also in prose, entitled *Le Haut Livre du Graal* (or *Perlevaus*) which follows the successive quests of Chrétien's heroes, Gauvain, Lancelot and Perceval after the death of the Fisher King. Perceval joins Arthur's Round Table and eventually becomes Keeper of the Grail. Between 1215 and 1235, a vast Arthurian sequence in prose, the Vulgate Cycle, built a bridge between the time of Christ and the accession of Arthur, and dealt in a variety of registers with the exploits of the knights of the Round Table. In the long *Lancelot-Graal*, Perceval is demoted in favour of Lancelot and his adulterous love for Queen Guinevere. *La Queste du Saint Graal*, written by a Cistercian *clerc*, deals with the more spiritual and less dramatic adventures of Perceval, Bohort and Galahad, son of Lancelot and the daughter of the Fisher King. But it is Lancelot's illicit love for Guinevere which is central to *La Mort le Roi Artu*, for it is the reef on which the Christian ethos of the Round Table finally founders. The first branch of the saga, *Lancelot del Lac*, is courtly in tone, the *Queste* ascetic and mystic (with Galahad presented as a Christ-figure) and *La Mort Artu* dominated by a doomed conflict of human loyalties. But the death of Arthur did not end the legend, which continued to proliferate. The *Prose Tristan* (begun after 1230 and attributed to Hélie de Boron) fused two traditions: Tristan joins Arthur's court before meeting his inevitable fate with Iseut. Its mixture of adventure, love and human salvation proved lastingly popular.

Yet the mysticism was not to every taste, nor was the image of a settled world projected by Arthur's court convincing at a time when the fall of Constantinople (1204) revealed deep rifts in the unity of both Europe and Christendom. A new generation of non-Arthurian romances explored realistic themes in contemporary settings. Like the grail stories, they reflected the decline of court influence and the rise of urban values. Their subject was love which encountered obstacles closer to human experience: parents, social class and separation. The *Chastelain de Vergi* (written some time between 1203 and 1288) told a tale of tragic passion which had no roots in legend. Jean Renart (*c.*1180–*c.*1250) found his material in his own times and his *Roman de Guillaume de Dole* established a realistic approach to both psychology and manners. Two romances (*c.*1240–*c.*1270) by Philippe de Rémi also show young love tested by adversity, while the late thirteenth-century *Chastelain de Couci* is a solidly plotted tragedy of deception.

But the most enduring and influential of non-Arthurian romances, and the cause of the first of France's literary *querelles*, was *Le Roman de la Rose*, of which 300 manuscripts have survived. Begun between 1225 and 1230 by Guillaume de Lorris, it was expanded (1269–78) by Jean de Meun. Presented as a dream, it tells of the narrator's conquest of the rose which represents the woman he adores. Lorris traced the stages of the growth of love in what was intended as a platonic, idealized *ars amandi*. Jean de Meun's continuation is a digressive, encyclopaedic compendium of many points of view which subvert courtly love: his rose is not the symbol of the ideal woman but of sexual desire. The allegorical figure of Nature shows the artificiality of *amour courtois* and Reason sets friendship above love.

Meun's provocative views, and especially his perceived misogyny, were challenged before and after 1400 by a number of writers, including Christine de Pizan and the chancellor of the University of Paris, Jean Gerson. The quarrel stirred elements of a permanent debate. But the *Roman de la Rose* also popularized the dream as a major vehicle for both personal and didactic poetry. More important still, it established secular allegory as a method of explaining man's relationship to the world. Allegory was more literal than simile or symbol or an expression of causality. It was a direct correspondence between the structures of the concrete universe and states of mind and soul, between the macrocosm and the microcosm.

Although the *chanson de geste* had been eclipsed by the rise of Arthur, both traditions survived in rewritten, updated versions which turned the epic champion into a more human hero. In time, as new enemies of France appeared, fundamental changes were made in the eternal war between good and evil: in the late fifteenth century, Saladin, once the Saracen scourge of Western Christendom, becomes a model of chivalry and conquers England. Written (or rather rewritten) in prose, these new versions mark a movement in taste away from myth and the Christian marvellous towards love and its casuistry, magical perils, monsters and fairies and a more direct representation of the palpable world. The *roman d'aventure* drew on narrative traditions of all kinds. In the thirteenth century, *Joufroi de Poitiers* revisits the court of Guillaume IX, while Adenet le Roi (d. *c.*1300) returned to Charlemagne's mother and the gestes of his knights. The vast *Perceforest* (1314–40) took up the story of Alexander, linked it to the grail and thence to Merlin and the birth of Arthur. A patchwork of different tones – from farce to tragedy – it, too, minimized the importance of religion and placed its emphasis on love and adventure. The last Arthurian romance was Froissart's *Meliador* (1383–8), though in different forms the heroes associated with both Charlemagne and Arthur survived into the Renaissance and would continue as part of the stock-in-trade of the *Bibliothèque bleue*.

Comic realism

The taste for moral reflection was not the exclusive preserve of the Church. Ancient writers (like Cato) were respected as interpreters of human experience, and classical fables were familiar to the eleventh-century weavers of the Bayeux Tapestry who incorporated the tale of the crow robbed of its cheese by the flattering fox. Though Aesop gave his name to collections of fables – the *Isopet* – he was not read but survived through his disciple, Phaedrus. Marie de France drew on a Latin compilation, the *Romulus anglo-latin*, for her 103 lively, pointed fables (*c.*1170). *Exempla* which used animals to illustrate human truths remained popular, and Reynard the Fox acquired a unique following. The sprawling *Roman de Renard* was as popular and enduring as the *Roman de Tristan* or the *Roman de la Rose*, and his fame was such that the standard word for fox (*goupil*) was ousted by *renard*.

Le Roman de Renard

Reynard first appeared about 1175 in a verse tale by Pierre de Saint-Cloud based on a Latin source, *Isengrinus* (1149). His adventures proliferated rapidly and reached their peak in 1200. By then, 15 of the surviving 26 'branches' of the fragmented Reynard epic had been completed by multiple authors, and the remainder were composed before 1250. Occasional additions were made thereafter but they never recaptured the lightness and humour of the originals.

Once dismissed as 'popular' or 'bourgeois' literature, the *Roman de Renard* is now seen as the reverse image of the chivalric epic. The saga sets Reynard against King Noble, the lion, and their struggle, enacted in field, farm and village, is an extended satire of feudal values. In this sense, Reynard is a rebel baron who encapsulates aristocratic corruption. But the satire is also directed elsewhere – specifically at churchmen whose gluttony, lechery and opportunism are regularly lampooned, and more generally at the follies and frailty of human nature. For although Reynard encounters a range of non-aristocratic types (occasionally bourgeois, but mainly peasants, clerics and pilgrims), the animals express a consistently unflattering view of sly, selfish, arrogant humans who are either too stupid or too clever for their own good. Reynard fools the foolish, dupes the dupers and bites would-be biters. The humour is savage and the cruelty is relieved only by the grossness of the comedy. Reynard is cunning, and predatory, but also quick-witted, resourceful and, when on his best behaviour, an engaging rogue.

His disrespect for authority made him a popular hero who voiced widespread criticism not so much of principles and institutions as of those invested with authority. He was exploited by later writers for more serious ends. In *Le Couronnement de Renard* (*c*.1251–88) he becomes king and inaugurates a reign of vice. Rutebeuf in his *Renard le bestorné* (*Reynard the Hypocrite*, *c*.1260) uses him to attack the mendicant orders. The allegorical *Renard le Nouvel* (*c*.1289) makes him a personification of the devil and through him denounces evils of contemporary society, a task repeated at greater length in *Renard le contrefait* (*c*.1320–40), a comprehensive attack on universal corruption.

The *fabliau*

If the Reynard saga is the burlesque obverse of the chivalric epic, the verse *fabliau* ('little fable') is the antidote to romance which, as it grew more fantastic, invited criticism and mockery. Charlemagne and Arthur might represent authority, but their actions at times fell well short of the ideals they enshrined. Moreover, the obsession of their knights and ladies with delicate feelings sat ill with the adultery and violence which, paradoxically, were the narrative face of courtly love, chivalric prowess and the perfection of womanhood. The courtly ethos and aesthetic were challenged by growing urban values which preferred satirical humour to sentiment, the real world to fantasy and action to psychology. The *fabliau* reflected the new, urban outlook. About 150 from the late twelfth to the early fourteenth centuries have survived. Some are attributable to writers like Bodel and Rutebeuf but most were written by anonymous *clercs*.

The *fabliau* was short (rarely exceeding 1,000 lines), tightly plotted, used non-aristocratic characters and settings, and worked in a farcical register which extended from the suggestive to the bawdy and the obscene. An obsession with the functions of the lower body replaces the courtly interest in the emotions of the heart. Like the fable, they often concluded with a truth ('son tens pert qui felon sert': 'he wastes his time who helps a villain') but though most express a moral of sorts, they are more ironic than edifying. They include a great deal of cruelty but few sympathetic characters or situations. Wives routinely deceive their husbands with a priest, monk or student, though not all these tales centre on adultery. A range of non-aristocratic types – churchmen, lawyers, doctors, merchants, students and peasants – trick and are tricked. The settings are urban and much of what is known of town life in the thirteenth century derives from their clearly described streets, costumes and customs. But their main purpose was to entertain (they appealed to the same audience as the romances they undermined) and they gave no quarter, least of all to women who, duplicitous and lustful, are first in the line of satirical fire. It is as though the wars of epic and romance had been replaced by a battle of the sexes and social conflict, with participants exchanging lance and mace for quick wits.

The literature of devotion, moral reflection and information

From its liturgical beginnings to the age of Villon, literature maintained its central moralizing mission to guide souls and correct manners. Latin remained the language of theology, but pious tracts aimed at a wide audience were among the first vernacular texts to appear in the twelfth century. *Le Livre de manières* by Étienne de Fougères (d. 1178) and verse sermons such as *Li Vers des Juïse* (Judgement) warned that salvation lay in rejecting worldly temptation, while the themes of the brevity of life, the vanity of human affairs and the need to repent (*Le Poëme moral*, c.1200) were repeated endlessly, with lurid pictures of heaven and hell serving as carrot and stick. In time, authors added further graphic scenarios to Biblical, hagiographic and other Christian traditions, dramatizing the story of Eden, the Flood and the early life of Christ in narrative and, later, staged Passions. The same imaginative input colours the cult of the Virgin – intercessor and inspiration – which was expressed in verse compilations like Gautier de Coinci's *Les Miracles de Notre Dame* (1214–27).

But devotional literature was not only evangelical, it was admonitory. *La Bible de Guiot de Provins* (c.1206) denounced hypocrisy and materialism just as, a century later, Gervais de Bus's acronymic *Le Roman de Fauvel* (written 1301–14) attacked Flatterie, Avarice, U/Vilenie, Variété, Envie and Lâcheté. More positively, *Des quatre tenz d'âage d'ome* (c.1260) by Philippe de Novare described the moral conduct appropriate to each of the 'four ages of man'. Symbolic representations of human behaviour gravitated towards allegory, which was well established as a central device of Christian and moral writing by the time Guillaume de Digulleville wrote his three *Pèlerinages* (1330–58).

But the emphasis on man in his relations not only with God but with other men also gave a new urgency to his place in the world. New genres sprang up to accommodate a new spirit of curiosity: the 'bestiary' (in which animals conveyed Christian truths and moral lessons), the *miroir*, which gave advice to princes, women and soldiers, didactic *songes*, moralistic *chastiements*, collections of sententious *proverbes au vilain* and compilations on all manner of subjects. There were collections of canon and civil law and encyclopaedias, the most famous early example being the *Speculum maïus* of Vincent de Beauvais (1194–1264), which summarized what was known of the natural world, history, art and doctrine. In the thirteenth century, to devotional texts, manuals of penance, instructions in charity and virtue and moral treatises, were added manuals of education, cookery, chivalry and hunting, and commentaries on profane subjects. Drawing at first on classical sources and later on the reports of travellers (real, like Marco Polo, and imaginary from the *Vie de Saint Brendan* onwards), writers described the cosmos, mapped the three known continents, defined the four elements, explored mathematics, ascribed influences to the planets, and tackled practical issues, from medicine to education. By the fourteenth century, political matters were being raised. An anonymous *Songe du verger* (1376) examined the relationship between ecclesiastical and secular power. In *De Moneta*, Nicole Oresme (1320/5–82) reflected on the dangers of the money economy while Philippe de Mézières's *Le Songe du vieux pèlerin* (1389) reviewed French institutions and proposed reforms. The most significant, Alain Chartier's *Quadrilogue invectif* (1422), took France to task for failing to resist the conquering Henry V, and allowed *Peuple* to speak of its poverty, the Nobility to lament its decline and the Clergy to outline a plan for national revival.

These developments reflect a change in the concept of history. Knowledge of the past was derived initially from Latin sources and the first histories were written by monks, like Raoul Glaber (c.950–1046), who compiled chronicles of military, political and ecclesiastical events: the 'universal' history told the story of the world since Adam. For the first vernacular chroniclers of the twelfth century, history was inseparable from myth, fable and fiction, as the legendary nature of Charlemagne and Arthur makes clear. Like Geoffroy de Monmouth, Wace was less of a historian than a story-teller, as were most Anglo-Norman authors of biographical romances. The same element of invention makes the *cycle des croisades*, begun in the twelfth century and alleged to retrace the life of Godefroi de Bouillon (d. 1100), a variant of hagiographic fiction. Although Latin sources were used in the thirteenth century for less fanciful portraits of classical figures like Alexander, Hector and Julius Caesar, both chronicle and historical biography were committed to the general apocryphal and hortatory approach to all kinds of writing. The *Histoire de Saint Louis* (1309) of Jean de Joinville (b. 1225) was still locked into the hagiographic mode, though it conveys a view of Louis as a man and reflects in its vivid detail its author's experience of the seventh crusade (1248–75).

Geoffroi de Villehardouin (c.1150–c.1216) also wrote from personal observation. *La Conquête de Constantinople* (c.1207), one of the first prose works extant, tells how the fourth crusade (1202–4) was diverted from its objective of freeing the Holy Land and instead besieged Constantinople. Sparely written and deferential to the mighty, it gives 'treachery' and 'covetousness', not political differences, as explanations of the loss of purpose. Not all history dealt with the Orient, however. Robert de Clari's Anglo-Norman *Histoire de Guillaume le Maréchal* (1219–26) used eye-witness evidence to cover British history between 1186 and 1219. *Les Grandes Chroniques de France*, a vast sequence originating in the thirteenth century and continuing into the sixteenth, began by recycling old myths but later used documents and written testimony to tell the nation's history. Jean Froissart (1337–1404?) also relied on personal knowledge and eye-witnesses in his *Chroniques* which continued the account of the first years (1326–56) of the Hundred Years War, composed by Jean le Bel (c.1290–1370), to the end of the century. Froissart has a good eye for feats of arms, is dismissive of commoners, and adopts French or English points of view according to patron. He is no analyst of the events he describes and yet he does project an attitude to wars which are seen as an effect of dynastic rivalry, personal ambition and money, the only *patrie* of the mercenary soldiers who fight them.

Though Froissart's *Chroniques* were continued more reliably but less interestingly by Enguerran de Monstrelet in the first half of the fifteenth century, the focus had by then begun to shift from the events of war to its social and economic consequences. Knightly heroes like Du Guesclin (d. 1380), even Joan of Arc, lost their glamour in the anonymous *Journal d'un bourgeois de Paris* (1405–49) which expressed a much more intimate style of history already in evidence in *Le Ménagier de Paris* (*c*.1394). Written by a wealthy Parisian *bourgeois* as a manual for his young wife, it is a detailed record of daily life which reflects the impact of civil war on ordinary people. The *Chronique scandaleuse* of Jean de Roye also painted social reality – plague, crime, generalized immorality – 'from below'. Great events, however, continued to be recorded in the *Mémoires* of Philippe de Commynes (*c*.1447–1511) who covered the period 1464–98. Commynes wrote of what he knew in fluid, non-Latinate French and did not limit himself to reporting: he casts a gloomy, ironic eye on war as politics by another means and is a shrewd observer of the men who make history.

Learning and ideas

The learning of the ancient world survived in French Gaul in monastic institutions. Familiarity with antiquity continued to be identified with a learned class after Charlemagne gathered scholars at his court in the ninth century. Knowledge was transmitted through compilations, paraphrases and commentaries produced in monasteries and cathedral schools which also studied sacred and patristic texts and refined theological doctrine. By the death of the theologian and philosopher Pierre Abelard (1079–*c*.1142), Paris was already a great centre of learning. Teachers of grammar, logic, and theology opened schools from which the first universities emerged at the start of the thirteenth century. They were run like religious communities, with teachers privately paid by their pupils, and learning was separated into Faculties: Arts, Law, Medicine and Theology. Arts students were required to master core texts by Aristotle, who was read in Latin translations influenced by ancient and Arab commentaries, notably those of Avicenna and Averrhoes. It was accepted that, outside the truths revealed by Holy Writ, Aristotle's logical texts (but not his writings on natural science, ethics and metaphysics, all judged 'pagan') contained the best of what human reason, uninspired by Christianity, could produce. Both teaching and study were conditioned by respect for the authority of ancient writers and the church fathers. Even so, thinking was a rigorous process, and the scholastic method, proceeding by question and answer, created a large corpus of philosophical, scientific, legal and theological knowledge based on what human reason could infer from self-evident premises.

But the uses to which reason could be put were often controversial. From Carolingian times, thinkers were divided about the status of objects. Do they have a real, objective existence, or are they merely inventions of the mind? If things are no more than the names we give them (the Nominalist view), then the Trinity, the Incarnation, the existence of angels were abstractions and the truth of revealed religion was in doubt. Nominalism smacked of heresy and in the twelfth century the Church gave its approval to the Realists, though Nominalism eventually triumphed with William of Ockham (c.1270–1349). The history of scholasticism is inseparable from the conflict between the two opposing parties which would last four centuries. The scholastic method remained as a central teaching tool into the seventeenth century and, though scholasticism was derided from the time of the Renaissance, the arguments of the schoolmen laid the basis for rational enquiry based on experiment and induction, an approach which would be generalized by 1750.

Theatre

A similar development towards secularism is observable in the growth of theatre which, without losing its celebratory function, began inside the Church and ended as a realistic reflection of the changing world of men. Though the earliest literary forms were closely associated with performance, there appears to have been no unbroken theatrical tradition from Roman times. Theatre had been denounced as sinful by some of the early church fathers, yet the earliest extant

forms of theatre (as of hagiography) were vernacular extensions of
the liturgy which first appeared in the ninth century and developed
around the same time as the *Chanson de Roland* and the first poems of
Guillaume IX. *Le Mystère d'Adam* (mid-twelfth century) was still closely
associated with the Church, though specifically Biblical subjects (such
as *Le Courtois d'Arras*, c.1230, the story of the prodigal son) were rare
into the thirteenth century. It was rather around the Virgin and the
saints that the first theatrical forms took root. Bodel's *Le Jeu de Saint
Nicolas* (1200–1) is the earliest surviving example of the miracle play.

Vernacular theatre, which had left the orbit of the Church by the
end of the thirteenth century, was a product of urban development
and had no links with either the *chanson de geste* or romance. The first
surviving secular play is a short farce, *Le Garçon et l'aveugle*, written
between 1266 and 1282, which shows, in the manner of the *fabliau*,
how a smart youth meets his match. In the 1270s, at Arras, Adam de
la Halle broke new ground with *Le Jeu de la feuillée* (which adds
fairies to social realism in an extended *congé*) and *Le Jeu de Robin et
Marion*, an elaborate *pastourelle* which allows Marion to reject the
Knight and return to Robin.

Secular theatre made little headway, though Rutebeuf's *Le Miracle
de Théophile* (1260) included elements of social realism. The major
dramatic form remained the miracle. The cult of the Virgin provided
material for the succession of Marian miracle plays staged annually
between 1339 and 1382. Much more elaborate was the mystery play
of which 200 were performed between the late fourteenth century
and 1548, when the genre fell foul of religious and political pressures
and was banned. The mystery was designed to present the passion of
Christ in visual, human terms. A few examples on profane subjects
have survived, like *Le Mystère de la destruction de Troie la Grant* (1452),
the first theatrical representation in French of the ancient world. But
the mystery proper showed the whole life of a saint or a Biblical
story or, more frequently, as in Arnoul Gréban's *Le Mystère de la
Passion* (c.1450), the life and death of Christ. Performed, often over
several days, to commemorate saints' days and mark religious festivals, they had huge casts, complex staging and special effects (fire-
works, trapdoors, machinery). They included apocryphal material,
scenes of daily life and comic episodes involving devils, and were
financed by civic authorities or, in Paris, by the Confrérie de la Passion, first licensed in 1401.

Other forms of fifteenth-century theatre, broadly classed as 'comic', were performed by regular but non-professional companies which survived into the Renaissance. The Basoche was made up of students and lawyer's clerks, while the bourgeois laity formed the Enfants Sans Souci, though the two often overlapped. Between them, they were responsible for devising and staging a kind of play more appealing to urban audiences: the morality. The morality personified the battle fought between virtues and vices for the soul of Everyman, the World or the 'Povre Peuple'. But some of the 80 extant moralities also reflect current social and even political concerns and on occasion come close to the comic *sotie* which used a cast of fools whose costume (asses' ears, cap and bells) grants them the licence of their folly to launch outspoken attacks on establishment values. Farce dealt more generally with human failings and used plots and characters from the *fabliau* tradition: deceitful wives and biters bit. The most sophisticated of them, *La Farce de Maistre Pierre Pathelin* (1461–69?) has solid characterization, a consistent if patchwork narrative structure and a level of psychological observation which points to later developments.

Later lyric poetry

If theatre remained attached to its Christian mission and history clung to the glamour of chivalry, lyric poetry after Rutebeuf kept faith with courtly love and built on its semi-fixed forms. The lover's *congé* became at Arras a more general farewell lyric; the *tenso*, a dialogue about love, turned into the more tightly organized *jeu parti*; the *ballade*, originally a dance lyric, found a place beside the more relaxed *rondeau* and the formal *chant royal* before being annexed permanently for French prosody by Machaut and Villon. By the middle of the thirteenth century, others had been added: the *chanson de toile* (which expressed a female point of view), the farcical *fatrasie*, the *virelai* (another dance song) and the versatile *dit* which, until the fifteenth century, expressed love, satire and spirituality through a first-person narrator.

Poets still wrote of love in allegorical visions and argued points of courtly casuistry. But the fourteenth century saw formal developments, mainly in the versatile *dit* and the *ballade*, which allowed poetry to become more personal and poets to be more than names. Froissart wrote a quantity of courtly verse which recycled myth, moral digression and love debate, though his allegorical *Espinette amoureuse* (1369) is cast in an autobiographical mode. But a new level of pathos was reached in *Le Voir dit* (1364) by the prolific poet and musician, Guillaume de Machaut (*c.*1300–77), which projects the image of an ageing poet clinging desperately to love. Machaut's ornate *dit* counts his lady's virtues, pronounces on amorous doctrine and rehearses old love debates. Yet he also projects a clear poetic persona which confirmed the authority of vernacular lyricism. In historical terms, his major achievement was to establish a hierarchy of fixed verse forms which connect him with the vigorous poetic activity of the fifteenth century.

Machaut was much admired by Eustache Deschamps (1346–1407) who called him a *poète*, a term hitherto reserved exclusively for Latin versifiers. Deschamps wrote not only of love but of more mundane matters (he left a *ballade* on baldness) which comment on daily life and satirize courtiers and social groups. Although an unexciting versifier, he too left a significant legacy. His *Art de dictier et de faire chansons* (1392), the first treatise of versification in the vernacular, distinguished between 'natural' and 'artificial' music, that is, between poetry and music proper. The future development of French verse would depend on efforts to distance words from music. Machaut's example was also followed by Christine de Pizan (1364–*c.*1431) whose first writings included *ballades*, *rondeaux* and *virelais*. She wrote of adulterous love, as courtly tradition required, but showed how easily it led to unhappiness. Yet she also wrote of herself and particularly of her reaction to the death of her husband. She generates an authentic sense of loss and she handles both her verse and her feelings with considerable delicacy.

Fifteenth-century 'modernism'

Though poets continued to rehearse courtly themes and styles, courtly love was in decline. As growing economic activity changed the social landscape from feudal to urban, literature turned away from exalted modes and addressed more immediate subjects. The reaction against courtly values is clear in the polemic surrounding *Le Roman de la Rose* launched by Christine de Pizan in her *Epistre au Dieu d'amours* (1399) and the *querelle des femmes* which followed. Christine was a 'modern' woman, a widow who made her living as a 'vray homme' and an early exponent of the new literature of information. Between 1400 and 1410, she wrote commissioned works on a variety of subjects – government and law, peace, history, war and faith – which drew on her considerable erudition. But she stoutly defended the moral character of women in *La Cité des dames* (1404–5) where, advised by Reason, Rectitude and Justice, she selects women to inhabit her ideal city. Although her choice here falls on the Virgin and well-born figures from classical antiquity and French history, *Le Livre des trois vertus* (1405) is a compendium of duties offered to women of all classes. She also diagnosed the moral decline of France in *L'Avision Christine* (1405) and after 1410 commented more directly on the state of the nation, ending her career with a *Ditié de Jehanne d'Arc* (1429) who brought 'honneur au feminin sexe'.

Chartier

Christine's apology for women must be set against a larger quantity of misogynistic verse of which Deschamps's long poem, *Le Miroir de mariage*, written around the turn of the century, is an example. But the issue remained on the literary agenda. Alain Chartier (*c*.1385–*c*.1430) wrote courtly and pastoral lyrics but soon reached the limits of the now fading courtly love. His *Livre des quatre dames* (1416) sensitively conveys the feelings of four ladies left desolate by the battle of Agincourt. He is mainly remembered, however, for his controversial *Belle dame sans merci* (1424) which showed an *amant martyr* spurned by a Lady so fiercely independent that Chartier was accused of defaming women. A new phase of the *querelle des femmes* ensued in which he argued that courtly love had degenerated into an insincere game.

Charles d'Orléans

Chartier's injection of psychological realism into the conventions of ideal love found a subtler reflection in the work of Charles d'Orléans (1394–1465). Captured at Agincourt, he spent 25 years a prisoner of the English and, after his release in 1440, lived quietly at Blois, far from court and politics. In England, he wrote not of his captivity or the state of France but of his feelings. He began in courtly mode, but courtly abstractions are personalized in *ballades* which project a new awareness of the passage of time as a source of regret and sadness. At Blois, he preferred the *rondeau* and wrote wistfully and simply of his uneventful life: hunting, festivities, the seasons. But if he reflects the sunset of a tradition, he renewed the tired metaphors of courtly love and showed allegory interacting with a distinctive personality dominated by nostalgia and melancholy. Although he said little that was new, his more intimate manner, plainer vocabulary, subtler shifts in register and silky rhythms ('Le vent a laissé son manteau . . .') raised interest in poetic form and related poetry to a wider range of human experience.

But courtly modes also came under attack from less well-born quarters. By 1400, theatre, prose and verse, less idealistic now and more keenly conscious of death and the horrors of life, turned increasingly to the state of society, the human condition and itself. If romance remained popular, it was rooted in the past, unlike theatre which reacted to change. All prose narratives became more personal, and history and didactic writing of all kinds were increasingly drawn to the present. The new spirit is most clearly reflected in the *nouvelle*. The impetus was given by Boccaccio's *Decameron* (trans. 1400) though the mood is older and traceable to the *fabliau*, farce, and hostile attitudes to love and women generally.

The anti-courtly reaction

Around 1400, the anonymous *Quinze joies du mariage*, an ironically titled collection of prose tales, showed cunning women as the cause of marital misery. Against such conciliatory texts as *Le Champion des dames* (1440–2) by Martin le Franc (1410–61), the *Cent nouvelles nouvelles* (1464–7), a collection of bawdy anecdotes, showed men invariably outwitted and tricked by sly females. More measured were the *Arrêts d'amour* (1460–6) of Martial d'Auvergne (*c*.1435–1508), 51 'cases' heard before a Court of Love, most of which set an *amant martyr* against a *belle dame sans merci*. Short work is made of courtly values in the more substantial and psychologically credible *Petit Jehan de Saintré* (1456) by Antoine de la Sale (*c*.1385–*c*.1460), which has been called the first French novel. Jehan, a page, is favoured by his Lady who, after toying with his affections, abandons him for a priest. But instead of pining in the approved manner, Jehan takes his revenge by exposing her duplicity. The values of courtly love are shown to be empty and the vulgarity of modern lovers is intended as a criticism of the perfection expected by *amour courtois*. The message is clear: the *nouvelle* is truer and more moral than the vanishing rituals of the courtly creed.

'Rhétoriqueurs'

Even so, poetry remained connected with noble courts where, between 1450 and 1530, the 'art de seconde rhétorique' (as poetry was defined) gave rise to new formal experiment. Charles d'Orléans at Blois resisted the trend which flourished over several generations at the Courts of Bourbon, Brittany (Jean Meschinot, 1420–91) and Burgundy (Georges Chastellain, 1415–75; Jean Molinet, 1435–1507). This first generation of 'rhétoriqueurs' born between about 1420 and 1440 occupied court positions and their duties are reflected in their verse which was not always lyrical or concerned with love but ceremonial and designed to reflect the prestige of their patron. Though they never consciously formed a school, they claimed to follow Chartier who had raised political issues and opposed courtly love. But the common denominator was their interest in literary expression which they codified in treatises of versification (as in Molinet's *Art de rhétorique*) and practised in poems long and short. Unconstrained by fixed forms, they experimented with fuller stanzas and intricate rhyme schemes and displayed a technical virtuosity which pushed verbal dexterity to extremes where feeling seems stifled and clarity suffers. Though they were mocked by the Pléiade, their example was to have a crucial impact on the poetry of the Renaissance.

Villon

Such formal experiments are an essential part of the 'modernity' of the fifteenth century. But the age was modern especially in the steady decline of aristocratic and courtly values and the rise of a literature more in tune with the contemporary urban world. It was the city which produced François Villon. Born François de Moncorbier in about 1431 in modest circumstances, he was raised by an uncle who gave him a name and enabled him to obtain his MA in 1452. He killed a priest in a brawl in 1455, escaped punishment and spent some time at Blois, where he participated in the *puys* organized by Charles d'Orléans. He spent the next eight years in and out of jail for theft and other crimes before being condemned to death. The sentence was commuted to exile and after January 1463 there is no trace of him.

Villon's output was small. *Le Legs* (1456), *Le Grand Testament* (1461?) and a handful of *ballades* and *rondeaux* (1461–2) amount to some 3,300 lines. Yet no other medieval poet communicates a sense of shared humanity with such immediacy. *Le Legs* is a superior *congé*, a list of burlesque legacies left to friends, enemies and public officials. The tone is ironic (Villon is not the owner of what he bequeaths, except his heart which goes to the woman who broke it), self-mocking, but resilient. The *Testament* is darker, reaching beyond pathos to despair. The first part reviews his misspent youth, his poverty, failing health and the awareness of death. The second is a further catalogue of bequests interspersed with *ballades*, some satirical, others intended as homages to legatees, like his mother, to whom he dedicates a prayer to the Virgin. Villon's poetry has roots in the thirteenth-century *dit* and his themes (nostalgia, regret, death) were commonplaces of the well-established 'testament' genre. But the emotion is genuine (for his mother, for his uncle, his 'plus que père') and has a wider range: Villon moves from the courtly to the *sotte chanson*, from the 'Belle dame sans merci' to Grosse Margot, from the language of piety to thieves' cant. He was remembered, as he predicted, as a clown. But his real legacy was to express, within a Christian world view, the common ties which make all mankind – the saints and sinners, the long-dead, the still living and the yet-to-be-born – 'frères humains' deserving of God's (and our) mercy.

Conclusion

By 1500, solid foundations had been laid. France recovered from the Hundred Years War which had threatened its very survival, and acquired a solid political, administrative and legal framework. The principle of centralization was an accepted fact and the concept of absolutist royal authority was under consideration. France had a language which, if still fluid, was fixed in its basic structures and the French had a clear sense of their identity both as members of a nation and as individuals capable of moral and social choices. Though it is too early to speak of 'public opinion', the emergence of the urban economy created the beginnings of a cultured public.

The Middle Ages did not stop: the evolutionary process which had begun simply continued. Though hagiography, the epic and romance survived into the print age, they had run their creative course. Lyric poetry was firmly established. Prose was identified as the vehicle of serious discourse, and a notion of prose style had emerged. Prosody, based on the syllable, formal rhyme schemes and the alexandrine, provided a flexible framework for poetic expression of all kinds, and a long experience of theatre paved the way for later developments. And just as the author had been born, so the concept of genres became clearer. The *lai*, *fabliau* and *nouvelle* pointed to the later growth of the novel. Epic and romance, which were perpetuated in stilted forms, contained the seeds of the popular literature hawked by the *colporteurs*. Lives of saints, kings and heroes, abetted by chronicles and memoirs, were the forerunners of history, biography and auto-biography. In terms of mentalities, chivalric values would survive in the *courtoisie* of the sixteenth century and the ideal of *honnêteté* of the seventeenth. *Fin'amor* began the habit of psychological *analyse* which has remained a major French preoccupation, while the dawning of individual consciousness – the *moi* – is detectable in the lyric poets and the chroniclers. Though satire was not a literary form, it was a spirit which would thrive and prosper and, because it looked outwards at the world, nurtured the growth of literary realism. In philosophy, conceptual thinking outside the theological tradition had been established. But above all, the literature of the Middle Ages linked France, on the verge of a Renaissance, to its Latin past.

2

The Renaissance

The Age of François I

The assimilation of Burgundy into the kingdom of France after the death of Charles the Bold (1477) confirmed the authority of the crown, which finally acquired Brittany in 1532. But the strong leadership given by François I (ruled 1515–47) and Henri II (1547–59) was not maintained by the last Valois kings, and between 1562 and 1598 France was ravaged by religious and civil war. Even so, by the time of Henri IV, who added Navarre to the royal domain and imposed an uneasy peace, the centralized power of the monarchy had been considerably strengthened and a clear idea of France as a major European power and 'mère des arts' had emerged. Though provincial cities, such as Lyons, were centres of lively literary and artistic activity until after the middle of the century, Paris was, by 1600, the nation's undisputed cultural heart.

The nineteenth century defined the Renaissance as a clean break with the outlook and practices of the Middle Ages. Then it was argued that the introduction of printing in 1450 heralded a cultural revolution, explorers expanded the known world, Copernicus reshaped the cosmos and, by setting classical wisdom against church dogma, the Renaissance discovered Man. In reality, there was no such break in the continuum. The new presses long continued to reprint medieval texts, the Copernican revolution made little impact on the dominant theological perspective, and it was not until the last third of the sixteenth century that writers like Montaigne and Jean de Léry began drawing sociological, ethical and generally relativist lessons from the tales brought back by travellers, few of whom were

French. The sixteenth century was, of course, a time of transition from one set of structures and values to another, when secular history challenged sacred history and lived experience competed with abstract systems of thought. But it is now related to a much longer cycle of cultural renewal: there had been 'renaissances' at the court of Charlemagne, in the twelfth and thirteenth centuries, and, on a European scale, in fifteenth-century Italy. The extreme limits of the French Renaissance are marked by the mounting pressure for change perceptible in the last third of the fifteenth century, and the reign of Henri IV at the end of the sixteenth. But its high point covers the years 1515–62, between the coronation of François I and the start of the Wars of Religion.

The word 'Renaissance' was unknown to its makers, who spoke rather of a revival or 'restitution' of learning and faith. Rejecting the scholastic erudition of the Middle Ages, scholars rediscovered ancient writers who, though without the benefit of Christian revelation, had expressed truth and beauty. The realization that human intelligence was capable of generating lasting moral and spiritual values undermined medieval theology which claimed that its doctrine, defined over the centuries by ecclesiastical councils, was definitive and capable only of further, increasingly subtle refinement. The rise of the *disciplinae humaniores* together with a reaction against the rigid dogma and the corruption of the Church (the abuse of indulgences, the scandal of certain monastic orders, the ignorance of the clergy) led to pressures for moderate reform. The new spirit was embodied by Erasmus, a pivotal figure who influenced a generation of French writers. During the first third of the century, Humanism co-existed with the Reformation movement, comfortably at first but then in an atmosphere of growing tension.

Just as early Humanists were Christian believers who favoured religious reform, so most Reformers were infused with the spirit of scholarly Humanism. None saw a conflict between ancient philosophy and Christian piety, for both groups were informed by a similar spirit of intellectual enquiry. After 1517, however, Luther's uncompromising revolt against the papacy raised the spectre of heresy, which was duly denounced by Rome and the Faculty of Theology of the Sorbonne. A precarious truce ended after the 'Affaire des Placards' of 1534 when a pamphlet denouncing the mass was posted in Paris and, at Amboise, on the door of the King's chamber. François I reacted strongly and in the years that followed Humanists and Reformers were required to choose. Some opted for the new Protestantism and joined Calvin in Switzerland. Most hesitated, recanted and rejected the reformist doctrine, now judged heretical. By the end of the reign of François in 1547, the break between Humanism and the Reformation was complete.

The restitution of letters and the renewal of faith

The first printed books, which appeared in France in 1470, did not abruptly curtail the Middle Ages. Medieval theology remained dominant, scholasticism was permanently rooted in the universities and writers continued to work in established genres. The traditional moral, edifying vocation of literature survived well into the sixteenth century. Old debates, like the *querelle des femmes*, would be revived and the persistence of allegory is attested by the enduring popularity of *Le Roman de la Rose*, of which some 20 editions were published before 1540. Medieval romances were reissued in printed form, and in the theatre, especially comic theatre, the Middle Ages did not end until about 1550. Mysteries, moralities, *soties* and particularly farces (of which about 150, written between 1500 and 1540, have survived) were renewed and recycled. But change was in the air.

The impact of Italy

The dawning realization in intellectual circles that the Middle Ages had conveyed only a partial view of classical antiquity was confirmed by the example of Petrarch and the work of scholars of the Italian Renaissance who, reverting to original manuscripts, edited and translated writers of antiquity, discarding the glosses and interpolations which had, over the centuries, obscured the wisdom of the ancients. The result was a rich storehouse of scholarly texts which formed the basis of the new *studia humanitatis*, the 'Humanism' which, in different forms, would influence the tone and temper of the French Renaissance. Contact with Italy increased after the start of the Italian wars in 1494, which lasted sixty years, and remained part of the cultural landscape of France. If Dante was neglected, the French *nouvelle* plundered Boccaccio and Bandello, while romance-writers echoed the manner of Ariosto, a model too for social satirists. Castiglione's *Il cortegiano* (1528; trans. 1537) was merely the most celebrated of Italian books of manners to promote the new *courtoisie* which transformed the noble from a philistine soldier and hunter into, at least in theory, a courtier versed in the cultured arts. By 1550, Petrarch would emerge as a dominant poetic model and literary theorists would borrow heavily from their Italian predecessors: Du Bellay's *Defense et illustration de la langue française* (1549), for example, drew on Speroni, and Jean de la Taille's *Art de la tragédie* (1572) was indebted to Castelvetro.

Philology

At the outset, the Italians gave French scholars a tool: philology. For the first generation of Humanists, like Guillaume Fichet (*c.*1433–*c.*1480) and especially Robert Gaguin (1425–1501), the most eminent French intellectual of his day, Latin was the key to all knowledge. They translated ancient texts, applied the new methods of exegesis in preference to medieval interpretation, composed treatises of rhetoric and produced encyclopaedic compendia from mainly Latin sources. Tentatively at first, then with growing confidence, Hebrew gained support as a central element of Biblical studies. Greek authors, neglected by the Middle Ages, were rediscovered and acquired a new authority, though the first book published in Greek did not appear until 1507. The writings of Guillaume Budé (1468–1540) on political, legal and economic affairs made the link between ancient learning (including Greek authors) and modern experience. His *Commentarii linguae graecae* (1529) made him the foremost Greek scholar in Europe and this work, together with his influence in persuading François I to appoint royal 'readers' in Latin, Greek and Hebrew at the Collège royal in 1530, placed Hellenism high on the list of Renaissance concerns. Like many of his generation, he was anxious to show that there was no contradiction between ancient philosophy and Christianity. Thus *De transitu hellenismi ad christianismum* (1535), published at a sensitive moment, argued that Greek learning tutored the mind while Christianity formed the soul.

The new philological tools were put to a variety of uses. They yielded translations of both classical texts and sacred writings, despite protests from the Faculty of Theology at the University of Paris (the Sorbonne), keeper of orthodox ecclesiastical tradition, which feared that learned exegesis would undermine faith. Coinciding with Gallican reservations about the power of Rome, the new approach also gave the new learning a distinctive national flavour. Writing in French, Claude de Seyssel (1455–1520) associated classical culture with France's past (*Louanges du roi Louis XII*, 1508) and Lemaire des Belges (*c.*1475–?1524: *Les Illustrations de Gaule*, 1510–13) revived the thesis that the French were descended from the Trojans. But Lemaire (*La Concorde des deux langages*, 1511) also argued in favour of cultural harmony, a lesson many times rehearsed by scholars at pains to demonstrate that the new learning posed no threat to Christian belief.

Neoplatonism

But the Italians had not only furnished a set of scholarly techniques: they had also opened new intellectual horizons. Lessons were drawn from the commentaries of Plato and Plotinus undertaken in Florence by Marsilio Ficino (1433–99), which affirmed the power of human will and asserted the primacy of love over reason. Ficino's synthesis of Platonism and Christianity was first transmitted in Latin by Fichet and in French notably by Symphorien Champier (*c.*1471–1540: *La Nef des dames*, 1503) and Lefèvre d'Étaples (*c.*1460–1536) who linked it to orthodox theology. This Neoplatonism took many forms but its main impact stemmed from its association of love with mystical spirituality. Love, though it did not exclude sensuality, meant love of beauty, and the contemplation of beauty led to truth and ultimately goodness. This concept of a spiritual ascent from desire to ultimate virtue generated an ethic and a metaphysic which, though contested, survived in part because they underpinned the links between the moral philosophy of the ancients and Christian belief, but in part too because Neoplatonic ideas enhanced the courtly image of women and validated their cultural activities. Neoplatonism is detectable in various forms in the writings of Marguerite de Navarre, in the Pléiade's concept of poetry as a 'divine madness', and persisted into the poetry of Desportes at the end of the century.

Neo-stoicism

Another legacy of the ancient world transmitted through the Italians (though it would evolve significantly) was the neo-stoicism associated with both Ficino and Pico della Mirandola (1463–94) who projected a view of human autonomy through the example of Socrates, the embodiment of pre-Christian virtue. According to this doctrine, man could control both his will and his passions and use his reason to make moral choices, regulate his conduct and thus create his own happiness.

The new learning

This optimistic view of human nature was one source of the confident approach to man's ability – always subject to God's mercy – to advance through reason and take responsibility for his sublunary affairs. Hence the outlines of ideal states (Thomas More's *Utopia*, 1516, or Rabelais's Thélème) based on the toleration of human choices, and the new emphasis on education, a matter of concern not only to the many who continued to furnish *miroirs* for princely conduct but also to some of the greatest writers of the age: Rabelais and Montaigne. Humanists set about devising a pedagogical approach to counter scholastic Aristotelianism with more human-based concerns: the study of history and moral philosophy, with eloquence and rhetoric treated as practical arts. In 1530, at the behest of Budé, François I created a Collège royal, first mooted in 1517, which was seen as a challenge to the authority of the Sorbonne by its encouragement of free enquiry through the medium of the ancient languages. Though the new learning was not welcomed in the universities, it made rapid progress in the *collèges* which by the 1530s had ceased to be institutions devoted to training clerks for holy orders and were educating a wider social range. The recruitment of eminent scholars helped to raise a new generation conversant with French and Latin and familiar with the goals of Humanist learning. Montaigne was taught by George Buchanan at the Collège de Guyenne at Bordeaux, while the Pléiade emerged from the Collège de Coqueret, where Jean Dorat (1508–88) taught Latin and Greek to Ronsard, Du Bellay and Baïf, and the Collège de Boncourt, where Jodelle, Grévin and Belleau were introduced to the classics by Buchanan and Marc-Antoine Muret.

Erasmus

Though Italian influence remained strong, French scholars were also open to the Humanism of the north, represented by the Dutch scholar and theologian Erasmus (*c.*1469–1536) who marked an entire generation. His *Adagia* (1500–34) linked the proverbial wisdom of the ancients to contemporary life and his *Moriae encomium* (*In Praise of*

Folly, 1511) established a mode of wit and irony which would direct the growth of French satire. Although he lived mainly outside France after 1501, he maintained a numerous correspondence with French scholars and his religious writings (notably his Greek New Testament published in 1516) exerted a major influence on the moderate reforms favoured by the Evangelical movement which looked to the spirit of the Gospels.

The Evangelical movement

The Evangelicals sought to reform religion by returning to the textual basis of the Church's founding spirit. They called for simplified forms of worship, a more enlightened clergy and the spread of divine revelation by preaching and new translations of the scriptures from original sources. The lead was given by Lefèvre d'Étaples (*c.*1460–1536), who published commentaries on the Gospels (1522) and translated both the New (1523) and the Old Testaments (1529). He was encouraged by Guillaume Briçonnet (1472–1534), Bishop of Meaux, who established a strong Evangelical base in his diocese in the early 1520s. Although supported by Marguerite de Navarre and, through her, by her brother, François I, the group broke up in 1526: Lefèvre sought refuge at Marguerite's court at Nérac and Georges Farel (1496–1565) left for Geneva where he became one of Calvin's most energetic supporters. The Evangelical movement was undermined by the hostile reaction to Luther's 'heresy' and the opposition of the conservative Sorbonne, led by Noël Béda (d. 1536). Béda accused Erasmus of departing from orthodoxy by applying the critical and philological methods of Humanism to Holy Writ and was instrumental in sending his translator, Louis de Berquin, to the stake in 1529. He also attempted, unsuccessfully, to block the founding of the Collège royal in 1530, but was himself banished in 1533 for questioning the religious writings of Marguerite de Navarre. Although moderate reformers took heart from these signs of royal favour, their hopes were dashed after the 'Affaire des Placards' when François I reversed his policy of tolerance and threw his weight behind a return to orthodoxy. The crisis was precipitated by specific events, but in a sense it was waiting to happen. For Christians, faith was underwritten by the teachings of the scriptures and the traditions of the Church. In attempting to revitalize the first, it was inevitable that the Evangelicals would sooner or later run foul of the second.

Poetry

Though the early years of the century laid the basis for approaches, ideas and values which directed so many subsequent developments, they were, in literary terms, barren. The focus of intellectual effort was scholarly not imaginative, and the language of scholarship was mainly Latin rather than the vernacular which, unstable and limited in its range, was judged incapable of expressing matters of weight. By 1515, of the books which had been printed since 1470, a third were works of Humanist erudition written in ancient languages and half were volumes of theology, also in Latin. In 1528, books written in French still accounted for only 20 per cent of all new titles. Not until the mid-century would books in French make up over half the total production of the Paris presses and literary works constitute a significant proportion of that figure.

The 'rhétoriqueurs'

Latin, however, was not universally understood, and books in French, in both prose and poetry, were produced in modest numbers. Poetry was dominated by the second generation of 'rhétoriqueurs' who had transferred their loyalties from the ducal courts to the King. They were aware of Humanist principles and the new ideas imported from Italy. But their outlook remained late medieval and to the Italian poets they preferred Deschamps, Chastellain and *Le Roman de la Rose*. They continued the tradition of publishing treatises on the art of poetry in the wake of Jean Molinet, and the popularity of *Le Grand et Vrai Art de pleine rhétorique* (1521) by Pierre Fabri (*c*.1450–*c*.1535) is attested by its six reprints before 1544. 'Rhétoriqueurs' discussed poetry as craft and technique, commenting on issues of versification and defending the traditional fixed forms: the *ballades, chants royaux, rondeaux, pastourelles* and *lais* of their predecessors. As poets, they made bold experiments and in the process laid certain ground rules for subsequent poetic expression. Octavien de Saint-Gelais (1468–1502), for example, is credited with establishing the *alternance* of masculine and feminine rhymes and Jean Lemaire des Belges with introducing the *terza rima* from Italy. As a group, they enriched the vernacular by naturalizing words and structures derived from Latin, and Lemaire's *Concorde* may be seen as one of the first 'defences' of the French language. But they also pushed verbal agility to extremes, building puns and wordplay into rhymes – *batelées, couronnées, enchaînées, équivoques* – of distracting complexity. Never wearing their erudition lightly, they practised acrostic and pattern verse which often reads like stylistic exercises devoid of anything resembling a distinctive personality. They wrote of fortune, death, love and religion but, as court poets, they also celebrated the renown of their patron and treated patriotic themes. As chroniclers, they were happy to draw on medieval lore which they updated by making history a source of moralizing instruction for the guidance of princes.

Although their poetry often chokes on its gratuitous inventiveness, the 'rhétoriqueurs' were republished well into the second half of the century and, despite being mocked for their 'gothic' taste for archaisms and allegory, served as a rich storehouse of ideas and images for the poets who followed them. Recent estimates of them have been revised upwards. Yet the contemporary fame of Guillaume Crétin (lampooned as Raminagrobis by Rabelais) now appears exaggerated, and it is Lemaire who seems the more progressive. His openness to the new learning, his readiness to diversify and attempt new registers (as in the playful *Épîtres de l'amant vert*, 1505) shows him moving away from the rigid 'rhétoriqueur' concept of poetry as technique and ornamentation towards a new sensibility. Among transitional figures, Mellin de Saint-Gelais (*c.*1490–1558), a court poet who published little, preferring to perform his witty, satirical ephemera to an audience, similarly turned to newer forms such as the *chanson* and the *épigramme* and may have been the first to write a sonnet in French (1533–4), though the first to be published, in 1538, was signed by Marot.

Marot

Clément Marot (1496–1544) was the son of the 'rhétoriqueur' Jean Marot and, like him, a court poet. His early work, between about 1515 and 1526, suggests that he was the last of the medieval versifiers. He edited *Le Roman de la Rose* and Villon, was comfortable with the old fixed forms of *complainte, ballade* and *rondeau*, and his early allegorical poem *Le Temple de Cupido* (1515) fully reflects the goals and style of the 'rhétoriqueurs'. But his interest in Humanist learning (he translated Virgil and Ovid) and his later work cast him as the first of the Renaissance poets. His fluid rhythms, engaging humour and easy, often sensual manner, shorn of 'rhétoriqueur' excess, enabled him to emerge as a writer to rank with the Italians. He adopted new forms (the epigram, the elegy, and above all the *épître*, some in the form of wittily turned begging letters) and he revived old ones (like the ludic *coq-à-l'âne*). *L'Adolescence clémentine* (1532) and its *Suite* (1533) delighted the court and confirmed him as a poet with a personal voice, urban in outlook, playful and satirical, sometimes savagely so. For a deeper note is struck by his sympathies with the Reformers (he was jailed in 1526 for breaking the Lenten fast and fled Paris twice fearing ecclesiastical pursuit) which led him to focus on the wretchedness of the poor, denounce prison conditions and attack abuses tolerated by the Church. His lyrical talents extended from a *blason* celebrating 'le beau tétin' to much more sophisticated and serious reflections on death and, above all, to his translations of the Psalms (1541, 1543) which, many times reprinted, became part of the Protestant tradition.

After his death, 'marotique' poets (like the anti-Neoplatonic Bertrand de la Borderie (*c*.1507–after 1547) and Charles Fontaine (b. 1514) who made 'gayeté naturelle' an essential part of the poet's make-up) attempted to imitate his manner and achieve comparable success. But they lacked his wit, charm and craft and did nothing to perpetuate his reputation which declined dramatically. Within ten years, though he was admired by Ronsard, the Pléiade poets had dismissed him as the representative of an outmoded ideal of poetry. Yet, in historical terms, he played a crucial role in renovating versification, exploring new themes and genres, and injecting movement, personality and everyday experience into the world of poetry

Latin verse

While Marot's 'élégant badinage', to use Boileau's misleading term, dominated the 1530s, Humanist learning gave verse written in Latin a high profile, for only in Latin could the French hope to compete on equal terms with the Italians. Although this might appear a retrograde attitude, neo-Latin poetry between the 'rhétoriqueurs' and the Pléiade proved a springboard for many later developments. It explored new themes and genres which proved attractive to vernacular poets. Salmon Macrin (1490–1557) adopted the Horatian lyric metre in his *Odes* and neo-Latin poet-teachers like Muret, Buchanan and Dorat conveyed an enthusiasm for new subjects and forms – not least classical tragedy – to two generations of *collégiens*. All the Pléiade poets save Ronsard wrote Latin verse partly in the belief that by so doing they stood a better chance of posthumous fame than by the poems they wrote in French, still an evolving language.

Scève

An example of the interpenetration of classical and French cultures is provided by Étienne Dolet (1509–46), printer, scholar and neo-Latin poet. In the 1530s, he encouraged a *sodalitium* at Lyons, which had long been an important channel for Italian ideas and a significant publishing centre: between 1500 and 1599, against the 25,000 books printed in Paris, 15,000 were published at Lyons, including Rabelais's *Pantagruel* and *Gargantua* and the 1538 edition of the works of Marot. Maurice Scève (*c.*1500–60), himself a Latin poet, had strong links with the Lyons group and his French poetry uses imagery derived from classical mythology. But he also drew on the 'rhétoriqueur' tradition and was for a while a 'marotique' before finding his inspiration in the Italian, and specifically Petrarchan, past. *Délie, objet de la plus haute vertu* (1544) is the first French *canzionere*, a sequence of 449 *dizains* on the theme of love, ostensibly written to a woman, possibly Pernette du Guillet, but also capable of being read symbolically: it has been given Platonic and mythological interpretations ('Délie' as an anagram of 'L'Idée', but also as a daughter of Delos, birthplace of Apollo). But whatever Délie ultimately represents (she is evoked in mystical, sometimes surreal terms and the organization of the *dizains* was intended to have a numerological significance), she stands as an emblem of Beauty and reflects the virtue of which she is the 'object'.

The Lyons poets

Neither Scève's hermetic vision nor his densely textured language pleased all his contemporaries and his modern reputation began only with the Symbolists at the end of the nineteenth century. Yet he was respected by Pontus de Tyard, Du Bellay and Ronsard and, in historical terms, was instrumental in moving poetry away from Marot's focus on the ordinary to a more aristocratic vocation. Scève not only anticipated the programme of the Pléiade but helped confirm the status of French as the language of poetry. By 1550, vernacular poetry was well represented at Lyons by Claude de Tallemont (*c.*1504–after 1588) and in the early career of Jacques Peletier du Mans (1517–82).

Significant, however, was the contribution of cultivated women (Sybille Scève, Marguerite du Bourg, Claude de Bectoz) most of whom were indebted to Italian sources. The *Rimes* (1545) of Pernette du Guillet (*c.*1518–45) are lyrical expressions of unfulfilled love expressed in mystical, Neoplatonic terms. Louise Labé (*c.*1520–66) left a prose allegory, the *Débat de la folie et de l'amour* (1555), but is mainly remembered for two dozen intense, passionate sonnets which evoke emotion and sensuality in unambiguous terms. These themes are echoed in her three elegies on the theme of unhappy love and her desertion by, it is believed, Olivier de Magny (1529–61) who, in the 1550s, would publish several collections of love poetry in the manner of Ronsard.

The defence of women

Labé prefaced her volume with an epistle urging women to abandon feminine pursuits and asserting their capacity to compete with men in cultural activities. It was a rousing contribution to the long-standing *querelle des femmes* which was pursued in prose and verse throughout the Renaissance. The argument, which had its roots in the Middle Ages, turned on 'proofs' adduced from theological, medical and legal authority, and the century is punctuated by learned, sometime pugnacious statements for and against women. But the quarrel spilled over into literature: woman was a theme of 'rhétoriqueur' poetry and Rabelais raised the issue in the *Tiers Livre*. Yet before Du Guillet and Labé, the only noteworthy woman poet was Marguerite de Navarre who, though she defended her sex in her *nouvelles*, restricted her verse, save for a handful of profane poems, to spiritual and devotional themes derived largely from her links with the Evangelicals.

The *querelle des Amyes*

In the 1530s, when Neoplatonic ideas raised the status of women, Castiglione's *Courtier* accorded them an honourable place at court. The new *courtoisie* countered clerical misogyny and cast women as objects of respect and veneration. Prose writers furnished catalogues of famous women and female virtues (Henri Agrippa's *Précellence du sexe féminin*, written in Latin (1507), published in 1529 and translated in 1537, was a popular source book) but in the early 1540s the debate was taken up by poets. The *querelle des Amyes* opened with Bertrand de la Borderie's *Amye de court* (1542), which resisted the current idealization of women. Ripostes were published by Charles Fontaine (*Contr'amie de la court*, 1543) and Antoine Héroet (1492–1568) whose popular *Parfaicte amye* (1542) formed part of the Neo-platonic flow and defined love as divinely inspired but unachievable in this vale of tears. The *querelle* lasted some ten years and, though unremarkable in literary quality, it drew attention to issues (the relationship between love and marriage, the link between love and religion and the importance of courtly values) which widened the remit of literature. Thereafter, the argument reverted to the older gender divide and Desportes's anti-feminist 'Stances du mariage' (1571) provoked strong reactions, among others from Marie de Romieu (?1545–90) in 1581. By that time, the first *salonnières* – Sophie (*c*.1520–87) and Catherine (*c*.1542–87) des Roches at Poitiers and the Maréchale de Retz in Paris – had begun the long association between women and the arts which would continue into the eighteenth century.

Conclusion

By the death of François I in 1547, poetry had begun to break new ground. Old verse forms went into decline and were replaced by new ones inspired by translations of ancient authors and the neo-Latin poets. French versification was acquiring a fixed character and there was growing confidence in the vernacular as a vehicle of poetic expression. The range of suitable themes had been widened and the poetic voice of the 1540s is markedly more individualistic than during the previous generation: real personalities replace the old literary personae. Though allegory remained strong, its use was tempered by the growth of imagery (simile and metaphor) drawn from a variety of sources, notably classical mythology and the natural world. The next phase of its development would be inaugurated by the Pléiade poets.

Prose

As was the case with poetry, Latin was considered the appropriate vehicle for the discussion of serious matters in prose. Publications in the vernacular were mainly translations of books written in other languages, from the sacred texts furnished by the Evangelicals to works of Humanist erudition by way of old Latin chronicles, like the

Histoire de l'Église de France of Grégoire de Tours. Italian authors – of fictions (Boccaccio or Caviceo's *Peregrino*, 1527), but also of treatises defining *courtoisie* – were given a French voice, as were a smaller number of Spanish writers. Antonio de Guevara's *Livre d'or de Marc Aurèle* (trans. 1531) influenced moral and political thinking while his *Mépris de la cour* (trans. 1542 and many times reprinted) was both anti-courtly and anti-*Amye*. On the other hand, as we shall see, a number of Spanish novelists contributed significantly to maintaining and developing the concept of idealized love. At the other end of the literary scale, the trade in popular chapbooks had begun.

The rise of French

Although the cultural climate was dominated by the religious question, the first work of theology published in the vernacular was Calvin's *Institution de la religion chrétienne* (1541), a translation of his *Christianae religionis institutio* of 1536. Thereafter, as part of the Protestant policy of making the reformed word accessible to the faithful, Calvin used French to attack corrupt church practices (*Traité de reliques*, 1543) and denounce the spread of irreligion (*Traité des scandales*, 1550). But just as Evangelicals and, later, Protestants made devotional writings (including sermons) available in French, so the spiritual tendency of the early Counter-Reformation found expression in the vernacular, as in Béda's *Internelle consolation* of 1542.

Chronicle, epic, romance

Even so, nationalist feeling was strong enough to stimulate an interest in France's past, and new works of history, albeit still strong on legend, began to appear. Lemaire's *Illustrations* were written in French as were Corrozet's *Antiquités de Paris* (1531) and the *Annales d'Aquitaine* (1524) by Jean Bouchet (1476–1557), one of the first writers to criticize Luther in the vernacular. For similar reasons, there was a demand for 'classic' texts of the nation's literature and, in particular, for prose versions of epics like *Huon de Bordeaux* and *Fierabras*, and chivalric romances such as *Florimont* and those associated with the Round Table. The most popular of all was *Amadis de Gaule* which first appeared in four books in 1540 in a translation from the Spanish by Herberay des Essarts. It tells of Amadis, who confronts giants, enchanters and divers perils to serve his lady. The episodic form allowed for the addition of new adventures and insertions, and by 1591 the text had swollen to 21 books. Although a major target of Cervantes in *Don Quixote*, the vogue for Amadis did not finally decline until the 1640s.

Fiction

Initially, however, fiction was not highly regarded by French authors, though it featured in the chapbooks which would later turn into the *Bibliothèque bleue*. Its popularity with the public is attested by the translation of Spanish novels of sentiment. Diego de San Pedro's *La Prison d'amour* (1526) and the *Petit traité de Arnalte et Lucenda* (1539) were regularly reprinted. *Le Jugement d'amour* (1520) and *La Déplorable Fin de Flamette* (trans. by Scève in 1535), both by Juan de Flores, were also stories of unhappy passion. The latter was based on Boccaccio's *Fiammetta* which appeared in a new translation in the early 1530s along with his *Filocolo*. A new version of the *Decameron*, commissioned by Marguerite de Navarre, was published in 1545. These foreign imports helped shape home-produced fiction by defining two sets of narrative models (long and short fiction) and modes: sentiment and *analyse* from Spain, and the more realistic tradition of the *Cent nouvelles nouvelles*, of which Philippe de Vigneulles provided a new version in 1515.

Jehan de Paris (1533) prefigures these developments. Written in the 1490s, it tells how a king disguises himself as a Parisian merchant and wins the hand of the Spanish *infanta* from his rival, a witless king of England. To Jehan's chivalric adventures is added a vein of satirical comment and feyness, also observable in *Le Petit Jean de Saintré*, first printed in 1517. A deeper psychological note is struck in the first part of Helisenne de Crenne's *Angoisses douloureuses qui procèdent d'amour* (1538) which describes the fate of a wife who, for loving a man younger than herself, is imprisoned by her husband.

At about the same time, shorter fiction began to attract authors. To Bonaventure des Periers (1510–44), a secretary to Marguerite de Navarre, is attributed a collection of tales, the *Nouvelles récréations et joyeux devis* (c.1538; publ. 1558), which have their roots in the *fabliau* and Boccaccio, though the satire is muted. A more lasting impact was made by the *Heptameron* (written in the 1540s; publ. 1558), a collection of 72 tales (100 were planned) of varying length. A framework presents five lords and five ladies, their journey through the

Pyrenees halted by a broken bridge, who pass the time by relating adventures in a variety of registers ranging from the bawdy to the elevated. Marguerite draws on Boccaccio (a score of stories are about lewd clerics and she shows more straying wives than faithless husbands) but also provides *exempla* linking Neoplatonic ideas with her Evangelical beliefs to show that human love is the first spiritual step to salvation. Though there is a topical defence of women against male predatoriness, the collection largely accepts the male view of woman's inferiority. If the tales are uneven in quality, they reveal distinctive gifts of dialogue and narrative control. The social background to the tales is lightly sketched, but a clearer picture emerges of the narrators, and the *Heptameron* may still be read as a picture of contemporary life and manners.

Rabelais

Although the use of vernacular prose grew during the second quarter of the century, the prose writing of the period is dominated by one writer, François Rabelais (?1484–1553), who exemplifies the choices facing the first generation of the new century. Part of him remained at ease with the late medieval world-view. He retained certain scholastic habits of mind (his mock fastidiousness in argument, for example) and his fiction builds on both the chivalric epic and romance and old tales and farces. He was also marked by the verbal acrobatics of the 'rhétoriqueurs' who confirmed his appetite for words – archaisms, puns, lists, coinages – and inspired his own verse which Marot, for one, rated highly. Yet his commitment was to the new Humanism. A monk who was also well versed in law and the new learning, he was also a doctor of medicine and one of the leading anatomists of his age. He translated Herodotus and Lucian and corresponded with Budé and Erasmus. He argued that medical progress meant abandoning medieval habits of mind and adopting the new spirit of free enquiry. To this end he published an edition of the aphorisms of Hippocrates in 1532, while from Sir Thomas More he took the notion of an ideal realm enshrined in the Abbaye de Thélème. Sympathetic to Neoplatonic ideas, he also shared the Evangelicals' urging of moderate church reform – hence his pungent satire of the 'Papimanes' in the *Quart Livre* and the mocking eye which he turned, at every opportunity, on the Sorbonne, monasticism and practices such as the pilgrimage and the cult of saints. He

supported calls for new pedagogies and echoed the growing nationalistic spirit which led him, in *Gargantua*, to vanquish a tyrannical
invader who has been identified as the Holy Roman Emperor, Charles
V. Rabelais was not only an 'abîme de science' but an enthusiastic
advocate of the 'rebirth' of ideas and letters.

In 1532, he published three learned volumes but also the first
book of the exuberant fantasy for which he is remembered. Modelled on a popular tale which told how a family of giants was created
by Merlin to help Arthur overcome his enemies, *Pantagruel* parodies
the structure of Arthurian romance with its burlesque version of the
marvellous birth, youth, education and military exploits of its hero.
Pantagruel's father, the giant Gargantua, an enemy of scholastic ped-
agogy, raises his son in the Humanist manner to be a man of learning and judgement. In Paris Pantagruel meets Panurge and together
they do battle with the king of the Dipsodes. The narrative moves
from subjects of high seriousness (education, war) to farce, from the
mock-seriousness of Rabelais's pedantic exactness to frank scatology.
But above all, *Pantagruel* releases a formidable comic imagination.
Rabelais extracts humour from the size of his giants but also draws
on the tradition of university *facéties*, particularly through the trick-
ery of Panurge. Yet he never strays too far from the real world and
tilts at its absurdities in his satire of monks, lawyers and the forces of
obscurantism.

Gargantua (1534/5) takes a step back one generation and, in a
more orderly manner, follows Gargantua through similar stages from
birth, youth and education to Paris and thence to war, this time with
Picrocole. Though the internal chronology rules out the appearance
of Panurge, the lusty Frère Jean shoulders a comparable anarchic
role. A liminary poem ends: 'Rire est le propre de l'Homme', as
though to define what follows as comic invention. Yet the prologue
invites the reader to 'rompre l'os' and seek the 'substantifique moëlle'
contained within the text. But although this suggestion that there is
a hidden sense is contradicted by the following paragraphs, there is
no doubt that Rabelais's purpose was serious. No friend of the 'gothic',
he ends the volume with an account of the Abbaye de Thélème.
Inspired by Evangelical Humanism, it is anti-monastic, opposed to
Christian asceticism but committed to 'la foy personnelle', the home
of learning and polite manners, where the freedom of both men and
women is underwritten by an acceptance of the progressive principles

which were opposed by Sorbonne theologians, monks, lawyers and the tribe of hypocrites who are specifically excluded.

In succeeding volumes, the *Tiers Livre* (1546), the *Quart Livre* (1552) and the posthumous (and possibly inauthentic) *Cinquième Livre* (1562–4), the size of Rabelais's giants is largely forgotten and instead of the 'horribles . . . faits et prouesses' of 1532, he offers 'les faicts et dicts de Pantagruel': thus, against Panurge's praise of lenders and debtors, he affirms that it is work which makes people independent and societies healthy. In these later books, Panurge, no longer a cunning prankster but a poltroon, becomes the focus of the narrative. Unable to decide whether to marry or not, he seeks help through divination, is advised by authorities who provide further opportunities for anti-clerical and social satire before, at Pantagruel's suggestion, resolving to consult the *dive bouteille* of Cathay which ultimately gives its verdict.

Rabelais's narrative proceeds erratically (a coherent plot was not a priority) and offers endless opportunities for his fascination with language, his opposition to the conservatism of the Church and the professions and his alertness to current debates. He courted danger (the third and fourth books ran foul of the censors) with an attack on the practice of Lenten fasting and, more pointedly still, on the Church of Rome, which he wrote at a juncture when France seemed set to reject papal authority. Through Rondibilis, the physician, he intervened in the *querelle des Amyes* by attributing the inferiority of women to incurable physiological defects. This may or may not represent Rabelais's own position. Certainly, his female characters act out the traditional 'malices des femmes' and loving relationships do not figure in his recipe for Humanist happiness. Indeed, apart from an ideal of male friendship, Rabelais skips the affective side of human nature altogether. Yet it seems unlikely that he would risk offending Marguerite de Navarre, to whom he dedicated the *Tiers Livre*, by endorsing anti-feminism so openly. But if Rabelais provoked, his true legacy lies elsewhere, in his comic exuberance and his gift for imaginative fantasy. His travellers hear frozen words thaw and discover in the person of 'Messer Gaster' (the stomach) the master of all arts and the sole motor of human progress. This earthy reminder of the basic humanity of man in no way contradicts the answer given by the *dive bouteille*: 'Trink!'. Drinking is 'le propre de l'homme' and Rabelais's wine is a joyous, life-enhancing draught of truth, knowledge and intellectual curiosity which are the duty of man.

Rabelais has been badly served by the word 'Rabelaisian' which evokes the image of a carousing monk obsessed with bodily functions who knew more words than was good for him. But neither should he be seen only in historical terms and his work read as a commentary on contemporary issues which have long since gone cold. For Rabelais embodies a spirit which transcends his times. His 'philosophy' is not a closed system but a set of open attitudes: a hostility to establishment ideas, an assertion of human curiosity and mental discipline, doubts about the ability of words to express realities, and an exhortation to seek out truth dispassionately. Moreover, beyond the scatological irreverence and lack of restraint, Rabelais encapsulates a festival spirit which celebrates the community of man and looks forward to a future when human beings will live at ease with the world, each other and themselves. An exuberantly contrary man, Rabelais wraps perennial questions (what should we think? how should we live?) in fantasy, rumbustious humour and unshackled invention.

The Generation of the Pléiade

The defence of the language

By the end of the reign of François I, French as the language of learned and literary discourse had made considerable ground. The position of Latin was fiercely defended in the old universities and the new Collège royal, and many scholars, alarmed by the threat to what had become the *lingua franca* of European learning, continued to believe that French was too raw and unformed to compete with the expressive resources of ancient tongues or modern Italian. Others, however, took a more progressive view. The sense of national pride among early Humanists, Gallican opposition to Rome and the Evangelicals' proselytizing zeal all helped further the case for the vernacular which was strongly urged by Lemaire des Belges, Claude Seyssel and the scholar and printer Geoffroy Tory (*c*.1480–after 1553), whose *Champ fleury* (1529) urged France's writers to use their own language. Charles de Bouelles (*c*.1480–1533), though conceding the superiority of Latin, argued that French was capable of significant development (*De gallici sermone varietatae*, 1533). With such support,

French proceeded to move into areas from which it had hitherto been excluded. After 1550 it grew in stature as the language of learning (philosophy, science, mathematics, history and argument generally) and although the Church remained loyal to tradition, French intruded into the theology of the Counter-Reformation and, by 1550, was standard in Protestant France and Switzerland.

Royal intervention

The rise of French was made possible by a number of developments, not least of which was the active policy adopted by successive monarchs. Since the 1490s, the crown, anxious to unify its domains, had promoted the vernacular as an administrative language. A crucial step was taken in 1539 when the Ordonnances of Villers-Cotterêts decreed that court proceedings were henceforth to be recorded 'en langage maternel françois, et non autrement'. The spread of printing helped confirm royal policy. Latin, the idiom of the learned and governing elite, was far from universally understood and the demand for books in the vernacular could not be resisted.

Standardization

There resulted calls for the codification of the written conventions (spelling, punctuation) but also of the language itself. Though practical manuals intended for foreigners had circulated since the Middle Ages, it was not until 1532 that the first French grammar aimed at the French was published, in Latin, by Jacques Dubois. The first grammar written in French, Louis Meigret's *Tretté de la grammere françoeze* (1550), also called, as it title indicates, for orthography to reflect pronunciation, an argument he had first put forward in 1542. The issue was taken up in 1548 by Guillaume des Autels (1529–81), Peletier du Mans (1549), Claude Taillemont (who adopted a phonological system in *La Tricarite*, 1556), Baïf (*Etrènes de poèsie fransoêze an vers mezurés*, 1574) and Honorat Rambaud who devised an entirely new alphabet in 1578. This interest in the mechanics of language was also reflected in the growing popularity of dictionaries, for the most part polyglot (such as Ambrosius Calépinius's *Dictionarium*, 1502, many times revised) or bilingual (of French and Latin or another modern language). The Latin–French lexicons (1531, 1538) of the erudite printer Robert Estienne (1503–59) were published in 1539 as was a Latin–French dictionary (1539) which, when suitable equivalents were not available, provided definitions in French in the manner of later monolingual dictionaries, of which the first was not published until 1680.

The role of translation

No less far-reaching was the impact of translation which, since the start of the century, had stocked the vernacular with words and structures imported from classical and foreign languages. In addition to its role of making knowledge available to a wider readership, translation was highly valued as a literary exercise and an essential form of linguistic apprenticeship. The principles laid down in Dolet's *Manière de bien traduire d'une langue en une autre* (1542) were echoed in the many similar statements published before and after the mid-century. The goal was to produce a French version which was worthy of the original in dignity and quality. Few authors were not also translators and some, like Du Bellay, published Latin versions of their own work, though on the whole the Pléiade was hostile to translation as such and preferred creative imitation. In the middle third of the century, texts rendered from other languages represented a large percentage of published books, and translation was a highly respected art. Jacques Amyot (1513–93), bishop of Auxerre, turned Heliodorus and Longus into French but was especially admired for his versions of Plutarch (*Les Vies des hommes illustres grecs ou romains*, 1559) which were regarded as models of style. By using other languages as a springboard for its own development, French proved to be as versatile as its early defenders had claimed it could be.

Which French?

Despite the progress made, French was still evolving and Montaigne, for one, still considered it to be fragile. The language debate, which accelerated after 1540, had generated an argument about whose French should be adopted as the norm. Scholars, the court, administrators and lawyers, and the disparate mass of the population all had claims. In practice, literary usage was defined in the atmosphere of the court, the ultimate source of the preferment and honours which most writers sought. While most agreed that French should have the dignity and full range of Latin and Italian, others were aware of the paradox of making the independence of French dependent on other languages. Some argued that French had become too Latinate and syntactically over-complex. A similar reservation, about intrusive Italian influence, was expressed by Henri Estienne (1531–98), printer, scholar, Protestant polemicist and author of a grammar (1554). In *De la précellence du langage français* (1579), he argued that Greek was superior to all other languages but that French was nearest to it. Despite certain reservations, then, the late Renaissance placed its faith in French, though it would take another generation, after the esoteric flourish of the baroque had been digested, before Malherbe established the principles of simplicity and clarity of expression.

The new poetics and the Pléiade

The 'rhétoriqueur' concept of the craft of poetry, set out by Pierre Fabri in 1521, was steadily overtaken as the neo-Latin poets turned to themes and genres borrowed from antiquity. Newer practices and principles were also suggested by the Italian poets and theorists like Marco Girolamo Vida, whose influential treatise on the art of poetry appeared in Latin in 1527. In 1541, Peletier du Mans translated Horace's *Ars poetica* and reminded French poets of the ancient origins of their art. In 1548 Thomas Sébillet (1512–89) published an *Art poétique français* which, though anchored in traditions respected by Marot's generation, was not unsympathetic to the Humanist view of poetry. Sébillet discussed verse forms, rhyme and rhythm, and defined poetry as the result of divine inspiration, creative imitation and technique. In many areas he anticipated the theories of the Pléiade poets whose success prompted an outbreak of theoretical writings on language and the art of poetry. The Protestant Théodore Bèze and Barthélémy Aneau (*c*.1505–61), probably the author of the satirical *Quintil Horatien* (1550), attacked the rejection of French genres and warned that the vernacular was becoming over-Latinized. Ronsard continued to champion the new ideas in the 'avertissement' to his *Odes* (1550), his Pindaric ode to Michel de l'Hôpital (1553), an *Abrégé d'art poétique* (1565) and the prefaces to his epic, *La Franciade*. The case continued to be put in treatises (such as Peletier du Mans's *Art poétique* (1555) and statements by Pontus de Tyard and others, the last being the preface to the *Diverses poésies* (1605) of Vauquelin de la Fresnaye (1535–1606).

The *Défense et illustration*

The debate had been ignited by Du Bellay's *Défense et illustration de la langue française* (1549). In a sense, Du Bellay was preaching to the converted, for the battle for French as a literary language was largely won and the concept of poetry which he defined had been several times anticipated, by Peletier du Mans and, in Lyons, by Scève and Pontus de Tyard. The *Défense* is therefore best understood less as another 'art poétique' than as a pamphlet and call to action. Part I, borrowing heavily from Sperone Speroni's *Dialogo delle lingue* (1542), makes a vigorous case for French as a vehicle for poetry. Enriched by technical terms, periphrasis and a vocabulary renewed by interpenetration with Greek and Latin, French could compete with the languages of the ancient world and modern Italy. In Part II, Du Bellay dismisses the national poetic tradition (with a few exceptions, notably *Le Roman de la Rose* and Lemaire des Belges, judged more erudite than poets like Marot, who were on the whole too simple, too vulgar) along with the *ballade, rondeau*, 'et telles autres épiceries' in favour of classical and Italian genres.

The Pléiade

The *Défense* was the manifesto of the 'Brigade', a group of young poets of which Ronsard emerged as the undisputed leader. Most members of the Pléiade, a term first used by Ronsard in 1556, had met at the Collège de Coqueret, of which Dorat was appointed principal in 1547, and the Collège de Boncourt. There they were exposed to classical authors and genres which ranged from the ode to ancient theatre. Ronsard, Du Bellay, Baïf, Pontus and Jodelle were permanent members, but also included at different times were Peletier du Mans, Belleau, La Péruse, Des Autels, Magny and others. The major period of their activity covers the decade 1550–60 and their influence lessened after 1562 when the religious and political climate created a new mentality. But Ronsard continued to develop and write until 1585 and Baïf until 1589, and their example was not lost on the generation which followed them.

Its aesthetic

They agreed that natural talent needed to be nurtured by long study. Translation and imitation of good models were the essential tools which would produce a new poetic language and lay the basis for a learned, aristocratic style of poetry. By imitation was meant not naturalizing Latin and Italian poets but competing with them creatively as equals. They regarded inspiration as a Neoplatonic 'fureur divine' to be achieved within a strict discipline of style and metre. Rhetorical and mythological figures, hyperbole and periphrasis were sources of nobility and dignity and were recommended as a means of developing a form of poetic expression which was ornate, visual and musical.

The hierarchy of genres

The Pléiade poets adhered to a hierarchy among genres based on the classical tradition. On the one hand were minor genres and modes – *épigramme*, *épître*, *élégie* (a form of love poetry), satire and the pastoral *bergerie* and *églogue*. At the other extreme were the 'noble' forms of lyric poetry, the drama and epic. The ode, developed from Pindar and Horace, was launched by Ronsard in 1550. With its complement, the *chanson*, it was considered suitable for subjects located below the heroic level and was one of the major vehicles for lyric expression. For *L'Olive*, Du Bellay took the *canzionere*, a sequence of love sonnets, from Petrarch. The form had been pioneered by Scève's *Délie* and was taken up by Ronsard, Baïf and others. The sonnet was eventually divorced from the *canzionere* and emerged as a free-standing form suitable for other subjects, as in Du Bellay's *Antiquités de Rome* and *Les Regrets*. Du Bellay recommended Ariosto, not Homer and Virgil, as a model for the epic which was to speak of French heroes like Lancelot and Tristan. Few heeded his call and even Ronsard abandoned his national epic about France's Trojan origins, *La Franciade* (1572), after writing only four of its planned twenty-four cantos. The epic strain is, however, represented in several kinds of long poem: the *discours*, which proved sufficiently flexible to accommodate topical subjects, and the *hymne*, which projected lofty thoughts inspired by a hero or an idea.

Its themes

The themes of the Pléiade reflect the high idea the group formed of poetry. The poet spoke the language of the gods and saw things hidden from mortal gaze. But he also dispensed glory to his subjects and himself, for art conferred lasting fame. This last was an article of faith and it was expressed through a constant preoccupation with the impermanence of the world, passing time, and death. Though only Jodelle was an unbeliever, few sought consolation in religion. Most, even Du Bellay, the most Christian of the group, were more conscious of this world than of the next and their confidence that the French could surpass the ancients at least provided a non-metaphysical belief in a future which had little to do with politics, a sense of history or their own experience. Their mood was defiant rather than optimistic and the realization that a youth devoted to study and a life of labour will end in a death which might or might not be redeemed by posthumous fame sometimes produces a pre-baroque preoccupation with mortuary images offset by exhortations to make the most of the passing moment, youth and love.

Love and the court

Love was one source of their anguish and a major theme. The love poetry of the Pléiade is not confessional, though neither is it divorced from personal experience. It is an 'imitation' of what Love is according to the Petrarchan mode: sublimated and resigned. But if poets sang mostly of ideal love, they also wrote satirical, misogynistic portraits of faithless, deceitful, cruel mistresses, which express an ironic attitude to spiritual love and fidelity. Against the stability of Petrarchan love was set the *carpe diem* of Horace and the Pseudo-Anacreon which was published in 1554. A similarly bitter taste is left by the Pléiade's paradoxical attitude to the court for which they wrote ceremonial verse to celebrate royal occasions and famous victories. The court might be the centre of art and intellect, but it was also a place of corruption, deceit and enslavement. An escape was found in nature, and Pléiade poets left many vivid glimpses of rural life and country peace which are exploited in imagery or serve as backdrops to idylls of love. In so doing, they provided intimations of the pastoral which would reach its height half a century later in *L'Astrée*.

Nature

But their spiritual vocation also led them to use poetry to describe and unveil the forces of nature. The 'scientific' poetry to which Pléiade poets took after 1555 was didactic and philosophical rather than investigative, a celebration, not an explanation, of creation. The universe they described was Ptolemaic, not Copernican, and their astronomy a mixture of the cosmos as it was believed to be and as it

had been presented in ancient mythologies. Natural history was codified and the analogical and symbolic properties (medicinal, spiritual,
moral) of minerals, precious stones and plants were defined in verse,
with anthropomorphic commentaries. Beneath the surface were references to hermetic knowledge, alchemy, astrology, numerology, the
four elements and the pagan concept of fortune as the shaper of
human destinies. Though Ronsard's *Hymnes* reached heights of lyrical
description, the most interesting 'scientific' poems were written by
poets who were not members of the Pléiade, from Scève's *Microcosme*
(1562), which follows Man from the Creation and his Fall and catalogues his achievements, to Lefèvre de la Boderie and Du Bartas in
the 1570s.

The impact of the Pléiade

The ambitious programme of the Pléiade was not without internal
contradictions. It equated imitation with innovation and required art
to be reconciled with nature, polished writing with simplicity, and
hostility to the court with personal ambition. Even so, the example
given by the Pléiade poets was followed in Paris and the provinces,
and their influence on the language was significant: Antoine Foclin
illustrated his *Rhétorique française* (1555) largely from their work. If
the Pléiade epic left no imitable models, it stimulated both the philosophical *discours en vers* and the growth of drama. The themes of
death and spirituality point to the baroque poets, and the new engaged mood of satire to Regnier and the *satiriques* of the age of Louis
XIII. The use of the *je* softened the learned, aristocratic tendencies of
Pléiade verse and made the poetic voice less distant and more accessible. In aesthetic terms, the group established the sonnet, the *stance*
and other fixed forms, confirmed the shift from allegory to symbol
and imagery and, by adopting the *alternance* of masculine and feminine rhymes and the alexandrine, which they made the standard
poetic line, left a permanent mark on the rhythm and tone of French
poetry. But if the impact of the Pléiade poets was significant, their
achievement collectively and individually was also considerable.

Pléiade poets

Jacques Peletier du Mans (1517–82), a major pioneer and theorist,
extended Petrarchism by relating it to science. In his *Amour des amours*
(1554), he showed love in the wider context of nature, the cosmos and

eternity and thus linked two essential Pléiade themes. Jean-Antoine de Baïf (1532–89), a poet unequal to his ambitions, attempted all the genres promoted by the Pléiade and was perhaps the group's boldest experimenter. The work of Rémy Belleau (1528–77), at his best as a descriptive poet of the pastoral, is marked by a strong pictorial sense which was admired by other members of the group. Pontus de Tyard (1521–1605) wrote love and lyrical poetry mainly in the 1550s, but more significant are the philosophical poems on a variety of subjects – time, poetry, music, the cosmos – which were collected as *Discours philosophiques* (1587). Étienne Jodelle (1532–73) was the only Parisian of the group and the most urban in outlook. Although best remembered as a playwright, his poetry, emotionally charged, metrically interesting (he was an early exponent of the *vers rapportés*) and generally sombre (as in the savage *Contr'amours*), was greatly admired by the baroque poets.

Du Bellay

The most significant of the group after Ronsard was Joachim du Bellay (*c*.1522–60), author of the *Défense* and several collections of verse which embodied its principles (1549–50). In 1553, he left for Rome, hoping to renew his poetic inspiration in Italy and probably to further a career in diplomacy. He was disappointed on both counts. He found corruption and decay, grew nostalgic for France and was embittered by the cultural and social climate of Rome, the life he led, poor health and, if his Latin poems can be believed, an unhappy love affair. He returned to France in 1557 where, in the year before his death, he published three major collections of verse, *Les Antiquités de Rome*, *Les Regrets*, and the *Divers jeux rustiques*, together with the Latin poems of the *Poemata*.

Although portrayed as secretary to the 'Brigade' (he signed the *Défense*, their collective statement) and Ronsard's lieutenant, Du Bellay was in fact a lyrical poet of considerable originality. The spirited, impetuous style of the *Défense* was characteristic of the early Du Bellay, and it was he who not only published the first Petrarchist *canzionere* in French, but freed the sonnet from both its association with love and its links with cycles and sequences. But the extravagant idealization of woman expressed in *L'Olive* (1549) was also accompanied by the sarcastic, misogynistic *Antiérotique de la vieille et de la jeune amie* and subsequently by several blasts aimed at the Petrarchists.

In his translation of Book IV of the *Aeneid* he inveighed against the neo-Latin poets, but then proceeded to write four volumes of Latin *Poemata*. Similar contradictions are found in the *Regrets* which paint a nostalgic view of France which, when rediscovered, is abused and pilloried for its decadence and philistinism, a point of view trenchantly expressed in *Le Poète courtisan* (1559). These apparent inconsistencies reflect the tension between aspiration and reality expressed through a personal voice which grows in strength after about 1552. Against his melodic lyricism must be set the melancholic, elegiac mood of his later poetry. Though he was the most spiritually conscious of the Pléiade, he was also one of its major satirists and fiercely critical of the moral world in which he lived. He may have lacked a broader vision, but he expressed a distinctive sensibility in strongly rhythmic verse, rich in evocative images.

Ronsard

The major poet and leader of the Pléiade was Pierre de Ronsard (1524–85). Sent as a page to the court of François I in 1536, he was forced by illness to abandon his hopes of a military career and in 1543 he was admitted to minor orders. The same year he met Peletier du Mans, who encouraged his poetic ambitions, and from 1547 he studied at the Collège de Coqueret where he absorbed Humanist principles and helped shape the ideals of the 'Brigade'. His first collection, the *Quatre premiers livres d'odes* (1550), was inspired by Pindar and Horace, while the sonnets of *Amours* (1552), dedicated to Cassandre Salviati, drew on Petrarchist themes and manner. Subsequently, influenced less by Pindar than by Horace and Anacreon, he augmented the *Odes* and *Amours*, composed a new love cycle (the *Continuation des Amours*, 1555–6) written for an unidentified 'Marie' and published verse in a variety of metres and registers and on a range of subjects, from the *Livret des folâstries* (1553) to the sober *Hymnes* (1555–6), which reflected on moral and other issues and sometimes struck an epic note, and the lighter poems of the *Mélanges* (1556). In 1560 he published the first *Édition collective*, but in the changed political climate his work to the mid-1560s turned increasingly ceremonial and public, as in the *Discours* (1562–3) which deplored 'les misères de ce temps' from a Catholic standpoint. He replied vigorously to his Protestant critics but also published the buoyant *Nouvelles poésies* (1563–4).

By the mid-1560s, he was at the height of his fame, the 'poet of princes'. For the fête organized in 1564 by Catherine de Médicis at Fontainebleau, he wrote the courtly, pastoral entertainments of the *Élegies, Mascarades et Bergerie*, and his *Abrégé de poétique française* appeared in 1565. He became the favourite poet of Charles IX, who awarded him ecclesiastical livings and encouraged him to write the patriotic, 'national' epic *La Franciade* (1572), which he left unfinished. He revised and augmented his earlier work for six further *Éditions collectives* (1567–87) with which he hoped to ensure his posthumous fame. Notable among the additions were the *Sonnets pour Hélène* (1578), a new Petrarchist cycle, which were written perhaps to compete with Desportes, the court favourite of Henri III, and Du Bartas, whose reputations threatened to eclipse his own. During his final illness, he wrote of his physical decline (*Derniers vers*, 1586) with unsentimental directness.

Ronsard's reputation, which he had nurtured so carefully, faded within decades. Malherbe reacted against his ornate language and Boileau would damn his 'extravagant pedantry', allowing him at most a 'beau désordre' and dismissing his Muse for speaking French with a Graeco-Latin accent. Forgotten for two centuries, Ronsard was rehabilitated by the Romantics who heard in him one of the great lyric voices. Since then, new generations have found much to admire in the range and variety of his imaginative world. His political commitment and his philosophy (a complex preoccupation with human destiny) may have lost their immediacy and the erudition and artifice of his early work can make him seem distant and uninvolved. But the soaring eloquence of the *Discours* – the evocative imagery, the precision of his expression, the grandiose rhythms – is irresistible. Yet it is as a love poet that he strikes the most resonant chords. He can be sensual, fey, intimate, but he also explores the deepest feelings, linking love to nature, time, old age and death. Ultimately, it is Ronsard's lyrical gifts which remain in the memory: the delicacy, harmony and simplicity of his melodic line, the images which surprise and illuminate, and the graceful rhythms which carry the reader towards intimations which lie beyond mere sounds and words. Ronsard was the most versatile of the Pléiade poets, unmatched in his range, vision and technical mastery.

Theatre

After 1500 French drama remained faithful to the moralities, mysteries, farces and *soties* developed in the fifteenth century. They were performed by the non-professional *confréries*, the Basoche and the Enfants Sans Souci. There were no fixed theatres and stages were erected in towns, at court and in noble houses as the occasion arose. New additions to the corpus of texts were made, at dates often difficult to ascertain, but apart from a small advance in psychology and topical reference, there was little innovation. Most writers were anonymous, though a few names stand out, such as Jehan de Pont-Alais, Pierre du Val, or Jehan d'Abondance, author of *La Moralité pour personnages sur la Passion de Jésus*, a *Mystère joyeux des trois rois* and *La Farce de la cornette*. Pierre Gringore (*c.*1475–1538) worked closely with the Enfants Sans Souci in Paris devising and producing moralities (*La Vie de monseigneur sainct Loys*) and especially satirical *soties* in verse and prose (*Folles Entreprises*, 1505; *Le Jeu du prince des sots*, 1512; *Les Fantaisies de Mère Sotte*, 1516). The plays of Marguerite de Navarre, intended to be performed at court, dealt with religious and spiritual themes.

The Hôtel de Bourgogne

Audiences remained loyal to established genres throughout the century, though the appeal of the miracle play and the *mystère* declined against the continuing popularity of the morality and farce. In 1548, the first fixed theatre, the Hôtel de Bourgogne, was built for the Confrérie de la Passion which had the monopoly for staging religious plays in Paris. The same year, the performance of sacred *mystères* was banned in the capital, and thereafter the Confrérie leased out its premises to other companies, notably to the Comédiens du Roi at the end of the century when the climate was more favourable to the development of modern drama.

Humanist drama

But theatre was no more immune to change than other literary genres. The early Humanists rediscovered the playwrights of antiquity and tragedy first made its appearance in Latin. Erasmus included it in his interests and George Buchanan (1506–82), the Humanist scholar and teacher, made versions of *Médée* (1544) and *Alceste* (1556) before composing two Latin tragedies of his own. *Jephthé* (1544) and *Baptista* (1577) were based on Biblical subjects and drew on the practice of Euripides and Seneca and the theories of Aristotle. Marc-Antoine Muret (1526–85), who taught at the Collège de Boncourt from about 1550, published *Julius Caesar* in 1552. The subject was adapted from Plutarch and the structure (five acts and chorus) was modelled on Seneca. These Latin tragedies were not intended for public performance and remained within the confines of the Collèges, where they were sometimes staged by pupils: Montaigne recalls taking part at the age of twelve in productions at the Collège de Guyenne in Bordeaux. Even so, they marked an important step forward. They fired the imagination of a new generation and established two dramatic models, Greek and Latin, and two broad thematic areas: secular and classical, and religious and Biblical.

Growth of tragedy

Progress was accompanied by theoretical considerations, slowly at first, then with growing insistence. At the start of the century, a preface written by Josse Bade, printer of the works of Seneca, made use of Aristotle's *Poetics* and Horace's *Ars poetica*. But their principles had little impact even in the writings of Peletier du Mans and Du Bellay who, in his *Defense*, called upon French authors to restore dignity to comedy and tragedy which had been usurped by farce and the morality play. Meanwhile, tragedy defined itself by imitation of classical models and by the 1550s, the structure of five acts in verse leading to a climax was well established. Practice was codified by Jules-César Scaliger (1484–1558), whose posthumous *Poetices* (1561) would have a far-reaching effect on French classical theatre. Scaliger broadly commended the emerging pattern but insisted that the unities of time, place and action be observed, that *vraisemblance* be respected and in general that plays should conform to a regular model which corresponded to the prescriptions of both the ancients and the written *commedia erudita* of the Italian Renaissance. A similar position was adopted by Jean de la Taille (*c.*1533–1608) whose *Art de la tragédie* (1572) defended the five-act structure and the unities and made the subject of tragedy the noble but harrowing actions of the great: he called for 'de piteuses ruines . . . des inconstances de la fortune, larmes et misères extrêmes'.

Neo-classical tragedy

The birth of French neo-classical tragedy was signalled by the performance of Jodelle's *Cléopâtre captive* at the Collège de Boncourt in 1553. Though undramatic by later standards, it gave notice of what the genre would become: it offered a formal model (it was a verse play in five acts which respected the unities of time and place), took its subject from history, used only noble characters, and gave a moral and philosophical colour to Cléopâtre's decision to commit suicide. A number of authors, many with connections with Boncourt and the Pléiade, followed Jodelle's lead, like La Péruse with *Médée* (1556) and Jacques Grévin (1538–70) with *La Mort de César* (1561). The first tragedy on a modern subject was *La Soltane* (1561) by Gabriel Bounyn (1535–c.1586) which was set against events at the court of Suleiman the Magnificent. In Lausanne, *Abraham sacrifiant*, 'tragédie française', was performed in 1550 by the pupils of Théodore de Bèze (1519–1605), the eminent Protestant Humanist who had opted to join Calvin in Switzerland. Drawing less on classical models than upon the morality play, Bèze provides an early example of the propaganda play which would be taken up during the Wars of Religion. The first regular tragedy in French on a Christian theme was Rivaudeau's *Aman* (1566), which was based on the story of Esther.

These first halting steps show little concern for the main business of tragedy which is the irresistible power of fate. Static and lyrical, they are untheatrical and fail to engage the sympathies of the audience save at the level of words. In the decades which followed, the poetic character of tragedy in French remained pronounced and the accent falls less on action (minimal) and character (perfunctory) than on long monologues and commentaries delivered by a chorus. Authors continued to borrow from classical playwrights, while Protestant sympathizers exploited the genre for edifying or polemical purposes, taking their subjects from the Bible and their technique from Seneca (Jean de la Taille's *Saul le furieux*, 1572, and *Les Gabaonites*, 1576) or from a mixture of classical models and the French *mystère*, as in the *David* trilogy (1566) of Louis des Masures (c.1515–74).

Garnier

A significant advance, however, was made by Robert Garnier (1545–90), the most productive playwright of the Pléiade entourage. His early tragedies (*Porcie*, 1567; *Hippolite*, 1573; and *Cornélie*, 1574) reflect the inflated rhetoric and static nature of the genre. But *Marc-Antoine* (1578), *La Troade* (1579) and *Antigone* (1580) show a growing interest in character and dramatic action which culminates in *Les Juives* (1583), the best example of Renaissance tragedy. Garnier relates his subjects to topical concerns and draws parallels between dramatized events and the civil wars of France. He portrays tyrants who persecute the defenceless, praises kings who care for their subjects, and shows the sufferings of people in time of war. His versatility is evident in *Bradamante* (1582), based on Ariosto, the first tragicomedy written in French. This political dimension was also exploited by Pierre Matthieu (1563–1621) whose *Guisade* (1589) was written in support of the Catholic League. The only playwright to compete with Garnier was Antoine de Monchrétien (*c.*1575–1621) whose six tragedies were taken from classical sources, the Bible and, in *La Reine d'Écosse* (1601, 1604), recent history. His style is lyrical but lacking in dramatic tension and his achievement, though it marks a considerable advance on the dramatic practices of most of his predecessors, shows how far tragedy still was from its classical future.

Comedy

Comedy, perhaps because of the enduring success of farce, made an even slower start. Its earliest, Humanist stirrings were associated with the Collèges and its models were Plautus and Terence, and rarely the Greeks. The first French comedy, Jodelle's *Eugène* (1552), contained comic strokes drawn from the tradition of farce within a classical framework. The Boncourt stable and the Pléiade produced a number of comic plays – Belleau's *La Reconnue* (*c.*1563; publ. 1576) and Baïf's *Le Brave* (1567) and *L'Eunuque* (1573), the first adapted from Plautus and the second from Terence – of which Grévin's *La Trésorière* (1558) and *Les Ébahis* (1561) are the best examples. The first neatly works love and money into a love triangle and the second, also on the theme of love, develops character types (the amorous greybeard, the boastful soldier, the cunning lawyer) which would become fixtures in the landscape of French comic theatre.

At first, comedy was written in verse, but Jean de la Taille in *Les Corrivaux* (1560) and *Le Négromant* (1573) used prose, which quickly became standard. Although the most accomplished example is perhaps *Les Contents* (1584), on the ancient theme of the go-between, by

Odet de Turnèbe (1552–81), the most consistent comic writing is found in the nine comedies (1579–1611) of Pierre de Larivey (c.1540–1612). Not an original writer, Larivey adapted Italian originals, though there are traces of Plautus and Terence in his best play, *Les Esprits* (1579), the tale of a miser from which Molière may have borrowed for *L'Avare*. In the last decades of the century, a comedy normally consisted of a prologue, a love tangle and long speeches, and was probably intended to be read not seen, though there were performances in student milieus and small, court circles. This bookish quality plus the lack of contact with a live audience gave late Renaissance comedy its literate character. Its reliance on Italian models (the written *commedia erudita*) would inform many later developments, but it would also learn from the *commedia dell'arte*. After seasons in 1576 and 1588, a company of Italian actors settled permanently in Paris in 1600. Their energetic improvisation and reliance on fixed types (Pantaloon, Harlequin and so on) would bring a new dimension to accepted comic practice.

Literature during the Wars of Religion

Introduction

After the 'Affaire des Placards' of 1534–5, the divisions between the Protestant Reformation and orthodoxy deepened. The crown, increasingly sensitive to the threat of sedition, maintained its Gallican policy of resistance to the papacy (almost, in 1551, to the point of breaking with Rome). But at the same time it took strong measures to curb dissent, instituting a *chambre ardente* in 1547 and an index of forbidden books (1559) which formalized censorship as the combined responsibility of Church and state. Militant popes, the active role played by the crusading Jesuits (founded in 1540) and the inauguration of the Council of Trent (1545–63) hardened opposition to the heretical supporters of Luther and Calvin who, however, continued to recruit high-profile converts like Coligny and Condé and held a secret synod in Paris in 1559. Tension increased in 1560 with the failed attempt at Amboise by Protestant sympathizers to remove the young François II from the influence of the Catholic Guise family. At the Colloque de Poissy (1561), moderate Protestants and Catholics vainly sought a compromise, but the January edict of 1562, favourable to Protestants, was followed by the massacre of Protestant worshippers at Wassy.

The Wars of Religion

These events sparked a series of eight Wars of Religion which plunged France into civil conflict for nearly forty years. In the 1560s, the Chancellor, Michel de l'Hôpital, attempted in vain to reconcile the parties and after his resignation in 1568, the moderate, mainly Catholic *politiques* reacted against a policy of religious cleansing which threatened to destroy the nation. But moderation was regarded with suspicion by both sides. Pitched battles were fought and in 1572, on Saint-Bartholomew's Day, 1,500 Protestant nobles who had gathered in Paris for the wedding of Marguerite de Valois and Henri de Navarre, were slaughtered. In the week that followed a further 30,000 died in Paris and Protestant towns in the provinces: by the end of the century, the 2 million Protestant faithful of 1560 had dwindled to 1.25 million. In 1584, The Catholic 'Ligue', building on earlier extremist tendencies, set out to prevent what now seemed inevitable: the demise of the Catholic Valois dynasty and the accession of the Protestant Henri de Navarre to the throne of France.

Henri IV

Henri III, murdered in 1589, was duly succeeded by Henri de Navarre. In 1593 he took the mass, and established an uneasy peace after 1598 when he signed the Edict of Nantes which recognized, under strict conditions, the separate existence of the Calvinist religion. But few regarded him as the champion of tolerance which Voltaire would later see in him. Catholics suspected that his motives for converting were more political than religious and Huguenots felt betrayed. Although a truce had been imposed, the struggle was far from over. The ideological divide between the two faiths remained unbridgeable. For Protestants, Biblical teaching was superior to ecclesiastical tradition and they believed that salvation lay in faith. The Counter-Reformation stressed the importance of good works, insisted on doctrinal authority and defended the traditional Latin mass. These principles, together with measures designed to strengthen church discipline, were established by the articles of the Council of Trent which, however, were never officially received in France. At the States-General of 1614, Tridentine doctrine was formally rejected by the nobility and the bourgeoisie, despite the urging of the clergy.

Counter-Reformation

The Counter-Reformation was not a movement defined only by its opposition to the Reformation. It was rather a 'Catholic Reformation' or 'Renewal', an attempt to modernize the Church which was part of an older movement begun in the Middle Ages. It lasted beyond 1600 and would dominate the religious landscape of the seventeenth century through the work of reforming bishops and the rise of Jesuit education. Its insistence on uniformity and ecclesiastical discipline set it at odds with Jansenism and its greatest success was the revocation of the Edict of Nantes in 1685 which ended the toleration of Protestantism.

Literature

After the start of the Wars of Religion, in 1562, literature inevitably grew more committed. Protestant authors in verse and prose defended justification by faith, predestination, the role of the Church and the love of Christ. Catholic writers championed good works, the received wisdom of doctrine and the authority of the ecclesiastical hierarchy. But for all, the measured Humanism of the Pléiade was not enough and the ideal of *courtoisie* was also undermined by the new brutalized aristocracy, though Montaigne, for one, maintained his objectivity and anticipated the *honnêteté* of the classical age. But as the chaos deepened, literature grew less intellectual and more emotive in character. Argument gave way to vilification, satire turned vituperative, the language of love was replaced by images of violence and horror, and religious poets became obsessed with sin and death. The final decades of the century, dominated by the themes of the mutability of things, decay and metamorphosis, are indelibly marked by the spirit of the baroque.

Poetry

Despite the success of the Pléiade, neo-Latin poetry continued to thrive and, until the end of the century, a minority of writers continued to believe that posthumous fame would be denied to those who used the vernacular. Meanwhile, poets continued to produce didactic verse (the *sentence*) and moralizing works (sermons, satires, *discours*), and love poetry was well received at the Italianate court where the poem-sequence was still appreciated. But the major developments were in the 'scientific' epic and religious verse.

After the Pléiade

The influence of the Pléiade lasted several decades and is noticeable in the love poetry of Amadis Jamyn (?1540–93), one-time secretary to Ronsard who also inspired d'Aubignac's early lyrical collection, *Le Printemps* (*c*.1571–3; publ. 1874). None, however, matched the 'prince of poets', though in his lifetime Philippe Desportes (1546–1606) was better rewarded by Henri III and found more favour in the salon of the Maréchale de Retz. His neo-Petrarchist sonnets and *stances*, mostly written by 1573, wove elegant but self-conscious variations on the theme of love and the psychology of sentiment which link him, distantly, to the preciosity of the next century. His *Sonnets spirituels* (1577) dealt with religious themes and, after him, court poets like Jean Bertaut (1552–1611) worked a vein of silvery but sterile lyricism which may lack the fiery commitment of the Protestant baroque but in certain ways foreshadows the cooler voice of classical verse.

Poetry and religion

But from the middle of the century, lyrical poets had begun to look outside paganism to the Christian tradition for their inspiration, as in the *Cantique du premier avènement de Jésus-Christ* (1553) by Nicolas Denisot (1515–59), who adapted Pléiade objectives for spiritual purposes, or *La Christiade* (1559) by C. Babinot. After 1562, as anarchy grew, poetry turned increasingly to religious themes and subjects which were expressed in two major forms: the epic and the personal meditation.

Epic

Building on the example of Scève, Peletier du Mans and Baïf, Catholic poets wrote of creation, the greatness of God and the role of Christ and the saints in rescuing man from his sinful nature. In the *Encyclie des secrets de l'éternité* (1571), Lefèvre de la Boderie (1541–98) provided a 'scientific' account of the spiritual ascent of man from his beginnings to higher knowledge, and also set out the case for France's cultural superiority in his encyclopaedic *Galliade, ou la Révolution des arts* (1578–82). *Les Trois Livres des météores* (1585) by Isaac Habert (b. *c.*1560) was also a profession of orthodox faith expressed through the glory of God as it was reflected in His creation

But the best of the long scientifico-religious epics were produced by the Calvinist camp. *La Muse chrétienne* (1574) by Saluste du Bartas (1544–90) had harsh words for court versifiers who ignored the loftier vocation of poetry and wrote only of love. The same year, he published the first of his long religious poems, but became famous for *La Semaine* (1578), an epic which describes the seven days of creation in alexandrine couplets. An unfinished *Seconde semaine* was published in 1584. A polymathic compendium of existing knowledge, *La Semaine* is a structurally and stylistically uneven celebration of God's glory, though it reaches heights of rhetorical grandeur much admired by Goethe and Byron. But the greatest of the century's epic poems was *Les Tragiques*, in seven cantos, by Agrippa d'Aubigné (1552–1630). After a neo-Petrarchist debut, quickly repudiated, d'Aubigné became one of the most militant Huguenot apologists and a scourge of monarchs. Begun in 1577 and published in 1616, when it made little impact in the new age of Malherbe, *Les Tragiques* is a savage denunciation of the enemies of the Reformation and shows the triumph of the true faith over centuries of persecution, and ultimately of God over Satan. Sometimes speaking with the apocalyptic voice of an Old Testament prophet, at others sustaining a high level of dramatic vituperation aimed at tyrants and oppressors, d'Aubigné seizes the reader by the collar and never lets him go. His rhythms are strong, his images graphic and brutal, and his language low, elevated or vituperative according to his subject. Lyrical, bitterly satirical and, at the end, mystical, d'Aubigné's fiery poetry marks one of the high points of French baroque.

The personal meditation

A similar spirit marked a late revival of smaller-scaled devotional poetry which grew out of civil turmoil, Christian and particularly Calvinist faith, the neo-stoical current and the example of classical authors like Seneca, Epictetus and Cicero. The *Emblèmes* (1571) of the Calvinist Georgette de Montenay (b. 1540) inject a strong visual element into the didactic tradition and the *Sonnets spirituels* (1573) by Jacques de Billy (1535–81) use images of death and putrefaction to express the alienation of the soul from the world where all is vanity. Verse of infinitely superior quality was produced by Jean de Sponde (1557–94), a Huguenot who converted at the same time as Henri IV. His *Amours* (*c*.1598) and particularly a dozen sonnets on death have been compared with the best of the English Metaphysical poets. His sonnets are densely packed and intricately constructed but have an irresistible drive and a vitality which mirrors his confidence in the final victory of God over the world, the flesh and the devil. The baroque themes of life's transience, decay and the inevitability of horrible death are powerfully worked in *Le Mépris de la vie et consolation contre la mort* (1594), a sequence of 434 sonnets and short poems by Jean-Baptiste Chassignet (*c*.1570–*c*.1635). The gap which separates the vanity of appearance and the inevitable power of reality (*paraître* and *être*) is a recurring motif in this strongly rhythmic, graphic poetry which, for all the horrors of living, states its confidence in Christian salvation. Such is also the thrust of the several collections of Antoine Favre (1557–1624) and of Jean de la Ceppède (*c*.1548–1623), whose devotional sonnets (*Les Théorèmes*, 1613–21) reflect Counter-Reformation themes. By the time they appeared, such vivid, violent poetry, vibrant with extravagant conceits and lurid metaphor, had been challenged by the pre-classical taste for simplicity.

Prose

By 1550 the case for French as the language of prose had long been made. It was the language chosen to disseminate the results of the first experimental scientists, like the physician Ambroise Paré (1517–90: *Méthode de traiter les plaies faites par harquebutes*, 1545), the naturalist and traveller Pierre Belon (*c*.1517–64) and Bernard Palissy (*c*.1510–*c*.1590) whose *Recette véritable* (1563) established observation as the primary tool of his scientific investigation of anatomy, geology, architecture and astronomy. The emerging literature of travel, also rooted in observation, made extensive use of French, from the logbooks of the exploration of Quebec by Jacques Cartier (1491–1557) to the quarrel surrounding Villegagnon's failed attempt to establish a French colony in Brazil: *Les Singularités de la France antarctique* (1557) by the Catholic cosmographer André Thevet (1516–92) and the *Histoire d'un voyage en la terre du Brésil* (1578) by the Protestant Jean de Léry (1534–1613). These and other works, like the popular travels (1595) of Jacques de Villamont (*c.*1560–*c.*1625) in the Holy Land, laid the foundation of the *relation de voyage*.

Chronicles

French was thus associated with the reality of the world rather than with the abstract analysis of traditional learning. It graduated logically to history which began to lose its faith in legend and looked rather to documentary and other kinds of verifiable evidence. Étienne Pasquier (1529–1615) rewrote medieval history from official sources in his *Recherches de la France* (1560) and Claude Fauchet (1530–1602) used archive material for his work on ancient Gaul. Blaise de Monluc (*c.*1502–77) drew on his own active service for his military history, while Brantôme (*c.*1540–1614) used personal experience to paint a diverting if tendentious portrait of court life. After 1562, accounts of the times, often based on daily journal entries, provided, in varying degrees of reliability and objectivity, a kind of chronicle nearer to journalism than to traditional history. A vivid picture of France during the Wars of Religion emerges from the journals, memoirs and registers of d'Aubigné, Philippe Duplessis-Mornay (1549–1623) and Pierre de l'Estoile (1546–1611) who report on events and comment on the motives and character of those who made them. Latin, however, still in some quarters the vehicle of theology and philosophy, was the language of the fullest of these chronicles. Written by a Paris magistrate and covering the years 1543–1607, the *Historia sui temporis* of Jacques-Auguste de Thou (1553–1617) was published in 138 volumes between 1604 and 1627 and was not translated in its entirety until 1734.

Political writing

But French prose also gained strength as the medium for debating issues of the day. Anti-Italian feeling, prompted by the 'Machiavellian' court of the Valois, was articulated by Innocent Gentillet (d. *c.*1595) whose *Anti-Machiavel* (1576) also unleashed Protestant anger against the Saint Bartholomew's Day massacre which others, like Guy de Pibrac (*c.*1529–84), had no less pugnaciously justified. As the crisis deepened, political writing developed beyond satire and vituperative propaganda towards the beginning of political theory. In *Franco-Gallia* (1573; trans. 1574), François de Hotman (1524–90) argued that monarchy should be elective and constitutional. This view of popular sovereignty was contested by Jean Bodin (1530–96) who also rejected the Machiavellian model of royal absolutism. His *Six Livres de la République* (1576) defended the hereditary principle but proposed modest checks on monarchical power. Bodin also promoted an early form of natural religion and warned of the dangers of sorcery, generally perceived as a threat to society, but his major achievement was to have laid the basis of political science.

Pamphlet literature

Matters of faith and politics were raised, in an age which had no press, by a substantial pamphlet literature, in verse and prose, which ranged from the modest and mildly irreverent to the venomously polemical and incendiary. Little of it has survived the events which inspired the pamphleteers, but certain texts rise out of the mass. One example is d'Aubigné's *Confession catholique du sieur de Sancy* (1598–1600; publ. 1660) which shows no mercy for abjuring Protestants. But the most celebrated was the *Satire Ménippée* which was published in its definitive form in 1594. It reflects the spirit of the *politiques* of the 1570s and was collectively written in prose, with occasional verse, by six moderate Paris *bourgeois*. A series of monologues which ridicule the speeches given by the 'Ligueurs' (the 'zealous' Catholics) at the States-General of 1593, it mocks foreign influence, sets out the need for a clear distinction between temporal and spiritual governance and makes the case for the political peace promised by Henri IV. The inventive irony and the barbed wit, which operates on a variety of linguistic levels, set new standards of pointed, intelligent satire.

Prose narrative

Fiction was held in thrall by the proliferating *Amadis* cycle, and few long narratives independent of its endless ramifications were published before the end of the century. Translations of Italian romances and Spanish pastoral and sentimental tragicomedies satisfied demand for long periods. The French novel made little headway, though Béroalde de Verville (1558–1612) published a rambling romance, *Les Aventures de Floride* (1594–8), and the versatile d'Aubigné turned his hand to the picaresque, anti-papal *Aventures du baron de Faeneste* (publ. 1617–30).

But if long fiction stagnated, there was a lively vogue for *contes* and *nouvelles*. The tales of Marguerite de Navarre and Des Periers were first published in the 1550s and they found many imitators. A narrative framework was retained in some collections, but most authors published unconnected tales linked by mood and tone. Some drew on folk sources, others on foreign models and the treatment ranged from the bawdy to the pastoral. Noël du Fail (*c.*1521–91) published three collections of 'propos rustiques' (1547, 1548, 1585), probably drawn from his Breton youth, which mix a satirical, mildly scatological glimpse of rural life with nostalgia for lost country values. Among the most popular stories were the *Histoires tragiques* translated in 1559 from the Italian of Bandello by Pierre de Boaistuau (1517–66), an enthusiastic compiler and translator. The work was continued by François de Belleforest (1530–81), who supplied further marvels, monsters and melodramatic adventures, and by Raymond Poissenot (*c.*1558–*c.*1586) with his *Nouvelles histoires tragiques* (1586). The five tales of *Printemps* (1572) by Jacques Yver (1520–*c.*1571) reverted to the narrative framework of Marguerite de Navarre and in turn provided a model for Poissenot's *Esté* (1583). Relying heavily on translation and adaptation, such authors were in danger of surrendering to the anecdotal and the current fascination with ghosts, monsters and other 'unnatural' phenomena. This is the case with Étienne Tabourot (1549–90), author of *Bigarrures* (1583) and other collections, or the largely borrowed *Facétieuses journées* (1583) of Gabriel Chappuys. The three books of *Les Sérées* (1584–98) by Guillaume Bouchet (*c.*1514–94) are more structured, with narrators relating and commenting on stories on a variety of themes. It was a strategy also adopted by Nicolas de Cholières's *Neuf matinées* (1585) and *Après-dinées* (1587) which recycle similar satirical themes and materials without breaking new ground.

Moral reflection

Prose also emerged as the language of moral reflection which, after 1570, turned against earlier, positive readings of stoicism which had stressed man's ability to decide his destiny. A more sceptical generation of writers, forced to confront the current anarchy, turned to neo-stoicism as a means of managing human suffering. A new alliance was forged between faith and the stoic philosophers (Seneca, Epictetus and the Christian Boethius). The trend is evident in the

work of Juste Lipse (*De constantia*, 1583), Pierre de La Primaudaye
(1546–1619), Guillaume du Vair (1556–1621) and dramatists like
Garnier, who in various ways were attracted by the cardinal virtues
of the stoic ethic: courage, justice, wisdom, moderation and each
man's debt to the general. One of the most influential summaries of
the sceptical, neo-stoical view was compiled by Pierre Charron (1541–
1603), whose eclectic *De la sagesse* (1601) was reprinted some fifty
times by 1672. Learning is made subservient to practical wisdom
which locates ethics in a personal response to existential problems.
Charron borrowed freely from ancient and modern writers, but is
most indebted to Montaigne, who transcends the late Renaissance
concern with moral problems by treating the human condition with
a tolerant shrewdness which has not dated.

Montaigne

After receiving a Humanist education at the Collège de Guyenne in
Bordeaux, Michel de Montaigne (1533–92) studied law, served as a
magistrate in the city's *Parlement* for a dozen years and became its
mayor between 1581 and 1585. To the bustle of public life, however,
he preferred the peace of his study where he read, reflected and
composed the first two books of his *Essais* which appeared in 1580.
He was virtually unknown, though he had translated Raymond
Sebond's *Theologia naturalis* and, in 1571, edited a number of the
writings of his friend, the moralist Étienne de la Boétie (1530–63).
The *Essais* made little impact. But when, in 1588, a new edition
amplified the first two books and added a third, they were enthusiastically received. Thereafter, without adding new essays, Montaigne
continued to expand his text in the margins of a copy of the 1588
version and these accretions were incorporated into the posthumous
edition of 1595 where they added a quarter to the text previously
published. By comparing editions, scholars have been able to trace
the evolution of Montaigne's thinking.

At the outset, his interests lay in history, war and the lives of great
men. The first essays follow no clear order and are strong on illustra-
tive anecdotes and quotations. The tone is more impersonal than
it would later become, though it has a sceptical edge and assumes
the superiority of Catholicism over Protestantism which Montaigne
regarded as an error: it encouraged intellectual presumption and was
therefore a recipe for disorder and atheism. As this indicates, his

opposition was less theological or metaphysical than practical for, from the start, his primary concern was with man and his actions: why we behave as we do, how we should conduct ourselves and how we might judge well.

From compiling anecdotes and examples, Montaigne turned to the ills which threaten us and thence to seeking ways of overcoming them. His neo-stoic phase lasted until about 1576 when he conceded that we are at the mercy of passion, imagination, reason and pride which erect barriers between us and truth. We cannot know God, penetrate the mysteries of nature or understand man in relation to himself and others. But human will is too weak and human nature too strong to allow us to rise above the self, and stoical austerity was therefore no answer. Man is 'ondoyant et divers', a mixture of virtues, vices and variable motivations. Yet while our inconsistencies cannot be defended, they are nevertheless part of our human frailty and must be taken into account. In his most sustained piece of systematic argument, the 'Apologie de Raymond Sebond' (II, 12), Montaigne turned away from dogmatic philosophy towards Socrates and Pyrrho who avoided final judgements and replaced theoretical Reason by a more practical Reasonableness. It was a position which undermined both Protestantism and modern stoical Humanism.

His question 'Que sais-je?' was not a confession of impotence but an acknowledgement of the mutability of things and the multiplicity of paths human beings choose in their search for happiness. He noted that the untutored (animals, beggars, savages) are most contented when they follow their inclinations. It followed that the body, appetite, most emotions, common sense and judgement are all ingredients of the happiness we seek, while imagination and abstract reasoning lead to fear, unsatisfied desire, avarice, presumption (pride) and *gloire* (our awareness of the opinion of others). To acknowledge our less noble parts is therefore the beginning of wisdom, though instinctive behaviour alone is insufficient as a guide. If Reason which defines, orders and categorizes is a source of anxiety, Judgement enables us to control our impulses. Judging well means being not so much rational as reasonable. It means taking nothing on authority, regarding doctrine as borrowed truth, accepting the power of chance and fortune, and enlisting the support of diversion, custom and habit, so that instead of teaching men how to die, philosophy will teach them how to live.

Montaigne's rejection, through doubt, of theoretical reason led him to set the highest value on lived reality. The great test came in 1578 when he suffered the first major attack of the kidney stone to which he remained a martyr for the rest of his life. He turned against strategies designed to arm us against future ills and concluded that positive lessons may be drawn from adversity. Experience is the best educator and from it Montaigne derived his title. His *essais* are not 'essays' but tests and trials of his judgement. In taking himself as 'theme and subject' he did not project himself as an exemplary case but developed a method of critical self-scrutiny of which all are capable.

By 1580, Montaigne had turned the *essai* into a form and a method of self-exploration and self-portrayal. Thereafter, contact with others (through travel and in his work as mayor of Bordeaux) helped release him from the confines of his self and made him aware of the common denominators which make the social experience a part of the business of living. His individualism broadened as he acquired a sense of human solidarity. Thus the word 'vulgar' ceases to mean a class of people but a state of mind: he observed goodness to be most common among the humble while the clever and the privileged are not more virtuous because they are educated and rich.

But his priorities did not change. His ideas were less important than his approach to thinking, and his 'philosophy' was, at root, a set of mental attitudes: a mistrust of vanity and ambition, a constant effort to master the self which must remain free to develop and judge. His goal was the 'resjouissance' which brings satisfactions beyond the reach of material things. In religion, he preferred the weight of Church tradition to Protestant rationalism and populism, though he was no Christian apologist. He accepted that God is unknowable and the *Essais* raise no issues of belief and deal only with the problems faced by God's creation: Man. In politics, his conservatism is no less evident. Governments provide stability and order but they invariably interfere in the lives of individuals, rarely for the better. Indeed, Montaigne doubted whether politics could improve the inner lives of the governed, though he observed democratic rule to be the most equitable of systems. On the other hand, he believed that the sound judgement of which all men are capable but rarely display could be fostered by education. Unlike Rabelais, who preferred a 'tête bien remplie', Montaigne favoured a 'tête bien faite'. He set learning by doing above learning by rote as a means of establishing the primacy of experience, of developing judgement and promoting the basics of his ambition for all men which was to 'vivre à propos'.

Though Montaigne's ideas are unsystematized, he claimed: 'Mon livre est toujours un.' The *Essais* may not follow a carefully structured argument yet they are unified by the continuum of Montaigne's evolving personality. As he grew older, he spoke increasingly of himself, recording his noblest thoughts but also speaking freely of his less admirable but no less revealing personality. More interested in learning about himself than in teaching others, Montaigne, invariably stimulating and regularly self-mocking, draws us good-humouredly into illuminations of ourselves.

Montaigne is the most accessible of philosophers. 'Je parle au papier', he said, 'comme je parle au premier que je rencontre.' His choice of this intimate register is consistent with his preference for nature over art. It was logical that just as he mistrusted borrowed truth and rational categories, so he should dispense with the rules of formal rhetoric and adopt the tone of relaxed conversation. He moves constantly from the general to the concrete and to what is common to writer and reader. If he inserts quotations, he did not intend them to confirm his arguments by reference to authority, but to start a train of thought, like the many anecdotes which are offered as material on which our judgement may be tested. The *Essais* speak with one voice, that of an applied moralist whose honest self-scrutiny placed the *moi* at the heart of man's attempts to come to terms with himself and the world.

Conclusion

Montaigne's sceptical resistance to ideologies is symptomatic of the uncertainties of the last third of the century which could no longer share the confidence and optimism of the early Humanists, Rabelais and the Pléiade. Intellectual positions which had seemed unassailable (from the authority of Latin and the ancients to the truths of revealed religion) were questioned. As the boundaries of the known retreated, so the knowable expanded and knowledge itself became problematic. The dominant role of faith as the ultimate certainty was challenged by a growing awareness that ideas can come from within man, from his senses and his imagination. Nature was, of course, the handiwork of God. But nature was observable and those who observed it saw that it operated according to consistent laws which, though divine in origin, were open to human understanding. Naturalists who classified plants, geologists who grouped minerals, physicians who used tourniquets, and alchemists and necromancers who meddled with the elements of the created world, all took heart from the predictability of natural phenomena.

If their contribution to philosophy and science was modest, they nevertheless generated durable attitudes, not least of which was a new conception of nature and of man's place in it. To know the observable world meant judging well, and judging was an effect of comparison. A new relativism set the Now against the Then of the classical world and helped define a clearer concept of France and Frenchness. Comparisons of the Here with the There of new worlds provided a means of measuring the present against a Golden Age which, it was believed, had once existed in the past and, it was dimly seen, could be rebuilt in a distant future. But the comparatist mode of thinking also throve on contradiction. If literature, ideas and even the French language triumphed, they did so on the back of foreign influences ancient and modern. If the court, glory and women were revered, they were also derided and the wisdom of fools was used to mock the understanding of the wise. But such inconsistencies, left unresolved, started the taste for paradox and irony which is not the least of the century's legacies.

But the greatest of the achievements of the Renaissance were artistic and literary. It set the ground rules for French poetry, marked the beginnings of classical theatre and presided over the emergence of individualistic authors with distinctive personalities. The general broadening of ideas and the growth of an educated reading public widened the remit of literature, redefined the relationship between writer and both religion and antiquity, and gave a new importance to personal and collective experience. Sharpened on the social and political realities of a world which grew more threatening, literature processed knowledge and made it a guide to living. But if the century ended with a belief in Man's ability to change that world, there was as yet only a faint awareness that it is not Man who moves things on, but men, each in his hour.

3

The Classical Age

In the aftermath of the Wars of Religion, strong centralized monarchy slowly emerged as the best safeguard against the ambitions of the old feudal aristocracy and the threat posed by religious factions. The fragile peace achieved by Henri IV was consolidated by two royal ministers, Cardinal Richelieu (1585–1642) and his successor, Cardinal Mazarin (1602–61). The first kept Catholics favourable to Spain in check and forced the Protestants to surrender important privileges in the wake of the siege of La Rochelle in 1628. After the death of Louis XIII in 1643, Mazarin faced a sterner challenge from both the *parlements*, which sought to limit the fiscal powers of the crown, and the nobility which opposed royal absolutism and now attempted to regain its political independence which had been trimmed by Richelieu. The civil wars of the Fronde (1648–53) resulted in a victory for the monarchy which was thereafter secure. Louis XIV (1638–1715) did not replace Mazarin and from 1661 ruled as absolute king of a modern, centralized state incarnate in his person. He governed not through the nobility or the *parlements* but directly, through strong but subordinate ministers like Colbert (1619–83) and Louvois (1641–91), and he suffered no opposition. The Gallican party in the Church supported him, he ended the toleration of Protestants by revoking the Edict of Nantes in 1685 and, especially after the court moved to Versailles in 1682, he finally broke the aristocracy. The warring noble turned into a courtier dependent on royal favour to the point where court life seemed in danger of choking on its ceremonial etiquette. During his last years, under the influence of Mme de Maintenon (1635–1718) whom he secretly married in 1683, he and the court turned devout and France embarked on a series of disastrous

European wars which emptied the state coffers and laid up debts which would fall dramatically due in 1789.

The Fronde is a useful point of reference, for in broad terms it marks a watershed between the first turbulent half century and the less ebullient, more disciplined decades which followed. The consolidation of royal power is reflected in the growing centralization of culture which was progressively absorbed into a new uniformity and acquired a higher status as a symbol of the greatness of the Sun King. Just as the palace of Versailles was the visible emblem of his power, so art, literature, even the French language, advertised the *grandeur* of his reign.

Writers and Their Public

The growing concentration of power and influence made the culture of the new age a centripetal phenomenon. Paris eclipsed provincial centres of learning, like Lyons, and literature was increasingly managed by the crown which controlled the number of authorized printers, issued *permissions* to publish and claimed for itself the censorship role of both the *parlement* and the Sorbonne. The vast majority of the king's subjects had no access to books, disenfranchised by illiteracy, economics and linguistic variations which meant that even late in the century Parisian travellers encountered communication problems south of the Loire and even in Normandy. Yet though Paris had a population of about half a million, its market for culture was small. Rarely were more than 1,000 or 1,500 copies of a book printed and by 1700 the combined audience of the capital's theatres was somewhere between 10,000 and 17,000.

Rewards and favour

If the reading public was too restricted to support authorship as a profession, writers also faced other problems. When poets and novelists sold a book, the publisher acquired perpetual copyright and further payments for new editions were rarely made. Plays were bought by theatre companies along with the monopoly of performing them, and theatre managers were reluctant to allow them to be printed and thus made available free of charge to rival troupes: the Hôtel de Bourgogne authorized Alexandre Hardy to publish only 34 of the

600 plays he claimed to have written. But if publication continued to bring small rewards (though some, like Corneille, were able to make money in the theatre), other sources of income became available. Throughout the century, the Church effectively subsidized many writers who accepted livings without necessarily discharging the duties which went with them. If Henri IV despised authors and Louis XIII on the whole preferred hunting, official attitudes grew more encouraging. By the 1630s, writers began to appear in a more favourable light and rewards were given to those who served the right causes. Richelieu discovered their usefulness to the crown, Mazarin recompensed those who defended the independence of the monarchy, and Louis XIV viewed the artist as a jewel in his crown and was appropriately generous. Princes of the blood and the aristocracy, anxious not to be outdone, emerged as important patrons as did, after the Fronde, a new breed of financiers eager to acquire the trappings of nobility. The award of royal pensions and gratifications, institutionalized in 1663, together with an increase in court appointments (as secretary, *gentilhomme ordinaire*, royal historiographer and so on) not only supplemented earnings from authorship but enhanced authorship itself. If Montaigne had feared to be mistaken for an author who wrote for money, writing as such became socially respectable and posed no such problems for those with private means, such as Descartes and Pascal.

As the century progressed, nobles like Voiture, La Calprenède and La Rochefoucauld felt able to commit their thoughts to print without staining their honour as gentlemen by stooping to the 'métier d'écrivain'. Even so, the distinction between the aristocrat who wrote for his own amusement and the author who published for money was strictly maintained. Racine was ennobled, but he was given to understand that his blood had not become blue overnight, and Boileau was beaten by footpads hired by his social superiors to whom he had given offence.

The status of authors

But if their collective image improved, writers, despite their educated, middle-class backgrounds, remained at most a kind of superior servant in a hierarchized system which exacted a heavy price. Patronage ran the risk of creating a literature written to order, intended to please a paymaster or at least not to offend him. Royal patronage posed an even greater danger, that of making literature an arm of government. No less significant in determining the focus of literature was its appropriation by polite society as a fashionable occupation. Following the lead given by the *salonnières* of the late Renaissance, informal groups met in private houses to discuss books and ideas. Out of these 'academies' grew two kinds of influence, one official and male, the other unofficial and dominated by women.

The socialization of literature

To exploit intellectual effort for the benefit of the nation, a number of publicly funded bodies were established, the most important being the Académie Française (1635), charged with overseeing linguistic and literary standards, and the Académie des Sciences (1666) which encouraged and publicized scientific enquiry. But the salons of the Marquise de Rambouillet, Mme de la Sablière and the Marquise de Sablé, each with its own identity, proved no less authoritative in defining taste, the ultimate measure by which art of all kinds was judged. By linking literature to salon conversation, they gave a high profile to forms of writing which reflected the vogue for urbane spoken discourse. Eloquence and oratory (the sermon, *éloge* and the funeral oration) were judged as much by style as content, while the *dialogue, discours, entretien, conversation* and *lettre* were a preferred choice for writers who developed didactic or polemical ideas. These ranged from the *Lettres* of Guez de Balzac on good style which began appearing in 1624, through the *Lettres provinciales* (1656–7) in which Pascal defended the Jansenists, to the *entretien* used by Malebranche and Fontenelle to express ideas in accessible form, and the moral but increasingly political *dialogue des morts*. The portrait, which began as a salon amusement, developed into a major form of social satire and found its way into fiction, which also reflected the epistolary habits of a society committed to correspondence. Private letters were written with an eye to their limited circulation within a group of like minds, and journals and diaries recorded life in salon and court circles. Those who aspired to acquire the manners of refined society could turn to the many manuals which taught the art of conversation, correspondence and *civilité* in general.

Taste

The modernization of literature proceeded slowly to 1630, then gained momentum until 1660, when it dominated the landscape unchallenged for two decades before a more restive generation caused cracks to appear in the smooth façade of classicism. Along the way, it absorbed a number of more popular, or at least less regimented elements. Theatre, which had begun as a popular amusement, became a fashionable entertainment, and the novel, which had few antecedents in the ancient literatures, was preferred by many noble and bourgeois readers to the high culture and Latin tomes of learned authors. The scholarly Humanists of 1600 had not been concerned with amusing the reader – a duty now imposed on authors by a sophisticated society which refused to be bored. Outside the court, nobles were more interested in war, hunting and *galanterie* than in books and wore their ignorance defiantly. But under Louis XIII, they began to acquire softer manners and even Henri IV's brash *méridionaux* who continued to serve the monarchy were gradually 'dégasconnés', though there were no aristocrats in the group which founded the Académie Française in 1635. Between 1620 and 1640, the influence of the aristocratic Hôtel de Rambouillet on manners and genteel literary exchanges laid the basis for the new taste which, after the Fronde, was also taken up in middle-class salons where discussion centred on the casuistry of love and the appropriateness of language. That this was so was in no small part due to the influence of preciosity.

Preciosity

In the early decades of the century, a conscious effort was made to refine language and literature as means of countering the coarseness of society after a generation of civil war. The salons encouraged verse and prose which were light rather than profound, and set a higher value on technique than on genuine feeling and experience. Taking their lead from Malherbe, they insisted on 'correct' usage, banned 'impure' words and expressions and established a linguistic code which opposed both the dullness of learned discourse and the extravagance of the baroque poets. Between the end of the Fronde and the beginning of the personal rule of Louis XIV, preciosity was a major force in shaping the language and forms of French culture. The new taste was defined by the leading salons and their mostly male devotees and correspondents before and after the Fronde. But in the 1650s, the movement, widely regarded as an in-group, attracted hostile comment and salon women were directly targeted. The over-refined *précieuses* were regularly satirized as bluestockinged prudes whose taste, like their language, was pure affectation. In reality, their impact on language, literary modes and cultural preoccupations was profound and enduring. Their interest in the reform of family and marital law raised the status of women, who were emboldened to take up their pens. The old *querelle des femmes*, conducted mainly by reference to historical or legal authority and 'galleries' of women famous and infamous, continued to about 1650. But writings of this kind, such as Alexis Trousset's *Alphabet de l'imperfection et malices des femmes* (1617), were overtaken by a more modern view of women. Montaigne's adopted daughter, Marie de Gournay (c.1566–1645), moved the argument forward by raising the question of the education of women (*Égalité des hommes et des femmes*, 1622), a position developed later in the 1670s by Poulain de la Barre (1647–1723) who used a Cartesian argument to support his view of 'woman' as a social construct capable of being changed.

The *Précieuses*

A number of high-ranking women, like the Duchesse de Montpensier, the Duchesse de Chevreuse and the Duchesse de Longueville, played courageous, if sometimes irresponsible roles in the Fronde. But the influence of women continued to be felt most clearly through their domination of literature and taste. The immense success of the novels of Mademoiselle de Scudéry gave a high profile to the analysis of feeling and made psychological realism a major concern of fiction, long and short. Although the salons continued to function as testing-grounds for new attitudes and collective ventures, preciosity declined after 1661, when the court and the king emerged as the ultimate arbiters of taste: in 1670, no one dared applaud *Le Bourgeois Gentilhomme* until it was observed that Louis's reaction was favourable. But authors, however dismissive of the *précieuses*, remained permanently marked by the need to respect the new codes which they had made socially dominant.

The evolution of taste

The residue of vulgarity which had given Régnier, Sorel and Scarron a place beside Malherbe, d'Urfé and the decorous writers of the salon côteries, did not endure much beyond Furetière's *Roman bourgeois* (1665). By then it was clear that the public of aspiring authors was the 'nobles esprits' and the 'honnêtes gens' of court and town.

Occasionally, they spoke in prefaces of 'le peuple', an ambiguous term which designated a non-noble public which excluded the populace who, at best, were restricted to the wares of the *Bibliothèque bleue* and the theatrical entertainments of the Foire Saint-Laurent in winter and the Foire Saint-Germain in summer. The Pléiade's learned audience disappeared with the decline of readers bilingual in French and Latin and in the 1660s authors complained of the court's hostility to learning, which it dismissed as 'pedantry'. But their options were limited. Bound by patronage and hopes of preferment, and wary of upsetting the authorities – Vanini was burned alive in 1619 for impiety, Théophile was jailed in 1622 for his free-thinking and Claude le Petit went to the stake in 1662 for *Le Bordel des muses* – they were also obliged to respect the values of their public. Their audience was no longer captive but free to choose from an expanded range of literary productions. And since readers and audiences did not always abide by the high cultural values they claimed to revere (Molière's comédie-ballet *Les Fâcheux* was often performed at the court which never asked to see *Le Misanthrope*), authors began to grapple with the very modern problem of interesting a public and winning an audience. 'Notre premier but est de plaire à la cour et au peuple', observed Corneille, a view shared by both Molière, who considered that his prime object was to 'plaire', and Racine: 'La principale règle est de plaire et de toucher.' But pleasing the public meant negotiating a way through a complex framework of moral, social and aesthetic precepts.

The Elaboration of the Classical Ideal

The exuberant imagination and style of the post-Pléiade generation maintained a hold on poets and playwrights until the 1630s and is detectable until the 1660s. The doubt, anxiety and violence of the baroque poets were expressed in adventurous lyrical forms and brilliant, mannered imagery, while tragedy and the newly popular tragicomedy offered horror, illusion and paradox.

Malherbe

But there was a positive reaction to the order and discipline recommended by François de Malherbe (1555–1628), the reformer of poetry and pioneer of the classical ideal. With his authority as official court poet, Malherbe spoke against the 'extravagance' of Ronsard and Desportes, and set technique above inspiration, and control above imagination. Though he published relatively little, his ideas were publicized by friends and disciples (Honorat de Racan, 1589–1670; Pierre Deimier, 1570–1618; and François Mainard, 1582–1646) and taken up in influential salon circles by poets like Claude de Malleville (1597–1647) and Vincent Voiture (1597–1648). Malherbe's ideal of formal simplicity and soberer themes had gained wide currency by the 1620s and his principles would be further refined and developed by a series of commentators whose number and variety convey some idea of the range and urgency of the debate: La Ménardière (1610–63) and Jean-François Sarasin (1614–54) on tragedy in 1639, Vaugelas (1585–1650) on language (1647), the *Pratique du théâtre* (1657) by the *abbé* d'Aubignac (1604–76), the *Art poétique* (1658) of Guillaume Colletet (1598–1659), the *Traité de la beauté des ouvrages de l'esprit* (1659) by Pierre Nicole (1625–90), Corneille's *Discours* (1660), the *Réflexions sur la poétique de ce temps* (1675) by Nicolas Rapin (1621–87), René le Bossu (1631–80) on epic poetry (1675) and above all *L'Art poétique* published in 1674 by Nicolas Boileau (1636–1711), the fullest and most authoritative statement of the classical ideal culled from more than four decades of argument and practice.

The classical doctrine

Although Boileau self-deprecatingly called himself 'le législateur du Parnasse', classical doctrine was not formally established by law-givers but in most cases grew out of literary polemics and *querelles* which generated theoretical positions. Just as Malherbe had reacted against Desportes, so Chapelain's role as principal author of the critique of Corneille's *Le Cid* had more impact than his theoretical writings (like the *Lettre sur la règle des vingt-quatre heures*, 1630). Out of the controversy surrounding epic poems in the 1650s grew a new concept of the epic (but no readable epics) just as, a decade later, the *Tartuffe* affair set limits on dramatic expression and the rivalry between Corneille and Racine clarified the nature of modern tragedy.

The view that classicism, developed from older theorists like Scaliger, was imposed by *diktat* is therefore as false as the idea that it secured a clear-cut victory over the brash, irregular baroque. Not all Malherbe's supporters jettisoned the Pléiade poets and many of his opponents reacted positively to his stress on poetry as a craft. 'Regular' poets continued to indulge the monstrous and the bizarre and even when the battle seemed won baroque imagery continued to reverberate and loomed large in admonitory church oratory. The growth of classical taste proceeded by often bad-tempered debate and was imposed by a consensus which was as much social as literary.

Malherbe's call for the simplification of the language of cultural discourse met with a positive response. At court and in the salons, the new urbane fashion looked unfavourably on both *latiniseurs* and 'jargons' of all kinds, popular and erudite. Whereas the Pléiade had freely watered vocabulary and syntax, enlarging and expanding the expressive base of the vernacular, Malherbe, in his commentary of Desportes, sought clarity and simplicity through hard pruning. Archaisms, neologisms, regional and technical words were excluded and grammatical structures made simpler and more regular. The threat that the higher learning would grow remote from the concerns and capacities of polite society was thus removed and easy access was provided to literary and intellectual matters. Descartes's *Discours de la méthode* replaced scholastic jargon with a plainer, exact prose style and Pascal adopted forms of expression which owed nothing to the language of theology.

Language

Latin remained the language of both the schoolmen and scholars committed to the cosmopolitan 'republic of letters': Gassendi published nothing in French. But it was undermined by the growing use of the vernacular in Jesuit and Oratorian schools and by the efforts of lexicographers and grammarians to codify the French language. Latin–French inventories and *trésors* (Nicot, 1606; Monet, 1635) continued to appear, as did modern-language dictionaries, like Randle Cotgrave's *Dictionary of the French and English Tongues* (1611). But Ménage's *Origines de la langue française* (1650) branched out into etymology, and the first monolingual dictionary was published by Richelet in 1680. Furetière's *Dictionnaire universel* (1690), which included technical terms, was followed by the *Dictionnaire des arts et sciences*, edited in 1694 by Thomas Corneille for the Académie Française, which in the same year published its own long-awaited dictionary.

Running in parallel with the disciplining of the lexicon, norms for written French were defined in numerous descriptive grammars. The *Grammaire générale et raisonnée* (1660) by Arnauld and Lancelot, known as the 'Grammaire de Port-Royal', was the first to analyse language through parts of speech. No less influential were linguistic commentators like Balzac, who defined written style as elegance and simplicity, or Vaugelas who, in his *Remarques sur la langue française* (1647), pronounced on 'correct' usage by reference to the 'plus saine partie' of the court and the best contemporary authors. Vaugelas's rulings were regarded as authoritative and his lead was followed by other linguistic adjudicators, like Ménage. But he also set standards for translation, still regarded as an essential apprenticeship for aspiring stylists. Other translators, like Perrot d'Ablancourt (1606–64), helped shape classical taste, and models of rhetoric were provided by eminent orators, like the lawyer Olivier Patru (1604–81) and churchmen like Bossuet. A spate of manuals, such as *De l'art de parler* (1675, 1688), known as the 'Rhétorique de Port-Royal', by Bernard Lamy (1640–1715), codified best practice. When the French Academy was founded in 1635, Nicolas Faret (1596–1646) had dared hope that the French language 'pourrait enfin succéder à la Latine, comme la Latine à la Grecque'. By the 1670s, it was widely believed that this momentous step had been taken.

The language of classicism

The triumph of order and discipline in language initiated by Malherbe and embraced by court and town is a central feature of classicism. It demanded conformity to agreed rules of syntax, cleansed the lexicon, and directed the spoken and written word towards abstractions which were judged best for the communication of universal truths. Progress, however, was not uniform, for writers and readers were aware of other registers. Scarron rewrote Virgil's *Aeneid* in low language, and his example was followed by d'Assoucy and Furetière. The language of La Fontaine was close to everyday reality and La Bruyère was no stranger to the current of burlesque which was also adopted by Boileau, the guardian of classical purity. In *Le Lutrin* (1674), he reversed the usual pattern by making his squabbling monks speak like epic heroes. But if the momentum of classicism was strong enough to absorb the *travesti*, it also naturalized foreign influences. The authority of Aristotle and Homer, Virgil and Horace was unchallenged until late in the century and the ancients were widely used as both source and model. But if England was ignored, Italy exerted a powerful influence on poetry and comedy, and Spain helped shape both theatre and fiction.

The result was a model of excellence which defined not only the language of culture but the nature and form of literature.

Principles and rules

Few challenged the view that poetry should be, as Rapin remarked, 'une leçon de bonnes moeurs pour le peuple'. But it was no less true, as he further observed, that 'la morale doit se rendre agréable pour être écoutée'. But pleasing did not mean surrendering to the imagination, a source of wild fancy irreconcilable with order, gravity and control, but imitating nature, the only sure route to universal truth. The poet uses his knowledge of love not to recall a personal experience but to show Love itself. If history gives us Alexander, a great man, tragedy delivers the essence of greatness. The role of reason is to seek out such general truths and establish the principles by which they are best rendered. 'On ne peut plaire sûrement que par les règles', warned Rapin, though the view that classical literature was rule-bound is not tenable. While poetic metre and fixed forms evolved according to Malherbe's doctrine, the rules remained, to some extent, flexible. Half of Molière's plays do not respect them and they were avoided by La Fontaine who worked in a genre, the fable, which was scorned by theorists. But most authors worked happily within the limits set by self-appointed arbiters of literary excellence and the requirements of the salons. *Bienséance* meant respecting the manners and outlook of modern audiences: the author who failed to observe the proprieties of rank among his characters could scarcely hope to preserve the dramatic illusion. *Vraisemblance* was indispensable since, as Boileau affirmed, 'L'esprit n'est point ému de ce qu'il ne croit pas'. To be *vraisemblable* meant respecting the prejudices of the public, though Corneille's definition of it also included the *vrai*, that is, what history asserted was true, however implausible it might appear to modern minds. The three unities required that the action of a play take place within one day, in one place and with no distracting sub-plots, and their point was to concentrate the drama and intensify its impact which, according to various definitions of Aristotelian catharsis, meant creating fear, pity, admiration and pathos.

Honnêteté

But pleasing audiences also meant avoiding monotony by varying the literary menu. Within classicism existed a constant drive to renew art, build on tradition and create new tastes. The hierarchy of fixed poetic forms was reinvigorated, new genres were developed to reflect the vogue for conversation and, above all, theatre and fiction prospered signally. But at all times literature was linked to the new social ideal of *honnêteté* which defined the author's ultimate public. Renaissance *courtoisie* had long ceased to be seasonable, though it was mediated for the seventeenth century through the example of Montaigne who rejected pedantry and set the standard for good conversation. The traditional ethic of valour, honour and military service was widened for the benefit of the new *noblesse de robe* (wealthy *bourgeois* ennobled by appointment to judicial office or by the purchase of titles sold by the crown as a means of generating revenue) who, before braving the salons, could acquaint themselves with good taste, wit, sound judgement, and lightly worn learning in any number of guides to *politesse*, from Faret's *L'Honnête Homme, ou l'art de plaire à la cour* (1630) to the *Nouveau traité de la civilité* (1671) by Antoine de Courtin (1626–85), the *Conversations* (1668) and *Discours* (1677) of Antoine-Gombaud de Méré (1607–84) and the *Réflexions sur la politesse des moeurs* (1698) by Morvan de Bellegarde (1648–1734). For authors, *honnêteté* meant respecting the taste of readers and spectators, a form of courtesy which called for self-criticism and the constant polishing recommended by Boileau before any work could be deemed worthy of being set before the public.

The Rise of Rationalism

Reason, invoked by the champions of classicism as the surest means of pursuing and identifying universal truths, was also used by others to question religious and philosophical traditions and advance the new scientific ideas. In 1600, despite the doctrinal disputes of the Reformation and the growth of scepticism, man's view of the world was still dominated by faith. By the death of Louis XIV, the growing secularization of thought would offer new ways of approaching the natural world and man's place in it.

Jesuits and Jansenists

By maintaining the independence of the crown from Rome, the French Church gave its support to absolute monarchy based on divine right. It broadly adopted the Gallican thesis set out in 1611 by Edmond Richer (1559–1660) who argued against the ecclesiastical hierarchy and for the view that the Church was a body whose ownership was shared by all its members. The Jesuits embraced the Counter-Reformation with enthusiasm, acquired considerable influence at court and developed a network of schools. Measures were taken to train the clergy and new religious orders were founded, some contemplative but others devoted to working in the world, like the Benedictine Maurists (1618), who produced scholars and historians, or the Oratorians (1611), whose educational initiatives rivalled those of the Jesuits. The Compagnie du Saint-Sacrement, founded in 1627 for the relief of the poor, acquired an odious reputation for its inquisitorial methods, but generally the new developments helped to spread the faith. The religious revival generated a large literature of devotional poetry, spiritual counsel, like the *Introduction à la vie dévote* (1609) of Saint François de Sales (1567–1622), and accessible works of theology based on Scripture and the patristic tradition which aimed at explaining doctrine to the faithful.

The state continued to be the active defender of the faith. Protestants were kept in check until finally, by revoking the Edict of Nantes in 1685, Louis XIV ordered the destruction of their churches and the forced conversion of such Huguenots as did not flee abroad. Heretics of all sorts were pursued, from intellectual atheists who overstepped the mark, to those involved in intermittent outbreaks of witchcraft which sent Urbain Grandier (1590–1634) to the stake at Loudun and produced an epidemic of denunciations of sorcery which Colbert restrained by law in 1682. But Catholicism itself was divided internally by two competing doctrines. The first derived from the Spanish Jesuit, Molina, who in 1588, had reacted against the Protestant view that man, innately sinful, can only be protected against his wickedness by strict obedience to God's commandments. He argued that human will can cooperate with divine grace which is available to all: salvation is determined by the willingness and ability of the believer to do good and avoid evil. The search for redemption through the will and 'sufficient grace' required both faith and tenacity, and Corneille's *Polyeucte* shows how it could lead to Christian heroism. Yet the Jesuits were accused of laxism, since intention alone could seem the test of salvation, an argument used by the cynical Tartuffe to cover his immorality. Their opponents, drawing on Saint Augustine, argued that man exercises his will for invariably selfish ends, that goodness is beyond his reach without the intervention of God's mercy which, however, extends grace to only a minority. Human destiny is determined by forces outside man's control, a view endorsed, in ways which have been variously interpreted, in the tragedies of Racine.

This counter-view was associated with the Augustinianism of Cornelius Jansen (1585–1638) who, with the abbé de Saint-Cyran (1581–1643), attacked Richelieu in 1635 for equating the interests of religion with those of the state. His posthumous Augustinus (1640) set out the new principles, which were identified with the abbey of Port-Royal, known for its austere discipline, the success of its 'petites écoles' (Racine was a pupil) and the brilliance of its scholars. Saint-Cyran, who became its spiritual adviser in 1635, was jailed and the Augustinus was condemned by the Pope in 1643. In 1653 five of its propositions were pronounced heretical. Jansen was defended by the most eminent Jansenists, Antoine Arnauld (1612–94), Pierre Nicole (1625–95) and Pascal, whose Lettres provinciales mockingly demolished the Jesuit case. Even so, Arnauld was dismissed from the Sorbonne and the clergy were required to sign a statement rejecting Jansenist doctrine. Many refused but Port-Royal continued to be supported by influential patrons at court. A compromise solution brought an uneasy peace in 1668. A decade later, Louis, who suspected Jansenism of republican leanings, renewed the attack and many of its leaders fled abroad to avoid persecution. Port-Royal was closed in 1709 and its buildings were razed in 1711. But a new controversy broke out in 1713 when 101 propositions made by Quesnel (1634–1719) in his Nouveau Testament en français avec des réflexions morales sur chaque verset (1692) were declared heretical by the Papal Bull, Unigenitus, which ensured that the argument continued into the Enlightenment.

These divisions raised issues with implications which went further than doctrinal feuding for they strayed into political territory. The Jesuits acquired influence at court, were identified with the rule of Louis XIV and attracted powerful intellects: the fullest statement of the absolutist principle in politics, the Politique tirée des propres paroles de l'Écriture sainte (1709), was made by one of the century's greatest historians and polemicists, Bossuet (1627–1704), bishop of Meaux. On the other hand, the Jansenists questioned absolutism, asserted the legitimacy of conscience and personal conviction (at least for themselves), and produced some of the finest minds and the most influential books of the age: the *Grammaire* (1660), *Logique* (1662) and *Rhétorique* (1675) of Port-Royal set the highest scholarly and intellectual standards. But Jesuits and Jansenists did not merely fight with each other but had also to contend with the spread of secular ideas.

The new science

The Renaissance search for truth in the writings of the ancients was perpetuated on many levels, not least in the theatre which broached modern problems through the mediation of Greek and Roman literature. Moralists who revived the figure of the pre-Christian sage began to separate morality from religion, and philosophers who built on lost truths recovered from antiquity stimulated scientific interest in the nature of the universe: Pierre Gassendi (1592–1655), borrowing from Epicurus, argued in favour of the atomic structure of matter but also, as an astronomer himself, responded positively to Copernicus, Tycho Brahe and Galileo. Although the proposition that the earth circled the sun met with hostility from the Church (Galileo was censured in 1616 and faced the Inquisition in 1632), mathematicians attempted to explain in rational terms what had been observed experimentally: Desargues and Pascal developed new geometries and Descartes and Fermat laid the basis of algebra. The idea that nature operates through physical laws was extended to other areas of enquiry. Although Harvey's discovery of the circulation of the blood (1628) was contested into the 1670s when 'anti-circulationist' theses were defended in the Faculty of Medicine, vivisection was performed on cats, the bodies of criminals were opened, and in 1667 a semi-public dissection of the corpse of a woman in the new Académie des Sciences, caused an outcry.

The *libertins*

New ideas were not welcomed by either Church or state and the *libertin* drew fire from both. In 1600, the term, derived from *libertinus*, a freed Roman slave, was applied pejoratively both to men who led immoral lives and to writers and thinkers who were indifferent or fractious in matters of faith. Examples of the first were numerous, and typified by the entourage of Louis XIII's brother, Gaston d'Orléans. But more significant were the philosophical sceptics. By the 1620s, they were associated with 'blasphemous' Italian writers implicated in the clandestine *Traité des trois imposteurs* (Moses, Christ, Muhammad) and were denounced for their dissoluteness and atheism by the Jesuit François Garasse (1585–1631) in 1623. His targets were poets like Théophile de Viau and Saint-Pavin (1595/1600–1670) and any who contradicted theological truth by rational argument. Not all *libertins* were atheists, though La Mothe le Vayer (1588–70) doubted that the order of the world was divine, as did Gabriel Naudé (1600–50). But all were committed to the principle of free intellectual enquiry and many, including Nicolas Peiresc (1580–1637), Gassendi, Marin Mersenne (1588–1648), and the physician Guy Patin (1601–72) were able to reconcile rational ideas with at least a tolerance for orthodox faith. Yet collectively, their *libertinage érudit* undermined the concept of an anthropomorphic God, Adam's sin, the immortality of the soul and the Resurrection, a 'miraculous' occurrence which defied the laws of reason. Their conclusions led to a pessimistic view of a world without direction, governed by chance, in which man was as base as any other creature.

Yet their defence of the spirit of free enquiry was to reach far beyond their discussions of the new astronomy, materialism and mechanistic philosophy. They are the link which connects the Humanism of the Renaissance to the *philosophie* of the Enlightenment. Their irreverence had a more immediate impact on literature and is detectable in the bawdy, sometimes obscene collective volumes (the *parnasses satiriques*) published in the 1620s, the sensual poetry of Théophile, the anti-religious verse attributed to Des Barreaux (1599–1673), the low-life realism of the *histoires comiques* of Sorel and Tristan l'Hermite, and the open contestation of Cyrano de Bergerac. But the challenge of scepticism, posed by Montaigne and reiterated by Du Vair and Charron, was met more effectively by the two greatest minds of the age who, though retaining a Christian world-view, laid the foundations of modern science and philosophy.

Descartes

René Descartes (1596–1650) answered Montaigne's question, 'Que sais-je?', by seeking a way of turning common sense ('la chose du monde la mieux partagée') into a process rooted in rigorous analysis of evidence. The *Discours de la méthode pour bien conduire sa raison et chercher la vérité dans les sciences* (1637) defines the proper use of reason, which begins with the only truth of which we can be certain, that we think, and, abandoning all previous knowledge, builds new ideas, rising from the simple to the complex. Stepping carefully from one certainty to the next, he described the planets as swirls (*tourbillons*) of matter in the cosmic sea of ether, and the human body as a mechanical assemblage of nerves and muscles directed by a soul which prompts reflex actions which we are able to control by acts of will. Neither using religion to justify its propositions nor denying faith, *Le Traité des passions* (1649) argued that if our will is free, it is so constituted that it seeks always the best, 'ce qui est parfaitement suivre la vertu'. Although Descartes's account of the universe was later overtaken by Newtonian gravity and his explanation of the physiological origin of the passions has long since been superseded, his influence was immense. In cultural terms, Cartesianism implied a new definition of literature as the imitation of life, not of ancient models, and directed attention towards the analysis of psychological states and moral dilemmas. His promotion of truths achieved by disinterested 'longues chaînes de raison' made received wisdom unreliable and the principle of authority suspect, so that even religious and political assumptions were opened up to critical examination by the end of the century.

Pascal

Descartes's aim was to make us masters of ourselves and of nature through the proper use of our mental faculties. Blaise Pascal (1623–62) similarly adopted an experimental approach to thinking, drawing his conclusions from observation rather than from established authority. But he doubted the Cartesian assertion that knowledge thus obtained is objective, since the result of any experiment is inevitably influenced by the input and assumptions of the experimenter. He chose, therefore, as his starting point the needs and nature of man. After his mystical conversion to Christianity in 1654, he defended Jansenism and attacked Jesuit laxism in the *Lettres provinciales* (1656), one of the finest polemical pamphlets written in French. In 1658, he began collecting notes and fragments for an apology of Christian faith but did not live long enough to organize them into a coherent whole. The form given to his *Pensées* by Port-Royal sympathizers in 1670 has many times been contested but by tradition subsequent editors have accepted a broad division into two parts: 'la misère de l'homme sans dieu' and 'la grandeur de l'homme avec dieu'. Pascal started from the premise that man's needs and nature must be placed in a spiritual context, since salvation is a problem which all must face. Man exists in a state of physical and moral wretchedness, overwhelmed by the infinitely great (the universe) and the infinitely small (its atomic structure), constantly misled by his own errors and weakness, and incapable of coming to terms with his inevitable death. Yet he is capable of *grandeur* through his capacity for reason, which yields many arguments to show that Christianity alone can explain the human condition and offer a solution to our anguish. To convince the *libertins* and the indifferent, Pascal used the illustration of belief as a safe wager. If there is no God, nothing has been lost. But if there is, the prize is salvation.

While Pascal aimed to show the reasonableness of faith, Descartes used reason to advance from the known to the unknown, though neither solved the problems posed by Montaigne's Pyrrhonism. However, both brought the debate into the public arena where their literary qualities were greatly admired. Opponents of Descartes were impressed by his clarity and Pascal's doctrinal opponents acknowledged the force of his irony, his persuasive gifts and his style. But while both were to exert enormous influence on future thinkers, their immediate impact lay less in convincing their fashionable public of the truth of their philosophical and scientific arguments than in making ideas accessible to the non-specialist public. In this, they contributed to the process by which secular reason widened the proper domain of literature.

Literature

Poetry

Poetry continued to be regarded as the nobler branch of rhetoric and the most prestigious form of literary expression. It was the only possible vehicle for epic, tragedy, serious comedy, devotional verse and formal satire, and it reached a wide audience in numerous collections by individual poets or groups of poets who expressed party and aesthetic affiliations. But the classical ideal progressively collectivized the poetic *moi*. The individual lyric voice of the Pléiade, like the urgent tones of the baroque, found no echo in the society verse of the century. Though such poetry had qualities – fluency, lightness of touch and formal control – it rarely escapes the narrow limits set upon it. Indeed, the century's best poetry is found not in its poets but in the tragedies of Corneille and Racine, the satires of Boileau and the fables of La Fontaine.

After the turn of the century, the themes and manner of the Renaissance poets proved too demanding for courtly tastes, which took readily to Malherbe's reform of language, versification and themes. As befitted a court poet, his own verse was largely ceremonial and lacked both originality and sincerity. But the example he set of well-made poetry appealed to 'regular' disciples like the even stricter Mainard or Racan who was at his best describing the countryside. The pastoral was taken up in the 1620s by a group known as the 'Illustres Bergers' (Colletet, Malleville, Ogier) who also applied the new poetics to devotional translation, the elegy and love poetry. Certain fixed forms survived but were made part of the literary exchanges which were at the centre of salon life. In 1638, two sonnets, by Benserade (1613–91) and Voiture, led to a minor literary argument which divided society into 'Jobistes' and 'Uranistes'. Like them, La Mesnardière, Pellisson, Sarasin and the *abbé* Cotin in a later generation were admired for carefully worked but empty *stances*, *énigmes* and madrigals which reflected the dominant ethos but were derided for their affected preciosity. Molière regularly mocked salon poets (Cotin was the model for Trissotin in *Les Femmes savantes*) and clearly shared Alceste's distaste for the insincere flummery which passed as poetry.

So strong was the decorous poetic mode that more serious kinds of poetry found only a limited audience. Although the epic was in theory the noblest of the genres, it enjoyed only modest favour. As France emerged from the Fronde, the genre, drawing less on Greek and Latin models, and ignoring the forgotten Ronsard's splendid failure, *La Franciade*, sought inspiration in Tasso rather than Homer to draw attention to France's religious tradition and past greatness. In the 1650s, Pierre le Moyne (*Saint-Louis*, 1653) set out to establish a new national Christian epic, an objective echoed by poets who drew on the Old Testament (as in Saint-Amant's heroic idyll, *Moïse sauvé*, 1653) and found heroes in France's historico-religious past: Chapelain (*La Pucelle*, 1655), Desmarets (*Clovis, ou la France chrétienne*, 1657) and the three epics devoted to Charlemagne by Le Laboureur (1664) and Nicolas Courtin (1666, 1687). Although the genre was codified in Le Bossu's *Traité du poème épique* (1675), it was honoured mainly in the breach. Boileau's famous line, 'Un sonnet sans défaut vaut seul un long poème', intended as a defence of the craft of poetry, did little to improve the image of the epic which was judged too learned, too earnest and too long.

Other initiatives which departed from the fashionable consensus met with a similar fate. Bolder forms were used by Théophile de Viau (1590–1626) to express more personal feelings and baroque anguish. An identifiable personality emerges from the even less 'regular' Tristan l'Hermite (*c*.1601–55) and from the varied output of Saint-Amant (1594–1661) who wrote in many moods, from the satirical to the gently pastoral, from brooding meditation to the macabre. After the 1630s, the reputation of the *libertin* poets collapsed under the weight of the new orthodoxy which kept idiosyncrasy and free thought out of poetry for a generation until their sensuality and intellectual independence were revived by La Fare (1644–1712) and the *abbé* de Chaulieu (1639–1720). To these freer spirits were preferred the salon poets who remained faithful to a narrow range of themes (decorous love, nature, and rhetorical but excessively deferential addresses to great persons and to Louis XIV in particular) and the predictable and interchangeable odes, elegies, *chansons*, eclogues, madrigals, *rondeaux*, *ballades*, *épîtres*, idylls, portraits, *prières*, *lettres* and *billets*. The most admired lyric poet was Madame des Houlières (1638–94), author of a tragedy, *Genséric*, and winner of the first poetry prize awarded by the Académie Française in 1671. Detached in tone even when in playful mood, she rarely rises above the formal thematic conventions, being fulsome in her praise for 'great Louis', attentive to nightingales and in poems like her epistle on gout ('Fille des plaisirs, triste goutte') vicariously sensitive to human decay. She too followed the fashion for ingenuity, concocting verses around rhyme-schemes supplied in advance (the *bouts rimés*) and rising to the challenge of producing poems built on 'difficult' rhymes in *-ouille, -ille* and *-aille*.

Sometimes ranked with the early *libertin* poets, Mathurin Régnier (1573–1613) was as revealing as a mirror of his times as d'Aubigné. He set out to restore the moral purpose of satire as exemplified by Horace, Juvenal and the Pléiade, and asserted his independence from the prescriptions of Malherbe: 'J'approuve que chacun écrive à sa façon.' Although a man of dissolute habits, Régnier was a cultured moralist. Yet his thirteen *Satyres* (1608–13) made little impact on the vogue for coarse vituperation which then passed for satire, from Sigogne (*c*.1560–1611) or Sonnet de Courval (*Satires contre les abus et désordres de la France*, 1622) to the several thousand *Mazarinades* which, during the Fronde, heaped abuse on France's much-hated first minister.

Boileau

Literary *querelles* and salon rivalries raised the tone but were generally stronger on venom than wit. It was left to Boileau to revive Régnier's view of satire as the public administration, in formal alexandrines, of strong medicine. For Boileau, reason and truth were moral imperatives and his *Satires* (1660–1708) move from the portrayal of modern life, through literary criticism (he defended Molière and mocked empty vessels like Chapelain) to a consideration of human folly and social abuses in more general terms. Reluctant to expose his limitations as a writer by tackling the 'great' genres, he was nevertheless a considerable stylist, capable of a wide range of tones. Passages from the *Satires*, together with his contributions to the *Chapelain décoiffé* and his satire of the heroic style in *Le Lutrin*, reveal a mastery of the burlesque, while his *Épîtres* (1670–83) cover moral and spiritual matters, topical subjects and literary concerns with admirable control of rhythm and verbal precision. To these qualities, *L'Art poétique* (1674), his definition of the classical ideal, adds a facility for striking formulations ('Ce que l'on conçoit bien s'énonce clairement') which would not be contested until the time of the Romantics.

La Fontaine

Jean de la Fontaine (1621–95) wrote for the theatre, in the epic vein and conformed to the taste for *galanterie* and mythology (*Adonis*, 1658) and allegorical narrative (*Les Amours de Psyché et de Cupidon*, 1669). More 'boldness' and 'licence' are detectable in the *Contes et nouvelles en vers* (1665–75) which reworked tales drawn from the tradition of both Italian (Ariosto, Boccaccio) and French (Marguerite de Navarre, Rabelais) bawdy. Though admired for their sprightly style, the *Contes* substituted an earthier 'nature' for the artificial *naturel* so admired in the salons. Judged immoral, they were banned in 1675. Less controversial and enthusiastically received were the twelve books of *Fables choisies mises en vers* published between 1668 and 1694. La Fontaine's originality lies less in his invention of new fables than in his treatment of tales freely borrowed from Aesop, Phaedrus and, occasionally, the Oriental tradition.

In his hands, the flat moralizing narrative becomes an economically staged drama enlivened by sharp dialogue and neat reversals. The mood ranges from the heroic to broad farce, from the burlesque to the lyrical cadence, but rarely loses contact with the cynical sententiousness in vogue in the 1660s. His animals and peasants behave according to type and inhabit a precarious world dominated by power against which prudence and a ready wit seem the best defence. Although apparently working within a popular tradition, La Fontaine confronts issues as grave as those raised by tragedy, and there is more cruelty and death in his fables than in the plays of Corneille and Racine combined. His insight into human drives and his meditation on the vanity of things make him the most lucid moralist of his century, and, with his teasing ironies, by far the most engaging. At a time when poetry was dominated by the systematic celebration of the reign of Louis XIV, La Fontaine showed the vulnerability of social consensus to the subversive power of human individuality.

Fiction

Whereas the major literary genres were codified by reference to ancient models, there were no rules for the novel, a form of writing without respectable classical precedents. Nor did it suffer from the prejudice against the imagination which, on the contrary, was its main attraction for its growing public which included minds as judicious as those of La Fontaine, Racine and even Pascal. Yet novelists refused to take full advantage of their freedom and yoked fiction to aesthetic and social trends. Though they had difficulties with *vraisemblance*, most accepted *bienséance*, used the language of 'court and town' and respected the unity of time which generated narrative strategies such as the intercalated story. They also avoided contemporary settings while at the same time ensuring that their characters and plots transparently reflected current preoccupations. Readers knew that Cyrus was Condé and Sappho Mademoiselle de Scudéry, and regarded fictionalized love dilemmas as extensions of their own salon talk.

The pastoral novel

Not all novels were so well-behaved. For example, the taste for the myths of chivalry was maintained by the continuing popularity of the *Amadis* saga until the 1630s. But a new tone was established by the culmination of the pastoral tradition, the unfinished *Astrée* (1607–27) by Honoré d'Urfé (1567–1625). Set in ancient Gaul among shepherds and shepherdesses who discuss their feelings rather than their sheep, it tells how Celadon is banished by his mistress, Astrée, who believes he has been unfaithful to her. Endless ramifications involve disguises, misunderstandings and perils which all centre upon the theme of love and its allied states (jealousy, timidity, pride) as a Neoplatonic route to spiritual virtue. Despite the publication of a number of pale reflections (e.g. Gomberville's *Carithée*, 1621, or Du Verdier's *La Diane françoise*, 1624) and related ventures such as Gombauld's allegorical-mythological *Endymion* (1624), d'Urfé had no successor. Yet *L'Astrée* set the mode and reflective dimension of fiction for two generations. It was the founding text, a source-book of situations, characters and themes as essential to novelists as Roman and Greek authors were to the tragic playwrights.

The heroic novel

The traditions of medieval romance did not disappear (the tireless Du Verdier compiled an immense anthology of them, *Le Roman des romans*, in 1628). But the heroic temper of the 1630s directed the novel away from the timeless abstractions of the pastoral towards livelier adventures in pseudo-historical settings. The multi-volume *Polexandre* (1619–37), by Gomberville (1600–74), unfolds in a vague past and moves implausibly from the land of the Aztecs to Senegal and from Copenhagen to the mysterious Île Inaccessible. The novels in ten or twelve volumes of La Calprenède (*c.*1610–63) (*Cassandre*, 1642–5; *Cléopâtre*, 1646–57; and the unfinished *Faramond*, 1661–70) mixed spectacular anachronism with opportunities for their heroes to achieve 'sublime' feats of courage and generosity. Madeleine de Scudéry (1608–1701: *Ibrahim, ou l'Illustre Bassa*, 1641; *Artamène, ou le Grand Cyrus*, 1649–53; *Clélie, histoire romaine*, 1654–60) filled up to 15,000 pages with kidnappings, duels and battles but also found space for psychological reflections, most famously the 'Carte du Tendre', a map which guides lovers to 'Tendre-sur-Estime' by way of the villages of 'Sincérité', 'Générosité', 'Respect' and the like. It is a graphic example of the new interest in the classification of affective states. But many such fictions were also taken to be *romans à clefs* and identifying 'models' was not the least part of the appeal of such fiction to their small but exclusive readership.

The *roman d'analyse*

Scudéry moved the focus of the novel away from adventure to interiority, and the predicaments and dilemmas of her characters were enthusiastically discussed in the salons. But the implausibility and anachronism of long fiction alienated readers after the Fronde. Mme de la Fayette observed that the Romans of history were a good deal less interested in love than Romans in novels, a point developed both by Segrais (1624–1701: preface to *Les Nouvelles françaises*, 1656–7) and Sorel (*De la connaissance des bons livres*, 1671) who sought to make fiction a more direct reflection of modern life.

By 1660, the multi-volume novel was unfashionable, the *nouvelle* had revived and authors turned to history not as a source of dramatic action (of which the Fronde had produced a surplus) but of moral reflection. The *abbé* de Saint-Réal (1639–92: *De l'usage de l'histoire*, 1667) argued that history should be less a record of events than an attempt to understand the motives of those who were responsible for them. Though his own novels (like *Don Carlos*, 1672) were not successful, his argument was supported by the growth in the 1660s of memoirs and correspondences, some authentic but others invented, which helped steer the novel towards the near-contemporary chronicle and thence to accounts of the private lives of great persons, usually on the theme of the 'désordre de l'amour'.

The distinction between fiction and reality was blurred. The *Lettres portugaises* (1669), a short epistolary novel showing death by unrequited love, is now attributed to Guilleragues (1628–85) but was in its time believed to be an authentic correspondence. Readers wrote in large numbers to the *Mercure galant* offering their thoughts on the moral issues raised by *La Princesse de Clèves* (1678), the most enduring of the century's novels. The other fictions of the Comtesse de la Fayette (1634–93: *La Princesse de Montpensier*, 1662; *Zayde*, 1670; *La Comtesse de Tende*, publ. 1724) exemplify the trend towards brevity, linear plots, and the intensity of lived experience. Madame de Clèves offers a dignified response to the temptation of adultery and her unostentatious struggle with her inner conflict made the novel the focus of a deepening interest in motive and behaviour. Absorbing the salon taste for portraits and maxims (notable by their absence in *L'Astrée*), La Fayette established the tradition of moral and psychological *analyse* which has remained a central preoccupation of French fiction. More immediately, by giving her sixteenth-century settings a palpably contemporary resonance, she encouraged readers to relate their own experience to the lives of her characters. This reaction stimulated an interest in historical novels and the *nouvelle galante*, written mainly by women in the last decades of the century – Mme de Villedieu (*c.*1640–83), Madame de la Force (*c.*1646–1724), the Présidente Ferrand (1657–1740), the Comtesse d'Aulnoy (*c.*1650–1705) and Madame de la Roche-Guilem (*c.*1644–1707) – though none equalled her lucid dissection of tormented hearts.

The *roman réaliste*

From the start, however, the dominant pastoral romance, with its allegorical and mythological offshoots, had been challenged by more realistic fictional modes, one tragic and the other comic. Both dealt with lesser personages in modern settings, offered more action and avoided the 'noble' style. The first, overtly didactic, is represented by the *Histoires tragiques de notre temps* (1614) by François de Rosset (*c.*1570–*c.*1619) or the thirty romances by Bishop Camus (1584–1652) whose titles (*L'Amphithéâtre sanglant, Les Spectacles d'horreur*, both 1630) clearly indicate his purpose: drawing on baroque sensationalism, he warned of the threat represented by profane love for the life of the spirit. The *histoire comique*, on the other hand, was essentially satirical. It set out to unmask the vices of the age at every level and, as in the Spanish picaresque novel and Rojas's *Celestina*, used an alternative cast of characters drawn from the populace, the middle classes, the acting profession and the disreputable nobility. *La Vraie Histoire comique de Francion* (1623) by Charles Sorel (*c.*1599–1674) set its hero at odds with a range of social types but rose above the current satirical mode, exemplified by Mareschal's *La Chrysolite* (1627) or Gougenot's *Roman de la fidèle Lucrine* (1634), by its imaginative manipulation of narrative conventions and styles, and its *libertin* sympathies. An early admirer of Cervantes's *Novelas ejemplares*, Sorel parodied the pastoral in *Le Berger extravagant* (1626) and remained an opponent of salon-approved fiction. Like Sorel, Paul Scarron (1610–60) set out to parody the fashionable novel, not to give a realistic portrait of society. His unfinished *Roman comique* (1651–7) relates the often farcical adventures of a company of travelling actors and their dealings with the local population of Le Mans which includes Ragotin, an undersized lawyer, who becomes the butt of physical and usually cruel practical jokes. Scarron's social satire is less marked than his burlesque of the heroic style which enabled him to rewrite tavern brawls as epic conflicts.

With the decline of heroic fiction, the *histoire comique* on which it depended, lost its point, and *Le Roman bourgeois* (1666) by Antoine Furetière (1619–88) went largely unremarked. Set in the Place Maubert in the lower reaches of the legal profession, it tells of the love of Nicodème for pretty Javotte. These 'anti-novelists' (to use Sorel's term) were aware that their descriptions of low life were of little interest to a polite readership but they remained in touch with mainstream tastes not only through their pastiches of recognizable targets but also in their promotion of the tales of Cervantes, a dominant figure in the growth of the *nouvelle*.

The philosophical novel

However, they failed to respond to the subversive possibilities of the Spanish picaresque, nor did they explore the fictional potential of ideas. The anonymous Huguenot utopia, *Le Royaume d'Antagnil* (1616), had few imitators, though Sorel projected *libertin* ideas into an ideal society in an episode of *Francion*. The boldest philosophical novelist was the versatile Cyrano de Bergerac (1619–55), a political polemicist with a reputation for atheism. *L'Autre Monde, ou États et empires de la lune* (1657) and the *États et empires du soleil* (1662) use extraterrestrial travel to subvert religion, defend the new astronomy, satirize society and promote relativism. Though intended to provoke, his mixture of progressive ideas and startling invention (Cyrano has an honoured place in the history of science fiction) was not followed. Ideas, however, crept into the nascent imaginary voyage which would be more enthusiastically adopted by the Enlightenment. With *La Terre australe connue* (1676), Gabriel Foigny (*c*.1630–92) described utopian social organization and broached natural religion. In *L'Histoire des Séverambes* (1677–9), Denis Veiras (d. *c*.1700) projected an alternative view of society: an elected ruler, state-owned property, religious tolerance, and an enlightened approach to marriage and education.

The *conte de fée*

Such developments were largely ignored in the numerous prescriptive and polemical writings on the novel published by Segrais and Saint-Réal, nor were they catered for in Boileau's attack on the *roman héroïque* (*Dialogue des héros de roman, c.*1666), Daniel Huet's *De l'origine des romans* (1670), which defended the modern novel, and Sorel's exposure of its weakness (1671). Nor did such authors rule on two other developments which, however, grew out of the tastes and concerns of the polite society for which they wrote. In the 1690s, the *conte de fée*, launched by Charles Perrault (1628–1703) and taken up notably by Madame de la Force and the Comtesse d'Aulnoy, though ostensibly intended for children, acquired sophisticated readers through their mixture of magic and morality.

First-person narrators

More far-reaching in its effects, however, was the renewed interest in brief lives and the private journal inherited from Renaissance models, the recollections of notable figures like Montluc, and the self-examination of Montaigne. The autobiography of Saint Teresa of Avila (trans. 1601) set the confessional tone which was followed, for example, by Jean-Joseph Surin (1600–65), one of the Loudun exorcists, who chronicled his spiritual odyssey from error to grace. Soldiers, like Bassompierre (1579–1646), recounted their exploits and many participants in public affairs, notably the Fronde, justified their role in events (Madame de Motteville, La Rochefoucauld). Travellers compiled journals and those placed close to the centres of power kept detailed diaries: from 1684, the Marquis de Dangeau (1638–1720) made a daily record of public happenings which was extensively used by the Duc de Saint-Simon (1675–1755). Relatively few such writings were published (some were banned) but many circulated in manuscript form and they helped to accustom readers to first-person narration and marked the modern beginnings of both biography and autobiography. By the mid-century, the old hagiography had been replaced by a secular equivalent and thereafter demand remained high for the lives of notables, writers and philosophers. Gassendi wrote his life of Peiresc (1641) in Latin, but French was used by, among many others, Baillet (*Vie de Descartes*, 1691), Madame de la Fayette in her account of Henrietta of England (publ. 1724), and by Grimarest in his *Vie de Molière* (1705).

Fictitious memoirs

Novelists exploited this trend by developing the semi-fictional memoir, initially as a form of burlesque. The first notable memoir-novel was *Francion* and its success, together with Théophile's *Fragments d'une histoire comique* (1623) and *Le Page disgracié* (1642–3), a brisk, picaresque account of his adventurous life by Tristan l'Hermite, helped to establish an interest in real, as opposed to imagined, lives. If Cyrano's first-person journeys to the moon and sun were highly fanciful, reality plays a stronger role in the autobiographical *Aventures* (1677) of his friend, d'Assoucy (1605–77). By 1660, novelists had begun to set fictional characters against historical personages (Madame de Villedieu's *Mémoires de la vie d'Henriette Sylvie de Molière*, 1672) and authentic settings (*La Princesse de Clèves*), but they also wrote the pseudo-memoirs of real persons. *L'Histoire amoureuse des Gaules* (1665) by Bussy-Rabutin (1618–93) was a *chronique scandaleuse* of life at court, a genre attempted by Courtilz de Sandras (1644–1712) before he moved on to writing the largely romanced lives of notable personalities, such as his *Mémoires de d'Artagnan* (1700). In the same way, Anthony Hamilton (*c*.1646–1720) mixed court chronicle and the army experience of his brother-in-law in the *Mémoires du Comte de Gramont* (1713).

These autobiographical romances and romanced (auto)biographies confirmed the move from public to private history, created a taste for authenticity underwritten by a measure of realism (as opposed to *vraisemblance*) and validated subjectivity against the standardized *moi*. The way had been opened for the exploration of a wider range of human experience and the creation of subtler and more complex characters.

Theatre

Of all the century's literary activities, drama grew most rapidly. Although plays continued to be staged in Latin in the new Collèges, theatre was still, in the first decades of the century, a popular entertainment provided by itinerant players who toured the provinces and made short-lived assaults on the capital. Crude farces were also performed at Paris's two permanent *foires* where they competed with acrobats, jugglers and the patter of quacks and charlatans. Yet by 1660, theatre had acquired permanent stages, authors, actors, a public, a hierarchy of genres, and was a profession, a respectable social recreation and an art.

The theatres

In 1600, Paris boasted only one fixed theatre, the Hôtel de Bourgogne. There Valleran le Comte attempted to establish his Comédiens du Roi. He staged plays by Hardy, launched Bruscambille, whose satirical prologues were published in 1610, and above all gave the public the 'trois farceurs': Turlupin (Henri Grand, d. 1637), Gautier-Garguille (Hugues Guéru, d. 1633) and Gros-Guillaume (Robert Guérin, d. 1634). But audiences were small and unpredictable and the building's owners, the Confrérie de la Passion, demanded a too-large share of the receipts for it to be economically viable. The premises were let to a succession of companies, including groups from England and Italy, until about 1624 when the actor Bellerose (Pierre le Messier) acquired a legal hold on its stage. He attracted the best actors and authors, and steadily purged its fare of crude farce and sensational tragicomedy. The Hôtel de Bourgogne became the home of tragedy and its actors (Floridor, Montfleury, La Champeslé) were acknowledged to be the most accomplished.

In 1631, a new company, led by Charles le Noir and Montdory (Guillaume Desgilbert), was permitted to set up in the Hôtel du Marais on the right bank of the Seine. Between 1634 and 1646, with Corneille as its star attraction and helped by ambitious productions involving complex stage machinery, it competed successfully with both the Hôtel de Bourgogne and the popular Italian actors who, in 1653, acquired a permanent base at the Petit Bourbon, near the Louvre. Richelieu, who took a keen interest in drama, included a theatre in the new Palais-Royal which he intended for Parisian audiences. In 1660, it became the permanent home of Molière. Thus in the 1660s, in addition to the *foire* and the Italians, Paris boasted three well-supported playhouses: the Hôtel de Bourgogne, where Racine made his name, the Marais, which specialized in lavish spectacles and 'machine' plays, and the Palais-Royal, where Molière staged his own comedies and works by other hands. Jean-Baptiste Lully (1632–87) acquired the monopoly of performing musical plays in 1672 and began performing operas (which he called 'tragédies en musique') at the Palais-Royal. After Molière's death, his company joined forces with the Marais at the Hôtel de Guénégaud. In 1680, a further reorganization, ordered by Louis XIV, merged the new company with the Hôtel de Bourgogne to create the Comédie Française. It was given a new theatre in 1689 and the company acquired a distinctly official character, with its actors now virtually employees of the state. Topical and satirical *parades* continued to be offered by the Italian actors who were licensed to use French in 1684. Expelled in 1697 for lampooning Madame de Maintenon, they were not recalled to Paris until 1716.

The players

In the public mind, actors and especially actresses (boys were not used for female roles) were dissolute by definition. They were regarded with suspicion by the Church who, in exceptional cases, refused them burial in consecrated ground. But with the growing refinement of theatre and the encouragement given to dramatists by Richelieu in the 1630s, actors became public personages who contributed significantly to the success or failure of their companies. Some created comic characters – the white-faced 'Jodelet' (Julien Bedeau, *c.*1595–1660), 'Sganarelle' (Molière), 'Crispin' (Belleroche, pseud. of Raymond Poisson, 1630–90) – or were associated with types developed from the *commedia dell'arte*, such as Arlequin, Pierrot and the immensely popular 'Scaramouche' (Tiberio Fiorelli, 1606–94). As their confidence grew, actors like Hauteroche (1617–1707), Montfleury (Antoine Jacob, 1639–85) and Baron (Michel Boyron, 1652–1729) turned their hand to writing plays. But in the 1690s, after Louis XIV turned pious, official and ecclesiastical attitudes hardened against them.

The staging of plays

The development of drama was not uninfluenced by basic practical considerations: an act of a play could not last longer than it took footlight candles to burn down. From the beginning, audiences were noisy and, to be heard, actors developed a strong, declamatory style of delivery which would later be attacked as 'unnatural' by critics and playwrights like Molière. Stages were small, and made smaller still by the spectators who paid the highest prices to sit on them, and were ill suited to the rumbustious nature of farce and tragicomedy. With time, comedy grew accordingly less physical and the noble immobility of actionless tragedy was to some extent conditioned by the cramped conditions in which it was performed. In the same way, the unity of place was established, in part, by the retreat from the *décor simultané* of tragicomedy (which enabled characters to move from the part of the stage that was 'Europe' to 'Africa' in two steps) to simplified sets which showed a single location, thus strengthening the dramatic illusion. The new style of theatre was cheaper to stage, satisfied the theorists, and enabled authors to concentrate the drama. But such refinements were also intended to please the changing audience.

Audiences

Initially, spectators were drawn mainly from the popular classes (pages, lackeys, soldiers) with a sprinkling of young bloods, professional men and even respectable *bourgeoises*. Theatres also attracted pickpockets and troublemakers. Louis XIII never went to the theatre (though he commanded royal performances at Fontainebleau of plays currently staged in Paris), nor in his time was it a venue for the aristocracy and the upper middle classes. In the 1620s, attempts were made to raise the tone. Plays grew less crude and spectators who carried weapons were not admitted. By 1630, the wide social mix began to change and thereafter the rising cost of admission together with the growing sophistication of drama ensured that by the time of Molière and Racine, the pit was filled, not with groundlings, but with writers, students, merchants and professional men, and the *loges* with prominent persons of both sexes. Playwrights were obliged to take account of the requirements of their changing public. For a while, in the 1630s, tragicomedy suited both the popular and the sophisticated audience. But later authors were forced to choose between them. For most the choice was simple, for a summons to play at court or in aristocratic houses brought significant rewards. Though Molière remained faithful to the pit, Racine chose the taste of the court and thus ensured that the popular interest in serious theatre declined further.

Tragicomedy

Inaugurated by Garnier in 1582, tragicomedy acquired a strong following by 1620 and dominated the Parisian stage in the 1630s and 1640s. A verse play of love and adventure, it was the theatrical equivalent of the heroic novel. Its complex plots turned on evil deeds, cruel tyrants and bitter family feuds, but the threat to life and love was resolved in the happy, or at least optimistic ending which distinguished it from tragedy.

Early tragicomedy ignored the new rules of drama, spread the action over many years and several continents, and exploited baroque horror to the hilt: in Alexandre Hardy's *Scédase*, a father pulls the corpses of his daughters from a well where they had been thrown after being raped in the previous act. Hardy (*c.*1572–1632), an actor employed as a playwright by various companies, dominated the Paris stage for the first two decades of the century with his violent, muscular theatricality. By the time of his death, however, his 'irregularity' had been challenged and a case was being made for *vraisemblance*, *bienséance* and the unities. In 1628, François Ogier prefaced Jean Schelandre's revised ten-act *Tyr et Sidon* (1608) with a spirited attack on the new ideas which was taken up in *La Généreuse Allemande* (1630) by André Mareschal (*c.*1603–50). But more frequent were expressions of support for regularity and greater discipline. Jean Mairet (1604–86) gave the lead with a pastoral tragicomedy, *La Sylvie* (perf. 1626) and his preface to *La Sylvanire* (1631) defended the unities. The new generation of playwrights attuned the tragicomic mode to the new rules – Pierre du Ryer (*c.*1600–58), Georges de Scudéry (1601–67), Boisrobert (1589–1662), Jean Rotrou (1609–50) – and even Corneille's *Le Cid* (1637) was at first deemed to be a tragicomedy. In the 1640s, the genre became better behaved and drew closer to the *comédie héroïque* before being domesticated and absorbed into more regular genres. Yet its appeal lasted beyond 1660, for its commitment to the decaying baroque established theatrical subjects (violence, oppression, love) and techniques (resuscitated characters, disguises, sharp changes of pace) which helped define the permanent grammar of melodrama.

Comedy

Although farcical entertainments attracted popular audiences throughout the century, literary comedy was slow to break free of ancient models. The stimulus was provided first by the Italian pastoral and then by Spanish novels and plays which were adapted to the French taste. Elements of tragicomic action fed into plays based on both foreign models and on *L'Astrée*, as in Mareschal's *Inconstance d'Hylas*

(1630), and a new emphasis on character began to emerge. By 1630, farce was in retreat and pastoral preoccupations were turning into a new comedy of manners which located modern love intrigues in Parisian settings. Plots reflected the continuing baroque taste for complexity, and authors manipulated the conventions of theatre, as in *L'Illusion comique* (1636) by Corneille, the most original of the new comic dramatists. The fashion for the ironic presentation of social types is exemplified in *Les Visionnaires* (1638) by Desmarets de Saint-Sorlin (*c.*1600–76), while Corneille's *Le Menteur* (1644) laid the basis for comedy of character, and Mairet's *Les Galanteries du duc d'Ossonne* (1636) confirmed a taste for the sprightly comedy of intrigue. Neglected by theorists, 'high' comedy, like fiction, was left largely to define itself within the parameters of the new classical ideal.

Strongly marked by Italian comic theatre and especially Spanish *comedias* (adapted 1639–46 by d'Ouville, *c.*1590–*c.*1657), French comic theatre quickly achieved its definitive form of a five-act play in verse. Both Jean Rotrou (1609–50) and Thomas Corneille (1625–1709) used piquant Spanish models and Scarron (*Jodelet, ou le Maître valet*, 1643; *Dom Japhet d'Arménie*, 1652) used substituted characters in an exuberant dramatic style which indicated that comedy had still to be purged of its baroque enthusiasms. After 1660, it was refined by Donneau de Visé (1638–1710), Racine (*Les Plaideurs*, 1668), Philippe Quinault (1635–88), actor-playwrights like Montfleury and above all by Molière who combined a number of traditions into a new style of comedy which appealed to both court and town. His comedy-farces and comedy-ballets had the widest appeal, yet commentators like Boileau concentrated on his 'serious' plays with the result that comic theatre was defined as essentially comedy of character. In the hands of Molière's successors, this became less the study of human than of social *caractères*.

The subsequent direction of comedy as a mirror of society rather than of human nature may be judged from the titles of the best plays (*Le Chevalier à la mode*, 1687; *Les Bourgeoises à la mode*, 1692) of Dancourt (1661–1725), another actor-turned-playwright. No less topical and satirical was Dufresny (1648–1724) who began by adding music and dance to shorter comic pieces at the Comédie Italienne before turning his attention to personal and social corruption through character types for the Comédie Française. Such, too, were also the targets of *Le Joueur* (1696) and *Le Légataire universel* (1708) by

Jean-François Regnard (1655–1709) and of Lesage's *Turcaret* (1707), which dissected the new upwardly mobile but vulgar *bourgeoisie*. Such developments were a reflection of the late seventeenth-century social revolution but also paved the way for the wider social contestation which lay in the future. Paradoxically, the legacy of Molière, the greatest French comic playwright, was to chain comedy to decreasingly dramatic representations of social types and public vices.

Molière

Jean-Baptiste Poquelin (1622–1673) abandoned his legal studies for the stage, took the name 'Molière' by 1644 and spent thirteen years touring the south of France with a company of itinerant actors. In 1658, he returned to Paris and established his reputation as both author and actor with *Les Précieuses ridicules* (1659). Between 1658 and 1673, in addition to staging and often performing in some 70 plays by other hands, he acted in 24 of the 29 comedies he wrote and directed himself.

His output can be classified in various ways, none entirely satisfactory. However, three phases seem clear: a period of apprenticeship to 1662 when he persisted with farce but also experimented with tragicomedy and the 'comédie-ballet' (*Les Fâcheux*, 1661); a 'serious' phase when he wrote his least comic plays, *Tartuffe* (1664), *Dom Juan* (1665) and *Le Misanthrope* (1666); and a late harvest of franker entertainments which mixed the theatrical styles which he had already tried: farce (*Le Médecin malgré lui*, 1666), the comedy of monomania (*L'Avare*, 1668), the 'comédie-ballet' (*Le Bourgeois Gentilhomme*, 1670), a 'tragicomedy and ballet' (*Psyche*, 1671) and the satirical comedy of manners (*Les Femmes savantes*, 1672).

An actor-manager with a theatre to fill, Molière never lost faith with farce and sought ways of combining it with a more sophisticated comedy of character and manners suitable for his royal, aristocratic and Paris publics. Though he did not deliberately seek controversy, he made enemies: at court, among doctors, religious zealots, and the Faculty of Theology. A 'comic war' surrounded *L'École des femmes* (1662) which was construed as an insult to the 'holy mystery' of marriage. A play 'written against the hypocrites' in 1664 was halted by the Compagnie du Saint-Sacrement and was not finally staged in its definitive form, as *Tartuffe*, until 1669. *Dom Juan*, which prompted accusations of atheism, was withdrawn in 1665 and was not performed again in its original form until 1847. Molière continued to lampoon the extravagances of preciosity and offended the doctors with the first of his medical satires: *L'Amour médecin* (1665), a comedy with music by Lully, and *Le Médecin malgré lui*.

He was supported by friends like La Fontaine and Boileau and enjoyed royal favour. But his best defence was his success. He was not afraid of vulgarity and relied heavily on broad comic strokes which are visible in his soberest character studies: *Le Misanthrope* is, at a basic level, the tale of a man who cannot have an uninterrupted conversation with a woman. But by combining traditional forms of comedy, he created a new kind of comic play which drew its unity from a consistent concern with human behaviour and social foibles. He repeated plots, situations and characters from play to play – fathers who force their children to marry against their will, servants who plot against their masters, stagy dénouements which save the day – because they worked well in theatrical terms. But even his broadest comedy always has a point: to highlight the folly of his monomaniacs or to show some social failing in an absurd light.

But from the start, he also drew on his own observation. *Les Précieuses ridicules* owed less to tradition than to his knowledge of people and their ways. His 'high' comedies are original creations, for no two of his obsessives are the same. Their depth of characterization prevents them from being caricatures and raises them to the level of permanent types. It is through character that Molière castigates society. By drawing self-incriminating *précieuses*, prudes, zealots, philosophers, doctors, lawyers and self-obsessed *bourgeois*, Molière attacks what they represent. When the mismatch between self-image and reality is finally exposed, a mask falls and Tartuffe, Béline, doctors, poets and *précieuses* stand before us to be judged.

Molière believed that theatre had a moral vocation, though what he wanted his public to learn is far from certain. His social attitudes are clear: he attacks the self-interest of the professions, the hypocrisy of bigots, the snobbery of *précieuses* and the intellectual pretentiousness of court and salon. His literary ideas are equally unambiguous. While the purpose of comedy is to correct manners, the greatest rule of all is to please and his plays stray routinely from the path of 'regularity'. But Molière's philosophy is less clear-cut.

His 'raisonneurs', usually middle-aged men who preach 'le juste milieu', cannot be said to express his position but are functional figures designed to mark norms against which excess and folly may be judged. He does not recommend automatic obedience to authority, for his servants insult their masters and children defy their parents. Rather than defending a 'golden mean', the plays promote an elastic notion of 'natural' behaviour: tolerance, spontaneity and the rights of exuberant youth. Nor was Molière a politically committed author. He does not seek to undermine the structures and moral assumptions of his society, but instead shows that, without common sense and affection, marriage, the family and the social hierarchy do not make people happy. Even his attacks on preciosity are less than whole-hearted, for he puts 'precious' language and sentiments into the mouths of his lovers and defends 'precious' ideas on marriage and female education. Molière's target is not the *précieuses'* call for the purification of manners and language as such, but their foolishness and prudery which exist as much outside 'nature' as Harpagon's avarice or Argan's hypochondria. Against them women like Elmire in *Tartuffe* or Henriette in *Les Femmes savantes* stand out. They are intelligent, unimpressed by fashion and modestly self-assertive.

Most controversial of all is Molière's attitude to religion. He was called an enemy of the Church and an atheist, and the Enlightenment regarded him as an anti-clerical deist. Because he associated with *libertins*, he has also been turned into a defender of the new philosophical rationalism. Though not a bookish man, Molière was certainly aware of the scientific and intellectual debate going on around him. Yet there is nothing to suggest that he shared the atheism of Dom Juan who, despite certain admirable traits (his courage, for example), is portrayed as an unredeemable hypocrite. In this, Dom Juan is no different from Tartuffe who hides behind a façade of religious zeal as a way of serving his own interests.

The modern consensus is that Molière was probably sceptical in his own beliefs and as opposed to extremism in faith as he was to any other kind of private or public excess. His plays treat religion evenhandedly, for they attack both the laxity of the Jesuits, which gave comfort to Tartuffe, and the puritanism of the 'cabale des dévots' which was another name for intolerance. His perennial targets were the 'impostors' who exploited those foolish enough to be duped by them. By this account, Molière was a moral rather than a philosophical writer and his enemy was hypocrisy, that 'vice privilégié'.

He was not, however, a closet pessimist. He judged people and manners sternly, but he remained amused by the follies he castigates. His comic effects range from the gross to the sophisticated, from dreadful puns to a new kind of integrated comedy of observation. At its heart lies the individualized character-type rooted in the old, physical style of comedy: the cuckold as a figure of fun, the misunderstanding which sets characters at cross-purposes, the plan which backfires. In his lifetime, his public preferred the farces to the 'great' comedies and his greatest successes were *Sganarelle* (1660), *L'École des maris* (1661) and his comedy-ballet, *Les Fâcheux*. Changing tastes have long since altered these priorities and it is the comedies of monomania which are now considered to represent the best of the humane, enduring talent of a master of stagecraft.

Tragedy

In the early 1600s, the static model of Renaissance tragedy received, at the hands of the likes of Hardy and Schelandre (*Tyr et Sidon*, 1608), an injection of furious pace, drama and violence. Religious tragedy was attempted in Pierre Troterel's *Sainte-Agnès* in 1615. But as a distinctive genre, tragedy was almost obliterated by tragicomedy until its revival in the 1630s when systematic efforts were made to 'regularize' it. In 1634, Mairet's *Sophonisbe* and Rotrou's *Hercule mourant* came close to the later classical model and the *querelle du Cid* (1637–8) was preceded and followed by prescriptive statements and plays which sought to implement the new rules. Violent action was not abandoned but it became more discreet. Tragedy was opened up to religious subjects (Du Ryer's *Saül*, 1639) and especially Corneille (*Polyeucte*, 1641–2; *Théodore, vierge et martyre*, 1646) who was also one of a number of authors who gave the genre a political dimension by justifying the 'reason of state' and absolute rulers. But like contemporary novelists, playwrights found a rich storehouse of subjects in history. Du Ryer looked to Rome (*Scévole*, perf. 1630), Corneille drew on Spanish, Roman and Greek sources, and Rotrou's greatest successes (*Le Véritable Saint-Genest*, 1645; *Venceslas*, 1647; and *Cosroès*, 1649) were located in a more or less remote past. History provided a necessary distance which enabled dramatists to portray grandiose actions as part of the eternal war between good and evil and, during the Fronde, to reflect the political struggle between divided factions. But the Fronde saturated the public with politics and when tragedy returned after a brief eclipse, it made its primary subject the conflicts and tribulations of love. *Timocrate* (1656) by Thomas Corneille, the century's most-performed tragedy, reflected the mood of the novel (it was in fact based on an episode of La Calprenède's *Cléopâtre*) and inaugurated the move away from the virile 'dureté' and 'admiration', considered by Corneille to be the essence of tragedy, to the pathos of characters trapped in an affective predicament.

The heroism of Corneille was a form of optimism: human beings can surmount all obstacles by acts of will. But heroic ideals became unseasonable in a society which now preferred the analysis of feeling and psychological states. And if tragedy had no longer to compete with tragicomedy, it had to contend both with the popularity of comedy and the spectacular 'machine play'. In the wake of *Timocrate*, Quinault (*Astrate*, 1665) replaced the 'pity and fear' of Aristotelian catharsis with situations and characters whose plight produced tears. Racine, far from making audiences marvel at examples of courage and resilience, encouraged them to weep for helpless humanity. Corneille, still active, lost the battle (*Suréna*, 1674, is a very Racinian tragedy) and no serious competitor emerged to challenge the dominance of 'le tendre Racine'. Nicolas Pradon (1632–98) failed to equal him in a public contest: his *Phèdre et Hippolyte* (1677) was judged inferior to Racine's treatment of the same subject. But after *Phèdre*, Racine retired from the Paris stage and none of his successors were able to develop tragedy as a form. Quinault turned to writing *libretti* for the new 'tragédie en musique' of Lully. Campistron (1656–1723), who saw himself as Racine's heir, produced pale, sentimental imitations. After 1680, Longepierre (1659–1721), La Grange-Chancel (1677–1758), or even Crébillon *père* (1674–1762), much admired for his gory tragedies which began with *Idoménée* (1706), were unable to match the invention of *Esther* and *Athalie*, Racine's two last plays which directed the genre to a spiritual purpose and, in their form, took account of the rise of opera.

Though tragedy was brought to the highest pitch of excellence in the 1670s, the burden of classical aesthetics would play a significant part in hampering its further evolution. Established as a five-act play in alexandrine couplets, it drew on approved sources, subjects and themes, and was required to conform to the unities, *bienséance* and the *vraisemblable*. Its form and ethos were fixed – forever, it was assumed – by a succession of theoretical writings which left future tragic poets with little room for manoeuvre. The rules, however, do not alone explain the subsequent ossification of tragedy. They were devised to bring order to the chaotic stage of the early years of the century and, though they were made exclusive and immune to change, they still offer a perfectly reasonable model of dramatic art. Indeed, the century's two greatest tragedians worked within them, Corneille uneasily at times, and Racine effortlessly.

Corneille

Pierre Corneille (1606–84) wrote almost as many comedies as tragedies, and until 1650 was regarded as the unrivalled master of both. He was also the century's greatest theatrical innovator. He separated the tragic from the comic definitively with Le Cid (1637), perfected sacred tragedy with Polyeucte, invented the comedy of character (Le Menteur), anticipated a modern style of drama in Don Sanche d'Aragon (1650), and in the complex plots and surprise reversals of plays like Rodogune (1645) or Héraclius (1647) he produced a breathless but controlled kind of superior melodrama.

His long career began as the age of the baroque was fading. Apart from Clitandre (1630), a tragicomedy, his early plays (1629–36) were comedies. He staged his first tragedy, Médée, in 1636 and then produced in quick succession four tragic masterpieces: Le Cid, which made him famous, Horace (1640), Cinna (1640/1) and Polyeucte. After two comedies (Le Menteur and its Suite, (1644), he wrote four Roman tragedies, a pièce à machine (Andromède, 1648) and three plays which echoed the tense political climate of the Fronde. When the last of these, Pertharite, failed in 1651, he gave up the stage until 1659 when he returned with Oedipe. But having been in many ways the voice of his generation, which had now passed, he found it difficult to compete with Racine. Corneille, a victim of changing tastes, finally abandoned the theatre in 1674.

His first plays turned the pastoral into a more realistic comedy of urban manners which centred on love and marriage and 'une peinture de la conversation des honnêtes gens'. The most inventive of these early comedies, L'Illusion comique (1635/6), turns on a piece of skilfully managed theatrical trompe-l'oeil. More significant, however, was Le Menteur, whose hero is almost pathologically unable to tell the truth. A satire of manners, it is also the first comedy of character of the kind Molière, who admitted his debt, would later make his own.

Although *Le Cid* was the subject of one of the major literary *querelles* (its form was 'irregular' and Chimène's love for the man who had killed her father was judged 'immoral'), Corneille's tragedies set the standard in the 1640s. Yet his inventive, physical theatrical style which pushed human will and emotion to their limits was later held against him. If set against Racine's subtle analysis of eternal human passions, Corneille's theatre may seem cold, remote, and irretrievably male, a series of variations on the struggle between love and duty. Yet he nowhere suggested that his characters were a race apart, though he did insist that they were in some way exceptional and intended to astonish and provoke admiration as examples of the human potential for good and evil. Nor is their impact to be defined in the writhings of characters required to choose between love, public obligation and a sense of honour. Their heroic self-affirmation, reached through stern self-scrutiny, implies many different and conflicting values. They bear the mark of their times: their spirit is that of the militaristic nobility of the 1630s and 1640s. Yet they also project a timeless celebration of human will and the individualistic ideal of *gloire*.

Corneille was drawn to plots and situations which lent themselves to the exploration of the connection between the rights and duties of subject and ruler, and the relationship of individuals to practical politics. Horace's duty leads him to kill his sister because she prefers love to Rome, and Cinna's dilemma is eased by Auguste's clemency. At first, Corneille's rulers defend reasons of state and are admirable when they are just, like César in *La Mort de Pompée* (1643/4), but repulsive, like Cléopâtre in *Rodogune*, when they are not. After 1659, they follow their interest more ruthlessly and set political realities above natural and human justice. In his last play, *Suréna* (1674), royal ambition can no longer accommodate the hero, even though the monarch owes his throne to the victories he has won.

Corneille's tragedies define the conditions and nature of man's heroic potential. But they are not simply lucid character studies or abstract meditations on the conflict of loyalties but urgent, vivid dramas. Though Corneille had disciplined the melodramatic tendencies of his predecessors and achieved a new simplicity, he remained faithful to the violent action favoured by predecessors such as Hardy. Although, in response to the new ideal of classicism, he banished bloodshed to the wings, he was not afraid of horror. Rodrigue kills

Chimène's father, Horace stabs his sister and Cléopâtre, like Médée, murders her children. But if he shocked, he also surprised. Unexpected twists and reversals (like the false report that Horace has fled) heighten the tension to the point where, as in *Othon* (1664), the plot achieves a complexity which can disorientate the spectator. Suspense and high drama were Corneille's conscious stock-in-trade. He was proud of his ingenuity and by preference chose subjects from little-known episodes of classical history which allowed him to exploit the dramatist's licence to the full. The prefaces to his plays and his *Discours* affirm that his purpose was to 'éblouir' and 'étonner'. He did not fully accept Aristotle's definition of tragedy, for he considered wonder and admiration to be as much part of catharsis as pity and fear. Nor was he prepared to abandon the *vrai* of history merely because it was not *vraisemblable*.

He possessed an instinctive feel for the language of theatre. He could be direct and dramatic, as in the angry confrontation between Rodrigue and the Comte, intimate as in *Andromède*, and rhetorical at all levels, from the silky speeches of his kings to the emotional power of the tirades and lamentations which express the fury or despair of characters at bay. After 1660, despite the tragicomedies which offer more hopeful endings, his mood turned more sombre. Yet Corneille never finally chose between his monsters and his grandiose heroes, but left his audience to marvel at depths of ruthlessness and heights of exaltation which they so graphically incarnated.

Racine

Educated in Jansenist schools, Jean Racine (1639–99) abandoned all thought of an ecclesiastical living for which he felt unsuited and embarked on a literary career in 1663. A man of unforgiving temper, he was at his least attractive in his dealings with Molière and his Jansenist teachers, whom he betrayed, and in the bitter feud he waged with the ageing Corneille. He staged his first tragedy, *La Thébaïde*, in 1664 and successfully attempted comedy with *Les Plaideurs* (1668), a satire of the legal profession. Between 1667 and 1677, he staged seven tragedies in rapid succession, drawing on Greek mythology (*Andromaque*, 1667; *Iphigénie*, 1674; *Phèdre*, 1677), Roman history (*Britannicus*, 1669; *Bérénice*, 1671; *Mithridate*, 1673) and, in *Bajazet* (1672), the more recent Oriental past. Success brought advancement and in 1677 he was appointed historiographer royal.

He abandoned the theatre and followed the king's court and campaigns. He wrote two Biblical tragedies, *Esther* (1689) and *Athalie* (1691), for performance by the pupils of Saint-Cyr, a charitable foundation begun by Madame de Maintenon in 1686. He raised his seven children in strict piety, wrote a quantity of religious verse, and was ennobled, but lost royal favour for defending Jansenism in the historical *Abrégé de l'histoire* (1698) of Port-Royal, where he asked to be buried.

Corneille showed how men and women confront events and use their will to master their passions. Racine shows not admiration for heroism but compassion for human fragility, a 'tristesse majestueuse' rather than the 'grandeur majestueuse' of Corneille. The action is 'chargée de peu de matière', the drama arises from 'les intérêts, les sentiments et les passions des personnages' and the art of the playwright lies in his ability to 'faire quelque chose de rien'. Racine's tragedies are driven by character, not plot. His casts are small and situations are simple and clear – will Andromaque marry Pyrrhus? will Iphigénie be sacrificed? – and answers are not shaped by events but by passions which, long repressed, are finally acknowledged and can no longer be contained.

Racine is not concerned to show how his characters have arrived at the point of crisis but how they react to it. The circumstances which have precipitated the moment when they must choose are summarized in the exposition which sets out a predicament and a state of mind. There follow monologues, rational discussions and confrontations which do not advance the plot but make the situation clearer by uncovering the attitudes of the characters to others and especially to themselves. The tension may be heightened by events (the return of Orestes) and pseudo-events (the rumour of the death of Thésée, Athalie's dream). But the drama stems from a process of revelation: a blindness to reality (ignorance or self-deception) is replaced by full knowledge of an unbearable truth. Here, too, is the source of the cruel irony which allows characters to hope in vain, for whatever they do is invariably opposed by a force greater than themselves.

By showing so many men and women who are in some mysterious way doomed, Racine, however shrewd his understanding of jealousy, hate, love and pride, becomes far more than the author of psychological dramas. His characters are pursued by the implacable

Fate of the Greeks (*La Thébaïde, Andromaque*), by amoral or jealous gods (*Iphigénie, Phèdre*) or the vengeful deity of the Old Testament (*Athalie*). Even when they escape, their relief is precarious and does not alter the certainty that further pain and bloodshed will continue to be part of their human destiny. This preoccupation with fate has been interpreted in various ways, in psychological terms, for example, which range from Freudian analysis to physiological determinism, or as an illustration of Pascal's analysis of the 'wretchedness' of godless man, an argument which draws on Racine's own Jansenist leanings. But however it is viewed, the tension between human desires and the spoiling power of existence is a chilling reminder of how feeble our hold is on the life we believe we own and direct.

Nor is it clear that there is a moral centre of gravity in Racine's bleak universe. No characters represent an authorial voice and none are wholly good. Their passions are often destructive and love, especially in his heroines, does not inspire heroism but is subversive and a source of crime, misery and forgetfulness of duty. Even Phèdre, who nobly tries to conquer feelings constantly provoked by Venus and her human passion, is 'neither wholly innocent nor wholly guilty'. But she wears the face of culpable love as Andromaque encapsulates maternal feelings in fundamental ways which still seem wholly true. Their doubts and disarray are captured in verse which is perfectly attuned to their inner turmoil. If the public rhetoric of Corneille matches the confidence and self-mastery of his characters, Racine adopts a more natural patterning of the alexandrine which uses exclamations and broken utterances to express half-formed thoughts too dreadful to be articulated. Racine's tragedies are static, but his characters are feverish and the dramatic tension derives ultimately from what they feel, not from what they do. And what they feel is exposed with a clarity which conveys the danger of lives lived on the brink of insanity and death.

Racine believed that the primary rule of literature was to 'plaire et toucher'. He achieved the first by the elegant simplicity and deceptive understatement of his dramatic style which we sense may explode at any time into extremes of anguish and violence. The second he managed by his ability to involve us emotionally in moments of crisis which take us into the depths of human despair. Though he was no slave to his sources, making 'something out of nothing' meant adding little to them but eliminating all that was inessential and preparing and illuminating the moment of crisis with fluid, lyrical, elegiac, rhetorical verse of compelling beauty. Racine, far from being constrained by the unities of time, place and action, worked with them to achieve a degree of passionate formality which makes his view of the human condition so irrefutably and so unbearably true.

The Crisis of Confidence

The classical doctrine, formulated between 1620 and 1660, disciplined literature and linked it to the aspirations of a self-confident, hierarchical society. Only universal truths were valid and they were to be achieved by subordinating the particular of individual experience to the general of the collective viewpoint. Between 1660 and 1680, authors broadly accepted the consensus which represented the aristocratic ideal of *honnêteté*: it was not their role to challenge it. Yet while the new exclusiveness banished originality and all that was unorthodox – Ronsard remained in permanent limbo, tragicomedy was eliminated and the realistic novel of low life was shamed into oblivion – it needed the constant stimulation of novelty. This did not mean exploring new areas of life or society (the poor scarcely register and nature was rarely shown unimproved by artifice) but turning a fresh eye on the familiar and approved contents of the classical world. To be sure, the literary creator was expected to conform. But classicism, far from coercing or suppressing individuality, demanded that his approach be in some way personal and new, for otherwise his work was uncreative imitation.

Moral reflection

Thus La Fontaine was much admired not because he invented new fables, but for reshaping them as sly verse and providing a *faux-naïf* commentary on the power which gave the decorous regime its shape and character. In his *Réflexions, ou Sentences et maximes morales* (1665), the Duc de la Rochefoucauld (1613–80) developed the salon aphorism as a defence of true *honnêteté* and a warning against the dangers of self-love. Yet his disillusionment is so strong that he appears to describe rather than denounce the spiritual emptiness of his age, and his barbed, disabused formulations express a cynicism which has not dated. Far less sardonic and more moderate was Jean de la Bruyère (1645–96) who, using Theophrastus as a pretext, developed the salon portrait into a gallery of types. His *Caractères* (1688–94) painted a largely unflattering picture of human folly and the abuse of power. A defender of old values against the corruption of the new, he surveyed literature and the human condition with a shrewdness and elegance of style that preserve the spirit and manner of high classicism, which nevertheless already seems to exist in the past. No less lucid was Madame de Sévigné (1626–90) who maintained a vast correspondence (some 1,100 letters have survived) over half a century. She observed the court, public affairs and, in a more intimate register, conveyed the private life of a woman aware that comedy and tragedy were not simply literary genres.

The critical spirit

In varying degrees, these writers echoed the 'misère de l'homme' described by Pascal, the moral and spiritual scepticism of Molière and Boileau, and the pessimism of Racine. But taken together, they also suggest that the classical consensus was far from monolithic. Their reflections undermine royal despotism, authority of all kinds, and the belief that man is neither capable of good and redeemable through faith, nor in control of his reason and emotions, which are driven by self-love, pride and hypocrisy.

The press

A related restiveness is discernible in the fledgling press. The first newspaper, the weekly *Gazette* (1631), founded by Théophraste Renaudot (1586–1653), was officially sponsored. But in the verse *Muse historique* (1650–65), Jean Loret commented on public affairs in a manner taken up more cynically by memorialists like Bussy-Rabutin or Tallemant des Réaux (1619–92) whose *Historiettes* (publ. 1834) showed the gap separating the refined ideals of the age from the scandals of reality. Among the many journals which appeared in the 1660s, the *Journal des savants* (1665) provided a forum for scientific debate and, in its reviews of foreign books, opened a window on disturbing developments outside France's borders. The *Mercure galant*, founded by Donneau de Visé in 1672, was a literary review which published verse and fiction, but it also allowed readers to express a wider range of opinion than that sponsored by the court. In the

1680s, Jansenists and Huguenots were driven into exile and a stream of newspapers smuggled into the country from Geneva and especially Holland marked the beginnings of the subversive press. In 1700, forty periodicals were being published, some anodyne, but many critical of the regime.

History

Historians too, having abandoned the invented speeches and fanciful set-pieces of their Renaissance predecessors, developed approaches which demythologized the past and promoted ideas which were relevant to the present. Some were useful to the regime. Louis Maimbourg's *Histoire du calvinisme* (1682) helped justify the expulsion of the Huguenots in 1685. Bossuet showed that history was guided by God's Providence (*Discours sur l'histoire universelle*, 1681) and his *Histoire des variations des églises protestantes* (1688) demonstrated that Rome and ecclesiastical tradition were the sole defence against the horrors of schism. But drawing unorthodox lessons from history could be dangerous. François Mézeray (1610–83), best known for his solidly documented and strongly narrative *Abrégé chronologique* (1667), forfeited the protection of Colbert for decrying French kings who raised excessive taxes. Yet the point and nature of history began to change. In 1667, Saint-Réal argued that its purpose was to understand the motives of its makers, a view enthusiastically endorsed by novelists, who could now consult better-researched encyclopaedias and compilations, like *Le Grand Dictionnaire historique* (1674) of Louis Moreri (1643–80). In 1681, Jean Mabillon (1632–1707), one of the greatest Maurist historians, devised scientific methods for the study of documents and Claude Fleury (1640–1723) made rational enquiry the basis of the skills of the historian who should also be equipped to bring a knowledge of economic and political matters to the analysis of events.

Quietism

Fleury's Gallican *Histoire ecclésiastique* (1691–1720) was admired for its judiciously critical approach. Yet it was imbued with the dominant Counter-Reformation spirit which was, by then, under attack from various quarters. After the *Tartuffe* affair, the persecution of minorities intensified and, following the flight of the Jansenists and the expulsion of the Huguenots, was extended to Quietism, a mystical tendency within Catholicism. Championed by Madame Guyon (1648–1717), 'pure love', which required an 'inactive' soul and raised contemplation above petitionary prayer, was denounced by Bossuet who identified Quietism with passivity in matters of faith and used argument and influence to secure its condemnation by the Pope in 1699.

Fénelon

A major casualty of the Quietist affair was Fénelon (1651–1715), archbishop of Cambrai, who was exiled to his diocese. Admired at court for his opposition to Jansenism and his *Traité de l'éducation des filles* (1687), he was appointed in 1689 tutor to the king's grandson, for whom he composed both the *Dialogues des morts* (publ. 1700–18) and *Télémaque*, a continuation of the fourth book of Homer's *Odyssey*. The first was designed to remind his pupil of the vanity of human affairs, the danger of power and the responsibility of kings. The second was a modified prose epic which continued the lesson and included a view of the imaginary kingdom of Salente where the aim of government is the good of the people, not the greatness of the monarch. Published surreptitiously in 1699, it confirmed Fénelon's downfall. Although he accepted his disgrace, he continued to develop his opposition to absolutism (outlined in the *Tables de Chaulnes*, 1711) but the hopes of his supporters that royal power might be made more accountable were dashed in 1711 with the death of his pupil, heir to the throne, who greatly admired him. The marginalization of Fénelon is an indication of the treatment dispensed to any who opposed Louis's repressive regime. Yet *Télémaque* marks the shift from the didactic romance to the philosophical novel and its long-term political influence was enormous: no other fiction was more frequently reprinted by the Enlightenment.

Bossuet

The Quietist controversy also illustrates the power wielded by Bossuet who, as defender of Gallican Catholicism, was moved to challenge attacks which came from many directions. Some campaigns brought easy victories. Thus he demolished the defence of theatre as a theologically permissible recreation argued by the *père* Caffaro in 1694. His steamrolling reply, the *Maximes et réflexions sur la comédie* (1694), refigured the stage as a dangerous place where passions, better left sleeping, were unwisely stirred. This hostile stance was officially maintained by Church and state in the following century. But other divergent tendencies, which derived from the spread of rationalism, were more difficult to contain.

Malebranche

Nicolas Malebranche (1638–1715), the most original French thinker of his age, discovered a rational order in the created world. Creation was not autonomous and mechanical but coincidental with God: everything, from miracles to human motivation, is explicable by a theory of perception and a proper understanding of causality, the first cause being divine. *De la recherche de la vérité* (1674), despite its theocentrism, drew the fire of Bossuet who argued that Malebranche's view of creation made faith redundant. No less powerful was his reaction to the application of scholarly exegesis to Holy Writ by Spinoza in Holland and at home by Richard Simon, whose *Histoire critique du vieux Testament* (1678), which publicized doubts about the authorship of the early books of the Bible, he ensured was banned.

Relativism

But if a new mood of controversy was in the air, it was not restricted to Paris or even France. Travellers to Persia, India, China, Africa and the Americas brought back detailed accounts of societies, some primitive, others sophisticated, which managed to be orderly and virtuous without being Christian. In 1703, La Hontan (1666–?1715) described the natural religion of native Canadians and reported the wisdom of a noble savage. Herbelot de Mollainville (1625–95) compiled an encyclopaedic compendium (1697) of Eastern lore and Antoine Galland (1646–1720) translated both the Koran and the Arabian Nights (1704–17) and thus prepared the ground for the Enlightenment's fascination with Orientalism.

The new ideas

The impact of relativism, which undermined France's assumption of its intellectual and cultural superiority, was compounded by the work of foreign thinkers. The new mathematics of Isaac Newton (1642–1717) undermined Cartesian rationalism and John Locke (1632–1704) brought a new empiricism to the study of both government and human understanding. The logic of Spinoza (1631–77) alarmed Cartesians and theologians alike with the implications for morals and faith of its materialistic denial of free will. While most of these developments were restricted to a small circle of European intellectuals, an older spirit of philosophical dissent prepared the ground for their reception in France. Home-grown *libertinage* progressed modestly in the deism of Foigny or the tolerance which Saint-Évremond (1613–1703) recommended as the only rational response to the uncertainties of faith and reason. The sensuality of Chaulieu and La Fare, together with the appearance of obscene fictions (like Chorier's *L'Académie des dames*, 1660), steered the word *libertin* towards the sense it would have in the Enlightenment. The effect was to widen the limits of rational debate and even atheism (though for many it still meant the Calvinist heresy) ceased to be a taboo subject but an intellectual position susceptible to analysis.

Bayle

From Rotterdam, the Huguenot moralist Pierre Bayle (1647–1706) waged war against the religious intolerance which had driven him from France. He sought support for a non-aligned community of scholars in a periodical (the *Nouvelles de la république des lettres*, founded in 1684) and compiled a *Dictionnaire historique et critique* (1697) of the major philosophical and religious ideas from antiquity to modern times. He raised new issues (is it conceivable that atheists could construct a harmonious, even virtuous community?), offered sceptical comments on the Bible (he cast doubts on the morals and politics of King David) and raised ideas which would be taken up by others: the article 'Manichéens', which discussed the problem of evil, inspired Leibniz (1646–1716) to write the *Essai de théodicée* (1710). That Bayle was attacked by both the arch-Catholic Bossuet and the Calvinist Pierre Jurieu (1637–1713) is a testimony to his non-sectarian stance which was his legacy to the Enlightenment, of which he was the major precursor.

The spread of science

These fierce debates, conducted in large, learned tomes, although they set the terms of the eighteenth-century 'philosophic' debate, scarcely impinged on the non-scholarly reading public. In the public mind, orthodoxy was the voice of Bossuet and the divine right of kings. However, the last decades of the century anticipated another 'philosophic' activity, the *vulgarisation* of scientific knowledge. Bayle became famous with his *Pensées sur les comètes* (1682) which used rational arguments to denounce the superstitious belief that heavenly phenomena are portents of earthly disasters and, in the process, undermined unquestioning faith, both pagan and Christian. Much more accessible to the current taste was the urbane demonstration of the uses of reason by Fontenelle (1657–1757). His *Entretiens sur la pluralité des mondes* (1686), couched in the form of a salon dialogue, popularized the new astronomy and the mechanistic philosophy of Descartes and, by defining Earth as a point in a vast universe, contributed to the spread of the new relativism. The *Histoire des oracles* (1687) denounced credulity as *De l'origine des fables* (1724) would puncture pagan beliefs, though both implied that if judged by the same standards, aspects of Christian faith might fare little better.

The *querelle des anciens et des modernes*

While Bossuet feuded with Moreri, Spinoza, Malebranche and Bayle, and Maimbourg quarrelled with Bayle and Jurieu, a less arcane but no less bad-tempered argument, which had been smouldering since the time of the Pléiade, burst into flame. It centred upon the relative merits of modern and ancient cultures. The Ancients pointed unwaveringly to classical antiquity which had thought the best thoughts, perfected literary forms and produced mighty minds which posterity could only admire and humbly follow: all subsequent generations were but pygmies perched on the shoulders of giants. The Moderns replied that tradition is a gift and should not be a burden, and that if Homer or Virgil were indeed giants, anyone perched on their shoulders should be able to see further than they could. Classical literature was to be honoured for its human concerns, but ancient minds were at a disadvantage for the simple reason that knowledge is cumulative.

The argument had resurfaced in the 1650s in attempts to move the epic beyond mythology towards a national, Christian model, and again in the 1670s when it centred on the use of Latin versus French for inscriptions on public monuments. By then, La Rochefoucauld, Bossuet, Racine, and above all Boileau had declared their support for classical simplicity against modern confusion. Against them, claims were made for the spirit of enquiry and the right to break new ground. When, in 1687, Perrault rose in the French Academy to champion modern authors, he unleashed a battle of the books which, with a coda centred upon whether Homer was a man or a collection of texts, and whether it was proper to adapt ancient writings to modern taste, lasted until 1715.

That the Ancients' cause needed such stout defending was a measure of the ground made by modern perspectives not only in science and philosophy but also in theatre, fiction and poetry. The universal truths of high culture were yielding to a more subjective interiority, and the lofty pathos of Racine mutated into a more direct engagement with the language of the heart. *Sentiment* began losing its meaning of 'opinion', *affection* ceased to be only a medical term, and *émotion* was uncoupled from its political sense of 'unrest'. But faith in the modern was also a vote of confidence in the human capacity to master nature, in other words to make progress.

By initiating the shift from the general to the particular, from human nature to human beings, and by freeing science and philosophy from the bonds which chained them to the past, the *querelle des anciens et des modernes* illustrates the retreat from the classical worldview and marks a clear turning point in the history of literature and ideas. The Moderns won the battle. Yet in a real sense, they lost the war because they allowed the conservatism of the Ancients to acquire a stranglehold on French institutional life. It was the traditionalists who, in the following century, would control education, fill the Academies, define taste and ensure that Church and state would oppose change until the Revolution and beyond.

The Legacy of Classicism

However, in a broader perspective, classicism continued to shape the culture and outlook of France. Its legacy still survives in the habit of sententiousness, the respect for exactness of language and economy of style, and the Cartesian fascination with abstract ideas: it remains at the heart of 'la clarté française'. Romanticism defined itself as a reaction against neo-classicism, yet it was to rediscover the power of classical theatre that Hugo broke with its rules. And in the twentieth century, it is possible to recognize something Racinian in Mauriac, trace the taste for psychological *analyse* to the cinema of Éric Rohmer, or glimpse Pascal at the shoulder of Malraux, Camus and Duras. In a sense classicism was still for the twentieth century what antiquity was for the seventeenth: not a model nor a goal but a spirit and a standard of excellence.

4

The Age of Enlightenment

Introduction

When Louis XIV died in 1715, the geometrical gardens of Versailles were already growing out, overtaken by time and unstoppable forces. They may stand as a symbol of the Sun King's precarious legacy of order and stability which had been maintained, in his last years, only by his pious and increasingly autocratic rule. During the reformist Regency (1715–23), the clock which had been stopped was set ticking briefly. But thereafter Louis XV (1710–1774), guided by ministers of uneven quality, managed his realm with a disconcerting mixture of inflexibility and weakness. If France acquired Lorraine (1766) and Corsica (1768), her military strength declined and all hope of an empire was surrendered to the English, who were left masters of India and Canada. After 1774, Louis XVI initiated reforms through enlightened ministers like Turgot and Necker, but was defeated by the forces of privileged reaction and his own political inertia. By 1789, the *ancien régime* had become, like Versailles, an expensive, unmanageable burden on the nation.

The eighteenth century was, of course, an age of elegance, with sets by Watteau and music by Rameau. But the social and cultural hierarchy became increasingly vulnerable to pressures from below. Royal absolutism was tested by the fractious *parlements*, the Church was infiltrated by doctrinal and even secular dissidents, and the aristocracy maintained itself only through royal favour and intermarriage with the energetic bourgeoisie, which progressively detached itself from the mass of the 'third' estate. The *honnête homme* ceased to be a courtier and mutated into an *homme d'esprit* and then into the *philosophe* who had emerged from the middle class through the merit which was urged as a better recommendation than birth. The French Academy, bastion of intellectual conservatism, had fallen to the philosophic party long before the election of d'Alembert in 1772 signalled the final defeat of the theological *bonnets* by the secular *chapeaux*. By then authors had long ceased to be presented at court and they now made their names in the salons and theatres of the capital. Just as economic and political power moved from Versailles to Paris, so the Town acquired precedence over the Court in cultural matters. In many ways, the Enlightenment was a middle-class reaction against the dominant courtly and aristocratic tradition, the revolt of money, energy and intellect against the conservatism of the establishment.

Beginning the century as a kingdom of 16 million royal subjects, France was, in 1793 when Louis XVI went to the guillotine, a republic of some 25 million citizens. Christian, monarchical, classical France maintained its outward pomp and shell but its authority was steadily eroded from within. The Church, the absolute state and the cultural consensus were all challenged by writers and thinkers who identified their target as theocratic and royal 'despotism' and fought both with a new creed of reason and tolerance. The past was darkness and they set out to dispel old, oppressive shadows with the *lumières* of intellectual Enlightenment.

At first, their struggle was defensive. Literary and aesthetic values remained linked to neo-classical taste, and ideas which challenged the religious and civil order circulated in clandestine manuscripts, not openly in print. But by 1750, the new ideas had broken cover but had now to contend with growing competition from a different direction: the cult of sensibility. Emotionalism was not new (it can be traced back to the 1690s) but it grew stronger after the publication of *La Nouvelle Héloïse* in 1761. Underwriting the idea that knowledge was 'useful' only if it contributed to human happiness, sentiment humanized the austere rationalism of the early *philosophes* so that the last phase of the *ancien régime* is marked by a new individualism and a spirit of practical charity (*la bienfaisance*) which turned philosophical ideas into personal concerns which demanded personal responses.

Writers and Their Public

Language

After 1700, French rapidly replaced Latin as the language of the new learning. It was used by the Europe-wide Republic of Letters and, after 1714, became the vehicle of international diplomacy. Frederick of Prussia made French the language of his Berlin Academy and its adoption by foreign authors like Casanova, Gibbon and Beckford was an acknowledgement of the 'universalité de la langue française' proclaimed in 1784 by Rivarol (1753–1801). Yet the taste and culture of France, so admired abroad, was, at home, available only to a small minority.

Education

Education continued to be a luxury beyond the reach of all save the wealthy elite. There was no state provision and many believed that no such initiative should be taken: to instruct the people was a potential threat to social stability. Private tutors, 300 residential *collèges* for boys run by the Jesuits and Oratorians and a smaller number of convents for girls educated only a small percentage of the population. Boys were given a classical-based training and girls were instructed in the *arts d'agrément* judged suitable for their future roles as wives and mothers. After the Jesuit order was expelled in 1762, the syllabus was steered away from theology towards French, history and modern languages, though Latin remained central. Below the moneyed elite, *curés* guided parish children through the Latin catechism, while for a few *sous* dame schools in towns and village *maîtres d'école* taught basic literacy skills. Despite the low level of provision, there were significantly more readers in 1789 than there had been in 1700. But schooling was not the only problem.

The reading public

In 1794, according to the *abbé* Grégoire, French was a foreign tongue to 6 million citizens who spoke only regional languages and patois. Although literacy rates rose by the end of the *ancien régime*, when half the male population and under a third of women could sign the parish register, there were in 1789 probably fewer than half a million

French men and women capable of reading a book. Of this number, most never progressed beyond the chapbooks of the *Bibliothèque bleue*, which ranged from tales of chivalry and magic to almanacs and basic manuals, with a strong leavening of saints' lives and devotional tracts. They were books without authors, the work of men associated with the printing trades at Troyes, Rouen and Caen, the major publishing centres. Although only about fifty new titles were added each year, old texts were regularly revised or updated. Issued in the traditional blue paper cover and printed (and more often reprinted) in editions of 2 to 5 thousand copies, with certain volumes on religious subjects reaching 40,000, a million copies were sold annually by itinerant *colporteurs*. The market in country areas remained largely what it had been in the seventeenth century: impoverished nobles, small independent farmers and village schoolmasters. But in towns, where basic education was more readily available and minimum literacy was now demanded of apprentices, its new constituency extended to skilled workers, barber-surgeons, lawyer's clerks and servants in wealthy households, that is, to the cultural elite of the lower classes.

The book trade

In comparison, the public for serious books was minuscule. Contemporary estimates suggest that in Paris, whose population was greater than that of all the other major cities combined, it did not exceed 30,000. Twenty or so performances of a play exhausted the theatre-going public which, however, grew with time: Beaumarchais's *Mariage de Figaro* (1784), the century's greatest success by far, was played 73 times in nine months. The number of copies printed of a book matched its potential market. Useful books, like Barrême's *Comptes faits*, a ready-reckoner, had huge print runs but serious books averaged 600–800 copies while plays and novels managed about 1,500–2,000. Anything more was considered a success which was denied to all save established authors like Voltaire (*Le Siècle de Louis XIV*, 3,000 copies; *L'Ingénu*, 4,000) or Rousseau (*La Nouvelle Héloïse*, 4,000). But even good sales did not make an author rich. Voltaire's wealth came from official posts and shrewd investments, not from writing, and Rousseau copied music for money. Sixteen editions of Laclos's *Liaisons dangereuses* appeared within eighteen months of the first, but of these fifteen were put out by pirate publishers.

Authors were still unprotected by a copyright law. In 1777, Beaumarchais set up a Société des Auteurs Dramatiques to defend playwrights against the power of actors, and measures to protect authors against pirate publishers were announced. But their rights were slackly enforced and publishers continued to exploit them, sometimes requiring them to contribute to the cost of paper or to accept multiple copies of other books in part payment. A manuscript was sold outright to a *libraire* (a publisher who was also a bookseller) whose exclusive property it remained for an agreed period. But publishers were themselves vulnerable to the activities of pirate printers who simply reissued books which had made a stir. Illegal books found their way to Paris from Rouen and Avignon but also from abroad, notably from Amsterdam and Neuchâtel in Switzerland. But clandestine printers also operated in the capital, despite the watchfulness of the authorities, always alert to any threat to religion, morality and the established order.

Censorship

The book trade was subject to strict controls. Print-shops were raided and offenders could lose their licence, premises, stock and type. The number of authorized publishers was set at 36, each publication required an official *privilège* and measures were taken to halt the circulation of clandestine books. Manuscripts were vetted by a growing corps of censors (there were 41 in 1730, 73 in 1745, 178 in 1789) and, although censorship was now the sole responsibility of government, Jesuits campaigned successfully against Jansenists and the *philosophes*, and the Paris *parlement* had the power to order books to be burnt by the public hangman.

In practice, however, the system was less repressive than it had been under Louis XIV. Censors discussed problems with authors who usually agreed to make the necessary changes to their text. After 1718 manuscripts which were refused the *privilège* were increasingly granted a *privilège tacite* which withheld official approval but allowed publication, an arrangement which gave authors a measure of legal protection. Although the authorities relied on a vast network of informers, attempts to police the book trade encountered widespread resistance. Publishers were prepared to take risks for money and ideological groups devised ingenious ways of eluding their pursuers: the *Nouvelles ecclésiastiques*, the much-persecuted mouthpiece of

Jansenism, appeared regularly between 1728 and 1792, despite all efforts to stop it. D'Aguesseau's ban on all save wholesome novels in 1738 did not survive public disapproval and not all *directeurs de la librairie*, a post created in 1699, were committed to enforcing the letter of the law: the *Encyclopédie* would have faced a much sterner test without the complicity of the most liberal of them, Malesherbes, who held the post between 1750 and 1763. And although capital punishment was available to curb outspoken authors, it was never invoked. Sentences were relatively mild, consisting of a brief spell in jail (Voltaire, Diderot) or a period of exile (Voltaire, Rousseau, Raynal). Even so, the threat to freedom was real and while writers continued to push back the limits of what was officially tolerated, few were prepared to defy the law openly.

Although the authorities continued to pursue authors and books, their ability and even will to control the trade were weakened by many factors which ranged from the ingenuity of authors and publishers to a growing sensitivity to public opinion. Ideas which had once circulated clandestinely found their way into print after 1750, and few banned books remained banned for long: Voltaire's *Lettres philosophiques*, for example, or Rousseau's *Émile*. In 1783, Louis XVI categorically refused Beaumarchais permission to stage *Le Mariage de Figaro*, which was nevertheless performed the following year. It is a telling example of the new power of authors who in many ways had come to constitute an unofficial party of opposition in a system in which all power resided with the crown.

The status of authors

For the status of authors changed dramatically throughout the century. Many continued to depend on noble, royal and ecclesiastical patronage: Voltaire and Marmontel were historiographers royal and the semi-detached *abbé* was ubiquitous. But with the slow spread of education and the leisure which followed the growth of the economy, the old courtly audience evolved into a paying public. To meet the demand, the number of books published each year tripled between 1700 and 1789. Against the 1,000 novels published to 1750, a further 2,500 had appeared by 1800. The growing market for information was met by endless compilations, dictionaries, encyclopaedias, travel books and works of scientific and philosophical vulgarisation, and at prices which made them accessible to more pockets than ever before. Although the first daily newspaper, Le Journal de Paris, did not appear until 1777, it was preceded by a rapid growth of the press. The twenty periodicals available in 1734 had become a hundred in 1789, and they covered a wide range of subjects: science, literature, medicine, music, theatre and fashion. The jobbing author, the book reviewer and the journalist now gained their first foothold, though the rewards for most were as small as those offered to hopeful authors with a manuscript to sell. The poet Malfilâtre (1733–67) starved to death but he was the exception. Most authors accepted that if writing did not pay, it could bring advancement indirectly in the form of a private patron or a public post. Although the eulogious preface had disappeared by 1780, patronage was offered by the new financial aristocracy which supplemented the old, and foreign dignitaries and potentates paid for regular news of France. The crown remained the largest benefactor and the various royal academies provided backing for scholars and scientists. But for most authors the best hope lay in a success in the theatre. A run of twenty performances brought its author about 3,500 livres and, more importantly, a degree of fame which might lead to a royal appointment, a generous patron or an entrée to the salons where reputations and contacts were made.

But up to 1750, not even playwrights, the best-rewarded of all authors, could live by their pens and even after that date some of the century's most famous names depended on sympathetic patrons. Though the proprietors of L'Encyclopédie made a fortune, Diderot, as its editor, was paid 120,000 livres over twenty years and achieved financial security only after he inherited a share of his father's estate and Catherine of Russia bought his library. It was rather from the ranks of the lesser writers that the first professional authors appeared. Marmontel and La Harpe were scholarship boys who infiltrated the establishment and were handsomely paid for editing literary journals.

Restif de la Bretonne, who remained an outsider, was one of a small number of authors who had emerged from the peasant class. Less rare, but still in the minority, were the nobly born. Montesquieu and d'Holbach were barons, but most aristocrats who wrote (Mirabeau, Condorcet, Sade) were either fractious younger sons or rebellious spirits out of sympathy with their class. Most numerous were the sons of the middle and lower-middle class (artisans, merchants, and liberal professions) who had been educated in Jesuit collèges: of the philosophes, only Diderot was university-educated. The social range is comparable among women authors: if the physicist and mathematician Mme du Châtelet was a marquise, the novelist Mme Riccoboni was an actress before becoming a writer. Women maintained and extended their role as cultural impresarios, but here, too, the impact of the upwardly mobile middle class was felt. The aristocratic salon tradition, represented in the first half of the century by the Duchesse du Maine and the Marquise de Lambert, gave way to the circles presided over by *grandes bourgeoises*: Mme de Tencin, Mme Geoffrin, Mme du Deffand, Mme d'Épinay, Mlle de l'Espinasse and Mme Necker, last of the 'precious' *salonnières*. Each developed her own style and *côterie* but all provided a forum for writers and *philosophes*, whom they encouraged and protected. Outside their fixed hours, authors also met in less formal settings, the clubs and especially the cafés which were popular after 1750.

Such gatherings generated a new sense of corporate identity. Factions might quarrel and rivals clash, but authors, united by their opposition to common enemies and impelled by a collective purpose, developed the characteristics of a new class which existed outside the existing hierarchy. No longer superior domestics dependent on court favour, they worked for a new master, the paying public. Though most readers were conservative in outlook, authors as a group gained in prestige and, since they represented an urban, middle-class perspective hitherto excluded by the courtly tradition, they were the focus of a new phenomenon: the growth of public opinion. In 1726, the 'upstart' Voltaire was unceremoniously thrashed by the Chevalier de Rohan; in 1778, famed for his resistance to oppression and injustice, he was courted by France's aristocratic elite and honoured by the world's finest minds. In the half century separating those events, writers acquired power, independence and status. They came to be regarded not merely as educators or even leaders of taste and ideas, but as men with the authority to advise monarchs, visionaries with a crusading zeal which aimed at nothing short of shaping the future of civilization.

The Rise of the 'Philosophic' Spirit

The eighteenth century did not invent the literary intellectual. Ideas which had been the preserve of Latin scholars were appropriated by the poets and essayists of the Renaissance. In the seventeenth century,

Descartes expounded philosophy in French, Pascal's *Lettres provinciales* discussed theological questions for non-specialist readers, and La Fontaine and La Bruyère adopted a critical stance to the society in which they lived. After 1680, the mediation of science and philosophy through literature accelerated. Fontenelle popularized astronomy and cosmology and the hammer taken by Pierre Bayle to received ideas spread a spirit of scepticism. They reached a public receptive to both information and the ideas which could be deduced from it.

The knowledge revolution

The knowledge revolution was fuelled by curiosity. The enthusiasm for technological advances (the microscope, improved barometers, ever-slimmer pocket watches) gave a new impetus to invention and experiment. Beaumarchais first became famous in 1754 for perfecting a new escapement mechanism, Diderot included practical crafts and trades (from tiling to silk-making via metal-casting) in his *Encyclopédie*, and persons of taste occasionally blew themselves up in the private laboratories where they meddled with chemicals and electricity with the same enthusiasm they showed for amateur theatricals. Travel literature described exotic flora and fauna and took the first faltering steps towards anthropology. Prévost's compilation, the *Histoire générale des voyages* (1745–59), was furnished with an index of the world's plants, animals 'et autres productions remarquables'. A 'système complet d'histoire et de géographie moderne', it reflected the passion for classification exemplified by Réaumur's *Histoire des insectes* (1732–42) and the *Spectacle de la nature* (1732–50) by the *abbé* Pluche (1685–1761). Readers were encouraged to observe phenomena for themselves (Rousseau, an enthusiastic *herborisateur*, published his drawings of plants) and they visited the Jardin du Roi superintended by Buffon (1707–88) from 1739 until his death. In his *Histoire naturelle générale et particulière* (1749–88, 36 vols), Buffon catalogued the natural world and from his study of earth history classified rocks and minerals, confirmed the primitive evolutionary theory sketched by Maupertuis (*Vénus physique*, 1746) and de Maillet (*Telliamed*, 1748), and freed the history of the cosmos and the earth from the time-span established by the Bible.

There was a comparable expansion in the life sciences. To practical advances in medicine and surgery were added investigations into the origin of life, the nature of perception and the connection between body and mind, between physiology and behaviour. Diseases could no longer be seen as a divine punishment for human wrong-doing but became problems to be solved: smallpox was preventable by inoculation. Educational theorists ventured beyond the contents of the syllabus and stressed the importance of child-rearing: Rousseau persuaded mothers to breastfeed their children and teach them to swim. By speaking frankly of sex, the *roman libertin* reflected the new curiosity about the body as an assemblage of analysable parts. Homosexuality and lesbianism were regarded as by-products of institutional pressures (the harem in *Les Lettres persanes* and the convent in *La Religieuse*) and the effects of sexual frustration are the root of the conflict between soul and body which kills Mlle de Saint-Yves in Voltaire's *L'Ingénu*.

The new spirit of enquiry was not restricted to man's place in the natural world nor to his relationship with his physiology, but focused also on the group of which he was part. 'Political arithmetic', that is, demography, fostered an interest in statistics (Buffon drew up life-expectancy tables) and informed the attention given to economics. Vauban (1633–1707) documented the plight of the nation's poor and urged a reform of the tax system. Though his *Dîme royale* (1707) was confiscated by Louis XIV, interest in economic and demographic problems grew. The 'Louisiana Bubble' which burst in 1719 and ruined many speculators, left a suspicion of credit which harmed the economy. But Montesquieu, Diderot and Voltaire took an interest in economic principles and practice, a major theme also of *L'Encyclopédie*, while in the 1760s the Physiocrats, underestimating industry, defined agriculture as the 'wealth of the nation'. But links were also made between economics and politics and the role and nature of government became matters of public discussion. Although there was no serious challenge to the principle of monarchy, political structures were examined, albeit prudently, in the wake of Fénelon's constantly reprinted *Télémaque*. A contentious historical case for aristocratic rights was made by Boulainvilliers (1658–1722), though his *Essais sur la noblesse de France* (1732) were not published until after his death. But with time, even political issues were discussed in print. The nature of authority and the legitimacy of power were analysed in Montesquieu's sociological survey of political systems (*L'Esprit des lois*, 1748), while Rousseau, like Mably, argued that social systems and political principles had been corrupted by private property. By the 1760s, the social sciences had created a more critical political consciousness which identified specific targets: oppression (governmental despotism and the legal system, symbolized by the arbitrary *lettre de cachet*) and injustice (from the unequal distribution of wealth to the unfair tax burden so resented by the *bourgeoisie*). It was in this less repressive climate that Voltaire defended Calas (a Protestant executed in Toulouse in 1762) and practical charity was offered to the poor by philanthropists like Piarron de Chamousset (1717–73).

The cosmopolitan connection

If the old dream of a 'republic of letters' was never a reality, the Enlightenment was nevertheless not a French but a European phenomenon. Foreign contributions, however, varied in weight and influence. Spain contributed to the French picaresque novel and Beaumarchais's comic vision. Italy, through Vico, helped establish the new history and Voltaire derived the legal principle that punishment should fit the crime from Beccaria. Despite notable exceptions like Leibniz or the archaeologist Winckelmann, the disparate Hapsburg Empire was a net importer of French ideas. But from Holland, home of Spinoza, exiled Huguenots in the wake of Bayle launched books and periodicals attacking royal absolutism and religious intolerance in France. Their militancy was not lost on the French who, however, owed most to the English.

England, respected as a maritime power and a dynamic trading nation, fascinated the French. Wars divided the two nations and periods of Anglomania alternated with intense Anglophobia. But, loved or hated, the English were admired for their intellectual energy. Newton's discovery of gravity overturned Cartesian science and Locke's *Essay Concerning Human Understanding* (1692) laid the basis of the sensualist approach to perception (which argued that ideas come from the senses) and epistemology generally. But Locke was also the theorist of the Revolution of 1688–9, when the English established a Bill of Rights, dismissed the Catholic James II and invited the Protestant William of Orange to take the throne. This bold action was interpreted as a lesson administered to kings and England thereafter was identified as a land of freedom and justice. Montesquieu visited England (1729–31) and found much to admire in its constitutional monarchy. Voltaire, exiled to London (1726–8), extolled English tolerance in the *Lettres philosophiques* (1734). Diderot was one of many who were influenced by the English deists who rejected Biblical revelation and postulated a 'Clock-maker God' as an all-embracing explanation of nature and the cosmos. Diderot, translator of Shaftesbury, also grew his *Encyclopédie* from an English model. Mandeville's defence of vices like ambition and greed (*The Fable of the Bees*, 1707) as an essential ingredient of economic prosperity fuelled both the long-running debate on luxury (that is, on nascent capitalism) and the defence of the human passions against the constraints of traditional morality. England was a model, a spur, an inspiration.

Science, religion and the material world

The knowledge revolution was not neutral. Buffon collected facts 'in order to have ideas'. But ideas which challenged the established consensus, whether home-grown or imported from abroad, were inevitably controversial.

Nature

By 1700, the belief that God was the mysterious creator and curator of the universe was already under attack. The old chain of being which made man king of creation had now to be extended. New technologies, like the microscope and the telescope revealed new worlds previously hidden from view. But wherever they looked, observers found order. Reluctant at first to jettison God, they persevered in their suspicion that the cosmos was a gigantic, self-perpetuating system. They called it 'Nature', allowed that it was divine but nevertheless began to analyse it on the assumption that the universe was an enigma only because the human brain did not understand it. By demonstrating mathematically that the planets hold their station by gravity, Newton did more than make an important discovery: he made the first discovery of the new age of understanding. Nature had been made to yield a great mystery. It was only a matter of time before other principles, no less comprehensive, would emerge and dispel the darkness of ignorance.

Scientific optimism

Thus was born the scientific optimism of an age which believed that everything was explicable. For if there were laws which governed external nature, then there were surely laws which controlled the world of man: physical laws governing his body and mind, and social, political, economic and moral laws directing his collective life. Instead of bowing to a divine order which could not be questioned, human beings need only ask enough questions to acquire a total understanding of Nature and man's place in it.

Le Bonheur

But understanding was not enough. Knowledge arms. With the power conferred by new discoveries, there grew a crusading spirit which identified a specific objective: human happiness. Knowledge was not to be disinterested but useful, an agent of change and not an end in itself. Fired by a belief no less strong than the faith of Christians, the new rationalists proclaimed a brave vision of the future. By rejecting the superstitious hold of revealed religion and accepting his place in the natural order, Man could perfect himself and his environment and, heir to a demystified world, ultimately inhabit a society without oppression, injustice, crime and poverty.

Pure and applied reason

A broad distinction is therefore to be made between knowledge and the uses of knowledge, between pure and applied reason, between the observation of phenomena and the inferences drawn from scientific discoveries. The *philosophes* were not patient researchers and experimenters, nor were they, with the possible exception of Rousseau, conceptual thinkers. They were committed intellectuals who used the findings of others to build networks of ideas and principles designed to secularize society. They opposed a priori thinking and all systems based on unproved foundations.

Philosophical optimism

At first, rapid gains were made. The cosmos was removed from the ownership of the Church and became a mechanism which, at least until it was fully explained, could still be seen as the handiwork of a creating, benevolent God. It was a confident stance and Alexander Pope, proclaiming that 'Whatever is, is right', spoke for the majority. Even the reality of earthquakes or man's enduring inhumanity could not dent the belief that evil is the name we give to what we do not understand. Philosophical optimism dominated the first half of the century until it was fatally wounded by *Candide* (1759). It was the heart of deism which combined belief in God with the practice of human reason. Its enemy was the superstition and obscurantism of the Church. But, despite the hostility of the ecclesiastical establishment, the Church was an easier opponent than the logic of knowledge. Science sets its own agenda, for solutions uncover new problems and further investigation generates new lines of enquiry which complicate simple patterns.

Materialism

The most intractable problems arose from speculations about the physical nature of the universe and of man. La Mettrie (1709–52) in the 1740s and, later, the circle of d'Holbach (1723–89) which included Diderot and Helvétius (1715–71) and influenced Sade, denied the hypothesis, first advanced by ancient philosophers, that there were two kinds of matter, one divine, the other gross. There was only gross matter and it followed that the universe and its contents were agglomerations, some simple, others complex, of atoms and molecules (the words were interchangeable). Matter, sentient and capable of movement, and linked in chains by 'hooks', chemical attraction or electricity, sufficed to explain the physical universe and the cycle of life and death. This extension of Newtonian science ran in parallel with the development of the sensualism of Locke who, arguing against Descartes, denied that we are born with a knowledge of good and evil or indeed any innate ideas. We come into the world a 'clean slate' on which the hand of experience writes. Ideas are determined by the operations of remembered sensations, the comparison of sense impressions and our ability to judge between them: we taste an apple, a pear, distinguish between them and learn to prefer the one to the other. Enquiries into the processes of human understanding – from perception to the origin of language – redefined man as a bundle of nerve-ends and the brain as a machine which processed whatever the senses fed into it. In one of his expressive images, Diderot likened the brain to the spider which processes information supplied by activity at the extremities of its web. If the human body, like the cosmos, was a machine, then so was the mind.

Determinism

Initial reactions were positive. Human nature could be trained to prefer good to evil and both man and society could be perfected by social engineering. But when the problem was investigated further, alarming implications appeared. The least of these was that God ceased to be useful even as a hypothesis to explain what was not understood. Far more disconcerting was the possibility that external reality was an invention of the brain and, most worrying of all, that if the soul was a part of the natural world and brains were machines, then men have no free will, no moral choices and therefore no control over their destiny. Deism offered some protection, for it gave the universe a moral purpose, and the postulation of a caretaker creator-God recommended itself even to Voltaire. But convinced atheists like Diderot struggled with the implications of philosophical determinism: can man be happy if what he thinks and does is the result of the operations of an automatic chain of cause and effect over which he has no control? The suspicion that ideas and intellect were not enough to make humans happy was not limited to the materialist thinkers but surfaced in more philosophical forms. By the 1770s, it fuelled an interest in the occult (mesmerism or the supernatural powers claimed by Cagliostro) and found literary expression in Laclos's *Liaisons dangereuses* (1782), which shows the limits of reason as an approach to human affairs, or in Beaumarchais's trilogy (1775–92) where Figaro's ability to direct events is relentlessly eroded. Only Sade took materialism to its logical conclusion by accepting its implications: morality, law, society itself are unnatural and therefore indefensible. What had started as an optimistic faith in the ability of science and philosophy to create human happiness thus ended with a declaration of the law of the jungle.

The Social Programme of the Enlightenment

The discovery of the material nature of life led to a philosophical impasse, but *philosophes* were more successful in establishing a social programme which aimed at ending institutional abuse and creating a new secular morality.

Deism

The combination of arbitrary royal power and religious intolerance, which had converged during the last years of Louis XIV's rule, presented restive spirits with multiple resentments. New ideas were discouraged (Quietist spirituality was silenced, Vauban's proposed economic reforms were banned, Fénelon's criticisms of the reign brought exile) and escape was the best option. Huguenots and *libertins* fled, playwrights avoided controversial subjects and fiction retreated into the *conte de fée* and Oriental tale which, though occasionally impertinent, carried a low political charge. More significant were new *voyages imaginaires* and utopias in the manner of Foigny and Veiras. Both *L'Histoire de Calejava* (1700) by Claude Gilbert (1652–1720) and *Les Voyages et aventures de Jacques Massé* (1710) by the Huguenot Tyssot de Patot (1655–1738) described ideal communities founded on rational principles. But whether liberal or strictly regimented, such utopian alternatives to present miseries were uniformly deist. Revealed religion (the Bible) and the Church (systematized superstition) were rejected in favour of natural religion, to which, in various forms and to different degrees, almost all the *philosophes* remained attached. Only the most rigorous materialists adopted atheism. Montesquieu, Voltaire and Rousseau all retained God, whose role as Nature's creator was recognized by Maupertuis, Pluche, Buffon and several generations of scientists, poets and thinkers of all kinds.

The problem of evil

Their stance was not without dangers, for the Church punished unorthodoxy, nor was it unchallenged. *Anti-philosophes* like Chaumeix (*c.*1730–90) or Le Franc de Pompignan (1709–84) marshalled counter-arguments against them. Far more worrying, however, were the intellectual difficulties inherent in their position, of which the greatest was the problem of evil. Natural disasters and human cruelty were the ultimate test of faith: since evil exists, God cannot be both good and all-powerful. At first, arguments were found to support Alexander Pope's confident assertion that 'Partial evil [is] universal Good'. Cruelty was attributable to human imperfections, soon to be remedied, and natural disasters, reduced to a minimum by a benevolent God, were to be accepted as regrettable but inevitable by-products of the clockwork universe. The Lisbon earthquake of 1755 shattered the consensus and confirmed what many had long suspected: man occupied no privileged place in the chain of being and was not the object of God's special Providence.

Natural morality

The problem of evil identified God more closely with nature and redefined man's place in the scheme of things. Since the universe was built on rational principles, it followed that natural religion was capable of yielding a natural morality based on the needs, qualities and defects of human nature as defined by science, history and philosophy. Man was made responsible for his own happiness: virtue would be achieved through knowledge. Goodness was no longer to be defined by the Church: Bayle had argued that even a community of atheists would develop a set of workable moral values. Morality was therefore separated from orthodox religion and the old ideal of poverty, chastity and obedience was replaced by an enthusiasm for luxury, pleasure and freedom. The passions, traditionally the antechamber to sin, were rehabilitated as the spur to activities which made individuals and the society in which they lived happy and fulfilled. Thus the personal ambition which drove scientists, authors and merchants to extend knowledge and increase the nation's wealth was revalued: it was the heart of the process for which Voltaire found a new word, civilization.

Tolerance

Central to the 'morale de la nature' was the rejection of church dogma and the promotion of religious toleration. Religion (and Catholicism in particular) was equated with superstition, obscurantism and fanaticism. In the *Lettres persanes*, Montesquieu viewed Islam and Christianity as different but equivalent religions and in the *Lettres philosophiques* Voltaire pointed to England, where many sects lived in harmony and an Englishman went to heaven 'par le chemin qui lui plaît'. Anticlericalism took many forms. The traditional satire of lecherous monks acquired a political edge: worldly bishops and the monastic system were presented as symbols of institutional corruption. Ecclesiastical courts which dispensed injustice and burned books came under attack. Abroad, missionaries enslaved and exploited the pagan peoples they claimed to Christianize. In 1762, philosophic pressures resulted in the expulsion of the Jesuits who had been tainted by the Paraguay affair.

Politics

Removing religious influence from political power was merely one part of the search for a political philosophy and a form of government which were 'conformes à la raison'. Endless *Réflexions, Traités* and *Vues* laid down principles which were implemented in *Systèmes, Plans* and *Projets*. Would-be legislators reformed the legal system by reference to 'le droit naturel' and they studied the nature of monarchical power, concluding in favour of moderate constitutional reforms or placing their faith in an enlightened despot. More radical ideas were canvassed by what Marx would later dismiss as 'utopian socialists'. The anti-Christian *curé* Meslier (1664–1729) outlined a form of rural communism and Morelly (*Le Code de la nature*, 1755) attacked private property and argued in favour of egalitarianism and common ownership, views shared in various degrees by Rousseau, Mably (1709–85), Restif de la Bretonne and Mercier, whose *L'An 2440* (1770) reached a wide audience through the trade in smuggled books. These ideal societies had in common the virtues of the 'petite république' drawn from models old (Sparta) and new (Geneva): a hierarchy based on merit, and virtue defined as moral and civic duty. But from the *père* Porée's plans for universal peace in the 1720s to Raynal's collaborative *Histoire des deux Indes* (1770), which drew philosophic lessons for the future from a study of colonialism and recent European history, and thence to the even blunter views expressed in the 1780s, politics moved up the century's agenda.

Limits of reform

Even so, it would be premature to speak of democracy in any recognizable modern sense. The *philosophes* claimed a share of political power, but showed little interest in passing any of it to their inferiors on the not always tacit assumption that the well-being of societies depends on intellectual leadership and a docile citizenry. For the most part, they ignored the plight of the poor and left the problem of poverty to individual philanthropists. Serious social issues (prostitution, public health, even slavery) were the province of minor writers. The *philosophes* denounced the Church's superstitious hold on the people but most were happy to allow it to educate the children of the nameless poor. Enlightenment was not as yet for all.

The 'philosophic' programme

But neither was it shaped by the realities of political power. Few *philosophes* held public office and for the most part lacked practical experience of government. Between 1774 and 1776, Turgot (1727–81) attempted to introduce 'philosophic' reforms but met with resistance from many quarters. His experience was not unique. Voltaire never became the *éminence grise* of Frederick II, and Catherine II, though she admired Diderot, dismissed his plans for Russia as 'paper ideas'. Enlightenment principles would not truly be tested until 1789. Even so, those principles were by then clear and constituted a comprehensive programme: a modification of the absolute basis of government; the secular state as the highest authority; universal equality before the law; a legal system which ignored social rank and abolished torture, arbitrary arrest and detention without trial; the right to property and security; equitable taxation; and multiple freedoms, of speech, conscience and assembly.

L'Encyclopédie

If any single work symbolizes the tenacity and achievements of the Enlightenment, it is *L'Encyclopédie, ou Dictionnaire raisonné des sciences, des arts et des métiers* (1751–72). Its 60,600 articles filled seventeen folio volumes of letterpress and the engravings a further eleven. It formed a treasury of subversive erudition with which, Carlyle remarked, 'only the Siege of Troy offers some faint parallel'. It covered all subjects, theoretical and practical, and wasted no opportunity to promote the new ideas. Thus a seemingly innocuous article devoted to 'Shrewsbury' turns into a denunciation of clergy who use the pulpit to mislead the ignorant for their own sectarian ends. The Jesuits rightly regarded it as a destabilizing influence and opposed it vigorously. The *parlement* succeeded, temporarily, in having it halted in 1759. Only with the help of influential supporters was the enterprise carried through to its conclusion. In many ways, the publishing history of the *Encyclopédie* is as revealing of the struggle for Enlightenment as its contents.

It was edited by Diderot and d'Alembert (to 1758) and its contributors define the wide constituency of philosophic thought: nobles and bourgeois, priests and teachers, artists and scientists, professional men and artisans. The philosophic ranks were stocked by Christians who struggled to reconcile faith with reason, rationalists who needed to understand before they could believe, unbelievers and *libertins* who undermined established beliefs and independents who followed where their thoughts led them. But while many *philosophes* laboured devoutly in the cause, four names stand out. Montesquieu invented sociological method and the written constitution. Voltaire's legacy was resistance to authority and, above all, the message of tolerance: the freedom to believe, think and speak. Child-centred education, the democratic principle and the rights of the individual are traceable to Rousseau. Diderot, the 'Encyclopédiste', invented art criticism and modern drama and started trains of thought of startling originality.

Montesquieu

A wealthy aristocrat, Montesquieu (1689–1755) was a lawyer who served as a member of the Bordeaux *parlement* until he resigned in 1725 to pursue his literary interests. By then, he was already a fashionable figure, known as the author of a satirical letter-novel, *Les Lettres persanes* (1721) which, inverting the practice of the *voyage imaginaire*, brings two Persians to Paris. From their perspective as outsiders, they report on government, the Church, the law, literature and the salons, which appear inconsistent, prejudiced and often absurd. Punctuating this ironical portrait of society are serious discussions of politics, law, war, religion and population which are not lost on the earnest Usbek. Yet he is unable to reconcile them with his efforts to maintain despotic control of his seraglio in Persia where his eunuchs, slaves and wives finally revolt and his chief favourite, Roxane, commits suicide. A tale given a point by ideas, a treatise leavened by fiction, *Les Lettres persanes* mixes *philosophie* and entertainment, propaganda and literature and set a new standard of *haute vulgarisation*. Other political tales and discussions followed which, though much slighter, confirmed the direction of Montesquieu's ideas. From a period of extended European travel (1728–31), he returned with a mass of documented observations (his stay in England left an indelible mark on his thought) which, supplemented by his study of history, formed the basis of *L'Esprit des lois* (1748).

Here, Montesquieu identified three kinds of government, each having its own constitutional framework and defining principle: a republic operates through *vertu* (civic spirit), monarchy through honour and despotism through fear. No less important are local factors (tradition, climate, size, population, economics and religion) which account for wide variations in constitutions and legal systems. No neutral observer, Montesquieu states his horror of despotism and defended forms of constitutional monarchy where authority is limited by intermediate bodies, for example by independent courts of law which rule on the legality of government actions. His preferred model established checks and balances and the separation of powers, for such systems offered the best defence against tyranny. Urbane, civilized and clear, Montesquieu wears the optimistic face of the first phase of the Enlightenment. Through reason, good government and far-sighted legislation, nations could manufacture the happiness of their peoples who would live lives free of intolerance, persecution and slavery.

Montesquieu was the most self-effacing of all the *philosophes*. Moderate by nature, he mistrusted introspection which led to self-indulgence and thence to intolerance. Instead, he turned to history and his own observations as a traveller in his ambitious attempt to define the nature of societies. Philosophically, he aimed to isolate the 'spirit of law', but his comparatist approach also enabled him to explain the 'spirit of societies' and the 'spirit of peoples'. His relativist sociological approach led to a polemical position which warned of the danger of despotism and showed the need to liberalize and humanize law. He sought to insert human happiness into social structures and believed that the task was possible: Europe was capable of enjoying freedom and prosperity at home, while colonial expansion should steer a course between conquest and commerce. It was a progressive philosophy of reason and tolerance and it justifies Montesquieu's reputation as father of liberalism, constitutions and sociology.

Jansenists and Jesuits attacked him. Voltaire complained of his 'labyrinthine' exposition. Rousseau rejected his analysis because only corrupt results could come of lessons drawn from corrupt societies which had long lost touch with nature. Radicals like Helvétius thought him too conservative. Yet his ideas fared better than his reputation. His influence was considerable (the written constitution of the United States owed much to him) and his finest hour came during the constitutional debates which preceded the States-General of 1789. Thereafter, revolutionaries like Siéyès and Condorcet came to view him as reactionary and feudal. History has not treated him more kindly, for his careful, lucid arguments still rate below those of his more charismatic contemporaries.

Voltaire

The son of a Châtelet notary, educated by Jesuits, François-Marie Arouet (1694–1778) became 'Voltaire' in 1718 on his release from his first spell in the Bastille, where a lampoon on the Regent had landed him. Precociously gifted, he had frequented *libertin* circles while still in his teens and with a flair for self-advertisement was famous at 24 for his tragedy *Oedipe*. He moved in the best circles, was awarded pensions, and shrewd investments had made him rich. A public quarrel with a nobleman led him back to the Bastille in 1726 and thence to exile in England (1726–8) where he published his epic, *La Henriade* (1728). On his return to Paris, he set about ousting Crébillon *père* as France's leading tragic playwright, published his first history, an account of Charles XII of Sweden (1731) and the *Lettres philosophiques* (1734) which, with its defence of political freedoms and message of religious toleration, was the first major challenge to the authorities. Before his book was publicly burned, he escaped to Cirey, in Champagne, home of his mistress, Mme du Châtelet. There he remained, immersed in natural science, philosophy and history. Content at first (his poem, 'Le Mondain' (1736) ends 'Le paradis terrestre est où je suis'), he grew increasingly concerned for his reputation, which, however, was boosted by the admiration of Frederick of Prussia and, after his return to Paris in 1743, by honours reluctantly granted him by Louis XV, who mistrusted him.

Meanwhile, he launched the vogue for philosophical poetry with the *Discours sur l'homme* (1738), unseated Descartes with his support for the philosophy of Newton (1736), continued to produce tragedies and comedies and became the centre of a vast European correspondence: some 15,000 of his letters have survived. Soured by his treatment by Frederick at Potsdam, he settled in Ferney in 1758 after nearly a decade of wandering. Widely regarded as France's greatest living Frenchman, he maintained his prolific output of plays, histories, philosophy and poetry, and continued to be a thorn in the flesh of Church and state. A committed anti-clerical, his mission was to 'écraser l'infâme', by which he meant opposing religious fanaticism and obscurantist resistance to 'la saine morale' of reason. After 1760, he embarked on the final, militant phase of his career. Promoting tolerance and attacking injustice, he intervened publicly on behalf of victims of civil and religious discrimination. He was feared by the authorities who kept him in exile but neither they nor age and ill health halted the flow of books, plays and polemical tracts. At Ferney, he set up workshops for the local community, received a constant

stream of visitors who counted it an honour to meet him, and conducted gleeful wars against his literary enemies. By 1770, the Patri-
arch of Ferney was a sage and his century was already known as 'le
siècle de Voltaire'. In 1777, he made a triumphant return to Paris
where his last tragedy was performed to wild acclaim. He died unrepentant in 1778 and was denied a Christian burial.

Voltaire, the archetypal man of reason, lacked a capacity for faith.
Yet God remained a necessary hypothesis to him and he valued
religion for its role in supporting the practice of civic virtue. Politically, he favoured enlightened despotism, preferring to be governed
'par un lion que par cent rats de mon espèce'. A stout defender of
order, he opposed violent upheavals and strove to bring about social
change through rational progress. He was the principal advocate and
propagandist of the secular, tolerant society which he equated with
civilization and whose onward march was the theme of his innovative historical writing.

His literary achievements, revered in his time, have long since
been revised downwards. He was a master of light verse, but lacked
a poetic vision. His plays are stronger on stagecraft than psychology
and make propaganda for causes in terms which chain them to their
times. But if none of his tragedies and comedies entered the permanent repertoire, his 26 brisk, sprightly, pointed tales remain fresh
and eternally topical. Some are brief squibs but the most developed
of them, *Zadig* (1747), *Candide* (1759) and *L'Ingénu* (1767), transcend
their times, for the 'méchants et méchancetés' and 'sots et sottises'
which he targeted are blots on every generation's landscape. Bound
by neo-classical taste, he was by policy and temperament closed to
anything resembling documentary and psychological realism. His characters are ideas on legs and ideas structure his plots which are intellectual quests, often taking the form of a journey which ends in a
teasing, unresolved climax. Voltaire, inventor of the *conte philosophique*,
was less a novelist than a maker of intellectual fables.

He had a low regard for these 'bagatelles' which teach how to
dissent and how to resist. He took more care with his correspondence, knowing that his pronouncements were likely to be published,
as many were. But together, his tales and letters show the best of a
master of irony and the shrewdest *vulgarisateur* of his times. Yet
beyond his books, the spirit of Voltaire, the indispensable enemy
of humbug and crusader for truth, razor-witted, caustic, unfair

and almost invariably right, survives as an essential ingredient of Frenchness.

Rousseau

Son of a Genevan watchmaker, Jean-Jacques Rousseau (1712–78) was apprenticed to the trade at 13. He left home in 1728, found a substitute mother (and more) in the charitable Mme de Warens at Chambéry and educated himself by wide reading. He moved to Paris in 1742, hoping to make a living through music, a life-long passion. There he met Diderot and contributed articles on music and law to the *Encyclopédie*. He became famous in 1750 with the *Discours sur les arts et les sciences*, which attributed the corruption of societies to intellectualism and technology. This essentially moral argument acquired stronger political overtones in the *Discours sur l'origine de l'inégalité* (1755) which defined history as a fall from innocence. Natural inequalities had been institutionalized by private property which gave the wily and the strong the power to oppress the good and the weak. His call for a return to nature did not mean a resumption of primitivism but a return to natural law.

Du Contrat social (1762) defined political authority in terms of an unwritten pact between citizens and the state. Citizens embody sovereignty and make laws which are executed by a government. Men are as free as is compatible with these laws which are the expression of the general will, a nebulous concept not to be equated with majority opinion. Intended as a statement of founding principles, not as a model constitution, *Du Contrat social* asserts the rights of citizens who, by obeying laws to which they have agreed, obey only themselves. Rousseau's emphasis on individual rights and the collective will were founding principles of Western democracy, though by asserting that dissenting citizens would be 'forced to be free' he also gave comfort to totalitarian dictators, always ready to inform the governed what their will really is.

Such paradoxes are not rare in Rousseau's work and they are blatant in his life. The author of a performed opera (*Le Devin du village*, 1752), he denounced theatre as a 'school for vice' (*Lettre sur les spectacles*, 1758). The man who invented childhood and wrote so influentially of education (*Émile*, 1762) deposited his five illegitimate children in the Paris foundling hospital, despite its reputation as an effective infanticide agency. The opponent of property accepted the hospitality of wealthy patrons. Such contradictions were exploited by his intellectual enemies and his behaviour alienated friends like Diderot whom he suspected of persecuting him. Alternating bouts of conspiracy mania and exaltation did not affect the lucidity of his mind and certainly heightened the intensity of his feelings. Between 1756 and 1762, his most productive period, he published books which changed the mood of his generation and, beyond it, altered the direction of Western civilization.

If his political views had a delayed action (*Du Contrat social* was little read before 1789), his ideas on child-rearing were widely adopted and *La Nouvelle Héloïse* (1761), his only novel, was a sensation. Booksellers hired out volumes by the hour and 72 editions had appeared by 1800. Its saga of unhappy love was so intensely felt that readers believed it was true and wrote requesting news of the survivors. The sense of loss, the threat to simple innocence by urban corruption, tears as the outward sign of a virtuous heart, sensitivity as both a life-enhancing blessing and 'un fatal présent du ciel': here France (and soon Europe) learned to love Love, weep, worship nature and invest in new spiritual values.

Rousseau's own deistic spirituality, expressed by the 'vicaire savoyard' of *Émile* (book IV), was less well received by the Paris *parlement* which banned the volume. Rousseau fled but found no welcome in Switzerland or England, though some (like David Hume) befriended him. His life became increasingly reclusive and his writing focused on self-justification and autobiography. His *Confessions* (written 1764–70; publ. 1782), an extraordinarily frank self-portrait of a man at odds with the world and often himself, was intended to forestall his enemies by revealing his faults before they did and to state his case for posterity. In 1770 he returned to Paris to face his tormentors but was forced to settle for a retiring life. The lyrical, autumnal *Rêveries d'un promeneur solitaire* (1776; publ. 1782), a meditation on his character, life, ideas and above all feelings, showed him in a calmer mood. He died in 1778, a month after Voltaire who, in death as in life, upstaged him.

Rousseau, an outsiderly, thin-skinned bundle of contradictions, was in his time regarded as an *anti-philosophe*. He shared the common philosophic resistance to oppression and intolerance, but rejected the experimental method of enquiry. He dismissed history and sociology because as evidence both were tainted by centuries of social corruption.

He generalized from his own personality which, warts and all, gave him better access to nature, and made emotion an equal partner in the study of the human and social condition. He inverted the idea of progress, which was not a rising curve but a downward spiral, a fall from nature which might yet be regained.

As a political thinker, he is tantalizingly elusive: the general will can seem altogether more metaphysical than practical, and democracy is sometimes a form of government and sometimes a form of sovereignty. Variously interpreted, he influenced the major strands of democratic thinking, representative, limited and direct, but he was also used to justify revolution and even terrorism. Yet to many, his message has been all too clear, for his striking paradoxes ('L'homme est né libre, et partout il est dans les fers') have the appeal of popular slogans which unite any who feel oppressed.

Much less controversial is his literary legacy. His projection of imagination as both solace and torment, his *rêverie* on time, memory and loss, his cultivation of the *moi* as a proper, indeed the only, subject of literature, constituted the fullest expression of a new sensibility. His 'unctuous' style was greatly admired and a generation of novelists and readers were marked by *La Nouvelle Héloïse. Les Confessions* remains one of the great literary self-portraits and a landmark in the development of autobiography. In dissecting himself, Rousseau released the multiple anxieties of a new age.

Diderot

Denis Diderot (1714–84), son of a master-cutler who intended him for the Church, duly graduated in theology in 1735 but drifted into the literary bohemia of Paris. He wrote sermons for clerics, gave private lessons and translated the English deists. In 1746, a publisher invited him to undertake, with the mathematician d'Alembert (1717–83), a French version of Ephraim Chambers's *Cyclopaedia* (1728). For the next 25 years, Diderot devoted himself to organizing, defending, editing and contributing to *L'Encyclopédie*. To his contemporaries, he was *le philosophe*, impresario of the Enlightenment, editor of its mouthpiece, champion of the new *drame bourgeois*, a sound trencherman and an indefatigable talker. Yet they saw only his public face, for Diderot kept a tight rein on his boldest ideas, out of prudence, arguing with himself in the privacy of writings which were not published until after his death.

After his *Pensées philosophiques* (1746), the scepticism which had led him from orthodox faith to deism deepened as he developed Locke's sensualist epistemology and Spinoza's 'single substance' into a form of atheistic materialism. In 1749, he was jailed briefly for publishing a satirical, licentious novel (*Les Bijoux indiscrets*, 1748) and a study of perception which made God redundant (*Lettre sur les aveugles*, 1749). As a condition of his release, he undertook to publish no more subversive books. Though he threw himself energetically into the battle for the *Encyclopédie*, he kept his word. He took less contentious aspects of his ideas a stage further without challenge. But between 1753 and 1778 his most daring thoughts remained unprinted.

As a reformer of drama, he was on safe ground. *Le Fils naturel* (1757) and *Le Père de famille* (1758) were written as examples of a new kind of play, the *drame bourgeois*, the case for which he made in the *Entretiens sur le fils naturel* (1757) and the *Discours sur la poésie dramatique* (1758). Tragedy, which spoke of kings and ancient heroes, had grown remote from ordinary experience, and comedy merely caricatured the bourgeoisie. The *drame* was designed to give serious attention to moral and social questions in middle-class settings. Diderot included new ideas on staging and acting which he developed in the *Paradoxe sur le comédien* (1773), where he distinguished between the technical and the instinctive actor. He recommended the pictorial freezing of the action in *tableaux* as a means of emphasizing moments of crisis, an idea borrowed from his interest in painting. Between 1759 and 1781, he reviewed art exhibitions for the handwritten *Correspondance littéraire* edited by his friend, Grimm, and his *salons* virtually created art criticism.

Privately, he followed new developments in mathematics, perception and natural science and, in *Le Rêve de d'Alembert* (1769), defined all life as organized matter graded by degrees of sophistication. He developed the implications of his materialism in dialogues which stressed the relativity of moral values (*Supplément au voyage de Bougainville*, c.1772), the relationship between natural and social law and the workings of perception. Ideas derive mechanically from our senses, yet we regularly reach faulty conclusions because our interpretation of the data is marred by laziness and bad thinking habits. 'The inconsistency of public judgement', that is, the misconceptions which arise from our mistrust and misuse of rational processes, is a major theme of his shorter fictions, which are as sharp and stimulating as his plays are dull.

His novels also reflect his interest in perception and judgement. He admired Richardson, who provided 'petits détails vrais' which not only anchored his fiction in reality but taught the reader to judge well: a gesture, a movement, a turn of phrase revealed character and situation dramatically and far more effectively than a page of authorial explanation. Our view of Rameau (*Le Neveu de Rameau*, c.1760) changes constantly, for many moods, some more admirable than others, make a man. *La Religieuse* (1760), his Richardsonian novel, offers 'petits détails' and *tableaux* which allow us to deduce Suzanne's virtues and faults (vanity, for example) but leave us no choice but to sympathize with her plight. Intended as a denunciation of the convent system, *La Religieuse* also carries a wider political charge: it is an eloquent and moving protest against all forms of coercion, for the loss of liberty dehumanizes and perverts natural instincts. Where *La Religieuse* is sombre, melodramatic, even pre-Gothic, *Jacques le Fataliste* (c.1765–84) is fey, digressive and disjointed, an 'anti-novel' which breaks the rules of fiction as cheerfully as Sterne had done in *Tristram Shandy*, its immediate inspiration. Giving at times a startling impersonation of Samuel Beckett's tramps, Jacques and his Master wander through a characterless landscape filled with adventures and memories which refuse to yield simple answers. Diderot intervenes directly, teasing his readers, challenging our interpretation of what we read and cheating our expectations of fiction, another bad thinking habit. Yet his purpose is serious: he explores the impact of fatalism on Jacques, his *homme moyen sensuel*.

Diderot was preoccupied by the implications of his philosophical materialism. His intellect was satisfied by the mechanistic definition of the universe. Yet he could not accept universal determinism which deprived humans of free will and made societies prisoners of the chain of cause and effect. A man is pre-programmed physically and culturally, and Jacques accepts that 'tout est écrit sur le grand rouleau'. Yet he thinks clearly, accepts that much of what we call destiny is the result of 'inconsistent judgement', and, like Camus's Sisyphus, is as happy as he can be. Societies, however, can hope for more. By instituting rational reforms (of government or education), men together can enter the chain, making decisions which then become the consciously intended causes of future effects which are thus willed, not directionless. To this end, in the 1770s, he outlined democratic reforms (*Mémoires pour Catherine II*, 1773) and radical political arguments (in his anonymous contributions to Raynal's *Histoire des deux Indes*).

The problem of materialism informs all his writing. It is central to his political, moral and aesthetic ideas, and explains his digressive manner and the constant challenges to his reader to think clearly. He has been accused of spreading himself too thinly, of being too curious, too diffuse, too inconclusive. Sade's response to the mechanistic nature of the world and man was clearer but brutal. Diderot's was liberal and expressed with easy humour and irony. Unidentified with a specific viewpoint (as Voltaire was with tolerance) and with his boldest works published piecemeal long after his death, he has appeared to many as the century's performing flea. It is only in the last generation that he has emerged as the most original and intellectually stimulating of all the *philosophes*, and the most engaging.

Philosophie and literature

The initial optimism of the Enlightenment was unsustainable, for the unknown, far from being overcome, merely retreated before the advance of knowledge. The generation of Voltaire and Montesquieu was able to place greater confidence in reason than that of Rousseau and Diderot, who had to contend with the complexity and ambiguity of their ideas. But if 'philosophic' discoveries have long since been superseded, the questions they were intended to answer have lasted: what is life? what it is for? how shall it be lived? Moreover, the century laid down the basis of modern scientific methodology. It discredited the enemies of free enquiry (the vested interests of religion and state) and honoured only knowledge that was open, free of systems and validated by evidence. The search for truth had become secular.

It was also committed to 'usefulness'. The principle that ideas should not be self-contained but serve the general good was accepted as a truism. But since the agreement and active support of those to be enlightened was an essential part of the process, it was logical that *philosophie* should enter into partnership with literature. Ideas were fashionable (salons held 'philosophical' as well as literary sessions) and the taste for elegant language was endorsed as defining quality of mind: 'le style est l'homme même', wrote Buffon in 1753. Theatre, poetry, fiction and history were used as vehicles for discussing and publicizing not only new ideas but new ways of thinking too. The experimental approach to scientific knowledge, generalized in intellectual circles by 1750, migrated to literature which helped to establish the habit of critical thinking among a wide public. Voltaire sends Candide into the real world to test the validity of the optimistic thesis that 'tout est bien', just as Diderot put the problem of determinism in his reader's lap by requiring him to 'judge consistently' the adventures of *Jacques le Fataliste*. Literature was the essential arm of the philosophic Enlightenment.

Literature

Neo-classicism

The seventeenth century cast a long shadow. The precepts of Boileau continued to define taste and style, and classical masterpieces were held up as models of excellence. The traditional genres – tragedy, comedy, epic and ode – retained their prestige (Voltaire owed his reputation as a 'great poet' to his epic *La Henriade* and his tragedies) and the maxim and the *portrait* perpetuated the habit of sententiousness. Maintained in the salons and spread by conservative educational practices, the classical aesthetic ensured that the Enlightenment was, in its literary manifestation, a neo-classical age. Even so, the modernist stance encouraged a measure of divergence which was compounded by the spread of science and *philosophie*. Classical writers had explored psychological and moral concerns, universalizing experience against a background of cosmic, social and human stability. The *polygraphes* of the eighteenth century, increasingly aware of the uncertainty of knowledge, could not share their confidence and gave a new prominence to the observation of social reality and the physical world. In so doing, they entered the realm of the relative and the individual.

The eighteenth century sought a greater engagement with man as a social, thinking, and ultimately feeling being. The novel abandoned the pastoral and reflected the growth of urban, bourgeois values which also found expression in the theatre. The formal memoir of a public life turned into the personal autobiography. But these developments occurred at different speeds and not all released the imagination.

Anglomania

The way had been paved in England, home of Newton, Locke and freedom. Both Marivaux and Prévost established periodicals in the *Spectator* style of Addison and Steele. Milton was admired as a modern epic poet, Voltaire imitated Pope and Swift, the 'domestic tragedy' of Lillo and Moore helped shape the *drame bourgeois*, and, after 1760, the 'poètes du tombeau' – Young, Thompson, Gray and Ossian – gave poetry fresh themes and a new, more introspective voice. In the novel, the highly moral Richardson and the feyness of Sterne struck responsive chords, but Fielding and Smollett did not, for they showed a regrettable interest in the lower orders which was only to be expected of a nation given to gambling and suicide. Novelists puffed their work by claiming it was 'traduit de l'anglais', though genuine translators adapted their originals to suit superior French taste. Shakespeare, discovered by Voltaire in 1734, was 'improved' in this way by La Place (1745–9). After 1770, Le Tourneur naturalized his style and Ducis squeezed him into suitable French dress. Even so, Shakespeare helped direct French tragedy away from its well-behaved platitudes towards excitement, passion and ultimately melodrama.

Poetry

Despite recent attempts at rehabilitation, the eighteenth century remains the least rewarding period in the history of French poetry. Written in sand, not stone, it has left few traces: its *poésies fugitives* have fled. Voltaire, the greatest poet of the age, is hardly to be ranked with Ronsard or La Fontaine, and the lyricism of Jean-Baptiste Rousseau (1671–1741), much admired in its day, would find few echoes until André Chénier (1762–94) put the poetry back into verse.

The salons continued to define poetry as a social accomplishment, but also encouraged a critical spirit and a degree of theorizing. During the first phase of the *Querelle des anciens et des modernes* (1688–1700), Fontenelle divided poetry into high (epic, tragedy) and low (lyricism and verse tales). The first aspired to the 'sublime' while the second aimed at 'le naturel'. To strip both of obscurity, he recommended a retreat from classical mythology, preferred images to reflect the natural and social worlds, and encouraged incursions into the realms of the 'intellectual' and the 'metaphysical'. A comparable trend towards the 'rational' in poetry emerged from the second phase

(1711–16) which centred on the translation of the *Iliade* (1699) by the Hellenist, Madame Dacier (*c.*1651–1720). In 1714, Houdar de la Motte (1672–1731) produced an abridged version which corrected Homer's 'implausibilities' and 'improved' the text to suit modern taste. Opposed by Mme Dacier and her admirers but supported by those who advocated a less reverent attitude to ancient authors, an inconclusive truce was arranged in 1716. La Motte, however, pursued his side of the argument in a stream of *Discours* on poetic forms, arguing that rhyme and reason did not mix, that verse was not necessary for tragedy (he wrote prose versions of Sophocles' *Oedipus* and Racine's *Mithridate*) or indeed for the customary subjects of poetic utterance. Fénelon or Montesquieu were inclined to agree: prose conveyed more accurately and directly what poets sought to say through 'vain ornament', strained epithets and the limitations of rhyme. Poetry was denied its role of building bridges, through rhythm, imagery and emotion, to new apprehensions of thought and feeling. Instead, it became the art of overcoming difficulty in communicating not passions but ideas, which were in any case expressed more clearly in prose.

Similarly, though the epic retained its prestige, many admitted with Malézieu (the Duchesse du Maine's literary impresario at Sceaux), that 'les Français n'ont pas la tête épique'. The remark was a comment on *La Henriade* (1728), Voltaire's homage to the 'philosopher king', Henri IV, but it also applied to the twenty or so epics published between 1745 and 1789. They divided more or less equally into celebrations of France's 'national' past, discussions of the rights and wrongs of the European presence in the New World, and reflections prompted by heroic figures drawn mainly from the Old Testament. Despite occasional lofty moments, they strove less to stimulate the imagination than to capture the 'clarity' and 'elegance' which Voltaire regarded as the natural domain of the French language.

But while the century at large spoke in prose, not all agreed that poetry meant only overcoming 'difficulty'. The devotional poetry of Louis Racine (1692–1763) aimed at communicating the poet's 'exaltation' and 'passion', and Voltaire defended rhyme and the music of prosody. His endorsement, backed by the general admiration for verse of the preceding age, was enough to guarantee the future of, if not poetry, at least of versification. Certainly, the century rhymed endlessly. It confined 'noble' subjects to the alexandrine, and for lighter subjects – *stances*, odes, *chansons*, elegies, *épîtres*, *prières* and the omnipresent satirical *épigramme* – used eight- or ten-syllable lines. The fable, popular at first, declined but recovered at the end of the century with Florian (1755–94). The best of the lyric poets, Jean-Baptiste Rousseau and Écouchard-Lebrun (1729–1807), struck graceful notes rather than genuine emotional fire and were as much admired for the teasing cruelty of their epigrams, of which both wrote large numbers. The ode drew on Pindar but strayed into the 'anacreontic' mode and thence into crude satire and ultimately obscenity.

Poets were heard in the salons but also congregated in taverns and cafés. Their themes were urban and they catered for cultured society which demanded respectful homages, witty badinage and undemanding reflections on moral and topical subjects. They also turned verse into a venomous weapon which they used in the fierce cut-and-thrust of literary life. Vadé (1719–57) popularized the *poissard* style, which sanitized vulgar Parisian speech and was used in parody and many kinds of insubstantial verse. But light, often satirical but invariably fashionable verse had many practitioners: Grécourt, Panard, the genuinely witty Piron, Voisenon, Gresset, author of *Vert-vert*, the cautionary tale of a parrot, the 'innocent' Gentil-Bernard, satirists like Gilbert and Ruhlière, sentimentalists like Dorat and Parny and many others who included worldly *abbés* and military men like Laclos. But with time the subject-matter of poetry was extended. Voltaire, after his visit to England, intermittently used verse to express ideas, encapsulating his early optimism in 'Le Mondain' and, with his dark poem (1756) on the Lisbon earthquake, striking a note, rare in his century, of personal anguish. But although with the *Poème sur la religion naturelle* (1756), for example, he attempted to dignify philosophy by clothing it in the nobility of the alexandrine, his philosophical verse is more diffuse and less sharply provocative than his prose.

Alexander Pope's *Essay on Man*, mediated through Voltaire's *Discours sur l'homme* (1738), attracted philosophical imitators, though English influence was not restricted to rationalist musings. Nature poets like Thompson (*The Seasons*, trans. 1760) and Edward Young (*Night Thoughts*, trans. 1769) inspired descriptions of mountain, field and storm which, pictorial at first, mutated quickly under the influence of the new sensibility made fashionable by Rousseau. The didactic mood of the age left its mark on long, descriptive, meditative poems, notably *Les Saisons* (1764) by Saint-Lambert (1716–1803), *Les Georgiques* (1769) and *Les Jardins* (1782) by Delille (1738–1813), and *Les Mois* (1779) by Roucher (1745–94). But they, like the shorter pieces published in literary gazettes and especially the *Almanach des muses* (1763–1833), also reflected the sentimentalization of the countryside by the German-Swiss poet Gessner (trans. 1762), who abandoned the shepherdesses of tradition for honest peasants, rural toil and a 'natural' version of the pastoral which, in its own way, was as synthetic as that projected by the Comédie Italienne. James Macpherson, the supposed mouth-piece of Ossian (trans. 1777), the 'Gaelic bard', injected melancholy and regret into his Caledonian landscapes and helped to confirm the fashion for a new range of themes: ruins, decay, death and the passage of time which made life a dream and love a consolation. Expressed often in macabre, pre-Gothic tones, the new *rêverie* on man's transience and the eternity of nature marked a shift from the general to a self-conscious, often stagy form of introspection.

Versification still followed neo-classical norms, images were for-mulaic and the poetic voice remained yoked to circumlocution and mythological allusion. But in the 1760s, the *je* of lived experience began to undermine the impersonal voice of poetic discourse. It is visible in the verse letters attributed to famous people which Colardeau (1732–76), after Ovid and Pope, popularized as the *héroïde*: the many outpourings attributed to Héloïse and Abelard turned them into icons of unhappy love. But the sentiments expressed in such verses were as artificial as the pathetic fallacy of the nature poets and none approached the grace and harmony of André Chénier who, in odes, elegies and his disciplined but flowing *Iambes*, written in the shadow of the guillotine, captured the truth and sincerity of a new spirit which, when his works were finally published in 1819, enthused the first Romantic rebels.

Theatre

In 1697, the Italian actors were expelled and Paris was left with two official theatres, the Opéra and the Comédie Française. The Italians returned in 1716 and formed a third while the best of the unofficial *théâtres de la foire* became the Opéra Comique in 1715. In 1762, it merged with the Comédie Italienne, which it finally absorbed in 1779. Each had its tradition and style. Opera was immensely popular but, in literary terms, is interesting mainly for the quarrel which divided the supporters of Lully and Rameau in the 1730s and the 'Guerre des Bouffons' which set Piccinistes against Gluckistes in the 1750s. The argument, which centred on the relative merits of French and Italian music, was symptomatic of the new cultural openness to aesthetic ideas discernible also in the plastic arts. The Comédie Française, regarded as France's national theatre, was charged with a dual role: to maintain the classical repertoire and stage new playwrights to the highest standards of performance, taste and diction. The Comédie Italienne, with a less clearly defined role, presented a wider range of plays, from farce to the subtle comedies of Marivaux. But it also acquired a *corps de ballet* and, until 1779, performed also in Italian and used the improvised style of the *commedia dell'arte*. Outside the official theatres, the two Paris *foires* catered for a more popular audience but also attracted elements of the refined public. Established authors like Lesage, Piron and Favart wrote for the *foire* which, more outspoken and less bound by the rules of theatre, contributed significantly to the renewal of dramatic forms in the second half of the century. By then the first fixed theatres began to appear on the Boulevards. Competition between theatre companies was never less than fierce and bitter corporatist struggles erupted at regular intervals.

Theatres and staging

Although new architectural designs were implemented in the provinces (the horse-shoe auditorium instead of the traditional rectangle, for example), the capital's theatres were notoriously vulnerable to fire and ill-suited to performance. At the Comédie Française, actors were jostled by spectators who, until 1759, had seats on the stage. Until 1782, there was standing room only in the pit, which grew better-behaved but was still home to disruptive cabals. Lighting, sets and stage machinery improved, but plays did not have directors, a function yet to be invented. A production was the sum of the performances given by the actors, though actor-managers, like Dancourt, gave some direction, and influential authors such as Voltaire and Beaumarchais involved themselves in the staging of their work. Stagecraft, however, was not entirely neglected by drama theorists (Voltaire and Diderot had firm views on the matter) though major practical reforms were left to the actors. In the 1750s, Mlle Clairon (1723–80) abandoned the hoop-skirt on the ground that costumes should reflect the period and rank of the character, not the taste of the actress. With Lekain (1729–78), she also introduced less formal acting styles, modifying the grand gesture and replacing the declamatory, sung mode of verse speaking with a more 'natural' diction.

The theatre debate

Acting, however, was still regarded by the Church as an infamous profession and the theatre was widely portrayed as an 'école du vice'. The arguments used by Bossuet against Caffaro in 1694 were rehearsed endlessly by opponents of the stage and dictated official attitudes. The government not only instituted a system of censorship in 1701 but maintained a special prison for erring players. Liberal opinion repeatedly countered the charge with the argument that theatre was useful, an 'école de vertu', an effective source of moral education, a view roundly rejected by Rousseau's *Lettre sur les spectacles* in 1759. Rousseau was supported by conservative moralists, but did not carry the day. Even those who conceded that most plays were as immoral as the players who performed them defended its educational potential. In 1726, the *père* Porée had argued for a state-run theatre with a heavy utilitarian role and custom-written plays which would help society progress through emulation: the spectator who was stirred left the theatre a better person. In 1770, this idea was pursued in Restif's *Mimographe* which argued that theatre should be deprofessionalized and made into 'une affaire d'état', effectively a free public service committed to promoting civic and moral virtues.

Théâtre de société

The case against the theatre had little impact on the public which was, quite simply, stage-struck. Attendances went up, especially after 1750, and the court, no longer the arbiter of taste, commanded royal performances of plays which had first succeeded in Paris. Amateur theatricals were fashionable in the châteaux and mansions of nobles and financiers, and Marie-Antoinette acted in productions of *Le Barbier de Séville* and Rousseau's *Devin du village*, thus reviving the tradition of court theatre. Wealthy amateurs, often supported by handsomely rewarded Paris stars, staged plays from the repertoire of the Comédie Française. But this 'théâtre de société' also attracted authors like Collé (1709–81) and Beaumarchais, who supplied short, mildly shocking farces known as *parades*, and Carmontelle (1717–1806) who between 1768 and 1781 published a hundred brief *proverbes dramatiques*, each an illustration of a well-known saying.

Tragedy

If innovation occurred on the fringes of the mainstream Paris theatres, in the *foire* and on the private stages of the wealthy, it was because conservative neo-classical taste demanded respect for the traditional genres. Of these, the most prestigious, tragedy, was encumbered by the formal and aesthetic constraints of classicism and limited in its range of subjects. Its home was the Comédie Française and, despite occasional attempts to change the formula, it remained a play in five acts, in 'noble' alexandrines, which showed great persons confronting an inner conflict provoked by actions which occurred off-stage and were reported in the *récit*. No authors matched the dramatic intensity of Racine and Corneille, who maintained a strong stage presence to 1750, and attempts to inject urgency into static situations took two forms: the addition of controversial *philosophic* ideas and growing elements of exoticism and melodrama.

Crébillon *père* (1674–1762) took the plots of his nine tragedies (1705–54) from mythology and ancient history and his manner from the 'grand siècle'. He set out to lead the spectator 'à la pitié par la terreur', and to this end did not balk at exploiting horrors which were justified by both his sources and his ambition of intensifying, for moral purposes, the cathartic involvement of his audience. His successors continued to find subjects in Roman and Greek authors, but they also scoured other times and places for heroes and tragic predicaments: Europe in the Middle Ages, Renaissance France, and the Orient. The public approved, if we may judge by the success of La Motte's *Inès de Castro* (1723), *Gustave Wasa* (1733) by Piron (1689–1773) and La Noue's *Mahomet II* (1739), none of which had classical sources. After 1750, when the Renaissance Wars of Religion were a prime site for *philosophic* and 'national' subjects, *Le Siège de Calais* (1765) by de Belloy (1727–75) was greatly admired, though Lemierre (1733–93) returned to the Greek ancients with *Hypermnestre* (1758). But the fate of his *Veuve du Malabar*, a denunciation of religious intolerance, illustrates the public's growing impatience with the tragic formula. In 1770, his widow expired on her husband's funeral pyre off-stage, tastefully, leaving spectators unexcited; when the play was revived a decade later, she was burned in full view of the audience, which applauded wildly.

Eighteenth-century tragedy is synonymous with Voltaire who was at least as well known as the author of *Zaïre* (1733) and *Mérope* (1743) as of *Candide*. He wrote 28 tragedies and invigorated the genre with exotic settings, special effects, and Shakespearean flourishes, despite his ambivalent attitude to the 'histrion barbare'. What he lacked in psychological insight he made up in his use of the genre to attack despotism and defend religious tolerance: he turned tragedy into a platform for philosophic ideas. But while the message was not lost on admirers like La Harpe (*Le Comte de Warwick*, 1763), the declining prestige of the king and his court opened a gap between heroic characters and modern concerns. The revolutions of Athens and Rome now meant little to authors less well grounded in Greek and Latin, and Diderot, Beaumarchais and Mercier dismissed tragedy as irrelevant. But habit and taste were not easily unseated. Tragedy kept its audience and survived beyond 1789: M.-J. Chénier's denunciation of royal despotism, *Charles IX* (1789), though openly revolutionary in purpose, was classical in form.

For some, however, the original purifying catharsis of tragedy had been lost and, after 1760, there was resistance to the stranglehold which the mandatory imitation of Racine and Corneille, Crébillon and Voltaire, exercised over the genre. Baculard d'Arnaud (1718–1805) attempted to revive tragedy with Gothic horror. *Le Comte de Comminges* (1764), set in a monastery crypt, was judged so alarming that medical help was made available to any spectator overcome by terror. His formula of violence, sensation and sentimental moralizing had few takers, though it marks a step towards the melodrama which flourished during the Revolution. Yet his reservations echoed developments in comic theatre which moved steadily closer to sentiment.

Comedy

In terms of performance, Molière was four times more popular in the eighteenth century than either Racine or Corneille. Yet his influence on the direction of comedy was small. His successors reacted negatively to his farces and between 1690 and 1720, Dufresny, Dancourt, Regnard, and Lesage gave his psychological *caractères* a social resonance. The satirical possibilities of this approach would be exploited throughout the century: a lampoon of pretentious poets, *La Métromanie*

(1738) by Piron and *Le Méchant* (1747) by Gresset (1709–77), which unmasks a mischief-maker, were regarded as models of the genre. But by the 1730s, the moralizing implicit in the now dominant comedy of manners was explicitly linked to the classical requirement that literature should show vice punished and virtue rewarded. Destouches (1680–1754) began with the exposure of types (titles such as *Le Curieux impertinent*, 1710, or *Le Médisant*, 1715, are self-explanatory) but graduated to plays which rescued essentially good characters from, mainly, their social failings: *Le Glorieux* (1732) deflates the snobbery of its hero. The middle-class characters of Nivelle de la Chaussée (1692–1754) have even more virtuous hearts and they are duly saved from compromising predicaments, but not until enough artificially induced suspense has reduced spectators to tears (*Mélanide*, 1741; *La Gouvernante*, 1747). Dubbed 'le révérend père La Chaussée', at first admiringly, for his moral 'sermons' and then ironically for the same reason, he launched the *comédie larmoyante* which made comedy in the 1740s far more sentimental than comic. The genre tempted authors as different as Voltaire (*L'Enfant prodigue*, 1736; *Nanine*, 1749), Mme de Graffigny (*Cénie*, 1750) and even Marivaux (*La Mère confidente*, 1735).

Marivaux

Marivaux (1688–1763), however, stands apart from the general evolution of comedy. Though a devout 'Modern', he did not share his contemporaries' interest in social types. His theatre owes less to Molière than to the tradition of psychological *analyse* which, in the salons of Madame de Tencin and Madame de Lambert, developed into a finely graded *métaphysique du sentiment*. His 34 plays, written for the most part between 1720 and 1740, also broke with formal practice and tradition. He used prose, not verse, and to the five-act play preferred, with one exception, those with one act or three. After the failure of his only tragedy, *Annibal* (1720), he entered into a close association with the Comédie Italienne which shaped his style and theatrical manner. He was never its resident playwright (he was also performed at the Comédie Française), but he played to the company's strengths, creating many of his characters specifically for its leading actors, the fragile but resilient Sylvia, and Thomassin, who played an increasingly French Arlequin. He wrote heroic and allegorical comedies which humanized the gods and civilized their creatures. He was at home with the comedy of character and the comedy of manners and did not avoid social and philosophical issues. In *L'Île des esclaves* (1725), the roles of masters and servants are reversed, while *La Dispute* (1744) conducts a somewhat heartless experiment designed to show which of the sexes brought infidelity into the world. But Marivaux was no social reformer. He endorsed the class structure, which was too entrenched to be changed, but judged his characters by an alternative ideal, the 'aristocracy of the heart'. For his subject was love. The obstacles faced by his lovers stem not from tyrannical fathers (Marivaux's fathers are kind and considerate) nor from differences of rank, but from themselves. Through disguises, ruses and misunderstandings they are made to confront feelings which, through pride or snobbery, they have resisted. When Silvia, in *Le Jeu de l'amour et du hasard* (1730), exclaims: 'Ah! Je vois clair dans mon coeur!', she enters into possession of her feelings and in so doing acquires a new understanding of herself and others.

In the first half of the century, Marivaux was France's most-performed playwright after Voltaire. Yet despite his popularity, his critics attacked him for constantly rewriting the same play, for creating characters who had 'trop d'esprit' and for developing not so much a style as a 'metaphysical (over-subtle) jargon': Voltaire remarked that Marivaux laid 'butterfly's eggs in a spider's web'. But *marivaudage* was more than a precious affectation. It meant a consistent point of view, subtly structured dialogue, deep feelings expressed with the lightest of touches and, if not outright laughter, the tolerant smile of human understanding.

The *drame bourgeois*

Comedy, like tragedy, kept its audience but grew less amusing and more earnest. It recycled the secret marriages, false identities and recognition scenes, often triggered by the *cri du sang*, which were also the commonplaces of fiction. In the 1740s, the *abbé* Desfontaines suggested that the fashionable *comédie larmoyante* might be better labelled *drame romanesque*. The idea that bourgeois settings could support tragic passion was roundly rejected by Voltaire and Rousseau who saw no merit in Diderot's proposals in the late 1750s for a new 'tragédie domestique et bourgeoise' which explored modern problems in middle-class hearts, replaced universal *caractères* with social types and, by appealing to emotion as much as reason, left audiences the better for their vicarious experience. Theoretical support for the *drame bourgeois* came from Beaumarchais (1767) and Louis-Sébastien Mercier (1773). The essentially conservative Parisian public gave a cool reception to Diderot's plays, were polite to Beaumarchais (*Eugénie*, 1767; *Les Deux Amis*, 1770) and applauded only *Le Philosophe sans le savoir* (1765) by Sedaine (1719–97). Mercier, author of some fifty *drames*, used the form for more direct forms of political comment and, with *La Brouette du vinaigrier* (1776), widened its narrow class range (merchants and financiers) by writing of the problems of the honest poor. But while its moral didacticism failed to make an immediate impact, its long-term repercussions were considerable. Its influence is detectable in Romantic drama and the *pièce à thèse* of the later nineteenth century.

Beaumarchais

Pierre Caron (1732–99: he became 'de Beaumarchais' by marriage in 1759) was a controversial figure in his lifetime and remains an enigma. From humble beginnings, he achieved wealth by means not always above suspicion, and his popularity was at least in part due to a talent for self-advertisement. Even his literary reputation seems tarnished. His fame rests upon *Le Barbier de Séville* and *Le Mariage de Figaro* but 'Beaumarchais' has long been a kind of brand name for a product reprocessed by Mozart, Rossini and the score or so of librettists and musicians who have perpetuated his plots and his characters, though not always his pugnacious spirit.

His interest in theatre began in the 1760s, when he contributed *parades* and *poissard* farces to the *théâtre de société*. In 1767, he gave his support to the *drame bourgeois* but earnest moralism does not make good theatre. Though his two *drames* were only politely received, he remained a committed *dramiste* and the final play of his Figaro trilogy, *La Mère coupable* (1792) is marked by the genre's sentimental humanitarianism. Embroiled in the early 1770s in a vexatious lawsuit, he became an anti-establishment hero with four combative memoirs ridiculing the judge, Goezman. From this platform, he launched *Le Barbier* in 1775. His intention was to restore 'la franche gaîté' to the stage and to this end reverted to the comedy of intrigue. He turned the most hackneyed of plots (young love, helped by servant, foils marriage plans of elderly guardian) into a dazzlingly crafted, exuberant celebration of youth and energy. *Le Barbier* is a bustling play, all pace and twists, and punctuated by wit as sharp as Figaro's razor. Behind the good humour and skittishness of the infinitely more complex *Mariage* lie darker moods of self-doubt and a new dimension of provocative social criticism aimed at defending merit against the privileges of birth.

His combative stance alarmed Louis XVI and much ink has been spilt on his role as a catalyst of the Revolution. Was his impertinent barber the Sweeney Todd of the *ancien régime*, the true begetter of the guillotine? 'Figaro killed off the nobility,' remarked Danton, and Napoleon saw in *Le Mariage* 'the Revolution in action'. His liberal credentials seem unimpeachable. He ridiculed the law, provoked the authorities and sold vital arms to the Americans in their war to free themselves from British rule. As a major investor in the *Courier de l'Europe*, he publicized the workings of British parliamentarism for the French and introduced words (*opposition, amendement, motion, popularité*) which gave dissent a vocabulary with which to fight the old regime. But he always ensured that he turned a profit.

For Beaumarchais was not so democratically inclined as this suggests. Though his opera, *Tarare* (1787), denounced despotism, his *drames* were much less politically outspoken than those of Mercier, the Goezman memoirs state the case for Beaumarchais not justice, and his barber clearly needs the system he has been accused of demolishing. Figaro admits that he fares badly when he is his own master and, the philandering apart, he has no political criticism of Almaviva who is a just magistrate, a sound estate manager and a pillar of a social system which is never openly challenged. The castle of Aguas Frescas is a hierarchical, liberal, constitutional, family-based but also well-heeled community, and Figaro's role is to ensure it stays that way. He puts spokes in wheels but never stops the traffic. It seems likely that Beaumarchais was an anti-authoritarian, radical but essentially bourgeois individualist who hated the tyranny of the people as much as the oppression of kings.

Yet Figaro's weakening powers parallel the accelerating slide of the *ancien régime* into revolution. In *Le Barbier*, all his plans work. In *Le Mariage*, he discovers he cannot control events and that chance works against him. In *La Mère coupable*, he is outmanoeuvred and needs a great deal of authorial assistance to overcome villainy. Such help was not available to his creator, for the Revolution turned on Beaumarchais and cast him as an enemy of the people. His reputation for subversion survived his death. Until 1870, *Le Mariage* was regarded as a dangerous play. During the Occupation of France, the Germans refused to allow it to be staged in Paris and Mussolini banned it in Italy. But if his biography is discounted and the plays are allowed to speak for themselves, the values he represents become clear. Beaumarchais, who is not Figaro but certainly his cousin, mocks not with the destructive comedy of derision but with a 'gaiety' rooted in the exhilarating spirit of joyful reconciliation – of men and women, of all with life – which crowns *Le Mariage*. His voice is unmistakable: pugnacious but vulnerable, embattled yet endlessly engaging, and still capable of drawing blood.

Although theatre had a central role in the cultural life of the Enlightenment, it bequeathed little to the permanent repertoire. Voltaire's tragedies, once so admired, and the socially conscious *drame bourgeois*, now have only an antiquarian interest. Only two playwrights remain theatrically viable: Marivaux and, above all, Beaumarchais, the only truly international theatre star the age produced.

Prose writing

The eighteenth century inherited a language which was fixed in its structures but in need of a lexical transfusion to meet the requirements of the new knowledge. The evolution of prose style similarly reflected the secular concerns of the age. The fires of seventeenth-century pulpit and funeral orators burned lower and eloquence was redefined as clarity. Flamboyance was regarded as a lapse of a taste which preferred language to be sparingly ornamented, rhythmic and direct. Voltaire set the standard with his sharply elegant prose. Writing which was turgid or mere *marivaudage* was despised while departures from the conventions of polite society were dismissed as *bas* and *rampant*. Only in the second half of the century did rule-breakers begin to develop individual voices. Rousseau, as famous for his paradoxes as for his lyricism, was greatly admired for his style, which was judged both *viril* and *délicat*. By requiring authors to mind their literary manners, the Enlightenment forged an adaptable tool capable of expressing the most abstract ideas and the intricacies of human emotion.

Observation

The range of prose writing widened as human curiosity expanded, but a firm emphasis was placed on the vulgarisation of new ideas. Scientific discoveries and philosophic arguments were made accessible to a non-specialist audience. Increasingly professionalized men of letters published *cours de littérature* (La Harpe, 1739–1803) and established the principles of literary history (Sabbatier de Castres, 1732–1807). An organized press alerted subscribers to new developments in all fields, fuelled literary arguments, began to report domestic and foreign news and mobilized opinion by exposing scandals and commenting on political issues: Linguet (1736–94) anticipated political journalism. The scientific emphasis on observation was now extended to a wider range of social and human phenomena. Books by travellers and explorers (from La Hontan to Bougainville, La Pérouse and Cook) found an increasingly receptive public which also acquired an appetite for news from France, still a foreign land to the Paris public. Life at court (Saint-Simon) and in the capital (Mathieu Marais, 1664–1737; E.-J.-F. Barbier, 1689–1771) was minutely recorded though not, in the main, published. In the last decades of the century, however, Mercier (*Le Tableau de Paris*, 1781–9) and Restif (*Les Nuits de Paris*, 1788–94) revealed lower-class life to middle-class readers who were also catered for by periodicals, like Métra's gossipy but well-informed *Correspondance secrète* (1775–93), or the numerous collections of scandalous revelations and 'anecdotes secrètes' which were an important part of the lucrative trade in clandestine books.

Historiography

The growing curiosity about the present was stoked by the lessons delivered by the practice of a new approach to history. With a few lay exceptions, history in the Middle Ages had been the province of monks and clerics whose concern was not the objective study of the past but the central fact of Christian revelation. By 1500, shaped by the Italian interest in historical remains and ancient models of historical writing, history began to yield more than theological truths. From it, the new learning derived secular principles of kingship, political theory, diplomacy and commerce, and the Renaissance established the importance of documents and archives and laid the basis for a science of chronology. But during the Wars of Religion, the nascent objectivity of history was replaced by polemics as Catholics and Protestants sought to undermine each other with arguments drawn from selected evidence. Four distinct kinds of history were written: memoirs, chronicles, national histories and universal histories. Of these, despite their bias, only the first, written by those who had taken part in events, had any lasting value.

Even so, by 1600, the use of history for political and moral purposes was well rooted as was the awareness that if the past was to be made useful scholars needed a solid base of organized knowledge. Between 1600 and about 1750, the age of Erudition, texts and documents were published in large collections by the Maurists and Benedictines, who developed scientific methods for authenticating and editing manuscript and other materials. This trend, reflected by secular writers, was consolidated by Cartesian rationalism which rejected what could not be verified. The importance of primary sources was enhanced both by theological battles and by secular investigations into forms of government, especially after 1700 when history was used to provide arguments for defending or limiting the powers of the crown: both the *thèse royale* (which justified dynastic monarchy) and the *thèse nobiliaire* (which asserted the political rights of the aristocracy) took history as their witness. The approach was not without its dangers. The conservative majority, both religious and political, continued to oppose the critical examination of tradition, judging it tantamount to blasphemy and treason. But the new mood was reflected even by historians affiliated to the Church. Fleury and Daniel (*Histoire de France*, 1696–1713) insisted on factual accuracy and in his *Méthode pour étudier l'histoire* (1713), Lenglet du Fresnoy (1674–1755) put the case for it in a less scholarly and more general context. But the most consistent support for what was called *le pyrrhonisme de l'histoire* was supplied by Pierre Bayle who, though not primarily a historian, bequeathed a fierce brand of historical scepticism to the Enlightenment.

After 1680, there was a growing awareness that nations and epochs were different, and accounting for their differences became part of the historian's function. Fénelon's 'Projet d'un Traité sur l'histoire' in his *Lettre sur les occupations de l'Académie française* (1714) argued that history should be impartial and based on authenticated sources, its objective being to identify patterns generated by the interplay of cause and effect. The telling *mot*, the anecdote which revealed character or motive were preferable to details of merely antiquarian interest and a work of history should have the same unity and climactic structure required of imaginative literature, and the epic in particular.

Fénelon gave comfort to two views of history, one popular and literary, the other scientific and philosophical. Most readers continued to seek in history a narrative of dramatic events which authors were happy to supply, though at the cost of blurring the line between history and historical romance. A popularizing historian like Mézeray showed almost as little regard for accuracy as Courtilz de Sandras, who posed as the biographer of real persons. Novels, roundly attacked by moralists for their corrupting influence, sailed under a flag of convenience. Calling themselves 'Histoires', they reflected the growing respectability of history as truth. In reality, however, even Daniel and Lenglet were uncritical and careless in their use of sources. Historical writing was more valued for its literary 'ornaments' and stylistic 'graces' than for its accuracy. Portraits, 'noble' speeches, maxims, narrative pace and a certain elevation of tone were preferred to any whiff of archival dust. Even the standard histories of France (Daniel was read until late in the century) and the ancient world (René Vertot, 1655–1735; Charles Rollin, 1661–1741) offered views and interpretations of the past which gave a large place to narrative, anecdote and 'ornament'. Nor were they impartial, for most belonged to the ecclesiastical or educational establishment: the ownership of history would not pass to the laity until after the Revolution.

In some cases, however, Fénelon's call for accuracy and impartiality was heeded: the *Nouvel abrégé chronologique de l'histoire de France* (1744) by the Président Hénault (1685–1770) was a judicious and well-informed survey of military and political history. The more specialized kind of 'scientific' history was read mainly by lawyers and *parlementaires* who had a professional interest in annals, rolls and registers. But by the 1730s, history was being annexed by the *philosophes* who used it as a vehicle for the new ideas. Montesquieu was as interested in the sociology of the present as in the facts of the past. As his title makes clear, the *Considérations sur les causes de la grandeur des Romains et de leur décadence* (1734) offered more analysis than narrative. Montesquieu contested Bossuet's view that history was directed by Providence, and explained the rise and fall of Rome and, by extension, of all empires and states, in terms of economics, population and the decay of institutions.

For Voltaire, too, history was a means to an end. A survey of man's past, based on primary and secondary sources and informed by a healthy scepticism towards both, revealed the stages and circumstances of human progress through the patterns of cause and effect, from undeveloped nature to enlightened civilization. His major histories (*Le Siècle de Louis XIV*, 1751, and the *Essai sur les moeurs et l'esprit des nations*, 1756) argued against both Providentialism and determinism and showed history as the struggle of reason to free itself from religious superstition and the repressive social structures which religions invariably generate. In the event, his documentation was less sound than he believed and impartiality hardly his strongest suit. Yet Voltaire widened the basis of history, which thereafter would include social factors, economics and, not least, ideas. Diderot's *Encyclopédie* made precisely this use of history as philosophic propaganda, as did the *Histoire des deux Indes* (1770–80), an account of European colonization overseen by the *abbé* Raynal (1713–96).

The creation of 'philosophic' history was one of the major achievements of the century. It demythologized the past, which was ransacked for lessons about the nature and processes of civilization as a form of evolution. It generated a new sense of time as a continuum, of societies as part of a chain of cause and effect, of a future which could be shaped by present actions. As Voltaire had intended, history ceased to be simply a record of what had been and became the description of patterns of development which could be harnessed for the common good. If time was a river, it flowed in one direction: onward. It was this belief that inspired the culmination of 'philosophic' history, the *Esquisse d'un tableau historique des progrès de l'esprit humain* (1795) by Condorcet (1749–94), who defined progress as the realization of human perfectibility through science and the intellect.

Biography

But if society had a history, so did each person. From its beginnings, literature had personalized the human predicament by putting human faces to abstract ideas. Out of the Latin *vita* grew the lives of saints which, cumulatively, created a framework (childhood, deeds and death) for accounts of kings and legendary heroes like Arthur and his knights. In the thirteenth century, the brief, formulaic *vida* honoured poets who, in the fourteenth, began to acquire individuality and finally, with Machaut or Villon, names. Well into the seventeenth century, however, works and deeds continued to be held in greater esteem than the circumstances of a particular life, unless that life could be seen as a work and made exemplary. Plutarch furnished a secular model, the *vie illustre*, which was used to offer lessons in chivalry, valour and honour, but in the late Renaissance summaries of the lives of artists and authors also linked works to their creators. After 1650, proto-biography acquired some of the habits of the new document-based history. Accounts of historical figures and writers like Descartes and Molière, though sketchy and unreliable, adopted a chronological sequence, assessed their subject's achievements and offered the same kind of categorized character judgements as the *portrait*. After 1700, interest in public figures continued to grow, though biographies were rare. But the impetus was preserved in the academic *éloge*, novels which encouraged readers to be curious about supposedly 'real' lives and philosophic writings which created a gallery of radically-minded precursors.

Autobiography

The practice of generalizing human experience remained part of the neo-classical outlook, and collections of maxims were supplied by Vauvenargues (1715–47) and the pessimistic Chamfort (1740–94). But the newer habit of scientific observation, which provided knowledge of the external world, was turned increasingly inward and became a means of knowing the self. The memoir of court, literary and political life, which focused on public events, remained the dominant mode. But the growth of individualism brought major developments. From being spectators of events, victims of oppression used personal experience to highlight abuses of power. Jean Merteilhe's *Mémoires d'un protestant* (1757), a graphic account of life in the galleys between 1700 and 1713, exposed the realities of religious persecution. At the other end of the century, the *Histoire d'une détention de trente-neuf ans* (1787) by Henri Latude (1725–1805) made a vivid case against the *lettre de cachet*.

More far-reaching, however, was the interest in the inner life (pursued in Mme Guyon's account of her spiritual odyssey, for example) which paved the way for the invention of the concept of private life. This was already sufficiently advanced for the *Mémoires* (1755) of Madame de Staal-Launay (*c*.1684–1750) to accord a prominent place to her impoverished childhood, her hopes, fears and struggles. The specificity of personal experience is clearest in non-aristocratic authors, like Jameray-Duval (1695–1775), a peasant who became librarian to the court of Lorraine, or Ménétra (1738–after 1802), a glazier, whose *Journal de ma vie* (published only in 1982) offers a rare view of a working-class life. Rousseau too was a commoner, but his achievement was not merely to record a life but to establish autobiography as a literary genre. His *Confessions* validated personal experience as history, self-discovery and self-justification, and his example was not lost on others who felt impelled to record experience which, though general in its import, was unique in its circumstances. Casanova (1725–98), Marmontel (1723–99), Restif (1734–1806) and Madame Roland (1754–93) reflected, each from a particular standpoint, truths about man, nature and society. But the most popular mirror was held up by fiction, which evolved more rapidly than either poetry and theatre and remains the most enduring of the century's literary achievements.

Fiction

From the beginning, the novel faced aesthetic, moral, intellectual and official opposition. It had not been dignified by Aristotle as a genre with rules, and the small number of ancient fictions (Apuleius's *Golden Ass*, for example) could scarcely be considered models of anything but bad taste. For the Church, the novel was frivolous and immoral, for by taking love as its subject, it taught forgetfulness of duty, undermined marriage, and roused passions better left dormant. From pulpits, in the pages of the Jesuit periodical, the *Journal de Trévoux* (founded 1701) and through hostile surveys like the *abbé* Jacquin's *Entretiens sur les romans* (1755), the Church attacked fiction as an assault on Christian society. The rationally minded raised different objections. They argued that by giving an enlarged role to the imagination, a suspect faculty, novelists undermined intellectual rigour and blurred the line between truth and invention. Rousseau, a novelist himself, damned novels with faint praise, for they were 'la dernière instruction qu'il reste à donner à un peuple assez corrompu pour que toute autre lui soit inutile'. The adjective *romanesque*, which was at first to *roman* what *tragique* was to *tragédie*, acquired a pejorative sense and was standard usage for those who deplored 'grotesque' and 'extravagant' fancy and 'extraordinary' adventures. Official censors denied a *privilège* to novelists who undermined morality and institutions, the police seized scandalous and subversive novels and a short-lived blanket ban on the genre was imposed in 1737.

Defence of the novel

In their defence, novelists pointed to Fénelon's *Télémaque*, which was commended by both the Church and the *philosophes* for its wisdom and literary qualities. It was a 'poème en prose' admirable in content and absolute in its respect for the classical aesthetic. Against the charge of immorality, Prévost went so far as to define fiction as a practical moral lesson. The rationalist objection was countered by Lenglet Dufresnoy (*De l'usage des romans*, 1734) who argued that fiction unveiled truths about life and love which were beyond the reach of history or philosophy, a view echoed in the prefaces of even the most *romanesque* novels. And despite the experience of Marmontel (*Bélisaire*, 1767; banned for its defence of the philosopher king) or Laclos (whose scandalous *Les Liaisons dangereuses* was seized by the police in 1782), novelists managed to operate within the official guidelines without being seriously inconvenienced.

Public demand

But the novel's best defence was the support it received from the paying public. Demand grew dramatically. The 150 titles published in the century's first decade swelled to 320 in the 1740s, and 550 in the 1780s. Readers were reassured by the more relaxed view of the passions which had been rehabilitated by anti-clerical *philosophes*. The decline of the old aristocracy and the rise of bourgeois individualism generated new levels of inquisitiveness about the behaviour of individuals who made up in merit what they lacked in birth. The aspiring middle class took their manners from novels which, for many, were not simply agreeable reading but manuals which taught social etiquette, taste and the ways and values of the fashionable world. But the greatest attraction was escape. Few things, as La Rochefoucauld had noted, are as enjoyable as the misfortunes of others and novelists played to the curiosity of readers who experienced vicariously the perils and tribulations of characters they could believe in and, even better, judge.

Literary strategies

Yet novelists remained in a state of siege and adopted an array of defensive strategies. They took care not to challenge neo-classical taste. The market might well prefer the *vrai* to the *vraisemblable*, but the novel respected *bienséance* by excluding the lower classes and eschewing vulgarity of language and sentiment. Portraits and maxims were supplied in the approved manner and the duty to 'plaire et instruire' was redefined as an obligation to show virtue rewarded and vice punished. But novelists also avoided drawing attention to themselves. Most remained anonymous or used pseudonyms, and few described their work as *romans*, preferring more compliant labels: *relation, anecdote, aventures, mémoires* and, above all, *histoire*. They wrote prefaces which insisted that their stories were not invented but true, and posed as intermediaries, not creators. Since what they wrote was history, they claimed to use the methods of the historian. They were transcribers of stories heard from the lips of real persons, translators of authentic manuscripts, and editors of journals, diaries and bundles of letters bequeathed by dead friends or found by chance. For the most part, readers were not taken in and accepted the convention.

Narrative modes

Yet if the link with history was spurious, it nevertheless determined the two major forms of long fiction: the *roman-mémoires* and the epistolary novel. Third-person narrators were not rare (especially in short fiction). But the dominant narrative modes echoed respectable forms of writing – autobiography and the vogue for published correspondence – and, more importantly, both invited the reader to peep into the secret lives of others. From the pseudo-memoirs of celebrated persons by Hamilton and Courtilz, novelists graduated to the memoirs of people who, though not famous, were said to be no less real. The letter-novel, taking its lead from Guilleragues's *Lettres portugaises*, also widened its scope. It exploited the monologue of the single voice, the dialogue between two characters and the chatter of multiple correspondents for dramatic, psychological and increasingly sentimental effects. It frequently strained credulity, however. Letters, often of excessive length, were written and sent in the strangest circumstances, and Mme de Graffigny (*Lettres d'une Péruvienne*, 1747) explained that her Inca heroine communicated not in writing but by coded knots tied in a silken thread. On the other hand, Laclos's *Liaisons dangereuses* realized the full potential of the epistolary form. Each character has a distinctive voice, letters are subtly ordered to maximize ambiguity and irony and correspondence even becomes part of the action: Tourvel is killed by a letter and letters bring about Merteuil's downfall.

Narrative genres

Narrative modes were not systematically linked to types of story, though in broad terms the epistolary novel dealt with a situation while the memoir-novel charted the broader growth of a life. For whether written in letters or by first-person narrators, the subject of the novel was love thwarted, tested, lost and regained. The *roman d'analyse* continued to define its nature and show it in conflict with moral duty and social propriety (Challes, Marivaux, Duclos). But the intellectual analysis of love gave way to the pleasure of feeling (in the 1730s, Crébillon *fils* distinguished clearly between 'le coeur et l'esprit') which was legitimized by the authority of Prévost, Rousseau and Bernardin de Saint-Pierre. It was an area which attracted women authors (Tencin, Graffigny, Riccoboni, Charrière) who created strong, independent heroines who refused to accept love and life on the terms offered by men. Moralists and theologians wrote novels of piety as antidotes to the 'poisons' spread by mainstream fiction. Rationalist arguments were spread through 'philosophic' novels, from *Les Lettres persanes*, to *Bélisaire* and *Jacques le Fataliste*, and ultimately Sade. Utopian reformers revived the *voyage imaginaire* and described ideal societies beyond the seas and on invented planets: between 1760 and 1780, there was an outbreak of flying men. They tapped a vein of unrealism exploited in more traditional terms in the *roman fantastique* from Lesage (*Le Diable boîteux*, 1707) to Cazotte's *Le Diable amoureux* (1772) which contained the promise of the Gothic mode of the 1790s.

Romans d'éducation

The versatility of the novel is well illustrated by the *roman d'éducation* which found a natural home in a century dedicated to mastering the world. In its classic form, it showed how a young man (rarely a woman) is matured by his adventures. In novels inspired by *Télémaque*, he is well-born and achieves wisdom: such is the pattern from Ramsay's *Voyages de Cyrus* (1727) to Barthélemy's *Voyage du jeune Anacharsis en Grèce* (1788). A variant, the *roman d'apprentissage*, focused on young men (and sometimes women) born with few or no social advantages, and followed their struggle to achieve respectability. At first the mood echoed both seventeenth-century French realists, like Sorel and Scarron, and the Spanish picaresque, as in Lesage's *Gil Blas* (1715–35). It took a more naturalized form in Mouhy's *La Paysanne parvenue* (1735–7) and Marivaux's two novels: *Le Paysan parvenu* (1734–5) and *La Vie de Marianne* (1731–42). For Jacob and Marianne, self-awareness leads to self-knowledge and both novels, though Marivaux left them unfinished, reach a satisfying conclusion when his characters acquire full mastery of themselves. Prévost (1697–1763) respected the *bienséances*, but by making his heroes vulnerable to their feelings helped shift the emphasis from the passive acquisition of knowledge to resistance to conventional wisdom. He made free with history and filled his narratives with adventure and perils. But his characters are constantly aware of what they feel and reflect at length on the ethical implications of their conduct. Prévost described *Manon Lescaut*, the seventh part of the *Mémoires d'un homme de qualité* (1728–31), as a practical demonstration of 'la morale en action'. It is a kind of prose tragedy which shows how circumstances alter cases. Though Des Grieux and Manon behave badly, their innocence is not in doubt, for what they do is directed by fate in the guise of social pressures, chance and events. The *Histoire d'une Grecque moderne* (1741) offered an equally sobering view of *amour-passion* and further undermined the absolute standards and taboos which defined ethical conduct. This habit of introspection continued to hang question marks over accepted social and moral values which, from black and white, became grey. The duty to conform turned into the search for emotional and spiritual fulfilment, and many novels in the wake of Richardson and *La Nouvelle Héloïse* explored the guilt which arises from the inability to reconcile idealism and worldly compromise. The *roman d'initiation*, a further variant, specialized in sexual rites of passage and was a staple ingredient of the *roman libertin*.

The *roman libertin*

Philosophical *libertinage* had entered into a tentative alliance with the traditions of common bawdy at the end of the seventeenth century. But after 1700, though the popular Oriental tale played with the mildly shocking habits of its many-wived sultans, public prurience was satisfied by the *histoire galante* which dealt with adultery in decorous terms. The *roman libertin* came into its own with the return of salon life in the 1720s and 1730s. At first, it spoke of the relations between the sexes with sententious worldliness. But the aristocratic heroes of Crébillon *fils* (1707–77) and Duclos (1704–72) were taught a social skill now more important than feats of arms: the art of seduction. In chaste and disembodied narratives, they learn to move in a closed world dominated by language systems and behavioural signifiers where a sigh, a glance and the right words do not so much wake a female heart but open her bedroom door, beyond which, however, the reader does not pass. Seduction was a sophisticated game and its point was style and wit. Its coded preciosity was regularly revisited, ambiguously by Laclos and enthusiastically by Vivant Denon (1747–1825), whose faultless *Point de lendemain* (1777) is perhaps its finest hour. Many, however, reacted against this essentially courtly amusement. La Morlière's *Angola* (1746) mocked its linguistic artifice and Dorat's *Les Malheurs de l'inconstance* (1772) pointed to the dangers of the philosophy of pleasure which was a denial of emotion, a point implicit in *Les Liaisons dangereuses* where the aristocratic *ars amandi* is exposed as a sterile and empty error.

But already in the 1740s, *galanterie* was being challenged by direct and earthy eroticism set in less exalted surroundings. Sex was not its only, or even main, concern. La Touche's *Portier des chartreux* (1741) updated the lewd monk of tradition by exposing the lust of modern churchmen. The same subject was treated more pointedly still by, probably, the Marquis d'Argens in *Thérèse philosophe* (1748) which resurrected the scandalous case of the Jesuit priest Girard, accused in 1731 of seducing one of his charges. Between orgies, Thérèse also manages to provide an outline of philosophical materialism far bolder than anything Diderot ventured to say the same year in his *Bijoux indiscrets*. The social range of the *roman libertin* was widened by Fougeret de Monbron's *Margot la Ravaudeuse* (1750) which sets the rise of a prostitute against a background of documentary realism rare in these novels. *Le Colporteur* (1761), Chévrier's contribution to the *chronique scandaleuse*, implicated influential nobles and wealthy financiers in the vice trade. Nerciat (*Félicia*, 1775), immune to the reservations of Dorat, made guilt-free hedonism a more than acceptable substitute for happiness. Conduct which does not injure society is not society's concern: the argument which had exposed Tartuffe's villainy ('to sin in private is not to sin at all') had been legitimized by the eclipse of religion. Sade would go much further and argue that conduct which is natural, whether or not it injures society or individuals, is legitimate.

Libertine literature was a form of resistance. Its authors showed scant respect for religion, morality and exclusive love. By translating *galanterie* into pleasure and sensuality, it delivered a body blow to the dominance of courtly values. The seducer's stratagems have less to do with honour than with winning and losing, profit and loss. The *roman libertin*, where bodies are 'possessed' and love is a 'commerce' which trades in feelings, reflected the *embourgeoisement* of aristocratic culture. But by defending the natural urges of both men and women in unambiguous terms, it also stated the case for the individual against the collective. It was a vessel into which was poured all the frustration of those who were not free to protest openly against the arbitrariness of an absolutist state. In this sense, *libertin* discourse was as political in its implications as the boldest *philosophie*. The French Revolution was sexual long before it became political in 1789.

Realism

The vast majority of eighteenth-century novels are now remarkable only for their tedium. They used stock characters, repeated narrative clichés and were conservative in outlook. The authority and wisdom of the king and Church were never questioned, fate was corrected by the workings of a benign Providence, marriage was the goal and honour its means, with the light of the *Encyclopédie* rarely penetrating its complacent darkness. Its literary failings were regularly pointed out. Marivaux parodied the grand style of heroic romance in *La Voiture embourbée* (1714), and the *Voyage merveilleux du Prince Fan-Férédin* (1735), Bougeant's 'anti-novel', defined the land of 'Romancie' as a place of absurd, escapist fantasy. Even reputable authors were not spared such strictures. Charles Bordes deflated the poetry of Saint-Preux's sentiments in *La Nouvelle Héloïse* by observing that, when considered objectively, its hero 'prend le pucelage de son élève pour ses gages'. In *Jacques le Fataliste* Diderot mocked the melodramatic implausibilities of Prévost to which he preferred the 'petits détails' of Richardson and the teasing 'conversation' of Sterne.

Whereas the English novelists observed reality directly and left a broad picture of social manners, the French, bound by taste, were most at home with the non-specific and the universal. The epistolary novel dated imagined correspondence as a proof of its authenticity, but letters headed 'Jeudi' or 'Paris, ce 9 juin 17**' were embedded in no precise time or place: only a stray remark that Gercourt is on manoeuvres in Corsica suggests that the *Liaisons dangereuses* might be set in 1769. Novels which ventured into the area of the non-genteel revealed most about everyday life. *Manon Lescaut,* set in 1720, is a very Parisian novel and money is an essential ingredient of plot and situation. But for the most part, characters were presented as *caractères* and they inhabited a world denied social and temporal reality. Even so, its cast of types reflected changing values. The outsiderly *pícaro* of Lesage and Marivaux was made clubbable as the representative of the new creeds of merit and sensibility. Churchmen grew more corrupt and aristocrats more arrogant, but the merchant lost his boorish image and earned respect as the upholder of duty, thrift, family, and moral worth. The place of peasants and the urban poor, however, was at the rich man's gate, objects of charity or a reminder of simple virtues which readers sampled at a distance. Modest asides on current abuses did not give the novel a social conscience and Diderot's attack on the convent system in *La Religieuse,* unpublished until 1796, was exceptional. No novelist took as a subject the persecution of Protestants, the peasant condition or the delays of the law.

Nouvelle and *conte*

But if the public had the patience to read long novels, it also devoured shorter fiction. The *conte* had slowly moved beyond its bawdy associations with the *fabliau* and Boccaccio to the sophistication of Marguerite de Navarre's *Heptaméron.* After 1600, however, it was eclipsed by the novel until about 1660 when the long *nouvelle* became the dominant fictional form. Before that date, only two volumes of French tales (Sorel, 1623; Segrais, 1656) were published. Thereafter, 24 collections had appeared by 1700, plus over a hundred separate short fictions of the type popularized by Mme de la Fayette.

By 1700, the amusing anecdote (the *conte*) had been subordinated to the longer *nouvelle* which took as its subject the psychological drama of its almost invariably aristocratic characters. It reflected the aesthetics of the novel and, in many cases, was indistinguishable from the intercalated narrative of the *roman à tiroir.* At the beginning of the eighteenth century, however, these *nouvelles historiques* and *histoires galantes* were challenged by new styles of short fiction. The seven tales of *Les Illustres Françaises* (1713) by Robert Challes (1659–1720) injected a new note of psychological and social realism into the form, but for the most part *nouvelle* and novel differed only by length. It was not until after 1750 that it eliminated sub-plots and reverted to a single adventure or situation involving a limited cast of characters.

More significant was the rise, after the turn of the century, of the *conte*. The Oriental tale mixed elegant titillation (the *frisson* of the harem) with oblique but often sharp social criticism. An extension of the adult fairy tales made popular in the 1690s by Perrault and Mme d'Aulnoy, it offered a screen behind which authors could hide. In settings perfunctorily decked out with exotic detail, despotic viziers and fanatical brahmins were used to mock and condemn despotism and fanaticism at home.

After 1750 both *conte* and *nouvelle*, if the differences between them narrowed, grew in popularity. Stories were published in periodicals and in collections, sometimes running to many volumes, which sold well. Traditional tales remained popular (*Le Cabinet des fées*, 1785–6, 41 vols, preserved several hundred) but as the *conte* gained ground, it diversified. Its raciness was perpetuated by the *conte badin* of Voisenon (1708–75), Cazotte and the Comte de Caylus (1692–1765), but in Voltaire's hands, it became the sharp-edged, ironic *conte philosophique*, which was more concerned with ideas than love and made no claim to realism. Though its mood was continued in Diderot's *Jacques le Fataliste* and Sade's *Les Infortunes de la vertu* (1787), the Voltairean short story proved less influential than the model popularized by the tales (1755–65) of Marmontel. Anchored in contemporary settings, the *conte moral* told stories which were closer to the preoccupations of ordinary readers. It raised moral questions and social issues and proved extremely flexible. Restif wrote over a thousand (*Les Contemporaines*, 1780–5, alone ran to 42 volumes) which offered 'mille moyens d'être heureux par le mariage'. With Baculard d'Arnaud (*Les Épreuves du sentiment*, 1772–80) and Loaisel de Tréogate (1752–1812), it exploited sentiment, horror and melodrama. The *conte fantastique* progressed from the folklore of Perrault and the magic of the Orient to more scientific marvels (interplanetary travel and exotic adventure) before surrendering to the devils and ghostly apparitions of the

Gothic imagination which Sade took up in *Les Crimes de l'amour* (1800), though he had first written bawdy tales in the manner of Boccaccio. The *conte* was as versatile and as unstoppable as the novel.

Beyond Enlightenment

Fiction proved to be a powerful tool of Enlightenment. It loosened the rigid structures of the neo-classical aesthetic and opened literature to a wider range of modern concerns. It was at its most progressive as a forum for the discussion of moral ideas. Even the most conservative novelists invited readers to judge their characters and in so doing encouraged independent habits of mind. By extending the reader's experience (by showing the circumstances which drive a sympathetic character to act badly), the novel undermined categorical moral verdicts. As swans swim in water without getting wet, so Prévost's Manon does wrong without being wicked. The idea was not new (Phèdre was neither innocent nor guilty) but it was now applied to contemporary people in modern situations. In the process, virtue was detached from religion and nobility of heart ceased to be the exclusive preserve of the aristocracy. In this sense, novels endorsed the message of tolerance preached by Voltairean *philosophes*. But novels also led a Rousseauistic reaction against rationalism. By asserting the rights of emotion, novelists made indirect propaganda for other rights which defended the individual against the power of Church and state. Utopian fiction established political alternatives to absolutism, and the *roman libertin* demanded freedoms for the individual which even the Revolution would not grant. This shift from the docile acceptance of monolithic values to contestation emerges forcefully in the work of transitional writers who had one foot in their century and the other in the next.

Mercier

In his 50 *drames*, Louis-Sébastien Mercier (1740–1814) raised social questions (war, equality). As a social observer, he showed the underside of the capital (*Le Tableau de Paris*, 1781–9); *Le Nouveau Paris*, 1793–8). But *L'An 2440* (1770), his picture of the future with its strong criticism of the present, articulated a level of political radicalism which fuelled discontent more actively: it was the most widely read title in the clandestine book trade. But his literary ideas also formed a bridge to the future. His writings on the theatre anticipated the principles and practice of Romantic drama, *Mon Bonnet de nuit* (1784) pointed poetry in the direction it would in fact take, and *La Néologie* (1801) was not merely a dictionary of coinages but a defence of the principle that language should not be constrained by taste but free to express the imagination and thought of the writer. It was a revolutionary position to which Hugo would return.

Restif

Restif de la Bretonne (1734–1806), son of a yeoman farmer, was apprenticed to a printer and earned his living as a typesetter until 1767, when he made a late start as a self-taught novelist. He admired Voltaire's 'saine morale' and from Rousseau he learned to explore his sensibility. He wrote moralizing novels and tales which endlessly recycled his own experience. But he also set up as a social reformer, starting with prostitution (*Le Pornographe*, 1769) before moving on to the 'reformation' of society and the 'regeneration' of human nature according to the values of the 'petite république', the laws of the cosmos and moral reciprocity. He was made famous by *Le Paysan perverti* (1775) and *Les Contemporaines*. But, an outsiderly figure, he was too diffident to be drawn into fashionable society and observed life from street level, ignoring high politics, of which he knew little, but leaving a vivid chronicle of small lives. His account of his love for Sara, *La Dernière Aventure d'un homme de 45 ans* (1783) conveys lived experience with raw immediacy. The source of his writing was his past, his thoughts, his feelings and he retreated progressively into a private world which fascinated him. He turned himself into a 'livre vivant', the 'homme entier' of *Monsieur Nicolas* (1796–7), a vivid self-portrait which was a 'supplement' to Buffon's *Histoire naturelle*. But Restif surrendered too easily to his subjectivity to be a detached observer and his strengths lie elsewhere, not least in an exploration of time and memory more sophisticated than anything attempted before Proust. Though he looked for himself in his past, his books pointed to the future. He thought with his imagination and his feelings, neologized from necessity and cultivated his *moi* with an intensity more readily associated with the 'personal' writing of the Empire and the poets of the 1820s. His utopian socialism influenced Leroux and Fourier, Nerval found a kindred spirit in him, and the seeds of the totalizing ambition of Balzac and Zola have been detected in his picture of society, which he saw from below stairs.

Laclos

Les Liaisons dangereuses (1782), the only novel of Choderlos de Laclos (1741–1803), has been interpreted in many ways. When it was published, its author was identified with the cynicism of Valmont, and Laclos's life and personality are still invoked to explain a book which has so many levels and facets that it yields no single meaning. Is it a neutral picture of manners based, perhaps, on real letters which may yet be discovered? An indictment of corrupt aristocrats motivated by the spleen of an army officer with insufficient birth to merit promotion, or alternatively by moral disgust for a society ripe for revolution? Yet if it is a moral book, it does not reward virtue and punishes oppressors and victims alike. If not any of these, then it is perhaps philosophically inclined: a study of human evil, say, or a proto-Existentialist revolt against the boredom of an existence so privileged that it is meaningless. Unless, that is, Laclos's essays on the education of women (1783) are added to the novel's criticism of convent education and marriage, in which case it is possible to speak, with different degrees of enthusiasm, of *Les Liaisons dangereuses* as a feminist book. Its literary stance is no less ambiguous, for it can be read as either a celebration or an impeachment of the *roman libertin*, an expression of cool irony or of controlled indignation. But if it is the most elusive of novels, most readers sense that Laclos is far from neutral, that he admires the style of Valmont and Merteuil but not their callous disregard for human values. The same ambivalence is reflected in his political life after 1789, when he served the Revolution but lacked the steel to be anything other than 'second dans tous les genres'. A man of science (he trained as a military engineer) and an admirer of Rousseau, Laclos expresses reservations about eighteenth-century rationalism which, when reduced to mere lucidity, denied the emotional side of human experience.

Bernardin de Saint-Pierre

An experienced traveller and friend of Rousseau, Bernardin de Saint-Pierre (1737–1814) achieved success with the *Études de la nature* (1784) which rejected philosophical atheism by arguing, from final causes, that Nature was designed by a benign Providence for man's use. Though his examples were sometimes absurd (the segments of a melon are marked for man's convenience), he made up in sentiment and painterly style what he lacked in scientific rigour. *Paul et Virginie*

(1788), set in Mauritius, constructs the idyllic world of Rousseau's natural man and expresses in poetic and tragic terms the loss of human innocence. In *La Chaumière indienne* (1791), the seeker of truth finds it not in European learning but in the simple hut of a pariah. Rural utopias, cloying sentiment and the primitive sage were hardly novelties, but Bernardin gave them a graphic, pictorial form. Colours, sounds and perfumes brightened the monochrome universe of fiction. His lyrical, melancholic, elegiac descriptions of sea and tropical landscapes would survive, abetted by Chateaubriand, as part of the arsenal of the Romantic nature poets.

Sade

From his reading of materialists like La Mettrie and d'Holbach, the Marquis de Sade (1741–1814) concluded that nature's purpose is the perpetuation of life; that nature renews itself by recycling matter, which is finite in quantity; that death releases atoms and molecules for re-use; and that there is no place in such a scheme of things for a God. But whereas atheists invariably found arguments to support moral values without which individuals would not be human and societies could not function, Sade made no such compromise. The only legitimacy is nature. Actions, however unspeakable, which furthered its purposes are crimes only in the eyes of society, a conspiracy mounted by the weak to contain the strong in whom urges burn most fiercely. We are made to desire what Nature wants by the same pleasure principle which makes bees pollinate flowers with the promise of nectar. If nature requires us to seek gratification, then no attempt to obtain it can be wrong. Because what we desire is natural, the only crime is the rejection of pleasure and virtue is its unrestricted pursuit. But since pleasure includes the enjoyment of the suffering of others, extreme cruelty must also be part of our programming. Sade, who asserted his right to be called a philosopher, did not claim to invent Sadism. He merely drew back the veil of hypocrisy which had kept it hidden from view.

He filled his novels with murder, theft, rape and all forms of sexual perversion, and justified them in repetitive tirades against religion, morality and tolerance, which he defined as the virtue of the weak. His arguments scarcely hold water, for they depend on a restricted view of human nature. He skips the affections which, since they exist, must also be as natural as the priapic rages of his heroes, who are enslaved by their insatiable desires. From *Les 120 journées de Sodome* (1785) through the three versions of *Justine* (1787–99) to *Les Prospérités du vice* (1799), Sade's obsessive fictions imprison his reader in a world of dark forests and subterranean labyrinths which have less to do with the Gothic than with the jails in which he spent a third of his life. They show none of the literary qualities of his tales and, in so far as they constitute a uniquely documented case-history, belong to medicine or law rather than to literature. Sade was born in a château and died in a madhouse. He was incarcerated by every regime, monarchical, revolutionary, republican and Napoleonic, under which he lived, and his books remained banned until the 1960s. Yet his place in the history of ideas is clear. By taking philosophic ideas to their logical conclusion, he showed that the humanitarianism of the Enlightenment was incompatible with its rationalism. But he also represented a new force of anarchy which was admired by Baudelaire and Apollinaire and made him, in the twentieth century, the permanent symbol of transgression.

Conclusion

Enlightenment and Revolution

The extent to which the Enlightenment prepared the way for Revolution remains a matter of controversy. Most *philosophes* were, of course, critics of absolute kingship and admired the English Revolution of 1688–9. That upheaval, however, had been 'peaceful' and it had led to a form of constitutional monarchy which fully met philosophic ambitions. Only Rousseau defended the people's right to insurrection and only Diderot, in a handful of late, unpublished writings, stated the case for republicanism. By 'forcing' citizens to be free, Rousseau might seem to justify the Terror to come, yet he was as firmly opposed to despotism as Montesquieu and Voltaire, who had spent too much time defending freedom and tolerance to accept tyranny in new clothes or approve of murder and, less still, of regicide. Revolt against injustice and the reform of abuses were different from revolution, a concept alien to Enlightenment thought, which learned from Nature that change must be a slow and measured process. After 1789, its surviving representatives adopted generally moderate positions and did what they could to curb the excesses of the Terror.

But however opposed they were to the principle of violent upheaval, the *philosophes* had nevertheless compiled a comprehensive case against the corrupt, still feudal *ancien régime*. They had also shown what needed to be done. They set out plans for correcting institutional abuses, denounced the links between the Church and civil power, gave men rights and urged social reforms which were consistent with reason and natural law. The Enlightenment sowed discontent and disrespect for the Church and the nation's leaders. If the philosophic spirit 'prepared' the Revolution it was in creating a climate in which ideas ceased to be abstract. After 1789, all shades of political opinion could be justified by reference to the vast body of philosophic writings which, by their cumulative effect, had made change inevitable.

Pre-Romanticism

The eighteenth century left a relatively small legacy of imaginative literature. Its strengths lay elsewhere, in its pursuit not of pure but of applied reason. Yet its concern with the realities of human existence opened new literary horizons. The rigid compartmentalization of genres was eroded and authors metamorphosed into *polygraphes* who both satisfied and created new publics. They annexed literature, turning it outward to reflect the order and logic which determined man's place in the natural and social world. Against scientific reductionism grew an awareness of human diversity. The focus of interest moved from classical antiquity to the modern countries of northern Europe, from Virgil's fields to Rousseau's Alps, and thence, via travellers and explorers, to the Indians of North and South America, the virtuous tribes of the tropics and the sages of China. This relativism in space was echoed in the discovery of alternative cultural values in the poetry and prose of the Middle East, Ossian's 'Celtic' outpourings and, in the 1780s, the vogue for the literature of the Middle Ages. The weakening of rationalism is graphically demonstrated by the rise of the 'English' garden which, less disciplined, challenged the domestication of nature represented by the geometrical French style.

But what was true of foreign lands or gardens was also true of human nature, a territory which had still to be explored. If man did not control his collective life (empires rose and fell despite him), it was also true that he was not in control of himself. He was vulnerable to passions which were not only unruly but disturbing. Incest was added to the standard arsenal of the sentimental novelist. Melodrama and the Gothic pricked darker regions of the psyche and superstition proved less easily eradicated than the *philosophes* had supposed. In the last decades of the century older beliefs in magic resurfaced. Cagliostro raised spirits, the Comte de Saint-Germain was believed by many when he claimed to be 2,000 years old, Lavater (1741–1801) invented the 'science' of physiognomy and the 'animal magnetism' of Mesmer (1734–1815) was a source of fascination. Such unphilosophic beliefs, codified by the Illuminists, were symptomatic of an anti-rationalist tendency which drew its power from the awareness that the individual was alone in a world which offered only the comfort of sentiment.

The crisis of confidence of the century's early years had been halted only temporarily by scientific optimism. By the 1770s, less sure of reason and open to sensation and sentiment, aware of the 'vanités du monde', the 'vicissitudes' of life, and the remorseless passage of time, the mood turned to introspective, tearful pessimism of which literature was the beneficiary. In the struggle to align 'le coeur' and 'l'esprit', the writer who used his imagination to exploit his sensibility acquired a new standing and became a new model. He wrote not for money or reputation but to put his readers in touch with their true natures, a task which meant abandoning the sterile tradition of academic classicism and striking out in new directions. Originality, centred on the cult of the individual, became an essential ingredient of the new aesthetic. What is called 'pre-Romanticism' (a word coined only in 1912) was thus more than a prelude to future developments: it was part of the evolving Enlightenment. It signalled a psychological shift, a move to new literary, social and cultural values which, however, would not find their full expression until the storms of Revolution and its aftermath had passed.

Literature and the Revolution (1789–99)

A decade of revolution transformed the social, institutional and cultural landscape of France. The nobility was abolished, the civil power of the Church was broken, and government became a matter for elected representatives. Limits were set on royal power but the Republic was declared before Louis XVI was guillotined in January 1793. The state, which had belonged to the king, became the *patrie* of citizens who were promised rights guaranteed by a constitution. But the struggle to establish a new regime was not conducted without violence and bloodshed. Even after the Terror ended in July 1794, conflict continued to divide the radical Left and the conservative Right, two permanent groupings which were not the least of the legacies of the Revolution.

In the dawn of the new age of liberty, the Déclaration des droits de l'homme et du citoyen (26 August 1789) made free speech a right and relaxed controls on its printed expression. The *privilège* required for the publication of books and newspapers was abolished and in January 1791 a simple declaration allowed any citizen to 'élever un théâtre public et y faire représenter des pièces de tous les genres'. Between that date and 1800, some 50 new theatres were opened in Paris and 1,500 new plays were staged. In 1793, the state recognized intellectual property rights. Such liberalizing measures, however, were temporary. New controls were introduced in August 1792 and freedom of expression was negated by the Terror when, for publishing 'unpatriotic' views, printers, journalists and authors were arrested and, usually, executed. Notable casualties were Condorcet, André Chénier and Chamfort. The principle of freedom was restored in 1795 and lasted until a failed royalist coup in September 1797 brought a return to strict press controls. Yet despite the dangers and constraints, a decade of Revolution produced mountains of print, fevered creativity, but little of lasting literary worth. If writers became politicians, politicians became writers. Théroigne de Méricourt and Etta Palm raised the voice of women until 1793, when it was made finally clear that the Rights of Man did not apply to the female sex: the pugnacious Olympe de Gouges (*Les Droits de la femme et de la citoyenne*, 1791) and Mme Roland both died on the guillotine.

For the first time, popular opinion was heard. The *Cahiers de doléances* (statements of grievances supplied by villages, guilds and municipalities to delegates of the States-General in May 1789) amounted to a book in many disparate volumes written by the People. But the People needed guidance and journalism supplied it. Two thousand newspapers, mostly short-lived, appeared in Paris during the decade (300 in 1790 alone) and a further 1,000 in the provinces. They were supplemented by a vast pamphlet literature of many hues which made carefully reasoned cases, launched crude, obscene satire, and delivered deadly denunciations. Eloquence, now a secular art, acquired a new vitality, for words made history and could be the difference between life and death. In 1789, Camille Desmoulins (1760–94) harangued crowds in the Palais-Royal before joining Mirabeau, Maury, Danton, Robespierre, Saint-Just and many more in the assemblies of the Revolution. Their speeches were reported verbatim in *Le Moniteur* from 1789 onwards. Although they forged a new political language of procedure and ideology, the Revolution's orators drew on older rhetorical models, the heroes of antiquity, the virtues of Republican Rome, the writings of Montesquieu and Rousseau. On the other hand, private correspondence, particularly 'last letters' written in the shadow of the guillotine, acquired a new simplicity. Between public oratory and the intimate exchange stood the personal journals and memoirs of those, like Condorcet and Madame Roland, who felt the need to leave a spiritual testament for posterity. The Revolution redirected the shape of France. But it also revealed the impact of politics on individual lives.

It also changed the nature of political discourse. Now that ideas were linked to power, Enlightenment projects could be translated into parties and policies. Not all philosophic ideas were well received, however. Atheism was resisted in favour of a deistic faith in Reason, egalitarianism ran counter to the right to private property and the Nation, now one and indivisible, fiercely opposed the individualism of the *philosophes* and set a higher value on the good of all. Factions, from the political clubs to the 'Conspiration des Égaux' of Babeuf (1760–97), were served by a new breed of publicist. But less specific intellectual positions were also defended. For the Illuminists, the universe was a divine emanation and man's task was to restore the harmony and unity of creation which had been lost through the Fall. A mystical, occult tendency, Illuminism fascinated social and religious thinkers in the nineteenth century and the view of the poet as a seer possessed of a symbolic vision, which was advanced by its most flamboyant representative, Saint-Martin (1743–1803), helped give a content to the Absolute sought by the Romantics and anticipated the hidden 'harmonies' revealed by Baudelaire. The Ideologues, on the other hand, were opposed to any such metaphysical speculations. Extending the sensualist epistemology of Condillac, they set out to define, not the nature of man, but the physiological processes which give rise to thought. Their 'science of ideas', most systematically defined by Destutt de Tracy (1754–1836), was a prelude to the 'science of man', who was to be perfected through education (Lakanal, 1762–1845), new standards of public health (Cabanis, 1757–1808, founder of modern psychology) and a methodology which could be applied to all human activities, government, morals and even the arts. They processed the atheistical humanism of the eighteenth century for the Directoire, which gave their journal, *La Décade philosophique* (founded 1794) semi-official backing. They were instrumental in the creation of the secondary *écoles centrales* (1795–1802) which eliminated religion from the science-based curriculum.

The new schools were one of the few educational reforms implemented by the Revolution, despite many official reports which argued that an elementary level of instruction was essential if citizens were to participate in the life of the Republic. Yet it is clear from the sheer volume of print aimed at influencing a popular readership that elementary literacy improved. And despite the departure of the mainly noble *émigrés*, of whom some 150,000 fled to escape the *enragés*, there was still a market for literary writers (Restif, Sade, Mercier, La Harpe) who moved from the old regime to the new, some with more ease than others. Established poets (M.-J. Chénier, Parny, Palissot, Lebrun, Delille, Florian) found it safest to write of love, but on occasions penned hymns to liberty or Revolutionary triumphs, with only André Chénier rising from the mass of mediocre verse. In the theatre, the classical genres survived formally intact, though they were coloured by the temper of their violent times. Tragedy maintained the alexandrine but was annexed for the Republican and 'national' cause; however, comedy declined, eclipsed as a popular genre by the upsurge of melodrama. In the hands of Ducray-Duminil and Pigault-Lebrun, the novel reached out to Gothic horror and, as we shall see, laid the basis for the growth of popular literature. But there were signs of literary renewal. Louis de Fontanes (1757–1821) and Joseph Joubert (1754–1824) kept faith with neo-classical values but were sufficiently flexible to catch the new breezes that blew. If Fontanes's didactic poetry faded quickly, Joubert's *Pensées* (publ. 1842) showed how the move from the general maxim to the 'personal' voice might be managed. More significantly, Mme de Staël, Senancour and Chateaubriand had all published books by the end of the old century and it was they who held the key to the future.

5

The Nineteenth Century

Introduction

During the Revolution, France, for centuries an absolute monarchy, had known anarchy and the Terror and had experimented with successive forms of constitutional and representative government. Discipline was reimposed by Napoleon after the *coup* of 18 Brumaire (9 November 1799). As Consul (1802), then Emperor (1804), he restored the Catholic Church on his conditions, laid the basis of France's modern administrative institutions and imposed French influence on continental Europe through a series of military victories and diplomatic initiatives. The Restoration of the Bourbon monarchy gave France, after the defeat at Waterloo in 1815, a limited parliamentary constitution but increasingly 'ultra' conservative government. Liberal hopes of the July Revolution of 1830, which installed the 'bourgeois' monarchy of Louis-Philippe, were disappointed, and the Second Republic was proclaimed in 1848 in the wake of another revolution. By the *coup d'état* of 1851, Louis-Napoleon, nephew of Bonaparte, became its president and, in 1852, as Napoleon III, head of the Second Empire. His authoritarian regime encouraged France's industrial revolution but ended humiliatingly in the rout of the Franco-Prussian War of 1870–1 which resulted in the loss of Alsace and Lorraine. The socialist insurrection of the Paris Commune of 1871 was quickly and brutally suppressed in May and the Third Republic was confirmed in August. Regarded by many as a prelude to the restoration of the monarchy, it would last until May 1940. Though it stumbled many times, it presided over France's emergence into the twentieth century as a modern nation.

After 1789, the pace of change accelerated. Within a century, France, though still hierarchical and predominantly agrarian, would acquire the beginnings of an industrial economy and democratic institutions, a transformation which brought unprecedented shifts in outlook, modes of thought and expectations. The growth of capitalism after 1830 consolidated the *bourgeoisie* and created a new class, the urban proletariat, while the growth of a French empire (Algeria from the 1830s and Central Africa and Indochina in the 1860s) widened national horizons. In cultural terms, a period of idealism and imagination, essentially a reaction against the conservative, classical past, was followed, after 1850, by a sharper focus on the present and its lessons for the future. Images of the pastoral gave way to a new imperative, the city, a place of marvels and a battleground for warring factions. But every generation was conditioned by an awareness that the French Revolution had left unfinished business. The monarchist Right remained committed to the values of the *ancien régime* which the Revolution had destroyed. The liberal (and later radical) Left attempted to implement the freedoms it had promised but not delivered. Socially, the centre of gravity was middle-class, not aristocratic. But the literary impetus was radical: the term 'bourgeois' now acquired a pejorative sense. After 1830 middle-class philistinism was the target of writers fired by ideals so varied that consensus was uneasy and fleeting. Romanticism, which had applied a revolutionary stamp to literature, continued to fuel aesthetic debates which led, often by reaction against what had preceded, to movements and, for the first time, 'schools'.

Writers and Their Public

Language

Over the century, French, challenged by Europe's new nation states and the growing power of the Anglo-Saxon world, declined as an international language. Population growth (30 to 38 millions) failed to keep pace with that of England and Germany and, although France acquired an empire, its colonized peoples adopted not French but varieties of creole. Internally, despite the rural exodus which supplied industry, the growth of communications (railways from the 1830s) and information (cheap newspapers after 1860), many areas remained diglossic or spoke only patois. But as the language of cultured discourse, French was codified in normative grammars, mainly for use in schools, and in authoritative dictionaries, from those of Boiste (1800, many times revised and reprinted) and Bescherelle (1843) to Littré's *Dictionnnaire de la langue française* (1836–72) and the two editions (1832, 1878) of the French Academy's dictionary. Pierre Larousse's *Grand dictionnaire universel* (1865–90) was part lexicon and part encyclopaedia, a formula extended to his illustrated *Larousse* (1898–1907).

Literacy

On its launch in 1905, the abridged *Petit Larousse* sold 200,000 copied. Its success is an indication of the dramatic spread of literacy. Despite the earnest intentions of the Revolution and the active promotion of education by the Ideologues, primary instruction had remained largely in the hands of the Church. Secondary education was supported by the need for administrators and technocrats but the *écoles centrales* of 1795, converted into *lycées* by Napoleon in 1802, remained the preserve of the middle class. Attempts to create a system of state elementary schools (by Guizot, for example, in 1833) were patchily implemented and were consistently opposed by the Church which claimed that the nation's moral fabric would unravel if unsupported by Christian teaching. It was not until Jules Ferry's education laws of 1881–3 made elementary education free, compulsory and secular that basic instruction was made available to both boys and girls. Even so, parish registers and army recruitment records show a steady rise in literacy rates before the 1870s. These increased rapidly in the 1880s and by 1900, 83 per cent of men and women were able to read and write.

The reading public

During the century, the People, revealed by the Revolution as a political force, turned into a market for manufactured goods of all kinds, including books. At first, wider access to printed matter was provided by the *cabinets de lecture* (subscription libraries) which, beginning in the 1760s, reached their height in the 1820s when there were 500 in Paris alone. *Littérature de colportage* reached a wider audience in town and country (9 millon chapbooks were sold in 1847) but, faced by increasing government controls and competition from popular newspapers, the *Bibliothèque bleue* finally ceased publication in 1863. However, though the book trade grew rapidly after 1789, it remained a largely artisanal craft until the 1820s when improved technologies began to transform it: by 1860, publishing accounted for 10 per cent of the industrial output of the Paris region. The number of titles published annually rose from the 4,000 of 1812 to 14,000 in 1913 and more meant cheaper books. In 1838, Charpentier more than halved the price of a volume to 3 francs (the average daily manual wage). This fell to 1 franc in 1855 and 'treize sous' (65 centimes) in the 1880s, when even the poorest homes could afford a modest library. The growth of the reading public implied by these figures is confirmed by the huge expansion of the press. In 1824, the combined circulation of Paris newspapers and periodicals, with an annual subscription of about 80 francs, was 60,000, a figure which had trebled by 1848. In 1865, using the new rotary press, *Le Petit Journal*, priced 1 sou, was selling 250,000 copies daily and by 1886 a million. In 1914, Parisians were buying over 5 million Catholic, socialist, popular and quality newspapers every day.

As access to reading matter widened, the reading public ceased to be restricted to the educated elite. New constituencies, each with its own demands, grew up around the *littérature de colportage*, popular newspapers, the fashionable Paris readership and the scholarly circles based on the universities. Literature, increasingly professionalized, adapted quickly to the new popular and semi-popular market. Most authors, however divided on aesthetic principles, aimed at the widest public. The Romantic poets raised the profile of poetry but after about 1850 readers were less prepared to follow where the Parnassian and especially the Symbolist poets led. In the novel, Stendhal was unread until the 1880s, but Dumas *père*, George Sand, and Hugo (especially with *Les Misérables*, 1863) achieved a huge following while Zola consciously wrote for a mass audience. Boulevard theatres catered for the working-class *public à 10 sous* but from Scribe onwards the mainstay of serious theatre was middle-class.

Censorship

Although new markets offered challenges and opportunities, authors needed to tread warily. Speech, freed by the Revolution, was severely curtailed by Napoleon, who closed most newspapers (just four remained in 1811) and in 1807 allowed only eight theatres to operate in the capital. The book trade was similarly monitored. Casualties included the Ideologues, whose liberalism clashed with the new order, Sade, who was jailed for an edition of *Justine* (1802), and Mme de Staël, whose *De l'Allemagne* was banned in 1810. That year, a third of the capital's print-shops were closed and printers were required to swear an oath of allegiance to state and emperor. Thereafter, official attitudes to censorship continued to follow the ebb and flow of politics. Liberal after a change of regime, they turned repressive and were often a cause of the next upheaval. The Charter of 1814 restored limited freedom of expression and the number of newspapers rose again. But dissident ideas were politically sensitive (Courier and Béranger were imprisoned) and in 1819 penalties were introduced for authors who offended against public decency, religion and morality. Lifted after the Revolution of 1830, controls were reimposed in 1835, relaxed again after 1848, but restored by the repressive Second Empire, which in the 1850s curbed *colportage*, imposed stamp duties on newspapers and prosecuted not only minor writers like Xavier de Montépin but also the Goncourts, Flaubert and Baudelaire. After a brief respite in 1870, the Third Republic reinstated prosecutions under the law of 1819 which was not repealed until new legislation in 1881 freed the press and henceforth made alleged offences against public morality a matter, not for the state, but for the courts.

Rights and rewards

The rights of authors, proclaimed by the Revolution in 1793, were extended in 1810 by Napoleon who outlawed pirated editions, and again in 1844, 1854 and 1866. The Société des Gens de Lettres (1838) protected playwrights against theatre managements and a Société des Auteurs was set up in 1884 to defend authors against publishers. Manuscripts deemed uncommercial were bought outright for a fee, though more common was a payment which, at first, allowed an agreed number of copies of a book to be published and then, by the 1860s, an unlimited number but over a fixed period. Only in the 1880s did something like a modern royalty arrangement give authors a fixed sum for every copy sold. However, it was not until the Berne copyright convention was signed in 1886 that French writers were given international protection. This had been a problem between 1815 and the 1860s when new technologies made cheaper books available. During this time, the French book trade was seriously compromised by Belgian publishers who reprinted works of note which might then be translated, all without payment to author or publisher. In the 1830s and 1840s, when the practice was at its height, Dumas, Balzac and others complained bitterly but to no avail.

At the outset, however, the issue of literary property was less a problem than the size and nature of the market for books. During the First Empire, novels, for example, were published in editions which rarely exceeded 1,000–1,500 copies, though large rewards were already available to authors with popular appeal. The fiction and stage adaptations of Pigault-Lebrun and Ducray-Duminil, like the melodramas of Pixerécourt (whose *Coelina* was staged 1,500 times in his lifetime), made their authors rich. By the 1840s, the 5,000 copies printed of a reasonably successful novel paled beside the huge readership of the *roman feuilleton* (Sue, Dumas, Féval) or the success of Boulevard playwrights from Scribe to Sardou. Although Dumas had triumphed spectacularly with *Antony*, *La Tour de Nesle*, and *Kean*, Romantic dramas rarely exceeded 40 performances. On the other hand, the audience for Augier, Dumas *fils* and the Boulevard playwrights grew rapidly after the 1860s. In 1893, Sardou's *Madame Sans-Gêne* was staged 300 times and Rostand's *Cyrano de Bergerac* (1897) ran for 18 months at the Porte-Saint-Martin. From the Second Empire onward, popular fiction, after the now standard first outing in newspapers, appeared in editions of 30,000 copies and provided a good, sometimes spectacular living: Ponson du Terrail earned a fortune with his pen. Cheap collections, vigorously promoted (like Hachette's 'Bibliothèque du Chemin de Fer', 1852, intended for travellers, a new category of reader, or the 'Collection Michel Lévy', 1856, which offered 1,414 titles 1887) gave a measure of financial independence to the growing number of professional authors.

Serious writers, however, fared less well. Writing did not make Chateaubriand or Stendhal wealthy and Balzac had eternal money worries. Vigny drew attention to the struggling poet ignored by the materialistic July Monarchy which created the image (later encapsulated by Murger) of the 'bohemian' writer of the Latin Quarter who lived for art and scoffed at money. Most authors, however, looked for some form of subsidy. Court patronage, revived by Napoleon and maintained during the Restoration, was managed after 1830 by ministries which, appropriately solicited, offered small pensions and minor posts to suitable candidates. Books did not become profitable until the second half of the century, but authors were increasingly able to finance grander projects through journalism and works of vulgarisation (from history to encyclopaedias) judged profitable by publishers. The rise of the popular press also gave them opportunities to sell stories, poems, and articles and make their names. Zola was one of many who graduated to literature through journalism.

Market forces

This new publishing climate helped make authors independent, but it also exacted a price. The development of literature was directly influenced by the choices made by the paying public. The appeal of the *vaudeville* and melodrama was reflected in both the excitement and sensation of Romantic theatre and the stagy plots and manner of later drama. The *cabinets littéraires*, a major outlet for books by the 1820s, created a demand for certain types of fiction at the expense of others, and authors (including the early Balzac) supplied a demand determined not by aesthetic considerations but by market pressures. Borrowers preferred novels which were sentimental, *gais* and, especially, historical: half the fiction consumed between 1815 and 1830 was set in the past. Following the success of the *feuilletonistes* after 1836, serious novelists saw the advantages of pre-publication in magazines and newspapers and thereafter most novels were serialized before being published in book form. *Madame Bovary* first appeared in the *Revue de Paris*, though its commercial success was due rather to its prosecution in 1857, a clear example of the new importance of publicity as an ingredient of literary fame. Nearly all serious novelists, from Balzac and Sand to Zola and Anatole France were pre-published. But serialization also imposed literary choices. Maupassant, for example, wrote different types of tales for different newspapers and literary fiction responded to the constant demand for historical sagas and dramas of modern life. It also drew on the less subtle but more eye-catching techniques of theatre which tempted authors who were not primarily playwrights. Since, as Zola calculated, a play could be 20 times more profitable than a novel, novelists not surprisingly adapted their books, allowed them to be adapted, or wrote original plays, though few of those who attempted it (from Balzac and Sand, author of 20 dramas, to Flaubert and Zola) did so successfully.

If fiction and drama reacted positively with popular culture, the market for poetry shrank over the century. Certain Romantic poets,

Lamartine and Hugo most obviously, Vigny and Musset to a lesser extent, were successful and were well, sometimes very well rewarded. In comparison, Nerval, Gautier and, after them, Leconte de Lisle and even Verlaine had a restricted appeal, nor did prosecution do for Baudelaire's *Fleurs du mal* what it did for *Madame Bovary*. Even so, such writers, however committed to Art and hostile to 'philistinism' they might be, did not turn their backs on the broad public and retreat into radical literary positions. This course, however, was later adopted by Rimbaud, Mallarmé and the Symbolists who aimed at only a small fraction of the many publics available. Here, no doubt, is the beginning of the lasting rift between avant-garde writing and literature intended for the mainstream and popular markets.

Status of authors

The birth of such an avant-garde is symptomatic of the new confidence of authors, who ceased to exist in the shadow of the ruling elite and were judged by a new power: public opinion. The salons survived into the Empire, the Restoration and beyond. But while they remained socially important, their claim to define taste was challenged by new commercial and aesthetic criteria. Writers no longer performed for a patron: they wrote for money or fame, and the true Artist rejected convention and obeyed a higher law. The antagonism between Art and 'philistine' society was confirmed by Romanticism, when outrageous behaviour was intended to 'épater le bourgeois'. But after 1830, writers felt a growing obligation to comment on society and change it. Some, like Chateaubriand or Lamartine, held high political office. Others used their pens to publicize causes and initiate action.

During the Restoration, Béranger (1780–1857), the 'poète national', had celebrated the Revolution, Napoleon, and the People, and Paul-Louis Courier (1772–1825) attacked oppression represented by Church, nobility and government. By 1830, social and political freedom was the dominant sub-text of the new literature whose champions claimed the moral high ground. Hugo defined the writer as a 'public educator', a man with a national, social, human mission which consisted of fighting oppression, promoting democratic ideals and directing progress towards a just and human goal. Hugo is the clearest example of the poet-as-prophet, but the invasion of literature by politics was general. Vigny gave his work a social charge and Sand's 'mystique de l'humanité' coloured her novels. For Balzac, the artist was at least the equal of the statesman, and his *Comédie humaine* contained a systematic, semi-scientific critique of society. The expression of political views was curbed during the Second Empire (Sand's publisher made it a contractual obligation that she keep her socialist views to herself) and if Hugo campaigned against Napoleon III, it was from forced exile in the Channel Isles. After 1870–1, when a few writers like Jules Vallès and Rimbaud actively sided with the Commune, literature was invaded by ideas and writers became publicists in the intense debate which set Progress, the goal of science and positivism, against the Order defined by monarchism and the Church. By the 1890s, novelists in particular were filling the ranks of what, after 1898, would be called 'intellectuals'. Léon Bloy (1846–1917), anticipating a new Catholic revival, denounced the materialism of society, Maurice Barrès (1862–1923) redefined nationalism, and Charles Péguy (1873–1914) promoted the 'universal socialist republic' in *Jeanne d'Arc* (1897). But none equalled the impact of Zola who, with 'J'accuse' (1898), ignited the Dreyfus Affair which closed the century and opened the door to the next. After 1900, literature, no stranger to polemic, would strengthen its role as an extra-parliamentary opposition and writers consolidated their role as propagandists of moral, social and political ideas and shapers of opinion.

Movements and Schools

Intellectual currents

Pure and applied science

The changes wrought by this 'century of revolutions' covered many fields. Biologists, entomologists, and zoologists refined and corrected earlier classifications of species, while geographers and archaeologists (like Champollion, 1790–1832, the first modern Egyptologist) expanded the world in space and time. Speculations formulated by the Enlightenment were taken up and developed. Transformism, contested by Cuvier and defended by Lamarck and Geoffroy de Saint-Hilaire, evolved into Darwinism. The old empirical, experimental approach to phenomena was turned into a systematic method of scientific enquiry by Claude Bernard (1813–78). Louis Pasteur (1822–95) developed principles drawn from inoculation against smallpox while the interest in mental states created by Mesmer was developed first by Cabanis and later by Charcot (1825–93), whose lectures were attended by Freud, into the discipline of psychiatry. On the other hand, new directions in pure science pushed at the limits of the known, from Ampère (1775–1836), discoverer of electromagnetism, to Marie Curie (1867–1934) who explored the phenomenon of radioactivity. Spectacular technological advances were made and steam drove locomotives, printing presses and progress itself. Photographic images were fixed by Daguerre in 1839 and made to move by Augustin le Prince in 1888 and the Lumière brothers in 1895. On a grand scale, engineers built railways, roads and canals, industry acquired factories and machines, and Haussmann, symbol of the energy and activity of the age, transformed the Paris of the Second Empire.

Literature and ideas

Imaginative literature remained largely unenthused by such developments. Balzac and Zola claimed to be social scientists, but authors were more likely to be attracted by pseudo-science (Balzac's generation was fascinated by the physiognomy of Lavater and the phrenology of Gall) or, say, the exotic possibilities of Egyptology (Mérimée, Gautier) than by science or industry. On the other hand, they shared the anxieties of an age which kept one foot in the past of faith, kings and aristocracy and the other in the future of reason, democracy and progress. In one form or another, the old debate between the claims of spirit and matter set the terms of the search for the meaning of existence and a direction for society. Few authors remained untouched by mystical impulses, not simply in unfocused spirituality or the swings between disillusionment and optimism, but more specifically in quests for all-inclusive theories, utopian solutions and the religion of Art. Yet there was also a widespread feeling that man was not the victim of history but its driving force. The debate about change, freedom and progress which found violent political expression in 1789 and continued throughout the century, drew literature into a symbiotic relationship with ideas. The process was under way by 1800 when the first attempts were made to come to terms with the Revolution which had generated far more history than could be accommodated comfortably.

Digesting the Revolution

Napoleonic France, hostile to progressive ideas, laid the blame for the disaster which had snapped the continuity of history at the door of the *philosophes*. Their heirs, the Ideologues, continued the search for a science of man in which the supernatural played no part: progress is achieved through reason and free enquiry. But although they laid the foundations of later scientific and liberal positions and left their mark on writers like Constant and Stendhal, they were ousted by 1815, victims by association of the sentence passed on the godless, irresponsible rationalism of the Enlightenment. While Mme de Staël's posthumous *Considérations sur les révolutions* (1818) defended the liberal spirit of 1789, Catholic apologists like Pierre-Simon Ballanche (1776–1847) denounced the regicidal Revolution in *L'Homme sans nom* (1820) and a vast epic, *Essai de palingénésie sociale* (1827–32), which showed how the past might be redeemed through expiation of the sins of 1789, and a new, more rational and just society be built.

Throne and altar

As the line adopted by Ballanche suggests, the anti-rationalist reaction took spiritual, often mystical forms. The Concordat of 1802 re-established the Catholic Church, but the religious revival, far from being the preserve of Christianity, embraced a range of occult tendencies. Varieties of neo-pagan and esoteric thought, from Pythagoras to Swedenborg via Osiris (revealed by nascent Egyptology), together with the interest in semi-scientific subjects like mesmerism and somnambulism, expressed attempts to reconcile the world of the scientist with man's inner life and social duties. For the Illuminists, the Revolution was a divinely inspired trial from which France, cleansed of impurity, would emerge regenerated. The direct influence of Providence on human affairs was also accepted by Joseph de Maistre (1753–1821) and Louis de Bonald (1754–1840), the major spokesmen of the counter-Revolution and the twin pillars on which the ideology of the Restoration would be built. Both welcomed the Concordat but regretted that legitimate monarchy had not also been restored. Their belief that Roman Catholicism and kings were inseparable set authority and tradition above the principle of individual rights, a position which would hamper attempts to reconcile Catholicism with the modern world for a century.

History

A less dogmatic position was adopted by Chateaubriand, the major publicist of the Catholic revival. Though a legitimist, his Christian reading of history convinced him that all nations were destined to evolve into democracies. He rejected the history practised by the Enlightenment for being tendentious, finding some truth in Montesquieu's observation that Voltaire's purpose was no different from that of monks who cared less for truth than for 'la gloire de leur ordre'. The hostility to the Ideologues reinforced the reaction against philosophical history which was judged too dispassionate and urbane, too preoccupied with 'society' and not enough with nations and the races of which they were composed. The way was shown in the 1820s by Walter Scott, who revealed how 'England' had been forged in the conflict between Normans and Saxons. But Scott had also made the Middle Ages exciting and his many French readers looked for similar, dramatic illuminations of their own tangled past. Publishers supplied surging demand by issuing multi-volume collections of journals, memoirs and correspondence which enabled the modern public to re-establish direct contact with the continuities disrupted by the Revolution. Historians like Barante, Mignet and Augustin Thierry responded by developing a vigorous narrative thrust, strong on local colour and dramatic detail, which projected the Middle Ages and the Revolution as stages in the growth of the idea of 'France'. It was an approach endorsed by Jules Michelet (1798–1874), the greatest historian of the century, who early in his career identified Revolutionary and Republican France with the onward march of humanity.

Historians continued to function strongly as chroniclers. But as their methods grew more analytical and they turned to documentary rather than narrative sources, they were also called upon to explain what they narrated. Guizot (1787–1874) used history to reflect on the processes of civilization and Thiers (1797–1877) emphasized the importance of economics as a historical determinant. Edgar Quinet (1803–75) stressed the role of religion in the unfolding of events and the shaping of nations (*Le Génie des religions*, 1842) and Louis Blanc (1811–82) gave his political account of the July Monarchy (*Histoire de dix ans*, 1841–4) a socialist interpretation. For Michelet, history was the 'integral resurrection' of the life, evolution and especially the communifying myths of a people, and his *Histoire de la Révolution française* (1847–53) was intended to turn the Revolutionary values of

1789 into the articles of a new republican faith. Influenced by the current of positivism after 1850, numerous 'philosophies of history' were generated and vast syntheses explained the future by distilling truths from the past. Fustel de Coulanges (1830–89) made the organic unity of societies dependent not on economic forces but on religion and shared political myths. Marx (*Das Kapital*, 1867) offered an explanation of history which stressed class conflict, showed culture and social relations to be dependent on the material conditions of production and made the ultimate victory of organized labour historically inevitable. Élie Halévy (1870–1937) rejected the materialist interpretation of history and pointed instead to value systems and common beliefs which direct the actions and reactions of nations. Positivist history processed all the great forces which shaped the century's ideas: romantic utopianism, revolutionary Christianity, a faith in science, the idea that revolutions are moments in the ascending curve of progress, the whole infused by, at times, a mystical belief in unstoppable, mysterious forces which were part of history itself.

Catholicism and the Right

By 1850, a gap had opened between two philosophies of history, one scientific and 'positivist' and the other rooted in conservative theology. After the trauma of the Revolution, the Concordat had provided the basis for a relationship between Church and state that was to last for a century. Meanwhile, Catholicism recovered some of the ground it had lost during the Revolution. By 1880, 400 new congregations had been established, the priesthood had expanded dramatically and the tenfold increase in the number of nuns gives the measure of the feminization of piety. The authority of Rome was defended by de Maistre (*Du Pape*, 1819) and in the early writings of Lamennais (1782–1854) who, in the 1820s, campaigned to end civil interference in religious matters. After 1830, the Gallican tradition withered. The bishops accepted the authority of Rome and the Church's campaign against irreligion, spread by science and positivism, was supported by the *loi* Falloux of 1850 which strengthened its role in education. Clerical authority opposed the godless Third Republic which, in the aftermath of the Dreyfus Affair, finally broke its grip on education in 1902 and, in 1905, separated Church and state.

The market for edifying religious books, buoyant throughout the century, reached saturation levels between 1838 and 1866 when the *abbé* Migne (1800–75), an unlikely entrepreneur, made vast collections of essential texts of the Catholic faith 'accessible and intelligible to all'. Until 1830, devotional writing concentrated on the spiritual value of suffering. Its mystical emphasis was echoed in the inspiration and vocabulary of poets – Vigny most obviously – who were marginal to Catholicism. But doctrinal authority was challenged by progressive elements within the Church itself. From the pulpit, Lacordaire (1802–61) asserted that faith was compatible with reason; A.-L. Constant (1810–75) graduated from devotional poetry to socialism and a view of society which linked ritual and magic; and Lamennais (*Paroles d'un croyant*, 1834) proclaimed Christianity and democracy to be reconcilable and denounced war, oppression and capitalist exploitation in terms which earned the condemnation of Rome. He left the Church and embraced a form of republicanism based on the social virtues of Christianity. Such liberalizing tendencies were denounced by the reactionary Catholic newspaper *L'Univers*, whose editor, Louis Veuillot (1813–83), attacked capitalism, Jews, the free press and, in *Les Libres Penseurs* (1848) progressive ideas generally. The defenders of orthodoxy also opposed what they regarded as intellectual laxism within the Church itself. The even-handedness of Monseigneur Duchêne (1843–1922), an academic historian who applied the methods of historical criticism to sacrosanct ecclesiastical traditions, was not greatly appreciated. The *abbé* Loisy (1857–1940) was excommunicated for showing that religious dogmas are not definitive but subject to change. After 1900, the entrenched defenders of religious orthodoxy, supported by Pius X, developed 'integral Catholicism' which opposed all forms of modernism.

The defence of ecclesiastical authority was associated with illiberalism and a new breed of right-wing thinkers. Gobineau (1816–82) attributed the decline of empires not to economic and social decadence but to the debilitating role played by 'inferior' races (*Essai sur l'inégalité des races humaines*, 1853–5). After 1870, extreme right-wing publicists, like Henri de Rochefort (1831–1913) or the anti-Semitic Édouard Drumont (1844–1917: *La France juive*, 1886) defined narrow concepts of nationhood and campaigned loudly against the intellectual and social implications of science and rationalism. The rift caused by the Dreyfus Affair ensured that such extreme views were unlikely to moderate.

Positivism

By the 1820s, the critique of Enlightenment materialism had produced definitions of human nature and society based on historical
forces which, if they were not divine, were at least mysterious. Even
an Ideologue like Maine de Biran (1766–1824) moved to a more
spiritual interpretation of man and his affairs. Spiritual alternatives,
often with a political dimension, were offered by Jouffroy (1796–
1842), Royer-Collard (1763–1845) and Victor Cousin (1792–1867)
to both liberals and religious moderates apprehensive of Catholic
support for reactionary royalism. Auguste Comte (1798–1857), applying the methods of the natural sciences to society, identified
three steps in the history of human understanding of the world.
During the first, 'religious' phase, phenomena had been explained
as the action of supernatural forces; the second 'metaphysical' stage
converted superstitions into abstract ideas; in the third 'scientific'
age, the physical sciences had extracted certain ('positive') knowledge from experiment, observation and rational deduction. The
human sciences had not yet advanced to this 'scientific' age and
Comte formulated the principles of 'social physics' (for which he
coined the term *sociologie* in 1830) as the pathway to a form of
collective organization which would be consistent with man's
nature and the laws of history. Comte's *Cours de philosophie positiviste*
(1830–42), markedly less mystical than his later writings, nevertheless expressed a 'religion de l'humanité' which exerted a powerful influence before, but especially after, 1850 when the term
'positivism' acquired a more general meaning: it signalled the rejection of untested theories and defined knowledge as ideas verified
by experience.

Positivism in this sense powered the rationalist, scientific, and generally progressive tendencies of the post-Romantic age. It attracted
minds as varied as the philosopher Renouvier and Toqueville (1805–
59), champion of liberal democracy, Edgar Quinet who saw society
as the expression of a religious idea realized through the freedom
and individuality of its members (a qualification which hardly endeared him to the Church), and the influential sociologist Émile
Durkheim (1858–1917) in whose wake theories of mass psychology
were developed. Hippolyte Taine (1828–93), a fierce critic of spiritualist philosophers like Cousin, used history to explain human and
social phenomena as predetermined 'products' of the interaction of

three forces: 'la race, le milieu et le moment'. Less uncompromising, anti-democratic and determinist and considerably more influential was Ernest Renan (1823–92). Renan trained for the priesthood but, unable to accept the truth of the Biblical miracles, lost his vocation and, as a historian of ancient languages and religions, arrived at his own *loi des trois états*. Man's first perception of existence was intuitive and religious. A 'Hellenic' phase promoted science as a means of understanding nature. It was now possible to predict a Messianic union of religion and science which would propel man more swiftly along the path of progress. Renan achieved a huge following. *La Vie de Jésus* (1863) sold 170,000 copies in four years and his autobiography (1883) made him as famous as Hugo. A kindlier Voltairean sceptic, he never reconciled his belief in scientific method with the seemingly ineradicable pull of faith, a dilemma posed in *L'Avenir de la science* (1849; publ. 1890) which contained the seed of philosophic tensions which would erupt at the end of the century. By 1900, the natural sciences had become unassailable. But the human and social sciences had yet to throw off the spiritual and mystical tendencies which continued to inform the lessons of history, the concept of France as a nation with a civilizing mission, and the moral, economic and political principles best designed to achieve its destiny. It was thus that positivism, which acquired a strong hold in academic circles, dominated the writing of histories of science, of literature and the French language.

Socialism and the Left

If positivism, rational, anti-clerical and deterministic, grew out of eighteenth-century experimental *philosophie*, socialism was the heir of the Enlightenment utopianism and the Revolution. But which Revolution? The Rights-of-Man constitutional liberalism of 1789, or the muscular revolutionary republicanism of 1793?

After 1800, the ground between the extremes of Catholic royalism (Maistre, Bonald) and fading Ideologue rationalism was occupied by many shades of opinion which gave a mystical colouring to the view that history is made not by Providence alone but by man's readiness to align progress with his spiritual nature. Such was the motivation of social utopians like Charles Fourier (1772–1837) whose *Théorie des quatre mouvements* (1808) first set out his concept of the *phalanstère*, a small community which channelled unruly passions and created the harmony visibly lacking in modern inegalitarian society. The Comte de Saint-Simon (1760–1825), the most influential left-wing thinker of the first half of the century, developed a theory of social organization based on science and a progressive view of history. He classed useful citizens as scientists, industrialists/workers, or artists/priests, each with separate functions. They would work by category and ability, unimpeded by notions of either equality or individualism. Improved productivity, secured by state support for social and industrial development, would bring true fraternity. Though closer to Restif and Bonneville than to later communism, and discredited by more extreme disciples like Prosper Enfantin (who, as leader of a utopian community at Ménilmontant, was jailed for immorality in 1832), Saint-Simonism left its mark on social Romanticism and influenced writers as different as Comte and George Sand.

During the July Monarchy, public unrest and the first workers' strikes helped move political thought away from abstract principles towards specific social issues. Toqueville's *De la démocratie en Amérique* (1837) proposed an alternative social model based on freedom, economic liberalism and plural democratic institutions. But the human cost of France's industrial revolution created a new social conscience and a new breed of political activists who, through parliament, direct action or their pens, campaigned vigorously and sometimes faced prison and exile. Auguste Blanqui (1805–81), an advocate of armed rebellion, was jailed for long periods for his role in the revolutions of 1830, 1848 and 1871, and Henri-Alphonse Esquiros (1812–76), a religious poet who made violence the *Évangile du peuple* (1840), spent the Second Empire in England. A *littérature de combat* emerged which departed from the traditional preoccupations of literature. Graphic accounts of working-class hardship, like Agricol Perdiguier's *Livre du compagnonnage* (1839), documented a case which was promoted noisily in inflammatory newspapers and more systematically by Louis Blanc, who attributed to the state a responsibility for organizing industry and providing employment. Étienne Cabet (1788–1856) argued in favour of common ownership in his utopian novel, *Voyage en Icarie* (1840), and cast Christ as a communist in *Le Vrai Christianisme* (1846), a view which echoed Lamennais's Christian socialism. Pierre Leroux (1797–1871) defended the principle of equality, opposed individualism and defined mankind as a collective being whose historical destiny was communal (*De l'humanité*, 1840).

Such statements of principle quickly gave way to programmes of action. Flora Tristan (1803–44) denounced the social conditions of the oppressed and called for working-class solidarity and women's rights. In 1840, Pierre-Joseph Proudhon (1809–65) answered his question *Qu'est-ce que la propriété?* with the word 'Theft!' He denounced capitalism – and God for allowing it – argued for economic reform and the organization of labour, and inspired the first International in 1864. After 1870, his libertarian, anti-state socialism rooted in economic determinism was opposed by Jules Guesde (1845–1922), popularizer of Marx and supporter of his class-based reading of history. Constantly opposed by Church, state and writers as different as Taine and Drumont for sowing the seeds of anarchy, the rise of the Left was inexorable. Jean Jaurès (1859–1914) unified the divided socialist parties in 1905 when the Section Française de l'Internationale Ouvrière (SFIO) was established. But the internal argument was not settled and, after 1920, Proudhon's influence continued to be felt in the Socialist Party while French communism was marked by Guesdiste tendencies. The terms of the debate between reform and revolution which continued to divide the twentieth century were thus set by the nineteenth.

Ideas and literature

Less directly committed to ideas than it had been during the Enlightenment, literature nevertheless added its own perspective to the adversarial climate of ideas which set spirit against matter, religion against science, faith against reason and, in social and political terms, Right against Left. In one sense, the intellectual debate had been launched not by philosophers but by imaginative writers: liberal ideas had their roots in the literary revolt of the first decades of the century. Authors who had helped unleash a revolution in 1830, acquired a social conscience by the 1840s, resisted the repressive Second Empire and thereafter threw themselves into religious, philosophical, political and social quarrels which lasted beyond 1900. Along the way, they developed a belief in Art as Truth and a view of the artist as its inspired, priestly mouthpiece. Most authors, hostile to social injustice or cultural philistinism, took up broadly progressive positions. But like philosophers and sociologists, they too acknowledged the mystical as they reflected on man's spiritual nature and the workings of the world. But literary forms were also influenced by the battle of ideas. History, the focus of so much philosophical activity, was a major preoccupation of novelists, playwrights and poets who developed new genres and intellectual ambitions. From the historical novel of the Romantics to the Naturalists' attempt to subordinate fiction to the discipline of science, literature continued to respond to the challenge of ideas. But just as ideas were controversial, so literary principles became a subject for divisive and often acrimonious debate.

Aesthetic doctrines

The growth of schools

The baroque, classicism, even the modernism of 1700 were broad tendencies and did not generate literary 'schools'. Even 'Affaires', like the polemic surrounding *Le Cid*, had been relatively localized arguments. The nineteenth century, however, is remarkable for its literary *côteries* and groups, each with its theorist, revue, leader and disciples, which proclaimed its exclusive dogma in a blaze of publicity and with the intensity of theological disputes. Literary controversy reflected the habit of confrontation set by the Revolution, and its often extreme adversarial nature scarcely supported the general view of art as the expression of civilized values: in 1809, a spectator died during a riot sparked by the irregularity of Lemercier's *Christophe Colomb*. Beginning as the affirmation of post-Revolutionary sensibility, the doctrinal tendency developed its factional habits after 1815 and thereafter modernity was constantly redefined as a reaction against the dominant literary ethos.

Chateaubriand

François-René de Chateaubriand (1768–1848), began his long career with an *Essai sur les révolutions* (1797) which held out little hope for Christianity. Yet *Le Génie du Christianisme* (1802) argued that man has an ineradicable hunger for the absolute which only religion can satisfy. This he had already demonstrated in 1801 in his short novel, *Atala*, and would confirm with *René* (1805). *Le Génie*, a wide-ranging historical survey, defined progress as the product of Christianity which, however, was not merely a civilizing force but the inspiration for beautiful works of art which satisfy man's emotional and imaginative needs. Chateaubriand demonstrated God's goodness not only through the marvels of nature but through his own artistic sensibility. By communicating the beauties of Dante or medieval literature, he established a new aesthetic complete with literary models: here, in tangible form, was the 'spirit' of Christianity, the only possible antidote to René's *mal du siècle*. Similar arguments had been put by Ballanche (*Du sentiment considéré dans ses rapports avec la littérature et les beaux-arts*, 1801) who concluded that if the Moderns were superior it was because they had over the Ancients the advantage of Christian revelation. But Chateaubriand's sensuous prose style and mystical appreciation of love and nature caught the mood of his time. His opposition to Napoleon's restrictions on free speech gave him unimpeachable liberal credentials, but it was his poetic expression of *le vague des passions* which would make him an inspirational figure for the first generation of Romantic poets.

Madame de Staël

A comparable movement towards cultural renewal centred on Mme Germaine de Staël (1766–1817). In the mid-1790s, from the Château de Coppet on Lake Geneva, she worked with Benjamin Constant (1767–1830) in the cause of moderate republicanism which was threatened by the rise of Napoleon, whom she regarded as a military dictator. She was forced into exile in Germany after the publication of *Delphine* (1802) which contested the new puritanism. No less liberal in its stance was *Corinne* (1807), which also illustrated her contention, first outlined in *De la littérature* (1800), that ideas and literature are conditioned by social institutions. France was a 'southern' country and its culture, with its emphasis on control, clarity and form, reflected its Graeco-Roman origins. On the other hand, the countries of the Christian north had inherited different cultural traditions which stressed imagination, enthusiasm and feeling. In *De l'Allemagne* (1810), she accordingly introduced modern German literature (notably Goethe and Schiller) to French readers. Though her comparatist approach to culture now seems rudimentary, her conclusions, developed at cosmopolitan, ecumenical Coppet, confirmed the spirit of *Le Génie du Christianisme*, not least in her analogy of the mystic and the poet who both operate in a state of creative inspiration.

Her devoted but not always favoured companion, Benjamin Constant, located the origin of religions in a universal 'sentiment religieux' which was an aspiration 'vers l'inconnu, vers l'infini' (*De la religion*,

1824–31). It was as impossible to deny as the equally mysterious 'sentiment amoureux' which he explored in *Adolphe* (1816). A comparable subjectivity had already been displayed by the alienated, indecisive hero of Senancour's *Oberman* (1804). Dissatisfaction with the present, and unquenchable longing for the unattainable and an inability to find spiritual peace in action defined new values which would fire the literature of the 1820s.

Romanticism

Chateaubriand, Staël, Constant and Senancour were the major channels of the new 'Romantic' sensibility. First used to describe the state-of-soul English landscapes and gardens of the late eighteenth century, the word was imported in 1804 from Germany, where it referred to writings which rejected classicism and took their inspiration from the chivalric and Christian values of the medieval troubadours. During the 1800s, France eagerly absorbed cosmopolitan influences. Italy gave Dante, and England 'Shakespearean' grandeur, Gothic sensation and the atmospheric melancholy of Ossian. Through Charles de Villers (1765–1815) and Mme de Staël, France discovered Kant and, above all, Goethe who poeticized irresistible themes: impossible love, the rejection of society, the consolation of nature and the attraction of suicide. Primarily an acutely felt form of alienated subjectivity, the *mal du siècle* also had a complex social dimension. In the 1800s, 'Romantic' values were liberal and anti-Napoleonic; after 1815, they nurtured the Napoleonic legend which recast Staël's 'dictator' as the archetypal hero felled by destiny. And while Romanticism continued to centre on the crisis of the self, it also generated a crisis of belief and directed the search for new value systems and philosophies.

There was no such dramatic change in the forms of literary expression. La Harpe in his *Lycée* (1799–1805) and Barante in 1808 defended classical tradition while M.-J. Chénier's *Tableau* of literature since 1789 (1809) openly attacked the Romantic tendency. True, new aesthetic principles were implied by Chateaubriand's promotion of the imagination and more clearly stated by Staël who, applying the methods of the human sciences to literature, enjoined authors to replace taste by subjectivity, and classical mythology by nature, passion and philosophical *rêverie*. But linguistic and formal experiment did not keep pace with the growth of sensibility. The old literary forms persisted (exponents of the epic included Chateaubriand, Alexandre Soumet and Quinet, and still attracted devotees in the 1860s), the separation of genres was respected and even the language of poetry remained highly disciplined: Lamartine's *Méditations poétiques* (1820) was classical in prosody, register and imagery. Yet by then, the Romantic mood was spreading rapidly. For its opponents, it was 'irregular', a largely foreign import, given to the 'fantastic', idiosyncratically inclined to locate beauty in the eye of the beholder and unhealthily addicted to introspection. For its supporters, it expressed the ideals of youth and its hopes for the future.

But it was not until the 1820s that the battle to free 'genius' was truly joined. At first, the new poets (Lamartine, Vigny, Hugo) echoed the spirit of legitimist, Catholic Chateaubriand. But in *Le Conservateur littéraire* (1823–4) and from Nodier's *cénacle*, they also developed his confessional tone, defining the new 'genre romantique' as the exploration through the imagination of personal and spiritual uncertainties. The tenets of classical literature were challenged more directly by Stendhal (*Racine et Shakespeare*, 1823–5) who set out the terms for the 'combat à mort' to come. There followed a spate of prefaces and declarations proclaiming the liberty of poets and playwrights to present humanity in all its complexity with whatever means they chose. Among them, Hugo's *Préface de Cromwell* (1827) was a comprehensive manifesto of the aims and means of the new 'school' which, by 1829, had brought together both the personal and liberal strands of Romanticism. The following year, the 'bataille d'*Hernani*' brought a famous victory which ended the centuries-old domination of culture by the establishment and gave responsibility for the future of art to authors.

To this point, the Romantic revolution had been predominantly literary. Its themes were personal: *le vague des passions*, spiritual yearnings, the vanity and transience of life, and the obsession with love and death. After 1830, the critical stance which had fired the struggle was extended by marginal groups which set no limits on artistic freedom and expressed, in self-consciously provocative terms, their contempt for the bourgeois values of their materialistic age. The 'Jeunes France', a literary avant-garde, behaved in a manner designed to shock public opinion, the 'Bousingots' pressed literature into the service of republican ideas, and the 'Frénétiques' produced morbid, nihilistic texts which focused on madness, death, suicide and despair. More significant was the rapid growth of social Romanticism, a reaction against the philistinism of the regime and a response to calls made by Stendhal, Saint-Simonians, Fourierists, and *Le Globe* (1824–32), the organ of liberalism, for writers to engage directly with contemporary realities. Awareness of the plight of the working classes and the immorality of capitalism fuelled sympathy for the poor and created new social religions. Hugo exposed the horrors of capital punishment, novelists were obsessed with prisons and prisoners, and feminist writers, encouraged by utopian socialism, demanded the extension of civil rights to women. Popular literature caught the mood, with Eugène Sue in particular spreading the socialist message and contributing to the humanitarian pressure for reform.

Schools of poetry

The Romantic 'school' was more adventurous in its themes than in its experiments with form. The language and prosody of Lamartine and Vigny mark little advance on Chénier. The alexandrine remained the point of reference and the retention of traditional imagery and figures (antithesis, periphrasis) reflected a general acceptance of established diction and metrical discipline. Hugo pushed harder at the constraints than most, varying the alexandrine with ternary rhythms and bold *enjambements*. Yet his claim to have put 'un bonnet rouge au vieux dictionnaire' was hardly justified by his own linguistic practice. A more 'natural' tonality was achieved by Musset, the purest lyric voice of the 1830s.

The Parnassian school

Not all Romantic poets, Musset especially, were convinced that art should have a social function. In the preface to *Mademoiselle de Maupin* (1835), Théophile Gautier set out the case for non-utilitarian art which was impersonal, defined by its aesthetic qualities and indifferent to passing social and political preoccupations. His proclamation of 'l'art pour l'art' and his linking of poetry with the plastic arts was taken up by Théodore de Banville, who retreated from the ugliness of modern life into the formal purity of French verse which he ultimately codified in his *Petit traité de la poésie française* (1872). During the 1860s, a group of younger poets gathered round Leconte de

Lisle (1818–94), leader of the Parnassian school, so called after the publication of the first collective *Parnasse contemporain* in 1866. Disillusioned by the failure of the Revolution of 1848 to deliver the progress which committed Romantic writers had promised, he rejected both their obsession with self and their didacticism. Progress and action are not the concern of Art, which neither echoes current concerns nor issues directives. Beauty and usefulness are antagonistic, and Beauty, synonymous with Truth, achieves its moral purpose through impersonal, formal perfection. The poet abandons inspiration, seeks new sources of poetry in erudition and 'scientific' method and expresses ideas indirectly, through words, sound and images.

Baudelaire

The Parnasse rejected both the sentimental, personal side of Romanticism and its socio-political commitment. But its emphasis on formal aesthetics would also clear a path to Symbolism. Baudelaire (1821–67) reflected all three tendencies but refused to chain either poets or poetry to a system. Beauty is not eternal and final but 'bizarre', multiple and particular to its age, and the poet strives to capture it by exploiting his own individuality. The Romantics had found the essence of 'l'art moderne' in a new way of feeling, but had squandered their discovery on large human and social themes. Gautier's 'dilettantist' anti-didacticism was a positive but over-categorical step. The Parnassian concern with form was well founded. Yet after 1860 Baudelaire largely abandoned verse for the prose poem. He opposed all exclusive tendencies and general principles: poets must remain free to explore their own temperament. Poetry has no specific civilizing mission but Beauty elevates and provides access to hidden truths which, obscured by the confusion of daily life, exist in a 'forêt de symboles' which the poet decodes through the free exercise of his imagination. It was Baudelaire's non-aligned but precisely targeted prescriptions which made him a pivotal figure in his time – Hugo detected a 'frisson nouveau' in him – and a crucial influence on the evolution of poetry in the twentieth century.

Symbolism: the first phase

During the 1870s, the century's third poetic generation was alienated by the triumph of positivism, realism and naturalism and the bleak impassivity of the Parnassians. Like Baudelaire, Verlaine, Rimbaud and Mallarmé stepped outside doctrinal conformity. For Verlaine, poetry was less like painting or sculpture than music, suggestive not explicit, fluid not static. Rimbaud made the poet a hallucinated 'Voyant': not a seer who proclaimed religious or philosophical truths, but the visionary of a transcendental world of 'êtres parfaits, imprévus' hitherto beyond the reach of poetry. As lead turns to gold in the crucible, so base words are transformed by the 'alchimie du verbe'. They cease to be channels of meaning and become concrete realities which live through their vowels and consonants. Mallarmé, too, set out to 'donner un sens plus pur aux mots de la tribu'. He also gave a high priority to the psychological responses that can be obtained from the suggestive possibilities of words and groups of words. But whereas Rimbaud's consciously cultivated disorientation of the senses could not be contained by structured prosody, Mallarmé made the assemblage of images and sounds of the poetic line a Word which was non-verbal, a music which, allusively, not directly, suggested an abstract, intellectual or affective Idea. Mallarmé did not use words to express a previously existing thought or emotion: words were both the subject and object of poetry. His starting point was therefore not experience or some perceived truth but words which could be rearranged to release forms and ideas, as a cigar may be made to generate circles of smoke. Hence his commitment to 'peindre, non la chose, mais l'effet qu'elle produit'.

Décadisme

After 1880 appeared a plethora of literary movements which gave forms of revolt an aesthetic dimension, from the satirical and absurdist humour of the *Hydrophathes* or *Zutistes* to Decadents who reacted against the starchy solemnity of the Parnassians and, over a longer period extending to the First World War, embodying a mood if not exactly a movement, clung to an elitist concept of culture and opposed the threat posed by socialism and feminism. In 1884, Verlaine introduced Rimbaud and Corbière in his *Poètes maudits* and Huysmans extolled Mallarmé in *À rebours* whose hero, Des Esseintes, epitomized the archetypal Decadent. To the rebel poets of the 1870s were now added influences from abroad: German Romantics and philosophers, the music of Wagner and his 'synthesis of the arts', and Swinburne and the English Pre-Raphaelites.

The Symbolist movement

Décadisme as such was quickly overtaken by Symbolism which was proclaimed in 1886 by Jean Moréas. The new Symbolist school claimed to replace Parnassianism as Parnassianism had replaced Romanticism. Rejecting the many competing poetic systems which clamoured for attention, Moréas hailed as its masters Baudelaire who had established 'correspondances' between the concrete world and abstract ideas, Verlaine who had made 'mystery' and the 'ineffable' the heart of poetry, and Mallarmé for lifting the stifling constraints of strict prosody.

The new doctrine looked beyond appearances and deciphered the symbols which concealed an ideal world of which reality is merely a representation. Baudelaire's 'forêt de symboles' was explored through verse which aspired to the condition of music, exploited the evocative power of rare vocabulary, preferred *vers libre* to the regular cadences of the alexandrine and replaced large themes with intimate musings and states of soul. The poet pursued the 'universal analogy' of things through a merging of the senses, creating hieroglyphs which suggested a mysterious, secret idea through themes which centred on death and the twilight mood of the century.

Symbolism renewed the Romantic idea of the poet as mediator between the human and the transcendental and drew on the impersonality of the Parnassians and their cult of form. But during its brief span – as a school it had dispersed by 1895 – the Symbolist impetus also migrated to painting, music and theatre. Its poetic principles were refined (René Ghil contended that rhythm is meaning and words are to be played like musical instruments) and much attention was given to the form which the new elusive poetic spirit should take. The retreat from classical prosody was confirmed. The rise of the 'poème en prose', beginning with Chateaubriand and continuing through Aloysius Bertrand to Baudelaire, Rimbaud and Lautréamont, had indicated an alternative: only Hugo remained loyal to traditional metres. After his death in 1885 and following the example set by the anti-Parnassians of the 1870s, consistent attempts were made to modify syllabic regularity and the tonic accent. The looser *vers libéré*, the *vers impair* (which used an odd number of syllables) and blank verse, together with a willingness to trade rhyme for assonance, led to the *vers libre* which was defined by rhythm and musicality. Defended by Gustave Kahn, François Viélé-Griffin, but best exploited by Jules Laforgue, it was at first restricted to the expression of personal feeling. Claudel later extended its use, arguing that we think 'par intermittence'. Thoughts and emotions are not ours to command for they rise unbidden into our consciousness. The free *verset*, liberated from the artificialities of metre and rhyme, gives its content an opportunity to 'coagulate' in the air. Better attuned to the 'natural' processes of perception, *vers libre* stimulates our sensibilities and imagination through rhythm, sounds and those images of concrete things which are the symbols of universal realities.

The evolution of Symbolism

The impetus of the Symbolist revolution, launched by the generation of Moréas and Henri de Régnier, was maintained in the 1890s by the input of American (Stuart Merrill and Viélé-Griffin) and especially Belgian poets (Émile Verhaeren, Charles Van Lerberghe and, though better known as a playwright, Maurice Maeterlinck). Around them, and for long after the movement was considered to have ended, variations on Symbolist principles were woven by Georges Rodenbach, who wrote moodily of lives enclosed by flat landscapes, the mannered Henri Bataille, the aesthete Robert de Montesquiou, and in the prose poems of Saint-Pol Roux. By 1895, however, a reaction had set in against the taste for subjective, impalpable and insubstantial themes and destabilized poetic forms. In 1891, Moréas founded an École Romane which regarded Romanticism and its aftermath as errors and sought to reconnect French poetry with its medieval, Renaissance, national and above all Latin past. Rejecting the amorphous and the deliquescent, a mild neo-classical spirit sought to make poetry more direct and regular. Reflecting a need for order and stability against the political turmoil of the *fin de siècle*, it aimed to refurbish the image of France's national muse. The new 'classicized' Symbolism is exemplified by Albert Samain but, like Francis Jammes, 'post-Symbolists' found more solid themes in the realities of nature, the landscape and the local patriotisms publicized by the 'réveil des provinces'. A new generation of regional poets, led by Frédéric Mistral and the Félibrige, also reflected ancient classical culture but showed a firmer commitment to the sufferings and hopes of mankind not as individuals but as brothers.

Post-Symbolism

By the end of the century, Symbolism was turning into a one-winged bird. Around 1900, the need to renew the content of poetry and to relate it to broader human concerns prompted an alliance of inspiration and technique with the social vision of Zola and Verhaeren, who, in *Les Villes tentaculaires* (1895) and *Forces tumultueuses* (1902), wrote idealistically of the problems of urban life in the new industrial age. The 'Naturists' expressed this mood of social humanitarianism which also extended a welcome to regionalist and women poets, notably Anna de Noailles and Lucie Delarue-Mardrus. The 'Humanism' (1902) of Fernand Gregh, also a reaction against obscurity, demanded that symbols be clear and poetry directly life-enhancing. But despite both the classical revival and a renewed interest in things pagan, the anti-Symbolist reaction handed poetry to dull Romantico-Parnassian versifiers. More significant was the Groupe de L'Abbaye (1906–8), a short-lived community of writers and artists who sought to provide an alternative to industrial capitalist society. Its members included Charles Vidrac, Georges Duhamel and Jules Romains, whose collection *La Vie unanime* (1907) linked the group with Unanimism which took Naturist principles, stripped them of their rhetoric and expressed a more accessible lyrical and fraternal concern with common humanity. Yet, despite appearances, Symbolist theory and practice were far from done. Jean Royère, founder of *La Phalange* (1906), had some success in developing a form of neo-Symbolism (Mallarmé modified by Laforgue), but it would fall to Valéry and Claudel to transmit the Mallarméan 'Verbe' to succeeding generations who would continue to untangle its knots.

The Symbolist revolution

Symbolism evolved through three generations, with Baudelaire as pioneer, Verlaine and Mallarmé as leaders and, in their wake, a large number of poets who first rallied to a more or less precise poetic before breaking away to form new tendencies which continued, in various ways, to bear its mark. Yet its fragmentation was the sign of a greater achievement. The Symbolist adventure secured what the Romantics had sought: creative liberty for art and artists. Its essence was individualism, the primacy of idealism and, not least, the liberation of technique.

The final decades of the century thus saw a level of reflection upon the nature and technicalities of poetry unparalleled since the Pléiade or the generation of Malherbe. The Romantic poets, Nerval apart, had remained within the oratorical tradition. Faithful to the logic of prose and making only a mild assault on the bastion of versification, they used poetry to express what they knew, believed and felt. With Baudelaire, Verlaine, Rimbaud and Mallarmé, however, poetry acquired a new function. The poet discovered knowledge and feelings through writing: poetry ceased to be a mode of expression and became a mode of discovery. The Symbolist movement faded quickly but it had brought about a revolution which, relayed through Claudel and Valéry, would reverberate into the twentieth century. However, it received a cooler reception from the public which after about 1880 felt increasingly alienated from the elitist culture of poetry and its wilful obsession with the 'art of the difficult'. On the other hand, the novel, though no less thoroughly subjected to scrutiny, maintained and increased its readership.

Schools of fiction

Unlike theatre or poetry, the novel in 1800 did not carry a large baggage of classical doctrine. It remained free of the battles which divided the new Ancients and Moderns, largely because, as a form, it had already broken the classical embargo in the eighteenth century. For at least two decades, the new generation unadventurously followed the practices of the old. The epistolary novel and the memoir-novel flourished, maintaining the tradition of psychological *analyse*, mainly in the area of sentiment. Yet changing taste grew dissatisfied with fiction committed to general moral truths in non-specific settings. Novels should be 'useful' in a wider sense, rooted in what Stendhal called 'les petits détails vrais', closer to contemporary life and, said Hugo, less analytical and more 'dramatic' in presenting action and character. The preference for the colourful and the particular against the uniform and the general was expressed through new themes and modes. The Gothic novel generated excesses which reflected the anxieties and excitements of the age. First-person narratives, given a fresh autobiographical and confessional character by Chateaubriand, Senancour, Staël and Constant, moved away from the universal and public to personal and private experience. The historical novel told France about itself and showed *grandeur* in action. By 1830, the novel was beginning to adapt to a new age.

Balzac

Le Rouge et le Noir, Stendhal's 'chronique du XIXe siècle', represented a documented view of the modern world, free of the standard clichés, through the history of Julien Sorel. For Balzac too, the novel had a future only if it relinquished *romanesque* invention in favour of observation, abandoned introspection and adjured the excesses of melodrama. His approach was vindicated, he believed, by the natural scientist Geoffroy Saint-Hilaire who argued that there is only one type of animal which had, through many centuries, developed different characteristics through the influence of environment. In the case of man, this environment is society which, though it shapes people, does not make them the same: their varied passions and intelligence are too useful for its many purposes. While common denominators are all too visible (avarice, paternal love, social ambition), they are infinitely graded. The inner life of individuals is externalized in clothes, speech, habitat and physiognomy which are helpful pegs on which the novelist may hang the range of characters which define the spirit of an age. Fiction could thus aspire to the 'philosophic value' of history and, in the preface (1842) to the *Comédie humaine*, Balzac claimed to be the 'secretary' of society, the recorder of its manners.

Realism

Balzac, who justified his undertaking retrospectively, was the practitioner rather than the theorist of Realism which was given its name and its doctrine by Champfleury (pseudonym of Jules Husson, 1821–89). From 1843 onwards, he took up arms against the preachiness of 'social' fiction, the excess of sentiment, poetic idylls and the populist tendencies of the *roman feuilleton* which was the negation of art. In the 1850s, with Edmond Duranty (1833–80), he defended the cause of Gustave Courbet, leader of the 'Realist' school of painting, who adopted a controversial, anti-academic stance by limiting himself to modern and popular subjects. In a series of essays published as *Le Réalisme* (1857), Champfleury linked Courbet's ideas to fiction. Using a minimum of imagination and avoiding intrusive comment, the novelist studies the appearance, behaviour and environment of 'l'homme d'aujourd'hui dans la civilisation moderne'. What Balzac had done for French society between 1815 and 1835, the Realist novelist would do knowingly, and more scientifically, in the 1860s.

Ordinary lives, set against social, economic and generally material reality, would be photographed through a process which demanded a discipline as great as that required by the rules of versification. Strict objectivity and meticulous documentation were the only means of identifying human, social and historical truths.

Flaubert, often considered to be the ultimate Realist, despised such arguments and their aesthetic implications. In his view the novel had no business with moral views or political, social and religious theses. It was an art in the way that poetry was an art for Baudelaire and the Parnassians. Like them, he believed that perfection of form created Beauty which was in itself a moral force. To achieve it, the novelist eliminated his own emotions, abandoned inspiration and strove for objectivity. Impassive as a scientist and dispassionate as a judge, his goal was not to show the trials of extraordinary heroes (as the Romantics had done) but to reveal characters neutrally as accurate images of a human group or general type. But in practice, his *roman artiste* needed the concreteness of the *roman réaliste*: the search for the true facts, typical details or the revealing gesture was as important as the quest for the 'mot juste' and the subtleties of art. Flaubert might dream of a novel which was pure form, whose material content was a mere pretext for a harmonious assemblage of style and construction, but he never attempted such a 'livre sur rien'. Instead, he achieved something new: he combined the objectivity of the realist with the idealism of the pure artist.

Naturalism

Zola too regarded subjectivity with deep suspicion. In his view, the sentimental deism of Rousseau, transmitted through Chateaubriand, Lamartine, Hugo and George Sand, had been made redundant by the intellectual and social evolution of society. Stendhal, Balzac and Flaubert, however, were descended from Diderot, the 'ancestor of modern positivism'. They had abandoned Romantic rhetoric, broken with the classical aesthetic, and engaged directly with the new age of democracy and science. In the preface to *Germinie Lacertaux* (1864), the Goncourts committed fiction to the discipline of science, and after 1866 Zola showed how scientific methods and knowledge were to be applied to literature. He had in mind recent work on heredity, Darwin's *On the Origin of Species* (trans. 1862), Taine's explanation of societies as the product of 'la race, le milieu et le moment' and especially Claude Bernard's systematization of the experimental method of enquiry (1865). For the novelist was not merely an observer but an experimenter. He released characters into a situation and allowed them to follow the logic of the laws of heredity and environment: his Rougon-Macquart cycle was accordingly subtitled 'the natural and social history of a family'. Zola's approach assumed that the human world is subject to the same mechanistic determinism as the rest of nature. The novel was not, however, simply a mirror which reflected its inevitable processes. Its moral role lay in identifying the laws governing existence, which would enable politicians and reformers to intervene and modify social life according to principles of justice. Nor was fiction the anonymous notation of reality. Passive observation produced sterile results: imagination was required to invent 'true' experience and rescue it from banality. The use of the methods of science to promote social morality did not therefore require the novelist to disappear. On the contrary, Zola quoted with approval Alphonse Daudet's remark that a work of art is 'un coin de la création vu à travers un tempérament'.

Zola systematized his views in *Le Roman expérimental* in 1880. By then, he was the focus of the Naturalist doctrine which marked the extreme point of the view that the goal of the writer was Truth not Beauty. The group which had rallied around him during the furore unleashed by *L'Assommoir* (1877) collaborated on *Les Soirées de Médan* (1880), a collection of stories of the war of 1870, though not all contributors applied strict Naturalist principles. Nor, despite the flood of Naturalist texts which appeared in the 1880s and the migration of Naturalism to the theatre, did they remain unquestioning disciples. Zola's approach worked best when applied to the naked drives of unsophisticated individuals and groups where 'nature' had not been masked by worldly values. The result not only brought charges of immorality but limited the social range of literary subject-matter to the lower classes and marginalized subjects. In 1887, the 'Manifeste des cinq' reacted indignantly to the excesses of *La Terre*, and Maupassant's preface to *Pierre et Jean*, while agreeing that life could be recreated only on the basis of observed fact, argued that the aim of the novel was to provide not a 'banal photograph' but a vision more 'probing' than reality itself. By the early 1890s, Naturalist doctrine was dead and its adepts had gone their separate ways. Daudet, Barbey d'Aurevilly and Villiers de l'Isle-Adam had added their own brands of fantasy to the Naturalist recipe. Maupassant linked manners with psychology, and Huysmans's 'spiritualist' naturalism was a 'parallel route' which Zola himself explored in his final trilogy. While it was agreed that there was more to life than biology, the vein of pessimism opened up by Flaubert, and confirmed by Schopenhauer and embryonic psychoanalysis, was mined by writers as different as Bourget, Marcel Prévost and Gyp who explored the disillusionment and frustrations of modern life in 'psychological' novels which focused on morbid states and pathological sexuality among the rich. By 1900, fiction had been profoundly marked by Naturalism. Its social and psychological sphere of reference had been widened and observation had renewed the study of the inner and collective life of men and women. Like Symbolism, to which it was profoundly antagonistic, it freed the creative artist from 'literature' defined as a system of agreed aims, objectives and approaches.

Literary criticism

But literature was not the exclusive property of creative writers. Claims upon it were also made by academic institutions and individuals who defined its function and set its standards. Around 1800, La Harpe judged literature against an absolute, unchanging idea of Beauty. After 1830, literature ceased to be universal but was relative, the expression of a given society (as Bonald had put it) or the product of particular circumstances (Sainte-Beuve related books to their authors and the groups to which they belonged), or historical determinism (Taine) or the Darwinian evolution of *genres* (Ferdinand Brunetière, 1849–1906). After 1870, literary history, subjected to the methods of positivism, was divided into Periods and equipped with a canon of Great Authors. Academic criticism acquired the trappings of science, with critical editions, philology and bibliography providing the basis for authoritative analysis, evaluation and surveys like the ultra-magisterial *Histoire de la littérature française* (1895) of Gustave Lanson (1857–1934) which defined the institutional approach for half a century. After 1880, literature, the finest expression of France's national heritage, was made part of the republican, democratic education of the young, who learned to think, feel and express themselves through contact with the best of what had been thought, felt and expressed. The Frenchness of French literature was a communifying force which clarified the idea of France as a Nation. Yet what by

1900 had been institutionalized as the Great Tradition was less a definition of literature than a reflection of contemporary social and moral values. It excluded what was deemed unclubbable (subversive trends, lapses in taste and immorality in general) and cast literature as the product of the conscious mind at the very moment when the new psychoanalysis suggested that literary creation was an altogether more mysterious process. It was against this entrenched conservatism that the twentieth century would rebel.

The press

Public taste had by then, however, also been shaped by the rise of opinion-forming magazines and newspapers, home of the reviewer and essayist. Some were short-lived mouthpieces for schools and groups. Others aimed at the cultured elite and, according to their lights, defended the old or championed the new. But the rapid expansion of the popular press brought news and views of literature to the general public. In the 1820s, Geoffroy's strictures on Romantic excess were limited in their influence by the small circulation of *Le Globe*. Francisque Sarcey (1827–99), appointed drama critic of *Le Temps* in 1867, publicized and judged new plays for a wide readership, tempering his conservative views by taking account of the enthusiasms of the public. By the end of the century, however, professional critics like Anatole France and Jules Lemaître (1853–1914) expressed less dogmatic and more impressionistic views as the gulf between academic criticism and literary journalism widened.

Foreign influences

The concept of the 'Frenchness' of French literature was not so exclusive that it failed to recognize the growing interpenetration of cultures. During the Enlightenment, foreign influences had been mediated largely by books and by fashions like *chinoiserie* or the English gambling habit. After 1789, they were experienced directly by the 150,000 émigrés who fled the Revolution, by the countless soldiers enrolled in Napoleon's campaigns and thereafter by French travellers and visitors from abroad. The literature and thought of France were, accordingly, far from insular. Romantic writers readily exchanged ideas with their counterparts in other countries. Mme de Staël's taste for 'Nordic' literatures created a lasting vogue for German poetry (Goethe), theatre (Schiller) and philosophy from the

Idealist school to Schopenhauer. The English Gothic defined horror, Ossian embodied the new *mal du siècle*, Shakespeare was grandeur, Scott was history and Byron achieved mythical status. Italy was rediscovered by Chateaubriand, Stendhal and Musset, though by 1850 its glamour had dwindled to little more than a setting for novels of adventure and romance. Spain, too, made a picturesque location for fictions like Mérimée's *Carmen*, but poets from Gautier and Hugo to Hérédia also experimented with Spanish themes and forms (like the *romancero*). But by 1850, the post-Romantic generation had begun looking further afield, to the mysterious Russia revealed by Custine (*La Russie en 1839*, 1843), by Dumas *père* who travelled there in 1859, by Turgenev who resided in Paris and by *Le Roman russe* (1886) by Melchior de Vogüé who first revealed Tolstoy and Dostoevsky to the French. Fenimore Cooper, a transatlantic Walter Scott, had chronicled the birth of the American nation. Toqueville publicized its democratic style, Gustave Aimard linked its dynamism to the myth of the Far West, Baudelaire championed Poe, and Mark Twain helped shape the direction of French humour in the 1880s. By then Belgian poets were prominent in the Symbolist movement and the exotic had been widened to include the Far Eastern and North African outreaches of France's empire. But while literature had absorbed many cosmopolitan influences, France's culture continued to generate its own dynamism which, in turn, it exported to many lands where it was admired for its clarity, boldness and supremely civilized values.

Literature

Poetry

Between La Fontaine and Chénier, poetry had surrendered to neo-classical taste and the climate of intellectualism. After 1800, it continued to modulate conventional harmonies and respect the precepts which gave prosody its discipline and each poetic genre its appropriate vocabulary, imagery and register. But the subjective note struck by pre-Romanticism was confirmed by the *mal du siècle* and the spiritual values attached by the new generation to love and nature. Solitary glens, mountain crags, running brooks, lost youth, dead loves, memory, in other words the major Romantic themes, feature, in muted tones, in the work of transitional poets – Chênedollé (1769–1833), Millevoye (1782–1816) and Pierre Lebrun (1785–1873) – who built a tentative bridge between the old conformities and the new sensibility. A more distinctive and personal lyrical voice was heard in the first collection (*Élégies*, 1819) of Marceline Desbordes-Valmore (1786–1859) who wrote of her tragic life directly and without self-pity. She spoke of remembered love and precarious joys not as abstractions or absolutes but through exactly observed impressions of the natural and everyday world. Her unself-conscious, intimate confidences, expressed unemphatically and with a rhythmic mastery which Baudelaire and Verlaine would later admire, achieve a spontaneity unmatched by the grandiose Romantic poets who overshadowed her.

Lamartine

Alphonse de Lamartine (1790–1869), an elegiac poet with mystical tendencies, brought a new emotional intensity to poetry. His diction, stately rhythms and literary frame of reference came from the past and some considered him the spokesman of a new classicism. Yet there was no mistaking either his tone or his personal engagement with life and creativity. His four major collections, beginning with the *Méditations poétiques* (1820), tackled the great lyrical themes of love, nature and religion, relating them directly to recollected feelings and his spiritual uncertainty. While frequently anthologized poems like 'Le Lac' or 'Le Vallon' express the anguish of lost love and passing time through intensely remembered experience, many of his poems deal, from the same melancholic standpoint, with man's soul, prayer and the question of immortality. After 1830, he came to view poetry as an instrument of social progress and his more portentous verse, exemplified by *Jocelyn* (1836), an epic with a social message, was the counterpart of his gifts as a political orator.

Vigny

Alfred de Vigny (1797–1863) adopted a similarly unadventurous aesthetic approach to poetic renewal. He never quite freed himself from the manner of Chénier but as he moved from lyrical to philosophical narrative, his voice became deeper and articulated a vision whose pessimism is relieved only by pity for the tragic destiny of man and a stoical code of resigned fortitude. From the *Poèmes antiques et modernes*

(1826) to *Les Destinées* (posth., 1864), he wrote of the indifference of God and nature and the solitude to which great men are condemned. He saw himself as 'une sorte de moraliste épique' and, armed with an impersonal but dignified 'plume de fer', he turned Moses, Christ, the dying wolf which suffers in silence or the sailor who, like the poet, casts his message into the sea with no hope that it will ever reach a shore, into majestic, allegorical figures. His 'symbolism', however, in no way anticipates that of Mallarmé, for his symbols do not decode the world at large but are hooks from which a philosophical idea is suspended. Yet his refusal to be consoled, and in particular his disdain for material progress as an answer to spiritual anguish, connects him with Baudelaire.

Hugo

Whereas Vigny retreated into private life, Victor Hugo (1802–85), poet, dramatist, playwright, philosopher and rebel, lived in almost perpetual limelight. His precocious *Odes* (1822), classical in manner and royalist in their sympathies, were quickly overtaken by a new allegiance to the liberal and aesthetic values of the new literature. His subsequent claim to have dislocated the alexandrine and revolutionized the vocabulary of poetry was premature, but *Les Orientales* (1829) revealed a metrical virtuoso and a master of picturesque, exotic colours. Yet there is a certain shallowness in the poetry he published before 1830, as though he had perfected a technique before he had much to say: his first battles were less about life than about literature. But after that date, the social conscience displayed in his fiction found its way into the collections he published between 1831 and 1840. His place, he said, was 'au centre de tout comme un écho sonore', a reflection of the joys, hopes and fears of common humanity. To his personal lyricism he now added philosophical and metaphysical *rêveries* which reached out for an understanding of the interconnectedness of things, which he saw as the basis of cosmic unity. In the 1840s, his poetic output fell while he pursued political ambitions which brought him, after 1851, into conflict with Napoleon III. He lived in exile in Guernsey until 1870 and there wrote his greatest poetry, giving Romanticism its finest expression long after it had disappeared as a movement. *Les Châtiments* (1853) breathe invective and irony for France's new emperor who had betrayed the Napoleonic dream and the nation's destiny. *Les Contemplations* (1856), unfashionably personal, were mystical, metaphysical 'mémoires d'une âme' and *La Légende des siècles* (1859) offered an epic view of the struggles of mankind as individuals or as elements in a grander design. His final incarnation, after his triumphant return to Paris in 1870, was as the nation's spiritual leader. He had long regarded the poet as a priestly 'mage' who announced moral truths. The prophetic Hugo, who spoke with a 'bouche d'ombre', has worn much less well than the poet who, whether in thunderous or intimate mood, still startles the reader with an electrifying image or a vivid apprehension of a mind which still vibrates. The poetic revolution promised by his contemporaries was delivered by Hugo who vastly expanded the vocabulary of poetry, gave new life to its fixed forms and turned the rigid alexandrine into an arrangement of free-flowing rhythms. The last and most complete Romantic poet, he also ventured into territories later explored more systematically by the Parnassians and the Symbolists and remained, in the twentieth century, a force to be reckoned with.

Other Romantic poets

Although intellectual revolutions and literary 'schools' continued to direct the broad progress of literature, it would be wrong to assume that all authors conscientiously followed the beliefs and practices of the groups to which they belonged. Romanticism, like the movements which followed it, was a collective sound made up of highly individual voices. Among these, Alfred de Musset (1810–47), more a man of the theatre than a poet, avoided the grand humanitarian themes of the 1830s and took as his subject the hurts of bruised love. *Les Nuits* (1835–7), a long confession of anguish and rejection, contains, despite declamatory moments, some of the best-loved Romantic verse. Intimate, personal themes were also explored in the three collections (1829–37) of Sainte-Beuve (1804–69) and *Les Myosotis* (1838) of Hégisippe Moreau (1810–38). On the other hand, others, like Edgar Quinet or Maurice de Guérin (1810–39), kept faith with philosophical and epic poetry. Many poets, however, had been permanently marked by the revolutionary fervour of 1830 and at first wrote to further its political objectives. Pierre-Jean de Béranger (1780–1857), a *chansonnier* with popular appeal, had no need to be reminded what these were, for his rousing verses and songs had played a part in the Revolution. In contrast with his optimism, Auguste

Barbier (1805–82) struck a note of acerbic satire which, however, had few imitators. If Alphonse Esquiros (1812–76) maintained his political impetus, many 'frantic' and anarchist poets such as Pétrus Borel (1809–59) or Philothée O'Neddy (1811–75) soon generalized their adversarial stance and set about shocking France out of its growing complacency by renewing the old traditions of fantasy and the supernatural.

Gautier

By 1840, the retreat from Romantic excess was signalled by a short-lived classical revival and the emergence of new moods, themes and aesthetic forms. Xavier Forneret (1809–84) injected a novel note of black humour into poetry and Aloysius Bertrand (1807–41) experimented with the prose poem in his collection of 'fantaisies à la manière de Rembrandt et de Callot', *Gaspard de la nuit* (1842). An indication that personal poetry would move to more 'symbolic' forms of expression was provided by *Les Chimères* (1854), a dozen strange, obscure sonnets by Gérard de Nerval (1808–55). More influential in the short term, however, was the example of Théophile Gautier (1811–72) who had begun as a disciple of Hugo but came to find more to admire in the external world than in his own soul. He claimed to have missed his true vocation, which was painting, and set the poet the task of evoking in words what the painter depicted in images: a poem is a vision made permanent by craft and form. His *Émaux et camées* (1852) mobilized the full range of colours, tones, intricate rhythms, ingenious rhymes and painterly metaphors within the severe constraints of the compressed octosyllable. Offering little to the emotions, Gautier's appeal is to the eye and Baudelaire's description of him as a 'poète impeccable' gives the measure of the quality of his craftsmanship but also indicates how little often lies beneath his polished surfaces. Gautier's example was followed by Théodore de Banville (1823–91) who, in two collections (*Les Cariatides*, 1842, and *Les Stalactites*, 1846) directed poetry to the 'serenity' of pure form. By allowing discreet, half-ironic glimpses of his sensibility and adapting the rhythms and forms (*ballade* and *rondel*) of medieval and Renaissance poetry, he achieved considerable success among contemporary readers who greatly admired his more ludic *Odes funambulesques* (1857).

Leconte de Lisle

Gautier's doctrine of 'art for art's sake' recommended itself to Leconte de Lisle (1818–94), a Fourierist and republican intellectual disillusioned by the rise of Napoleon III. In the preface of his first collection, the *Poèmes antiques* of 1852, he declared war on all poetry inspired by personal emotion. In an age of positivist, scientific knowledge, enlightenment was not to be found in subjectivity nor in an attempt to understand the present, for the modern world is ugly, man is vile, religions a fleeting creation of the human mind and all didactic art ephemeral. The truth about man and society was best sought by studying the cultures of the past civilizations in which art and science were joined. Evocations of ancient Greece or exotic India could deliver this truth and, mediated through harmonies and images, give it the permanence of the infinite. Leconte de Lisle's poetry is metrically disciplined, highly visual and rooted in strong sensual impressions of heat, light, sun, ice and shadow. In one sense, it is not impersonal, for it carries a strong positivist message. Yet, though it is far less detached and antiquarian than his detractors claimed, his poetry is a cool, finished product which invites us to look and admire but fails to release the imagination.

Parnassian poets

By the early 1860s, Leconte de Lisle was the acknowledged leader of the post-Romantic generation of poets. Many followed his creed of craftsmanship and impersonality which set art above its content and promoted much scientific musing on the history of civilization. Of his many disciples, José-Maria Hérédia (1842–1905) would become the acknowledged master of the finely honed sonnet with *Les Trophées* (1893). But most of his admirers settled for weaving variations on a narrow view of poetry which disciplined emotion, made spontaneity suspect and set the highest value on polished, marmoreal form. Though Flaubert's friend, Louis Bouilhet (1822–69), Léon Dierx (1838–1912), the Hellenist Louis Ménard (1822–1901), and François Coppée (1842–1908) rise above the crowd, the award of the Nobel Prize (1907) did not prevent Sully-Prudhomme (1839–1907), the most philosophic of the Parnassians, from sinking beneath the weight of his stately, academic dullness. Nor did Leconte de Lisle himself fare better. His reputation had stood higher than that of Baudelaire

and the major Symbolists. Yet there can be few poets in any literature who had less effect on the subsequent development of their art.
For a new direction, we must look elsewhere, to Charles Baudelaire
(1821–67), translator of Poe and De Quincey, art critic, essayist, and,
in *Les Fleurs du mal* (1857), painter of modern life.

Baudelaire

Baudelaire was the essential link between the old and the new in
poetry. He shared the Romantic poets' thirst for the absolute, but
rejected their facile rhetoric, indulgence of the self and earnest social
moralizing. His poetry is no less personal than theirs, but it is not
confessional. When Baudelaire speaks of himself, he does so as the
victim of a new malady which he was the first to diagnose and
describe. He is the poet of the city. He articulates the spiritual apathy
induced by modern, materialistic society which brings neither peace
nor fulfilment but applies the whip of pleasure and offers the prospect of addictive sensations which enslave and leave appetite unslaked.
He did not observe society as the Realists did and he punctures the
sentimental view of Lamartine and Hugo, who still linked the Beautiful and the Good: Beauty is also to be found in evil. Everywhere he
saw 'correspondances' between things and 'innombrables rapports'
in the seemingly unconnected experiences of modern life. He set out
to locate and decipher the 'universelle analogie' not in philosophical
verse but by exploring general themes (art, death, beauty, time)
through the duality of 'spleen et idéal', the two contradictory tendencies, 'l'une vers Dieu, l'autre vers Satan', which defined *homo
duplex*. He saw through the sham of the modern wasteland and conveys the self-disgust, guilt and aimlessness of mankind's spiritual
poverty. His 'spleen' is self-flagellating, misogynistic and derisive and
looms larger than the 'idéal' in which he invests his despair. Yet he
never abandoned his belief in the redemptive power of poetry and
this explains why in Baudelaire's secret garden, vice and sin came
up looking like flowers. Despite his own contradictions (he lost his
faith but counted himself as damned; an enemy of progress, he was
fascinated by the modern city), he pursued the 'unité intégrale' of
things and the 'centralisation du Moi' through images and metaphors which readily mutate, through sense impressions which melt
into each other, into symbols which suggest an idea. Baudelaire was
an essentially tragic figure, a modern Dante (as T. S. Eliot called him)

squelching through city mud and occasionally glimpsing an inaccessible star.

His pessimism, however, is relieved by a bracing moral irony which is underscored by the contrast between the intensity of his feelings and the cool control with which they are expressed. Baudelaire's alexandrine is classical, as is his stanza, and his rhythms, harmonies and rhymes reflect his admiration for the craft of poetry exemplified by Gautier. A lucid dissector of his emotions, he was also an acute literary analyst, a 'poète-critique', in Valéry's phrase, whose art criticism, literary essays and varied reflections on writing led him to a resonant urban aesthetic and a new form of poetic expression. After the second edition of *Les Fleurs du mal* (1861), he wrote little verse, having discovered, in the wake of Aloysius Bertrand, 'le miracle d'une prose poétique, musicale sans rythme et sans rime' which, displayed in *Le Spleen de Paris* (1869), would be perfected by Lautréamont and Rimbaud.

Verlaine

Like Baudelaire, Paul Verlaine (1844–96) was a contributor to *Le Parnasse contemporain* of 1866. But he was temperamentally incapable of writing 'des vers émus, très froidement' and quickly abandoned the stiff-backed aesthetic programme of Leconte de Lisle and his disciples. No thinker, he avoided large, abstract themes and worked in an intimate register, evoking inner landscapes and states of mind through half-tones and languid, melancholy impressions and sensations. His short poem, 'Art poétique' (1874, published in *Jadis et naguère*, 1885), rejected rhetoric and intellectualism and required poetry to be 'de la musique avant toute chose'. He gave syntax the cadence of speech, shifted stress and accent and unbalanced standard rhythms. Rich Parnassian rhymes were 'cheap baubles' and he preferred simpler echoes and the effects of alliteration and assonance. His fluid, delicate rhythms, subtly toned harmonies and unemphatic images were intended to be 'soluble dans l'air', to pluck strings which released unplanned resonances. It was a manner anticipated in his nostalgic, sardonic evocation of the Watteauesque world of lost grace (*Fêtes galantes*, 1869) and was perfectly attuned to the impressionism of *Romances sans paroles* (1874) or the search, which he never abandoned, for the innocence and irresponsibility of childhood. Though his last collections, from about *Parallèlement* (1889) onward, are marked by a sentimental, insistent religiosity, perhaps a morbid legacy from Baudelaire, Verlaine remains the most accessible of late nineteenth-century poets.

Rebels of the 1870s

Verlaine was not alone in challenging the rhetorical tradition of French poetry. *Les Amours jaunes* (1873) of Tristan Corbière (1845–75) used the rhythms of popular speech and real experience to deride the grandiloquent rhapsodizing of the Romantics and Parnassian regimentation which drilled the poetic line not like fighting men but like so many lead soldiers. The same targets were also savaged by Lautréamont (pseud. of Isidore Ducasse, 1846–70) in his *Poésies* (1870). While most rebel poets moved to the *vers libéré*, few broke with structured prosody. Charles Cros (1841–88), though spurned by the Parnassians, was as controlled a technician as any of them, though, as with Germain Nouveau (1851–1920), his simpler melodic line and more intimate tone helped change the poetic climate. Lautréamont's unclassifiable *Chants de Maldoror* (1868–9), which looks back to Gothic horror and fantasy and the cruelty of Sade but also forward to Surrealism, took poetic prose several highly original steps forward.

Rimbaud

But even Arthur Rimbaud (1854–91) began in Parnassian mode with poems which expressed his hatred of religion, the bourgeoisie and his compassion for the poor ('Les Effarés') and the victims of the war of 1870. Yet a sonnet like 'Le Dormeur du val' pushes at the constraints of form. But Rimbaud's transformation of the poet into a 'voyant' led him to break with the 'vieillerie poétique' and took him beyond the liberated verse of 'Le Bateau ivre' and even the *vers libre* to the hallucinatory prose of the *Illuminations* (written 1872–3; publ. 1886) and *Une saison en enfer* (1873).

   Rimbaud's early poems engage with the external world not as a form of social criticism but with a directness of emotion uncomplicated by thought. They possess an innocence and a spontaneity which he protected by resisting, in his reckless life and unruly art, all compromise. His determination to retain the absolute clarity of childhood vision has been given spiritual, Christian, even political interpretations. As he expressed it, it was certainly mystical: he sought 'pouvoirs surnaturels' in a vast attempt to embrace 'l'âme universelle'. But whereas the ascetic aspires to spiritual planes by the denial of the self, Rimbaud reached trance-like states through excess, by the deliberately cultivated 'dérèglement de tous les sens'. He travelled from the known to the unknown, which was not a destination but the gateway to new apprehensions of what connected him to the universe. In 'Le Bateau ivre', his visions are mediated in part through literary reminiscences in which the reader may share. In the *Illuminations*, they break free and rise out of sensations which allow objects, experience and impressions to merge and communicate both the nature of the creative process ('voyance') and the expanded sensibility which lies beyond the conscious self. But if he surrendered to his inner eye, he remained a very conscious artist. As late as 1872, he used resonant alliterations and bold metaphors to reach out to the reader. Thereafter, to 'fixer des vertiges', he developed a poetic language which not merely associated disparate sense impressions but made 'parfums, sons, couleurs' interchangeable. The explanatory links, the images which normally relay meaning through a shared frame of reference, are omitted and we are exposed directly to unfiltered, unexplained, fantastic pictures. His hallucinations are not described as memories, nor are they mediated by thought: we see what he sees at the moment he sees it. There is no distance between Rimbaud, his visions and the reader. 'L'alchimie du verbe', which refines gross experience into magical and immediate knowledge, is a form of exploration.

Mallarmé

The poetry of Stéphane Mallarmé (1842–98) is also less a vehicle for the transmission or discussion of knowledge than the means of its discovery. Committed to the pursuit of the Ideal (that is, the essence of things which lies beyond their contingent forms), his 'grand oeuvre' pursued the absolutes which lie hidden beyond existential appearances. But if the musical resonance of the word 'flower' can evoke a Flower too absolute ever to figure in a bouquet, the effort to decode the existential world of representation may reveal higher, metaphysical realities ('l'explication orphique de la Terre'). Romantic idealism was a delusion, for God was dead and the sole means of capturing a reflection of the 'supreme fiction' which might redeem the contingency of life was language, because language is not fixed but in constant conversation with itself. But the task was jeopardized by its limitations which made it an imperfect instrument for translating concealed harmonies. Mallarmé, less concerned with the problems of existence than with the mysterious life of language, turned the arithmetic of vocabulary and syntax into algebra. Words, not the poet's experience of life, are the raw materials of poetry. By removing the varnish which has dulled their brightness, he released their ancient power. By changing their normal order, multiplying appositions and omitting articles and links (like 'comme'), he maximized their effect and hoisted signs and symbols which, by their power to suggest a 'tiers aspect fusible et clair', gestured towards a 'central unity' and the 'azure' of infinity. He saw no need to reject regular metres and fixed forms like the sonnet (until *Un coup de dés jamais n'abolira le hasard* (1897) which was set typographically to resemble a musical score) and pursued his difficult art at the level of the play of language, its sonorities and strange rhythmic collisions, which rejuvenated old words and enfranchised rare vocabulary. It should be no surprise that such poetry should be hermetic and emotionally arid nor that Mallarmé would remain very much a poet's poet. Limited in its range of themes, it is dense, obscure and elliptical, and Mallarmé would not have it otherwise. Poetry was a sacred language and, as its high priest, he wrote only for the initiated. Money and fame did not concern him (his first collection, *Poésies*, appeared only in 1887) but he was aware that poetry as he defined it was perhaps doomed to the incommunicable and to silence: 'Mon art est une impasse.' In this he was wrong. His verbal and visual discoveries were to feed the curiosity of twentieth-century successors who, as they pondered the workings of language and the function of poetry, would return to his formulation of poetry as 'l'expression par le langage humain ramené à son rythme essentiel du sens mystérieux de l'existence'.

Laforgue

Jules Laforgue (1860–87) moved quickly from Hugolian verse, adopted a more relaxed attitude to rhyme and gravitated to rhythms which owed less to standard metre and Verlainian 'music' than to the natural pulsations of *vers libre*. His technical innovation and vision of spiritual emptiness were more highly regarded abroad, notably by Ezra Pound and T. S. Eliot, than in France, although he formed an essential link between the Rimbaud/Mallarmé tandem and Apollinaire and the 'Fantaisistes'. Technical considerations apart, Laforgue, regarded in his brief time as a Decadent, still startles with his combative irony and wry self-deprecation. As despairing as any Romantic poet, but more bitter, he tracks the banality of existence ('que la vie est quotidienne!') with rhythmic sprightliness, nimble verbal inventiveness and unglamorous images (sunsets are red as butchers' aprons). Like life, the cosmos is a form of sarcasm and Laforgue responds in kind. The last of the great nineteenth-century poets, Laforgue offers a gently fading pessimistic shrug in answer to the great problems which his predecessors had raised but not solved.

Poetry to 1914

The renewal of poetic expression of the 1870s gave courage to the Decadents of the 1880s who were quickly absorbed into Symbolism which, after about 1895, had begun to break up. But nineteenth-century poetry did not come to a stop in 1900 but sailed on, like a slowly deflating, parti-coloured *montgolfière*. Its passenger list included Naturists, Humanists, neo-classicists and post-Symbolists of subtly differentiated persuasions. Many regulars and irregulars gravitated to other genres. The reputation of Jean Richepin (1849–1926), poet of vagrants (*Les Chansons des gueux*, 1876), was made as a playwright (*Le Chemineau*, 1897), and Alfred Jarry (1873–1907) moved beyond the Symbolist poems of *Les Minutes de sable mémorial* (1894) into the novel and, famously, the theatre, laying time bombs under the structures of language and society which would explode during the avant-gardism of the 1920s. But most turn-of-the-century poets outlived their passing fame. François Coppée, sentimental observer of the urban poor and one of the best-known poets of the 1870s and 1880s, survives mainly as a pre-populist witness. Henri de Régnier (1864–1936) turned to neo-classicism but never abandoned his Symbolist openness to the mystery of experience. His was a careful, pondered art, like that of Jean Moréas (1856–1910), who achieved a sustainable compromise between the Symbolist and the classical in *Stances* (1899–1920). It was also the time of Albert Samain (1858–1900), harmonious and delicate, who captured the *fin-de-siècle* mood, and of Francis Jammes (1868–1938) who wrote lyrically of hill and field before turning to the faith he had rediscovered. Paul Fort (1872–1960), man of the theatre and editor of *Vers et prose* (1905–14), developed assonanced, rhymed, rhythmic prose in *ballades* which extended from 1896 to 1958.

Conclusion

The nineteenth century was the glittering age of French poetry. Ideas and sensibilities locked out by classicism were released first by the Romantics who established personal, social and mystical themes which were taken up, with increasing formal adventurousness, by poets who wrestled with the human condition in an age still poised between belief and science, tradition and progress. Their reflection on the visible and the invisible, on man, the world and what lay beyond it, continued after 1900 on a less anguished and, with the Unanimists, more prosaic note. Yet the uncertainty of mankind's destiny had grown no less urgent and, by 1910, out of the forest of Symbolists and their 'classicizing' successors, three broad answers were proposed: Christian, with Péguy and Claudel; positivist, with Valéry; and radical and anarchic, with Apollinaire and, soon, the Surrealists.

Theatre

Napoleon's strict control of the Paris theatres was relaxed after the Restoration when small playhouses catering for popular audiences sprang up on the Boulevard du Temple, known as the 'Boulevard du crime' for the gory melodramas they staged. Restrictions, lifted briefly after the Revolution of 1830, were restored in 1835 and relaxed in 1848. After 1853, new plays again required an *autorisation préalable* but in 1864 theatres were deregulated and numbers multiplied rapidly. By 1875, there were about 60 in Paris and more than 100 in 1900, when they attracted half a million spectators weekly. Although theatre censorship ended in 1906, public morality continued to be protected by powers invested in local police and civil authorities who worked through the courts. As with other forms of culture, the demands of the new paying public helped determine success and failure. But theatre was also vulnerable to the drawing power of star actors whose new status allowed them to influence the course of drama. Talma (1763–1826) enabled tragedy to survive beyond its natural life; Marie Dorval (1798–1849) and Fréderick Lemaître (1800–76) were vital to the success of Romantic drama; Virginie Dejazet (1797–1875) and Réjane (1856–1920) helped to impose the modern repertoire after 1850; and Sarah Bernhardt (1844–1923) internationalized France's theatrical traditions.

1800–50

During the Revolution, theatre was a public focus of the new age of liberty. Its successes were celebrated and its enemies denounced on stage. Actors ceased to be outcasts and became 'educators of the people'. New and more popular theatrical forms prospered – *vaudeville* and melodrama in particular – and tragedy and comedy were given a revisionist, republican facelift. The *drame bourgeois* proliferated in a variety of hybrid forms and the calmer mood of the Directoire encouraged a revival of classical genres.

Tragedy

Late eighteenth-century tragedy had choked on the mechanical application of the classical rules. Yet it had an ideology – hostility to despotism and fanaticism – which preserved it from extinction. In the hands of M.-J. Chénier and others, it served the Revolution, which created a new tragic hero: the warrior-patriot. After 1800, dull tragedies about great men (William the Conqueror or Peter the Great) were intended to reflect the glory of Napoleon, but authors also added medieval, 'national' and exotic subjects to their still-classical arsenal and experimented mildly with the unities. François Raynouard (1761–1836) and Marie-François Baour-Lormian (1770–1854) were suitably imperial but failed to renew the genre which, by remaining faithful to the *récit*, banished action to the wings at a time when audiences demanded excitement. Though *Tippoo Sahib* (1813) by Étienne Jouy (1764–1846) attempted to build on the *drame bourgeois*, the controlling spirit remained neo-classical.

After the Restoration, tragedy was artificially prolonged by the reputation of Talma and the politico-literary quarrel between the defenders of classicism and the emerging Romantic rebels. Jacques-Arsène d'Ancelot pleased the royalists with *Louis IX* (1819). On the other hand, with *Les Vêpres siciliennes* (1819), which defended the revolt of Palermo against the house of Anjou in 1282, Casimir Delavigne (1793–1843) expressed the resentments of Bonapartists and liberals hostile to Louis XVIII, and Michel Pichat won the support of the liberals for *Léonidas* (1824), which echoed the Greek struggle for independence. But most tragedians in the 1820s, drawing on classical, Biblical, and historical themes, expressed a broadly conservative point of view while at the same time straining at the constricting rules. In 1820, Pierre Lebrun's *Marie-Stuart* departed from the unity of place by setting scenes in different rooms of a castle and, offending against the purity of classical language, dared say plain *mouchoir* for the noble *tissu*. Alexandre Soumet scorned the *récit* and allowed Mlle George to be burned on stage in *Jeanne d'Arc* (1825). But even the boldest playwrights stopped well short of a break with tradition. The sense of tragic fate emigrated to other genres and tragedy as a genre was dead long before 1830.

Comedy

Between 1791 and 1800, two-thirds of new plays staged were comedies, *vaudevilles* for the most part. Classical comedy, diverted into the sentimental mode during the Directoire, had few exponents. Comic authors were expected to follow the classical rules if they were to be staged at the Théâtre Français and the Odéon and their options were further limited by the moral climate which protected the Church, feminine virtue, the new aristocracy and middle-class parvenus, and thus denied them access to the mainstay of comedy: the satire of human and social foibles. Louis-Benoît Picard (1769–1828), author of some 100 plays, succeeded with *La Petite ville* (1801), the first of many satirical treatments of provincial manners. Charles Étienne also found a safe subject with *Brueys et Palaprat* (1807), a satirical account of two *ancien régime* poets, though *Les Deux gendres* (1810) showed two sons who ruin a father against a well-observed portrait of the social elite of the Empire. Technically, the most adventurous of these mild iconoclasts was Népomucène Lemercier (1771–1840). Beginning with a 'Shakespearean' tragedy (*Agamemnon*, 1797), he attempted, in *Pinto* (1800), to show 'des personnages parlant et agissant comme on le fait dans la vie'. *Christophe Colomb* (1809), another *comédie historique*, caused a furore by flouting the dramatic unities and daring to rhyme *coquin* with *requin*. With hindsight, Pinto, a valet who leads an attempt to free Portugal of the Spanish yoke in 1640, might seem to anticipate Ruy Blas. But the limits of Lemercier's adventurousness are demonstrated by his later hostility to Romantic drama.

During the Restoration, when political subjects remained taboo, comedy returned to its traditional assault on manners: money, marriage and social ambition. Delavigne's *L'École des vieillards* (1823) reversed a stock situation by showing a *coquette* married to a sympathetic greybeard. Édouard Mazières, in *Le Jeune Mari* (1824), revealed that 100,000 francs could persuade a young man to take a wife aged fifty, while *L'Argent, ou les Moeurs du siècle* (1826) by Casimir Bonjour confirmed that love was not needed in a modern marriage. Such plays pushed satire to a broader cynicism which prefigured the *demi-monde* of Auger and Dumas *fils*. Though Carmontelle was revived by Théodore Leclercq (*Proverbes dramatiques*, 1820–30), comedy increasingly reflected the growing mood of anti-aristocratic liberalism. After 1830, however, verse comedy in the classical mould also reached the end of its natural life.

Romantic drama (1827–43)

Although the new Romantic spirit won its first skirmishes in poetry, the major battle took place in the theatre. The rise of Romantic drama was made possible by a number of factors.

First was the discovery of history, no longer a source of anguished tragic heroes nor of the 'national' subjects of the *drame bourgeois*, but of personality struggles, grand conflicts and turning points. This kind of anecdotal history abandoned the focus of traditional tragedy which had neglected events and concentrated on the psychological reaction of heroes to a moment of crisis. By showing the dramatic events which created the crisis, the new playwrights overturned the unities of time, place and action. Nor was the old 'nobility' of language adequate for their purposes. How, asked Stendhal, could the fate of peoples be shown if the word 'pistolet' was outlawed? The new historical drama replaced the *récit* by action, created new heroes, and added local colour and a new authenticity of costume and decor.

The second major impetus was the discovery of foreign drama – the publisher Ladvocat issued 25 volumes of *Chefs d'oeuvre des théâtres étrangers* in the 1820s – which expressed a wider range of emotions and dramatic action. Schiller, Calderón and Lope de Vega were seen as very imitable models, but Shakespeare was a revelation. Performed by English actors to great acclaim in 1827, he offered naked passion, horror, and soaring imagination. Moreover, the natural English acting style made the French tradition, represented by Talma, seem stilted and lifeless. A younger generation of players would breathe passion into dramas which mixed comedy and tragedy in a blazing, epic style. Stendhal (*Racine et Shakespeare*, 1823–5), Hugo's *Préface de Cromwell* (1827) and Vigny's *Lettre à Lord**** (1829) provided its theoretical base. Although plays were written according to the new precepts, such as Mérimée's *Théâtre de Clara Gazul* (1825) or Hugo's unperformed *Cromwell*, it was not until Alexandre Dumas (1802–72) presented *Henri III et sa cour* (1829) that Romantic theatre scored its first triumph. Its victory was confirmed with the controversial staging of Hugo's *Hernani* in February 1830. Set in Renaissance Spain, it showed Hernani, an outlawed noble, competing for the love of Dona Sol with the king of Spain and a reactionary grandee of the court. The *enjambement* ('escalier / Dérobé') in line 2 was a deliberate provocation and led to fighting in the auditorium.

The 'bataille d'*Hernani*' established Romantic drama. Yet the struggle had been less a quarrel about theatre than a clash of generations and aesthetic systems, and the literary revolution was to have more lasting effects in poetry and fiction than on the stage. The year 1831 marked the peak of the new drama. To historical subjects (Hugo's *Marion Delorme* and Vigny's *La Maréchale d'Ancre*) were added plots drawn from contemporary manners (Dumas's *Antony* and *Richard Darlington*). In 1832, the cholera epidemic emptied theatres, Hugo's *Le Roi s'amuse* was banned and only Dumas's *La Tour de Nesle* maintained the momentum of the movement which by 1835 showed signs of flagging. Neither Dumas's *Kean* (1836) nor Hugo's *Ruy Blas* (1838) could save it.

Romantic dramatists had freed theatre from the stylization imposed by the unities, the classical alexandrine and the sharp distinction between genres. Henceforth, 'tragedy' and 'comedy' would give way to the more flexible 'drama' which used more 'natural' prose and mixed moods in an altogether freer and more creative manner. The focus was on 'modern' passions, local colour and heroes who did battle on two fronts: they faced their metaphysical destiny but also struggled against their oppression by society. The claim that theatre had an educative, uplifting mission acquired a political colouring which reflected the concerns of social Romanticism. It was expressed, however, not in directly didactic terms but through the convulsions of 'extraordinary' individuals. Hugo's first prose drama, *Lucrèce Borgia* (1833), revealed the dealings of the rich and powerful but also, like many plays of the period, the precariousness of life. Vigny, suspicious of the excesses and 'surprises enfantines' of Romantic drama, stood up, in *Chatterton* (1835), for poets and genius against the materialism of the age. The groundswell of ideas was liberal and committed, and history was used freely as a stick with which to beat the present.

Hernani showed the corruption of monarchical government, an issue increasingly relevant to a generation alienated by Louis-Philippe's bourgeois rule: Musset's *Lorenzaccio* (1834) reflected the disappointment at the failure of the July Revolution and *Ruy Blas* anticipated the coming of the common man.

Romantic playwrights freed the stage from its constricting aesthetic, created a taste for technical innovation and redefined theatre both as lavish spectacle and as a forum for ideas. But the movement had more leaders than followers. The brilliance of Hugo and Dumas was inimitable and, as a form, the new drama suffered from its own ambitions. It offered truth, grandeur and art to increasingly materialistic audiences and it confused the 'Shakespearean' with the sensational. It relied on extravagant *coups de théâtre* and on the talents of the *monstre sacré*, like Frédérick Lemaître who was always tempted to turn what he was given to perform into melodrama. Few plays survived their period, and only Alfred de Musset (1810–47) has remained in the permanent repertoire.

Musset

After the failure of *La Nuit vénitienne* (1830), Musset's plays, published as *Un Spectacle dans un fauteuil*, were intended to be read, not performed. He wrote delicately of dawning, capricious, unhappy love enacted through characters who are spontaneous and cruel rather than perverse. They inhabit a world of imagination and fantasy and Musset's subtle analysis of their feelings places him close to Marivaux. With *Il ne faut jurer de rien* (1836; perf. 1848), he reverted to the eighteenth-century *proverbe*, while some of his plays, like *Un Caprice* (1837; perf. 1847), are basically conversation pieces. Others (*Fantasio*, 1835; perf. 1866) have stronger plots while *Les Caprices de Marianne* (1833; perf. 1852) or *On ne badine pas avec l'amour* (1834; perf. 1861) lie half-way between comedy and drama. Musset's 'armchair theatre' plays to the imagination and captures the poetry of dream. But there is anguish in his theatre too. *La Coupe et les lèvres* (1833) defines to perfection the tragic, Romantic hero, in love with his lost purity and aware that money and worldly success will not rid him of his *mal du siècle*. The same figure resurfaces in the magnificently brooding Lorenzaccio, one of the most complex characters in French theatre. Though he kills the tyrant of Florence, his motives, a mixture of personal and political idealism, are as tangled as Hamlet's.

Indeed, *Lorenzaccio* (performed abridged in 1896, and uncut by Jean Vilar in 1951) was the nearest any Romantic playwright came to producing a full-blown 'Shakespearean' play.

Vaudeville

In the 1770s, *vaudeville* was the name given to the comic, usually irreverent couplets sung to popular tunes at the Théâtre de la Foire and the first Boulevard playhouses. During the Revolution, it lent itself to political comment. After 1800, from its base at the Théâtre du Vaudeville (one of Napoleon's officially approved playhouses), it meant short plays, anecdotally rather than narratively structured, with a strong element of comic and satirical song. Subsequently it acquired a greater dramatic consistency and until 1850 was the major supplier of comedy. Between 1836 and 1846, for example, *vaudevilles* accounted for 1,900 of the 2,800 new plays staged.

Scribe

The most prolific *vaudevilliste* was Eugène Scribe (1791–1861). He began with a verse comedy in 1810 but by 1830 he had written 148 *vaudevilles*, sometimes in collaboration, as was then the common practice. Some, like *Une Nuit de la Garde Nationale* (1815) or *L'Ours et le pacha* (1820), are remarkable for their farcical energy. Yet Scribe also turned the basic sketch formula into the light, satirical comedy of bourgeois and petit-bourgeois manners in one or two acts. From 1818 onwards, he developed more consistent plots (*Le Diplomate* of 1827 was a 'comédie-vaudeville') which enabled him to drop the *couplet* and move out of the popular theatres and into the prestigious Comédie Française where he staged the satirical *Bertrand et Raton* in 1833. By *Le Verre d'eau* (1840), a historical comedy, or *Une Châine* (1841), a domestic drama, the *vaudeville* had been redefined by its well-structured plot which Scribe regarded as the essential ingredient of dramatic art. He expressed no consistent philosophy and from play to play moved easily between liberal and conservative points of view. The author of some 400 plays and *vaudevilles*, he also supplied libretti for, among others, Rossini and Meyerbeer. He had many imitators, but few matched his technical skills. After 1850, the *vaudeville* acquired an increasingly music-hall image and reverted to the loosely connected sketch with catchy *couplets* which did not survive the First World War.

Melodrama

The proposition, championed by the *drame bourgeois*, that theatre should teach civic virtues, was most effectively implemented not by Diderot, Sedaine and Mercier, but by popular melodrama. The term, coined in seventeenth-century Italy, designated a 'play with music', both sung and danced. Rousseau used it in this sense to describe *Pygmalion* (1770). During the Revolution, however, it emerged as a popular entertainment which adopted the primary colours of the Gothic and delivered Manichaean judgements on the enemies of the people. After 1795, the musical element was dropped in favour of sensational dramatic action. It was a form which suited the times. The Revolution operated in an aura of theatricality and accustomed ordinary citizens to horror, blood and amazing reversals of fortune. If events had changed the political landscape, it also created a new theatrical audience: the People.

Melodrama was firmly established by the time Pixerécourt staged *Cœlina* (1800), an adaptation of the novel by Ducray-Duminil. Thereafter, playwrights furnished industrial quantities of high-impact drama for the popular theatres. Louis Caigniez (1762–1842) was known as the 'Racine des Boulevards' for his treatment of Biblical subjects and maternal anguish, though he is best remembered for *La Pie voleuse* (1815) which provided Rossini with the libretto for his opera. The gory style of Jean Cuvelier de Trye (1766–1824) made him the 'Crébillon des Boulevards'. But the outstanding practitioner of the genre – and the 'Corneille des Boulevards' – was Guilbert de Pixerécourt (1773–1844), author of more than 90 melodramas. By 1810, he had achieved star status, which he maintained by adapting easily to the darker mood of the 1820s and, with *Latude* (1834), competing successfully with Romantic drama. He impressed the young Hugo and Nodier admiringly christened him 'Shakespirécourt'. A skilled dramatic craftsman, he also adopted a didactic stance, offering role models and lessons in heroism and loyalty to the class of society which had most need of them: he wrote, he said, 'pour les gens qui ne savent pas lire'. Not all, however, welcomed the conservative moral line taken by melodrama. In 1814, Jean-Baptiste Hapdé, himself a successful exponent of the genre, warned that it had become an instrument of propaganda for establishment values.

For melodrama was committed to the victory of virtue and the defeat of vice. It showed innocence threatened, undone and restored,

a tripartite structure which called for the unavoidable trinity of heroine, hero and persecutor. Aristotelian catharsis had purged passion
through terror: here it was sentiment that purified. It taught the
value of suffering and put Providence firmly on the side of the right-
eous. But it also moralized and politicized forms of persecution which
it regularly updated. During the Consulate and Empire, it promoted
the family and patriotism and underwrote the hierarchy of authority.
But in 1823 Frédérick Lemaître turned Robert Macaire, the scoun-
drel of *L'Auberge des Adrets* (1823), into a sympathetic villain and
created a cult figure who symbolized popular resistance to the old
moral order. In his wake, the innocents of the Boulevard du crime
appeared increasingly as society's victims, and their tormentors as
authority figures. After the July Revolution, melodrama found more
incendiary targets: the wealth and power of the bourgeoisie, corrupt
churchmen and politicians. With time, it turned more specifically
socialist. Villains became even more visibly capitalist and their victims more working-class. Philanthropic doctors and lawyers redefined moral worth by showing solidarity with the poor against the
establishments which oppressed them. New sensational twists were
added to the repertoire of plot and situation: lovers who discover
they are brother and sister, the murderer who kills the wrong person, the father who is misled into cursing his blameless children.
Dark deeds, situated as often in the past as in the present, were
perpetrated in sequestered farms and inns built on the edge of preci-
pices. After 1836, melodrama and the *roman feuilleton*, feeding off
each other, projected the same heightened theatricality and the same
view of ordinary people as victims of a heartless society. Their public
was the same and, in many cases, their writers were simultaneously
mélodramistes and *feuilletonistes*.

Though the appetite for new sensations made great demands on
the ingenuity of authors, some showed considerable staying power.
Victor Ducange (1783–1833) remained a Boulevard favourite for
twenty years and *Trente ans, ou la Vie d'un joueur* (1831), starring
Frédérick Lemaître and Marie Dorval, was one of the great successes
of the Romantic period. Joseph Bouchardy (1810–70), author of
Gaspardo le pêcheur (1838), defined 'style' in terms of the number of
harrowing and astounding effects he could produce. Adolphe Dennery
(1811–99) was known for his ability to devise sensational plots which
other hands (who would later include Labiche and Jules Verne)

translated into dialogue, and thus shared the credit for over 250 melo-dramas. Auguste Anicet-Bourgeois (1806–71), a success for fifty years, wrote 300 in various modes. Félix Pyat (1810–89) set up firmly on the side of widows and orphans oppressed by an unending stream of predatory industrialists and corrupt establishment persecutors. *Le Chiffonnier de Paris* (1847) struck an overtly revolutionary note and gave some credence to the view that the 'cradle of socialism' was not the writings of Proudhon but melodrama which sensitized the public to political realities and social injustice.

The classical revival

The failure of Hugo's *Les Burgraves* in 1843 confirmed the demise of Romantic drama. The public mood had changed and was better captured in 1843 by *Lucrèce*, a Roman tragedy by François Ponsard (1814–67). His Lucrèce was not an anguished Romantic heroine facing insuperable odds, but an honest woman caught in a domestic crisis. Conservatives hailed the play as a return to classicism, though in reality, its success was attributable less to its ancient source than to its reflection of modern life and its partial abandon of 'tragic' language. A number of playwrights, including Augier, author of a 'comédie grecque', *La Ciguë* (1844), rallied to Ponsard and formed the 'École du Bon Sens' which offered 'antic' plots and tedious 'verse'. They set out to rescue theatre from the excesses of Hugo and Dumas, combat foreign influences and reassert the rights of the majority which had been usurped by the struttings of the extraordinary indi-viduals spawned by Romanticism. They stood for order and reason and denounced the Revolution of 1848. Ponsard later recanted, admitting that it was Hugo who had art, right and life on his side. Yet though it was short-lived, the classical revival helped shift literary theatre to a position right of centre which it was to occupy for the rest of the century.

1850–1914

By the middle of the century, French theatre was looking for a new direction. Though the classical repertoire was maintained at the Comédie Française, tragedy and comedy were long dead, the *vaude-ville* was being challenged by comic opera, and melodrama, though popular, was trapped in its own formulaic sensationalism. The legacy of Romantic drama – spectacle, lofty subjects drawn from history and legend, the 'mélange des tons' – was rejected in favour of a more accessible human and social realism rooted in contemporary middle-class manners, written in prose, not verse.

The moralizing school of manners

Émile Augier (1820–79) cultivated a moral stance far removed from the nihilism of the Romantic hero. He found a public receptive to the defence of middle-class values (honesty and the family) against the disruptive influence of the dowry system, the courtesan and the seducer, all threats to marriage and therefore to the social and economic order. *Le Gendre de Monsieur Poirier* (1854) is the best example of both his manner and his attitudes. Wittily written and neatly plotted around a cast of firmly differentiated types, it mocks both the ant (personified by the grasping bourgeois) and the grasshopper (the feckless aristocrat) and situates 'common sense' somewhere between the two. Pitting the impoverished nobility against the newly rich and eternally vulgar middle class, he proceeded to show the evils of financial speculation and the insidious influence of churchmen before turning, after 1870, to divorce, the rights of illegitimate children and the arranged marriage (*Les Fourchambault*, 1878). Augier's taste for happy endings reflects his intrusive didacticism. Yet his technical mastery of a limited range of characters and situations made him a dominant figure in the theatre of conventional realism which expressed the conservative, moralizing mood of the Second Empire.

Augier competed for the moral high ground with Alexandre Dumas *fils* (1824–95). Dumas's artistic goal was to combine the social analysis of Balzac with the theatrical skills of Scribe. In practice he used theatre as a platform for social reform and his obsessive interest in two issues of intense personal concern: the problem of the illegitimate child (he himself was born out of wedlock and suffered cruelly for it) and divorce, which he came to regard as the solution to adultery. His solidly constructed plays dealt with the dangers of extramarital sexuality (*Les Idées de Madame Aubry*, 1867), and his themes may be deduced from the titles he chose: *Le Demi-monde* (1855), *La Question d'argent* (1857), *Le Fils naturel* (1858), *Un Père prodigue* (1859). His views hardened after 1870 and in his hands the *pièce à thèse* became preachily moralistic. Yet his ability to write dramatic dialogue together with his sense of stage technique make him a precursor both of the social-realist play and of the intellectual and analytical theatre of Shaw and Ibsen. However, he remains best known for what he came to regard as a youthful indiscretion. His first play, *La Dame aux camélias* (1852), adapted from his own novel, created one of the world's most enduring myths, Marguerite Gautier, the courtesan who sacrifices herself for love. The type was well known. Dumas drew heavily on *Manon Lescaut* and the subject had been treated by Hugo in *Marion Delorme*. But Marguerite is drawn with a touching directness which has still to lose its appeal.

A more firmly comic presence was maintained by Ernest Labiche (1815–88) who, between 1837 and 1877, wrote 173 plays, of which he thought only 57 worthy of inclusion in his *Théâtre complet* (1878–9). Author at first of *vaudevilles*, which taught him how to plot, he reacted against the school of Ponsard, whom he thought dull and earnest, and adopted a critical but essentially good-humoured view of middle-class *rentiers* who get into trouble spending their unearned incomes. Though Labiche could be moral (he had harsh words to say about arranged marriages), his plays wink at adultery and sexual irregularity which he exploited for comic ends. His technique of ridicule anticipates Bergson's later definition of comedy (the mechanical imposed on the real) for he specialized in showing how familiar types behave when placed in unfamiliar contexts: hence his fondness for the theme of travel. Labiche began where Scribe left off, though his dialogue is wittier and he indulged a more systematic taste for farce. Both are best exemplified in *Un Chapeau de paille d'Italie* (1851) and *Le Voyage de Monsieur Perrichon* (1860) which prefigured Feydeau and Courteline and whose pace and invention have earned them a place in the active repertoire.

Between 1850 and 1870, serious theatre had been a product for middle-class consumption. The repercussions of the Franco-Prussian War, the Commune and the arrival of the Third Republic, did not attract playwrights. Though an acerbic note was occasionally struck, satirical social realism in the manner of Augier and Dumas dominated the stage. This, plus his inventiveness and flair, goes some way to explain why the last of the nineteenth century's theatrical phenomena, Victorien Sardou (1831–1908), was not only able to make the transition from the Second Empire to the Republic, but also to encapsulate Belle Époque values.

His first success, *Les Pattes de mouche* (1861), dealt frothily with adultery and set the tone for a torrent of plays offering mild rebukes to the indulgent morality of their materialistic times. His forte was the comedy of manners and one of his greatest mid-career successes was a *vaudeville, Divorçons!* (1880), which dealt in frivolous terms with marriage. He attempted a political theme with *Patrie* (1869) but subsequently tempered social and historical subjects with farce – when the Commune was safely over, *Rabagas* (1872) offered audiences a chance to laugh at a stereotyped revolutionary bogeyman – and pathos: *La Tosca* (1887) was used by Puccini for his opera. *Madame Sans-Gêne* (1893), a *vaudeville historique*, the tale of a pretty laundress who marries one of Napoleon's generals, was his greatest and most enduring triumph. Part of his success derived from his collaboration with Sarah Bernhardt, whom Shaw dubbed 'the Queen of Sardoodledum'. His characters are shallow and his formula now seems contrived and mechanical. Yet his technical skills and ingenuity within his narrow compass qualify him as a supreme professional of the theatre.

The continuing domination of Paris stages by Dumas, Labiche and Sardou blocked the path of the new generation of playwrights. Verse drama kept a low profile with François Coppée, Jean Richepin (1849–1926) and Henri Bornier (1825–1901), whose *La Fille de Roland* (1875) was one of the few plays to deal directly with the loss of Alsace-Lorraine. For theatre turned its face away from such overtly sensitive subjects and audiences were far more comfortable with the familiar and by now highly stylized observation of bourgeois life and values exploited in the 1870s and 1880s by Édouard Pailleron (1834–99) and others.

Boulevard theatre of the Belle Époque

In the 1890s, of the varied bill of fare offered to the capital's half million regular spectators, 'Boulevard' theatre captured the frivolous mood of the Belle Époque most fully. It was above all an atmosphere and a style. Its subjects were love and money and its milieu was middle-class with an aristocratic leavening. While lawyers, bankers and financiers had money, counts and duchesses had glamour and status, and the exchange of bourgeois wealth for noble titles through marriage (predictably hampered by romantic love) was a perennial subject. Wives were domineering or wronged, husbands fools or philanderers, artists were respectable, servants docile, and the working class was represented exclusively by the pretty ingénue (a florist or seamstress) who made up for her background by a naturally noble soul. Facile answers were provided to serious questions and audiences willingly indulged authors who connived at the amoral complacency of the times. The great stars of the stage (Bernhardt, Sully-Mounier, Lucien Guitry, Réjane) were admired for their ability to 'carry a play' and the theatre was frequently little more than a showcase for their talents. Boulevard plays were written in different inks – sentimental, dramatic, satirical, titillating and shocking – and presented life neatly packaged in strong situations culminating in telling curtain lines. But all gave the same glossy picture of sophisticated society life which drew audiences denied access to it in reality. Maurice Donnay (1859–1945), Alfred Capus (1858–1922) and Henri Lavedan (1858–1940), the most popular craftsmen of a minor art, have long since vanished along with the unreal world of the Belle Époque. Even the immensely successful Henri Bataille (1872–1922), who wrote almost exclusively of adultery among the rich, had turned into an object of derision by 1918. Henry Bernstein (1877–1953), a force in mainstream theatre for fifty years, established himself as the author of sensational dramas which exposed the predatory machinations of politicians and financiers, but made no serious effort to temper the ethics of capitalism by reference to morality and justice. What was called the *pièce à thèse* featured tailor's dummies dressed up in abstractions.

If Boulevard theatre survives at all, it is in the area of comedy. The duo of Robert de Flers (1872–1927) and Gaston Arman de Cailhavet (1869–1915) specialized in mild satire laced with pungent one-liners. The gentler comedy of journalist and novelist Tristan Bernard (1866–1947) may be judged from the sketch, *L'Anglais tel qu'on le parle* (1899) which is still revived occasionally. But the most rustproof 'boulevardier' was Georges Feydeau (1862–1921) who turned broad farce into an art form. *Une puce à l'oreille* (1907), *Occupe-toi d'Amélie* (1908) and *On purge Bébé* (1910), the most durable of his 39 plays, deal with the preposterous antics ('Ciel, mon mari!') of cardboard characters but work supremely well as theatre in terms of furious pace, manic action and technical brilliance. But in the two decades before 1914, the most popular comic talent was Georges Courteline (pseud. of Georges Moinaux, 1858–1929). Both as novelist and playwright, his strength lay in observation rather than in plot or character and he freely admitted to being good for one act only, as in the lastingly popular *Boubouroche* (1893), the tale of a gullible cuckold, or *Les Gaietés de l'escadron* (1895) based on his sketches of army life, which was to give its name to a sub-genre of plays and, later, films.

However, the greatest success of the Belle Époque was provided by Edmond Rostand (1868–1918), who reacted against the oppressive tone and matter of serious comedy. In his day he was declared superior in theatrical talent and human truth to Ibsen and Strindberg, though of his modest output only the evergreen *Cyrano de Bergerac* (1897) has survived. His long-nosed hero was a mix of Corneille's Rodrigue, Molière's Alceste, Hugo's Ruy Blas and Dumas's d'Artagnan, artfully stirred into a late but full-blown Romantic drama. *Cyrano* and *L'Aiglon* (1900) were the last plays in verse to reach a wide audience. *Chantecler* (1910), a satirical and symbolical transposition of human foibles into the personality of farmyard animals, however, failed to give the public a lasting taste for poetic drama.

Naturalist theatre

The technical brilliance of the Scribe-Labiche-Sardou tradition and the didactic realism of Augier and Dumas created a respect for both the *pièce bien faite* and the *pièce à thèse*. Yet the dominance of formulaic drama impeded the development of theatre. The first sacrificed psychology to plot and manner, while the second was in permanent danger of drowning in its own moralizing. In comparison, the novel had been altogether more adventurous in its presentation of human and social issues. Balzac and Flaubert (*Le Candidat*, 1874) had failed as playwrights, but their example as novelists had played a part in alerting the theatre to its social and realistic vocation. But it had not been enough. In 1879 Edmond de Goncourt predicted the collapse of theatre under the weight of its conventions. In 1880 Zola, author of a number of plays (*Les Héritiers Rabourdin*, 1874) and adaptations of his novels (beginning with *Thérèse Raquin*, 1873) which had met with only limited success, publicly denounced the facile technique and indulgent morality of the Paris stage. Yet in the event, the Naturalist theatre which he had defined in 1878 was to be imposed less by theory and argument than by the example provided by Henri Becque (1837–99).

Becque's early success, *L'Enfant prodigue* (1868) was a *vaudeville* in the manner of Labiche, but the darker-toned *Michel Pauper* (1870), with its working-class hero and concern with specific issues such as low pay, was a failure. Yet it was the first instance of what would become known as the *tranche de vie*. Instead of virtuoso plots, imbroglios and happy endings, he offered a simpler narrative line and showed more individualized characters reacting to an evolving situation. It is the remorselessness of the 'crows' of the title (the partners of a dead husband who cheat his widow and daughters of their inheritance) which, in *Les Corbeaux* (1872–6; perf. 1882), gave a familiar situation a deeper and more sombre twist. Like *La Parisienne* (1885), which exposed the emptiness of adultery, it rejected the social and moral conventions and established a new tone of savage irony. Becque revealed the naked, cruel greed which lies just beneath the surface of man's social character.

Becque's influence was greater than his success. He appealed less to the public than to professionals of the theatre, who recognized his originality. He impressed André Antoine (1858–1943), manager of the Théâtre Libre which, in a plainer production style, cultivated the 'Naturalist' tendency. Conventionally decorated sets and lavish costumes gave way to exact reproductions of dress and social milieu. Acting techniques were simplified and the dominant position of the 'monstre sacré' who for decades had determined theatrical programmes and dictated production styles, was challenged by the new authority of the artistic director.

Between 1887 and 1896, Antoine gave a platform to poetic drama, the sardonic *comédie rosse* of Georges Ancey (1860–1917) and stark *tranches de vie* which showed vice unpunished and virtue unrewarded. Between 1906 and 1913, he pursued his ideas at the Théâtre de l'Odéon. Although his Théâtre Libre lasted barely ten years, its influence was far-reaching: Antoine was the father of modern *mise en scène* and subsequently playwrights and actors learned to work with a director. But in the short term, he signalled the arrival of a new spirit which put seamstresses and miners on to stages hitherto reserved exclusively for financiers and aristocrats.

The 'Naturalist' aim of exposing the power of instinct in determining human destiny was explored, without lasting success, by Henri Céard (1851–1924) and Léon Hennique (1851–1935). But Antoine also encouraged a stream of playwrights working in the spirit, if not to the letter, of Naturalism, such as Francis de Curel (1854–1929) whose psychological studies of criminals (*L'Envers d'une sainte*, 1892) and grim social studies showed society as a flimsy surface covering a deeper barbarism. Antoine also launched Georges de Porto-Riche (1849–1930) who specialized in frustrated desire in what he called his 'théâtre d'amour', and depicted love as a physical enslavement (*La Chance de Françoise*, 1887). The *tranche de vie* is psychological in the case of Jules Renard (1844–1910: *Le Pain de ménage*, 1898; *Poil de carotte*, 1900; *Monsieur Vernet*, 1903) but tended more frequently to social realism which revealed the ills of society in a mood which combined cynicism with strong moral judgements. *La Vie politique* (1901), by Émile Fabre (1869–1955), was a savage attack on electoral scandals. In *Les Affaires sont les affaires* (1903), Octave Mirbeau (1850–1917) unveiled the workings of money. Naturalist theatre, though it traded in character types and such jaded ploys as the misdirected letter, was solidly constructed and its frank treatment of contemporary issues (divorce, class antagonism, the illegitimate child, the evils of capitalism) guaranteed it a steady audience. From the showing of social abuses to attempts to remedy them was a short step, and Naturalist theatre was soon overtaken by a more overtly didactic impetus. The taste for socially conscious theatre encouraged a return to the tradition of Dumas *fils* and Henri Becque. The new *pièce à thèse* was Naturalist theatre spiked with often intrusive moral and social propaganda. Eugène Brieux (1858–1932) and Paul Hervieu (1857–1915) dealt preachily with subjects as varied as feminism, the corruption of the legal system and the family. Brieux's *Les Avariés* (1901) scandalized with its frank discussion of syphilis.

Symbolist theatre

In the 1880s, the repercussions of the Symbolist movement provided a solid focus for an avant-garde revolt against the conventional realism of commercial theatre and the bleakness of Naturalist drama. Theatre had beckoned to Symbolist poets since the 1860s, though the most ambitious text, Villiers de l'Isle-Adam's *Axël* (1874), with its subordination of sex to spirit, was not performed until 1894. The new mood of mystical spirituality struck a responsive chord in Paul Claudel (1868–1955) who developed an epic, lyrical style of theatrical non-realism. From *Tête d'or* (1890) and *La Ville* (1893) to *L'Ôtage* (1911), Claudel pursued exalted, spiritual themes in much-rewritten texts of which the first to be staged, in 1912, was *L'Annonce faite à Marie*, the third version of *La Jeune Fille Violaine* (1892).

Symbolist drama, rooted in the intuitive, the evocative, and the ritual, was first nurtured in the short-lived Théâtre d'Art founded in 1892 by Paul Fort (1872–1960) which in 1893 became the Théâtre de l'Oeuvre, directed by Aurélien-François Lugné-Poë (1869–1940). Fort staged Shelley and Marlowe and adapted poems by Rimbaud, Mallarmé and Laforgue, with music by Debussy and sets by Gauguin, Bonnard and others. The new drama first attracted attention in 1893 when Lugné-Poë produced *Pelléas et Mélisande* by Maurice Maeterlinck (1862–1949), set in a zone of legend where a ring dropped in a fountain may lead to the death of love. Maeterlinck dealt poetically with the mysterious forces which direct human destiny. His dramas of 'inaction' (like the more conventional *Monna Vanna* of 1902) project sleep-walking figures in more or less indeterminate landscapes and, with the exception of *L'Oiseau bleu* (1908), have not survived. Yet his example was not lost at home on Claudel, Joseph Péladan and Édouard Dujardin and abroad, on Yeats and d'Annunzio.

Maeterlinck's aim, like that of Symbolist drama generally, was to rescue theatre from the Naturalist obsession with instinctive drives by focusing on the soul. Though his grandiloquent unreality made large demands on audiences, Lugné-Poë's understated sets, specialized lighting and use of actors as emblems or symbols of their roles, were well suited to its allegorical, state-of-soul pessimism. Under his guidance, the Théâtre de l'Oeuvre remained the home of Symbolist drama until 1914.

But Lugné-Poë's eclecticism also accommodated the grotesque satire of *Ubu Roi* (1896), the most durable of the four Ubu plays of Alfred Jarry (1873–1907). Jarry's early poetry and working relationship with Lugné-Poë has led him to be associated with Symbolist drama, though he is unclassifiable. Fascinated by puppet theatre, he took farce to epic lengths and his chronicles of the sinister Ubu were to make a deep impression on later generations of writers. Jarry supplied a model for bizarre theatre but also came to be seen as a far-sighted prophet: Ubu points to the murderous dictators of the twentieth century. In Jarry, creator of 'la pataphysique' ('the science des solutions imaginaires' which denied all rationality), were the seeds of much subsequent political, anarchic and surreal theatre, and he was revered by the avant-garde of the next generation who found in him the first expression of a truly modern consciousness.

Melodrama

After 1848, Pyat's *Chiffonnier* was one of a number of melodramas banned as inflammatory. But as political tension eased and France settled into the bourgeois Second Empire, the public of all classes returned to the Boulevards to cheer and hiss. But melodrama never regained its former popularity. It now had to compete with the operettas of Offenbach and his imitators and the *café-concert*, ancestor of the music hall. Even so, historical melodramas continued to draw the public. Paul Meurice (1820–1905) wrote the engaging *Fanfan la tulipe* (1858) around a seventeenth-century swashbuckler who is first cousin to d'Artagnan. Paul Féval scored a resounding success with a dramatization (1862) of his novel, *Le Bossu* (1857), set in the Regency, while the spectacular battles and startling effects devised by Victor Séjour (1821–74) delivered all the thrills which the genre promised. Around 1870, there was a revival of the patriotic and military melodrama which by the 1880s would spawn sensational reflections of France's colonial ventures in North Africa and the Far East.

But melodrama also found subjects in domestic life and treated, in cruder terms, the same 'social' problems as Augier and Dumas *fils*: marriage, adultery, wills, and offspring lost and found. During the Second Empire, the mood was conciliatory and constructive. Audiences were directed to weep for the sufferings of the poor rather than rail against the social injustice which caused them. In the wake of Murger's *La Vie de bohème* (adapted 1849), melodramas about the lives of artists exploited the vicarious joys and sorrows of poetic young people in love with art, starving in garrets. Yet if the popular playwrights of the 1850s and 1860s damped down their old political fires, the persecution which was at the heart of melodrama was not without a social edge. There were exposés of the oppression of the defenceless. The hero of Octave Feuillet's novel, *Le Roman d'un jeune homme pauvre* (adapted 1858) is well-born but poor, and he faces the same prejudices as Georges Ohnet's self-made man would meet in *Le Maître de forges* (adapted 1883). By that time, Dennery's *Les Deux Orphelines* (1874) had built on the post-Commune experience and relaunched melodrama, which grew closer to the aims and methods of Naturalism, as a major vehicle for socialist ideas in the 1880s and 1890s.

But the continuing appeal of the genre lay in its capacity to provide sensational thrills (from sadism to hair-breadth escapes), spectacle (fire, flood and volcanic eruption), fearsome settings (prisons, sewers, low taverns) and the strongest emotions. Less socially committed was the interest in adventure (Anicet-Bourgeois's *Les Pirates de la Savane*, 1859) and exploration, of which the adaptation of Jules Verne's *Le Tour du monde en 80 jours* (1859) set the trend. Playwrights shared such themes with the *roman feuilleton* – of which many were adapted for the stage – and they discovered crime at the same moment: the first crime play, Dennery's *L'Aïeule* (1863), coincided with Gaboriau's *L'Affaire Lerouge*. Yet as with crime fiction, audiences were slow to take to the *mélodrame policier* before the 1890s. Xavier de Montépin (1823–1902) dramatized his novel *La Porteuse de pain* (1884; adapted 1889), in which a factory girl is unjustly imprisoned by a wicked industrialist, while in *La Policière* (1890), the sleuth is female and the criminal her own son. The greatest success of Pierre Decourcelles (1856–1926), *Les Deux gosses* (1896), gave the old theme of abandoned children a new twist by showing them viciously exploited in a criminal milieu. The puppet shows of the Cercle Funambulesque and Henri Signoret's Petit Théâtre des Marionnettes, which both opened in 1888, and even more so the Théâtre du Grand-Guignol (1897), offered audiences from all social levels further outlets for blood-curdling horror. But melodrama, now established as a 'school for socialism', was to reclaim a more specific role in productions which, in the run-up to the Great War, turned aggressively 'revanchiste'.

Though defended by Romain Rolland in his plea for a *Théâtre du peuple* (1903) and, after 1918, by others anxious to create a 'popular theatre' movement, melodrama never became intellectually or artistically respectable. Gradually, its practitioners drifted into silent cinema, and melodrama as a theatrical form disappeared. Yet the taste for sensation survived not only on the Boulevards but also in plays by literary dramatists like Cocteau, Salacrou and Camus, whose *Le Malentendu* reverts to the stock situation of the stranger murdered in a lonely inn. Classics of the genre such as *Le Bossu* and *Les Deux gosses* were revived during the Occupation and others resurfaced in the cinema in the 1950s and 1960s. Like tragedy and comedy, melodrama was dispersed but found homes in other popular fictional modes – romantic and historical fiction, the *roman policier*, cinema, the *bande dessinée* and the television soap.

Conclusion

After Hugo's *Les Burgraves* (1843), a gulf appeared between literary and commercial drama. 'Good theatre' was thereafter defined not in terms of fine writing and universal truths but more narrowly as a reflection of contemporary society which it set out to mirror, entertain and sometimes shock. Even at its most serious, its staple subjects – the 'social' question, love and topical moral issues – echoed the preoccupations of a conservative and largely inward-looking society. Gone were the soaring imagination and the passionate engagement with life which the Romantics had at least attempted. If melodrama aimed at the lowest social denominator, middle-class theatre appealed increasingly to the fashionable audience which did not care to have its moral withers wrung too hard nor its aesthetic sensibilities tried too far by experiment.

Although the nineteenth century was even more stage-struck than the eighteenth, its legacy was almost as small. No imperial tragedy or verse comedy entered the repertoire, and Romantic drama was eclipsed within a few years of its birth. The mid-century *comédie honnête* now seems impossibly self-righteous, Naturalist drama too stagy and the Symbolists gassily grandiloquent. Yet the *fin de siècle* was far from stagnant. Jarry and Claudel stood waiting in the wings; both the *pièce bien faite* and the *pièce à thèse* were far from exhausted; popular theatre was kept alive by melodrama and the new music-hall entertainments; and the base of French theatre was extended from Paris to the provinces where, on the eve of the Great War, there were 62 well-established playhouses. Not the least important of these developments, perhaps, was the gradual demotion of both author and actor: by 1914, there were clear signs of the director's theatre to come.

The novel

In his preface to *Les Crimes de l'amour* (1800), Sade reviewed the history of the novel and concluded that 'l'imagination épuisée des auteurs paraît ne pouvoir plus rien créer de nouveau'. In this, as in much else, he was wrong. Although long undermined by its reputation as a popular amusement and an entertainment for women, fiction would dominate the new century, during the course of which some 10,000 novels were published. Such 'rules' as had existed for the form were replaced by the modern concept of technique, and constant improvements of technique established the 'traditional novel' which, despite

Proust, Gide, the *nouveau roman* and postmodern avant-gardism, remains the standard against which alternative types of fiction are still measured. Until 1820, fiction looked inwards, focusing on the hopes and pains of human types beset by troubles, often of the heart. Thereafter, it looked outward to the world before returning, at the end of the century, to a more systematic examination of the human psyche and the mechanisms of society. At first, moral truths were sought through the imagination. But after the Romantics the concept of truth was widened to include the lessons of a reality which drew closer to the contemporary world. The novel became a mirror of the manners, style and mood of society. Its heroes and heroines, once victims of love, turned into individuals at odds with life and circumstances who, in their struggle to find an accommodation with both, may lose their illusions and even their lives. Sustained by an expanding public, fiction maximized its potential and proved to be the most adaptable and versatile of all available forms of literary expression.

1800–30

At first, the burgeoning *cabinets de lecture* classified novels under three main heads: the *roman d'intrigue sentimentale*, the *roman noir*, and the *roman gai*. The first, frequently epistolary in form, was the territory of a dozen or so women novelists of aristocratic extraction. Mme de Guénard de Méré, Mme de Souza, Mme de Krudener and others wrote in unrosy terms of contemporary marriage and the unhappy effects of divorce. Sophie Cottin (1770–1807) specialized in heroines riven by passions which conflicted with social constraints, ground also covered in a dozen statuesque novels by Sophie Gay (1776–1852). The standard for the *roman noir,* heavily influenced by the English Gothic novel, was set by Ducray-Duminil (1761–1819), prolific author of *Victor, ou l'Enfant de la forêt* (1796) and *Cœlina, ou l'Enfant du mystère* (1798), whose heroes face brutes and knaves in a world of dark deeds spiced with injections of the supernatural. The *roman gai* was associated with Pigault-Lebrun (1753–1835) who reacted against both the sentimental and Gothic trends. He exploited a brand of below-stairs realism and social observation combined with picaresque adventures recounted at high speed. His first novel, *L'Enfant du carnival* (1796), mixed autobiography and adventure with a virulent denunciation of the Terror. But *Les Barons de Felsheim* (1798) and a stream of regularly reprinted novels were lighter in tone, pitting beleaguered lower-class heroes against foreign agents, convicts, money-men and conspirators who oppress the vulnerable. Between them, Pigault-Lebrun and Ducray-Duminil gave popular fiction an armoury of enduring clichés: murder, poison, foundlings, stratagems and spoils.

The 'personal' novel

Literary novels were a rarity and reflections on the novel rarer still, with only Sade and Mme de Staël (*Essai sur les fictions*, 1796) raising broader formal issues. But pre-Romantic themes and moods established before 1789 were revived and developed. Mme de Charrière's *Caliste* (1787), the story of an independently minded woman and her indecisive lover, prefigured a handful of novels which raised 'sentimental intrigue' to a new plane. Mme de Staël's epistolary *Delphine* (1802) challenged the strict morality of Napoleonic society and defended individual freedom. No less liberal was *Corinne* (1807), which told of the doomed love of its passionate Italian heroine for a brooding Scottish aristocrat. While Constant's largely autobiographical *Adolphe* (1816) drew on two established fictional modes, psychological *analyse* and the *roman libertin*, its stance was new. Adolphe's inability to leave Ellénore, through pity, guilt and embarrassment, captured the new fascination with social taboos and unassuageable feelings. Disillusionment with the self and life infects the reclusive hero of Senancour's *Oberman* (1804). Disappointed in marriage, he retreats into solitude and cultivates his inability to find reasons for belief or action, enacting a drama of alienation from both society and the self in which personal experience and philosophical meditation are inseparable. But the author who best caught the new mood of introspection was Chateaubriand. *Atala, ou les Amours de deux sauvages dans le désert* (1801), an episode detached from his North American saga, *Les Natchez* (unpublished until 1827), was a tale of fatal passion set in exotic surroundings and infused with sentimental, spiritual yearnings. The melancholy hero of *René* (1805) showed the gulf between man's infinite aspirations and the paltry goals he can achieve in this life: no future hope can rise from the ruins of the past. *Les Aventures du dernier Abencérage* (1810; publ. 1826), a 'troubadour' novel, was a no less poetic evocation of frustrated longings. Indecision, introspection and a yearning for spiritual satisfaction not to be found in either the self or life defined the *mal du siècle* which, in different forms, would leave its mark on several generations to come.

Mainstream fiction

While such 'personal' novels exploited the unique experience of their authors, most novelists preferred to work in the cliché-ridden mode of fiction demanded by the *cabinets de lecture*. Gothic melodramas were supplied in abundance and, despite the strict moral climate, mildly shocking novels proved popular. Aimed to titillate (the degree of bawdy may be judged by their titles), these risqué novels were usually the work of men (like J.-P.-R. Cusin's *Clémentine, orpheline androgyne*) but not exclusively so. Between 1799 and 1824, the Comtesse de Choiseul-Meuse kept up a steady output of indelicate novels which included *Julie, ou j'ai sauvé ma rose* (1807). But the most enduring of the breed was the ultra-prolific Paul de Kock (1794–1871). Beginning in 1813, his pictures of Paris life amused France for half a century with tales of concierges, artisans, and amiable *rentiers* who pursue accommodating *grisettes*. Dismissed in some quarters as fodder for 'portières, cuisinières et femmes de chambre', he appealed to a wide range of tastes and social classes and his spirit continued to fuel the *grivois* mood of many satirical novels to come.

After the return of the Bourbons, the novel reflected a certain nostalgia for the old aristocracy and the 'noble' values of honour and duty. The lower-middle classes moved up at the expense of the comfortable bourgeoisie which had gained most from the Revolution, and Pigault's resilient 'enfant du peuple' turned into a more sharply challenging figure. Such realignments were reflected in the vogue for history. Between 1815 and 1832, almost half of all novels were set in the past, a sign, no doubt, of the nation's need to come to terms with change which had been a permanent feature of the French political and social landscape since 1789. But it was also an early indication of the popularity of imported authors. Walter Scott may have packaged tradition and modernity in a manner which satisfied both bourgeois and aristocratic ideologies, but for most readers Scott, like Fenimore Cooper, was a page-turner. Their high standing is reflected in the catalogues of the *cabinets de lecture* which kept readers of the 1820s supplied with authors old and new. There Mme de Genlis and Mme Riccoboni rubbed shoulders with Mme Cottin, Kock, Mrs Radcliffe and, of course, Pigault-Lebrun and Ducray-Duminil.

Romantic fiction to 1830

In the 1820s, the battle for literature was waged in the field of poetry and theatre. But the rejection of classical restraint and the new taste for the exalted and the grotesque were also reflected in fiction which, less heavily freighted by rules, offered more scope for the extravagant imagination. Charles Nodier (1780–1844) began in 1803 with a Wertherian tale of suffering love but is best remembered for nightmarish tales (*Smarra*, 1821; *Trilby*, 1822) which exploited the fantastic already attempted in the *Manuscrit trouvé à Saragosse* (begun in 1797; full text publ. 1989) by Jean Potocki (1761–1815) and which Balzac would take up with *La Peau de chagrin* (1831). Until Hugo (*Le Dernier Jour d'un condamné*, 1829; *Claude Gueux* 1834) raised contemporary social issues directly, it was left to minor novelists like Victor Ducange (1783–1833) or Ancelot (1794–1854: *L'Homme du monde*, 1827) to contest the political morality of the Restoration. And while Stendhal struggled with modern characters who failed to be the heroes of their own lives (*Armance*, 1827; *Vanina Vanini*, 1829), most Romantic writers followed fashion by taking their subjects from history which Vigny described as 'un Roman dont le Peuple est l'auteur'. He set *Cinq-Mars* (1826), a study of the solitude of the man of destiny, around a plot mounted against Richelieu in 1639. But though he planned other historical novels, he quickly turned to more contemporary settings for fictions (*Stello*, 1832; *Servitude et grandeur militaires*, 1835) which constituted 'une sorte de poème épique de la désillusion'. Prosper Mérimée (1803–70) reacted strongly against novelists who used history to grind philosophical or literary axes. He offered his *Chronique du règne de Charles IX* (1829), set at the time of the Saint-Bartholomew's Day Massacre of 1572, as no more than an accurate portrait of the manners and characters of the period, not an illustration of some illusory view of the inevitable march of progress and freedom, though his anti-clericalism is barely disguised.

But Mérimée was in the minority. The protagonists of Balzac's *Les Chouans, ou la Bretagne en 1799*, also published in 1829, represented points of view (royalism *versus* the myth of the Revolution) and made history part of the 'science des moeurs'. Balzac planned a sequence which would constitute an *Histoire pittoresque de la France* from 1380 to 1815 which, however, never materialized; its elements were absorbed into the *Comédie humaine*. But from the historical novel, Balzac learned to document the time and place which shaped character and to create social and psychological types which expressed general attitudes. Hugo, too, with *Notre-Dame de Paris* (1831), set in medieval Paris, used history for larger ideas which are carried by types rather than individuals: Frollo represents the Church, Phoebus the Army and Quasimodo the People. As characters, they are dwarfed by his visionary, epic sense of destiny which here reveals the fatal power of dogma just as *Les Misérables* (1862) shows Jean Valjean relentlessly pursued by the law and *Les Travailleurs de la mer* (1866) sets man against the forces of nature. Hugo never turned his back on the lurid appeal of the Gothic novel which he used from his first historical fictions (*Bug-Jargal*, 1820; *Han d'Islande*, 1822) to the last. *L'Homme qui rit* (1869) evoked the sixteenth century and *Quatre-vingt-treize* (1874) the Revolution, but the struggle of flawed but noble souls to overcome fate remains unchanged.

After about 1830, however, the literary novel fell out of love with history. The two great novelists of the Romantic age, Stendhal and Balzac, steered it towards modern life and contemporary manners. However, it remained a staple part of the *roman feuilleton* and Flaubert, Gautier, and other literary novelists would revisit it, abetting Michelet's invention of modern history and confirming the new tendency, declared after 1840, towards Realism.

1830–48

Until the rise of the *roman feuilleton* after 1836, popular fiction remained a hostage to the *cabinets de lecture* which required authors to write in the genres and formulaic styles defined by public demand. It also minded its manners, for the new regime remained watchful. The *roman gai* in the manner of Kock was one safe area. Émile Cabanon's *Le Roman pour cuisinières* (1834) satisfied the appetite for earthy dreams of love and Maximilien Perrin, author of some sixty novels to 1856 and a mainstay of the *cabinet de lecture*, specialized in suggestive, anecdotal fictions. The publication of *Monsieur Mayeux* (1831) by Auguste Ricard, Kock's main rival, was heralded by an unprecedented publicity campaign of posters and caricatures. Sentiment and adventure were also non-controversial, and Eugène Sue first made his name with tales of the sea (*Atar-Gull*, 1831). But most novels were *romans de moeurs* set in elegant drawing rooms (balls, gambling, conversation) where dramas of finance and adultery were played out. The staple conflict between noble hearts and cruel predators was resolved by duel, murder, suicide, madness and retribution. Though much was made of love, duty and honour, the motor of most society novels was money.

The *roman libertin*

In *Armance*, Stendhal had raised, in very oblique terms, the problem of impotence and Custine's *Loys* (1829) that of homosexuality. In *Mademoiselle de Maupin* (1836), Gautier expressed, not without scandal, his aesthetic ideal in the personality of his hermaphrodite heroine. But sex as a subject barely registered. The late eighteenth century had marked the high point of the *roman libertin* which declined rapidly after 1800 when vigorous action was taken against obscenity. Even so, the Garnier brothers published licentious texts, though the modesty of their operation indicates that the demand for pornography was specialized rather than general. They continued to supply this small market discreetly and, after 1848, stepped up production until 1853 when, having decided to abandon this side of their business, they were prosecuted for obscenity. Thereafter, fiction continued to deal sensationally with sex (rape, abortion, prostitution) but never overtly, probably, however, less because of official disapproval than through the resistance of conservative taste.

Colonial fiction

In any case, there were ample opportunities for sexual thrills in safer contexts. The taste for local colour combined with France's new colonial ambitions revived the sensual exoticism of the perennial Bernardin de Saint-Pierre. Dumas's *Georges* (1843) revisited Mauritius and Soulié chose the West Indies for *Le Bananier* (1843). But it was Joseph Méry (1798–1867) who opened the largest windows on foreign parts. Of his forty novels, the most successful were his well-documented tales set in far-flung places, and notably his Indian trilogy which began with *Héva* (1840). Whereas Gobineau would argue for the supremacy of the white races, Méry publicized a more progressive view of colonial development: the future of mankind lay in mixed marriages which alone would secure the union of the races.

Foreign imports

But for the growing reading public, the exotic was less a place than a province of the mind: it was to be found close to home, in the

Gothic, in social fiction and, of course, in the past. Hugo's *Notre-Dame* quickly acquired a mass following which helped to ensure that historical novels outsold both Stendhal and Balzac. Before finding fame as a *feuilletoniste*, Frédéric Soulié (1800–47) wrote sombre, sensational novels (*Les Deux Cadavres*, 1832) before turning to a sequence of *Romans historiques du Languedoc*. Charles de Bernard (1804–50), whom Thackeray recommended to his English readers as superior to Balzac, had also begun as a historical chronicler before turning out highly coloured novels of contemporary life featuring convicts, adulteresses, aristocratic persecutors and lily-white victims. But if by 1830, basic themes, moods, narrative strategies and stereotypes were firmly in place, new horizons in fiction had been opened with Scott and Cooper. Subsequent generations were no less curious about foreign literature and welcomed Poe, Harriet Beecher Stowe's *Uncle Tom's Cabin* (1852), the many *Robinsonnades* derived from Rudolf Wyss's *Robinson suisse* (1812), and Conan Doyle who, in the 1890s, helped redirect the embryonic *roman policier*.

Most of these developments, however, would affect the course of the popular rather than the literary novel. By 1840 the *roman feuilleton* had taken root and new commercial factors favoured the rise of popular and middle-brow novelists who are considered in the next section. Serious fiction evolved in less predictable ways, through the fiercely argued aesthetic debates of the Realists and Naturalists, and as the product of what George Sand in 1831 described as 'the vision of nature and humanity observed through the prism of genius'. Her observation is amply confirmed in the work of the two major novelists of the period.

Stendhal

Henri Beyle (1783–1842) was far too sceptical to be taken in by the ideologies, utopias and religiosities of his overheated times. A part of him remained anchored in the eighteenth century and he accepted its view that thought is the product of sense-impressions and that motive is determined by self-interest. Yet he was also a man of the new age, viscerally aware that behaviour is dictated by the passions, and he championed the new literature against the perspective and methods of neo-classicism. He redefined happiness, the Enlightenment's goal, in highly personal and contradictory ways. A liberal who despised the greatest good of the greatest number, a radical with aristocratic sensibilities, he invented 'Beylism', a lifeplan devoted to the fey, even eccentric but relentless cultivation of the self as the only value. He possessed a wide culture, but as travel writer, art critic, biographer or opera reviewer, he remained a spectator primarily of himself. He started 'a history of my life' at 18 (his unfinished autobiography, the *Vie de Henry Brulard* was written in 1835) and became the Egotist, an exceptional individual, an eager Narcissus who, however, is appalled to discover that he is not as admirable as he would wish. Yet he is so frank and self-mocking that he persuades us that we too, with a little effort, could join his elite company of superior souls, the 'Happy Few'.

Stendhal is nowhere more engaging than in his novels which capture the spontaneity and amused irony of their author. They were largely unplanned, for Stendhal performed well for only as long as his improvisatory mood was on him. As adept at the 'double register' as Marivaux, he is both the hero and observer of the odysseys of Julien Sorel (*Le Rouge et le Noir*, 1830), Lucien Leuwen (protagonist of the abandoned novel (1835) which bears his name), Fabrice del Dongo (*La Chartreuse de Parme*, 1839) and the heroine of the unfinished *Lamiel* which he began in 1839. Like them, he dreamed heroic dreams which he deflated with dry irony. But while his heroes may despise their own weaknesses, their urge to live in harmony with their discoverable selves is a positive function of their energies. They share his hates (of power, hypocrisy, vulgarity and Romantic self-indulgence). They admire boldness and honesty, and display that mixture of cynicism, generosity and self-deprecating humour which makes their creator the most English of all French novelists. They, too, pursue happiness, which Stendhal defined as the cultivation of feeling and the appreciation of the rare and the beautiful. But they also behave with an uncompromising lucidity which makes death, suicide and sacrifice the ultimate nobility. Happiness could be glimpsed through love (*De l'amour*, 1822), music, art and literature, yet it was ultimately elusive. Julien Sorel is much happier being in love in prison than he ever was strutting his way to worldly success. At the end of *La Chartreuse*, Fabrice, purged of ambition, is deliciously fulfilled as he surrenders to 'sensations of the soul'. Stendhal was a wounded spirit, made wretched by love, a failure in life who breathed youth and energy into his books. He admired Napoleon and grand gestures but disclaimed any political intentions which, he said, are always as intrusive in fiction 'as a pistol fired at a concert'. His contemporaries, who did not mind where pistols were fired as long as they made a noise, ignored him and Stendhal's original, comic, subjective realism, as he anticipated, was not appreciated until he had been dead for half a century.

Balzac

In the 1820s, Honoré de Balzac (1799–1850), a late developer like Stendhal, supplied formulaic novels for the *cabinets de lecture* under a variety of pseudonyms. A disastrous business venture saddled him with debts which, after 1829, he attempted, in vain, to expunge by writing. His contemporaries saw him as just another novelist of manners, Sainte-Beuve disliked his work and in the 1840s Balzac grew envious of the success of the *feuilletonistes*, whose popularity he could not match. Yet he was the architect of the modern novel and in a sense, as Oscar Wilde observed, the inventor of the nineteenth century.

His decision to remake his life through fiction reflected his belief that the will is a material 'fluide vital', a form of capital to be spent in passion, ambition, obsession. The shrinking ass's skin of *La Peau de chagrin* illustrated its workings, which were analysed in the philosophical *Louis Lambert* (1832–5). Human beings are graded by the use they make of their volitional energy to shape their existence. Some act instinctively and disastrously, others reach accommodations with their milieu, while a minority are capable of the intuitive, mystical, second sight of genius and a few acquire an 'angelic' dimension. Such was the 'Christ de la paternité', the martyr of *Le Père Goriot* (1834), the first of the novels to feature recurring characters.

Convinced that there was a direct relationship between outer appearances and inner reality, Balzac set his characters in their habitat and dwelt on the distinctive behaviour, voice and clothes of individualized types which, taken together, would express the hidden nature of society. At first, proceeding with no overall plan, he had pursued his materialist metaphysic in novels which dealt more or less randomly with all classes and all ages in country, provincial and Parisian settings during the Consulate and Empire, the Restoration and the July Monarchy. But re-using characters like the upwardly mobile Rastignac meant inserting them into the flow of history, following their fortunes in different situations and settings, varying the point of view and showing them in their three-dimensional reality.

They came to seem as real as Napoleon or Talleyrand, as though, by observing society so exactly, he had created a separate one of his own. After 1837, he began to organize this invented world. His novels would show, in a series of *Études*, the 'effects' of society, their 'causes', general 'principles' and ultimately the 'lois psychologiques' which explained human nature, the collectivity and the forces of history. He found scientific confirmation for the project in the work of Geoffroy Saint-Hilaire who, by showing that there is no more equality in society than there is in nature, justified his own vertical, hierarchical view of people and groups. He found a general title for his enterprise in 1840 and in 1842 set out his aims, casting himself as its reporting 'secretary'. He completed 85 of the 115 projected volumes of *La Comédie humaine*, each 'un chapitre du grand roman de la société' which eventually featured some 4,000 characters.

Balzac's technique was determined by his ideas. The detailed, highly visual descriptions of places, buildings, clothes, gestures and speech patterns which made many of his readers impatient (some thought nine adjectives to describe a chair excessive), were intended to establish individuals within general types and against solidly constructed backgrounds. But once the plot is launched, it proceeds briskly to a dramatic crisis which, if Balzac had further plans for his characters, may not end conclusively. His writing is energetic rather than elegant and his snobbery is sometimes intrusive. But Balzac was a master of dialogue and the forcefulness of his narrative style creates an intensity which reveals the visionary nature of his Realism.

Mérimée

Since the early nineteenth century, the novel, like melodrama, had regularly featured brigands, heartless villains and outlaws. Nodier's *Jean Sbogar* (1818) or the hero of the frequently reprinted *Le Solitaire* (1821) by Arlincourt (1789–1856) had fuelled a taste for terror, cemeteries and prisons exemplified by Jules Janin's gruesome *La Femme guillotinée* (1831) and the garish inventions of the 'Frénétiques'. With Prosper Mérimée (1803–70), violence and horror take more muted forms. The finest short-story writer before Maupassant, he used irony and understatement as distancing devices to show impossible, often tragic situations moving remorselessly to their inevitable conclusion. His first collection, *Mosaïque*, appeared in 1833, and thereafter he developed his fascination with the relationship between primitive and civilized codes, love and death, in *Colomba* (1840) and *Carmen* (1852), his best-known tales. Théophile Gautier also tried his hand at short fiction, though his stories are anecdotal, low in both human interest and dramatic impact. He was also drawn to the historical novel with *Le Roman de la momie* (1858), set in the time of the Pharaohs, and *Le Capitaine Fracasse* (1863), which engagingly relates the adventures of a troupe of seventeenth-century actors with a wealth of often distracting documentary detail.

Sand

Gautier was not the only poet to diversify into fiction. Sainte-Beuve, with *Volupté* (1834) and Musset, with *Les Confessions d'un enfant du siècle* (1836), moved beyond the 'personal' novel into autobiographical territory. It was there that George Sand (pseud. of Aurore Dupin, Baronne Dudevant, 1804–76) situated the first of her eighty or so novels. *Indiana* (1832), a protest, based on her own experience, against the constraints of marriage, helped ignite the feminist campaigns of the July Monarchy. *Lélia* (1833), part fiction, part 'essai philosophique', raised the same issues which soon, through her links with Lamennais, Leroux and her lawyer-lover Michel de Bourges, led her to 'communalist' and, after 1840, socialist ideas. *Consuelo* (1842) and its sequel, *La Comtesse de Rüdolstadt* (1843), set in the eighteenth century, promoted egalitarian and republican principles which had already figured in *Le Compagnon du tour de France* (1841). Its preface also indicated how the 'eminently revolutionary' muse of Romanticism might be reinvigorated: 'il y a toute une littérature nouvelle à créer avec les moeurs populaires'. Between 1844 and 1853, she made good her case in half a dozen *romans champêtres* which made her a pioneer of regionalist writing. Meanwhile, she continued to express strong reservations about the political regime and contemporary values, defending feminist positions and parliamentary republicanism but drawing the line at violent revolution. During the Empire, she published historical, psychological and 'realistic' novels but was for long identified as the author of rustic tales deemed suitable for the young. After her death, she was remembered more for her colourful life and proto-feminist stance than for her uneven fiction which, always written at high speed, recycles sentimental clichés but also strikes original chords. Even her modern feminist readers prefer her *Histoire de ma vie* (1864), which breathes courage, iconoclasm and the spirit of independence.

1848–90

Sand's interest in folk traditions was shared by both Gérard de Nerval (1808–55) who, however, achieved darker tones in oneiric and only partly fictional texts (*Sylvie*, 1853; *Aurélia*, 1855), and Barbey d'Aurevilly (1808–89). After a début as a 'Frénétique' in the 1830s and a *roman mondain* (1841) with its backdrop of aristocratic manners, Barbey set out to be the Walter Scott of the Cotentin. In six novels published between 1849 and 1881, he invented a lurid cast of strong, passionate characters, satanic priests and witches, saints and sinners, who are catapulted into highly coloured, melodramatic situations. His shorter fictions (*Les Diaboliques*, 1874) were made in the same mould. Barbey's baroque, fiercely anti-democratic imagination allowed Romantic excess to survive long enough for it to seem modern to the generation of Huysmans and Villiers de l'Isle-Adam. He was joined on the Right by Gobineau (1816–82), better known now than during his lifetime for historical novels and especially his ironical, sharply observed shorter fiction. The principles advanced in his *Essai* on racial inequality (1853–5) inspired *Les Pléiades* (1874), a stolid novel about three friends, which rejects positivism and democratic progress and pins its faith on the emergence of natural elites. Gobineau anticipated not only Nietzsche but the 'action heroes' of Malraux and Saint-Exupéry of the interwar period.

The Goncourts

Les Pléiades is an early example of the right-wing turn the political novel would increasingly take after about 1880. Until then, the reverberations of social Romanticism had ensured that the sympathies of most novelists attacked the establishment and defended a vague entity called 'the people'. In practice, however, with a few exceptions like the outspokenly republican, anti-clerical Sand, most novelists focused on meritorious individuals who were the victims of the injustice of law, class or religion. This was particularly true of many popular fictions from Octave Feuillet's *Le Roman d'un jeune homme pauvre* (1858), for example, to the rewards for honest toil doled out in the 1880s by Georges Ohnet. More systematic were Edmond (1821–96) and Jules (1830–70) de Goncourt who developed the implications of Realism and anticipated Naturalism by unveiling the lives of the underprivileged in solidly documented 'clinical' studies. The novel, they said, was 'the history of those who have no history'. They showed *Soeur Philomène* (1861) battling against horrific hospital conditions and turned *Germinie Lacerteux* (1864) into an early 'pathological' case-history of a servant-girl. After the death of Jules, Edmond continued with *La Fille Éliza* (1877), one of the century's many prostitute novels, and *Les Frères Zemganno* (1878), set in a circus. This approach yielded more cool, document-based accuracy than imaginative understanding, a dichotomy which is echoed in the gap between their below-stairs characters and their fondness for rare vocabulary, high-profile subjunctives and the *écriture artiste* further developed by Edmond in late studies of neurosis, *La Faustin* (1882) and *Chérie* (1884).

Flaubert

The post-Romantic generation of novelists, though far less extravagant in manner and already turning to less assertive heroes, remained marked as much by a sentimental attachment to love as to society's victims. *Dominique* (1862), an unemphatic study of frustrated feelings by Eugène Fromentin (1820–76), with its painterly style and crepuscular melancholy, was the most complete example of its type. Gustave Flaubert (1821–80), however, felt confident enough to publish only when he had banked down the treacherous fires of Romantic lyricism and ideology. He believed in very little. If he despised the bourgeoisie, he also hated the populace. He was contemptuous of those in power but rejected republican and socialist dogma and equated equality with slavery. He retained a belief in the potential of human nature, but saw little evidence that it had delivered what it promised. He did, however, believe in art which was truth distilled from reality and made permanent by beauty of form. Casting aside his early writings, he remained true to Romantic creativity but pursued it through the craftsmanship of the 'l'art pour l'art' movement and the scientific observation recommended by the Realist school.

Flaubert's pessimism, even nihilism, is translated into a bleak fatalism which dooms ancient Carthage (*Salammbô*, 1862), blights the lives of his modern characters (*Madame Bovary*, 1857; *L'Éducation sentimentale*, 1869), leaves the questing protagonists of *Bouvard et Pécuchet* (posth., 1881) with the certainty that all knowledge is uncertain and Félicité (*Trois contes*, 1877) clinging to the vision of a transmogrified parrot. Human *bêtise* is savaged and *idées reçues* are exposed as the bogus wisdom of a vulgar age. Flaubert's heroes collapse under the weight of their unsustainable dreams, with Frédéric Moreau, brother to Emma Bovary, dwindling into a failed Rastignac and learning nothing from his 'sentimental education'. Yearning, acting (in both senses of the word), achieving only their own downfall, they remain spectators of themselves and the shabby world they hope to overleap. They are constantly exposed to Flaubert's irony, the chink in his impassivity, which suggests a point of view. In a novel by Balzac or Stendhal, the narrator both narrates and speaks directly to the reader: author and storyteller are one and the same. Flaubert's indirect interventions steer us more subtly. The *monologue intérieur* expresses the flow of consciousness and the unspoken reporting of the 'style indirect libre' conveys a sense of detachment from reality which is reinforced by the characteristic use of the imperfect tense, 'le temps de l'incohérence', as Valéry termed it. The result is to disconnect characters from themselves and their world which, for all its carefully documented reality, is described impressionistically. Flaubert's universe is the setting for tragic banalities sharpened by farce. But it is also relieved by a macabre optimism and a comic sense which soften the bleakness of his vision and convey a kind of impatient, desperate compassion for ruined dreams and a protest against life's spoiling power.

Zola

If Flaubert was a fatalist by temperament, Émile Zola (1840–1902) was a philosophical determinist persuaded by contemporary science that character and action are the products of heredity and environment. He applied his ideas in his fourth novel, *Thérèse Raquin* (1867), but both his theories and his approach to them, which he termed Naturalism, called for a much fuller treatment. His 20-volume sequence (1871–93) of interrelated novels purported to be the 'natural and social history' of the Rougon-Macquart family during the Second Empire. Whereas Balzac had organized his *Comédie humaine* retrospectively, Zola sketched the family's tree in 1870 and proceeded to work through its various branches which yielded contrasting psychological types in four main groups: working people, the shopkeeper class, the bourgeoisie, and high society, with glimpses of a less orderly world inhabited by whores, murderers, priests and artists. He worked in terms not of traditional *caractères* but through socially defined types (peasants, clerics, miners, sober bourgeois) whose characteristics, like their lives, are determined by physiology, which cannot be avoided, and milieu, which few can escape. Zola documented each novel meticulously and revealed areas of society hitherto rarely explored in fiction: the new department store (*Au Bonheur des Dames*, 1883), coal mines (*Germinal*, 1885) and railways (*La Bête humaine*, 1890). Yet as an experimental scientist, he did not avoid the error of allowing the observer's point of view to affect his results. The determinism which he took as his guiding principle produced above-average levels of violence and neurosis and an overly mechanistic view of human relationships. It also persuaded him that the future would be the outcome of the titanic Darwinian 'struggle for life' between Capital and Labour. His sympathies were with the latter and the Rougon-Macquart is marked by strong socialist sympathies. After 1893, a trilogy (*Les Trois Villes*, 1894–8) proclaimed a new 'religion of humanity' and his last series, *Les Quatre Évangiles* (1899–1903), set out a utopian view of progress.

Yet Zola's fiction is more than the sum of his Naturalist ideas and manner which could not control an imagination that was more poetic than scientific. Objects acquire a symbolic presence and turn into powerful allegories. The mine of *Germinal*, like some ravening mythological beast, demands a tribute of human sacrifice and Paris is an omnipresent crouching monster which devours its population to feed its cruel appetites. Zola's science acquires the face of Destiny, documentary realism breeds a visionary mission and the novel turns into a modern form of the epic. The heavy-duty style is relieved by its sheer power (Zola is the ultimate painter of crowds) and its capacity to generate vivid pictures from words. Zola's vast chronicle of the failure of the Second Empire is enormously varied, urgent and intensely dramatic, and its lurid colours and committed stance drew far more readers to socialism than Marx ever achieved.

Zola's totalizing social fresco, more consciously planned and ideologically committed than Balzac's *Comédie humaine*, set the scene for what Romain Rolland would call the *roman fleuve*, practised well into the twentieth century. Meanwhile, Zola inspired the Médan group, which included Léon Hennique and Paul Alexis, and influenced a new generation which, though some rejected Zolaesque 'littérature putride' in 1887, continued to focus on the working classes, army life and in general society's victims (Lucien Descaves, Paul et Victor Margueritte, J.-H. Rosny).

Maupassant

Among those who moved beyond Naturalism, Guy de Maupassant (1850–93), who contributed *Boule de suif* to the *Soirées de Médan* (1880), remained loyal to Flaubert, whose influence looms large in the theoretical preface to *Pierre et Jean* (1887), the fourth of his six novels of broken lives. His greatness, however, lies in his 300 short stories which, oddly, have always been rated more highly abroad than in France. Though not philosophically inclined, Maupassant accepted Flaubert's 'l'éternel néant de tout' and Schopenhauer's view of life as struggle and torment. Man has no free will but is the plaything of urges dictated by a mechanistic universe. Love is not the best part of us but the most insidious of nature's snares and, like friendship and idealism, it is an illusion. But we are not merely the victims of nature but her instruments. Unwittingly or by design, we make others as miserable as ourselves. Maupassant's picture of humanity is unflattering to an extreme. His characters are rapacious, egotistical, obsessive, unfeeling and cruel. Yet even in the tales of the morbid, and the macabre and disturbing glimpses of madness (*Le Horla*, 1887), what was called in his day his 'emotional impotence' is modified by a sense of human solidarity. For while pessimism was his natural pitch, his range included satire, farce and the comic which at least disguise his cynicism. But even at his most sardonic, his irony is relieved by that compassion for 'l'humanité saignante' expressed so movingly in the lingering kiss planted by the chastened Chenal on the lips of the dead Miss Harriet (1883).

The retreat from Naturalism

In 1877, Joris-Karl Huysmans (1848–1907) sprang to the defence of Zola's *L'Assommoir*. His first novels (*Marthe*, 1876; *Les Soeurs Vatard*, 1879) were written according to the Naturalist prescription, which he abandoned in *À rebours* (1884). Its aristocratic, neurotic hero, Des Esseintes, expresses the refined taste of Decadence in a fiction which, having neither plot nor dialogue, also broke with the aesthetics of the novel. After 1890, Huysmans, without losing his fascination with the macabre, produced a series of largely eventless, autobiographical novels inspired by his conversion to Catholicism (*Là-bas*, 1891; *En route*, 1895; *La Cathédrale*, 1898). The idea that the artificial was superior to nature, encapsulated by Des Esseintes, was also pursued by Villiers de l'Isle-Adam (1838–89) in *L'Ève future* (1880–6), which has the inventor, Thomas Edison, creating a female robot superior in every way to a woman of flesh and blood. Villiers, however, is better remembered for his volumes of *Contes cruels* (1886–8) which reflect his contemporaries' renewed interest in the occult, the supernatural and abnormal states of mind. Like Villiers, Léon Bloy (1846–1917), sometime secretary to Barbey d'Aurevilly, reacted against the impoverishment of the spiritual. He spoke out against atheism and rationalism in two angry, autobiographical novels, *Le Désespéré* (1886) and *Une Femme pauvre* (1897), which, with his polemical journalism, made him a precursor of the Catholic Revival. Octave Mirbeau (1848–1917), on the other hand, misogynistic and violently anti-clerical, chronicled his own disillusionment with the Church and the state which it supported (*Le Calvaire*, 1886; *L'Abbé Jules*, 1889; *Sébastien Roch*, 1890) before exposing bourgeois hypocrisy in the novel (*Journal d'une femme de chambre*, 1900) and the theatre (*Les Affaires sont les affaires*, 1903).

In the 1880s, a certain impressionism of style, from the racy to the ironic and sensational, and a taste for solidly documented social, psychological and physiological fiction were established. Like Mirbeau, Jules Vallès (1833–85) developed a form of personal commitment in the largely autobiographical Jacques Vingtras trilogy (1879–86). Alphonse Daudet (1840–97), the humorous painter of Provence and creator of Tartarin de Tarascon, had already drawn heavily on his life and particularly on his childhood (*Le Petit Chose*, 1868), territory also explored by Paul Arène (1843–96), Anatole France (1844–1924: *Le Livre de mon ami*, 1885) and Jules Renard (1864–1910) in the bitter *Poil de carotte* (1894). It was an area of human experience which had been very much neglected by the major novelists, but the deficiency would soon be made good.

1890–1914

By 1890, Zola's 'miry' novels, 'lifeless photographs' and over-mechanistic determinism had alienated the new generation which took *À rebours* as its Bible. Zola had confused the real with the visible and it now seemed that Flaubert had captured reality more truthfully. But so had Stendhal, pioneer of the egotistic psyche, who was discovered in the 1880s, as were Russian, English and Scandinavian authors who drew attention to the complex workings of the soul. But the intellectual climate, too, was changing. Rationalism was in retreat. New work in psychology by the neurologist Charcot (1825–93) and then Freud placed question marks over human motivation, while Henri Bergson (1958–1941) undermined the traditional representation of time, threw new light on consciousness, and promoted intuition, the 'élan vital' and more open definitions of morality. Aesthetic principles were also reviewed, rather disconcertingly. The neo-classical revival was offset by the rise of Cubism which completed what Impressionism had begun: the artist could no longer be a copier of reality. Anti-clerical pressures, which had been building for a century and a half, finally secured the Separation of Church and state in 1905. Yet it was a pyrrhic victory for science and reason, for the burgeoning Catholic Revival attracted new converts among those alienated by the secular education system and the intellectual press. Politically, the Dreyfus Affair, which divided the nation, was reflected by novelists of Left and Right who used fiction to defend Justice and the Rights of Man and, on the opposite side, to promote a new spirit of nationalism.

But although socialism was now a force and workers had begun to express their discontent in the streets, the novel remained the domain of the social elite. On the other hand, the Belle Époque showed a resistance to fictions which tested its patience. Symbolist aesthetics were applied to the novel, without marked success, by Paul Adam (1862–1920), Édouard Dujardin (1861–1949), and, most effectively, by Georges Rodenbach (1855–98) whose *Bruges-la-morte* (1892) conveyed his love for his dead wife through the misty, atmospheric landscape of Bruges. Until the eve of the Great War, there was no major initiative to renew the novel which, in historical and literary terms, continued to belong to the nineteenth century. But if aesthetic options seemed exhausted and few novels of the Belle Époque have survived, fiction nevertheless continued to display considerable vitality.

Les psychologues

The 'psychological' novel associated primarily with Paul Bourget (1852–1935) modernized the venerable *caractère*. Bourget was interested in the pressures exerted by modern intellectual and moral ideas on the individual and normally shows the effects to be harmful. Early novels, like *Un Crime d'amour* (1886) or *Le Disciple* (1889), solidly constructed and acutely observed, show vulnerable individuals at the mercy of systems they cannot control. After the 1890s, his reservations about the new ideas led to *romans à thèse* which stressed the value of Catholic, monarchical and generally conservative values which were the individual's best defence against unhappiness and alienation. A trilogy, *Le Culte du moi* (1888–91) by Maurice Barrès (1862–1923), made the case for disciplining the self and promoting 'le sens social' and the concept of 'la patrie psychique'. Focusing on the land and those who had shaped it, he illustrated a doctrine of *enracinement* in *Les Déracinés* (1897) which showed the disintegration of a group of *lycéens* who, detached from their roots in Lorraine, find only misery in modern, cosmopolitan Paris. Barrès campaigned for the return of Alsace-Lorraine (*Colette Baudoche*, 1908) but also defended, often in mystical terms (*La Colline inspirée*, 1913), the political and spiritual continuities of the French tradition in a spirit of conservative nationalism which made him the leading intellectual figure of the Belle Époque and after. A comparable trajectory was followed by the prolific Anatole France, an observer of *caractères* (*Le Crime de Sylvestre Bonnard*, 1881) who used the amiable but foolish Monsieur Bergeret, hero of the four-volume *Histoire contemporaine* (1897–1901), to lampoon current attitudes. After the Dreyfus Affair, however, adding acerbic satire to his humour, he tackled larger subjects like human progress (*L'Île des pingouins*, 1908), the revolutionary spirit (*Les Dieux ont soif*, 1912) and the Christian tradition (*La Révolte des anges*, 1914). For the rest of the world he was by then the symbol of 'civilized' French values and his non-aligned, sceptical humanism became a rallying point for those alarmed by the rise of both the political Right and the Left.

Le roman de l'enfance

The 'psychological' novel, like fictions tracing spiritual or political odysseys (Huysmans, Bloy, Mirbeau) or reflecting the struggles of the first generation of state-educated working-class literary hopefuls, found a new impetus in the autobiography of their authors. More specifically, the lead given by the likes of Daudet and Vallès gave rise to an interest, fuelled in some cases by the new psychology, in childhood as both a crucial formative influence and a world of lost innocence. From the gentle Trott books of André Lichtenberger to the unsentimental glimpse of children at school by Léon Frapié (1863–1949: *La Maternelle*, 1904), novelists proceeded to draw closer to the world of the child with Louis Pergaud (1882–1915: *La Guerre des boutons*, 1912) and, one of the best-loved of all such books, *Le Grand Meaulnes* (1913) by Alain-Fournier (1886–1914) whose 'creed in art and literature' was childhood. It was there that Proust began, though others preferred to focus on adolescence as both a *rite de passage* and the age of revolt. Barrès's *lycéens*, Colette's four Claudine books (1900–3) and Jules Romains's *Les Copains* (1912) were early examples of a genre developed between the wars around the rebellion, *angst* and pranks of pre-adulthood by, among others, Radiguet, Cocteau, Giraudoux, Lacretelle and Pagnol.

Decadents

The reaction to Naturalism included a rejection of its fascination with the lower orders. But if bankers and duchesses were as interesting as miners and serving girls, their problems were defined in Decadent circles by the relationship between art and sexuality. Rémy de Gourmont (1858–1915) explored the link in *Sixtine* (1890), while the self-styled dandy Jean Lorrain (1855–1906) raised eyebrows with novels (e.g. *Monsieur de Bougrelon*, 1897) which expressed the interest of *fin-de-siècle* Decadence in alternative forms of love. The eroticism of Pierre Louÿs (1870–1925) was more discreet and veiled by a cloak of Hellenistic propriety (*Aphrodite*, 1896) but, with Lorrain, he helped to prepare the way for franker discussions of homosexuality by Proust and Gide. Eroticism straight and bizarre also featured in the *louche* novels, sometimes passed off as studies in 'pathological neurosis', of Marcel Prévost, Gyp and Rachilde.

Le roman de moeurs

Most novels, however, were *romans de moeurs* which explored every class and reach of society. The army, the Church, medicine and the law all had their chroniclers, but the centre of gravity was located in the fashionable *quartiers* of Paris which yielded limitless variations on the themes of money, marriage and morality. Novelists adopted no general ethical or political stance, though by endlessly recycling familiar situations which set the individual against social and moral imperatives, they broadly endorsed conformism while allowing their heroes and heroines a certain latitude. None defended bourgeois values more consistently than Henry Bordeaux (1870–1965). Repetitive, often thoughtful and generally competent, the novel of bourgeois manners dominated the market and allowed Edmond Jaloux (1878–1948), author of some 300 volumes of well-observed fictions, the darker-toned Édouard Estaunié (1862–1942) and Abel Hermant (1862–1950), the reporter of cosmopolitan society, to acquire considerable reputations.

But the definition of manners was quickly extended after 1890 to include new varieties of the exotic. Regionalist novels dominated the new literary prizes in the first decade of the new century and the first stirrings of the populist novel, which would come into its own between the wars, acquainted Parisian readers with both the way of life of the poor who lived unseen on their doorstep and the seafaring men of Brittany evoked in *Pêcheur d'Islande* (1886) by Pierre Loti (1850–1923). For the novel had begun to look further afield. Before abandoning fiction for the travelogue in the 1890s, Loti had successfully mixed autobiography and foreign settings in engaging novels set in North Africa, Turkey, Polynesia (*Le Mariage de Loti*, 1880) and Japan (*Madame Chrysanthème*, 1888, the source of Puccini's *Madame Butterfly*). It was inevitable that France's emerging empire should generate a new genre of colonial fiction which expressed a variety of moods. In *Biribi* (1890), Georges Darien used his military service in North Africa to expose the brutality tolerated by the authorities, while Henry Daguerches's *Le Kilomètre 83* (1913) told of the human cost of building the Siam–Cambodia railway. On the other hand, the 'civilizing' impact of French colonialism was defended by Louis Bertrand and the Tharaud brothers (Jérôme, 1874–1953, and Jean, 1877–1952) at a time when Anglophobia was helping to give a new definition to French imperialism. While Louis Hémon (1880–1913) provided Quebec with a formula for survival in *Maria Chapdelaine* (1914), Claude Farrère (1876–1957) began his long career as the urbane but somehow bloodless reporter of, mainly, the exotic Orient. But France failed to produce a Kipling.

Short fiction

After 1800, moral, gallant and historical tales remained popular, but by 1830 the distinction between the anecdotal *conte* (*oriental, allégorique, philosophique*) and the psychological *nouvelle* had become blurred. Romantics, Realists, Naturalists and Symbolists better known as poets, novelists and playwrights wrote short fiction for periodicals where length was an important consideration. Over the century, they widened the range of the form, which became sombre and oppressive (Vigny, Balzac), touchingly sentimental (Musset), violent and dramatic (Stendhal), strange (Nodier, Gautier), exotic (Gobineau), terrifying and bizarre (Barbey d'Aurevilly, Villiers de l'Isle-Adam). The terms *nouvelle* and *conte* became more or less interchangeable, though in practice the *conte* retained something of its old oral character: typically, the narrator recounts to an audience an incident of which he or she, or an acquaintance, was the hero or witness, thereby gaining an immediacy denied to the third-person voice. The *nouvelle*, on the other hand, tended to designate stories which were less anecdotal and charged with some wider significance inferred from narratives which generally claimed to be 'true'. This was the case not only with the many realistically described stories of ordinary life but of the extraordinary too: tales of the supernatural, of horror and mystery inspired in large part by foreign authors (Pushkin, Poe, Gogol). Even writers who distanced themselves from the outlandish and the strange identified the form with some intense, exceptional experience: hence the large numbers of stories about war, revenge, violence, madness, sex and blood. The French *fabliau* tradition survived in the comic tale, from Balzac's consciously parodic *Contes drôlatiques* to the many entertaining anecdotes which revolved around a farcical situation and the discomfiture of ridiculous protagonists. Most authors did not set out simply to amuse but to widen the reader's horizons by turning a *fait divers* or some banal situation into the drama of an exceptional experience. To maximize impact, a brief episode, pared to its basic essentials, was sharply articulated to heighten the intensity of the tale, which was encapsulated in a strong, reverberating finale. Such *nouvelles* operated on principles quite distinct from the discursive novel. On the other hand, the long short-story (like Mérimée's *Carmen*) accumulated more in the way of incident and diverse points of view, but nevertheless maintained the stress on the forward movement of the central situation. Such tales sailed close to the novel: it is possible to imagine Stendhal's *Vanina Vanini* fleshed out into a more substantial fiction just as Maupassant turned his brief *Yveline* into the much fuller *Yvette*. Yet more than length separates even such *nouvelles* from the novel. The subject is more contained and where the novelist expands, the *nouvelliste* condenses, so that, as Bourget observed at the end of the century: 'La matière de la nouvelle est un épisode, celle du roman une suite d'épisodes.' One significant development was Maupassant's interest in the instant (*Promenade, Les Tombales, Le Baptême*), a plotless tale built around an incident which confronts characters with an illumination of their self or their life. Its minimalism, like its rejection of time (so essential to the novel), would be renewed by his successors after 1950.

Conclusion

Around 1900, it seemed to many that the novel had lost its way. Its worldliness was a pose, its values false and its political stance, which set Zola and Anatole France on the Left against Bourget and Barrès on the Right, a distraction. Many novelists reached their peak of fame at a moment when the new generation had consigned them to the past. Advances in philosophy and physics, together with the rising profiles of Marx, Freud and Bergson, identified urgent problems which could not be solved by exoticism, eroticism and the recycling of clichés demanded by the publishing industry. Yet new avenues were being explored. Regional writers of quality (Eugène le Roy, Émile Guillaumin, Marguerite Audoux), together with Charles-Louis Philippe (1874–1909), chronicler of the rural and urban poor and observer of childhood (*La Mère et l'enfant*, 1911), renewed the tradition of social and psychological realism and pointed to the democratization of fiction. Others, with different priorities, considered that the imagination had been devalued and forms of 'anti-fiction' were preferred by Marcel Schwob (1867–1905) and Gide, whose aesthetic principles were opposed to the novel and turned him to alternative forms: the prose poem, allegory, the fictitious journal. For Valéry, the future of the novel was as the history or biography of a mind which observed itself. *La Soirée avec Monsieur Teste* (1896) was the first instalment of a cycle which he conceived as 'le roman d'un cerveau'. Proust, on the other hand, separated the writing and existential selves and, with the first volume (1913) of *À la recherche du temps perdu*, rediscovered his lived past through involuntary memory. But if modern forms of sensibility were pioneered before 1914, the phenomenon of the best-seller, institutionalized by the Prix Goncourt (1903), emphasized the gap separating serious from commercial literature, which also had a history.

The roman feuilleton and the growth of popular fiction

The Revolution of 1789 invented the People but it was left to the nineteenth century to give the concept a content. To a large extent the objective was achieved less through concerted social engineering or government action than as a by-product of capitalist enterprise. Thus the People read little until the 1830s, when economic and technological change began its own work of modernizing France. The rise of popular literature was a function of the development of the press, increasing prosperity and rising literacy.

1836–48

By the 1830s, some publishers, like Barba and Charpentier, were beginning to issue novels in cheaper editions, though printing technology was not yet sufficiently advanced to lower retail prices for a mass market. But when the July Monarchy relaxed the rules controlling newspaper start-ups, the battle for readers was joined. In July 1836, Émile de Girardin founded *La Presse* and Armand Dutacq *Le Siècle*, and both ran advertisements as a way of halving the cover price. The move had an immediate impact on circulation which was consolidated by the drawing power of serialized fiction. The earliest success was registered by Frédéric Soulié, whose *Mémoires du diable* (*Journal des Débats*, 1837–8) revived the Faustian theme against a backdrop of macabre episodes of murder and mayhem. But Soulié was quickly overtaken by Eugène Sue (1804–57) who, with *Les Mystères de Paris* (1842–3), set a new standard. Rodolphe de Géroldstein, a prince in disguise, moves through the Paris underworld expiating his past, righting wrongs and saving the helpless from their oppressors. Marx denounced its capitalist paternalism in a famous essay, but Gautier reported that 'des malades ont attendu pour mourir la fin des *Mystères de Paris*'. Sue's equally rambling *Le Juif errant* (1844–5), which tells how the descendants of the Wandering Jew reassemble the family fortune appropriated by the Jesuits, specialized in cliff-hanging episodes but also confirmed the taste for crime, melodrama, social comment and the super-hero, a mixture which had an immediate impact on the circulation of *Le Constitutionnel*, in which it appeared: the number of subscribers rose quickly from 3,600 to 24,000.

Rival newspapers could not afford to stand idly by and offered huge sums to Sue, Soulié, Alexandre Dumas and any author who could turn out eye-catching novels at high speed. The queens of the *cabinets de lecture* failed to adapt to the new demands but others, like Paul de Kock, successfully reinvented themselves as *feuilletonistes*. Literary novelists like Balzac and Sand were serialized, but because they were too cerebral or lacking in melodramatic immediacy, they failed to equal the success of the market leaders, who acquired the status of media-stars.

At a time when a serious novel might be published in an edition of 1,500 copies, serialized fiction acquired a vast readership which in 1847 Michelet estimated at 1.5 million. After serialization, novels were republished in 'library' editions (7–10 francs) for the nation's 1,500 *cabinets de lecture* before appearing in cheaper reprints (3–4 francs) with runs of 25,000 copies, and finally in inexpensive, collectable parts or *livraisons* (reaching editions of 50,000 to 100,000 later in the century). Denounced in 1839 by Sainte-Beuve as 'industrial literature', the *roman feuilleton* was despised for its crudeness and denounced for promoting imagination and emotion at the expense of reason and thought. Where literature instructed and improved, sensational fiction poisoned minds with lurid oversimplifications. It was accused of undermining morality and of spreading political subversion. Such fears were justified. Sue's socialist ideas reached a wider audience than those of Proudhon or of utopians like Cabet, while in the novels of Dumas, the battle between d'Artagnan and Richelieu symbolized the aspiration to liberty against the dead hand of Louis-Philippe's oppressive regime. For whether Dumas wrote of the Renaissance, the seventeenth century, the French Revolution or the stultifying, bourgeois world of Louis-Philippe, he projected the same heady defence of freedom and independence. He divided humanity into roundheads (Richelieu, Mazarin, Colbert) and cavaliers (Fouquet, d'Artagnan, Monte Cristo, and himself), the former symbolizing the creeping bureaucracy of modern society and the latter individualism, male friendship and enterprise. But whereas his rivals, like Sue, were too marked by their times to outlive them, Dumas, by casting the conflict of good and evil in human rather than ideological terms, has continued to speak to the youth of every generation. He has survived not simply because he was a master story-teller, but because he encapsulated his own boisterous optimism in four-square heroes who occupy a permanent niche in the culture of France and the wider world, which still admires d'Artagnan's flashing blade, holds its breath while Edmond Dantès escapes from the Château d'If and thrills to the cry of 'All for one and one for all!' Stendhal, Balzac and Flaubert are admired: Dumas, a lesser artist, is loved.

Reflecting the Romantic aesthetic which willingly mixed tragedy with comedy, and history with social comment, the serial novel was short on psychology but strong on melodramatic types (the innocent victim, the *justicier*, the black-hearted villain), and women were given roles as either freebooting *femmes fatales* or defenceless, dewy-eyed creatures perpetually in need of rescue. It traded in suspense, high drama, quests (to right a wrong or redeem a tainted past) but invariably aimed to strike an epic note. The vogue for history ensured that the historical novel dominated production. The *roman de moeurs contemporaines*, in favouring Paris low life, echoed the philanthropic concerns of social Romanticism. Aristocratic virtues were admired, the middle classes were caricatured and the urban underclass was regarded with suspicion and fear, though it too was capable of noble honour and bourgeois energy in selected individuals. Money was generally shown to be evil except in the hands of heroes like Rodolphe or Monte Cristo who, as Marx pointed out, were individual opportunists who usurped society's obligation to correct social evils. But whether set in the past or in the present, the serial novel offered a world of adventure and provided a home for heroes.

1848–70

The *timbre* Riancey, a short-lived tax levied in 1850 on newspapers which ran serials, temporarily slowed the progress of the *roman feuilleton*. But a market had been created and, despite the censorship of the Second Empire, editors supplied it. New publicity and distribution methods (the news-stand now made its appearance) together with improvements in the rotary press, reduced cover prices and pushed circulation to new heights in the 1860s. In the climate of fierce competition, newspapers continued to invest in serials. Public demand was so high that *journaux romans* appeared which published nothing but serialized fiction. These developments, together with the rising circulation of high-brow magazines like *La Revue des deux mondes* (from 5,000 in 1851 to 25,000 in 1868), ensured that until the end of the century, fiction popular and serious was pre-published in newspapers and reviews, an arrangement which suited established authors, who were better rewarded, and new novelists who, if successful, were assured of seeing their work appear in book form.

At first, Sue and Dumas, still hyper-active, remained the market leaders, the former providing a stimulus for the 'populist' social novel and the latter for the enduring historical saga. But the momentum of the 1840s was also maintained by Paul Féval (1817–97), who wrote seventy novels in different styles: satirical, fantastic, historical, with a hint of the *roman policier* to come. Vicomte Pierre-Alexis Ponson du Terrail (1829–71), known as the 'Alexandre Dumas des Batignolles', published 5,500 thrilling episodes (10,000 pages a year) in the two decades before his death. But there were new trends. The exotic tradition of Fenimore Cooper was developed in the 'trapper' novels of Gustave Aimard (1818–63), who popularized the myth of 'le Far West' for French readers. Tales of suspense, high adventure and dark deeds continued to be set in a largely fanciful past, but increasingly invaded the present. Henri Murger (1822–61) sentimentalized student life (*Scènes de la vie de bohème*, 1851) and Alexandre Dumas *fils* wrote disapprovingly (but enticingly) of the *demi-monde* of genteel prostitution in a series of exposés beginning with *La Dame aux camélias* (1848). Less moralizing and unashamedly escapist were novels which introduced readers to the criminal underworld and robber gangs. But socially conscious authors showed, in politer surroundings, the same greed and violence in the nefarious activities of financial swindlers, unscrupulous lawyers and shady speculators, with the good using the weapons of the wicked to defeat evil. When in doubt, authors reverted to the staple ploy of the innocent who is cheated of an inheritance (always restored in the fullness of many episodes) and their stock-in-trade included poison, magnetism, cataleptic trances, predatory females, wilting heroines and fantastic escapes, often from dark dungeons or across roof-tops. In the 1860s, Jules Verne (1825–1905) took up the travel theme and transformed the traditional *fantastique* with an injection of science. But while his 62 novels were immediately popular, the vogue for science fiction was slow to gain momentum. Similarly, the *roman judiciaire* exploited the public's taste for crime and criminals – Émile Gaboriau's *L'Affaire Lerouge* (1865) has claims to present the first French detective – but without achieving spectacular success.

Seeds were also sown at this time for other kinds of fiction with a future: the regionalist novel, pioneered by George Sand in the 1840s, made a tentative appearance, while Hetzel's weekly *Magasin d'éducation et de récréation* published 'instructive and dramatic' tales for younger readers who were more sternly schooled by the Comtesse de Ségur (1799–1874) in Hachette's *Bibliothèque rose*, the home also of many of the 83 improving novels of Zénaïde Fleuriot (1829–90). The Church, anxious to protect the nation's moral fibre, launched periodicals like *L'Ouvrier* (1861) and *Les Veillées des Chaumières* (1877), which ran wholesome serials that showed virtue rewarded, deceivers unmasked, and the ravages of the demon drink, all presented with appropriate Christian guidance.

Reactions to the unstoppable *roman feuilleton* were mixed. Moralists believed that the danger represented by the moribund *littérature de colportage* (the *Bibliothèque bleue* disappeared in 1863) had been transferred to serialized fiction. The authorities remained vigilant and authors and newspaper proprietors accepted a high degree of self-censorship. Even so, Xavier de Montépin was taken to court for *Les Filles de plâtre* in 1855, as was Adolphe Belot in 1869 when *Le Figaro* refused to continue serializing *Mademoiselle, ma femme*, though the novel was published in volume form the following year. On the other hand, the forerunners of the Naturalist movement admired the energy of *feuilletonistes* but regarded them as rivals for the mass audience they themselves hoped to conquer and enlighten. Critics continued to complain of the form's aesthetic crudeness, but a few observers saw it as an interesting sociological phenomenon. Readers were not concerned by such matters and relished the exciting fare which writers produced quickly and with considerable powers of invention.

By 1860, *feuilletonistes* were supplying wares of appropriate quality to more precisely targeted sections of the market. Fiction destined for the mass readership of the cheapest newspapers recycled tested formulae, but more sophisticated and thoughtful novels were aimed at the discriminating mainstream public which had outgrown perils and crude emotion but had not graduated to Balzac or Flaubert. The yarns and social dramas of Edmond About (1828–84), like the patriotic historical novels of the team of Émile Erckmann (1822–99) and Alexandre Chatrian (1826–90) (who, unusually, were able to bypass serialization), are representative of a new intermediate level of fiction. Designed neither for the crowd nor the refined aesthete, it remained in touch with both and pointed to the vast expansion of the middle-brow novel which, well written but disinclined to take risks or push its readers too hard, defined the form for the general public in 1900. 'Popular' fiction, in the modern sense, has its roots here.

1870–1900

The liberalization of the press at the start of the Third Republic created a new generation of cheap newspapers. In 1870, the 1.5 million readers of the capital's dailies created a demand for serials so great that some papers ran two or three simultaneously. 'Classics' like Dumas were reprinted and imitated: Paul Malahin and Jules Lermina were adepts of the 'Sons of the Musketeers' school of writing. But new stars emerged. Émile Richebourg specialized in social dramas featuring converted adulteresses and orphans (still being cheated of their inheritance). Montépin developed a line in persecuted innocence and criminal investigations which righted wrongs and punished evil. Jules Mary wrote highly charged tales of soldiers, policemen, passion and sentiment while Pierre Decourcelle kept *revanchisme* alive in stirring serials which dealt with the loss, after the Franco-Prussian War, of Alsace and Lorraine. The dominant note was now moral and sentimental, and more pity was generated for the weak than exultation in the fall of the wicked. Although the limits of decency were sometimes tested (in 1890 Oscar Méténier was found guilty of outraging public morality in *Madame la Boule*), self-censorship ensured that the tone was broadly conservative. The last third of the century saw the retreat of the hero, who grew less enterprising and decisive and became more sensitive and hesitant. Victims (of sexual predators, ruthless capitalists and corrupt authority) continued to be rescued, but their salvation was now achieved not by the bold actions of a fearless champion but by society in the guise of a paternalistic legal system. The classical thesis that literature means vice punished and virtue rewarded, long since exploded by serious novelists, survived happily in this modern form.

The educational reforms of the Third Republic created a new, enlarged reading public which was eagerly courted. Two books aimed at children (*Le Tour de France par deux enfants*, 1877, by G. Bruno [pseud. of Mme Alfred Fouillée] and Hector Malot's *Sans famille*, 1878, which showed how the orphan Rémi finds a place in society), quickly became classics and ideal school prizes. The exotic yarns of Aimard and About and the 'scientific' fictions of Verne were reclassified as 'novels of youth', and they, along with tales aimed at the younger market (rarely, as in England, about school-days) appeared in 'juvenile' magazines before being republished in collections like Hachette's *Bibliothèque rose illustrée*. Crime fiction, as yet unboosted by the Holmes phenomenon, was kept in *judiciaire* rather than deductive mode by Eugène Chavette and Pierre Zaccone. The prevailing taste until about 1900 was for the novel of manners which underwrote the bourgeois values of the Third Republic: work, marriage and patriotism. The upwardly mobile hero of *Le Maître de forges* (1882), the most spectacularly successful of the novels of the prolific Georges Ohnet (1848–1918), demonstrated the triumph of middle-class honour over aristocratic decadence. New heroes and villains appeared. The *femme fatale* gave way to the persecuted woman. The swashbuckling adventurer was overtaken by the worthy but impoverished young provincial who makes his way (and finds love) against the hostile establishment. The poor ceased to be shown as knaves and thieves and even peasants were admitted to be, on occasion, human. The ranks of the wicked were stocked by villains from the 'dregs' of society, or were heartless money-men, duplicitous lawyers, sinister churchmen and haughty aristocrats with expensive tastes financed by mortgaged estates. Formulaic and repetitive, they wrung withers, stimulated tear-ducts and made hearts beat faster.

1900–20

By 1900, the brash, high-impact *roman feuilleton* had grown to such proportions that critics feared for the future of the novel as a form. However, at a time when 'universités populaires' were spreading ideas and culture to the working population, the educational potential of the serialized novel had its defenders. It might peddle sensation rather than instruction, but it reflected current social trends such as the pro-regionalist 'réveil des provinces', the decline of anticlericalism which followed the Separation of Church and state in 1905, and new xenophobic tendencies: the villainous English imperialist and, in the wake of the spy-mania which had stoked the Dreyfus Affair, the German agent defeated by the French counter-spy. The Nietzschean Superman helped revive the tradition of the omnipotent hero who might be a force for good or, almost as often, a figure of evil. Socialist ideas added a new dimension to social justice, psychiatry opened doors to new oneiric fantasies, and technology was a source of gadgetry but also of a new menace: the insane genius who symbolized a growing feeling that science was a danger to civilization.

Sherlock Holmes and 'scientific' police methods turned the old *littérature judiciaire* into crime fiction which yielded anarchic heroes and sinister power figures like Fantômas. Judex, the masked avenger, was an updated version of the Romantic hero, but public enemies carried the day. The 'master-criminal' was as power-crazed and ruthless as the mad scientist of the now hugely popular science-fiction yarns which featured space voyages and alien invaders but also looked to prehistory (the 'Darwinian' novel) and Egyptology. Heroes found scientific ways of becoming invisible and immortal; they sought the secret of creation and attempted to control nature. And so new twists were given to old stories: medieval romances were rewritten in suitably 'modern' forms.

But the reading public was now a divided province. The 'juvenile' end of the market demanded exotic adventure (trappers and castaways) and science fiction (death rays and space travel). A mixed readership, though predominantly male, required crime novels and still warmed to history as retold by Michel Zévaco (1860–1918), the last author to make his name on the strength of his *feuilletons*. Women preferred sentiment and social dramas which continued to show widows and orphans evicted by inheritance-stealers, though the new psychology and the raffish mood of the Belle Époque allowed a more open (but still discreet) treatment of sexuality. Stories of sentimental love made their mark in 1908 when Delly (Frédéric (1879–1949) and his sister Marie (1875–1947) Petitjean de la Rosière) published the first of their phenomenally successful romances laced with enjoyably and modestly perverse entanglements. At the same time, Marcelle Tinayre (1872–1948) raised sentimental and moral problems from a mildly feminist perspective, and the Claudine novels of Colette provided role-models for the non-conforming modern girl.

Newspaper serialization remained dominant until the Great War, by which time the economics of the book trade had changed dramatically. In the 1890s, the *roman à treize sous*, blotchily printed on poor-quality paper, was standard. But in the early 1900s, publishers began to offer low-priced 'collections' of novels, complete or abridged and often illustrated, which offered a challenge to the *feuilleton* and the *livraison*. But the growing appeal of cinema also lured *feuilletonistes* into script-writing and during the War the success of Hollywood film serials helped to turn Fantômas and Judex into super-heroes to rival Zorro. They not only acquired a vast public following which crossed the boundaries of class, age and gender but also revealed to the Surrealists the potential of cinema as a laboratory of dreams. After the war, the appearance of the *cinéroman* (brief text plus stills) confirmed the assimilation of the *roman feuilleton* into the newly emerging mass media. Novels continued to be published in newspapers but serialized fiction had lost its drawing power by the 1920s, which saw the rise of its successor, the 'collection' which grouped and thus defined genres which would continue to dominate the mass market: the *roman d'amour*, the *roman policier*, the *roman historique* (increasingly in the guise of the family saga), the *roman d'anticipation* (already turning into *la science-fiction*) and the varied branches (western, thriller, spy-story, and so on) of the *roman d'aventures*.

Conclusion

With few exceptions, the *roman feuilleton* has long since been unreadably melodramatic, for it was designed to catch current preoccupations and passing fashions. Even so, it shadowed – at a distance – the evolving taste and techniques of serious fiction. Most *feuilletonistes* were educated and middle-class and many began as aspiring poets and *littérateurs* who hoped to launch serious careers with money earned in the marketplace. Slowly, but without abandoning the violence, sensationalism and emotion which were their permanent arsenal, they retreated from the early narrative sprawl of Sue (who, like others, readily adopted suggestions from readers and brought his unstructured chronicles to an end for commercial rather than artistic reasons) and gave popular fiction a firmer shape and greater realism.

Yet they also played a significant role in the evolution of literary taste. The *roman feuilleton* encouraged the reading habit and enabled many to graduate from the thin gruel of the serial to the stronger meat of literary fiction. Serious novelists were not above borrowing its energy and dramatic directness, and the 'literary' novel would have developed differently without it. Zola, for instance, may have consciously used science as the rationale of his Rougon-Macquart chronicle, but his audience had been prepared in advance by the likes of Sue, who had shown the brutality of life outside the salons, Dumas *père*, who had used history as a weapon against the present, and the many authors who had shown how the rich prey eternally on the poor. Avant-garde poets like Apollinaire, Cendrars and Cocteau regarded Fantômas as a great creation of the imagination. The young Pagnol read Aimard alongside Virgil and Racine. The Sartre of *Les Mots* confessed that his aesthetic sense and imaginative awakening came not from Chateaubriand but from the 'magic box' opened by Paul d'Ivoi and Jean de la Hire. Conversely, the *feuilletonistes*, like their soap-opera successors, incorporated elements of the formal and intellectual concerns of their betters into their own tales. To this extent, they mediated high art for the unlettered, who could be as deeply stirred by this new, manufactured popular culture as the cultured reader by the subtleties of Stendhal, Flaubert or Proust. If the chapbooks of the *Bibliothèque bleue* mark the first stirrings of mass culture, the *romans feuilletons* of the nineteenth century constitute its prehistory.

6

The Twentieth Century

Beneath the self-confident optimism of the Belle Époque, political and social tensions threatened urbane, middle-class, turn-of-the century France. In the aftermath of the Dreyfus Affair, Left and Right adopted more aggressive postures and centuries of ecclesiastical involvement in the political and administrative life of the nation ended with the Separation of Church and state in 1905. The Great War introduced the world to the horrors of mechanized death and robbed heroism of its dash and glory. It also marked the end of an era. Alsace and Lorraine were regained, but the style and self-confidence of the Belle Époque had long evaporated by 1920, when new dangers loomed. The Russian Revolution of 1917 and the emergence of the USA as a world power launched opposing economic and political models and two conflicting ideologies: communism and capitalism. The Wall Street Crash of 1929, and the recession which followed, showed the vulnerability of national governments to world events. France's democratic, republican institutions withstood the threat of civil war in 1934, but the rise of the fascist dictators destabilized the postwar order, which the League of Nations was unable to maintain as Europe slid into a new conflict. When the *drôle de guerre* ended in May 1940, France was overrun within weeks. To the humiliation of defeat were added four years of Occupation. Liberation in 1944 was followed by an *épuration*, one of the most shameful episodes in French history, but also by a remarkable thirty-year period of economic growth which made France prosperous once more.

But after 1945, despite the *trente glorieuses*, France faced new onslaughts on its battered self-image. At home, the Fourth Republic bred unstable governments until 1958 when de Gaulle inaugurated the Fifth, which proved resilient enough to survive both the Algerian crisis and the events of May 1968. But France had to come to terms with the loss of empire and lived, as the Cold War intensified, in the shadow of the Bomb. Yet the technology which produced nuclear weapons and gave genocide fearsomely efficient tools also modernized agriculture and industry and underwrote the affluence of the sixties. France embraced the information revolution with enthusiasm and found a new role as a leading member of the European Union. After the departure of de Gaulle in the wake of the events of 1968, internal divisions slowly cooled. The consumer society and the expanding welfare state deflated the class war and the French Communist Party (PCF), with the fall of the Berlin wall in 1989, was left with a small power base. The threat posed by the extreme Right was contained, though many problems posed by the new multi-cultural, multi-ethnic society remained. In the last decades of the century, French politics acquired an uncharacteristic pragmatism as ideology declined and Left and Right were defined by their relation to a shared centre which assumed a commitment to public spending and private enterprise, but feared the cultural imperialism of the USA and the globalization of the economy. France entered the twenty-first century with a sound economic base and stable institutions.

Writers and Their Public

French in the world

Over the century, French as an international language lost further ground, outdistanced by Spanish, Mandarin and English: in 2000, of just over 100 million French speakers worldwide, over half lived in France. For over a century, governments have actively sponsored the propagation of French language and culture through the Alliance Française (founded 1883) and its network of Instituts Français. Since the 1960s, private associations and publicly funded agencies have promoted the ideal of *francophonie*, a term coined in 1880 to describe a French-speaking commonwealth. By 2000, it had over 50 members mainly in Canada, the West Indies, North and Central Africa and the Far East. While in francophone countries French may be the language of government and often of education, it is, with a few exceptions (Quebec and areas of Belgium and Switzerland), spoken by the educated social echelons which first articulated the case for decoloniza-tion, defended national cultures and generated a body of work which has been a major feature of writing in French for several generations.

Language

The francophone initiative helped maintain the status of French in the wider world but was only one element in the renewing of the language in a century which presided over a linguistic revolution. The clarity, elegance and abstract purity bequeathed by the classical tradition remained the admired qualities of literary discourse until after the Great War. Before that time, the *style noble* had occasionally been challenged by writers who found it inadequate to express 'mod-ern' and especially urban realities, but even the *roman feuilleton*, lexic-ally more adventurous, did not disdain the imperfect subjunctive. *Argot*, *patois* and 'popular' French, on the other hand, were spoken forms of the language which were excluded both from literature and, after 1880, from the new *école communale*. Most French citizens, who had learned to use one register in the classroom and another in the playground, lived in two linguistic codes: formal when they read and informal when they spoke. By 1930, however, the process by which the oral language would invade normative usage had already begun, stimulated by radio, the growing supply of popular fiction and, soon, talking films which validated Raimu's Marseilles accent, Arletty's Parisian *gouaille* and Jean Gabin's working-class directness. Literary authors drew on the spoken language no longer as a form of local colour but as an integral part of the worlds they created. Such was its role in populist fiction, the snarling novels of Céline or the film scripts and verse of Jacques Prévert. In *Le Chiendent* (1933), Raymond Queneau experimented with a register which was neither noble nor vulgar but a 'néo-français' which combined the old virtues of clarity and precision with the inventive energy of spoken French to give literature a new, versatile and endlessly resourceful voice. Such arguments hardly needed to be pressed in the more democratic postwar world where readers encountered *argot* in crime fiction and found non-conventional French legitimized by Boris Vian or Antoine Blondin. By 1959, when Queneau gave the fullest demonstration of his 'néo-français' in *Zazie dans le métro*, departures from the old standard were routine in regionalist, autobiographical and many forms of popular and journalistic writing.

Further pressures were exerted by the influx of technical and specialized vocabulary which drew attention to changing linguistic values. In the 1960s, René Étiemble (b. 1909) waged war on intrusive Anglicisms and Pierre Daninos mocked the proliferating jargons of business and administration. After 1970, Jacques Cellard (b. 1921) defended *argot* by reconnecting it with the tradition of Rabelais and Marot, and Claude Duneton (b. 1935) popularized the reaction against the 'imperialism' of cultured French. By the time a new dimension was added by feminist hostility to gendered language, authors had long been faced with a fundamental problem: should they use the French of the educated elite and perhaps alienate the public, or a version of 'néo-français', and risk the wrath of the literary establishment? Further pressure was exerted by the emergence in the 1970s of the *argot de banlieue*, a mix of traditional *verlan* (back-slang) and vocabulary drawn from an eclectic, multi-cultural social base. Used by urban youth as a badge of group identity, it has entered the speech of the young professional class via cinema and rap music and invaded the language of the novelists who write for them. The older generation refused to compromise (Marguerite Duras remained a classical stylist) but new writers have proved more flexible.

The Académie Française remains the official arbiter of usage, but its authority has been undermined since the 1960s by successive governments which introduced protectionist measures (foreign film quotas, glossaries of approved usage) designed to maintain the integrity of French against the encroachments of *franglais*. Such holding operations have met with mixed success and despite the high status still accorded to *le beau parler*, literary French has retreated significantly from the formal elegance of Proust or Valéry. Responding to the postwar rise of the mass audience, the French of literary and intellectual discourse, no less disciplined but lexically and syntactically more inclusive, has ceased to be the tool of an elite and become a looser, more speech-based and less abstract instrument which speaks directly to voters, consumers, and the mass paying public whose requirements now challenge those of the educated middle-class readership.

The public

For the literary public changed as society developed more democratic forms and economic progress extended privileges once reserved for the few to the many. At first, the pace of institutional change was slow. The majority of citizens did not proceed beyond elementary schools and secondary education was not made free to all until the early 1930s: at that date, loans from Paris's municipal libraries stood at just over half the 1902 figure. After 1945, however, postwar reconstruction initiated a dramatic expansion of educational opportunities at all levels and included significant support for the arts, with the regional Centres Dramatiques Nationaux of 1946 being followed in the early 1960s by Malraux's Maisons de la Culture. Educational reform closed the gap between the sexes and official cultural policy undermined the domination of the exclusive 'high' art of the elite in favour of the interests of the mass of citizens.

It was the continuation of a long-standing trend. Popular culture first laid claim to its territory from the 1840s onward. After the First World War it gained momentum and, after the Second, accelerated dramatically. Following the rhythm of falling social barriers and rising technological innovation, the book was challenged in the 1920s by cinema and radio, to which were added, in the 1960s, television and the *bande dessinée*, and, in the 1990s, the word-processor, the internet and the playstation, with sport and other activities also competing for what, a century earlier, was both the citizen's reading time and the creative hours of writers who had once penned Symbolist poetry and Naturalist novels but now produced advertising material, popular songs and scripts for screens large and small.

The book trade

Even so, the book market remained resilient, though there is a clear correlation between its performance and war, recession, prosperity and social change. Until 1940, about 8,000 titles were published annually. Since 1945, the figure has risen steadily to 12,000 (1965), 23,000 (1973) and 41,000 (1993), of which a fifth were classed as 'literary'. Sales were helped by the paperback revolution which began in 1953 with the first Livre de Poche (there were some 200 such imprints at the end of the century), by the spread of book clubs and by the availability of alternative retail outlets, such as supermarkets. Publishers studied market trends and acted accordingly. By 1990, the industry accepted that its economic core was the mass market, set the number of middle-class, mainstream book buyers at 100,000–200,000, and put the elite audience at 25,000. In the latter category, a serious essay or a literary novel which sold 4,000 copies was a success, though even this figure was beyond the reach of poets who competed for the nation's 2,000 regular poetry buyers.

In the first half of the century, an author's name was made less by means of advertising than through the intermediary of literary society: influential critics, enlightened readers, and café and *salon* society. Writers from Proust to Sartre acquired their reputations in this way. But after 1945, 'literary society' was dispersed and verdicts were delivered by more impersonal publics. The *nouveau roman* owed its success to the faith placed in it by Les Éditions de Minuit, but by then the days of the autonomous, risk-taking publisher, like Gallimard or Grasset, who nurtured authors and acted as literature's mid-wives, were no more, cut short by the realities of a harsher business climate. After 1960, the expansion of Hachette, begun before 1939, served as a model for the reorganization of the industry which was achieved through mergers, takeovers and the modernization of distribution. In the last half century, the trade has become streamlined, with two-thirds of the turnover now attributable to a handful of dominant imprints owned by large groups and conglomerates for which books are a commodity like any other. The small independent publisher survives but cannot compete with the power and publicity machine of the large companies which, for example, accounted for the bulk of the winning authors of France's 'Big Six' literary prizes in the last decades of the century.

Yet just as Paris, despite the rise of the regions, remains the centre of French cultural life, so the book is still the primary vehicle for the expression of ideas and literary culture. It continues to be supported by an abundance of literary reviews. Between the wars, *La Nouvelle Revue Française* (1909), *Les Nouvelles littéraires* (1922), or *Esprit* (1932) kept readers abreast of new developments. After 1945, some lost ground but others appeared like *Les Temps modernes* (1945), *La Table ronde* (1948) and (for followers of the avant-garde) *Tel Quel* (1960–83) and its successor, *L'Infini*. Since the 1970s, the line has been continued by *La Quinzaine littéraire* and *Le Magazine littéraire* while influential book reviews and literary analysis appear in quality dailies and general-interest magazines. The number of Paris-based daily newspapers may have fallen dramatically (from 80 in 1914 to 31 in 1939 and just 11 in the 1990s), but they remain authoritative, and the regional press, which represents 70 per cent of the national readership, also carries news of the world of books. Literary culture is also underwritten by a long tradition of serious book programmes on radio and television. Furthermore, the role of government in organizing the nation's cultural and artistic life since the war has encouraged the growth of public lending libraries and, especially since 1981, has offered financial support for academic publishing, the showcase *salon du livre* and festivals which promote women's writing and popular genres like crime fiction and the *bande dessinée*. On the other hand, while there is still a world demand for French books, the home market has, since the 1930s, absorbed an above-average quantity of imported books in translation. But although the publishing industry maintains an army of translators, no successor to Amyot has emerged, nor a French equivalent to Scott-Moncrieff, who gave Proust his English voice.

Censorship

The press law of 1881, like the 1906 ruling on theatre, made censorship a matter for the courts, not government. Except in times of national crisis, notably the Great War and the Vichy regime, state intervention was limited to ensuring that laws concerning public morality, obscenity and personal privacy were upheld. Occasional prosecutions for obscenity (Victor Margueritte's *La Garçonne*, 1922; Dominique Aury's *Histoire d'O*, 1954) reminded authors of the limits. But publishers were also sensitive to the political climate which, for example, made collaborationist novelists like Drieu la Rochelle and Céline difficult to market after 1945 and led to a form of pre-censorship practised by the book trade. In 1957, Jean-Jacques Pauvert was charged with the offence of issuing a scholarly edition of Sade. Although he was fined for obscenity, the trial opened a debate which was ended not by argument but by the permissive climate of the 1960s, and writers thereafter were rarely troubled. Film-makers fared less well. Roger Vadim was taken to court for *Les Liaisons dangereuses* (1959), judged to have brought France's literary tradition into disrepute, and Rivette's film of Diderot's *La Religieuse* (1966), deemed offensive to the Catholic faith, was not distributed. But the government intervened to ban Godard's outspoken *Le Petit Soldat* (1960) during the Algerian crisis and Gatti's play *La Passion du général Franco* during the troubles of 1968. In the early 1970s, legislation targeted the expression of racist views but in other areas censorship was relaxed. Pierre Guyotat's *Éden, Éden, Éden* (1970) and Bernard Noël's *Le Château de*

Cènes (1971), both prosecuted for 'outrage aux moeurs', overstepped the new tolerance, which was cynically exploited by pornographic cinema to the point where government intervened in 1975, not by introducing legislation but by withdrawing subsidies for such films. While the state left the protection of morals to the legal system (Éric Jourdan's gay novel, *Les Mauvais Anges*, was banned in 1984), the controversial *loi* Gayssot, enacted in 1990, made denial of the Holocaust a criminal offence, a measure considered by some to infringe the right to free speech. On the other hand, censorship by another name strengthened its hold as profit-conscious publishers became inclined to judge the risks posed by new, experimental or controversial manuscripts by commercial criteria.

Writers' rewards

In 1900, the expansion of the publishing industry gave rich rewards to writers who pleased the popular public, like Michel Zévaco, last of the super-*feuilletonistes*. But serious authors could not live by their pens, for few benefited from the new literary prizes which, after 1910, boosted sales from the 10,000 to 12,000 copies, which had until then represented success, to above 100,000 for best-selling titles like Barbusse's *Le Feu* (1916). Though some, like Proust or Gide, had private means, most relied on other employment. Duhamel and Céline were doctors, Valéry lectured for money before finding a home in the Collège de France, and many worked as teachers, civil servants and journalists. There was little state support for writers, though the Ministry of Education occasionally awarded small sums to suitable candidates. In 1946, an ineffectual Caisse Nationale des Lettres, first mooted in the early 1930s, was established, but its replacement, the Centre National de Lettres (CNL) (1973) was more successful in providing grants and pensions. On the other hand, the relationship of authors with publishers and the law was clarified. After the First World War, a payment system based not on print-run but on copies sold, with an advance against royalties, became standard. In 1957, a new copyright law gave improved protection to intellectual property. By then, to the old Société des Auteurs had been added professional associations and, as a group, writers became an object of sociological study. In 1968, the Syndicat National des Éditeurs estimated the number of authors of all kinds at 40,000, though only a tiny proportion were able to make a good living from writing. Writing was a spare-time activity for the vast majority, who earned their living as teachers, academics, and sometimes farmers and businessmen, and increasingly through cinema and television which, still regarded in the 1960s as suspect, became after 1970 a respectable source of income and recognition.

The status of authors

Whereas the financial prospects of writers improved in general terms, writing as a career was, at the end of the twentieth century, as precarious and unpredictable as it was in the nineteenth. Popular stars shone more brightly than before, but the status of the literary author declined dramatically. In 1900, poets and novelists still commanded the respect which the public had learned to give the Artist who was teacher, sage and prophet. It was not a sustainable role. No authoritative literary voice interpreted the Great War and it quickly became clear that Art was under-qualified to explain modern humanity to itself. That function, in the wake of Freud and Marx, was steadily usurped by the experimental and analytical human sciences. Until 1940, literature retained control of the morality of personal action which it explored through the imagination. But by then, morality had long been problematic and literary writers were drawn into the political, philosophical and generally intellectual concerns of the postwar world. The new generation found more to interest it in collective questions than in personal psychology and individual choices which became the last refuge of the old literature. Literature was now made out of fascism, communism and colonialism and while its leading lights, from Gide and Bernanos to Sartre, had one foot in literary soil, the other was more firmly planted in ideas. In the 1960s, Structuralists announced the death not only of authors, who were products of socio-economc forces and the laws of the psyche, but of literature itself, a predetermined, predictable way of seeing, artificially preserved by a privileged social system.

Authors refused to die, though they found the climate of the last third of the century inhospitable. Playwrights were demoted by the *création collective* movement and theatrical publishing shrank significantly. Disquiet was expressed about the influence on the future of literature of the large profit-driven publishing corporations which discouraged experiment and, against new writing, backed winning formulae. Yet such commercial practices were the response to changes in taste and, more positively, enabled writers to reach a wider variety of publics than ever before. There were casualties and beneficiaries. Poetry, the form of writing the CNL subsidizes most frequently, continued to decline but the appeal of the singer-songwriter has strengthened. The individual voice of the dramatist was muted by collective theatre but found outlets in *auteurist* cinema. And if the novel has proved to be the mainstay of modern literature, it has done so by absorbing the mixed legacy of *nouveau réalisme*, popular sub-genres and (auto)biography. But what 'writing the self' gains in authenticity it loses in universality: it offers not Truth but plural truths from different perspectives. Authors, no longer teachers and guides nor the servants of their art, have been freed of the old didactic burden and have stepped down from their pedestal. In 2000, the writer knows no better than his reader, but is prepared to share the view from his corner of the fragmented world.

From Literary Doctrine to Critical Theory

To 1914

Between the 1890s and the Great War, post- and neo-Symbolists generated new 'schools' on what seemed an annual basis. The casualty rate was high, though the Unanimist engagement with modern urban realities would linger into the 1930s in the novels of Jules Romains and Georges Duhamel. More significant was the founding in 1908–9 of the *Nouvelle Revue Française* as a focus for the new writing which was replacing Symbolism, now judged to have been an aesthetic unsupported by an ethic. Uncommitted to any particular literary or political view, it promoted 'pure' creation and, in its long history, has reflected all the major literary trends of the century. The 'École Fantaisiste' which had formed around Francis Carco and Paul-Jean Toulet by 1912 reacted against lyricism and turned an ironic, disabused eye on the world and mined the 'fanciful' vein of French poetry which ran from Marot and La Fontaine to Verlaine. Its spirit did not survive the intellectual upheaval which, after the war, bred more radical movements.

Between the wars

In the 1920s, 'schools' based on agreed doctrines gave way to more loosely based tendencies, like the non-aligned 'poésie pure' promoted by *abbé* Henri Brémond in 1926 or the more socially committed 'littérature populiste' defined by André Thérive and Léon Lemonnier in 1929 which was intended to be less political than the 'littérature prolétarienne' proclaimed by Henri Poulaille in 1930. Such movements reflect the left-wing colouring of the new literary thinking which was partly a reaction against the bourgeois values associated with the late, disastrous war but, more generally, as a reflection of the lower social origins of the new generation of publicly educated writers. The 'Clarté' movement (1919–27), initiated by Barbusse, offered internationalism as an antidote to bellicose nationalism and capitalism. But the loudest reaction against the pointless carnage of war and the positivist belief in logic and progress which had produced it, was articulated by the Surrealists.

Surrealism

Dada, imported from Austria in 1919, was anarchical and nihilist but in France it generated a revolutionary avant-garde committed to demolishing the rationalism of the 'real' world and imposing a new way of seeing. Freud had shown how little control humans have over motives and ideas which are rooted in drives beyond the reach of the conscious mind. By exploring the subconscious, André Breton was confident of unveiling 'le fonctionnement réel de la pensée . . . en dehors de toute préoccupation esthétique ou morale'. Dream, the most direct manifestation of the subconscious, was fused with reality so that mind, imagination and perception could move uninhibitedly in zones of 'surreal' freedom which was expressed through automatic writing and its plastic equivalent: painted, photographed and moving images. All forms of art mobilize frames of reference, cultural, aesthetic, social and linguistic, which the reader/spectator interprets to make sense of what is shown. The texts of Surrealism disconcert with their random juxtapositions of fact and fancy; its cinema frustrates our expectation of what film should be; and Duchamp's 'ready-mades' dislocate our structural norms by de-contextualizing words and objects. But the point was not simply to disrupt the accepted frames, but to impose freer ways of perceiving the world. Destroying the better to construct, Surrealism aimed verbal and graphic collages at readers and spectators who were induced to unlearn old referential modes and change their perception not merely of Art but of reality. The goal was quickly extended to politics. The *clartéistes* introduced Surrealists to communism, but Party discipline proved a constraint too far for their anarchic spirit and the last card-carrying members had been expelled from the PCF by 1936. Nor did they, for the same reasons, function well as a group. Held together by André Breton, whose two *Manifestes* (1924, 1930) best define their purpose, they produced collaborative works and ephemeral magazines. But internal disagreements, though they led to splinter groups and individualist creation, constantly undermined the movement, which declined after 1932. When the Surrealist Exhibition was held in 1938, Surrealism had been betrayed by its works. Though it revived after 1945 and remained a powerful reminder of the attractions of iconoclasm, it never regained its former influence and was finally disbanded in 1967, a year after the death of Breton.

The 'Collège de Sociologie'

While para-Surrealist groups, like 'Le Grand Jeu' (1928–33), pursued the movement's strict radical goals, other tendencies found alternative ways of making literature serve the common weal. In 1937, dissident Surrealists unrepentantly committed to regenerating the world through conscious and unconscious revolution, created the 'Collège de Sociologie'. Conventional sociology dealt with 'profane' power structures which impose rational order at the expense of the 'sacred' which unites citizens around the national flag or individuals in an excited crowd which expresses a group 'totality of being'. Recommendations of how a new *sursocial* was to be achieved ranged from Georges Bataille's definition of revolt as 'abjection' (the acceptance of horror and disgust as a necessary purging of mind and spirit), to the communifying 'festival' spirit proclaimed by Roger Caillois (1913–78), and Michel Leiris's insertion of his own dreams into the collective consciousness. Though short-lived (the group broke up in 1939), its denunciation of literary tradition and bourgeois individualism would help to explode the idea of monolithic culture and deconstruct its artefacts, with Bataille, in particular, emerging as a guiding spirit of Postmodernism.

The Catholic revival

A different view of the 'sacred' had been advanced by turn-of-the-century liberal Catholics like Léon Bloy, Claudel and Péguy, who had reminded readers of the importance of faith in personal and social matters. In 1926, the excommunication of members of Maurras's right-wing Action Française gave rise to a Catholic revival. It was led by Jacques Maritain (1882–1973) who sought to reconcile Christianity with Enlightenment values, and publicized by *Esprit*, founded in 1932 by Emmanuel Mounier (1905–50) whose 'Personalism' attempted to install a practical social philosophy within the Catholic tradition. This more liberal climate found echoes in the novels of François Mauriac and Georges Bernanos and in the theatre, where Gabriel Marcel developed a Christian response to atheistic Existentialism.

Since 1940

Between the wars, literary doctrine had grown increasingly subordinate to political and philosophical concerns, a trend which grew after 1940. Theatre and fiction were readily annexed in their more or less naturalistic forms by the Existentialists, who regarded them as equivalents of the analytical treatise and eminently suited to the task of showing what existential choices meant in practice. But like the right-wing, anti-resistentialist 'Hussards' who opposed them, they argued more about content than form, and even the New Theatre movement of the 1950s grew out of practice rather than theory. Neither Beckett nor Ionesco, its major architects, published literary manifestos and they broke with precedent by launching no polemical reviews. On the other hand, although the principles of the *nouveau roman* were explained by its practitioners (Robbe-Grillet and Butor in paricular), the New Realism was as much defined in its first phase by its works as by its disparate principles. But its evolution after 1960 generated intense doctrinal debate by the members of the *Tel Quel* group. Yet the abolition of the once-sacred distinction between genres, justified by Maurice Roche who amalgamated *roman* and *poésie* and produced simply *textes*, was adopted without theoretical explanation by Duras who, in the 1970s, designated certain of her writings *roman-théâtre-texte*.

The Aesthetic rump

The venerable preoccupation with aesthetic literary doctrine survived the war, though it appealed now to a declining constituency. In 1945, Isidore Isou (b. 1925) launched *lettrisme* which made the single character the building block of poetry. The letter, preceding the word to which meanings have been attached, was used to redefine poetry as rhythm and sound. Essentially phonic in its reliance on onomatopoeia and neologism, it invited performance, though on the page it could also generate meaning through its typographical arrangement into ideograms and the like. By the mid-1950s, it had become voiceless and was extended to visual forms of expression and thereafter evolved into *schématisme* which was appreciated by the few. Less arcane but no less experimental was 'Cobra' (1948–51), an international art movement which stressed spontaneity, abolished barriers between artistic forms, took everyday life as its subject and expressed it through free-association imagery, linguistic play and the word-pictures of the *logogramme*. If such projects were related in various ways to Surrealist anarchy, 'Oulipo' (Ouvroir de littérature potentielle), begun in 1960, developed out of the Collège de Pataphysique founded to honour Jarry in 1948. It was designed to catalogue existing literary forms and extrapolate from them new structures of which their practitioners had been unaware: the only true literature, said Queneau, is 'involuntary'. Conscious lyricism and the old Romantic absolutes to which even Surrealism had remained committed were rejected and literature was redefined not in terms of what it had produced but of its 'potential'. Two categories of *lipo* ('*litt*érature *po*tentielle') were identified. A comparative analysis of detective fiction, say, or medieval poetry would yield an inventory of all the possibilities which, thus possessed, would enable them to be not imitated but exactly reproduced. To this transformational model was added the synthetic *lipo* which used a variety of artificial, constraining devices within which the writer worked. The lines of all ten sonnets of Queneau's *Cent mille milliards de poèmes* (1961) were printed as individual strips which the reader could turn separately and thus assemble a maximum of 10^{14} new poems. The structure of Jacques Roubaud's verse sequence, Σ (1967), followed the rules of an obscure Japanese board game and for his murder mystery, *La Disparition* (1969), Georges Perec dispensed with the letter 'e'. Though Oulipo writers set a higher value on the laws by which texts could be generated than on the finished product, they also struck a ludic note which ran counter to the fictional trends of the 1960s. But while they opposed Structuralism (the review, *Change*, founded in 1970 by Roubaud and others, was intended as a riposte to *Tel Quel*), their analytical model shared certain Structuralist assumptions which, from the 1960s onwards, would turn literary doctrine into critical theory. Narratology would also attempt to establish a descriptive (and not normative) grammar of literature. Oulipo was the last major literary movement of the century, for while *écriture féminine* and the promotion of gay and lesbian writing were suitably polemical, they were hardly inclusive and defined the rules of engagement of writing in general and not literary expression in particular.

Literary theory

Throughout the century, criticism, steadily losing interest in literature as a craft, swung periodically between two inescapable poles: text and context, the book itself and the life/mind/times of its author. Sainte-Beuve had used the biography and milieu of writers to explain their works, an approach institutionalized by the positivist, philological methods of academic criticism, exemplified by Gustave Lanson, which were standard before 1914. During the 1920s, Proust's distinction between the *moi social* and the *moi créateur* was one factor in encouraging, as in the case of Albert Thibaudet (1874–1936), a more intuitive approach to both books and authors. After 1945, rejecting both positive and intuitive approaches, a new generation looked to non-literary authority to explain both books and authors: psychoanalysis and Marxism. The search for the author's *moi profond* was led by Gaston Bachelard (1884–1962) who identified a new 'scientific' epistemology in the four elements which define the human imagination and organize our vision of the world. Discarding the traditional tools of criticism (scholarship, literary history, the 'life and work'), he redefined the text as a network of words and, especially, images by which the personal vision of the author is communicated to the collective psyche in which the reader participated. Bachelard's pursuit of the 'imaginary world' of authors was developed after the war by the Geneva School of criticism, which studied themes (time, space, sensation) as a means of entering the writer's creating self. On the other hand, Marxist critics like Lucien Goldmann (1913–70) and Pierre Macherey (b. 1938) related literature to the structures and contradictions of the society in which it was produced and made the imagination a function of a given economic and political system.

La nouvelle critique and Structuralism

Existentialist critics were philosophically committed to human subjectivity, the ultimate source of meaning. Sartre's studies of Baudelaire, Genet and Flaubert were indebted to psychoanalysis and Marxism but they maintained the reasoning individual who emerges from the totality of things by taking responsibility for himself and thus acquires an irreducible uniqueness. After 1960, however, the psychoanalytical and Marxist approaches were absorbed into a wider quest to define the laws of literature through an analysis of the structures of which literature is the product. The New Criticism rejected the old prescriptive universals and moved towards a 'science of literature' extrapolated from the forces which shape texts. These forces were stronger than an author's conscious purpose (the 'intentionalist fallacy') or the reliance on emotion, however sincerely felt (the 'affective fallacy'). Texts were the outcome of factors external to the conscious creative imagination: language and the autonomous formalities of literary expression. To these, Structuralist theorists added the 'discourse' of the psyche, the 'myths' which underpin all cultures, and the inescapable influence of the dominant socio-economic climate.

Post-Structuralism

After 1968, the Structuralist search for the 'science of literature' turned into the Post-Structuralist emphasis on the text, no longer a humanly engineered artefact attributable to an author but a phenomenon which could not be accounted for, since there were no universal concepts, like Beauty or Order, by which it could be measured. A written text could not be explained or interpreted: it was indeterminate, endlessly open and the property of no one, not authors, nor critics nor readers. Since all judgements are either misconstruals or misunderstandings, criticism could not be prescriptive or normative but simply descriptive. A text is not singular but multiple – it exists as many times as it is read – and all approaches to it must respect the full range of its endless 'difference'.

Deconstruction

Such a conclusion was a convergence of the complex arguments of many analysts, linguisticians and specialists in many fields: Georges Bataille (1897–1962) and Maurice Blanchot (b. 1909–2003), who had conceived literature not as a vehicle for ideas or a reflection of the world but as an effort to overcome language and to generate its own meanings; Roland Barthes (1915–80), who moved from semiology, through the 'death of the author' to the plurality of meaning; Jacques Lacan (1901–81) who defined the subconscious as a structured language operating independently of will; and Julia Kristeva (b. 1941), for whom subjectivity was the product of language and history. The major spokesman of 'Deconstruction', Jacques Derrida (b. 1930), argued that, of the two forms of language, speech and writing, the spontaneous *parole* has been associated with truth, meaning and ideas while *écriture* has been made suspect because it is a manipulation of language, a tool derived from *parole*. Reacting against the repression of the written, Derrida sought to reconfigure it as pluralism, difference and, above all, openness. As an approach to reading, it was less concerned with uncovering the author's argument or intentions than with the shifting, contradictory patterns which lie beneath the surface of the text. To detect them, the new ways of thinking and analysing which had emerged from psychoanalysis, physics, biogenetics and the social sciences, were central to any consideration of language and the things it signifies, even though the capacity of language to open new horizons always runs ahead of meaning. It is not merely that 'justice' means different things to human beings in a democratic society and in a totalitarian regime. The human subject is infinitely variable and democracy has not merely a past and a present but a future: deconstruction meant excluding nothing and remaining open to difference and otherness.

Postmodernism

By the 1980s, the idea that the practitioners of language could claim no privileged status in determining meaning and that analysis was an open-ended process of interpretation and reinterpretation, was firmly established in history and sociology as well as literary criticism. Yet avoiding 'closure' meant, in practice, being inconclusive. For Postmodernism, literature was no longer an end but a means of establishing the validity of pluralist, non-dogmatic thinking. To say that *Madame Bovary* was 'better' than the latest best-seller was meaningless because there were no absolute values on which such a judgement could be based: for whom, for what, is Flaubert's novel 'better'? For this and other reasons, such an approach took its place alongside feminist, reader-response, rhetorical, hermeneutic and other theories. From the 1960s onward, the New Criticism metamorphosed into Critical Theory which claimed that nothing, neither literature or anything else, can be finally accounted for. Destiny was redefined in personal terms by the power of the gene and in universal terms by the unaccountable rhythms of history. Writers could not claim to understand people nor historians to explain peoples. Yet the old humanist criticism, increasingly identified with human resistance, was not obliterated. The 'commonsense' view that politics and history do indeed have 'grand narratives' and that books are created by authors and may be made to yield meaning, continued to be held by traditionalist critics and newspaper reviewers who regarded the *nombrilisme* of high-octane intellectuals as the incomprehensible in pursuit of the unfathomable.

The concept of 'literature'

Even so, by the end of the century, the belief that literature was a complete diet which catered for the needs of all generations and classes, had been overturned by profound social and intellectual changes. France's decline as a world presence and the threat to its language sapped confidence, undermined the sense of unified national identity and dug up the neatly ordered field in which its liberal, humanist, civilizing mission had grown. The process of democratization created a tension between individualism and pluralism; secularism overtook spiritual concerns; and the progress of consumerism shifted attention to the present and away from both the past, which was irrelevant, and the future, which was conceived in materialistic terms. The classical base of literature – beauty, order, form, soul – was discarded, the old ideas of genius and the religion of Art were abandoned, and the imagination, no longer the means of transcending reality, was subverted, as Christophe Donner (*Contre l'imagination*, 1998) argued, by a reliance on pastiche and the taste for real as opposed to invented experience. Literature was replaced by Writing.

The old literary 'school', committed to generating creative works, was overtaken by the intellectual 'ism' which attached less importance to creation than to its deconstruction. Yet successive avant-gardes fared none too well. Apart from alienating large sections of the public with its excesses (from the scandals of Surrealism to the media-hungry provocations of New Philosophers and New Theorists), the literary vanguard was regularly overtaken by events and its challengers. Its revolutionary impetus was invariably absorbed into new audacities, and its theory and practices were domesticated by the public purse and the market forces which subsidized it, and by the educational establishment which made it an object of academic study. But if at the end of the century no group or tendency has a monopoly, the cumulative impact of France's literary avant-garde is not difficult to detect. The Surrealists failed to impose their vision but bequeathed their particular iconoclastic spirit, and generations of intellectuals helped pave the way for the *fin-de-siècle* pluralistic, mass culture in which the 'alternative' has become the new orthodoxy. Literature has lost its privileged status and writers are no longer matrix-breakers: they pick their way through a surfeit of meaning systems which they are no more able to master than their readers.

The Rise of the Intellectual

If the purpose of literary doctrine was the production of literary works, the object of critical theory was to provide approaches to the study of literature. It was the natural evolution of a tendency clearly visible in the last decades of the nineteenth century when imaginative writers were first drawn into the ideological arena where, wittingly or unwittingly, they served the aims and objectives of intellectualism. Literature in the twentieth century has been remarkable for the manner in which it was underpinned by philosophy and abstract ideas.

From Dreyfus to the Great War

While every society is directed and administered by an intellectual elite, the word 'intellectual' has a special meaning in France. It signifies a long tradition of independent philosophical reflection which subjects the dominant ideology to critical analysis. The Pléiade and classicism strove consciously to create a 'modern' idea of France, and the Enlightenment, the Revolution of 1789 and the positivists of the nineteenth century promoted progress against the established order. In the 1890s, conservatives and progressives were brought into open conflict when Alfred Dreyfus, a Jewish army officer, was found guilty of selling military secrets to the Germans. By 1897, doubts about the verdict divided France into two camps. For the Right, the security of the nation, enshrined in the army, outweighed any individual miscarriage of justice. For the Left, if the French Revolution meant anything, then the rights of the individual had to be defended in the name of justice which applied to all.

Dreyfusards and anti-Dreyfusards

The noun 'intellectual' first appeared in 1898, when it designated the supporters of Dreyfus. But their opponents were no less 'intellectual' and the term came to mean those who participated in public affairs not as elected politicians but as extra-parliamentary commentators who sought to influence public opinion through their writings. The Dreyfus Affair created opposing camps. The Dreyfusards defended a libertarian view of the French Revolution which attracted many to finely graded liberal positions. The anti-Dreyfusards defended conservative values, the army and the Church, and saw a threat to the nation in the activities of 'non-French' elements: Jews, Freemasons, socialists and Protestants. Personalities emerged, each attracting a following, a pattern which would recur throughout the coming century. Although the Dreyfusard Left had acquired a high profile during the Affair, the socialists, led by Jean Jaurès (1859–1914), stayed out of what they regarded as a bourgeois squabble, and it was the right which produced the first charismatic figures. Maurice Barrès (1862–1923) began with a belief in the *moi individuel* which made personal freedom more important than collective unity. However, he came to believe that individuals are not well placed to know where their best interest lies and offered the *moi social* as a more valid ideal: the best defence of the individual was society. As he demonstrated in his best-known novel, *Les Déracinés* (1897), the whole is more important than its parts. It was therefore an error to defend Dreyfus against society. Dreyfusard 'justice' was a 'metaphysical abstraction' which threatened the 'nation' and gave encouragement to its enemies. The defence of order and tradition was also undertaken by Charles Maurras (1868–1952), founder of *L'Action française* (1899) and the leader of the intellectual French Right from the Dreyfus Affair to the end of the Second World War. He too considered 'metaphysical abstractions' to be dangerous, but went further. Since the Third Republic tolerated, even encouraged, a degree of factional strife, the solution lay in 'integral nationalism' based on the discipline of monarchy, the hierarchical Church and tradition. A different kind of nationalism was expressed by Charles Péguy (1873–1914) who never broke either with the image of Christian France or with the lessons of 1789. He associated the cause of Dreyfus with a spiritual vein of patriotism but, disillusioned to observe how the mystical charge of the Affair dwindled into political manoeuvring, he set out the case for ethical socialism in the *Cahiers de la quinzaine* (founded 1900). Concerned by the destructive anti-clericalism which the socialists adopted after the Affair, he underwent a double conversion to Catholicism and the nationalism of Barrès.

Ideas to 1914

The intellectual argument was conducted in newspapers, magazines and books by leading literary figures. But fiction was also drawn into the debate. Anatole France, a mildly Voltairean sceptic before the Affair, turned into a champion of the modernizing potential of science and socialism. Paul Bourget adopted the ideas of Barrès while Maurras found support in Léon Daudet (1867–1942), novelist and virulent polemicist of the Right for thirty years. In *Jean Barois* (1913), Roger Martin du Gard traced the odyssey of a young man who rejects religion, adopts scientism, becomes a socialist after the Dreyfus Affair and finally returns to the faith. It was, for many, the history of a generation. Against the narrower nationalisms of Barrès and Maurras, Romain Rolland wrote from a European, pacifist perspective. *Jean Christophe* (1904–12), expressed an optimistic view of the future tempered by a pessimistic assessment of the present. Rolland criticized Kaiser Wilhelm's Germany as unworthy of its past greatness, which he celebrated. But he also judged France adversely for its refusal to face the 'truth' – its parliamentarism which meant rule by committee, and its republican anarchy which had been shaped by Freemasonry, humanist ideologies and Jewish influence.

The intellectual in 1914

By 1914, two conflicting views of the place of the intellectual in society had emerged. While both Right and Left defended the uses of the intellect, some argued in favour of limiting free enquiry in the national interest, characterizing the intellectual as detached from his roots and therefore unable to defend the France which tradition had constructed. Others argued that truth, however unpalatable, is truth. Thus while Barrès, Maurras and Bourget were clear that society was greater than the individual, a majority of literary 'Dreyfusards' argued that there could be no valid society which did not respect the rights of all citizens. The Dreyfus Affair had brought into the open a debate which had been simmering since the eighteenth century.

The interwar years

During the Great War, extreme positions were modified in the cause of national unity, but after 1918 the intellectual landscape was re-drawn. In the wake of the Russian Revolution, the Parti Communiste Français (PCF) was formed in 1920. While French socialists continued to defend working-class interests through parliamentary channels, the PCF was committed to revolution and took its doctrinal lead from Moscow. On the Right, Barrès modified his position and sought to re-concile differences of opinion. Maurras, more extreme, remained true to xenophobic, anti-Semitic, 'integral' nationalism, to the point where, in 1926, the Pope officially condemned the perversion of Catholic teachings expressed by its mouthpiece, *Action française*. But new con-cerns appeared. Gide brought homosexuality into the open with *Corydon* (1924) and exposed French colonialist policy as a form of oppression (*Voyage au Congo*, 1926). Pacifism resurfaced in the maga-zine *Europe* (1923) which set out to build international bridges, while the Surrealists preached their own idea of revolution through revolt against the bourgeois order.

Benda

However, not everyone shared the taste for demagogy, polemics and extreme positions. In 1927, Julien Benda (1867–1956) published *La Trahison des clercs* which argued that idealism was dead and only two banner-cries were permitted: Nation for the Right, and Class for the Left. Writers and thinkers (that is, the *clercs*) were failing in their duty. For the search for universal truths, they had substituted polit-ical realism. They created a binary opposition – the creed of race (anti-Semitism, xenophobia) and nationalism (jingoism, militarism) versus the dogma of class (*bourgeoisisme*, Marxism) – outside which no thought was possible. Reason had been abandoned in favour of passionate commitment to sectarian, partisan positions.

Capitalism

But the postwar Left also identified a new enemy: capitalism. The behaviour of the American trusts threatened societies with dehumanized industrialization symbolized by the production line. Capitalism overruled elected national governments which, instead of working to create a just order based on the good of its citizens, were increasingly forced to surrender to the tyranny of international finance. Both economic liberalism and parliamentary democracy were failing the nation, but so were Marxism and fascism, which demanded obedience to authority and offered little hope that freedom and equality were realizable goals for the individual. Urgency was added to these fears by the recession which followed the Wall Street Crash of 1929 and threatened the social fabric. There was no agreement about which path France should follow and by 1933 a number of positions had been adopted by new groupings. While the extremes were occupied by Maurras on the Right and by the PCF on the Left, between them stood the more moderate 'Jeune Droite', progressive Catholics and communist sympathizers who offered their support to the PCF but refused to commit themselves to membership. While all these groups differed, most equated economic and political liberalism with capitalism and France's duplicitous parliamentary democracy.

Fascism v. communism

In February 1934, an anti-government protest, prompted by the Stavisky Affair, a high-profile financial scandal, polarized opinion and brought France to the brink of civil war. International events – the arrival of Hitler in the Reichstag in 1933, the invasion of Abyssinia in 1935 and the outbreak of Civil War in Spain in 1936 – brought fascism into the open. The Right saw it as the only credible means of opposing communism, the intellectual Left and the parliamentary system, and of providing strong leadership, peace and stability. Fascism was opposed by the PCF, the socialists and uncommitted libertarian intellectuals. In the debate, the Church, once the pillar of the traditional Right and enemy of the anti-clerical Left, ceased to have a major institutional voice in the argument.

The Front Populaire

The divided Left saw that a collective response was required to meet the challenge of a common enemy. Anti-fascist groups and committees multiplied, but the full extent of the ideological conflict emerged during the 'Congrès des Écrivains' of June 1935, organized by the PCF. It was dominated by André Malraux, the embodiment of the committed writer, and Gide, who spoke of communion, justice and freedom, objectives which were identified with their current home, Stalin's USSR. But at the same time the PCF abandoned its policy of non-collaboration with bourgeois parliamentarism and communists took their seats in the new Popular Front government of Léon Blum which was elected in May 1936. Important social measures were enacted but the unsustainable increase in public spending, opposed by business and industry, led to defeat in the election of 1937. However, though it was short-lived, the Front Populaire generated considerable idealism and, as an example of how concerted action could achieve social and political goals, would live on in the mythology of the Left.

Realignments

Events at home and abroad forced many intellectuals to abandon their hesitations and choose. Gide visited Russia and returned with the message (*Retour de l'URSS*, 1937) that it was no Workers' Eden. Pierre Drieu la Rochelle abandoned his hope of reforming the bourgeoisie and saw the way ahead in a combination of nationalism and socialism. Malraux's ideas were expressed in his active participation in the Spanish Civil War. Georges Bernanos, a leading Catholic polemicist, denounced the evils of both communism and totalitarianism. The reaction to the events of 1934–6 was not limited to the high intelligentsia but was transmitted to a wider audience in more accessible forms: fiction, cinema and theatre. The 'Groupe Octobre' (a loose grouping of left-wing writers, playwrights and film-makers created to commemorate the October Revolution of 1917) undertook to popularize the cause of the Left for which Jean Renoir made a number of propaganda films, from *Le Crime de Monsieur Lange* (1935) to *La Marseillaise* and *À nous la liberté* (both 1937). Serious fiction moved away from its postwar interest in tortured psychology and bourgeois adultery and took up political and social issues: such was the itinerary of Roger Martin du Gard and Jules Romains. Left-wing writers like Louis Aragon and Paul Nizan embraced socialist realism *à leur façon*, but Céline lurched to the Right and embraced fascism and the anti-Semitism which grew in strength throughout the 1930s. As war loomed, fascists urged a rapprochement with Germany, liberals supported negotiation and appeasement, and the PCF argued that the cause of freedom was inseparable from the defence of communist Russia. This stance was thrown into disarray by the non-aggression pact signed by Germany and Russia in August 1939. Party officials explained that this unlikely alliance did not alter the fact that the true enemy of both was liberal democracy. But high-profile Party members, like Nizan, resigned.

Defeat, Occupation and Liberation

After the fall of France, ideology was dominated by the collaborationist Right. Communists, non-aligned intellectuals, liberal Catholics and Christian democrats were excluded by the Vichy regime, which defended 'French' traditions against their enemies abroad and at home. Yet despite the dangers, poets and novelists kept the fight alive in clandestine publications like *Les Lettres françaises* (1942). The most organized voice, however, was that of the communists who opposed the 'imperialist war' and de Gaulle, while stigmatizing Vichy. But the PCF did not enter the Resistance officially until Germany invaded Russia in June 1941: its primary aim was the defence of the USSR, which was equated with the defence of France.

'L'Épuration' and after

After the Liberation of Paris in August 1944, action was taken against publishers, actors, film-makers and writers who had supported Vichy and colluded with the German Occupier. The 'Comité National des Écrivains' (CNE) published lists of literary and intellectual collaborators who were now called to account. Drieu committed suicide, some were jailed (Henri Béraud, Maurras), while others (Châteaubriant, Céline, Paul Morand) fled the country. A few, like Georges Suarez and Robert Brasillach, were executed.

Épuration

The *épuration* has been seen as a culmination of the undeclared civil war of the 1930s or even as an new outbreak of Dreyfus fever, which itself has been traced both back to the Terror of 1793–4 and forward to the excesses of the Algerian War. But the *épuration* generated one of the first intellectual postwar debates. The morality of the death sentence passed on Béraud, which was later lifted, generated a clash between François Mauriac, the major Catholic writer, and the Existentialist spokesman, Albert Camus. Jean-Paul Sartre, on the other hand, was less concerned with such ethical questions. His experience of war led him to redefine the role of the intellectual in society as that of *engagement*. But what form should this commitment take?

Engagement

The options were limited. The Right, tainted by collaboration, was discredited. Gide, symbol of moral integrity, was marginalized and liberal humanism was identified with the weak democratic policies of tolerance which had failed France in the 1930s. On the other hand, the Left had been heroically vindicated by the Resistance which was presented as the finest hour of the PCF which had largely organized it. In the new climate, the intellectual had little choice but to take a position for or against communism. Those who wished to see their work in print chose, to varying degrees, the former.

Sartre and Camus

After 1944, Sartre and Camus emerged as the leaders of the new intellectualism. At first, they shared a number of views but they would come to disagree on fundamental issues of principle and policy. Both were associated with Existentialism which, insofar as it placed responsibility for actions on individuals, forced them to make choices, though without offering specific guidance on what those choices should be.

Existentialism

Existentialism was the name given to a synthesis of a number of competing 'philosophies of existence'. Two thousand years of philosophy had not translated absolute 'essences' (justice, freedom, and other universals) into universally agreed values and institutions. Abandoning 'essences', thinkers turned to Existence, which preceded Essence. If there are no essences, then God is an illusion of human reason. If God is dead, then, as Dostoevsky said, 'everything is permitted'. Political systems based on the assumption that God exists ceased to be valid, and along with them the supposition that the universe has a moral dimension and the belief that life has a purpose, which was man's salvation. The realization that life has no grand purpose or destination (it is arbitrary or 'Absurd') means that human beings are forced to give it meaning themselves. How this should be done elicited many different responses, but two influential routes to man's salvation in this world attracted wide attention.

Sartre

Before the war, Sartre was little interested in the political responsibilities of the writer and saw himself as an anti-bourgeois, individualist voice. But the defeat of France and his own captivity converted him into a 'social' being. He did not pledge himself to direct action but began his unfinished trilogy, *Les Chemins de la liberté*, staged the obliquely *résistant* play, *Les Mouches* in 1943 and published *L'Être et le néant* (1943) which made him, after 1945, the leading exponent of French Existentialism. If Sartre was not quite the Resistance hero he would have liked to be, he emerged, as editor of *Les Temps modernes* (1945), as the major exponent of intellectual commitment. The writer carries a burden of responsibility and has a mission to bring about necessary social and political change. By also publishing newspaper articles, making public comments and signing petitions, novelists, playwrights and poets engage with the fundamental issues of their age. For Sartre, history showed that humanism, democracy and economic liberalism were enemies of a freedom which could only be achieved through a version of Marx's workers' revolution.

Camus

Camus, more temperamentally than philosophically exercised by the Absurd, also sought a means of reconciling the individual's responsibility to himself with his human obligations to others. The evolution of his ideas is visible in the ground covered between the awareness of the absurdity of things (*L'Étranger*, 1942), man's duty to rebel against it (*Le Mythe de Sisyphe*, 1942), and *La Peste* (1947) which defines fraternal solidarity as a workable solution. Thereafter, opting for revolt (*L'Homme révolté*, 1951) in preference to revolution, which invariably leads to totalitarianism, he went on to pursue his concern with the human, from which he did not exclude a metaphysical dimension.

'Resistentialism'

By 1947, the division between the two most charismatic intellectuals was clear. As Sartre became more radical and committed to Marxist analysis, Camus turned moderate, reformist and committed to atheistic humanism. The terms of the intellectual debate were set by the Left, which occupied the moral high ground. According to the 'resistentialist' myth, the Right had collaborated *en masse* and were accordingly disqualified from offering a view on anything. Whereas capitalism, increasingly defined by American 'imperialism', was a bourgeois system, communism was an ethical idea. Dissent from this position met with denunciation, as though the real enemy was not fascism or totalitarianism, but liberal thought. At the start of the Cold War, the PCF was committed to the defence of the civilizing values of the USSR against the American threat. Most party members and fellow travellers swallowed their misgivings and gave Stalin the benefit of the doubt. Others considered the PCF too Stalinist by half and were expelled for anti-communism, a crime as great as heresy had once been and, for many, the punishment was the same: excommunication. Alternative views were not welcome in Paris, capital of ideas. Some dissenters were foreigners, like Arthur Koestler and Iganazio Silone, but there were home-grown examples too, like Bernanos, Léon Blum (1872–1950), the moral conscience of French socialism, and Raymond Aron (1905–83), who was sidelined for believing that it is possible to behave consistently without adopting partisan positions. Such non-aligned attitudes were anathema to the PCF and anti-communists alike, but also to Sartre's supporters who to some seemed committed to commitment for commitment's sake.

The 1950s

Sartre, though never a member of the PCF, was the leading spokesman of the intellectual Left. His commitment to the USSR remained intact and his attacks on capitalism, American imperialism, and bourgeois society became more outspoken. In 1951, he took issue with Camus's *'Homme révolté* and a definitive rift followed their bitter public argument. For the Left, Camus, a hero in 1944, had become a renegade for transposing political choices into a moral key.

The recovery of the liberal Right

Slowly at first and then with growing confidence, right-wing opinion regrouped and turned into a plausible extra-parliamentary 'National Opposition'. Survivors of the prewar Maurrassian Right, Vichy die-hards and anti-bolsheviks were joined by those who could not stomach the myth of the Resistance, the post-Liberation purge, the mediocrity of the Fourth Republic, de Gaulle who had fathered it and Existentialism which it had adopted. Mauriac continued to be a thorn in the flesh of the new orthodoxies, the satire of Marcel Aymé showed up the absurdity of thinking by numbers, Boris Vian lampooned Jean-Sol Partre, and the 'Hussards' stood up for flair and freedom against the grim orthodoxies of the postwar years. But their impact was small. The defence of communism and the USSR remained the dominant intellectual position and the Korean War (1950–3) provided an opportunity for further pro-Russian and anti-American propaganda. Even so, Raymond Aron mounted a liberal challenge to left-wing ideologies. L'Opium des intellectuels (1955) confronted pro-communist intellectuals with their illusions and punctured their founding myths and unquestioned beliefs which claimed to pursue high moral ends but used means of the deepest cynicism.

Doubts about the USSR

In 1956, Khrushchev denounced the crimes of Stalin, and Russia invaded Hungary. Here, for many, was proof that the Soviet regime did not represent democracy and they left the PCF. Those who remained did so because they believed that while communism had been betrayed by Stalin, communist ideology was still valid. Until the late 1970s, many French intellectuals continued to be enthusiastic supporters of the Left in many forms, from the anti-bourgeois stance of novelists like Marguerite Duras and the near-Marxist sympathizers of Catholic gauchisants, to the theorists published by Tel Quel magazine.

Colonialism

But with the Revolution still as distant as ever, attention gradually turned to the colonialist issue which, after France's humiliating withdrawal from Indo-China in 1954, focused on the war in Algeria (1954–62). For the Left, colonialism was an example of Western capitalism and ideological imperialism. But the Right protested against the loss of empire and in the acrimonious controversy which surrounded the Algerian War, the discredited Right emerged from the shadows. Yet it was de Gaulle, not the intellectuals, who imposed a solution in 1962 by granting Algeria its independence. By then, the intellectual landscape had changed. The intellectual Right had faded, but the PCF had also demonstrated its inability to begin the process of de-Stalinizing itself. The gap between left-wing intellectuals and the PCF widened further.

1962–68

During the 1960s, old-style political arguments continued, but with an increasingly fragmented commitment to the traditional ideologies. The economic boom and rising public expenditure drew the teeth of the class struggle and the revolution was once more postponed. Anti-colonialism, no longer able to feed off the now-resolved Algerian question, turned its attention to the Third World, where Western imperialism had found new countries to enslave. Cuba and Vietnam became what the USSR had once been – the hope of the 'avenir radieux' – and new heroes appeared, like Castro and Che Guevara, heirs of the old revolutionary struggle. For its part, the Right was forced to recognize the erosion of strict moral values by the general liberalization of attitudes most vigorously expressed by the 'permissiveness' of the popular media. But the extreme Right called the liberals to order by attacking American influence and deploring, on racial grounds, the rise of immigration.

A new intellectual order

During the 1960s, the traditional Left–Right ideological split, while still a source of reductive labels applied to persons and ideas, was challenged by alternative philosophical approaches to a range of issues. The dissatisfaction with old ideas is indicated by the vogue for the New Novel, the New Criticism and the New Wave in cinema. Guy Debord (1931–94), a founder-member of the *Internationale situationniste* (1957–72), sought to rescue art from the new consumerism and to make it a separate social activity to be 'situated' in everyday life. *La Société du spectacle* (1967) argued that social living was a 'show' which masked the reality of inequality and exploitation. The commodification of everyday life and the annexation of political argument by institutionalized political systems alienated individuals from reality and made them spectators of their own lives. Spiritual needs were addressed by Pierre Teilhard de Chardin (1881–1955) who, in *Le Phénomène humain* (1955), developed a theory of evolution which reassured Catholics by showing the compatibility of science and faith.

Structuralism

The philosophical debate, however, remained secular. A new line of enquiry, derived from the Swiss linguistician, Ferdinand de Saussure (1857–1913), began with doubts about the ability of language to mean what it says. From this beginning emerged Structuralism, which overturned Existentialism not by exposing its philosophical weaknesses but by denying its basic premise that Nothingness can be filled with Being, that the Absurd can be defeated by a conscious effort to give it a human, social and political meaning. On the contrary, all human activity is shaped not by reason and will but by pre-existing personal and collective forces. The anthropologist Claude Lévi-Strauss (b. 1908) argued that primitive societies are structured according to myths no less valid than those on which sophisticated nations are built. With *Mythologies* (1957), Roland Barthes revealed the codes, signs and signifying systems which order the world we live in and applied this semiological approach to social phenomena, including literature and language, which are not singular in their meaning but plural. For the influential psychoanalyst Jacques Lacan (1901–81), the unconscious is a language which 'speaks us'. The *Annales* school (founded 1929) turned history away from the study of events towards the search for collective phenomena and 'mentalities', in other words the structures which determine social change. Though never a 'school' of thought, the separate strands of the new thinking found a brand-image in *Tel Quel* (1960–83), its principal mouthpiece. Broadly speaking, Structuralism gave priority to the deep-seated forces which drive language, history and culture. We can say only what language allows us to say, and what we think and do is not merely coloured but determined (1) by our subconscious, and (2) by social, cultural and economic forces. The 'human subject' who claimed to think and act on the basis of pondered, conscious motives, had ceased to be at the centre of anything.

Alienation

Although the new theories were contested vigorously and individuality was defended on humanist grounds, the new synthesis seemed to be confirmed by the progress of consumerism which, though it offered choice, offered only the range of choices which suited the determining power of business and industry. The point was made in fiction (Georges Perec, *Les Choses*, 1965) and cinema (Jacques Tati, *Mon oncle*, 1958; *Playtime*, 1967). More analytical observers diagnosed a deeper malaise which created a 'société bloquée'. The progress of consumerism relegated those least able to participate in it to a condition of 'marginalization', most clearly visible in the growth of a disaffected underclass in city suburbs. Pierre Bourdieu (b. 1930) used the notion of 'cultural capital' to show how dominant groups perpetuate their superiority, for example by establishing an educational system which excludes the working class (*Les Héritiers*, 1964). Such ideas fuelled a climate of intellectual instability. Announcements of the death of the individual subject, sociological analyses showing the inevitability of standardization and uniformity, together with the complacency generated by the buoyancy of capitalism and the authoritarianism of de Gaulle's regime, created, especially among the young, a mood of alienation and dissatisfaction which turned into revolt.

1968–80

In May 1968, students demonstrated in the streets, factory workers struck, and intellectuals, wrong-footed at first, soon joined the fray. Raymond Aron viewed the 'Events' as a utopian psychodrama which did not threaten the *status quo*. Sartre castigated the PCF and the left-wing trades unions for not seizing the opportunity to turn revolt into revolution. The communist Left lost further ground when Russian tanks ended the Czechs' 'Prague Spring' in August and the PCF backed the 'normalization' of the Czech situation. The dream of revolution was again detached from the discredited USSR and was now transferred to Mao, Trotsky and Bakunin, who embodied goals which were to the left of the totalitarian PCF. Marxism had been overtaken by history. But so had de Gaulle, who resigned.

A new intellectual equation

In reality, there were two separate revolts in 1968: the students, with their broad cultural libertarianism, and the workers, who had a more specific agenda. A pay rise and the expansion of the welfare state placated the latter. The former, having secured de Gaulle's departure, waited for promised reforms to materialize. In the event, France settled back to enjoy its continuing prosperity under the avuncular presidency of Georges Pompidou. Yet in the wake of the events of 1968, the mood remained one of fierce contestation.

The *soixante-huitard* spirit

In the early 1970s, France awoke from the collective amnesia which had covered events of the Occupation with a blanket of silence: the novels of Patrick Modiano and films by Marcel Ophuls (*Le Chagrin et la pitié*, 1971) and Louis Malle (*Lacombe Lucien*, 1974) at last forced the French to confront their murky wartime past. The Arab–Israeli war and a new interest in the Holocaust raised the Jewish question in new forms. But more immediate problems clamoured for attention. Issues centring on military service, educational reform, prison conditions, psychiatric treatment, feminist questions, the communist domination of the unions, matters of race and immigration, the role of the state in radio and television, and the 'permissive' moral legacy of the 1960s, were discussed in an atmosphere of mistrust of the state.

A new 'Resistance'

Until 1974, left-wing intellectuals made the running. A new 'Resistance' opposed Americanization, state complicity with capitalism, and the conservatism of the electorally dominant Right. Demonstrators manifested against the slowness of university reform and in favour of abortion. If the PCF failed to win back hearts and minds, Mao now seemed to point the way ahead. His 'cultural revolution' had enabled China to establish the dictatorship of the proletariat which was served, not led, by the Chinese Communist Party, and the Chinese state was in the process of 'withering away', to use the term Marx applied to the fate of the *bourgeoisie*. It was a view championed notably by the *Tel Quel* group. But by 1974, it was apparent that the 'Asian Eden' was as much an illusion as Stalin's 'Workers' Paradise' had been, and the Maoist fashion did not survive the death of Mao in 1976.

Post-Structuralism

By then, the Structuralism of the 1960s had developed new forms and given birth to new intellectual leaders. The historian Michel Foucault (1926–84) argued that, by Descartes's time, language had already ceased to refer to real things but to systems of values and ideas. Words like 'madness' or 'prison' are shorthand for structures of repression which society uses to discipline the population. The effect is to objectivize the individual who, far from being free, is enslaved by normative pressures, for those who do not conform are 'sick', 'mad', 'deviant' or 'delinquent'. To the powerful influence of Lacan were added the ideas of Gilles Deleuze (1925–95) who argued that man's nature cannot be separated from his culture. The combined effect of such thinking was not only to undermine the authoritarian state but also to identify 'society' as an enemy. Communal attitudes rooted in a symbolic order shaped by factors outside the power of government (language, history, collective memory and so on) explained the marginalization and persecution of minorities and the denial of rights to significant sections of the population, in the workplace, for example, where the employed were seen as pawns in the capitalist game. In the same way the immigrant population was victimized by prejudice, and women were oppressed by the male order. The 1970s saw an upsurge of feminism of two distinct kinds: the 'materialists', who campaigned for measures to improve the material condition of women, and the 'reformists', who used psychoanalysis, language theory and other Post-Structuralist tools to challenge institutional ways of thinking defined by men. For a moment, Sartrean 'commitment' was revived and of all the left-wing movements of the decade, feminism was the most effective.

Feminism

After 1900, agitation in favour of women's rights – suffrage, the pay and conditions of women workers together with issues like contraception and abortion – met with little measurable success. But of whatever political colour, it was opposed by the generalized misogyny: women were subdued by the Church, exploited by the Third Republic, marginalized by virile fascism and ignored by Marxism. But prewar campaigns and the awareness of the part played by women during the war finally attracted the support of both the communists and de

Gaulle, and the right to vote was granted in October 1944. In the pressure of postwar reconstruction, women's lives did not change significantly. However, the feminist case was forcefully expressed by Simone de Beauvoir. *Le Deuxième Sexe* (1949) provided an intellectual argument based on Existentialist, historical and sociological analysis. But though it was later regarded as a founding text, its immediate impact was small and the 1950s provided no impetus for a feminist movement. Interest increased, however, in the 1960s with the wider participation of women in education and the economy. Pressure groups succeeded in bringing about practical reforms (a revision of the marriage laws, 1965; the liberalization of contraception, 1967) and further gains, including the right to abortion (1975), were made under Giscard d'Estaing (president 1974–81) who appointed a secretary for the condition of women. Since 1981, women have acquired further social and employment rights, although equality of the sexes, enshrined in law, has proved more difficult to apply in practice.

After 1968, encouraged by the example of militant American feminists, a more sharply focused form of feminism developed around the Mouvement de Libération des Femmes (MLF). The goal ceased to be absorption into a system created and run by men but the creation of a new consciousness which challenged a phallocentric domination so pervasive that it had annexed language itself: how was it possible to use words in a new sense when they were invested with male concepts? Remaining outside party politics (regarded as a male domain) and working through women's groups, periodicals and women's writing, the new feminism generated a wide range of literary and theoretical texts which explored questions of gender, class, psychoanalysis, language and history. It took issue with Marx and Freud but also with Structuralism and Post-Structuralism, which all viewed woman only in relation to the masculine order. Since the late 1970s, the new feminism has championed the notion of difference ('alterity') and attempted to give woman a new definition through the multiplicity of writings as the means of establishing a distinctive alternative to male attitudes, practices and institutions. The concept of *écriture féminine* has, since mid-1970s, appealed to a wide range of women who express themselves through theatre, the cinema, autobiography and fiction long and short.

The retreat from revolution

By the mid-1970s, the revolution had still not come. The intellectual Left maintained a faith in non-Stalinist communism through Louis Althusser (1918–90). For him, Marx's historical analysis was a historical break in the habit of ideological thinking, so that Marxism was not a form of ethical humanism but a revolutionary idea. But affluence and the more relaxed social climate eroded the inequality and injustices which political commitment was pledged to change. The class struggle grew less tense, women achieved significant material advances and the welfare boom gave the state and society a more human face. Manipulation there might be, but at least citizens were wealthier and felt less like victims. Moreover, while the enemy remained capitalism, capitalism was now a global phenomenon, not a specifically French issue. What problems remained (drugs, delinquency, race and immigration) hardly called for revolution.

The right-wing reaction

Not all intellectuals had been enthused by the events of 1968 and some regarded its libertarian aftermath as the imposition of the new conformity of 'correctness'. The ideological Right reacted against governments which had conceded too much to the clamouring Left. The liberal right, led by Raymond Aron, maintained its stance: it continued to resist both totalitarian ideology and the non-egalitarian, anti-democratic right. But more extreme views were expressed after 1974. These ranged from a hostility to equality to a detestation of the new multi-racial society which undermined 'Frenchness' by adding unassimilable foreign elements to the 'melting-pot' and threatened to produce an inferior sub-culture. Unlike the old nationalism of Maurras, which was based on the defence of native traditions, the new nationalism was Europe-centred and based on race. For equality, it substituted the 'right to be different' and adopted anti-liberal, anti-American and ethnocentric positions. Such views, formulated notably by 'the new Maurras', Alain de Benoist (b. 1943), survived and proved useful to the extreme nationalism of Jean-Marie le Pen. Their popularity was reinforced by the decomposition of Marxism and coincided with the union of left-wing parties which brought François Mitterrand and a socialist government to power in 1981. By then, the New Right was a significant player in the political game.

The *nouveaux philosophes*

Intellectual opposition to the ideological Left emerged around 1975 in the writings of the New Philosophers, most of whom had, in 1968, been militant supporters of Marx, Mao, revolution, and freedom. In *Les Maîtres penseurs* (1977), André Glucksmann (b. 1937) rejected abstract ideology, for all ideologies lead to oppression. Marxists, Trostkyites and Maoists could no longer argue that communism was intact and undamaged by its 'betrayal' by Stalin and Mao. His moral critique of ideologies and states was echoed by Claude Lefort (*Un homme en trop*, 1976), by ex-socialist Jean-François Revel (*La Tentation totalitaire*, 1975) who not only denounced Stalinism but also showed that intellectuals had been in part responsible for promoting its myths, and by Bernard-Henri Lévy (b. 1948: *La Barbarie à visage humain*, 1977; *L'Idéologie française*, 1981) who diagnosed fascist tendencies in the intellectual Left. The *nouveaux philosophes*, a very loose grouping, retreated from ideology as a way of thinking because abstract ideas invariably had the effect of producing injustice and enslavement. Because they were united in their resistance to one such ideology, communism, they were deemed by their left-wing critics to have crossed to the Right. Drawing on ideas first aired in the 1950s, they offered a kind of moral alternative, though their impact on the 1981 elections was small: the electoral victory of the socialists was not attributable to the intellectuals but to the political Left. By 1983, the 'de-Marxing' of the Left had turned most French intellectuals into fervent anti-communists. Thus the process which had begun in 1956, had slowed during the Algerian War, accelerated after 1968, and was boosted in the mid-1970s by revelations about Russia and China, seemed to have reached a conclusion at the time when members of the PCF finally accepted office in a French government in 1983.

Since 1980

In the early 1980s, the old intellectual guard – Sartre, Barthes, Lacan, Foucault, Althusser, Aron – died out and was replaced by a new generation of high-profile 'intellocrats' who wielded great influence from their base in journalism, publishing and the most prestigious university institutions. They were regarded in some quarters with suspicion. Yet while media exposure threatened to dilute ideas, it also presented a continuation of the *haute vulgarisation* which had started with Voltaire and identified ideology with personalities, from Barrès and Gide to Sartre's flair for publicity.

An intellectual mafia?

Around 1980, intellectuals themselves became an object for sociological study and their image suffered. Not only were they a 'mafia' but their validity as thinkers was questioned: they followed intellectual fashion, claimed changes of mind were part of their 'evolution', and relied on counter-argument rather than on new ideas. Positions which had been distinct now converged, notably the New Right and the New Philosophers. In the 1980s, rather as 'schools' had turned into 'isms', intellectual groupings mutated into 'networks'. Interest revived in right-wing authors like Drieu and Céline but the intellectual Right retreated as Le Pen's extremist politics gathered momentum and the New Philosophers failed to develop positive positions beyond their common denunciation of Marxist ideas. Meanwhile, the left-wing Catholicism of *Esprit* maintained a kind of social-democratic stance, though it found no spokesmen in the tradition of Léon Bloy, Bernanos and Mauriac. While the PCF continued to lose support, the old Left was represented by ex-communists, the anti-colonialist rump, and those who still clung to the spirit of 1968.

The retreat from dogmatism

By and large, the new generation of French intellectuals, characterized especially by their anti-communism, reflected rather than directed social trends. While suspicious of bourgeois humanism, they were open to anti-militarism, pacifism, ecologism and regionalism. They argued in favour of giving minorities a voice and abandoned dogmatic positions. Sartrean commitment became redundant and Aron's liberalism now appealed particularly to the New Philosophers. Glucksmann and Lévy, sceptical of all ideological systems, approached old problems from a moral direction, urging ethical foreign policies and aid for the Third World. But the old ambition of the intellectual (to identify universal principles in response to large questions) had ended in failure and now seemed impossible: Marx's belief that history leads to an unknown future goal collapsed with the Berlin Wall in 1989. The intellectual reaction to world catastrophes (from the Aids epidemic to massacres in Bosnia, Iraq, Rwanda and Kosovo) was rooted not in doctrine but in humanitarian interventionism. If this was hardly an ideology, it was at least an attitude. And it would become a form of politics.

History and philosophy

Meanwhile, intellectual activity continued on two major fronts, history and philosophy. The first maintained the impetus of the *Annales* school while the second continued to invest heavily in psychoanalysis, sociology, culture and the problem of language. But both tendencies confirmed the now generally held view that the rationalist tradition was suspect because its premises were false. Thus Pierre Nora (*Les Lieux de mémoire*, 1984–92) argued that ideas of 'identity' and 'nation' were rooted less in the historical 'narrative' built around Charlemagne, Joan of Arc and Bastille Day, than in the 'realms of memory', an amorphous, Darwinian but communifying awareness of the past which made the 'myths' of Versailles or the 'genius' of the French language the constant rallying points of Frenchness. The broad 'philosophical' current similarly pointed to the determinism which shapes and transforms attitudes, power structures and institutions, not by conscious dirigisme, but through deeper mechanisms. The sociologist Alain Touraine (b. 1925) emphasized the evolutionary nature of social forces. For Jacques Derrida, totalizing words like 'tolerance' or 'freedom' have no meaning outside history, for meaning derives from the 'metaphysics' of the speaker's present, that is, the particular point he or she occupies in the continuum. General concepts have no validity if they are not broken down (deconstructed) to allow for pluralism, difference and, above all, inclusiveness. All that is possible is a process of examination and re-examination which can have no end. Jean-François Lyotard (1924–98) diagnosed language and meaning as 'drift'. *La Condition postmoderne* (1979) took as its premise the death of absolutes, certainties and general principles, and therefore the impossibility of consensus through universal 'master narratives'. For Jean Baudrillard (b. 1929), the number and variety of forms of communication drown meaning, disrupt the relationship between signs (words, pictures, etc.) and the reality they are supposed to represent: the image of America (projected by Disneyland and cinema) is more real than the real America. The result is that human will and responsibility are threatened by the bombardment of information which Baudrillard viewed as a new phase of capitalism. 'Simulation' creates a 'hyperreality' designed to stimulate consumption but, in human and moral terms, it undermines our ability to know true from false and thus to make informed decisions about the world in which we live.

Postmodernism

Such ideas are at the heart of Postmodernism which is less the successor of 'Modernity' than its rejection. 'Modernity' (that is, the use and achievements, since Descartes, of reason) postulated certainties: knowledge is real. This assumption had allowed the Enlightenment to believe that science can master nature and deliver progress; it had enabled Freud to define the psyche, and Marx to describe the social process. Since such self-sufficient 'sealed' systems have failed to produce a convincing, overarching Order, it seems likely that all totalizing efforts will meet the same fate. Better, then, to concede that no universal vision is possible, concentrate on differences and resist the powers which seek to make the world conform to 'Modernist' assumptions and the 'stable' structures of hierarchy, thought, and culture. Universal concepts are illusions because all values are situationally determined.

A new pragmatism?

Some, like Alain Finkelkraut (b. 1949: *La Défaite de la pensée*, 1987), reacted against the defeatism of a point of view which denied general ideas and values, made a pair of boots as culturally significant as Shakespeare, and relativized all thought. But despite attempts to reject Postmodern nihilism by reverting to older forms of logic, the intelligentsia in the 1990s remained wary of adopting 'universalist' positions. Instead, on Left and Right, they adopted increasingly empirical positions on social and political issues. They worried less about Justice than about specific cases of injustice. They highlighted problems associated with *laïcité* (for a century the republic's defence against sectarian oppression), unearthed surrogate proletariats (the Third World, illegal immigrants), and followed a humanitarian line on crises at home and abroad. Thus by the end of the century, the distinction between Left and Right, once a yawning chasm, had been blurred. Battles were no longer fought over general principles by representatives of conflicting ideologies but over specific problems by pragmatically motivated democrats and republicans. Politically, communism has faded badly and the old Right of Maurras survives only in the National Front. That this is so is explicable by the fact that both wings of the new intelligentsia, liberal and conservative, have a common origin. The leading republican intellectual, Régis Debray (b. 1941), was once a revolutionary and Maoist activist, while the prominent democrat, Daniel Cohn-Bendit (b. 1945), was a leader of the student revolt. Republicans promote the idea of France as an autonomous nation state and the best defender of equal rights in the tradition of 1789. They champion the unity and sovereignty of the Republic against regionalism and decentralization at home and, abroad, dislike Europe, the global economy and the Americanization of culture. Democrats form a broad-based group which remains faithful to the libertarian spirit of 1968, is suspicious of the authoritarian 'nation' and supports the rights of citizens against bureaucracy, consumerism and all power structures. Supported by the New Philosophers and encouraged by the collapse of communism in 1989, they nevertheless include free-marketeers and anti-interventionists in their ranks. In January 2000, Cohn-Bendit formed a new tendency, the 'Troisième gauche verte', dedicated to the socialist proposition that peoples can liberate themselves by common effort and the non-socialist principle that they can best do so by adopting certain pro-market policies. This mixture of leftism, greenism, libertarianism, humanitarianism and economic liberalism was designed to appeal to the widest public.

Conclusion

In the last quarter century, the philosophical base of French intellectualism has weakened and political questions are framed less in terms of universal principles (denounced as myths by thinkers since the 1960s) than in practical responses to issues as they arise. Yet while it would seem that a new empiricism has contaminated the Cartesian tradition of rationalism, French politics has always operated on a basis of pragmatism. Considered objectively, the most successful intellectuals have not been Barrès, Gide, Sartre and the Structuralist tribe, but politicians with vision, like Blum or de Gaulle, who steered the country through real perils. But this would be to misunderstand the significance of France's intellectual elite, which has always formed an extra-parliamentary, unofficial opposition, impossible to ignore, a permanent source of ideas, argument and militancy which consistently raised the level of public debate. Yet its most recent manifestation, an uncharacteristic eclecticism, has marginalized literature, which has long since ceased to supply artists and seers offering prescriptions for all social and moral ills. By 2000, its territory had shrunk and its new home is the sectional group and real life.

Literature

Poetry

In 1900, poetry, still absorbing the lessons of Baudelaire, was dominated by three voices: Verlaine, the melodious poet of subjective emotion; Rimbaud, who had perfected the prose poem and bequeathed a new mythology of revolt; and Mallarmé, practitioner of a hermetic craft, who had pursued an absolute which he knew to be illusory and sought purity in the difficult, meticulous art of abstraction. The line from Verlaine was continued by Apollinaire and the Fantaisistes. Out of Rimbaud came Surrealism, which would leave its mark on so many poets, while the spirit of Mallarmé would survive through Valéry to Yves Bonnefoy and the formalist poets of the second half of the century.

Despite the controversy they provoked, these separate strands were acculturated by the retreat from entrenched literary doctrine, which steadily lost its hold on all forms of writing. The Symbolist revolution liberated the poem from formal rules and freed poets to pursue their impulses. Poetry was increasingly perceived not as a formal expression of thought or theme but as a quality, a way of seeing and feeling which not only crossed the boundaries of genre but was open to the interpenetration of all artistic forms. A poem could be an idea or mood articulated in conventional metrical form. But it could equally be the product, expressed with scant regard for 'literary' principles, of every conceivable state of the conscious or unconscious mind, taking every imaginable form and neither requiring nor seeking any kind of external justification. The poetry of the twentieth century lies between these extremes of regularity and irregularity, mind, spirit and sensation. Steadily abandoning its commitment to the old rhetoric, it favoured new registers in which to put its questions and suggest tentative answers.

1900–18

After 1900, poetry continued to build on the forms and ideas developed by the nineteenth century. But cracks soon appeared in the smooth façade of Belle-Époque self-confidence. The Dreyfus Affair, the gospel of *laïcité*, the growth of socialism, the arrival of the machine age and increasing urbanization alerted poets to the emergence of a new order. After 1908, Péguy, apostle of Christian socialism, identified Catholicism as a necessary continuity. His stylized, loosely textured litanies are marred by repetition which, intended to generate a mood of incantation, become tedious. Yet at his best he has a power of conviction and a simplicity which stand comparison with Hugo. Claudel, a greater poet, the last of the Romantics, latter-day psalmist or perhaps a reincarnation of the baroque, first made his mark with the *Cinq grandes odes* (1910). Against the hesitations of Baudelaire, Rimbaud and Mallarmé, he pointed to a triumphant certainty: the immanence of God in the wonders of the created world. The ceremonial solemnity of his epic vision was expressed through a more flexible poetic line. The *verset claudélien*, a semi-Biblical union of prose and verse, orchestrated pitch, stress and syllabic length, followed the rhythms of speech and proved attractive to later poets who rebelled against strict metres but were reluctant to adopt the deregulated *vers libre*. Both Péguy and Claudel defined the human spirit in Christian terms, but other poets explored alternative varieties of mysticism. While Anna de Noailles (1876–1933) perpetuated the self-indulgent pantheism of the Romantics, Oscar Lubicz-Milosz (1877–1939) looked to the Bible, the Kabbala and Einstein for a synthesis of poetry, metaphysics and science in an attempt to define 'le langage pur des temps de la fidélité et de la connaissance'.

World and mind

However, for Paul Valéry, the major disciple of Mallarmé, the spirit was of less immediate concern than 'le drame de la génération d'une oeuvre'. Fascinated by the processes of the mind, he sought an accommodation between action and contemplation, the artist and the philosopher, in a poetry whose virtuoso control of classical forms expressed (and on occasion fused) the abstractions of the absolute self with the sensations which bind the body to the world. Yet while *La Jeune Parque* (1917) and *Charmes* (1922) were greatly admired as the embodiment of a new classicism, Valéry's influence on his successors was small. Many of his contemporaries, abandoning Mallarmean abstraction, reverted instead to what Baudelaire had called 'la beauté moderne' and preferred to explore the world around them. Jules Romains and fellow Unanimists like Georges Duhamel, Luc Durtain (1881–1959) or Charles Vildrac (1883–1973) found their subject in the urban landscape, while the cosmopolitan component of Modernism was established by Valéry Larbaud (1881–1957) and Victor Segalen (1878–1919) before being taken up by Apollinaire and Blaise Cendrars (1887–1961). Léon-Paul Fargue (1876–1947) was the type of city *flâneur* who chronicled Paris and, increasingly drawn to the prose poem, wove engaging and often acerbic patterns around his childhood and youth. No less disabused were Fantaisistes like Francis Carco, Jean-Marc Bernard (1881–1915) and Jean-Paul Toulet (1867–1920) whose *Contrerimes* (1920), verbally agile, ironic and self-deprecating, defined a significant area of modernist sensibility.

The 'modern' spirit

But a more durable reaction against Symbolist decadence was provided by Guillaume Apollinaire (1880–1918), catalyst and symbol of the modern spirit. *Alcools* (1913) revealed him as a vibrant and accessible lyrical poet while *Calligrammes* (1918) contained the finest war poetry produced in France. Apollinaire was instrumental in extending Cubist and Futurist principles to poetry, which was no longer required to present everyday reality according to some external organizing principle but combined verbal fragments multi-dimensionally and discontinuously, as in Cendrars's 'livre simultané', *La Prose du Transibérien* (1913). *Alcools* abandoned punctuation and *Calligrammes* arranged poems on the page as fountains or falling rain. But Apollinaire's experiments were less bold than they seemed. For the figure of 'pauvre Guillaume', melancholy, engaging and nostalgic, was rooted in older lyrical traditions which have continued to attract readers. Around him, others, like Pierre-Albert Birot (1876–1967) or the precocious Jean Cocteau (1889–1963) who classed all his writings as forms of poetry, enrolled in the new avant-garde and took up the challenge. The most influential would prove to be Pierre Reverdy (1889–1960), a literary Cubist, who in 1918 in his review

Nord-Sud defined the poetic image as the fortuitous *rapprochement* of two unconnected realities, an idea which would become an article of faith for the Surrealists.

1918–40

Lautréamont and Laforgue had revolted against reason and Rimbaud's 'dérèglement de tous les sens' had opened a route to the unconscious. The anti-rational tendency had been continued in the anarchism of Jarry and the fantasies of Raymond Roussel (1877–1933), Max Jacob (1876–1944) and Apollinaire (both as poet and *conteur*). There was still a general assumption, however, that inner drives could be trusted and consciously directed. Before 1914, most poets adopted a sceptical attitude to the intellect but did not doubt the reality of the external world, nor did they believe that their instincts and feelings were unreliable.

Dada and Surrealism

But the shock of the Great War and the discovery of Freud revealed that the world was out of control and that the human spirit was as fragile as the mind on which it depends. Dada, which took root in Paris in 1919, savaged the cultural assumptions of humanism, which had produced, not truth and harmony, but violence, injustice and poverty. Boosted in 1920 by the arrival of Tristan Tzara (1896–1963), it mounted highly publicized exhibitions of non-art objects and gave recitals of anti-poems. Its 'grand travail négatif' produced little of lasting value but its impetus was appropriated by André Breton (1896–1966) who undertook a systematic exploration of the creative possibilities of the unconscious. Once freed of the censorship of logic, morality and aesthetics, the imagination could be released through hypnosis, automatic writing and other techniques, unmediated by the mind. The goal was the fusion of dream and reality into a *surréalité* which would overturn the bourgeois world and open visionary perspectives.

Surrealism was as much a social provocation as an artistic movement. It generated a literary polemic but developed no aesthetic, nor were its works superior to the productions of those poets, like Rimbaud and Lautréamont, whom it honoured as its spiritual begetters. Surrealists did, however, renew forgotten themes (childhood, the primitive, the strange) and revealed the possibilities of dream, which fascinated many poets who wrote within the group or in its shadow. The movement faded quickly and its achievements were more marked in prose than in verse. Even Breton, though committed to its essential *humour noir* and despite the disturbing quality of his imagery, was more cerebral and controlled in collections like *Clair de terre* (1923) than in prose texts like *Nadja* where he came closer to the 'convulsive' beauty he sought. Some remained steadfast, like Benjamin Péret (1899–1959), the fevered liberator of language, and Tzara, whose *L'Homme approximatif* (1931) packaged fantastic visions in startling images. But others, like Philippe Soupault (1897–1990), who had explored *Les Champs magnétiques* with Breton in 1922, left the group over doctrinal issues or went on to develop areas of Surrealism best attuned to their own sensibilities. Robert Desnos (1900–45), who had set sail on the 'vague des rêves' in *Rrose Sélavy* (1922), reverted to classical forms and the popular lyric. Both Jacques Prévert (1900–77) and Raymond Queneau (1903–76) took up the anarchical, satirical side of Surrealism, while René Char (1907–88), a group member until 1937, went on to express the elusive unconscious in consciously controlled language as meticulous in its way as that of Mallarmé. Even Paul Éluard (1895–1952), the most original Surrealist poet, never fully subscribed to the practice of automatic writing and both as a poet of sensual love and, later, of human fraternity, maintained a measure of conscious creative input.

Non-aligned poets

Although Surrealism and its reverberations dominated the poetic vision of the interwar years, many poets remained free of its spell. Catherine Pozzi (1882–1934) maintained the philosophical tradition and Marie Noël (1883–1967) published *Les Chansons et les heures* (1920), the first of many collections, classical in form, lyrical in rhythm and strong on simple charm, which made her the foremost Catholic poet of her generation. New themes emerged, from the diversity of creation and man's alienation from it, to the search for some way of transcending it, often with myth and mysticism as routes to the deep personal and collective self. Established poets, like Reverdy or the austere Pierre-Jean Jouve (1887–1976), continued to develop and new names emerged or were confirmed: Jules Supervielle

(1884–1960), with his message of reconciliation; Saint-John Perse (1887–1975), the epic observer of man's exile from himself and the world and celebrant of the cosmic power of nature's forces; Henri Michaux (1899–1984), who launched his defence of man against 'les puissances environnantes du monde hostile'; or Patrice de la Tour du Pin (1911–75), who opened his 'theopoetic' account with a volume, *La Quête de joie* (1933), which used legend to give point to spiritual concerns expressed with classical purity.

Matters of form

By 1940, the forms of poetry were as free as the matters which they expressed. Verse as a discipline had come under systematic attack in the 1880s by proponents of *vers libre*. By 1914, the absence of punctuation, the irregular spacing of lines and other graphic arrangements seemed to threaten strict metre. In fact, basic rhythms were not displaced. Apollinaire dispensed with commas but rang with octosyllables, and beneath the prose poems and *laisses* of Perse the Hugolian alexandrine rumbled on. Valéry maintained the formal conventions, though sense-rhythms often dislocate his line. Breton, who sought to revolutionize poetry, wrote with classical discipline and Jacques Audiberti (1899–1965) turned on 'le vieux robinet lyrique' in more or less regular, rhymed verse. The tonic accent no longer dominated, sub-accents were allowed to undermine measure, and rhyme – displaced, internal or merely associative – was used more flexibly to start resonances rather than impose echoes. Prosodic innovations were syntactical, stylistic and typographic rather than metrical and the major development was Claudel's *verset* which allowed moments of silence which are as necessary to speech as rests are to music. The adaptable, extensible *verset* illustrates the principle which still marks the limit of poetic expression: the rhythm of sentence structure and sense-units is regulated by the effect poetic expression is intended to have on the ear.

1940–45

The Second World War suspended aesthetic quarrels, restored a sense of mission to poetry and gave the public a taste for poems. In 1940, Louis Aragon (1897–1982), a founding member of the Surrealist movement, called for a return to the old prosody and rhyme and, with *Le Crève-coeur*, offered poetry as 'une arme pour l'homme désarmé'. Clandestine presses published *poètes casqués* as did reviews like Pierre Segher's *Poésie* (1940–8) and *Confluences* (1941–50). Poems circulated in roneotyped form and Éluard's 'Liberté', the most famous wartime poem, was dropped over occupied France by the RAF. Immediate, vivid and accessible, war poetry dealt with the tragic sense of life, the horrors of war, the dead and those who mourned them, captivity, and the plight of the nation. A focus for the spirit of resistance, it was, however, a *poésie de circonstance* which, once the conflict ended, turned into so many dried leaves: indignation and sincerity are not enough to make great art. Yet more than sturdiness of spirit was expressed in, say, the prison-camp poetry of Jean Cassou (1897–1986: *Trente sonnets composés au secret*, 1944) or Jean Cayrol (b. 1911: *Poèmes de la nuit et du brouillard*, 1945). It was also the experience of imprisonment which shaped *Les Rois-Mages* (1943), the first collection of André Frénaud (1907–73). But the war was equally crucial to the development of major poets like Éluard and Char, who wrote not only of abnegation, sacrifice and pain but also of the 'counter-terror' of love and humanity, while Pierre Emmanuel (1916–84) renewed the tradition of Catholic eloquence at a moment of history which set a low value on life.

The École de Rochefort

In 1941, the École de Rochefort(-sur-Loire), like Aragon, put aside the intellectualism and oneiric conceits of Surrealism and wrote instead of nature, love and human solidarity in directly lyrical terms. The original members included René-Guy Cadou (1920–51) and Jean Rousselot (b. 1913) but the group quickly attracted other poets committed to communicating everyday experience directly. They included G.-E. Clancier (b. 1914), Jean Follain (1903–71) and Maurice Fombeure (1906–81) who wrote of 'la terre végétale' (the subtitle of Cadou's best collection) in terms which were less regionalist than celebratory. The École de Rochefort was a focus for the most cohesive and varied group of poets operating between 1941 and 1961. Committed to more or less regular verse and friendly to rhyme, it rejected poetry which took language as its subject and made obscurity a virtue. It influenced poets as different as Frénaud, Eugène Guillevic (1907–97) and Jacques Réda (b. 1929) and dispersed only when overtaken by the formalist vogue of the 1960s.

1945–60

If Occupied France had responded positively to the return to direct feeling and regular form, it also saw a revival of verse that was sung: 'Maréchal, nous voilà!' was designed to rally the population to Pétain while the 'Chant des partisans' became the voice of Resistance. Most commercial songs aired during the war were bracingly cheerful or sentimental, and they perpetuated the popular view that poetry meant familiar rhythms and rhymes. Yet not all lyrics were banal. The war gave a new impetus to the old *chansonnier* tradition of protest and satire which, since the Belle Époque, had found new homes, first in the *café-concert* and music hall and then, since the 1920s, in the phonograph record, the wireless and the cinema. Aristide Bruant (1851–1925), the first singer-songwriter to be recorded, had sung of life in the streets of Paris, while in the 1930s singers like Fréhel and Édith Piaf (1915–63) turned the lyrics of their songs into personal dramas of hope, joy and despair. Most songs were technically proficient but depended both on the quality of the performance and the personality of the performer. A distinction, however, is to be made between prolific lyricists like Vincent Scotto or André Willemetz, and Charles Trenet (1913–2001) who, before and during the war, kept popular song in touch with the traditions of French poetry: he echoed the ludic vein of Charles Cros and Max Jacob but also preserved the nostalgic charm of Verlaine.

After 1946, while the success of the commercial song was a matter more of music than words, 'French' song was valued primarily for what it said. It secured a lasting place in the growing mass culture, its profile raised by performers like Yves Montand and Juliette Gréco. First heard in the cabarets and clubs of the Left Bank, it commented on life and love, society and politics, in terms which ranged from anti-bourgeois satire to protest and revolt. A form of committed writing, it maintained contact with the radical traditions of literature both in its choice and treatment of themes. It benefited from its link with popular music, a key ingredient of postwar youth culture, and from performance and electronic diffusion. Both Léo Ferré (1919–93) and Georges Brassens (1921–81) set poets from Villon to Rimbaud and Aragon to music but they also acquired a strong following with their own defiant verses. The line was continued by Boris Vian (1920–59), Guy Béart (b. 1930) and, in increasingly radical terms, by Jacques

Brel (1929–78) and Serge Gainsbourg (1928–92), whose provocations turned him into a cult anti-hero. By the 1980s, abetted by the audio-visual revolution, singer-songwriters, with albums which were the modern equivalent of the verse collection, had long been established cultural figures and for the wider audience offered a more palatable definition of poetry than the 'difficult' poets.

Continuities and renewal

Between these two extremes, a more intimate note was struck by Jacques Prévert, an established writer of song lyrics, who captured the flavour of ordinary life with quirky observation and verbal invention. In the hugely successful *Paroles* (1946) and the collections which followed, he managed to be both popular and sophisticated, qualities also achieved by Queneau and Oulipo poets like Jacques Roubaud (b. 1932). Although such verse could strike deeper notes, as with Jean Tardieu (1903–95), and achieve high levels of verbal dexterity, its success derived from its light touch, humour, and its air of improvised triviality. Greater challenges were laid down by the poets of modernity – Reverdy, Jouve, Éluard, Perse – who were at the height of their powers, while Surrealists like Breton and Péret continued to seek ways of fusing mind and imagination. Post-Liberation uncertainties gave an urgency to the dispossessed self projected by Armand Robin (1912–61) and the brutal reminders of man's inhumanity powerfully expressed in the *Apoèmes* (1947) of Henri Pichette (b. 1924). For La Tour du Pin, Pierre Emmanuel and Jean-Claude Renard (b. 1922), man's duty was to accept his essentially religious nature. Others were impelled to remind him of his political obligations. Communism, despite the talents of Aragon and Guillevic, failed to produce great poetry, however, nor did world events (Hiroshima, the Cold War, Indochina) inspire poets. The Algerian War did not produce, on the French side, any poet of stature, although intensely felt poetry written in the shadow of colonialism was supplied by Léopold Senghor (1906–2001), Aimé Césaire (b. 1913) and Édouard Glissant (b. 1928). Sometimes in fixed metres (Renard, Guillevic, Olivier Larronde), poets wrote of isolation, alienation and human solidarity. They explored the relations of man with himself, the world, and the sacred, extracting meaning and myth from things, and facing the eternal problem of the elusiveness of reality and the unreliability of language. Poets whose promise was already recognized in 1945 went on to build a considerable *oeuvre*, Char with the problem of how we should inhabit our world which is eternally under threat, and Michaux with a restless quest for ways of multiplying and escaping the self. Both favoured the prose poem, as did Francis Ponge (1899–1988) who explored the otherness of objects and the arbitrariness of language in detailed evocations of the matter and movement of things. André Frénaud used 'l'énergie du désespoir' (*Il n'y a pas de paradis*, 1962) to metamorphose reality and assert the humanity of man: his work is the profession of faith of a man who cannot believe.

1960–75

The lyrical revival born of the war expired with it and after 1945 poetry, dense, elliptical and 'difficult', attracted a diminishing readership. Its language, often hermetic and esoteric, was a factor in creating public mistrust of poets, who often wrapped their work in mysteries which were further deepened by the abstruse commentaries of critics who explained the 'New Novel' but served 'modern' poetry much less well. After 1960, direct reflections and celebrations of reality were undermined by the emphasis placed by Structuralism on linguistics and the human sciences. It was a time when poetry could no longer be a direct communication with a responsive public and became, very largely, a private experience. A wave of intellectual formalism washed over poetic expression and language was promoted as its proper study and true consummation.

From the offices of *Tel Quel*, Marcelin Pleynet (b. 1933) explored the workings of the language of poetry and promoted the group's view that a poem was the product of a writing act and its own and only subject. Michel Deguy (b. 1930) also sought to fuse poetry and poetic theory by exploring ways of inserting the signs and discourses of the modern world into a modern poetic. The review *Change* (1968–83) opposed *Tel Quel* doctrine, arguing that 'dismantling' forms was less important than changing them, and its anti-intellectualism was reflected by Oulipo writers who rejected personal lyricism, sought the laws of poetry and accepted new constraints. Opposition to abstract intellectualism also came from the writers associated with the review *L'Éphémère* (1966–72). All were in their forties and some were already regarded as the finest poets of their generation. The formalist concerns of André du Bouchet (b. 1924) are visible in his exploded syntax and experiments with typography, but his purpose was to capture mental and bodily sensations and give us access to who we really are. Yves Bonnefoy (b. 1923) had begun by accepting that words come between us and the material world, obscuring not clarifying, separating not joining. But the world is not 'excarnate', that is, susceptible only of being conceptualized into lifeless abstractions, but 'incarnate' and capable of being made ours. This he attempted to achieve through philosophical and theological explorations of the spiritual and the sacred which he related to our familiar and intimate experiences of objects and of each other. Bonnefoy converted existence into consciousness, and consciousness into beauty and, by the end of the century, was regarded as one of its great poets.

While Bonnefoy had remained immune to Surrealism, which ended as a movement in 1967, others continued to explore its possibilities, with Alain Bosquet (1919–98), for example, moving beyond it towards the muscular 'dérision fervente' of later collections like *Bourreaux et acrobates* (1989). Surrealist iconoclasm was now extended by the impact of the American Beat Generation. Franck Venaille (b. 1936), who had given a vivid response to the Algerian War, wrote forcefully of death, sex and memory in terms which borrowed from jazz, cinema and painting. Bernard Noël (b. 1930) aimed to make poetry a 'langue vivante' which encompassed the relationship between body, the word and identity. Eschewing such provocations, the Swiss Philippe Jaccottet (b. 1925) scrutinized natural signs for human and spiritual meaning, while Cairo-born Edmond Jabès (1913–91) continued to build his mystical synthesis of word and world. With others, like the Lebanese Salah Stétié (b. 1929), or Lorand Gaspar, born in Transylvania in 1925, they confirmed the growth of a cosmopolitan tendency which was also reflected in the space allotted by the growing number of little magazines to francophone poets and foreign poetry in translation.

The events of 1968 generated quantities of political doggerel but failed to build on the traditions of activist poetry. However, with *Oiseaux mohicans* (1969), Daniel Biga (b. 1940), co-founder with Venaille of the review *Chorus* (1962–74), and as *beatnikien* as he was *rimbaldien*, defended anarchy, opposed the work ethic, promoted the libido and sought to protect the *moi* which was defined by the language of media and advertising. Charles Dobzynski (b. 1929) wrote in committed terms of the displacement and enslavement of peoples and races. By 1975, however, this political impetus was exhausted and growing resistance to Structuralist *poétiques*, tartly denounced by Ponge in 1974, handed poetry back to the poets. But what poetry was in 1975 is not easily summarized. Extremely varied in its forms and subjects, it confirmed two broad attitudes or arguments which had emerged since the war. The first was the defence of the community of humankind, which for some was religious in character and for others meant human fraternity. The second aspired to universality. The poet was longer a Romantic hero intent on imposing his vision on the world, nor an arranger of words who made Art his only goal, but an isolated, even reclusive figure who offered himself as a witness and the apostle of unity.

Since 1975

Although in 1975 change was in the offing, there was no sharp break in continuity. Surrealist embers still threw off sparks, Oulipo members like Roubaud and Georges Perec (*Alphabets*, 1976) persisted with its verbal games and some, such as Lionel Ray, (b. 1935), maintained contact with the poets of modernity, many of whom remained active. But between 1975 and 1988, the deaths of Perse, Jouve, Aragon, Michaux, Ponge and Char signalled the end of an era: even Guillevic became 'Un souffle / Qui essaie de durer' (*Art poétique*, 1990).

Poetry and publishers

Although the market for new poetry was weak, anthologies edited by Robert Sabatier (1975–88), Alain Bosquet (1979), M. Décaudin (1983), Jean Breton (1992) and others proved commercially viable. Moreover, in the two decades after 1968 Baudelaire sold 1.2 million copies and Rimbaud almost a million in Livre de Poche. Major publishers like Gallimard maintained a poetry list, though the main outlets for new work were the small presses in Paris and the provinces and the large number of poetry magazines which showed no sign of fatigue: there were some 400 in 1985. Among the most influential, *Po&sie* (1977) welcomed verse in translation, encouraged discussions of poetic theory, and stressed the links between poetry and the plastic arts which had begun with the Futurist manifesto of 1909, had informed the Cobra movement and resumed in the 1960s. The objective of *Poésie*, relaunched in 1984 by Pierre Seghers (1906–87), was to publicize the work of contemporary poets most of whom, however, also wrote in other more profitable genres. Poetry remains more than ever a vocation, not a profession, and even France's major poets have been received support from public funds.

Matters of form

Poetry can no longer be grouped into two distinct categories: verse texts and prose poems. Classical metres and rhyme have not disappeared but free forms dominate. The melodic phrase and fluid imagery blur the boundary between the poetic line and poetic prose. Typographical arrangements on the page are designed to produce a desired impact and the *blanc* has emerged as a more pregnant comma. While grand rhetoric and epic have given way to more intimate forms of expression, the long poem is sometimes attempted and collections are usually meant to be read as entities. There are wide variations of register, ranging from classical clarity, to esoteric vocabulary and the most informal speech. On the other hand, the link with popular music has strengthened through a new generation of *chansonniers* led by Renaud (pseud. of Raoul Séchan, b. 1952) who, like Bruant, sings of street life which is now, however, marked by the drug culture and a mood of anarchy. The tradition of protest also generated rap, imported in about 1983 from the United States, which used insistent rhythm and rhyme to highlight racial and urban themes before falling prey in the 1990s to the commercial pressures of the entertainment industry. While the public continues to take its idea of poetry from such popular alternatives, the literary establishment sets a small value on them.

Themes

The ability of language to express reality and ideas remains a challenge. Claude Estéban (b. 1935) seeks a means of making the signs and sounds of language coincide with concrete experience, Emmanuel Hocquard (b. 1940) looks for new ways of transcribing the real and Patrice Delbourg (b. 1948) exploits a deconstructed form of verse, which uses *blancs* and unexpected juxtapositions. On the other hand, Jude Stéfan (b. 1930) remains faithful to a learned tradition of eclectic references, Latinate syntax and metres based on ancient models. But the business of poetry remains the observation of the world and man's relationship with it and himself. For Charles Juliet (b. 1934), introspection abolishes the *moi* while Jean Mambrino (b. 1923) gives a religious interpretation to the creation which he celebrates. The response of Claude Roy (1915–98) to the too-much-life of nature was a wry rather than anguished capacity for surprise which he expressed in simple, fluid rhythms which came to him via Éluard and the Chinese poetry he translated. Jacques Réda, the leading *intimiste*, looks beyond nihilism and materialism. While man may be uprooted from the world, there is nevertheless a hope of communion which is projected in 'les mots de tout le monde'. A clearer optimism emerges with Jacques Darras (b. 1939) whose wide-ranging *Autobiographie de l'espèce humaine* (1991) celebrates, in bouncing octosyllables, the abundance of human experience.

Regional poets

The links between poetry and language, philosophy and the spiritual remain major concerns, not as the expression of party doctrines and principles but as personal reactions to the contradictions and opacities of life. But two trends, both originating in the cultural revolution of 1968, are, however, observable. The first stemmed from the rejuvenation of the provinces which relaxed the grip of Paris and encouraged regional voices. Rarely pastoral, however, this non-Parisian strain uses observation of the natural world to release a feeling for place and looks at the world with fresh eyes. The sensual delight in the created world leads Paul de Roux (b. 1937) to an unaffiliated religiosity. On the other hand, Luc Bérimont (1915–83), a member of the École de Rochefort, was less sanguine about man's effect on the landscape and concluded that the ecological option was the only solution. More specifically still, poets like Jean-Paul Klée have adopted a militant anti-nuclear stance. The vigour of the regions indicates that, like the theatre, poetry is now more decentralized than at any time in its history.

Poetry by women

The second major development has been the growth of poetry by women to the point where, at the end of the century, there are probably as many female as male poets. Some developed feminist issues, expressed uncompromisingly by Thérèse Plantier (1911–90), which were explored in philosophical and cultural terms in the 1970s and 1980s. But others adopted a less doctrinaire view of what Annie

Scaliger (b. 1938) called 'féminie'. Andrée Chedid (b. 1920), with transparent lyricism, implanted a metaphysical concern with mortality into her record of lived experience. Marie-Claire Bancquart (b. 1932) explores modern anxieties, Esther Tellerman (b. 1947) captures delicate apprehensions of feeling, and Anne-Marie Albiach (b. 1937) developed a technique as demanding as any during the last quarter century.

Conclusion

The rift between poetry and its wider audience, which began in the 1870s, has continued to deepen. Its growing hermeticism alienated not merely the popular readership but large sections of the educated public too. Yet no other century produced so much poetic activity or thought so hard about poetry as the twentieth. By engaging in the major movements of the century – Surrealism, Existentialism, the postwar vogue for the 'New' and Structuralism – it signalled the strength of its commitment to intellectualism. By abandoning lyricism and traditional forms (like the narrative poem) and by adopting 'difficult' techniques, it opted for non-referential experience which set the reader at a distance. Yet the freedom it had been given by the Symbolist revolution ensured that it has remained autonomous. What most readers still think of as poetry – the lyrical expression of feeling – was perpetuated less by serious poets than by the entertainment industry. Shielded against commercialism, poetry has maintained the momentum of the avant-garde more effectively than any other genre. It has kept faith with Art and is now the purest aesthetic laboratory on the French literary scene.

Theatre

Theatre during the Great War continued in its Belle-Époque mode of *théâtre digestif* and *grand guignol*. But after 1918, more thought was given to the nature and purpose of theatre than for almost a century.

1914–39

Activity was concentrated on three broad fronts: the national theatres, the commercial stages of the Boulevard and, most significantly for future developments, the Studio movement.

The national theatres

The Comédie Française maintained the classical tradition of French theatre in its choice of authors and plays and in its production and acting styles. Under the direction (1922–30) of Firmin Gémier (1865–1933), the Théâtre de l'Odéon, of near-equivalent status, played fewer classics and more Labiche and Dumas *fils* with a sprinkling of new authors. The entrenched conservatism of both was undermined by a government reorganization of the state theatres in 1936. Édouard Bourdet, the new director of the Comédie Française, widened the repertory to include new authors like Lenormand and Giraudoux and modernized its style with productions mounted by the leaders of the 'Cartel des Quatre'.

The Boulevards

After 1918, commercial theatre kept its middle-class, middle-brow audience with the same stars in well-tried vehicles written by successful prewar playwrights and their heirs. The tone was superficial and serious subjects were treated melodramatically. To the social *pièce à thèse* were preferred the psychological effects of passion explored in the contrived, sensational plays of Porto-Riche, Bataille and especially Bernstein, who linked plot to the warring, usually sexual, elements in the psychology of his characters. Love, though in a very different guise, was the subject of the 130 revues, satires, musical biographies and frothy comedies of Sacha Guitry (1885–1957), actor-manager, matinee idol and the embodiment of the Boulevard spirit. A leader of style rather than an observer of manners, Guitry projected his own irreverent personality into plays which were admired for their cynical charm, sparkling linguistic invention and dramatic curtain lines.

Studio theatre

But the cause of theatre was served less by individual authors than by a remarkable group of actor-managers. The example set before 1900 by André Antoine and Lugné-Poë was followed by Jacques Copeau (1879–1949), founder of the Théâtre du Vieux-Colombier (1913), who introduced radical changes in production styles which subordinated actors, decors and lighting to the text. In the event, Copeau served the classics better than new authors, but his opposition to lavish theatricality and 'star vehicles', and his insistence that theatre was a collective enterprise exerted a powerful influence on a number of other actor-managers who had been associated with him. Louis Jouvet (1887–1951), believing that good theatre meant good writing, encouraged new playwrights and discovered both Giraudoux and, later, Jean Genet. Unlike Jouvet, who set out to revitalize conventional realistic drama, Charles Dullin (1885–1949) was committed to the imaginative use of all the technical resources of theatre to create not an image of reality but 'a world apart governed by its own laws'. Although his *Volpone* (1928) furnished the best instance of his plastic, balletic productions, he also offered openings to the talents of Salacrou, Passeur, Achard and others. Both Jouvet and Dullin were active teachers and left their mark on a generation of playwrights and actors. Georges Pitoëff (1884–1939) and his wife Ludmilla (1895–1951) helped make French theatre less insular: a third of their productions were of foreign plays (Ibsen, Pirandello, Strindberg, Shaw). They had no systematic views on staging, which they adapted to the 'secret truth' implicit in each play. Their taste was for non-realistic drama (from the neo-Symbolist Claudel to the mythologizing Cocteau) and their goal was to disengage theatre from ordinary experience and poeticize reality. On the other hand, Gaston Baty (1885–1952) was committed to an idea of 'total theatre' which emphasized production values over the text which, like acting and decor, was but one element of the whole.

The Cartel

In 1927, Jouvet, Dullin, the Pitoëffs and Baty formed the 'Cartel des Quatre', a loose grouping designed to oppose commercialism in the theatre and set high standards of acting, production and design. They published a manifesto and a revue (*L'Entr'acte*, 1927–34) and called for productions which aimed at poetic impact rather than spectacle. The Cartel played a central role in the interwar revolution in public taste and paved the way for many later developments.

The Surrealists

More extreme in its ambitions but less influential in the short term was the Surrealist concept of theatre as revolution. Indeed, the two playwrights who now appear most effectively 'Surrealist' – Jarry and Ionesco – do not even belong to the period. Of the fifty or so Surrealist plays, the most successful was Roger Vitrac's anarchic *Victor, ou les enfants au pouvoir* (1928), the story of Victor, aged nine but already six feet tall, who recognizes that the real world is squalid and proceeds to smash everything within reach. *Victor* was the fourth and last production of the significantly named Théâtre Alfred Jarry founded by Vitrac and Antonin Artaud (1896–1948) who were violently opposed to the philosophy of the Cartel. Artaud began his career as an actor in 1920 but quickly joined forces with the Surrealists in identifying art as the only effective antidote to the comprehensive decadence of Western civilization. Theatre did not mean plot, psychology, realism and human interest. It was a magical ceremony, a ritual of cleansing, and its function was to create a form of social communion which gave access to emotions normally buried under the habit of living. Hidden truths were to be communicated principally by scenic means rather than the spoken word, by actors who were 'moving hieroglyphs'. His 'Theatre of Cruelty' was a psychodrama which played in a redesigned auditorium which abolished the standard separation of stage and spectator. Artaud was a relatively obscure figure during the 1930s when, despite his startling but unsuccessful production of *Les Cenci* (1935), he was still known mainly as an actor. Even the publication of *Le Théâtre et son double* (1938), which set out his ideas, made little impact. When it was reissued in 1944, however, it struck multiple chords. But Artaud's tragic life ended before he was recognized as one of the most significant influences on theatre in the second half of the century.

Art and commerce

At its extremes, the gulf separating commercial theatre and the avant-garde was unbridgeable. But there was a great deal of cross-fertilization between the Studio movement, which sought greater box-office appeal, and commercial playwrights, who incorporated Studio insights and techniques into their work for the Boulevards. Some (like Achard) began as uncompromising avant-gardists and ended up as devout *boulevardiers* without entirely relinquishing their respect for 'art'. Others (like Cocteau) successfully packaged avant-garde theatre for commercial audiences. This interaction was beneficial to both sides of the argument and by the end of the 1930s had considerably raised the standard of writing, production and public taste. Within this middle ground, a number of tendencies are discernible.

Social comment   While the play of manners remained the preserve of older playwrights like Léopold Marchand, it was invested with a vein of satirical realism which attacked institutions, the press and the contradictions of sexual and social morality. The hypocrisy of post-war values was best exploited by René Benjamin (1885–1945), Bernard Zimmer (1893–1964) and Édouard Bourdet (1887–1945). Like many such 'well-made' plays of the period, Bourdet's *Vient de paraître* (1927), his fierce satire of literary circles, has a brilliant first act which is not quite matched by what follows. Marcel Pagnol (1895–1974) first made his name with a series of bitter satires of personal and social corruption and with *Topaze* (1928) scored the biggest box-office success of the interwar years. His 'Marseilles trilogy' (*Marius*, 1929; *Fanny*, 1932; *César*, film 1936; staged 1946) continued to explore the theme of innocence under threat, though in gentler and less acerbic terms. His sure comic sense, sharp dialogue and amused affection for life's victims transferred effortlessly to the cinema, which absorbed his energies in the 1930s.

Ideas   Pursuing the implications of Unanimism, Jules Romains reflected on the relationship between the 'common soul' and the groups which it animates. When properly directed, this 'soul' acts for the general good. His verse play *Cromedeyre-le-vieil* (1920) conveyed the spirit of a mountain village threatened by an alien order and with his film script *Donogoo Tonka* showed how willingly groups are duped. *Knock, ou le Triomphe de la médecine* (1923) demonstrated the ease with which the collective psychology can be turned into passive obedience by a leader who believes his own propaganda. It has worn well as a prophetic fable for it anticipates one of the most distinctive features of the twentieth century: the subjection of the human spirit by dictators, ideology and the herd instinct. Though a cerebral playwright, Romains carried audiences with his comic energy and sure-footed treatment of types and myths. Far less successful were the 22 published (but mostly unperformed) plays of Gabriel Marcel (1899–1973). Dramatically weak, they deal with the problem of existence in ways which anticipate the ideas of Sartre and Camus, and, after his conversion to Catholicism in 1929, gave a Christian answer to the problem of how the soul 'in exile' in a 'broken world' may be redeemed.

The psychologists   After the Great War, the Cartesian view of man as a lucid creature who makes rational decisions was undermined by Marx, Freud and Bergson, who had shown that human beings do not control their own destinies but are the victims of powerful internal and external forces. Playwrights showed occasional interest in the socio-economic determinants of personality, but most delved into the psychological springs of motive and action. This tendency reactivated the tradition of character *analyse*, but was updated by the current interest in the mask of the *commedia dell'arte* and Japanese Noh theatre which reduced human complexity to types. To such influences were added the input of foreign playwrights, the morbid intensity of Ibsen, for example, or, more fruitful, the distinction exploited by Pirandello between illusion and reality, between individuals as they really are and the faces they wear in society. Henri-René Lenormand (1882–1950), one of the few playwrights of the period to acquire an international reputation, took his lead from Bergson's distinction between the 'surface self' and the 'deep self' and concluded that fate is not outside but inside us. For his 'clinical' observations of complexes (like *Mixture*, 1927: a study of destructive mother-love), he developed a technique which parted company with the narrative structure of the 'well-made' play. His *tableaux* reveal different phases and moods of a neurosis or show characters from different points of view, the unity stemming from the revelations which yield the 'deep self'. Narrower in their defini-tion of subconscious motivation, the characters of the twenty plays of Stève Passeur (1899–1966) seek to dominate each other in ferocious, instinct-driven exchanges. Less openly didactic was the *théâtre intimiste* of exponents of the 'school of silence'. To stagy plots, they preferred the realistic observation of, usually, working-class characters unable to give verbal expression to their motives and feelings. In *Le Paquebôt Tenacity* (1920), Charles Vildrac (1882–1971) allowed the deep self of his characters to emerge from their reactions to events. A good example of the stratagem is provided by a study of frustrated maternal feeling. *Les Sœurs Quédonac* (1931), by Jean-Jacques Bernard (1888–1972), a classic of the genre. Among other 'playwrights of the unexpressed', Paul Géraldy (1885–1983): *Aimer*, 1921) and Denys Amiel (1884–1977: *La Souriante Madame Beudet*, 1921) specialized in exteriorizing hidden sufferings and tensions within marriage and the couple. The dialogue is indirect, and silences, monosyllabic replies and oblique comments release truths which are all the more painful for being unarticulated.

Poets of illusion   Not all dramatists reacted grimly to the shock of the postwar years. Some, like Guitry, turned to comedy. Others, taking their cue from Musset, sought escape in a world of illusion. Marcel Achard (1899–1974) played fancifully with clowns (*Voulez-vous jouer avec moâ?*, 1923) and types drawn from Italian comedy. His women are coquettish but never cruel, and the hero of *Jean de la lune* (1928) is a dreamy, vulnerable figure who is never quite allowed to escape into his imagination. More substantial were the characters of Jean Sarment (1897–1976) who showed the gap between ideals and reality, between self-image and the way others see us. But while he struck a note of neo-Romantic disenchantment, he remained more wry and melancholy than anguished.

Other playwrights

Much of the dramatic output of the interwar years has weathered badly. Leading literary figures (Martin du Gard, Gide, Mauriac, Giono) tried their hand at drama, but their work for the theatre has proved to be the least durable of their activities.

Salacrou   A firmer theatrical presence was asserted by André Obey (1892–1975). His significance, however, lies less in his recreation of national and Biblical myths (*Noé*, 1931) than through his connection with the 'Compagnie des Quinze' (1930–4) for which he pioneered the role of the resident playwright, a feature of the later collective, repertory mood. His range was much smaller than that of Armand Salacrou (1899–1989), who in the 1920s flirted with Surrealism and communism but found that neither provided answers to the 'absurdity' (he used the word long before Camus did) of a world marked by metaphysical and social evil. His first major play, *Patchouli* (1930), a study of disillusioned love, broke with the conventions of theatrical narrative and showed considerable technical originality. He outgrew realistic drama, experimented boldly with the flashback technique (*L'Inconnue d'Arras*, 1935) and attempted a metaphysical drama, *La Terre est ronde*, in 1938. Never far away was the sense of nightmare and the presence of a sleeping, unwakeable God who allowed the individual to be the eternal victim of injustice. After the war, he recommended a humanistic brand of collective solidarity as an answer to the indifference of a senseless universe (*L'Archipel Lenoir*, 1947). If Salacrou made good theatre out of metaphysical and existential

questions, he also questioned capitalism, the subject of his best political play, *Boulevard Durand* (1960).

Cocteau   The heyday of Jean Cocteau (1889–1963) lasted most of
the fifty years of his writing life. Though he wrote novels, poetry and
film scripts, his first home was the theatre, a form of 'graphic writing' which mobilized as many arts as it took to convey the relationship between the poetry inherent in life and life as it appears to be.
He wrote ballets, dramas, *mimodrames*, but systematically rejected
realism and commitment and sought instead to harness the power of
legend. *La Machine infernale* (1934) modernized the Oedipus myth
while *Les Parents terribles* (1938), only superficially a satire of bourgeois manners, confronts the spontaneity of youth with the calcula-
tions of old age in an atmosphere derived from Greek tragedy. 'Unreal'
glimpses of the 'real' world, they illustrate his view that Art is the
ordinary poeticized. Myth, fable and legend express recurring patterns of the struggle between free will and fate, and it was to their
structural symbolism that he turned to provide fresh statements of
old truths. In addition to drawing on Greek sources, he also exploited the folk tale (*La Belle et la bête* (film, 1945), and his historical
drama *L'Aigle à deux têtes* (1946) shows how wrong things may go
when the Sleeping Beauty is awakened. Cocteau never analysed the
forces which direct our inner lives (they seem more Racinian than
Freudian), and he preached no message save deference to the will of
the gods, scorn for man's petty concerns and the certainty that only
Art is real. Cocteau, the unrepentant middle-class iconoclast, sought
to return the theatre to the People to whom it belonged and for
whom it provided an illumination, religious in character if not in
form, of the human condition.

Claudel   Such was also the ambition of Paul Claudel (1868–1955),
whose definition of religion, however, was of an altogether more exalted order. He remained committed to rescuing humanity from the
idea that life is pointless: existence is given a meaning by the Catholic faith. His first plays, Symbolist in manner, dealt with the conflict
between man's temporal concerns and his religious destiny. *Tête d'or*
(1890), *La Jeune Fille Violaine* (1892), *L'Échange* (1893) and *La Ville*
(1895–8) all set pride, human desire and the call of the flesh against
submission to Providence and the promise of salvation. While he

gave *Partage de Midi* (1905) a contemporary setting, his trilogy (*L'Ôtage*, 1911; *Le Pain dur*, publ. 1918; and *Le Père humilié*, 1920) showed the continuity of faith against successive waves of nineteenth-century 'progress'. *L'Annonce faite à Marie* (a reworking of *La Jeune Fille Violaine* and his first play to be staged, in 1912) is a medieval 'mystery play' which shows humanity's predicament assuaged by faith, miracle and pardon. During the Great War, Claudel widened his range with two 'lyrical farces' but his newer, more expansive manner found its finest expression in *Le Soulier de satin* (written 1919–24; publ. 1930), a sprawling epic set in the Spanish Renaissance, rich in sub-plots which show the multifarious mechanics of divine deliverance. A lyrical drama, *Le Livre de Christophe Colomb*, was published in 1935, and *Jeanne d'Arc au bûcher*, an oratorio, in 1939.

Claudel provided a formidable challenge to producers and was for most of his life a largely unperformed playwright. It was not until the 1930s that he acquired a reputation which was at variance with his short list of staged works. In 1943, Jean-Louis Barrault produced an abridged *Soulier de satin* and Claudel had to wait until after the war to see first or notable productions of *Le Père humilié* (1947), *Partage de Midi* (1948) and *Le Livre de Christophe Colomb* (1953). Yet he was one of the few playwrights of the period to move the art of theatre forward. He found new ways of dramatizing timeless conflicts, enabled his characters to achieve mythical status and invented for them a ceremonial, incantatory language. Even those who do not accept that human destiny is a matter of submission to divine grace appreciate the power and variety of Claudel's dramatic imagination and poetic style.

Giraudoux   Jean Giraudoux (1882–1944) made his name in the 1920s as a novelist, but is better remembered for plays produced in a symbiotic partnership with Jouvet. *Siegfried* (1928), *Intermezzo* (1933) and *La Folle de Chaillot* (perf. 1945) have modern settings. A second group (*Judith*, 1931; *Sodome et Gomorrhe*, 1943) are drawn from the Bible. A third group (*Amphitryon 38*, 1929; *La Guerre de Troie n'aura pas lieu*, 1935; *Électre*, 1937) rework classical subjects. But the enigmatic tone and sleek craftsmanship never change, nor do the somnambular characters who exist between reality and idealism ever quite achieve the peace and wisdom of which they dream. The fairy-tale heroine of *Ondine* (1939) acquires human form but in so doing learns that to be human also means learning to be unhappy. In the same way, *La Guerre de Troie n'aura pas lieu* shows that there is no departing from the path of destiny: the war will happen because the gods always demand periodic displays of 'human brutality and madness', a chilling message in 1935. Giraudoux is saved from pessimism, however, by his lightness of touch which ranges through parody and paradox to exuberant fancy. Giraudoux, the exponent of the 'well-made play', also made a case for the 'well-written play' in his *Impromptu de Paris* (1937). His defence of consciously literary drama gave a new if short-lived respectability to 'fine writing' which, apart from a brief flowering around the time of Rostand, had been lost for a century.

Anouilh Jean Anouilh (1910–87), last of the 1930s playwrights, was also the first of the postwar generation. He labelled his early plays *roses* or *noires* and after the war, created other groupings: *pièces brillantes, grinçantes* and *costumées*. The rose-tint of optimism and the blackness of pessimism do not correspond to any consistent distinction between the comic and the tragic, though *Antigone* (1944) and *Médée* (1944) come closest to being modern tragedies. The adjectives refer rather to the variations in Anouilh's reactions to an obsessional proposition: how is the idealist to live with the insincerity, falsehood and collaboration on which society is based? The dilemma is repeated through recurring types and may be resolved by defeat (*La Sauvage*, 1938) or with the offer of a second chance (*Le Rendez-vous de Senlis*, 1942). But for the most part his plays affirm that purity is impossible in a world without justice. Characters from different classes and historical times look to their own narrow interests; the family generates divisions; military and political leaders are cynical or inadequate. Against them and generalized hypocrisy, the 'pure' (like the hero of *Becket*, 1960) pursue an increasingly personal ideal of integrity which can at times seem as remote as Cornelian *gloire*. Anouilh grew increasingly sceptical, and the revolt articulated in *Antigone* gave way by about 1950 to a resigned acceptance of what cannot be altered, even to the view that while idealism may be admirable, it is not (in, say, the controversial *Pauvre Bitos*, 1956) a warm or humanizing aspiration. *Le Boulanger, la boulangère et le petit mitron* (1967) confirmed Anouilh as a man of the Right, a position not significantly altered by three late series of plays described as *baroques, secrètes* and *farceuses*. It was with one of the latter, *Le Nombril* that Anouilh scored his last success, in 1982. Anouilh, sophisticated, Parisian, provocative and always determined to entertain, was one of the great stylists of twentieth-century theatre.

Conclusion

In 1940, the balance sheet of interwar drama showed more profit than might have been anticipated in 1918. The Studio movement had waged successful battle with *théâtre digestif* and helped revolutionize play-making, production and taste. By 1940, mental states had become an acceptable alternative to narrative action as the centre of dramatic interest. *Tableaux*, accelerated time, flashbacks and other devices imported from cinema were now as familiar as the obligatory five acts had once been. The interest in Greek myths was one indicator of the health of the literary play, and stage design had entered a new era. Drama had begun to give way to theatre in the modern sense: actors and authors became less important than the plays they helped to create. But if the avant-garde led the way, its appeal was limited and theatre-going remained a primarily middle-class pastime. A few attempts had been made to respond to the call made by Romain Rolland in 1903 for a 'people's theatre', notable among which were Gémier's experiment with drama as collective communion at the Cirque d'Hiver in 1919 and his creation of a 'Popular' theatre the following year; the attempts at open-air Christian drama; the activities of the more politically direct Théâtre d'Action Internationale; and the Popular Front government's encouragement of mass theatre. But the popular movement made little impact and the legacy of the 1930s was a written, literary theatre which provided entertainments for the middle-class audience of the capital.

1940–68

After the defeat of 1940, theatrical activity was curtailed. Writers, directors and actors departed into exile and tight restrictions were imposed. The Boulevards continued to bubble with thirties froth, serious playwrights played safe with historical subjects and the poetic vein, and producers took refuge in the classic repertoire and literary adaptations. But not all dramatic activity was illusion and escape. Revivals of the classics and plays about France's history and heroes (notably Joan of Arc, symbol of French fortitude) made theatre a focus for national pride and oblique resistance. But while drama helped maintain morale, it also showed signs of new vitality. Yet few in 1945 could have foreseen the far-reaching changes which, by 1968 would revolutionize the very concept of theatre.

The mainstream

The Boulevards continued to offer wartime audiences the familiar stereotypes involved in the same eternal triangles and melodramatic plots. Thirties idols like Sacha Guitry maintained their following but newer playwrights like Roger Ferdinand (*Les J 3*, 1943) also found a public. After the Liberation, the middle-class public welcomed the stage version of Pagnol's *César* (1946) but dropped other prewar favourites like Jean-Jacques Bernard and Stève Passeur in favour of Marcel Achard (who achieved his biggest success, *Patate*, in 1957), the twenty or so comedies of André Roussin (1911–87), a box-office favourite into the late 1960s, and the steady stream of commercially viable plays, like Alexandre Breffort's *Irma la douce* (1956), the engaging (and very exportable) story of a prostitute with a heart. But while the private stage drew spectators resistant to committed or experimental theatre, it also welcomed both the mime Marcel Marceau (in 1954) and the well-crafted play, more often than not written by established writers working in other genres. The novelist and short-story writer, Marcel Aymé (1902–67), made a second career as a man of the middle-brow theatre with, among many others, *Lucienne et le boucher* (1947), a farce on the theme of murderous sexuality, and *La Tête des autres* (1952), a savage attack on the legal profession. More interesting, technically, are the plays, often adapted from his own novels, of Félicien Marceau (b. 1913). The long-running *L'Oeuf* (1956) is an illustrated monologue in which a man reviews his life and concludes that we are prisoners of the 'system' of conventions. Middle-class *angst*, the clash of generations and the problems of innocence feature in the plays of Françoise Sagan (b. 1935): *Un Château en Suède* (1960) was an early example of the 'psychological games' drama. The public which went to see Aymé, Marceau and Sagan liked to be reminded that it had a conscience but insisted on being entertained.

The literary play

The major exponent of the 'fine writing' exemplified by Giraudoux and Cocteau was the novelist Henri de Montherlant (1896–1972), author of a dozen plays of uncompromising literary quality and widely regarded in his day as France's greatest living stylist. *La Reine morte* (1942), set in sixteenth-century Spain, articulated the vanity of life and action, the central theme of all his costume dramas (*Malatesta*, 1946; *Le Maître de Santiago*, 1947; *Port-Royal*, 1954) which he classed as 'Christian', as opposed to his plays in modern dress which dealt in similarly grim terms with matters 'profane' (*Fils de personne*, 1943; *Brocéliande*, 1956). He set his protagonists aristocratic goals of integrity and purity which were curiously at odds with the values of the new postwar democratic world. Indeed, it seemed to many that the cause of theatre was not served by the demands of 'culture' and 'literature'. A break with the classical traditions of the French stage was called for and one immediate casualty was the play which re-worked Greek myth, that product of a rational, orderly world which had no place in the chaos of modern Europe. The psychological study, like the old *pièce à thèse*, was no longer seasonable and the conflict of character gave ground to the conflict of ideas.

The philosophical play

The anguish of modern man abandoned in a senseless universe, expressed in varying degrees of intensity by Salacrou, Gabriel Marcel, Giraudoux and Anouilh, acquired a new immediacy in wartime Paris where the 'play of ideas' was pointed in a particular direction by Jean-Paul Sartre (1905–80).

Sartre Theatre, like fiction, was ideally suited to showing the mechanics of the choices imposed by Existentialist 'authenticity'. Accordingly, Sartre's plays are 'situations' which dramatize and test a philosophical position, though with time the 'commitment' which they recommended was to take on more specifically political over-tones. *Les Mouches* (1943) showed how the individual creates himself: in this reworking of the Greek myth, Orestes takes responsibility for his freedom and accepts its consequences. *Huis clos* (1944) showed the 'hellish' consequences for individuals of the refusal to assume their freedom. Here 'mauvaise foi' is shown as a personal and moral issue. But by the time of *Les Mains sales* (1948) and *Le Diable et le bon Dieu* (1953), Sartre had given 'commitment' a political meaning, and both plays trace the struggle of the intellectual to break free of per-sonal morality and graduate to forms of revolutionary action consist-ent with the requirements of 'good faith'. *Kean* (1954) returned to the problem of 'mauvaise foi' (Kean avoids making choices by retreating into his roles), and the theme recurs, set contrapuntally between the horrors of the Nazi past and the brutality of the contemporary issue of torture, in Sartre's last play, *Les Séquestrés d'Altona* (1959). Despite their philosophical radicalism, however, all Sartre's nine plays remain *pièces à thèse* of a traditional kind. Settings are realistic, plots are linear, characters are as lucid as those of Augier or Dumas *fils* (as they must be if they are to make conscious choices), and dramatic tension is generated by devices – murder, betrayal, death – many times exploited by mainstream playwrights who wrote of love and money as 'problems'. The priority he gave to ideas ensured that Sartre used the stage more as a thinker than as an artist.

Camus The four plays of Albert Camus (1913–60) illustrate his concept of revolt against the Absurd, but do so in ways which, when set against his more formally inventive fiction, are unadventurous. *Caligula* (1945) teaches the lesson of revolt against the constraints of the human condition. *L'État de siège* (1948) shows how dictatorship can be overthrown by collective revolt, on which *Les Justes* (1949) sets limits imposed by human solidarity. Camus may succeed in showing that there is life after the Absurd, but his plays are wordy and static when they are not spiked with mayhem and murder. Like Sartre's over-excited resistance drama, *Morts sans sépulture* (1946), Camus's *Le Malentendu* (1944) has links with the tradition of *grand guignol*, and this, together with the contrived point of crisis from which doctrinal truth emerges, lends Existentialist theatre a heavily melodramatic air. It has ideas which run ahead of its means to express them and, from a theatrical point of view, it was locked into forms which looked conservatively back, not radically forward. And so, abetted by Sartre and Camus, the play of ideas slipped comfortably into the commercial theatre where Anouilh became its chief exponent.

New Theatre

Existentialist thinkers assumed that the world, however bleak, was a place which might receive order and man a rational creature who, through understanding and an effort of will, could rise above the Absurd. But not everyone regarded these propositions as self-evident. To some, the world was more truthfully captured by Strindberg,

Kafka or Artaud than by the theatrical formulae which Existentialist intellectuals had inherited from the Cartel. The playwrights of the 'New Theatre' started with the certain knowledge that nothing makes sense. They accordingly withdrew the comforts – linear plot, realistic psychology, rational discourse – which had hitherto enabled audiences to stand outside a play and observe human simulacra imitating life. Spectators lost their privileges, were 'assaulted' in ways derived from the Surrealists and Artaud and became part of what they saw. They shared the bewilderment of the characters as they watched them endure the Absurd which was not explained but displayed in all its senselessness. Settings were minimal and symbol was abandoned: what was shown represented no hidden value or meaning but was simply its arbitrary and inconsequential self. Language was shorn of its claim to intelligibility, and words – the conventional signs of conventional meanings – were used as shock troops to show that, even if there were meaning in the universe, human language would still be inadequate to express it. Great play was made with 'literality', that is, the physical materialization of objects which conveyed the alarming, nightmarish reality of existence. Action had no latent content but a manifest and usually threatening immediacy.

New Theatre came in a variety of moods – from whimsy and Surrealist fantasy to the tragic by way of black humour and farce – but all marked a savage break with the classic, realistic tradition of drama. The first stirrings were heard in the late 1940s in plays by Jacques Audiberti, Boris Vian, Michel de Ghelderode (1898–1962) and Roman Weingarten (b. 1926), whose *Akara* was 'the *Hernani* of 1948'. They were soon joined by others who, though working in different registers (from the poetic to the consciously ludic), projected a view of humanity adrift in a world where nothing was certain: Jean Vauthier (1910–92), Georges Schéhadé (1910–89), Arthur Adamov (1908–70) and notably Jean Tardieu (1903–95), whose 'chamber theatre' played with language in a manner which would be exploited more systematically in Ionesco's remarkably long-lived *La Cantatrice chauve* which was staged daily for nearly half a century.

Confined to the small art theatres of the Left Bank, New Theatre remained a minority cult until 1953 when Beckett's *En attendant Godot* startled the world. Now accorded a higher profile, its grotesqueries were made to serve a variety of ends: to create worlds of play and dream, to satirize society, and to raise general issues of politics, language and even – though this ran counter to its fundamental ethos – metaphysics. To the favourites of the art theatres – Ionesco, Ghelderode, Schéhadé and Audiberti, in whose poetic style the future seemed to lie – were later added two refugees from radio: Roland Dubillard (b. 1923) and François Billetdoux (1927–91) who, in *Tchin-tchin* (1959), saw the abandonment of materialism as the solution to evil. The spirit of New Theatre, which survived its vogue years, proved to be a potent and lasting force in modern drama which has never quite abandoned its interest in the dispossessed, its questioning of human lucidity and rational explanations, its invention of 'literality' and the assault on the audience. But the 1950s are also remembered for producing three quite distinctive writers of world stature.

Ionesco Eugène Ionesco (1909–94) tackled the Absurd with the weapon of derision, his riposte to the tragicomedy of life which he defined as the solitude of man in a meaningless world. Constantly seeking ways of expanding the language of drama, from the first short nonsense plays (*La Cantatrice chauve*, 1950; *La Leçon*, 1951) to his more finished later work, Ionesco offered dislocated images of a permanently disintegrating reality through Surrealistic juxtapositions which defy logic and create a world of dream and nightmare. The audience is carried beyond logic to weird shores where language ceases to be an instrument of communication and things rise up – chairs in *Les Chaises* (1952), the expanding corpse in *Amédée* (1954), or the furniture in *Le Nouveau Locataire* (1957) – to challenge the assumption that life means something. During the 1950s, this brilliantly inventive use of the 'literality' of things and, more centrally still, of language, created a series of rumbustious metaphors for a world bent on violence and destruction.

For Ionesco, the human body is tragic and human tragedy 'derisory'. His characters are not social beings but isolated individuals, and relationships are more often than not hostile and disruptive. Before about 1960, his 'tragic farces' lack a specific social or political dimension. They focus on the individual who is crushed by the irresistible force of things and trapped by an inability to communicate intelligibly: the failure of language is its inability to express man's metaphysical dimension. However, a shift is noticeable with *Tueur sans gages* (1958) which marked the first appearance of Bérenger, Ionesco's *alter ego*, who was to reappear in a more positive role in his best-known play, *Rhinocéros* (1960). In his first incarnation, Bérenger fares none too well. But when confronted by multiplying rhinoceroses, he refuses to capitulate, no longer a victim but almost a hero. Some critics took the play to be a veiled account of the rise of fascism, though Ionesco defined his target as 'massification' (the pressure and willingness to conform), an altogether more generalized concept entirely in keeping with his preoccupation with the individual as a victim. Bérenger, who is potentially as 'massifiable' as anyone else, reappears in *Le Roi se meurt* (1962) which strikes a more personal note in this account of how he faces death by disintegration. Here is the *misère* but also the *grandeur* of man who is rescued by no God. Ionesco put even more of himself in his later work – his family, his health, his neuroses – but in plays which never quite recaptured his first anarchic manner, though *Macbett* (1972) plays like Shakespeare revised by Jarry. In his thirty-third and last play, *Voyage chez les morts* (1980), Jean meets up with his dead grandparents as though time has been abolished. The view of man's situation as a nightmare gave way finally to a gentler rumination which underscores Ionesco's place as a surviving representative of the old humanities.

Beckett Samuel Beckett (1906–89), claimed by both English and French literatures, was born in Dublin and settled permanently in France in 1934. His prewar writings in English projected a view of life as a tragicomedy relieved by irony and aesthetic pleasures. His experience of war appalled him and one climactic day in 1945, he saw clearly that writers had always tried to say everything: perhaps the aim of art should be to say nothing, to chronicle not the light but the dark. This he first attempted in a trilogy of novels (1951–53) and thereafter in other prose works in which form is determined by the increasing intensity of an interior monologue. But 'fogged down' by his trilogy, he turned to the theatre. *En attendant Godot* (written 1948–9, staged 1953) proved to be the greatest international success of the 1950s. From the 1960s onwards, in both his reading and performance texts (not only for the stage but for radio, film and television), he reworked his major themes, paring them down to a minimum of dramatic and linguistic expression but imparting to them a measure of ironic, defiant acceptance: when all is stripped bare, men and women still have language with which to communicate what they think and feel. They cannot be silenced. Life is an incurable but not terminal condition. Being alive means falling, not jumping, going downhill but also being already at the bottom, with no way up in sight. His beaten but undefeated characters cannot live either with or without each other or their past: remembering is part of imagining. Vladimir and Estragon, the non-heroes of *En attendant Godot*, wait, hoping in vain for some transcendental illumination of life which, it becomes clear, has no point but itself. It is a play without plot or psychology, and yet it is as close as Beckett would ever get to staging anything approaching 'realism'.

Thereafter, he proceeded to strip form to its expressive essentials, the better to reveal the emptiness of existence. In *Oh! les beaux jours* (*Happy Days*, 1963), the mindlessly content Winnie maintains a faltering grip on life as she rummages through her handbag while the mound of sand in which she is buried rises up her torso. Beckett was fascinated by tramps and other marginalized figures who are alienated (*Fin de partie*, 1957 / *Endgame*, 1958) or alone (*Krapp's Last Tape* / *La Dernière Bande*, 1959) but always at the last ditch and at the end of their tether. Beckett's performance texts grew shorter and denser, and increasingly dependent on language which is beaten down to the limits of syntactical intelligibility, as though a voice speaking into the void is the only affirmation of life possible. But when Beckett appeared to have reached the limits of minimalism, he staged *Not I* (1973) which consists of a hidden watcher and a woman's mouth pouring out a stream of desperation. Hopeless, sometimes limbless, his characters are remnants of humanity, though what remains is unalterably human. Beckett is the poet of the destitution of modern man. He left no philosophical or literary manifesto and merely affirmed that his work 'means what it says'. His plays create a world filled with grief and increasing silence relieved by black humour and a faith in language as a fragile bridge between people.

Genet   At the age of sixteen, Jean Genet (1910–86) chose to be what other people had decided he was: a criminal outsider. He explained himself in his *Journal d'un voleur* (1949) three years before Sartre saluted him as an authentic Existentialist martyr who had assumed responsibility for his acts and 'created himself'. Homosexual and a self-confessed thief, Genet turned his poetical and uncompromising trinity of theft, murder and betrayal into an arresting, shocking description of the Absurd world. His four major plays identify with the oppressed as they struggle to be free of a world in which they suffocate.

For Genet, theatre was not an arena for airing political problems but a ceremony, a rite as powerful as the raising of the host at Mass, a game as serious as children's play. He fully recognized the misery of existence. But while Beckett dwelt on its inevitability, Anouilh protested against it and Ionesco derided it, Genet experienced it as exaltation and a source of visceral pleasure. His characters find release in collaboration and self-debasement, in other words by playing the roles which have been written for them by others. In *Les Bonnes* (1947), the maids want to kill their mistress but also to become her. *Le Balcon* (1957) shows identities dissolving in the archetypes spawned by our fantasies, but also gives the lesson a social dimension: power needs theatricality, for the general who commands and the archbishop who blesses depend on the willing collaboration of troops and believers. The ritual enactment of murder in *Les Nègres* (1959) is used to show how easily men and women, far from being captains of their souls, gravitate towards other, imposed forms of being. *Les Paravents* (publ. 1961; perf. 1966) dealt in deliberately provocative terms with the Algerian War, but also developed Genet's obsession with illusion, fantasy and the elusive nature of personal identity: here appearances and imposture are instruments of domination. All his plays focus on types or groups which, having been deprived of their subjectivity, surrender to the image which others have imposed on them. Genet's theatre is rooted in acts of symbolic imagination and his purpose was to send his audience to their homes where, he said, they will find life no less false than in the performance they have just witnessed.

Institutional developments

After 1945, the capital's privately run theatres continued to define theatre as an entertainment in the Boulevard tradition, essentially melodrama and light comedy with star casts. The sedate image and classical repertoire of the Comédie Française were modernized in the 1950s under its new director, Jean Meyer, though after 1960 it lost ground, overtaken by more progressive views of what theatre should be. Even so, its institutional prestige remained high after 1968, when the number of national theatres was increased to five, not all located in the capital. 'National' no longer meant 'Parisian', for the decentralization of theatre, one of the most significant developments of the second half of the century, had grown out of the wartime spirit of cultural democracy.

The CDNs   In 1946, five centrally funded Centres Dramatiques Nationaux (CDNs) were set up in the provinces, with fixed repertory ensembles which also toured with new productions drawn mainly from the classic repertoire. A Théâtre National Populaire (TNP) was installed in Paris in 1951 and, during the 1950s, further CDNs were inaugurated. In 1959, André Malraux, Minister for the Arts, created the network of Maisons de la Culture which included theatre in their activities. During the 1960s, however, the state was accused of using subsidy as a means of controlling free expression and theatres became a focal point for the unrest of 1968. Many took the view that Malraux's policy had from the start been one of 'cultural imperialism'. Even so, throughout the 1970s, most companies continued to depend on public subsidies which were increased after the election of a socialist government in 1981. By the close of the 1980s, the number of CDNs had risen to 33, every middling-sized town in France had its own municipal theatre, and many boasted a semi-resident company. It was a far cry from the New Theatre movement which, despite its influence abroad, was an essentially Parisian phenomenon.

The institutional changes introduced after 1945 prompted renewed calls for a decentralized *théâtre du peuple*, a concept which has remained ambiguous. Should its priority be the People (that is, to reflect working-class culture) or the Theatre (that is, to educate working-class taste by making that product of the social elite, the national repertoire, accessible to all)? The challenge was taken up less by playwrights than by theatre directors who to their organizational role added an artistic input to the point where, by the 1970s, they had achieved equivalent status to that of the cinema director.

Vilar   The initial response was provided by Jean Vilar (1912–71), the inspiration of the Avignon Festival (1947) and director of the TNP (1951–63). Vilar shared Copeau's faith in the uplifting function of theatre and was committed both to renewing tradition (as he did with a notable production of *Le Cid* in 1953) and widening its remit. In 1954, he introduced Brecht, who provided a clear definition of 'popular theatre'. Instead of the small casts, strong plots and psychological analyses of the French tradition, Brecht offered movement, rapid scene changes, a wide social mix of multiple characters and provocative commentaries on socio-political issues. Steadily, the TNP moved to the Left and by the early 1960s was staging plays which commented on topical questions such as the Algerian War. Vilar resigned in 1963 to concentrate on the Avignon Festival, but by then he had set the standard for producers and *animateurs* who would develop his insights.

Barrault The approach of Jean-Louis Barrault (1910–94) was primarily that of a performer. But by 1935, he had developed a production style which included mime, dance and acrobatics, and his concept of 'total theatre' was ideally suited to the plays of Claudel, with whom he worked in a symbiotic relationship. After the war, the Renaud-Barrault Company encouraged new writing talent, but in 1959 he was given charge of the subsidized Théâtre de l'Odéon where he directed Ionesco and Beckett. Summarily dismissed for condoning the student occupation of the Odéon in 1968, he moved to a wrestling hall and staged spectacularly successful shows built around Rabelais (1968) and Jarry (1970) which used, as was his practice, the total resources of theatre. Further spells at the Théâtre d'Orsay (1972–80) and, beginning in 1981, the Théâtre du Rond-Point, confirmed Barrault and his wife, Madeleine Renaud (1900–94), as national institutions.

The New Theatre had drawn on the talents of directors like Roger Blin (1907–84), with whom Beckett worked closely, and Jean-Marie Serreau (1915–1973), who, after promoting Brecht in the 1950s, went on to encourage promising writers from North Africa (Kateb Yacine) and the West Indies (Édouard Glissant, Aimé Césaire). Their themes (self-determination, anti-colonialism) also appealed to French working-class audiences who, mistrustful of authority, were shown the advantages of community values. This subordination of the individual to the collectivity, the insistence that theatre was a communifying experience, was to be at the heart of the French, 'epic' version of Brechtian theatre.

Planchon Roger Planchon (b. 1931), the most committed exponent of 'popular theatre' in the 1960s, was an early admirer of Brecht. He abandoned theatre-as-illusion and his many productions (which included some fifteen of his own plays) were visually rich and vibrantly theatrical. Among his many successes were Marxist interpretations of the classics (Molière, Racine, Shakespeare), but between 1953 and 1960 he also participated in New Theatre, particularly with Adamov. His staging of Le Ping-pong (1955), with its mix of documentary material, film projection and ideological comment, not only helped to direct Adamov's early Absurdism into a more committed stance, but turned it into the first properly 'Brechtian' play written in French. Much of his best work, reflecting the decentralizing tendency of his times, was presented to provincial audiences. In 1957, Planchon was appointed director of the Théâtre de la Cité, situated in an industrial suburb of Lyons, to which the title of TNP was transferred in 1972.

Playwrights of the 1960s

Adamov, who politicized the Absurd, provides a good illustration of the choices which polarized attitudes in the 1960s. While most playwrights readily abandoned narrative and psychological realism, opinion was divided on the fundamental objectives of theatre itself. The Copeau-Vilar philosophy held that theatre belonged to the people who, given the chance, would become alive to its power. But to the new generation, the solitary playwright spoke only for himself and the only truly popular theatre consisted of plays which dealt collectively with the plight and experience of the working class. There were thus two main options: to develop the Absurd or to seek new and more directly political forms of expression.

Individualists and the conservatively minded (Ionesco became increasingly both) chose the former and found middle-brow audiences well able to cope with literality, the incommunicability of language and sharply angled fantasy. Established 'New' dramatists like Audiberti, Billetdoux, Dubillard, Weingarten and Vauthier maintained an enthusiastic following into the late 1970s. René de Obaldia (b. 1918) followed his first success, Génousie (1960), with a highly successful parody of the western, Du Vent dans les branches du sassafras (1965). But the Absurd, communicated in poetic, whimsical, and fantastic registers, had become domesticated and the avant-garde of the 1950s entered the mainstream.

The dominant influence of the 1960s was exerted by Brecht and Shakespeare, who was discovered once more. Brecht had buried the individual and presented the ideological forces of history through crowds, song, spectacle and movement. By 'Shakespearean' was meant a large theatrical style based on fragmentation and gesture which proceeded by contrasts and contradictions. Together, the strands combined to produce an 'epic' style. The effect on the decentralized theatres was remarkable and set the scene for the phenomenon of *création collective*, which demoted the author who became merely one member of a team. However, a number of personal voices continued to make themselves heard.

Gatti Gabriel Cousin (b. 1918), though faithful to the philosophy of old-style social drama, abandoned the time-honoured stratagem of showing common misery through the suffering of single, representative characters. Subordinating his text to movement, he developed a 'festival' style (masks, photographic blow-ups, mime, music) which dealt with large themes (war, famine, capitalism) in terms not of individuals but of groups. More uncompromising, Armand Gatti (b. 1924), the leading Marxist playwright of the decade and exponent of *théâtre éclaté*, chronicled the fragmentation of the individual in a context of revolutionary politics. Abandoning the Absurd, he resorted to theatre as a means of finding collective solutions to collective problems. Since 'art is always linked to a context', he used recent history to show individuals as the victims of both past and present, an approach which was not without controversy: *La Passion du général Franco* (1968: perf. 1976) was banned. Sensing that his personal success reduced his effectiveness, he thereafter sought to turn the passive spectator into an active participant. With *V comme Vietnam* (1967) he had encouraged post-performance debates with his audience and he enlisted members of the public to co-write *Les Treize Soleils de la rue Saint-Blaise* (1968). This proved the point of departure for a *théâtre sans public* which took the form of 'projects' designed to reveal the workings of the class war beneath the orderly surface of capitalist society. Considering himself more a catalyst than an 'author', he turned increasingly to community theatre projects and used 'self-expression' television, film and other means to enable ordinary people to dramatize their experience.

Arrabal For Fernand Arrabal (b. 1932), 'transgression' was the prime function of the artist. The evils he had found in Franco's Spain, from which he fled in 1955, also infected the West which he attacked through derision, cruelty and anarchical swings between tragedy and farce, vulgarity and poetry, which he christened *théâtre panique*. His first short Absurdist plays focused on the alienation of the individual, which was worked more forcefully in his most frequently performed play, *Le Cimetière des voitures* (written 1955; perf. 1965). His black humour emerged spectacularly in *L'Architecte et l'empereur d'Assyrie* (1967), a Freudian fable which reveals the erotic ingredient of power through two castaways who play sado-masochistic games before one devours the other. Though his nightmarish preoccupations turned increasingly political after 1967, he never lost touch with the Surrealist belief that theatre, by shocking and provoking, can change the world, a stance he maintained into the 1990s.

Theatre since 1968

The events of May 1968 produced deeper effects on French drama than on other forms of literary expression. Theatres were occupied and used as venues for revolutionary meetings, agitprop shows were hurriedly mounted and street theatre was invested with an aura of direct action. The radical mood persisted in progressive theatrical circles. The student cry 'Nous sommes tous des Juifs allemands' expressed a widespread feeling that individuals were helpless victims of the modern capitalist state. The slogan 'Tout le monde est artiste!' was also taken up in the form of the deprofessionalization of the performing arts. In many companies, directors exchanged their 'dictatorial' control for a looser, more comradely supervision, and playwrights were enrolled as equal members of a team. A new concept of 'popular' theatre overturned the Copeau-Vilar tradition of making high culture available to a mass audience. Instead, companies went into the work-place, identified and dramatized subjects of concern and performed at venues and times convenient to shift workers. 'Theatre by committee', sponsored by public funding, became the new avant-garde.

Boulevard and mainstream

The survival of Boulevard theatre into the new century indicates that there is still an audience for *digestif* comedies, farces, star vehicles, musicals and well-crafted dramas, new and revived, home-grown and imported. The classics, too, have fared well, shored up by the requirements of the academic syllabus and by the more general desire to maintain the best of France's heritage against the cultural imperialism of the Anglo-Saxons. On the other hand, the 1970s saw notable casualties. Surreal fantasy and 'literality' remain, but only as well-tried recipes for wrong-footing audiences. But the poetic play has fallen by the wayside and the vacuum in philosophical theatre left by Sartre and Camus has not been filled. Indeed, it is remarkable that the new intellectualism of the 1970s did not produce a single dramatist to represent it on stage. But theatre ceased to be a ghetto for the comfortable middle class. The social conscience of the 1960s consolidated the decentralization process and dispersed dramatic activity into suburban and provincial arenas. State funding and the habit of following rather than leading the public has helped live theatre to meet competition from cinema and television. It is unlikely that these changes would have come about had not the firebrands of 1968 consciously set out to attract new audiences.

La création collective

In the 1960s, drama had given way to theatre. In the 1970s, theatre turned increasingly into spectacle. The enthusiasm for group productions was exploited most effectively by the Théâtre du Soleil, begun in 1963 by Ariane Mnouchkine (b. 1934), whose *1789* (1971) showed how the landed nobility of the *ancien régime* had been replaced by a new aristocracy of money. Its thesis was less novel than its style, a dazzling display of the talents of the group which shared the responsibility for all aspects of production and performance, from script and design to lighting and sound and the use of multiple stages. 'Epic', 'Brechtian' and 'Shakespearean', it was performed in a disused factory at Vincennes and destabilized the conventional image of the theatrical venue. The play *1793* (1972), another reminder of the impotence of the people in a capitalist society, again dispersed the action to stages on three sides of the hall, while *L'Âge d'or* (1975) placed the argument in a contemporary setting. These productions were in a sense a development of the 'happenings' of the 1960s and, since scripts were less important than presentational styles which are evanescent by nature, they are now difficult to assess. They may be glimpsed, however, in the group's filmed life of *Molière* (1979) which, like *Mephisto* (1979), dealt in metaphorical terms with the function of theatre in a capitalist society. After 1980, Mnouchkine returned to the text-based play and, after 1984, began a collaboration with Hélène Cixous (*Sihanouk, roi du Cambodge*, 1985; *L'Indiade*, 1987) which dealt with the responsibility of the West for the problems of its former colonies. Their collaboration continued with *La Nuit miraculeuse* (1990), a film set in the French Revolution, while Mnouchkine returned to classical and Oriental-style productions with *Les Atrides* (1990), the *Oresteia* (1991) and *Tambours sur la digue* (1999) which drew on all the expressive resources of theatre.

Although it achieved the highest profile, the Théâtre du Soleil was but one of many companies which reinvigorated the theatre after 1968. In 1971, they formed a federation, 'Action pour le Jeune Théâtre', which called for state subsidies and made the case for political drama on contemporary issues. This ranged from the Théâtre de l'Aquarium's *Un conseil de classe très ordinaire* (1981) which caused a furore by shedding light on the way pupils were assessed in French schools, to the Nouvelle Compagnie d'Avignon's promotion of Occitan language and culture. The movement was strongly regional and often local. A collaborative production by the Théâtre Populaire de Lorraine, *Splendeur et misère de Minette de Lorraine* (1969), drew an unambiguous parallel between the exploitation of the local iron ore ('minette') and the capitalist exploitation of the whole region. Other productions highlighted racism, the press and the threat to the small shopkeeper posed by supermarket chains. However, not all groups were so politically committed. Jérôme Savary (b. 1942), creator of Le Grand Majestic Circus (1965), set out to renew the music-hall tradition. By 1988, Savary had produced nineteen 'spectacles' and directed eighteen operas and, in this way, helped to demystify the theatre for the wider public.

Directors and playwrights

'Collective creation' led to a radical reassessment of responsibilities. The star performer was demoted and set-designers (no longer *décorateurs* but *scénographes*) acquired a status consistent with the high emphasis on production values. The director became the overseer of a collective activity, though some acquired considerable financial and artistic power. To Planchon and Barrault were added Peter Brooke (b. 1925), Antoine Vitez (1930–90), Mnouchkine and Patrice Chéreau (b. 1944) who owed less to Copeau than to the Brecht/Artaud tradition. The 'director's theatre' of the 1960s and 1970s severely reduced the status of the writer: texts were merely a starting point and collaborative scripts were preferred to the single-author play. The 1970s were a difficult decade for playwrights, though after about 1975, some companies appointed resident writers who produced scripts based on collective research, discussion and preliminary improvisation. Writers were also disadvantaged by the growing economic recession which discouraged risk-taking by commercial managements and decimated theatrical publishing. Radio, television and the cinema, also facing financial and other problems, concentrated on the mass audience and did not encourage the experimentation essential to new writing. However, the Théâtre Ouvert (1970) was specifically directed at authors. It organized play readings and radio broadcasts and eventually set up both a publishing outlet and a small theatre where new plays, by the 'Beckettian' Philippe Minyana (b. 1946), Eugène Durif (b. 1950), Daniel Besnehard (b. 1954) and others were performed. While there has not been anything like a return to 'writer's' theatre, a number of individual voices have nevertheless made themselves heard.

Sarraute and Duras

The most successful new playwrights have combined elements of popular theatre, literalist New Theatre and the exploded Brechtian model. But notable too is the enduring influence of the New Novel of the 1950s which encouraged a minimalist tendency: disembodied voices, indeterminate settings and the deliberate rejection of a dramatic fiction which packages a 'meaning'. The plays of Nathalie Sarraute (1902–2000) articulate tensions between the oppressed and their oppressors in individual rather than political terms. *Le Silence* (1964) and *Le Mensonge* (1966) began as radio plays before being staged in 1967. Her other dramatic writings – *Isma* (1970), *Elle est là* (1978; perf. 1980), *Pour un oui ou pour un non* (1982) – are equally intimist and turn on the reactions of shiftingly adversarial characters to unexplained provocations. Marguerite Duras (1914–96), from *Le Square* (1956) onward, also gave dramatic form to her essential themes of escape from the present towards an 'impossible' liberation. *Les Viaducs de la Seine-et-Oise* (1962) gave a modified realistic treatment to a subject – a bizarre murder – which was repackaged in incantatory, understated terms as a novel (1967) and a further play (1968), both entitled *L'Amante anglaise*. By then, she was using the stage for more directly political purposes (*Yes, peut-être,* and *Le Shaga,* both 1968) but returned to her ceremonial fusion of impossible love and impossible revolution in *Détruire, dit-elle* (1969; also filmed). In 1971, she abandoned the formal distinctions between genres. Thus *India Song* (1973–5), designated 'texte-théâtre-film', began as a radio play but was filmed (in the event twice, with two distinct sets of images), though it was also intended to be staged and read. *Des journées entières dans les arbres* (1976), *L'Éden cinéma* (1977) and *Savannah Bay* (1983) wove strange arabesques around the enigmatic figure of her mother, while *Véra Baxter* (1983) conveyed the spiritual aspirations of a woman caught between desiring and the impossibility of desire. A Duras play is not concerned with narrative, psychology or ideas, and her recurring characters, recognizable but never the same, are anonymous figures in a neutral landscape. Through memories true and false, they enact semi-mystical rites of passage from what has been towards a freedom which is all the stronger for being non-specific. Time, space and drama are replaced by a voyaging present which is conveyed by the rhythms of Duras's poetic prose. Her refusal, after about 1970, to allow actors to act and directors to depart from her printed text and directions was at odds with the practices of collaborative theatre. Although relentlessly modern, Duras was less a survivor of the postwar avant-garde than a playwright in the classical mould. Her intensity, discipline and poetic control invite comparisons with Racine: the same 'stricte nécessaire' of decor, the same sacrifice of action to the 'récit' and the same high value set upon rhythm and the spoken word.

Playwrights since the 1970s

While Sarraute and Duras continued to mine the psychodrama, most playwrights of the 1970s showed the individual locked in more open conflicts with historical, political and institutional realities. For some, the alienation of the New Theatre remained a useful stratagem, though Georges Michel (b. 1926) had moved beyond his early Absurdism to the flat, clichéd dialogue which was a conscious feature of the new decade. More actively opposed to all forms of totalitarianism, the ten plays of the Belgian René Kalisky (1936–81) exploit a *surtexte*: the superimposition of images of social and historical oppression (fascism, the Holocaust) on contemporary forms of exploitation. Historical forces also lie at the heart of the prolific Cuban-born Éduardo

Manet (b. 1927). *Les Nonnes* (1969) used farce and horror to illustrate the Marxist thesis that socio-economic conditions determine behaviour and ideas and that culture is manipulated for political ends (*Un Balcon sur les Andes*, 1979). Jean-Claude Grumberg (b. 1939) deals directly with the violence born of racial hatred, intolerance and dehumanized modern society. The technocratic realists of *Amorphe d'Ottenburg* (1973) recommend the killing of old people as a logical solution to a growing economic problem. The parallel with Nazism is clear, but Grumberg's intention is rather to shock the audience by uncovering the Jarryesque collective cruelty which shelters behind seemingly rational propositions and is condoned by public apathy. The same idea, backed by his experience as a Jewish immigrant, informs *Dreyfus* (1974). *L'Atelier* (1979) covered similar ground in more naturalistic terms but *L'Indien sous Babylone* (1985) marked a return to his earlier manner. By juxtaposing different levels of reality (the collective and the personal) and language (Parisian *argot*, Yiddish humour and the clichés of ideology), Grumberg defends the individual against the forces of history and the state which acts with violence but speaks the language of reason.

Théâtre du quotidien

The suspicion that the consumer society meant not freedom but a new form of servitude fuelled the 1970s vogue for *théâtre du quotidien* which presented unexceptional, usually inarticulate and generally defenceless individuals in non-climactic, fragmented situations. The label has been applied to writers as different as Michel, Grumberg and Kalisky, though the name derived from the company created in 1975 by Jean-Paul Wenzel (b. 1947). For Michel Deutsch (b. 1948), individuals acquire definition through the pervasive images and language of politics and the media, so that the hero of *La Bonne Vie* (1976) is taken over by the image of Humphrey Bogart and even murders in character. The *théâtre du quotidien* built interestingly on the New Theatre (in its freer use of space and time) and the 'epic' vein (by fragmenting human experience in ways which emphasize society-as-fate). It also offered timely warnings against the advance of the social and more specifically capitalist Juggernaut. Yet in the long run, its relentlessly political stance has generated a pessimistic, even fatalistic view of human nature. If individuals are such easy victims of the linguistic clichés of economic and ideological systems, then they are helpless, creatures incapable of either resistance or moral choices.

Koltès and Vinaver

In the 1980s, the French stage remained more friendly to directors than to playwrights, and most maintained the general stance of the *quotidien*. However, with a shift from non-text to text-based plays, individual voices began to emerge. The four plays of Bernard-Marie Koltès (1948–89) dealt with topical issues (homelessness, family tensions) and showed individuals as customers of the ideological, cultural and commercial service providers which define the modern Western civilizing process. A similar but less symbolic reflection on modern values was provided by Michel Vinaver (b. 1927). His first forays into theatre in the 1950s presented ideology as a form of conditioning and *Iphigénie Hôtel* (written 1959; perf. 1977) was an effective satire of media disinformation. Vinaver's professional experience of the world of work – of takeovers, 'rationalization', and new marketing and management techniques – provided him with a solid documentary base for his most ambitious play, *Par-dessus bord* (written 1967–9; perf. 1973), the story of a French manufacturing company which beats American competition at its own game, though the outcome is not so much a victory as a comment on changing values. The same themes are treated in *Les Travaux et les jours* (1977) and *À la renverse* (1980) which, as in the plays which followed, make inventive use of multiple stages, varied registers of language and time scales. His approach was aimed at a 'marketing mix' which made progressive theatre appealing to the paying consumer. His subjects continued to reflect current concerns with the dehumanization of the individual in modern society, from life on a housing estate (*Les Voisins*, 1986) to the way the media packages reality (*L'Émission de télévision*, publ. 1989). Sharply observant but uncensorious, it is ultimately Vinaver's non-aligned ironic humour and his handling of ordinary human emotions which give him his personal voice.

Conclusion

Since the war, French theatre has been transformed. Decentralization has been achieved and institutional structures have created a national framework which has fostered experiment and left the commercial theatres with a predominantly entertainment role. Yet theatre remains a minority interest for just 1 per cent of the population, and of the 8–10 million tickets sold annually, half are still bought in Paris. Serious drama shed its role as an amusement and, in its publicly funded form, acquired a strong didactic and ideological vocation. The New Theatre of the 1950s abandoned the linear plot, the character study and the poetic, literary and philosophical play. The 1960s polarized activity into Absurdist and political camps. Since 1968, the Surreal has declined and the political has been expressed not through the resistance of heroic or ill-fated individualized victims but through attacks on consumerism, capitalism and the state, which overwhelm the citizen. Just as the single viewpoint of the unified character was collectivized, so the expressive resources of theatre were exploited to downgrade the written text in favour of a gestural, pictorial theatre which demanded the active participation of audiences. The avant-garde, protected by subsidy, has become part of the establishment it once attacked.

At the turn of the century, the major crisis facing the French stage, to which the success of collective and 'director's' theatre has contributed significantly, is the dearth of new writing, although there are exceptions, like Yasmina Reza's international success, *Art* (1998). Despite a tentative return to text-led theatre and alliances formed between certain directors and playwrights, the dramatic author has looked for alternative outlets for creative ideas in television and cinema. For the moment, the director and the *scénographe* are firmly in charge and no broad-based challenge to creation-by-committee has yet been mounted by those, like Vinaver or Valère Novarina (b. 1942), who call for a return to a theatre of authors and the restoration of the text.

Fiction

In the literary hierarchy of the nineteenth century, fiction was long ranked below poetry and theatre. During the twentieth, it not only displaced the other genres but invaded their territory. The novel annexed the personal, poetic voice, appropriated tragedy and, by abandoning word pictures, acquired proprietary rights over dialogue. But the novel also waged war on itself. Authors learned to discuss and use the codes of narrative with irony, implying that as a form of writing the novel was not stone to be carved but infinitely malleable clay. From the time of Valéry onwards many acknowledged that a work of art is never finished, merely abandoned, and that it consequently has a biography which may be as significant as its published form. Writers wrote fewer prefaces, but they kept journals of work-in-progress and explained themselves to literary journalists.

Unlike Balzac or Zola, they did not stand outside the world they created but were implicated in it. They could no longer lease their voices to their characters and distinguished between author, narrator and protagonist. Losing faith with both linear plots and linear time, they expanded their technical arsenal to include multiple viewpoints, the interior monologue, and the fragmented discourse of collage and montage, to the point of trusting to form to produce meaning: pastiche was both a comment and an advance on the aesthetics and values of novels validated by majority taste. Novelists ceased to provide neatly packaged tales for a passive audience, for they had not so much a story to tell or a lesson to give as an experience to share. Gide handed readers the responsibility for picturing his characters according to their own fancy and Barthes defined reading as a form of writing, the rival of creation.

But what was created moved out from the tradition of humanist, ethical observation towards concerns which were collective and increasingly intellectualized. From the outset, the novel entered into aggressive alliances with other disciplines – philosophy, politics, psychoanalysis, sociology, linguistics – which enabled it to respond to social change and public crisis. Taking many forms, from the multivolume *roman fleuve* to the *nouvelle-instant*, fiction charted the slow demise of the cultural values which had been shaped by the Judæo-Christian tradition and were steadily undermined by scientific progress, unbelief and indifference. Fine writing was one casualty. The individual was another. The combined impact of Freud, war, totalitarian systems and the invasion of private life by history made the behaviour of groups and social categories the focus of attention. The character study disappeared from fiction as did the portrait from academic painting. Interiority ceased to reflect the mind of man in his struggle to overcome the world outside him but focused on the confusion and turmoil of his inner life. Heroes, however vulnerable, had always risen above their circumstances. They now lost their self-belief and became victims. Confronting God or the Absurd, or swimming against the stream in their populist or *noir* manifestations, they no longer directed themselves, events and others (as the military hero had once done) but exchanged *gloire* and victory for impotence and defeat. They acquired a sense of guilt born of failure: they failed God, struggled vainly to be existentially free, and discovered that right and wrong, once clearly separated, had merged, overlapped and become problematic. They suffered punishments which had no palpable justification beyond the charge, against which there was no defence, that they were products of the same forces which filled the world with destruction. These defeated heroes inhabited a tragic universe driven by an unavoidable but unspecified fatality. Stripped of social or human identity, trapped in lives which did not fit them, they stumbled through a dehumanized world which was increasingly that of the city, no longer a place of moral corruption but an impersonal environment, a source of cynicism and alienation.

Just as the novelists of 1830 rejected the simplistic formulae of the eighteenth century which required fiction to punish vice and reward virtue, so their successors after the Great War began to reject both story as the main business of fiction and the realism which expressed it. The novel was no longer an exclusive, closed system; in the form of looser-boned fictions, it steadily became inclusive and open. But not all novelists were prepared to jettison the legacy of the nineteenth century and they carried the majority of readers with them. They kept faith with plot, psychology, heroes and mainstream standards of judging right from wrong, and in so doing they catered for the permanent demand for naturalistic fiction. The journeymen among them worked in popular categories (crime, fantasy, science fiction, romance, humour, adventure) which were aimed by the book trade at distinct constituencies. Many produced literate, technically accomplished novels which highlighted issues, illustrated liberal dilemmas and made human dramas out of moral choices. Yet however proficient, both popular and middle-brow authors continued to create closed worlds, working within a tradition rather than renewing it. In historical terms, they belong with the mainstream and will be considered in a later chapter as part of the widening definition of literary culture. How arbitrary such distinctions are, however, is demonstrated by their recuperation, after about 1970, by serious novelists who ceased to deconstruct the novel and steered it firmly back to the sub-genres of fiction they had once despised.

The novel in the twentieth century remained what it had always been, a mirror of the society which produced it. But while it reflected social and political crises, it acquired far stronger intellectual affiliations and was profoundly influenced by the rise and fall of ideologies. Four phases seem clear. Between the wars, it echoed post-1918 cynicism, the crisis of faith, political confusion, the uncertain self (even Proust's memory is involuntary) and the failure of action: the human condition was tragic. For two decades after 1940, confidence revived: meaning could be built out of chaos by commitment to just causes. By 1960, however, the mood had again turned negative and pessimistic: the *nouveau roman* exploded the myth of realism, and Structuralism insisted that meaning was defined not by human subjectivity but by the obscure conjunction of psychoanalytical and collective forces too diverse to be harnessed to a point of view. After about 1975, ideologies collapsed and confidence returned slowly: the 'human subject' became a person once more, an individual capable of making meanings which were right for the self if not always for others, while the author returned from the dead with the freedom to revert to story, explore 'post-literary' avenues and diversify into popular fictional forms.

1914–40

To many of the generation of 1880, the novel seemed too explicit and simplistic, and even before 1900 Gide (*Paludes*, 1895) and Valéry (*Monsieur Teste*, 1897) proposed anti-fictions which departed from the standard models. Though their impact was small, progress may be judged by the publication, in 1913, of Alain-Fournier's *Le Grand Meaulnes*, Martin du Gard's *Jean Barois*, and the first volume of Proust's *À la recherche du temps perdu*. The first supplied the imagination which had been lacking in the novel, the second experimented with form and engaged with pressing issues of modernity, and Proust explored new states of consciousness and engineered a new representation of time. But it was the Great War and the disillusionment that followed which gave fiction a new urgency.

The revolt of youth

Henri Barbusse (1873–1935: *Le Feu*, 1916), Maurice Genevoix (1890–1980: *Sous Verdun*, 1916), Roland Dorgelès (1886–1973: *Les Croix de bois*, 1919) and others returned from the trenches with graphic accounts of carnage, comradeship and sacrifice. But the novel of raw experience quickly acquired a point of view: while Georges Duhamel (1884–1966) showed the resilience of the human spirit, the Clavel novels of Léon Werth (1878–1955) were openly anti-militaristic. Against Henri de Montherlant (1896–1971) whose *Le Songe* (1922) exalted the virility of heroism, most novelists looked back on the war as a nightmare (Céline), a source of disillusionment (Drieu la Rochelle) or the best argument for pacifism (Giono: *Le Grand Troupeau*, 1931). The view that France's soldiers had been betrayed by the generals and politicians was extended to the older generation at large who had been responsible for the cataclysm which had claimed the lives of two million Frenchmen and writers like Péguy, Alain-Fournier and Apollinaire. In 1923, puncturing the mood of a mourning nation, Raymond Radiguet (1903–23) shocked readers with the cynical disaffection of *Le Diable au corps* (1923), the story of an adolescent who saw the war as an opportunity for sexual adventure. In *Thomas l'imposteur* (1923), Cocteau also gave short shrift to the postwar pieties and *Les Enfants terribles* (1929), a reworking of classical myth, encapsulated the rebelliousness of youth. By then, refractory adolescents and *lycéens* had acquired a high profile in the novel (Gide, Marcel Arland, Jacques de Lacretelle) and collectively they expressed resistance to authority and received values.

For revolt was in the air. Regional novelists defended the countryside against the soulless encroachments of the modern world. Individualists asserted their independence, with Giraudoux reaching out for a poetic view of self-fulfilment or Colette undermining the moral, and specifically male, conventions governing relationships and sexuality. The loudest protest came from the Surrealists who gleefully liquidated the past and moved fiction out of realism. Aragon's first novels (e.g. *Anicet*, 1921) were strong on pastiche and painted not nature but its 'photographic negative'. With *Le Paysan de Paris* (1926) he made fiction 'un lieu impersonnel, neutre, où tout peut arriver' and filled this new space with a fantastic vision of the capital. Dream and fantasy structure Breton's enigmatic *Nadja* (1928) which used episodes from his 'non-organic' life to project the spirit of Surrealism, and it was through somnambular, pataphysical and linguistic fantasies that those sympathetic to the movement, such as René Daumal (1908–44: *La Grande Beuverie*, 1938), sought to connect the human spirit with its roots.

Time and history

Although the proponents of revolt conceived negation as a positive act, a necessary prelude to refashioning social and cultural values, others took a longer view of the disruption which the war had brought. Before 1914, vast undertakings had revived the totalizing social panoramas of Balzac's *Comédie humaine* and Zola's Rougon-Macquart cycle. *Jean-Christophe* (10 vols, 1904–12) by Romain Rolland (1866–1944) offered idealism as a counter to the 'décomposition sociale et morale' of the times, and human destiny was the even grander subject of the *Histoire d'une société* (12 vols, 1904–59) by René Behaine (1880–1966). After the war, what Rolland had called the *roman fleuve* proved attractive to authors who, collectively, looked to the future by re-establishing continuity with the past. Duhamel's *Salavin* series (1920–32) highlighted the anxieties of the age while *La Chronique des Pasquier* (10 vols, 1933–45) expressed a disabused humanism in a family saga which asserted the rights of the individual against the collective. Roger Martin du Gard's *Les Thibault* (10 vols, 1922–40), originally intended to project into the future and end in 1940, was curtailed and turned into a chronicle of bourgeois society before 1914. It centres on two brothers, Jacques, who rebels against his father, symbol of an outmoded value system, and Antoine, a progressive but sceptical doctor, who fights disease and death as an affirmation of fraternity in a world of suffering. More resilient was Jules Romains's *Les Hommes de bonne volonté* (27 vols, 1932–46) which observes the lives of two *normaliens* between 1908 and 1933. Consistent with his Unanimist beliefs, Romains makes the group the focus rather than the individual and the sequence follows a fragmented pattern, perhaps adapted from American models, providing an impressionistic and not always tidy picture of a quarter-century of French history. Its multiple viewpoints, rejection of structured plot lines and use of discontinuous reality mark an advance on the linear technique of Duhamel and Martin du Gard and anticipate later aesthetic doubts about traditional realism.

Proust

A very different approach was adopted by Marcel Proust (1871–1922) who thought of *À la recherche du temps perdu* (1913–27) not as a *fleuve* but as a 'cathedral', a self-contained structure of mysterious essences waiting to be released. In a general sense, time is linear, for the states of Marcel's *moi* proceed towards the unveiling of a *moi profond*. But Proust's time is not forward movement but multi-layered, horizontal rather than vertical. It does not exist in the collective experience but in the narrator's mental processes. It is accessed through involuntary memory and is finally 'recovered' in an illumination when remembering transcends remembered moments and yields a reality which is universal and timeless.

Although Proust drew on his own experience, his novel is only incidentally autobiographical: it is not the story of a life but the history of a vocation. It is narrated by a double first-person voice, by the young 'Marcel', who has little understanding of the significance of what he relates, and his mature self, who with hindsight knows exactly what sensations retrieved from the past mean to him and to others. This duality is resolved only in the last volume when Marcel overcomes his fear of creation and accepts his calling as a writer. Finally mastering the mechanisms of time and art, he describes the book he will write. It exactly resembles the novel we have read, yet will be different.

Around this relatively simple structure, Proust orchestrated endless variations on his secondary themes of love, jealousy, the arts, and the changing social hierarchy which finally allows the *bourgeoise* Mme de Verdurin to become the Duchesse de Guermantes. It is the culminating irony of a vast tragicomedy where the comic is perfectly at ease with high seriousness. Proust's reflections on sleep, habit, and the 'intermittences du coeur' recall Montaigne, his gallery of portraits (above all of Charlus) ranks with that of Saint-Simon, and his sociological insights are as acute as Balzac's. Yet if his view of the subjectivity of love seems to look back to La Rochefoucauld, it also anticipates Freud, as did his own discovery of involuntary memory. In the same way, he drew on the themes and styles of the old fiction – psychological *analyse*, the novel of social and emotional initiation, the *roman de moeurs*, the 'double register' of Marivaux and Stendhal – but combined them into a new form capable of accommodating them all. Proust might appear to be the culmination of a literary tradition. Yet it is hardly an exaggeration to say that since the 1950s fiction has been defined by reference to him.

The relationship with history

Proust's immediate influence was small (though Gide the novelist was greatly indebted to him) and the *roman fleuve* continued to follow the linear model, as in Lacretelle's sequence, *Les Hauts Ponts* (4 vols, 1932–5), a chronicle of family decline. Such sagas and cycles were designed to explain people's relationship to history, but the lesson they drew gave no cause for optimism. Just as the Naturalist novel from which they sprang had shown how characters doomed by their temperament were herded towards their unpleasant destiny, so the *roman fleuve* pointed to the overpowering forces of history against which individual resistance is ineffective. The 'poetic' novel of revolt and fantasy denied this concept of causality by removing man from history through fantasy and dream. Jean Giono (1895–70) removed him from the city and placed him in a cosmic perspective. But while his novels, starting with *Colline* (1928), might make nature a living, healing force, the choices made by humans continued to be determined by its primitive, magical power.

The relationship with God

More orthodox metaphysical concerns elicited responses of comparable gloom. Marcel Jouhandeau (1888–1979) developed a 'mystique de l'enfer' which made the acknowledgement of the destructive power of evil a precondition of any approach to Christianity. Evil also occupies a central position in the fictional universe of Georges Bernanos (1888–1948). The priest of *Sous le soleil de Satan* (1926) fights the devil for the soul of his village, a struggle re-enacted with even greater personal anguish in the *Journal d'un curé de campagne* (1936). Innocence and heroism do not save: they make saints and martyrs of mild sinners. *Monsieur Ouine* (1945) unveiled the cynicism and violence which are the public face of evil which, in his polemical works, Bernanos had many times denounced. In the claustrophobic world of Julien Green (1900–99), paradise has been lost and there is little hope that it will be regained. His characters are isolated, desperate and tormented by the flesh. Abandoned by an inaccessible, unforgiving God, they plumb the depth of guilt and neurosis. Cast in more worldly terms but no less sombre in their implications, the novels of François Mauriac (1885–1970) paint an unflattering portrait of provincial manners with the traditional tools of realism and *analyse*. His target, however, was not the materialism or even hypocrisy of his characters but their attachment to both at the expense of their souls. They, too, exist in solitude, and for them love is not generosity but a form of appropriation of the other. Envy of those who dare to stray is barely concealed by characters who avoid sin for fear of the consequences. Spiritual poverty dominates the early novels, from *Le Baiser au lépreux* (1922) to *Thérèse Desqueyroux* (1927), but by the early 1930s the prospect of salvation gleams faintly on the horizon. But whereas Claudel's faith was a rock, Mauriac, like other Catholic novelists, was less confident of the outcome of the struggle between good and evil.

The problem of destiny

The deterministic tone of fiction left little room for chance or free will which, even though a person might choose wrongly, at least allowed them the dignity of choosing. André Gide (1869–1951), who had come to reject the sterility of sacrifice and the aridity of prayer, had made classically observed dramas out of such choices in his *récits*, *La Porte étroite* (1909) and *La Symphonie pastorale* (1919). But *Les Caves du Vatican* (1914), one of the 'ironic' fictions he called *soties*, explored the notion of an *acte gratuit* which restored the randomness of life. *Les Faux-Monnayeurs* (1926) pursued his ideal of 'vivre le possible', which meant living authentically and thereby safeguarding freedom in the present and for the future. The last sentence of the novel is, however, inconclusive. Far less hesitation was shown by muscular authors who found a more positive role for man in mainstream novels of empire or in cosmopolitan fictions like Cendrars's *Moravagine* (1926) and the fevered *Confessions de Dan Yack* (1929). Montherlant celebrated the virility of the bull-fight (*Les Bestiaires*, 1926) and, thinly disguised as Costals, misogynistic hero of *Les Jeunes Filles* (4 vols, 1936–9), made a virtue of rampant individualism. André Malraux (1901–76), adventurer and man of action, was also a thinker exercised by the death of God and the decline of Western values. But while his novels have an epic dimension, their heroism is shown as a struggle against overwhelming odds. The adventure of *La Voie royale* (1930) does not lift the oppressive weight of human isolation, nor is individual will sufficient to achieve revolutionary change. *Les Conquérants* (1928), *La Condition humaine* (1933) and *L'Espoir* (1937) situate an ideal of combative fraternity in collective political action. But while the idealism of his heroes may redeem their absurd deaths, it was hardly a complete answer to man's solitude, which might yet be cheated, however, through art and eroticism, an avenue explored by Georges Bataille in *Histoire de l'oeil* (1928) and *Bleu le ciel* (1934;

publ. 1957). Antoine de Saint-Exupéry (1900–44) chose the same fraternal ideal but in less exalted and more human terms. In *Courrier-Sud* (1930), *Vol de nuit* (1931) and *Terre des hommes* (1939), the battle to establish airmail routes bonds men in a common goal which is less utilitarian than heroic. Yet small gains required large sacrifices. Just as evil spread its wings over the good in the Manichaean world of Green and Bernanos, so the action hero with aspirations to Cornelian self-assertion was doomed to fail. As Cocteau observed: 'L'enfer existe: c'est l'histoire.' Service and the merging of self into a brotherhood of man were not responses calculated to impede the onward march of barbarism.

The human tragedy

Not all novelists felt quite as oppressed by the forces, historical or metaphysical, ranged against them. Colette continued to cast an acerbic eye on *louche* behaviour; Marcel Aymé (1902–67) satirized the current hypocrisies; Panaït Istrati (1884–1935) defended the freedom and dignity of his picaresque heroes; and Joseph Kessel (1898–1979) and Pierre Mac Orlan (1882–1970) gave their backing to adventurers. But the rejection of Belle-Époque values focused attention on new social constituencies, notably the provincial and urban lower classes which were now freed of the determinism of the Naturalist novel. Although Francis Carco chronicled 'picturesque' Montmartre in romanticized terms, Populists led by Léon Lemonnier observed the lives and struggles of the poor unsentimentally. Mac Orlan (*La Bandera*, 1931), like Eugène Dabit (*Hôtel du Nord*, 1931), accorded them the respect which the Front Populaire proclaimed was their right. 'Proletarians' grouped around Henri Poulaille gave poverty a sharper voice. Maxence Van der Meersch (1907–51) documented the crisis of capitalism from the workers' standpoint and expressed a paternalistic vision of society rooted in family values and good neighbourliness. Louis Guilloux (1899–1980) exploited his working-class roots in the *intimiste* vein before producing *Le Sang noir* (1935), which exposed the tensions that divided a northern town on one day in 1917. Against the cowardice of the bourgeoisie, it sets a socialist who, however, fails to secure the support of Cripure, a philosophy teacher too uncertain to act and too lucid not to be aware of the absurdity of action. Cripure is a Dostoevskian figure and one representative of a trend which implanted tragedy in ordinary lives. The same tragic sense resurfaced in crime fiction whose *noir* tendencies – the inevitability of events and the impossibility of escape – spread to the cinema, where Carné, notably, showed the death of hope and the power of fate through the iconic figure of Jean Gabin.

As the 1930s advanced, the conflict between Right and Left intensified and seemed to push Europe nearer to a war which could not be prevented. Pierre Drieu la Rochelle (1893–1945) struggled with an awareness of the pointlessness and mediocrity of existence and man's efforts to give it a rational form. His fiction expressed his disenchantment with society, politics and the 'drames minuscules' of his own life. After the crisis of February 1934, he opted for fascism, yet his characters, like their creator, continued to be paralysed by their lucidity. The hero of his finest novel, *Gilles* (1939), finally commits himself to Franco, but more out of despair than conviction. Drieu was a tortured figure unable to rise above the heroism of disillusionment. Louis-Ferdinand Céline (1894–1961) was motivated by a simpler reaction: disgust. His first novel, *Voyage au bout de la nuit* (1932) denounced war, nationalism, colonialism and the dehumanization of industrial society. With brash violence, burlesque irreverence and echoes of the proletarian novel, he demolished the ideological foundations of modernity in a manner acceptable to the Left. But *Mort à crédit* (1936) disconcerted his supporters with its absolute pessimism, obscenity and bare-knuckle anarchy. His literary reputation was long buried beneath the weight of the energetic fascism and rabid anti-Semitism which he adopted after 1937 and which underpin much of his later work. Yet he shared his generation's tragic vision of man, which he expressed with mocking, destructive glee. The nightmarish quality of his world has been validated by events and, though his reputation as a collaborator long made his name unmentionable, Céline is now recognized as one of the century's most original novelists. Not the least of his achievements was to overturn the humanist assumption that for art to be great it must be moral.

Forms of fiction

Between the wars, the tradition of realism (*analyse*, the omniscient narrator, the structured plot) were more enthusiastically endorsed by mainstream and popular fiction than by literary novelists, who experimented with new approaches to form. Proust redefined interiority and revolutionized fictional time. Gide's *Faux-Monnayeurs* adopted multiple viewpoints, allowed the story to develop out of what his characters say in letters and diaries and gave notice of the narratorial self-consciousness which would be taken up by the *nouveau roman*. The *vérisme* of the *roman fleuve* was challenged by enchantment and myth and overturned by the oneiric experiments of the Surrealists. Techniques of montage were suggested by American fiction and cinema to which Malraux was particularly drawn, and Céline simply threw away the rule-book. Paul Morand, Giraudoux and Cocteau may have created a distinctive *style d'époque* which was as urbane as their fiction. But the new prose style was urgent, eclectic and often unlovely. Less constrained by notions of taste and class, it was free to accommodate the urgent concerns of a fevered generation.

1940–60

If fiction in the 1930s caught the tragic mood of the times, it also saw the first stirrings of personal and group *engagement* which would dominate the 1940s. Aragon promoted communist solidarity in his *Monde réel* cycle (1934–51) which adapted socialist realism to a French cultural context. For Paul Nizan (1905–40), also a communist, the solution to personal and collective alienation was for individuals (*Antoine Bloyé*, 1933) and groups (*Le Cheval de Troie*, 1935) to take responsibility for themselves and face reality (*La Conspiration*, 1938). For Sartre the problem lay elsewhere, in the outcome of a systematic reflection on the arbitrariness of existence. Roquentin, hero of *La Nausée* (1938), experiences a feeling of sickness as he becomes aware that the world simply is: there is no transcendental power to give it point or direction. Sartre explored contingency as a philosophical problem in *L'Être et le néant* (1943) but made the fear of freedom the theme of *Le Mur* (1939), a collection of stories which illustrate inauthentic choices. Yet while his critical writings show an acute awareness of the technical possibilities of fiction, his uncompleted and heavily didactic sequence, *Les Chemins de la liberté* (1944–9), intended as a practical demonstration of the workings of *mauvaise foi*, remained set in the realistic mode.

After making inventive use of the first-person narrative in *L'Étranger* (1942), Camus also reverted to realism in *La Peste* (1947). In his 'cycle of the absurd', subjectivity is followed by solidarity before retreating into the solitude which emerges from Clamence's subversion of the confessional novel in *La Chute* (1956). Although by the early 1950s, Camus had doubts about the suitability of fiction as a medium for communicating ideas, his last novel, *Le Premier homme* (publ. 1994), was designed to be 'philosophical'. This modest interest in formal experiment is in part attributable to the movement's crusading ambition to reach the widest audience. It is equally visible in other 'committed' novelists, from Simone de Beauvoir, who dramatized ethical choices, to Emmanuel Roblès (1914–95), enemy of oppression and injustice, the pacifist Yves Gibeau (1916–94), Aragon (*Les Communistes*, 1949–51) and Roger Vailland (1907–65), who gave the individual responsibility for resisting the oppressions of society (*La Loi*, 1957). The same realistic conventions were adopted, and for similar reasons, by the 'Hussards', who fiercely opposed the commitment of the dominant left-wing hierarchy. Roger Nimier (1925–61), Antoine Blondin (1922–91) and Jacques Laurent (1919–2000) ostentatiously paraded individualism in terms which excluded innovative impulses. And if Françoise Sagan (b. 1935) captured the new spirit of youth, the cut and style of *Bonjour tristesse* (1954) were classical.

New departures

During and after the Occupation, regionalist writers, chroniclers of the war, collaborationist novelists (like Drieu or Robert Brasillach (1909–45), Existentialists and 'resistentialists' continued to insert individual destinies into history with the methods of realism. Their purpose was to persuade and the least of their causes was reshaping the novel, which they used as a practical tool: the most famous wartime book, *Le Silence de la mer* (1943) by 'Vercors' (pseud. of Jean Bruller, 1902–91), was a classically formed *récit*. But alternatives to fictions which created parallel worlds and created the illusion of ordinary life had been proposed at home by Proust and Gide and abroad by Kafka, Joyce, Dos Passos and Faulkner, and the reinvention of the novel proceeded apace. Paul Gadenne (1907–56) abandoned plot, abolished time and space and made the immediacy of existence the point of *Siloé* (1941) and there were more depths than surface in *Le Seau à charbon* (1940), the first of the wartime novels of Henri Thomas (1912–93). The heroes of Julien Gracq (b. 1910) inhabit a somnambulistic world and watch for signs which might mean the end of their exile from it. And if the postwar Giono reconnected with history and adventure, *Noé* (1947) told tales each of which is abandoned as the next begins, *Les Âmes fortes* (1949) gave two versions of the same story which are equally possible but contradictory, and *Un roi sans divertissement* (1953) disrupted the chronology of the discontinuous history of the death-fixated Langlois. Henri Bosco (1888– 1976) rejected the label of *roman*, with the exception of *Le Mas Théotime* (1945), but *Malicroix* (1949) met his criteria by using narrative to 'atteindre indirectement à la poésie'. More anarchic but no less serious, Boris Vian (1920–59) subverted the novel with his vein of disconcerting logic which is rooted in the unconscious and expressed through verbal slippage and the association of words. Language was also central to the novels of Raymond Queneau (1903–76), master of pastiche and clever nonsense: popular speech was not a threat to be resisted by literature but a resource to be exploited. After his 'roman cinématographique', *Loin de Rueil* (1945), his plots reject the rites of realism, events turn into anecdote, and dialogue, racy and naturally inventive, acquires a dominant role as the prime means of evoking character, relationships and the view that our connection with the world is essentially ludic.

Radical experiment

By 1950, many novelists had challenged the accepted practices of fiction by adopting multiple points of view, ellipsis, narrative disruption and expanded time, dissolving linguistic and literary borders, rejecting *engagement* and taking the view that the subject of a novel was itself and that fiction was not a statement but an 'act' (Leiris). Others went further and attacked the very foundations on which the genre was based. Adding texts like *Madame Edwarda* (1941) to his prewar *récits*, Georges Bataille used excess and perversion as routes to the abjection beyond which the 'impossible experience' of sex, death and life provides access to the 'sacred' communion of the human spirit: anonymous sex, described with icy detachment, acquires a metaphysical value. The humiliation of self as the condition of its emancipation was also the theme of the *Histoire d'O* (1954) by Dominique Aury (1901–98) and the short erotic novels of Pieyre de Mandiargues (1909–91). For Pierre Klossowski (b. 1905) the transgressions of Roberte, heroine of his trilogy *Les Lois de l'hospitalité* (1953–6), locate self-fulfilment not in transcendence but in the communion of transgression. Although obscene by any standards, these narratives wrap sex in philosophical abstractions, reduce psychology to desire and sacrifice plot to the moment. Transgression – betrayal, theft, homosexuality – was central to the spiritual itinerary of the heroes of Jean Genet's four novels (1944–7). They exist in a world of systems and rules which parody reality and the narrative codes with which it was conventionally expressed: the ordinary and the fantastic, normality and perversion, illusion and identity, masculine and feminine do not clash but merge.

For Maurice Blanchot (1907–2003), the novel was not 'la relation de l'événement, mais cet événment même'. When life is reduced to words, it dies, but words may yet be made to give life. Against committed literature and militant poetry, he defined writing not as an action on the world but as the only meaningful act. How this might best be achieved is the theme of his critical writings but also of novels which, from *Thomas l'obscur* (1941) onwards, set disembodied characters in indeterminate settings. The narrative voice is uncertain, limited, even false, yet it creates the space in which the real fiction is located. The same principle directs *Le Bavard* (1946) by Louis-René des Forêts (1918–2000), a monologue which claims to be a confession of the hero's greatest vice: his need to talk. But as he talks, he hides as much of himself as he reveals, and he is judged not by what he says but by what his unreliable voice says about him. Sincerity with the self was addressed by Jean Cayrol (b. 1911) in *Je vivrai l'amour des autres* (1947) which also uses a first-person narrator to negotiate a way through a world which contains more things than people. Voices dominate Samuel Beckett's trilogy (*Molloy*, 1951; *Malone meurt*, 1951; *L'Innommable*, 1953) and the shorter prose texts which followed: telling their tale is their protagonists' main business. They are so much 'word-dust' sprinkled over their decomposing, disintegrating, dispossessed selves. Yet, as in Beckett's theatre, they endure, stayed by humour and comforted by nothing.

The New Novel

Existentialist *engagement* had led to an aesthetic impasse. By failing to move beyond the realism required for its didactic purposes, the committed novel had beached itself. But as the tide retreated, it left pools teeming with anti-novels. Even so, it was not until the mid-1950s that concerted opposition to the conventions of realistic fiction was mounted. Alain Robbe-Grillet (b. 1922), Nathalie Sarraute

(1902–2000), and Michel Butor (b. 1926) had distinct writing agendas but, as authors published by Les Éditions de Minuit, they were linked as exponents of a *nouveau roman*, a term coined by a journalist in 1957. They agreed with Sartre that the function of the novel was to enlighten not to entertain, but rejected his insistence that enlightenment should take a political form. Instead, looking to Kafka, Joyce, Proust and Ponge, they set out to involve the reader in an apprehension of the world which was rooted in a theory of perception. The problem of perception revolves around our awareness of the external world and our hold on the inner reality of the mind which processes it. In phenomenological terms, no such distinction exists since the perception of reality is invariably influenced by the subjectivity of the perceiver. Butor accepted that objective description of either external or internal reality is not possible but believed that new fictional conventions would capture our waking dream: the contrapuntal diary of *L'Emploi du temps* (1956) or the train journey of *La Modification* (1957) which alters the false idea Léon has of himself. For Sarraute (*Portrait d'un inconnu*, 1948; *Le Planétarium*, 1959), the description of objects was a means of conveying her characters' fluctuating self-awareness, those minute shifts of the psyche which she called *tropismes*. Robbe-Grillet considered the external world to be alien to man and described it with detached precision in a neutral voice which excluded metaphor, the pathetic fallacy and any point of view which might dramatize the relationship of his characters to the world in which they moved. Their inner reality is rendered, in his early novels from *Les Gommes* (1953) to *Dans le labyrinthe* (1959), by what they see, an approach which identified New Realism as *l'école du regard*.

In practice, however, the *nouveaux romanciers* were united less by what they severally aimed to achieve than by their opposition to any utilitarian use of the novel which they regarded as autonomous. They rejected omniscient narrators, characters who represent human nature and plots which leave no loose ends. By showing, not explaining, they communicated a sense of the incompleteness of experience, a project more 'realistic' than the realistic novel of illusion. Both protagonist (who may be no more than a voice) and reader (who is given no privileged information) attempt to unpick the same puzzle. These broad principles were shared, in varying degrees, by Marguerite Duras, Claude Simon (b. 1913), Robert Pinget (1919–97), Claude

Ollier (b. 1922) and others, and, through Alain Resnais (b. 1922) and Jean-Luc Godard (b. 1930), gave a cerebral dimension to the cinema of the *nouvelle vague*.

1960–70

The age of the New continued into the 1960s. New Theatre, the *nouveau roman* and the *nouvelle vague* were followed by the New Criticism enshrined in *Tel Quel*, the flagship of French intellectualism for a quarter of a century. It took on the world 'as it is' not only by jettisoning systems but by questioning the means (the processes of the mind and society, the slipperiness of language) by which we define and express our apprehension of 'what is'. Literature was nothing if it was not uncommitted and free to follow its own logic. *Tel Quel*, rejecting humanism, political commitment and all forms of writing based on representation and psychological intentionality, backed the new realism of Robbe-Grillet and endorsed it through a variety of theoretical discourses which included fresh approaches to language, structures, signs, systems, psychoanalysis and the social sciences. By 1963, Robbe-Grillet's *nouveau réalisme* was suspected of subjectivism and the *Tel Quel* collection of novels promoted fiction which eschewed empirical psychologism in favour of a *nouveau nouveau roman* which aimed at formal rigour and acknowledged language as a 'phenomenology of perception'.

The *écriture textuelle* of Philippe Sollers (b. 1936), used geometric patterns (the chessboard of *Drame*, 1965) and allowed narrative identities to change puzzlingly, sometimes within the same paragraph. The approach – extreme fragmentation, disconcerting or absent chronology, and a flat, neutral narrative voice – was also adopted by Maurice Roche (1925–97), Jean-Pierre Faye (b. 1925) and Jean Thibaudeau (b. 1935). It was analysed and developed by many theorists, including Jean Ricardou (b. 1932) whose own novels turned 'l'écriture d'une aventure' into 'l'aventure d'une écriture': in *Les Lieux-dits* (1969) the fragmented narrative is assimilated into the painting which the protagonists, prompted by ambiguous clues, seek to recuperate. By 1970, the *nouveau roman*, non-referential and having no object except its own hermetic agenda, had dispelled the charm of fiction. Writing was a material act which generated texts from narrative codes, images and above all from language. Words do not represent thought; thought is already *there* and is merely revealed by words in a text. Anonymous protagonists, blurred identities and a non-expressive narrative style were common features of writings which were offered less as finished products but as a reflection of the processes of text-generation. By 1970, theorists like Ricardou urged the importance of codifying its practices into a prescriptive system.

The other major movement of the 1960s, the Oulipo, also turned against stories generated by the imagination. But far from retreating from the world, it engaged with it directly, though non-ideologically: if language was the source of their texts, it was at least the language of everyday reality. Narratives were to be generated from words and genre codes, as in Queneau's *Les Fleurs bleues* (1965), a dream within a dream within another dream. Jacques Roubaud would perpetuate Oulipo methods into the 1980s with his *Hortense* trilogy (1985–90), but the group's most illustrious member was Georges Perec (1936–82). *Les Choses* (1965) gave him a reputation as an acute sociological observer of the sixties generation. In fact, it expressed his obsession with things and with words which were not just signifiers but objects in their own right, to be piled in heaps and allowed to exude meaning. Oulipo provided a framework for his passion for catalogues (*L'Homme qui dort*, 1967, is a *pointilliste* confection) and he prospered within its atmosphere of playfulness disciplined by rules. He produced a murder mystery, *La Disparition* (1969), which avoided the letter 'e', and *Les Revenentes* (1972), which avoided all other vowels. *La Vie mode d'emploi* (1978), his masterpiece, links a hundred tales to the moves made by a knight on a chessboard and forms a vast interlocking network of stories. Perec was a maker of mosaics who proceeded by inventory and collage as a means of extracting sense from the banality of objects.

Despite the pressures on traditional fiction in the 1960s, the literary novel continued to evolve relatively free of dogmatic prescription. Jean-Marie le Clézio (b. 1940) broke with the 'goût vériste du public' in *Le Procès-verbal* (1963), but while he continued to focus closely on the material fabric of the world, his characters developed as emblems in a quest for identity, a theme central to the novels of Patrick Modiano (b. 1945), beginning with *La Place de l'Étoile* (1968). Des Forêts's *La Chambre des enfants* (1960) gave a new urgency to the conventions of realism which, if they were eschewed by Monique Wittig, remained at the centre of much of the writing published by women: Simone de Beauvoir's continuing deconstruction of bourgeois values, the autobiographical novels of Violette Leduc and Albertine Sarrazin, and the social observation of Christiane Rochefort. But if the intelligentsia derided the thoughtful novel of character and manners (the liberal humanism of Jean-Louis Curtis, 1917–95, was one of its targets), there were still those who stood above the fray and created worlds of their own.

Yourcenar

Marguerite Yourcenar (1903–87) had been writing since the 1920s but her reputation was made by *Les Mémoires d'Hadrian* (1951), a multi-dimensional portrait of the Roman emperor and his times. Yourcenar was no orthodox historical novelist. She used history to reach an understanding of values which are not attached to a particular time. Her high standing was amply confirmed by *L'Oeuvre au noir* (1968). Set in Renaissance Flanders, it projects Zénon as a hero of lucidity who, however, pays the price of Yourcenar's characters who rise above history: they become outcasts from the society which they master.

Cohen

During a literary career spanning nearly sixty years, Albert Cohen (1895–1981) remained deaf to the philosophical, aesthetic and cultural clamour which shaped the literature of his century. His cycle, *Solal* (1930), *Mangeclous* (1938), *Belle du Seigneur* (1968) and *Les Valeureux* (1969), is comic, tragic, and satirical, though its constant aspiration is an epic desire to reconcile Man with his lost humanity. His novels enact the conflict between assimilation and betrayal through Solal, who is incapable of choosing between Reason and Belief, East and West, Jew and Gentile, Love and Death. *Belle du Seigneur*, rich in high comedy, acid observation, social satire and allegory, traces Solal's doomed attempt to rescue the world through political action and, when this fails, to save himself through love, which proves to be his final illusion. He can no more live love than he can defend his people against the fascist threat in the Europe of the 1930s in which his quest is set. Cohen, a lucid, unsentimental idealist, allows him to die defeated but defiant.

Tournier

Michel Tournier (b. 1923), equally impervious to philosophical and literary fashion, found his themes in modernizations of familiar allegories and fables. On Defoe's island, Robinson, hero of *Vendredi, ou les limbes du Pacifique* (1967) discovers the solar dimension of the cosmos and chooses to stay while Friday opts to leave. *Le Roi des Aulnes* (1970) revived the predatory ogre, *Les Météores* (1975) explored the myth of the inseparable twins, and both the richly symbolic *Gaspard, Melchior et Balthasar* (1980) and *La Goutte d'or* (1985) focused on the cruelty and instability of societies and the vulnerability of the self which is rewritten for us by literature and our social existence.

Since the 1970s

Until the mid-1970s, the *nouveau roman* continued to occupy the aesthetic high ground. However, Ricardou's linking of any kind of realism to bourgeois ideology divided its exponents, notably Butor, Sarraute and eventually Simon, who repudiated all attempts to collectivize their separate practices. Anecdote, characters and personal reminiscence made an unexpected return. Robbe-Grillet's ostentatiously subjective trilogy of *Romanesques* (1985–94) was a hybrid form of autobiography, told by a narrating *je* which does not coincide with the author's self. The contradictions of the *moi* are expressed by the relationship to the documentable Robbe-Grillet with his fictitious but no less real double, Henri de Corinthe. Pinget continued to orchestrate voices which are experienced in performance, but also developed his talent to amuse with further tales of the pompous, gossipy Monsieur Songe. Sarraute crossed the boundary between conversation and *sous-conversation* with *Vous les entendez?* (1972) and turned her *tropismes* into a form of much more direct self-examination in later texts like *L'Usage de la parole* (1980) and the more overtly self-referential *Enfance* (1983). After *Les Georgiques* (1981), Simon offered a clearer narrative line and a stronger autobiographical presence. The defence of theoretical positions was left largely to Ricardou and his new *textique*. With *Femmes* (1983), even Sollers abandoned *texte* for satirical novels which commented directly on intellectual fashions and excesses of the consumer society. Kristeva's *Les Samouraïs* (1990) also broke out of the Postmodern impasse: it was a barely veiled autobiographical account of the adventures of feminism and the Parisian intelligentsia.

Duras

The highest profile of the old guard was achieved by Marguerite Duras, whose writing career lasted half a century. Duras reinvented herself several times. She moved beyond her early experimental realism and later disowned everything she had published before *Moderato cantabile* (1958). Her 'Indian' cycle, beginning with *Le Ravissement de Lol V. Stein* (1964), explored the private and collective psyche in novels and films which lacked warmth and human feeling and existed on the edge of the sanity which society equates with reason. Her attachment to libertarian causes (she supported the students in 1968, became a feminist in the 1970s, and wrote controversial articles on sensitive topical issues) alienated some readers but invariably found a regularly renewed younger audience. *L'Amant* (1984) brought her global fame. Although it begins: 'L'histoire de ma vie n'existe pas', she had by then already revisited it many times and in puzzlingly contradictory ways. Her 63 fictions, 20 films, 25 or so plays and theatrical adaptations explore obsessions – death, fear, love, freedom – through recurring symbols: her mother as the victim of 'colonial vampirism', the beggar woman who carries the weight of the century's public horrors, and Anne-Marie Stretter who encapsulates private transgression. 'Durassie' is a no-man's land which exists between memory and forgetting, past and future, sun and brooding forest, oppressive land and liberating sea. With time, her exact, understated prose style grew closer to poetry but continued to offer glimpses of an unattainable consummation which is all the more powerful for being as intensely felt as it is undefined. Love, like revolution, was 'impossible', although she knew that the 'impossible' she strove to reach was 'the history of the future'.

The legacy of the sixties

Spurred on by the success of Perec's *Vie mode d'emploi*, Oulipians like Roubaud and Marcel Bénabou (b. 1939) continued to deconstruct the novel. Ostentatiously jettisoning fiction as illusion, they played self-consciously with its conventions and the language of things, and intrigued readers with tantalizing anecdotes which replaced narrative structure. In *Le Directeur du musée des cadeaux des chefs d'État de l'étranger* (1994), Jacques Jouet (b. 1947) devised, around a perfunctory plot, a labyrinthine world capable of multiple readings. But the interest shown in the 'infra-ordinary' both by Perec and, notably, Sarraute, allowed *nouveau réalisme* to evolve. A number of authors, particularly women (Anne-Marie Garat, b. 1946; Régine Détambel, b. 1960) write of ordinary, anonymous, often interchangeable people at a moment of crisis, unexceptional individuals neutrally observed in hyperrealist detail. Clothes, common objects, routine actions (like rolling a cigarette) furnish a world in which adolescents fail to adapt to adulthood, personalities disintegrate and become ungovernable and a life may be rendered, as in *Adieu* (1988) by Danièle Sallenave (b. 1940), in a series of banal conversations. The same minimalist tendency is observable in parodic variations which replace the earnestness of the *nouveaux romanciers* with irony and comic detachment, where the humour lies in style, not in character or situation: *La Salle de bain* (1985) narrates the life of a man who rarely leaves his bathroom. Its author, Jean-Philippe Toussaint (b. 1957), was one of the 'Romanciers impassibles' (Christian Gailly, Patrick Deville) launched in 1980 by Les Éditions de Minuit which, under Jérôme Lindon (1925–2001), continued to encourage experimental writing. Their leader, Jean Échenoz (b. 1947) returned ostensibly to plot, character and genre (like his road novel *Un An*, 1997) but destabilized them with absurd and sometimes fantastic accretions which comment bathetically on contemporary realities.

Postliterary fiction

To these developments of New Realism could be added others: the *intimiste* novel which examines unexceptional, often marginalized lives and relationships in microscopic detail, or its annexation by forms of non-ideological *engagement* with social problems, such as *Impatience* (1998) in which François Bon (b. 1953) expresses the anger of the *banlieue* through silhouettes which are something more than just voices. What such novels have in common, however, is not so much their eagerness to abandon old narratives as their concern to extend the possibilities of story-telling. What has been called the 'postliterary' (or 'postcultural') generation has ceased to deconstruct fiction on principle and to experiment for experiment's sake. The last of the rules have been abandoned. The language of fiction may be elegant and clear or syntactically and lexically unliterary. Novels may deal in whole lives or move inside one head or more. They may be plotless or tell tales which have beginnings, middles and ends, and may incorporate diaries, newspaper cuttings, letters and essays. Two novels, *L'Extension du domaine de la lutte* (1994) and *Les Particules élémentaires* (1998) by Michel Houellebecq (b. 1958), illustrate the potential of the new approach: they freewheel through minds, exude sexual incorrectness, and tread a narrow line between provocation and responsibility. But whether they are set in the past, the present or the future, they reflect the *morosité* which afflicted France in the 1990s. Action is replaced by submission to the events of an erratic (as opposed to Absurd) world in which nothing may be judged except by existential (as opposed to Existentialist) fact. It was a form of writing perfectly attuned to the Postmodern condition. But its willingness to adopt new postures was prepared by two developments which occurred in the 1980s.

Autobiography

The reversion of the New Novelist of the 1950s to 'subjectivity' took a specifically autobiographical form which reflected the growing power of autobiography as a genre in its own right. Des Forêts (*Ostinato*, 1997), Annie Ernaux (b. 1940), Jean Rouaud (b. 1952) and others found their basic material in the self and the world which had shaped it. The literary imagination, long suspect, seemed no longer able to deliver truths to compare with the verities of writing which made the author's past and personality both its subject and narrative principle. But the autobiographical *je* is bound by facts and the obligation of sincerity, and is too limited to express a general experience. It could be freed, however, if harnessed to novels which packaged the lived experience of the *je* in ways which suggested that it belonged to a fictional character. *Autofiction* had already been practised by Perec and Modiano before Serge Doubrovsky (b. 1928) found a name for it in 1977. Thereafter it served not only individual sensibilities but the cause of identity for various constituencies, feminist, francophone, regionalist and gay (where it was best represented by Hervé Guibert).

Popular genres

The new freedoms claimed by the novel also had roots in the recuperation of popular fiction. It began in the early 1970s with Patrick Manchette's transformation of the formulaic *roman policier* into the *néo-polar*, strong on plot and character but capable of expressing more ambitious themes and ideas. In the 1980s, Échenoz inserted serious intentions into the spy and detective formulae and writers like Daniel Pennac, Tonino Benacquista, Didier Daeninckx and Philippe Djian moved out of the *Série noire* to create a new breed of *romans noirs*. Other pulp genres – science fiction, historical romance, espionage – have also been annexed as vehicles for comment, sometimes enlivened by sardonic humour, on racism, the marginalization of the *banlieue* and the corruption of business and politics. The element of pastiche has faded. What started as a form of parody has now outgrown the pulp styles and formulae it imitated and replaced them as superior, autonomous forms of story-telling.

The survival of tradition

The cannibalization of popular genres marked a return to heroes and structured narrative. But story and heroes had never disappeared. New Realism had been resisted for its elitist, theoretical approaches to fiction, and the more reader-friendly old realism of observation, the authorial voice, graphic images, fine writing and narratives with which the reader could engage found a ready response. The psychological, historical, philosophical novel prospered. Old-style adventure played with myth, and fantasy acquired an epic dimension. But even here, the influence both of the New Realism and popular genres has helped acculturize experiment, informal registers and imaginative individualism. But validation by the Académie Française and its endorsement by readers continue to ensure the survival of the classical model of fiction inherited from the nineteenth century.

Conclusion

Over the last century and a half, the novel, which at first offered a reflection on 'la condition sociale', changed its focus in the 1930s to 'la condition humaine' which, since the 1950s, has been expanded to include 'la condition sexuelle'. It has again proved its versatility, giving a voice to philosophers, social critics, the socially marginalized, women, the gay community and the francophone diaspora. It has fostered both introspection and sensibility and the dynamic contestation of ideas and the social process. In the last generation, its *engagement* has become non-ideological and its minimalism and parodic tendencies, together with the retreat from 'literary' writing, seem to be the basic essentials of its modern incarnation. Yet however varied its programme, the contemporary novel has reined in its ambitions, waiting perhaps for a makeover by the potential yet to be released by the information revolution. Doubtless, new names are waiting in the wings, but from this vantage point at least, the century remains Proust's, and Yourcenar, Cohen and Duras look like the last of the old-style Great Writers.

Short fiction

The nineteenth-century short story was characterized by its extreme diversity. Yet it acquired a name as a minor art. This was perhaps because, of its many practitioners, only Mérimée and Maupassant were *conteurs* by temperament. In 1900, Huysmans complained that stories sold as badly as poetry and André Breton was not alone, in the 1920s, in judging short fiction 'un genre périmé'. Before 1940, only Paul Morand succeeded in acquiring a following for his short fiction. For the most part, if the *nouvelle* was resuscitated it was for reasons foreign to the intrinsic interest of the form, by Sartre's revival of the *conte philosophique* (*Le Mur*), for example, or in Vercors's *nouvelle*, *Le Silence de la mer* (1943). Critical opinion, more hostile to the genre in France than abroad, did little to enhance the reputation of the French short story, though, paradoxically, foreign authors (from Chekhov and Katherine Mansfield to J. L. Borges and Julio Cortazar in the 1960s) were greatly admired.

Most authors continued to define the form as essentially a dramatic story. Established techniques survived: the framed tale, the 'oral' presentation by a narrator who recounts what he has experienced or witnessed, sometimes handing the narrative voice to an acquaintance. The *conte* continued to be associated with the comic, the disconcerting, the striking *fait divers* in the numerous collections of Marcel Aymé or La Varende. The *nouvelle* rejected fantasy and comedy and gave a realistic treatment to subjects taken from ordinary life (childhood and adolescence, conjugal strife, relationships). The limited scope of the episode and the brisk efficiency of its telling differentiated the genre from the more expansive novel. This may explain why major novelists like Montherlant, Céline and Saint-Exupéry left no collections of tales, though many (Colette, Julien Green, Drieu la Rochelle) did. After 1945, the bulk of short stories conformed broadly to the convention which made plot the vehicle for the mini-drama. This model continued to find an audience and has been perpetuated, in varying degrees, by Daniel Boulanger (b. 1922) or J.-M. le Clézio, who cast the tales in *La Ronde et autres faits divers* (1982) in autobiographical and colonial mode. Michel Tournier, beginning with *Le Coq de Bruyère* (1978), added the moralizing dimension of the fable to the realism of the traditional *nouvelle*.

Until about 1950, short fiction perpetuated nineteenth-century models. After that date, however, a number of more radical initiatives renewed the genre. In the 1950s, the *nouveaux romanciers* experimented with short fiction, though Robbe-Grillet, Sarraute and Beckett did not write *nouvelles* any more than they wrote novels. What were termed *récits brefs* or *textes courts* explored the modern preoccupation with perception and alienation in non-realistic terms, more at the level of language than of plot. The change in approach is visible if the near-naturalism of Duras's early collection, *Le Boa* (1953), is compared with, say, *L'Homme assis dans le couloir* (1980), which has neither action nor situation but evokes disembodied sexuality in impressionistic, voyeuristic terms. Such experiments are related to the major twentieth-century development in short fiction, the *nouvelle-instant*. The story is stripped of anecdote and incident and focuses on a single decisive moment which confronts a character with himself, his past, his system of values. This approach relies not on plot but on an emotional impact which makes the instant dramatic in a psychic rather than chronological sense. The dénouement ceases to be a conclusive event but an epiphany, and such tales do not aim for closure (one of the pleasures of the traditional story) but for the openness which allows the impact to reverberate long after the reader has stopped reading.

The *nouvelle-instant*, pioneered by Maupassant, was taken up before and after the Second World War by Morand, François Mauriac, Sartre, Camus (*L'Exil et le royaume*, 1956), and above all by Marcel Arland (1899–1986), one of the century's most gifted and prolific *nouvellistes*. His tales, broader-based than the *Nouvelles* (1945) of Beckett and Robbe-Grillet's avant-gardist *Instantanés* (1954–69), helped point the French *nouvelle* towards the model of the single moment. Other contributory factors have been the influence of foreign writers like Mansfield and Raymond Carver, who also avoided dramatic situations in favour of the understated discovery of feeling or the apprehension of some unexpected, life-changing truth. Since 1980, the disarray, solitude and desperation of ordinary lives have been chronicled through such brightly lit instants by a number of women writers (Christiane Baroche, Claude Pujade-Renaud, Régine Détambel) and above all by Annie Saumont. But the short story has still to achieve the glamour which attaches to the novel.

7

Beyond Imagination, Gender and the *Métropole*

The literature of France, unlike the First Republic, is not one and indivisible. Over a thousand years, many literatures have gone into its making. There have been literatures for warriors, Church and class, for court and town, for rational minds and delicate sensibilities, for conformists and for rebels. Literature has always been a movable feast and, in the twentieth century it kept moving.

In 1900, what was thought of as literature was the product of a cultural system rooted in privilege and inseparable from Parisian sophistication. Although it formed an exclusive club, its rules were sufficiently flexible to recognize and accommodate genius, the basic qualification for membership. Even a rebel like Rimbaud was admitted and many outsiders like Balzac, Dumas *père* or Zola were enrolled, assimilated and turned into acceptable approximations of *hommes de lettres*. By 1950, its social centre of gravity had been lowered by writers who had entered literature through a new door: the universal education installed by the Third Republic. Alain-Fournier, Pagnol, Duras or Camus did not enjoy the social advantages of Proust, Gide or Sartre, but they too carried literature forward. They were assisted by numerous factors whose action has accelerated dramatically since the Second World War: the democratic process, the decentralization of culture, the growing efficiency of the book trade, and, not least, the rise of the mass audience with an appetite for consumption of all kinds. There have been casualties. The fences which once separated genres have disappeared, literary style is less well-spoken, poets have lost their public and new roles have been found for the playwright. But change does not necessarily mean decay. Different constituencies have emerged with altered priorities and the result has been to give the concept of literature a more or less indefinitely extensible content. The forms of popular and para-literary culture will be dealt with in the final chapters. Here attention will be given to voices which have been heard only in the last half century: the voices of the subjects of lived experience, of women, of the gay community and of the many who inhabit the commonwealth of *francophonie*.

Biography

From its beginnings, literature personalized the human predicament by putting human faces to abstract ideas. Out of the Latin *vita* grew the lives of saints which, cumulatively, created a framework (childhood, deeds and death) for accounts of kings and legendary heroes like Arthur and his knights. In the thirteenth century, the brief, formulaic *vida* honoured poets who, in the fourteenth, began to acquire individuality and finally, with Machaut and Villon, names. Well into the seventeenth century, however, works and deeds continued to be held in greater esteem than the circumstances of a particular life, unless that life could be seen as a work and made exemplary. Plutarch furnished a secular model, the *vie illustre*, which was used to offer lessons in chivalry, valour and honour, but in the late Renaissance summaries of the lives of artists and authors also linked works to their creators. After 1650, proto-biography acquired some of the habits of the new document-based history. Accounts of historical figures and writers like Descartes and Molière, though sketchy and unreliable, adopted a chronological sequence, assessed their subject's achievements and offered the same kind of categorized character judgements as the *portrait*. After 1700, interest in public figures continued to grow. It is found in the academic *éloge*, novels which encouraged readers to be curious about supposedly 'real' lives and philosophic writings which created a gallery of radical precursors of the Enlightenment.

The Revolution identified events and parties with individuals who were praised and vilified in brief lives. After 1800 the vogue for history justified enterprises like Michaud's *Biographie universelle* (1811–28) and prompted a rush of biographers to feed the public's curiosity about great persons. Yet with a handful of exceptions like Renan's revisionist *Vie de Jésus*, the nineteenth century produced few biographies to rival, say, Southey's *Life of Nelson*. Even so, Sainte-Beuve's reliance on biography as a tool of literary criticism became standard. By 1900, historical and literary biography was the dominant form, with the demands of the syllabus favouring the 'life and work' and the 'life and times' of prescribed authors. Before and after 1914, collections of *grandes existences* and *grandes amours* were published for the general market. More serious was the 'intuitive' approach of André Maurois who, from the 1920s onward, used common sense and empathy to unlock the psychological complexity of Shelley or Chateaubriand, an approach developed more systematically throughout the middle decades of the century by psychoanalytical biographers who explained lives in terms of fixations and obsession, by Marxists who showed how socio-economic forces replaced the individual as the instigator of ideas and actions, or by chroniclers of the *Annales* school who made their subjects the expression of the 'mentality' of their epoch. Yet such approaches undermined the purpose of biography. What was there to admire in artists, heroes and history-makers if the psyche, social determinants and the network of structures denied any claim the human subject might have to individuality?

However, biography never lost its popular audience and even widened its remit to include, in addition to the illustrious dead, the currently famous: media-generated actors, politicians and personalities. Since the 1980s, to the dominant chronological sequence have been added variant approaches like the dialogue with the dead and other forms of discontinuity. The traditional function of the genre, which is to inform and celebrate, is sometimes subverted and serves another, more modern need: to topple heroes and expose corruption. Yet as a kind of writing, biography has still to be accorded the respect to which it has long been accustomed in the more empirical tradition of Anglo-Saxon culture.

Autobiography

Autobiography, on the other hand, has a shorter history but, by the end of the twentieth century, had achieved a higher profile. Its oldest form was the spiritual self-examination exemplified by Saint Augustine and Saint Teresa of Avila. But before 1750, the bulk of writing about the self took the form of the memoirs of soldiers, courtiers and other prominent figures who wrote of their public roles or left a record of events they had witnessed and important people they had known. Impersonal in character, they were directed outwards, away from the intimate personality of the writer. Even Montaigne, that most autobiographical of authors, had taken as his subject, not his narrative life but his cumulative self. In the last decades of the *ancien régime*, however, a cultural shift from the general of classicism to the particular of pre-Romanticism allowed a new kind of recollection to emerge, of which Rousseau's *Confessions* are but one example. Against the public persona of the memoir, it offered the inner life of social outsiders and exchanged discretion and self-effacement for self-justification and self-analysis, soul-baring and exhibitionism.

Quantitatively, however, it was dwarfed by the less confessional memoir which gave the facts of a life and rarely delved below its surface. But the chaos of the Revolution had fragmented human experience, and for those who had traversed it success did not mean acquiring a place in a secure social hierarchy but basic survival. Between 1820 and 1840, recollections of the leaders and victims of those terrible times stimulated an interest in struggles against adversity which soon widened to include other kinds of tests and trials. Travellers observed less and learned to speak more of themselves. Spiritual odysseys were traced by Quinet, Renan and Saint Thérèse of Lisieux (*Histoire d'une âme*, 1898). George Sand and Marie d'Agoult recalled the obstacles placed in the path of women on their road to independence, and writers, artists and musicians (Dumas *père*, Berlioz) retraced their battle for recognition. But autobiography (the word was lexicalized in the 1840s) was not confined to the world of bourgeois respectability. The *Cahiers du capitaine Coignet* (1851–3) related the career of a foot-soldier, and Agricole Perdiguier (*Mémoires d'un compagnon*, 1853) gave an insight into the lives of working people. The memoirs of criminals (Lacenaire, 1836) and policemen (Vidocq, 1828; Canler, 1863) were read for the light they threw on parts of society unknown to respectable readers. But the public was no less fascinated by the memoirs of those who made history, like Napoleon, and those, like Michelet and Guizot, who wrote it. Minor figures like Maxime du Camp (*Souvenirs littéraires*, 1881–2) published gossipy reminiscences of famous people and literary quarrels. The regularly kept journal (of the Goncourts; Marie Bashkirtseff, 1887) caught great authors off-guard and showed literature in the making. On the other hand, the *journal intime*, exemplified by Eugénie de Guérin (1862) and Amiel (1883), became a laboratory for introspection and self-analysis.

It is nevertheless surprising that the century which took so quickly to the 'personal' novel should not have invested more heavily in autobiography. Two exceptions stand out. Chateaubriand's *Mémoires d'outre-tombe* (begun 1809; publ. 1849–50) was not only an analysis of his times but of his *moi*, an insecure self vacillating between despair and hope. But the most original of all nineteenth-century autobiographies was Stendhal's *Vie de Henry Brulard* (written 1835). Like Rousseau, he dwells on his early years and moves freely between past and present, fascinated by the workings of memory as he attempts to distil from it an honest estimate of himself. It was an early intimation, against the positivist run of things, that individuals, who each inhabit a universe, are not necessarily at the centre of things. Nor can their experience be easily corralled into neat categories: private and public, personal and historical. Yet by 1900, Bergson's ideas on time, laughter and memory as mechanisms which enable us to reach an accommodation with existence, and the Freudian revelation of the uncontrolled workings of the subconscious, challenged the validity of the objective self-chronicle.

Until the Second World War, however, the self was explored for the most part not directly, in the chronicle which sought the truth of a life, but obliquely, in the guise of fiction. Proust and Céline are 'autobiographical' novelists in this sense, as was Gide. Gide's *Si le grain ne meurt* (1926), however, was a *récit d'enfance* and a new kind of confession: it culminates in the discovery and acceptance of his homosexuality. Meanwhile, public figures continued to evoke their lives to establish what they had thought or done rather than who they were. Politicians explained their actions and intellectuals (Beauvoir, Aron, Malraux, Claude Roy, Althusser) their part in the movement of ideas. Survivors of war and captivity wrote of their experience and some, like Robert Antelme (1917–90) or David Rousset (1912–97), used their ordeal to explain man's inhumanity. Regional writers revisited their past to record old ways threatened by the new world while the *récit d'enfance*, when not designed as an amusement, explored how an author became a writer (Sartre) or how he had lost the innocence of childhood (Pagnol). Working-class reminiscences, in addition to their value as social history, also throw light on popular reading habits and hardly confirm the modern view that great books have no intrinsic value, that they appeal only to an educated elite and that middle-class culture was a means of neutralizing the workers: *Robinson Crusoe* is rarely absent from any reading list and there is ample testimony that wide horizons were opened for the minimally educated by good books. Far less revealing were the autobiographies, often ghosted, of ephemeral personalities from the media-soaked worlds of sport, entertainment and topical affairs. Occasionally, there were experiments with form: Queneau's *Chêne et chien* (1937) and *Une vie ordinaire* (1967) by Georges Perros (1923–78) were autobiographies in verse. But on the whole, autobiographical writings were objective, untroubled memoirs which assumed that while a life is the sum of past moments it sits four-square on an unproblematic self.

A new form of self-portraiture emerged with Michel Leiris (1901–90), a distinguished Africanist, who, like Montaigne, found his subject in himself and, like Stendhal, was not the hero he would have liked to be. His artistic and political opinions were radical, but his life was conformist. Yet he remained convinced that poetic absolutes and social progress were related and he sought to define the links in his ethnography of the self. In *L'Âge d'homme* (1939) and the four volumes of *La Règle du jeu* (1948–76), he abandoned traditional chronological narrative and instead used Surrealist collages and free association to find his way about his being, perceiving deep desires and fears in his taste for opera or bull-fighting, extracting a 'mythological' self from the rules of a game which was his and ours. The result was not simply the century's most lucid, intelligent and honest autobiography. It changed expectations of what autobiography should be: a life could not be reduced to a smoothly unfolding story.

A similar mistrust of the falsifying conventions of the genre is visible in Jean Genet's *Journal du voleur* (1948), which adopts a looser approach to time and narrative. Beauvoir's *Mémoires d'une jeune fille rangée* (1958), like *La Bâtarde* (1964) by Violette Leduc (1907–72), were less formally adventurous and gave a higher priority to Existentialist themes such as revolt and *mauvaise foi*. Sartre's *Les Mots* (1964) was a *récit d'enfance* of a familiar enough kind which, however, beneath its serious frivolity, excavated his reasons for becoming a writer. By the time it appeared, the literary credentials of the genre were deemed simplistic and misleading and alternative ways of exploring selfdom were sought.

That this initiative should occur at a moment when Structuralism announced the death of the author and the autonomous self seems paradoxical. If the ego was an illusory construct (Lacan), subjectivity gendered (Cixous) and consciousness a product of multiple determinants, attempts to salvage individuality were clearly doomed. Yet since autobiography exists between fact and fiction, it was deemed to have a privileged place in giving individual experience an identity in the wider social and intellectual context. Non-literary materials (photographs, home movies) were equated with the 'archive', and journals preserved recoverable instants: both were concrete evidence of a life that had been lived. The mordant *Journal littéraire* (1955–66) of Paul Léautaud (1872–1956), a pungent and opinionated annotation of the literary scene between 1893 and 1956, was one such record. But a new fashion for seeing artistic creation less as a finished product than as the process from which a work emerges promoted interest in rough drafts, jottings and diaries which, once a private domain, were written with an eye to posterity and sometimes even published during their author's lifetime. Valéry's *Cahiers* (1957–61) explored his own mind, and journals personal and public were kept by major writers (Gide, Julien Green, François Mauriac, Marcel Jouhandeau).

But the pursuit of the self remained the dominant theme. However, by the 1970s autobiographers jettisoned narrative in favour of alternative strategies. For his significantly titled *Le Temps immobile* (1974–88), Claude Mauriac (1914–96) exchanged chronology for the juxtaposition of moments. Roger Laporte (b. 1925) defined his self in the pieces collected as *Une Vie* (1986) by its relationship with language. *Roland Barthes par Roland Barthes* (1975) was a sequence of fragments in alphabetical order which moved between first and third person while Georges Perec's *W, ou le souvenir d'enfance*, published the same year, interwove an autobiographical narrative with a fictional story. During the 1980s, Barthes's restitution of the 'human subject' stimulated surviving *nouveaux romanciers* to explore their past, Nathalie Sarraute with *Enfance* (1983), Duras with *L'Amant* (1984), and Robbe-Grillet with *Romanesques* (1985–94). Personal elements implicit in the novels of Claude Simon turned into clearer self-portraits (*L'Acacia*, 1989; *Le Jardin des plantes*, 1997).

At the same time, the novel was caught up by the vogue. Most novelists draw on their own experience, though few returned to defining moments of their lives as obsessively as Duras. But the ratio of personal experience to invention rose sharply from the 1970s and a new genre was proclaimed: the *autofiction*, in which the name of the author is also that of the narrator/protagonist. Cast as diaries which are authentic to varying degrees or mixing the narrative conventions of autobiography and novelistic techniques, the *autofictions* of Doubrovsky, Robbe-Grillet, Annie Ernaux and Hervé Guibert explored the self against the background of the *quotidien*, the 'everyday experience' already embraced by theatre, where the line between constraint and freedom was most visible. It was a development supported officially (an Association pour le Patrimoine Autobiographique was founded in 1992), by the academic analysis of the national memory led by Pierre Nora and, in a more general sense, by the interest in life stories and individual testimony which was reflected in the best-seller lists. But by then bearing witness had also become the new duty of women.

Women's Writing

Until very recent times, women in literature were the lovers and mothers of men. The medieval chivalric code granted them a high civilizing role but, by making them the inspiration for male deeds, cast them in a subordinate role which was confirmed by the Church, medicine, law and the institutions of the state. More honoured than respected, servants and only exceptionally the mouthpiece of the Muses, they were required to listen quietly while their virtues were sung and their *malices* exposed. Even so, from Marie de France and the *trobairitz* onwards, a corpus of writing by women accumulated until the first *querelle des femmes*, ignited by *Le Roman de la Rose* in the early thirteenth century, prompted Christine de Pizan to defend the excellence of women in terms which were perpetuated for four centuries. During the Renaissance, despite the arguments advanced by Louise Labé and participants in the *querelle des Amyes*, the debate continued to revolve around 'proofs' adduced by both sides from the lives of virtuous and infamous women. It was not until the seventeenth century that the controversy took a modern turn when Mademoiselle de Gournay made the education of women an issue and Poulain de la Barre argued that their supposed inferiority was determined by social attitudes, not by nature. By 1650, through their *salons* and as advocates of preciosity, they had secured a role in defining taste. They were not simply literary midwives, but poets (Deshoulières), correspondents (Sévigné) and above all, authors of romances (Scudéry) and innovative novels (Lafayette, Villedieu).

The eighteenth century

After 1700, the centre of power moved steadily from Versailles to Paris and gave women two theatres, court and town, in which to assert themselves. If France's queens remained invisible until the time of Marie-Antoinette, the royal mistress, from Mme de Maintenon to the Marquise de Pompadour and Mme du Barry, acquired celebrity and a high degree of unofficial political power, as did army and *parlement* wives, who were able to influence appointments and sometimes policy. Women also established a feminine space in the intellectual *salon*, where they directed the fortunes of the Enlightenment. A handful emerged as respected intellectuals (it was Mme du Châtelet who explained Leibniz to Voltaire) and a larger number produced novels, some, like Mme de Graffigny, Mme Riccoboni and Isabelle de Charrière, of a quality which has recently been revised upwards. The cause of women, a minor issue for the *philosophes*, was advanced by many treatises on the education of girls and, in the last third of the century, by reflections on the position of women in a society dominated by men. In 1772, Louis Thomas called them 'slaves' and in 1783 Laclos concluded that it would take a 'revolution' to make them free.

1789–1900

The Revolution he had in mind was not that of 1789, which granted rights to men but not to women. Olympe de Gouges, Théroigne de Méricourt and others protested unavailingly, but their arguments, based on equity and justice, would be taken up by their successors. To the generalized misogyny of society was added Napoleon's Civil Code (1804) which severely curtailed the freedom of women, who were left with the same legal rights as minors and mad persons. Some resisted. Mme de Staël, one of the century's founding figures, dared to defy Napoleon by promoting subversive, liberal ideas. The queens of the *cabinet de lecture* wrote of marriage in sombre fictions, and Marceline Desbordes-Valmore achieved a simple directness beyond the reach of the Romantic poets who eclipsed her. By 1830, however, 'the woman question' was on the agenda and the word 'feminism' entered the language in 1837. The July Revolution had not delivered the freedoms it had promised and women now claimed them in a vigorous campaign rooted in the principles of 1789. Encouraged by the disciples of Saint-Simon and Fourier, they organized a flourishing women's press which crossed the social divide. Suzanne Voilquin, a working-class journalist, proposed alternatives to patriarchy and Flora Tristan, daughter of an aristocrat, demanded practical reforms and a political voice. In 1848 women's clubs flourished briefly but the fires they lit were extinguished by the conservatism of the Second Empire.

Romantic writers codified male perceptions of women who thereafter were cast in three major roles: virgin (the embodiment of perfect, inaccessible love, the muse of poets), mother (a tender, forgiving figure) and the cruel *femme fatale* who made men unhappy. Refusing to accept the stereotypes to which the bulk of women in nineteenth-century life and fiction were required to conform, George Sand made independence her morality and, like Louise Colet and Marie d'Agoult, established the case for reform in both her writings and her rejection of respectability. But it was the growth of the publishing industry which allowed women, who played marginal roles in the rise and fall of literary schools, to emerge as writers. Proto-feminist positions were maintained by Clémence Robert and Marie Aycard in the 1850s, and between 1860 and 1880 the Comtesse de Ségur, Zénaïde Floriot and Mme Fouillée ('Bruno') established themselves as children's authors. But the next generation of female novelists (Marcelle Tinayre, Gyp, Rachilde and Colette) offered a bolder, racier view of modern womanhood, as did Renée Vivien (1877–1909) and Liane de Pougy (c.1870–1950) whose poetry ventured into lesbian territory. Symbolism attracted women poets like Anna de Noailles and Lucie Delarue-Mardrus while Marguerite Audoux, a beneficiary of the rise of universal primary education, won the Prix Femina in 1910 and gave working-class women a modern voice.

1900–45

Yet women continued to be sidelined. The feminist arguments advanced by Marguerite Durand (1864–1936) and Madeleine Pelletier (1874–1939) served as irritants rather than spurs to action, and poetry and fiction, theatre and cinema, like the Surrealist movement, remained predominantly male domains. Between the wars, no female writer won the Prix Goncourt and only five were rewarded by the all-woman jury of the Femina. The major exception was Colette (1873–1954) who, with *La Vagabonde* (1910), struck out on her own and, though no stranger to bohemian scandal, was admired for her independent spirit and feline prose, her insistence on the cruelty of love and her warmer defence of authentic being against the hypocrisy of the male-dominated Belle Époque which she had challenged.

1945–68

It was not until after 1945 that women writers began to emerge in force. Of the careers begun before 1940 and now resumed, Marguerite Yourcenar (1903–87) achieved the highest profile with *Les Mémoires d'Hadrian* (1951). Among women authors who began writing during the Occupation, the socialist-realist novels of Elsa Triolet (1896–1970), which recognized the role played by women in the Resistance, were greatly admired. But the conventions of realistic fiction or the historical novel (Zoé Oldenbourg, b. 1916) did not satisfy the postwar generation of women writers who, without opting for any single approach or form, questioned the assumptions of the world of men. The theoretical argument was made by Simone de Beauvoir in *Le Deuxième Sexe* (1949) and developed in her novels which pursued the Existentialist proposition that human beings are free to choose the lives they lead. During the 1950s, Marguerite Duras and Nathalie Sarraute were associated with the 'New Realism', Françoise Mallet-Joris (b. 1930) raised the question of lesbian love in *Le Rempart des béguines* (1951), and in *Bonjour tristesse* (1954) Françoise Sagan (b. 1935) invented a new heroine who, half innocent, half perverse, breathed the air of freedom.

The new habit of seeing the world from a female point of view was continued into the 1960s by Christiane Rochefort (b. 1917), Benoîte Groult (b. 1920), Claire Etcherelli (b. 1934) and others who linked women's lives to their social and political context. More radical were novelists who raised the profile of the desiring, transgressive woman. Violette Leduc (1907–72) and Albertine Sarrazin (1937–67) used their own experience to show women who attempt to assume responsibility for their marginalized, criminal lives. Their style of realism, however, and the prevailing cultural climate, ensured that revolt led more often to defensive rather than to liberated positions. Love does not bring happiness, and the weight of class and gender roles does not allow the heroines of the 1960s to transcend their predicament, which is laid at society's door. A more positive step was taken by Monique Wittig (b. 1935) who, in *L'Opoponax* (1964), wrote frankly of lesbian love and began her mission to reconstruct the language of patriarchy and demolish gender boundaries. Like Duras, Wittig experimented with form and genre and both were well positioned to grasp the opportunities offered by the events of 1968.

Since 1968

In tune with the times, feminism lost its defensiveness and developed a more aggressive, overtly revolutionary stance after 1968. It found a focus in discussion groups and pressure lobbies. Its profile was raised by the formation of the Mouvement de Libération des Femmes and in 1974 it acquired its own publishing house, Des Femmes, which launched new women writers. The new generation of intellectual feminists rejected Beauvoir's 'materialist' approach (which showed how women are defined by their material situation as daughters, lovers and mothers) which was at variance with the emphasis now given to women's 'difference'. Luce Irigaray (b. 1932) argued that gender identity is the product of a conflict between the male logical order and fluid female multiplicity. The first, being culturally dominant, imprisons women inside their bodies and enslaves mind and soul, culture and spirit. Julia Kristeva (b. 1941), also a trained psychoanalyst, developed the Structuralist emphasis on the role of language in the construction of the human subject and drew attention to the pre-verbal stage of human development when spontaneous reactions (such as laughter, associated with the mother) run counter to the logic of the world represented by the father. Unresolved tensions determine subjectivity, an argument which Kristeva applied to art in general and more particularly to women in *Des Chinoises* (1974).

Hélène Cixous (b. 1937) defended the concept of female difference and from it developed a theory of *écriture féminine*, an approach to writing which rejected the male perspective and the limitations of male language and exploited forms and expressions of desire particular to women. For Cixous, 'women's writing' was poetic not linear, open not closed, and better suited to accessing sexuality and the unconscious, an argument she developed and illustrated in essays and novels and through the Centre de Recherche en Études Féminines, which she helped found in 1977. Catherine Clément (b. 1939), from a Marxist perspective, endorsed these initiatives which, collectively dubbed *psych et po* (*psychanalyse et politique*), were opposed by the supporters of *Questions féministes* (1977). Its editor, Christine Delphy (b. 1941), revived Beauvoir's 'materialist' approach and criticized the concept of 'difference' for its elitism and disdain for economic realities. 'Otherness' was essentialist in nature and would ghettoize women, an argument supported by Michèle le Doeuf (b. 1948) who, while acknowledging women's exclusion from the philosophical tradition, promoted the less separatist principle of *mixité*.

Écriture féminine meant writing in other ways and about other things and may be identified in the work of established authors like Duras and Wittig (who both declared themselves feminists in the 1970s) and newcomers such as Chantal Chawaf (b. 1943), Jeanne Hyvrard (b. 1945) and Marie Redonnet (b. 1948). Their manner was allusive and fluid and their subject matter included identity, loss, alienation from patriarchal language and culture, and relationships between generations, persons and cultures. In the 1980s, its major theorist, Cixous, moved into theatre, where her concern with subjectivity focused first on the unconscious (what a psychoanalytical approach reveals of the feminine) and then transferred to the historical (which exposes the political nature of the patriarchal order).

Cixous worked in association with Ariane Mnouchkine, one of the major theatre directors who had harnessed the socially conscious *création collective* movement which had begun in the 1960s. Their collaboration was one indication of the rising profile of women in the arts which reflected their improving social status in the last decades of the century. They made their mark in genres which had been almost exclusively male preserves: theatre, cinema, *bande dessinée* and the *roman policier*. Women maintained their presence in poetry (Joyce Mansour, 1928–86; Annie Salager, b. 1938; Anne-Marie Albiach, b. 1938) but were most significant in renewing the traditions of fiction. Though they often brought a female perspective to their work, few were radical feminists. Indeed, the textual innovations of the feminist avant-garde, like its theory, alienated the growing number of women writers, though most agreed with the general proposition which favoured the insertion of the feminine into the symbolic order for the benefit of both sexes.

The bulk of women's fiction, like writing generally, remained faithful to the realistic, naturalistic tradition. While the *littérature à l'eau de rose* continued to supply romantic escapism, mainstream fiction by women dealt with relationships in historical dramas and the novel of contemporary manners. But the libertarian impact of feminism added more open attitudes to sexuality, franker discussions of the couple, and encouraged a new self-confidence. Feminist ideas had been popularized in the press and crusading *vulgarisations* such as Annie Leclerc's *Parole de femme* (1974), Benoîte Groult's *Ainsi soit-elle* (1975) and Françoise Parturier's *Lettre ouverte aux femmes* (1976). More women took up their pens and won a higher proportion of the major literary prizes. Marie Cardinal (1929–2001) and Annie Ernaux (b. 1940) achieved best-selling status for their autobiographical treatment of personal and class issues while Suzanne Prou (b. 1920), Michèle Perrein (b. 1935) and Sylvie Germain (b. 1954) gave a female perspective to regional writing. Social and psychological relationships, explored for a wide readership by Catherine Rivoire (b. 1921) or Christine Arnothy (b. 1930), are also given a more acerbic treatment by Catherine Rihoit (b. 1949).

After 1980, many women novelists were drawn to the *autofiction*, which mixed autobiography and invention in ways which inserted the *je* of the author into the *je* of readers who, as Marie Cardinal observed in *Les Grands Désordres* (1987), could feel that 'they were reading what was already written inside them'. The projection of personal experience into fiction, long practised by Duras, Sarraute and others, was not, of course, the preserve of women writers who, in the last twenty years of the century, also framed their narratives and priorities in other ways. Danièle Sallenave (b. 1940), after experimenting with structure and time, moved to a more objective observation of *le quotidien* as an alternative to commitment. Anne-Marie Garat (b. 1946) writes realistically of the fragmentation and disintegration of personality and Pierrette Fleutieux (b. 1941) analyses the crisis of adolescent lives. In the 1990s, the names of Amélie Nothomb (b. 1967?), Marie Ndiaye (b. 1965), Lydie Salveyre (b. 1959), or Marie Darrieussecq (b. 1969) were associated with a 'post-feminist' phase of women's writing which marked a return to less theoretical approaches to narrative, though it is too early to tell which of the decade's many women authors will win the respect of future generations.

Gay Writing

Throughout the *ancien régime*, inversion, particularly after the persecution of the Cathars, was linked to heresy and until 1783, when the last sodomite was burned alive, was punished as a form of blasphemy. Although male love was validated at different times by reference to the Greek ideal, homosexual writers (like the seventeenth-century *satirique*, Théophile, or the literary journalist Desfontaines in the eighteenth) did not generate a separate culture but operated within the intellectual and cultural mainstream. Denounced by the Church and, during the Enlightenment, by populationist economists and moral opponents of *libertinage*, sodomy and Sapphic *tribadisme* were relegated to society's darker corners. Those who ventured to defend same-sex love acquired *maudit* status which was modified only at the end of the nineteenth century by the nascent psychoanalysis. Regarded as a condition (had not Sade argued that it was 'natural'?) rather than a conscious choice, *homosexualité* (the word had entered the language by 1900) at last acquired a culture among writers born around 1850, from Verlaine and Rimbaud to Jean Lorrain, Gide and Proust. But society, as Oscar Wilde discovered, was not ready to accept inversion. While the closed circle which formed around the American, Natalie Barney, projected a more confident but still discreet image of lesbianism, male writing until the 1950s was defensive, apologetic and dominated by guilt. Proust regarded homosexuality, which crossed class boundaries, as a social dissolvant which threatened the hierarchy and, by drawing attention to itself, provoked oppression. Proust found salvation in art. Cocteau, who shared such reservations, saw his homosexuality as a spur to artistic creation, but Genet's 'authentic' self linked his to isolation and criminality.

A more positive attitude was advanced by Gide who justified his own homosexuality in *Corydon* (1924) and his autobiography, *Si le grain ne meurt* (1926). In the 1930s Bataille's efforts to reach spiritual self-fulfilment by exhausting all forms of sex was echoed in Jouhandeau's *Traité de l'abjection* (1939). More characteristic of the period, however, was the theme of adolescent sexuality, often presented through initiation by an older narrator. It was taken up by Green, Montherlant and, after 1944, by Roger Peyrefitte, in an atmosphere which grew more relaxed only in the 1950s. Even so,

Vichy legislation, designed to protect minors, remained on the statute book after 1944 and the law remained vigilant. If Pierre Hébart's homosexual novel *L'Âge d'or* (1953) went unchallenged, Jouhandeau prudently published his uninhibited *Tirésias* anonymously. The defence of *homophilie* mounted discreetly by the 'Arcadie' group founded in 1954 was a step to the greater permissiveness extended by the 1960s to sexual manners in general. It was not, however, until after 1968 that gay activism, boosted in theoretical terms by Foucault and Barthes, took more insistent forms. In 1981 the age of consent was lowered to 15 but the change in the law did not end prejudice against the gay community. The activists who had campaigned in favour of liberalization in the wake of 1968 continued to protest and mobilized around the issue of Aids, which threatened to return gays to their pariah status. Pressure was maintained throughout the 1990s and, at the turn of the century, the law gave limited recognition to same-sex partnerships.

After 1970, gay writing emerged as a recognizable, if rapidly evolving, literary category. The theme of adolescent sexuality, handled with wistful melancholy in Julien Green's *Jeunesse* (1974), received a more aggressive treatment from Tony Duvert (b. 1946), who made paedophilia an ingredient of a world of innocence (*Quand mourut Jonathan*, 1978). But by the 1990s, when Roger Vrigny (1920–97) published *Le Garçon d'orage* (1994), the novel of homoerotic initiation had revealed a capacity for raising more general issues of male relationships. This general evolution is reflected in the thirty novels of Yves Navarre (1940–94) which over twenty years moved closer to what Barthes called 'la quiétude insexuelle', an accommodation with his sexuality. Dominique Fernandez (b. 1929) showed homosexuality persecuted (*L'Étoile rose*, 1978) and threatened (*Une fleur de jasmin à l'oreille*, 1980) before concluding his cultural survey, *Le Rapt de Ganymède* (1989), with the argument that it can be a creative force only when freed from repression. History was also used inventively by Guy Hocquenghem (1946–88) and, after an experimental start, by Renaud Camus (b. 1946: *Roman roi*, 1983). But the most common thread was the vein of autobiography which runs through gay writing.

On the other hand, the violence associated with Bataille and Genet has been slower to disperse, sustained not least by the gay community's anger at its marginalization. It is visible from Pierre Guyotat's *Éden, Éden, Éden* (1970) to texts published in the 1990s by Éric

Jourdan. But it also figures in novels by Navarre and Duvert. A new phase opened with the Aids crisis. Although with hindsight the death of Rasky in Navarre's *Les Loukums* (1973) seems prophetic, the first Aids novel was Valéry Luria's *Babylon* (1986). The theme was taken up by older writers like Navarre and Fernandez, whose *La Gloire du paria* (1987) explored the human value of the suffering it brought. Far closer to the subject were its victims, many of whom died. Cyril Collard (1957–93) adopted an aggressive stance in his controversial *Les Nuits fauves* (1989), an approach which was echoed in part in the hallucinatory *Ludion d'alcool* (1990) by Jean-Baptiste Niel (1962–95), but stood at several removes from the clinical precision and fierce wit of the three novels of Hervé Guibert (1955–91). The response to the crisis took various forms: anger with the medical profession, bitter resentment at the renewed social ostracism of gays, a restatement of the value of friendship and for some, in the presence of death, an apprehension of the mystical.

If gay identity had still to be fully defined at the end of the century, gay writing, as a literary category, had acquired a consistency, not only in its themes, but through its long tradition of aesthetic inventiveness. Proust and Gide had reshaped the novel and Genet had made the *je* problematic by blurring the line between narrator and character. After 1970, the historical novel was renewed by Fernandez and Hocquenghem, and new uses were found for the *nouveau roman* by Duvert and Camus who, before also turning to history, had experimented with collage and the multiple viewpoint. Gay writing is not to be defined by its collective stance but by its varied style and manner.

Francophone Writing

France was expelled from India and Canada in the eighteenth century but maintained a presence in the Indian Ocean, the West Indies and the Pacific. After 1830, the French sought an overseas empire and moved into North and Central Africa and Indo-China. The subject territories brought economic benefits but were also exposed to a 'civilizing' mission which was underwritten by a mostly assimilationist colonial policy. French ideas and administrative practices were imported and in many colonies French became, at least for the administrative class, the language of instruction. Between the two world wars, there were signs of resistance to French paternalism, and reservations were expressed by Gide and others who drew attention to oppressive colonial rule. But France remained in control of its empire until the Second World War, when it was able to call on its loyalties. After 1945, the pressures which led to the disintegration of other European empires also terminated France's hold on its colonies and protectorates which gained their independence between 1945 and 1962. The change was managed peacefully for the most part and some ex-colonies became overseas *Départements* (DOM) or *Territoires* (TOM). But autonomy was won by Indo-China and Algeria only through armed resistance. Since 1960, successive French governments have supported the concept of *francophonie* partly to ease the sometimes painful process of decolonization and partly to maintain French influence in the international community. By the end of the century, the francophone community had over fifty members, and summits, beginning in 1986, convened to discuss issues of common concern.

Language

The common denominator of francophone writing is the French language, probably the major legacy of colonization. It provided a common tongue against a background of multilingualism and, by offering access to a mature written culture, has helped to forge new mentalities and habits of mind. Yet it has also been regarded as a deculturing force, the voice and tool of repressive colonialism, and a form of surrender to France. Moreover, its use may be restricted to the educated minority, and those who use it may seen to serve the *métropole* and the francophone community better than their home public. Linguistic decolonization has posed complex problems in countries lacking an extensive reading public, a mature publishing industry, a literary press and, in short, the infrastructures required by literature. Some authors have used *créole* or may write their novels and poems in Wolof or Arabic. Others write in their mother tongue, to capture a cultural specific, before translating the result into French. But even Quebec province, the strongest by far of France's former possessions, finds difficulty in promoting *joual* as a literary language and standard French remains the *lingua franca* of the francophone community. The major authors publish in France, sometimes in Quebec and Montreal, either by choice or through circumstances (usually forced exile) beyond their control. But while they operate within the cultural and linguistic atmosphere of France and raise issues of interest to *francophonie* in general, they write as Algerians, Martinicans, or Québecois. The problem is less acute in cinema which is far less dependent on language, though censorship, questions of finance and the 'cultural imperialism' of a specifically Western medium often raise serious obstacles.

Alternatives to *francophonie*

From the early nineteenth century onwards, French Canadians resisted the English language and British culture and found their identity in the language and culture of France. Other francophone countries, however, have also been suspicious of outside influences generally. During the US occupation of Haiti (1915–34), *indigénisme* rejected European values and looked instead to Haiti's indigenous culture. Boosted by the interest in black art (jazz), the black poets of Harlem and the strength of Latin-American literature, its case was forcefully stated by Jean Price-Mars's *Ainsi parla l'oncle* (1928), which attacked pro-French attitudes and defended Haiti's language and culture which was, at root, African. The Africanness of Haitian culture was endorsed by *Les Griots* (1938–40), mouthpiece of *noirisme*, a nationalist, racialist view of culture which would become the ideological basis of the Duvalier regime (1957–86).

Meanwhile, a group of Martinican students in Paris issued *Légitime Défense* (one number, 1932) which reacted against the alienation it detected in francophone black intellectual communities, rejected the French Parnassians and Symbolists and substituted Breton's Surrealism, psychoanalysis and Marxism as the means of relaunching West Indian writing. In 1935, the single issue of *L'Étudiant noir*, the result of contacts in Paris between West Indian and African students (who included Aimé Césaire, Léopold Senghor and Birago Diop), protested against the French policy of assimilation, which was hostile to local cultures. These developments, together with the publication of *Pigments* (1937), a volume of poems by the Guyanese Léon Damas (1912–78), mark the beginnings of *négritude*, a term coined by Césaire in 1939. The movement aimed to provide a common denominator for black peoples, irrespective of nationality, and to promote, in the words of Senghor, its leading publicist, 'le patrimoine culturel, les valeurs, et surtout l'esprit de la civilisation africaine'. Its origins coincided with the emergence of pan-Africanism, which had been growing since 1903 when *The Soul of Black Folk* by W. E. Burghardt du Bois urged the black populations of the USA and the West Indies to reconnect with their African roots. The idea became part of Price-Mars's argument and gained ground during the 1930s. It was given a concrete form after 1945 and international conferences demanded the right of black populations to self-determination. In the late 1950s, it acquired the essentially political role which it still plays. By then, however, the limitations of Negritude had been exposed by the Martinicans Césaire (*Discours sur le colonialisme*, 1950) and especially Frantz Fanon (1925–61: *Peau noire, masques blancs*, 1952; *Les Damnés de la terre*, 1961), who argued that culture could not develop freely in a colonial atmosphere and made resistance to the oppression of black peoples the first priority. Although Senghor continued to defend it, Negritude was not the answer to colonialism or metropolitanization. By the 1970s it was equated with the acceptance of servitude and was eventually abandoned. Even so, it produced major writings by Césaire, Senghor, Camara Laye, Ousmane Sembène and others and represented a crucial turning point in the history of *francophonie*.

Similarly inspired, but more limited in its resonance, was the *Créolie* defined in the 1950s by Jean Albany (1917–84), who advocated the rejection of French models and the assertion of the authentic consciousness of Réunion. More recently, Édouard Glissant (b. 1928: *Le Discours antillais*, 1981) put forward *antillanité* as an alternative to both Eurocentric assimilation and Afrocentric Negritude. It was taken up by *Éloge de la créolité* (1989) by Patrick Chamoiseau, Raphaël Confiant and Jean Bernabé. These theoretical positions have been of interest to francophone authors in other countries, and the process of cross-fertilization has helped clarify issues of identity and create a mood of self-confidence.

Problems of definition

French literature is stocked with writers who were born outside France, became French by adoption but do not qualify as francophone authors: Beckett and Ionesco are just two examples. On the other hand, it is far from agreed that *beur* writing, produced by the second generation of North African writers born in France, qualifies as properly 'francophone', though it too is concerned with its major themes: the politics of assimilation, ethnic difference, issues of personal and cultural identity, and the tension between the secular French tradition and Arab-Islamic values. What is meant by the term *francophonie* is further complicated by the inclusion of authors whose mother tongue is French but who are citizens of independent nations where several cultures co-exist, such as Belgium, Switzerland and Canada. Perhaps the answer lies in the point writers occupy in a scale which has, at one end, strong regional loyalties and, at the other, the aspiration to universality. Within francophone cultures, linguistic and literary advances occur at variable speeds. The first achievements are spontaneous rather than coordinated, but the next phase is marked by an assertion of geographical and personal individualism within a shared French culture. Subsequent generations may well distance themselves from their francophone role and seek to establish themselves as simply writers in French. The francophone nations of Europe have not had as far to travel as France's former colonies, which had an oral but no written literature, stories but not novels, poems but not alexandrines and no theatrical or confessional tradition. Yet they too face comparable problems of identity.

Belgium

A nation only since 1830, Belgium is, broadly speaking, bilingual, with Flemish spoken in Flanders and French in Wallonia in the south. This, together with the proximity of France, has prevented the emergence of a national French culture within the country. As a result, many authors have felt they had to choose between their provincial public and Paris. Most have chosen the second option and for over a century Belgian 'extra-territorial' literature has been drawn into the French tradition, to which it has made significant contributions. Belgians helped direct the destinies of Symbolism, Naturalism and Surrealism, while the creators of Maigret and Tintin were crucial to the development of French popular culture. In 1937 a manifesto signed by well-known writers proclaimed Belgian literature to be inextricably part of the literature of France. Yet writing produced inside Belgium, apart from its local frame of reference, is often credited with a measure of difference – it is less abstract and more pragmatic, more anxious and less assertive – though such distinctions are very fine. What has become clearer since about 1980 is the impact made by a new dynamism among Belgian publishers which, together with government initiatives, has enabled novelists like Jean-Philippe

Toussaint, Pascal de Duve, Amélie Nothomb, or Jean-Luc Outers to acquire visibility as specifically Belgian rather than French authors.

Switzerland

Given the fragmented nature of the Confederation and its three major languages (German, Italian and French), it is difficult to speak of a distinctive Swiss culture. 'La Suisse romande' comprises six French-speaking cantons which represent a quarter of the population. The battle for a national 'Helvetism' was lost eighty years ago with the Vaudois Renaissance led by C.-F. Ramuz, who sought to give writing in French a vernacular 'inflection'. Even so, if cultural identity has been most clearly defined in terms of canton rather than of nation, progress has been hindered by the drain of talent. For centuries, Swiss writers – from Calvin and d'Aubigné to Rousseau, Constant and Mme de Staël – were absorbed into the literature of France, of which Switzerland was viewed as a cultural province. In the twentieth century, the picture was complicated by the refugee or immigrant origins of many high-profile Swiss writers (like Albert Cohen) and the Parisian success of Cendrars, Pinget, Jaccottet and others (including Jean-Luc Godard) who lived and worked abroad. Those who have stayed write as individuals, not as part of groups, and are perhaps most clearly identified because they are published locally. Yet some, like Yvette Z'Graggen (b. 1920) or Janine Massard (b. 1939), chronicle social change and address clearly localized issues. Moreover, Swiss thinkers, like the linguistician Saussure, and critics (notably the postwar Geneva School) have exported ideas to France. Modern Swiss literature is now less marginalized by critics at home and abroad and has earned the right to feel comfortable in French on its own terms.

French Canada

French speakers account for just 2 per cent of the population of the American continent. Most are Canadian nationals and form concentrations in Acadia (the Atlantic provinces), Ontario and, especially, Quebec Province. This minority status has made them particularly vulnerable to the influence of the cultural traditions of France and, after 1918, the USA. The result has been a heterogeneous literature which centred first on the themes of survival and identity but which, since 1960, seeks to be an American literature which happens to be written in French. Acadia has a small reading public and its literature is the most recent. In the last thirty years, it has produced a quantity of fiction (notably by Jacques Savoie, b. 1950) and militant poetry. The celebration of the landscape and troubled history of Acadia, the alienation of its minority culture and the search for identity are the themes of poets like Ronald Després and Gérald Leblanc, while Herménégilde Chiasson has emerged as a leading French-Canadian experimental avant-gardist. But Acadian literature is most closely identified with Antonine Maillet (b. 1929) whose novels and plays have, since *La Sagouine* (1971), embodied its spirit and aspirations.

Ontario, on the other hand, has a longer literary tradition, dating back to the 1830s, and its larger population gave it a stronger cultural presence. In 1910 there were a quarter of a million francophone Ontarians whose cultural and linguistic difference was not recognized by the majority anglophone population. Their cause was advanced by Lionel Groulx's *L'Appel de la race* (1922) and by the law of 1927 which gave them the right to be educated in French. Until then, its poetry had a Parnassian ring and fiction a strong regionalist flavour. After 1928, both embraced the themes of nostalgia, revolt and self-assertion. In the 1960s the public purse supported institutional change and the universities led a new literary phase which linked Ontario to the linguistic French-Canadian community at large. But just as Quebec retreated into its province, so a more culture-specific literature has emerged, spreading from the north of the province. It is strongest in poetry (Paul Savoie, Patrice Desbiens) but novelists (Hélène Brodeur, Gabrielle Poulin) have revalidated Ontarian history and modern production styles have raised the image of theatre to the point where Jean-Marc Dalpé was able to stage *Le Chien* (1987) in the vernacular.

Quebec

In 1839, Lord Durham, in his report on the late Patriot Rebellion, observed that the half million French of Lower Canada were 'a people with no history and no literature'. In fact they had both, but their history was a largely unwritten chronicle of discovery and white-knuckle survival, and their literature was a literature of fact and faith: journals of exploration, descriptions of flora and fauna and devotional writing. They lacked a population large enough to sustain a culture of reflection or provide a sense of identity. Were they heroic pioneers or subsistence settlers? Should they mark time on the land in French or join forces with anglophone capitalism which threatened to overwhelm their culture and language? Since 1760, the 'British regime' had isolated French Canadians from their French roots. Though the Church defended French as a bulwark against Protestantism, it discouraged dissent. The bishops swore loyalty to George III, denounced the Revolution of 1789 and damned its secular legacy. By 1867, when the Federation was formed, there was nothing new about 'New France': the outlook and values of 'la vieille France' were stronger there than in the positivist, progressive *patrie*.

The first volumes of Quebec poetry and fiction were published in the 1830s and Garneau's *Histoire du Canada* (1845–52) promoted a 'national' view of Quebec's heritage. Even so, literature maintained its colonial status for a century. Unsupported by traditions of its own and lacking a literate public, writers settled for being 'our Fenimore Cooper' or 'the Quebec Hugo', though the haunting lyricism of Émile Nelligan (1879–1941) made him much more than a 'French-Canadian Rimbaud'. Even in the 1920s, when demographic growth, industrialization and rising literacy had changed the cultural landscape, it seemed that the place of Quebeckers was in the pocket of American finance, in the British imperial flow and in the servants' hall of the House of France. Their language (*joual*) was too crude to express things of the mind, and their image as a simple people low of brow and expectation was set out for the world to see – by a Breton.

Louis Hémon's *Maria Chapdelaine* (1914) was loathed by many for its false and sentimental image of Quebec. Others, warming to its sympathetic view of the 'heroic' Maria who prefers the ways of her ancestors to an easy life in the United States, spawned a succession of Maria types. However, the inward-looking *roman de la fidélité* – fidelity to rural labour and the conservative, Catholic moral values of family, marriage and the subordination of women – was derailed by Ringuet's *Trente arpents* (1938) which at last allowed Quebec peasants to be as brutal and rapacious as those of other literatures. By then, Lionel Groulx, novelist and historian, had mobilized nationalist sentiment and declared anglophone and francophone cultures to be 'racially' separate. By 1945, Quebec literature was outgrowing its parochial image, colonial dependence and even its cosmopolitan ambitions in favour of a more precise Quebec consciousness.

The centre of cultural gravity was still located in the conservatism of the Duplessis regime and in the Church. Yet the war and the booming city populations (especially in Montreal) created new aspirations. A market appeared for urban realism, often with a social or political edge (Gabrielle Roy, 1919–83; Roger Lemelin, 1919–92). In 1948, *Refus global*, a manifesto of artists, denounced the Church, Marxism and capitalism and made an impassioned case for artistic and other freedoms. During the 1950s, dramatists like Gratien Gélinas (b. 1908) developed a new social conscience and challenged the theatrical repertoire, which was still dominated by French imports and touring companies. Radio and television gave a platform to new playwrights (Marcel Dubé, b. 1930) who transferred after 1960 to the theatre where Jacques Ferron (1921–85) raised social and political issues. But it was poetry which created the greatest impact. Its progress was directed by the publishing house L'Hexagone (1953), founded by Gaston Miron (b. 1928), one of the major shapers of modern Quebec literature and the voice of poetry in the 1960s. By the late 1950s, poetry outsold fiction and a new generation had been made aware of an exciting programme of cultural and social renewal.

The Quiet Revolution, which hastened the demise of clerical and conservative influence after 1960, confirmed the democratic process as the sole agency of change. The state took charge of education, gave women rights, opened Quebec to modern capitalism, and faced demands for independence which ranged from terrorism to amendments of the constitution, which have yet to produce a solution. The new freedoms were championed by literature and its role was encouraged by public subsidy (to writers, publishers and universities) which at times made the arts seem like an arm of government policy.

Poetry acquired a more popular image with a new generation of *chansonniers* (Félix Leclerc, Gilles Vigneault), who transmitted the libertarian message to a new generation. By the 1970s, however, theatre was beginning to replace poetry as the spearhead of contestation and the new *indépendantiste* spirit. Dramatists moved into forms of activist, collective theatre which fought the cause of *joual*, feminism, nationalism and generalized revolt unimaginable before the Quiet Revolution. But the novel also developed a new momentum against a background of cosmopolitan and national influences: Anne Hébert, Hubert Aquin, Marie-Claire Blais, Gérard Bessette, Jacques Godbout, Roch Carrier, Jacques Poulin, and René Ducharme are among Quebec's 'modern classics'. After about 1970, feminist issues were defended in poetry and fiction (Nicole Brossard, b. 1943) and especially the theatre (Jovette Marchessault, *La Saga des poules mouillées*, 1980), with innovatory forms of drama being a notable feature of the 1980s and 1990s. Michel Tremblay (b. 1942), whose career began with *Les Belles Soeurs* (1968), remains Quebec's best-known playwright. The versatile Robert Lepage is the most notable practitioner of ensemble productions and Denys Arcand the most exportable of Quebec's growing number of film-makers.

In the post-1960 years, it was perhaps not good for literature to have been quite so protected by governments anxious to improve the image of Quebec. Nor was it entirely positive that writers should have been so receptive to outside influences, both French (Mauriac, Existentialism, the *nouveau roman* and, after 1968, the *Tel Quel* group) and American (from Hollywood, Hemingway and Tennessee Williams to the Californian 'New Culture' and Latin-American fiction). Until recent times, Quebec literature has adopted defensive attitudes, constrained by an obsessive need first to chronicle the saga of survival and then to define Quebec's identity.

Yet in the last decades of the century, the *nous* which voiced collective concerns has been overtaken by the *je* which speaks of wider human matters as Quebec writers move on after a generation of profound change. There is still some way to go, for a literature with no Modern tradition can hardly use the freedoms of the Postmodern condition. But Quebec has acquired the maturity to face the challenge of global culture and American consumerism like any other nation. If Quebec literature, contemporary, international, transgenerational and open in its formal practices, has not quite arrived, it has now come of age.

The Caribbean: Martinique, Guadeloupe, French Guyana

European and North American francophone literatures sprang from Western roots and have operated on the basis of shared institutional, economic and cultural assumptions. Elsewhere, *francophonie* developed in very different soil and the task of generating a cultural identity has been more troubled. In the West Indies in the nineteenth century, the dominant white class produced fiction and poetry which defended slavery against liberal opinion in France. But the *gens de couleur libres* were granted citizenship in 1833 and slavery was abolished in 1848. After 1870, both the white and mulatto middle class accepted the values of the Third Republic, modelled their sonorous verses on the French Parnassians and until 1945 preferred their poets to go on celebrating the beauties of 'Les Îles'. Until recent times, Caribbean writing was regarded as a regional extension of the literature of France, with the notable exception of Saint-John Perse who gave a universal resonance to memories of his *créole* childhood.

However, after 1920 Caribbean writers were prominent in questioning the assumptions of assimilationism and asserting a distinctive African identity. In 1921 the Martinican-born Guyanese René Maran (1887–1960) won the Prix Goncourt with *Batouala*, 'véritable roman nègre', which recorded village life in the Congo. Whites have walk-on roles only and for the first time natives were not presented to Western readers as curiosities. Maran's portrait of 'l'âme noire' was prefaced by a harsh and controversial critique of the systematic exploitation of the population by the colonial administration. In the 1930s, demonstrating that 'francophone' was not necessarily a synonym of 'francophile', Caribbean students in Paris, who included Aimé Césaire (b. 1913) and Léon Damas, helped shape the concept of Negritude and were active in validating West Indian language and culture. Between 1941 and 1945, Césaire co-edited *Tropiques*, a journal which collected folk and oral texts (his work was later continued by his daughter Ina, b. 1942) which helped shape a specific Caribbean cultural and psychological identity. Although he continued to assert its black African roots against colonial assimilation, Césaire approved the DOM status given to Martinique, Guadeloupe and Guyana in 1946. Until the 1950s, West Indian novels cast a backward eye on slavery, racism and colonialism, in a way that suggested that promotion to *départemental* rank had resolved the problems. But in the 1950s, Fanon made it clear that membership of the *métropole* created new difficulties, a view echoed in the poetry of Édouard Glissant (b. 1928) and by Césaire's departure from the Communist Party.

Since the 1960s, poetry has lost the prominence it enjoyed during the Negritude era. Similarly, despite the contributions of Césaire, Glissant, Vincent Placoly (1946–92) and Maryse Condé (b. 1937), Caribbean theatre (which, like poetry, has experimented with the use of *créole*) has been slower to develop than the novel. In the 1960s, fiction evoked the miseries of the colonial past but pointed to present gains. In the 1970s, the stirrings of an independence movement, mooted in Glissant's novel *La Lézarde* (1958) and promoted by Placoly and others, highlighted new pressures on the Islands: unemployment, immigration and the materialism imported from the *métropole*. The difficulties of a society based on limited production and over-consumption, which made it economically dependent and generated social and cultural malaise, were reflected in the increasingly pessimistic tone of novels like Jeanne Hyvrard's *Les Prunes de Cythère* (1975) and *Mère la mort* (1976). Since the 1980s, this more defensive mood has persisted. Daniel Maximin (b. 1947) has asserted the value of *créole* and Glissant has continued to champion *antillanité* and to argue that a modern world that is human must be based on the diversity of languages and cultures *(Traité du tout-monde*, 1997). Raphaël Confiant (b. 1951) expresses the disillusionment with the myth of Africa but, like Condé and Patrick Chamoiseau (b. 1953), has pointedly made use of *créole*. But experiment with form has not been limited to language. The novels of Xavier Orville (b. 1932) deal with the predicament of colonial and postcolonial peoples in terms of Latin American 'magic realism', also an influence on Placoly.

Haiti

Many Caribbean authors live and write outside the Islands. Since the late 1950s, this has been particularly true of Haitian authors who, however, worked from Paris, New York, Montreal or Dakar, more from necessity than choice. Haiti won its independence by the slave revolt of 1804. Liberation was not followed by social progress and by 1900 differences of colour and class divided the peasantry and the urban elite. Locally produced poetry and novels followed French models, but were nationalistic and anti-colonial in tone and, in the 1880s, Haiti produced several reasoned ripostes to Gobineau's theory of the supremacy of the white races. A review, *La Ronde* (1898–1902), in addition to developing a Symbolist aesthetic, attempted to steer literature towards the history and national life of Haiti, a tendency initiated before 1900 by novelists who had begun to produce more measured, realistic accounts of peasant and public life, sometimes with a satirical edge.

But the reaction to the American occupation (1915–34) fostered a climate conducive to *indigénisme* which was stated by Price-Mars in 1928 and thence, via Negritude, moved to the *noirisme* of *Les Griots*. In the 1940s, *indigénisme* was renewed by Marxism and Surrealism, both of which defined culture as a process of change rather than a steady state. Its principles were expressed in Haiti's most celebrated novel, *Gouverneurs de la rosée* (1994) by Jacques Roumain (1907–44), founder of Haiti's Communist Party in 1934. It was also the inspiration for poetry by Roumain, René Depestre (b. 1926) and others. At this time and after, intellectuals were divided over basic issues: over voodoo as obscurantism or as the symbol of resistance to imported religions, or the cultural value of *créole* as a viable alternative to French. In the event, the *noirisme* of François Duvalier, xenophobic and authoritarian, emerged triumphant and many poets and novelists fled the island before and after Jacques-Stephen Alexis (1922–61), a critic of the corrupt, dictatorial Duvalierist regime, was murdered by the Tontons Macoute. Those who stayed were forced into prudence or silence. In the late 1960s, *spiralisme*, which sedulously avoided political contestation, experimented with writing in *créole*. Those who left for Europe or America (Depestre; Édris Saint-Amand, b. 1918; Anthony Phelps, b. 1928) kept alive issues of Negritude versus universalism, the protection of Haiti's culture against outside influences, and opposition to the oppressive regime.

Indian Ocean: Mauritius, Réunion, Madagascar

France's association with the islands of the Indian Ocean dates from the seventeenth century. The annexation of Madagascar in 1896, far from ending nationalist resistance, left colonial problems unsolved. The uprising of 1947 was followed by independence in 1958 and a coup d'état in 1972 which made way for a Marxist regime that proved particularly unfriendly to writing in French. Mauritius, British since 1810 and independent since 1968, and Réunion, a DOM since 1946, have long been multilingual societies but boast a long literary tradition in French. In Mauritius, it runs from Bernardin de Saint-Pierre, a temporary resident, to Le Clézio, who reconnected with his roots in *Les Chercheurs d'or* (1985). Réunion can claim Parny, Leconte de Lisle, Léon Dierx, Mallarmé's successor, and others who followed them to France.

Until about 1950, the islands' exiles adopted French literary models: they were by turn Romantic, Parnassian and Symbolist. The Mauritian-born Loys and André Masson added the influence of Surrealism, and Negritude was reflected in the poetry, often written in exile, which appeared after 1960. *Mauricianisme* was promoted in essays and a novel by Marcel Cabon (1912–72), defender of *enracinement*, while Édouard Maunick (b. 1931) maintained faith with the ideals of Negritude, and Malcolm de Chazal (1902–81) pursued a more visionary course. Since the 1970s, a more committed, sharper edge has been noticeable in novels which reassess the colonial past, describe the impoverishment of the island and make full or limited use of *créole* as an affirmation of identity. The health of contemporary Mauritian writing may be measured by the emergence of women authors like the novelist Marie-Thérèse Humbert (b. 1940) and the growing strength of short fiction.

With *Zamal* (1951), Jean Albany, promoter of *créolie*, rejected the false but pervasive exoticism of the Parnassian faithful and marked out the territory of modern réunionnais poetry, which gives a consciously less Euro-centred picture of the landscape and the life of the islanders. In the 1970s, poets adopted a more militant stance, raising issues of autonomy and social deprivation, to the extent of preferring *créole* to French. The same concerns were reflected by novelists who wrote of the poor (Anne Cheynet, *Les Muselés*, 1977) or gave a genealogy to contemporary problems by exploring their historical, colonial origins. While metropolitan-based writers like Daniel Vaxelaire continue to use French, créole is strongly represented in fiction by, among others, Daniel Honoré (*Louis Redona*, 1980).

Madagascar first attracted the attention of French writers in 1913 when Jean Paulhan (1884–1968) published a collection of transcribed *hain teny*, a popular Malagasy form, which interested Apollinaire, Éluard and others. Between the wars, when poets found outlets mainly in literary magazines, one of the island's most famous writers, Jean-Joseph Rabearivelo (1901–37), made poetry out of the two quarrelling sides of himself, French and *malgache*. After the war, Damas's anthology of *Poètes d'expression française* (1947), published in the year of the uprising, raised the profile of the island's poetry, as did Senghor's *Nouvelle Anthologie de la poésie nègre et malgache de langue française* (1948), which was prefaced by Sartre's influential essay, *Orphée noir*. But after 1947, the political climate was unfavourable to literary activity and the militant nationalist Jacques Rabemanjara (b. 1913), and Flavien Ranaïvo (b. 1914), who developed *malgache* themes and styles first explored by Rabearivelo, eventually emigrated. In the 1950s most writers reverted to French models and subsequent political strife has given a low priority to literature. During the 1960s, poetry declined but the first *malgache* novel was published in 1965. Since 1972, the *malgachisation* of culture has further impeded francophone writing, though women writers have made their mark and the short story continues to gain ground.

Sub-Saharan Africa

The countries which now make up sub-Saharan francophone Africa (Benin, Burkina Faso, the Cameroons, the Central African Republic, Chad, the Congo, Gabou, Guinea, Ivory Coast, Mali, Rwanda, Senegal, Togo, Zaïre) have their several histories and have proceeded at different speeds. While all may claim a strong oral tradition, written fictional texts appeared only when French educational practices were introduced during the early colonialist era in the later nineteenth century.

The first authors were products of an education in French and in the 1920s they expressed admiration for the civilizing benefits of French colonialism: their gratitude was duly noted in the prefaces by French *notables* which endorsed them. René Maran's *Batouala* showed 'l'âme noire' and prepared the ground for Negritude, which developed in the 1930s into a form of black humanism. The first step to the creation of an authentic African literature was the preservation of the oral, folk tradition which was transcribed by Birago Diop (1906–89) and many others. Meanwhile, novels and poems told of legendary warriors and mythical figures but, as contacts with France and other francophone countries increased, Negritude acquired a more specific political dimension. From the 1930s onward, novels in the regionalist mode described real lives of toil, hardship and the colonial condition. Fiction which confronted the urban young with Western ways drew attention to the clash of cultures and made implicitly anti-colonial statements. The promotion of African identity was taken up by the influential *Présence africaine* (1947), published in Paris, which quickly became the mouthpiece of decolonization.

The 1950s were particularly fertile for the novel, which contested the colonial system in a variety of tones. The Cameroonian Ferdinand Oyono (b. 1929) managed it with humour in *Le Vieux Nègre et la médaille* (1956), the Senegalese Birago Diop continued to celebrate the African past, and the meeting of Africa and the West was handled soberly by the Cameroonian Mongo Beti (b. 1932) in *Ville cruelle* (1954) which showed the tension between the young and their patriarchal society, and the threat of social disintegration as a result of contact with Europe, a tension which has a tragic outcome in *Ô pays mon beau peuple* (1957) by the Senegalese Ousmane Sembène (b. 1923). There were limits to free expression, however: Beti's *Le Pauvre Christ de Bomba* (1956) was banned by the Church for linking missionary activity with the evils of colonialism. On the other hand, Guinea-born Camara Laye (1924–80) examined the phenomenon of cultural drift in thoughtful rites of passage novels like *Climbié* (1956) which were considered by some to be insufficiently committed to exposing the evils of colonialism.

The theoretical views expounded by Césaire and, above all, Fanon in the 1950s gave a new urgency to issues of assimilation, racism and the missionary hold on local belief systems. Even after independence, the climate remained pervasively colonial. Senghor's was the dominant poetic voice but Negritude poets also explored more personal aspects of identity: love, death, nostalgia and exile. Novelists developed a less defensive manner as they described a world that was absurd or poignant and sought ways of changing it. A more radical note, however, was struck by the Malian Yambo Ouologuem (b. 1940). *Le Devoir de violence* (1968) exploded the myth of black fraternity by showing the collapse of traditional values and the rise of totalitarian political figures who perpetuated systems which denied individual freedom. It was an early sign of the disillusionment which has subsequently been confirmed by a literature of anxiety, failure and violence. Such ideas were particularly relevant to women like the Malian Mariama Bâ (1929–81: *Une si longue lettre*, 1979) and Aminata Sow Fall (b. 1941) who linked the oppression of women to the constraints of Senegalese society in general. Much firmer feminist positions have been taken up by Calixthe Beyala (b. 1961: *Asseze l'africaine*, 1994) and Werewere Liking, born in 1950 in the Ivory Coast, who is as outspoken as she is boldly experimental with form.

In many cases, colonialism had been replaced by corrupt, tyrannical regimes which reacted with a violence which forced many authors into exile. After 1980, they were reaching beyond social realism, too redolent of Western models, and turned instead to fable, fantasy, allegory and parable, often with an injection of humour, to exorcize the dehumanization of Africa in fiction and theatre which denounced totalitarianism and corrupt dictatorships.

North Africa: Algeria, Morocco, Tunisia

As the oldest of France's North African colonies, Algeria had a literary image in France by 1900 as the setting of books by Fromentin, Daudet, Maupassant, Gide and others. It also had an established settler population of mixed European origin capable of sustaining a limited local literature: Musette (pseud. of Auguste Robinet) produced local tales liberally spiked with *pataouète*, the slang which had grown out of multilingual contacts. In 1921, the Association des Écrivains Algériens was formed. Though setting European values above those of the Muslim community, it stated the case for *algérianisme*, the belief that Algeria was capable of developing separately from France as a new cultural entity. In the 1930s, when the Muslim elite first began asserting their own nationalist vision of Algeria's future, the École d'Alger proved less exclusive, but its most famous representatives – Albert Camus, Jules Roy, Emmanuel Roblès – were Franco-Algerians.

Writing in French by Algerians of non-European origins was limited by restricted access to education, though both the novelist Abdelkader Hadj Hamou and the poet Jean Amrouche were associated with the *algérianistes*. It was not until after 1950 that native Algerian writers made their mark, particularly in fiction. Novels by the 'Generation of 1952' which included Mouloud Feraoun (*Le Fils pauvre*, 1950), Mohammed Dib (the *Algérie* trilogy, 1952–7), Kateb Yacine (*Nedjma*, 1956) and Mouloud Mammeri (*La Colline oubliée*, 1952) were often autobiographical in inspiration, sought to correct the view of Algeria presented by Franco-Algerians and raised issues of biculturalism and colonialism. During the Algerian War (1954–62), poetry grew strongly nationalistic (Henry Kréa, Anna Greki) and both nationalism and the war dominated much of the fiction written in the 1960s. After independence, most Franco-Algerian writers were repatriated to France with the rest of the settlers and the Algerian state committed itself to a policy of Arabization as an affirmation of the break with its colonial past. For a time it seemed that francophone Algerian writing had no future. Many authors, like Dib, emigrated permanently to France; others like Rachid Boudjedra (b. 1941) lived partly in Algeria and partly abroad, but some stayed: in 1971, Kateb Yacine (1929–89), the major Algerian playwright, chose to work in Arab dialect, and for a time after 1982 Boudjedra wrote only in Arabic. In the event, Algerian writing in French, far from collapsing, has grown and, despite the difficulties, more French than Arabic books continue to appear inside the country and publishers in France (and latterly Quebec) have provided outlets. The result has been the emergence of a wide-ranging literature of high quality. To it is sometimes added the *beur* writers who were born in France of immigrant parents, though their status is unclear. While they renew the 'ethnographic' trend of the 1950s, they write not of Algeria but mainly of the problems (racial intolerance, marginalization, biculturalism) which they encounter in France.

Before and after 1962, the 'ethnographic' impetus of the 1950s diversified and took many new directions. Not all exiles were exclusively preoccupied by the seemingly permanent crisis in Algerian affairs and their experiments with form (French New Realism was particularly influential) identified them with modern, cosmopolitan developments in literature. But many of the 1962 generation addressed their country's problems in a variety of tones. In *Le Muezzin* (1968), Mourad Bourboune (b. 1938) used a mixture of expressive modes to expose the hypocrisy not only of colonialism but of the anti-intellectualism of Islam. No less subversive was Boudjedra's *La Répudiation* (1969). The injustice, corruption and fanaticism of post-independence Algeria continued to be opposed into the 1980s by Rachid Mimouni (1945–95), and Tahar Djaout (1954–93), first of a series of intellectuals to be assassinated in the 1990s. Among the many women writers to emerge since independence, Assia Djébar (b. 1936) has remained committed to French, her *langue marâtre*, and to inserting the oral testimony of women into the written colonial discourse of Algerian history, giving them a voice (*L'Amour, la fantasia*, 1985; *Loin de Médine*, 1991) against the silence of the past and the tragedy of the present.

The French presence in Morocco, which was a protectorate between 1912 and 1956, was briefer and its impact accordingly smaller on its Arab, Berber and Judæo-Maghrebin cultures. Even so, by the 1940s, the small number of Moroccans trained by the Third Republic's education system were aware of the importance of French as a means of entering modernity. Ahmed Sefriou (b. 1915), the first novelist to attract outside attention, was a chronicler of ordinary life in the 'ethnographic' manner. This model, which normally drew on autobiographical experience to show the clash of cultures and the gap between a Europeanized son and his parents, especially an authoritarian father, was given a new iconoclastic charge by Driss Chraïbi (b. 1926). *Le Passé simple* (1954) expressed revolt against fathers, the closed society and the hidebound aspects of Islam. His later novels (like *La Foule*, 1961, with its Ubuesque hero) are socio-political fables which take humane positions on the relationship between East and West, modernity and tradition. Chraïbi was for long the best-known Moroccan writer. But in the 1960s, the review *Souffles* provided an arena for literary discussion and experiment and helped launch a new generation of poets and novelists who, however, were not always immune from the attentions of the state. Its editor, Abdellatif Lâabi (b. 1942), a socialist, was imprisoned for 'délits d'opinion' between 1972 and 1980. *Agadir* (1967), the first novel of the angry, iconoclastic Mohammed Khaïr-Eddine (b. 1941), was construed as an attack on the monarchy, and its author left the country. At the same time, Abdelkebir Khatibi (b. 1938) developed the aesthetic and psychic implications of his bilingualism in *La Mémoire tatouée* (1971), and Tahar Ben Jelloun (b. 1944) published studies of psycho-sexual states which are expressed against a background of the culture, imagery and traditions of the Koran and the Arabic language. His disturbing *La Nuit sacrée* (1987), which made him the first North African to win the Prix Goncourt, is an account of a girl raised as a boy who struggles to assume her female identity. Since the 1980s, new poetry on the themes of *errance*, identity and migration have renewed Morocco's strong poetic tradition, and fiction is well represented by Edmond-Amran El Maleh, Omar Berrada and Abdelhak Serhane and, though they are less numerous than in Algeria, a new generation of women novelists, like Halima Ben Haddou.

A French protectorate between 1881 and 1956, Tunisia managed the transition from colonialism to independence more smoothly than Algeria or Morocco. French remained the language of administration after 1956, but the bulk of Tunisian literature continued to be written in Arabic. Literature written in French has been relatively free of postcolonial trauma and has acquired a high reputation for its sophisticated engagement with contemporary aesthetic issues. Its leading figure, Albert Memmi (b. 1920), novelist and essayist, began writing in the 1950s and was the voice of Tunisian francophone literature, as Chraïbi was in Morocco. He explored the problem of colonization in dialectical terms, that is, by examining its effects on Jewish and Arab communities, the partners of mixed marriages, colonized and colonizer. But while major new novelists like Mustapha Tlili (b. 1937) have emerged since the 1970s, poetry has been the major vehicle of literary expression. The older generation of Abdelaziz Kacem (b. 1933) and Salah Garmadi (1933–82) continued to publish, but new voices were heard: the militant Moncef Ghachem (b. 1946), Tahar Bekri (b. 1975) who both expresses his culture and transcends it, and Amina Said (b. 1953), one of the new women poets who explores the self in the quest for wider identification.

Conclusion

The conditions from which francophone writing has emerged are as varied and complex as the histories of the countries which produced it. Allegiance is not always to France, nor even to the French language, which has been challenged as the vehicle of expression by both variants of it (*joual, créole*) and quite separate local languages (those of the Maghreb and Africa). Its central themes (cultural survival and identity) have often been maintained in an atmosphere of hostility to France, and if francophone authors write in French, they do so within their own Québecois, Mauritian or Tunisian traditions. Yet few would deny that both the language and the culture of France have played crucial developmental roles. The early struggle for nationhood vibrated to a common resonance which in many cases fell silent once independence was achieved. But the echoes reverberate still in the wider community and at the beginning of the new century the francophone phenomenon surely ranks among France's most successful cultural exports.

8

Beyond 'Literature'

In the 1960s, radical opinion contested the traditional place accorded to literature in the national culture of France. New Critics and Structuralists rejected the conventional wisdom according to which the literary 'canon' reflected universal values like beauty, order and truth and defined itself by the test of time through an evolutionary process which selected certain authors and genres and doomed the rest to oblivion. On the contrary, if literary Darwinism showed anything, it was the imperialism of a male cultural elite, the importance of market forces and the power of cultural institutions, of which the most powerful in recent times was the education system. There was no mystery, for just as culture was a product designed and packaged for the dominant class, literature, said Roland Barthes, 'c'est ce qui s'enseigne' and its survival was determined by its institutional framework. There were no universal aesthetic concepts by which literature could be separated from any other kind of writing. Nor was its creation separable from its reception. The act of reading was also an act of invention and forms of literary expression hitherto denied entry to the canon were recognized as valid cultural statements which could no longer be ignored. In other words, 'literature' died with the hierarchical society which had nurtured it and was replaced by 'writing', which obeyed new pluralistic and inclusive criteria.

Although such arguments were highly publicized in the intellectual community (Raymond Picard denounced the New Criticism as a *Nouvelle imposture* in 1965), they made little impact on the mass audience. Yet the status of literature was already changing independently of the cultural debate. For centuries, it had explained readers to themselves and defined their relationship with the world and the universe. But from early in the century, it had been upstaged by new and powerful authorities. Humankind was more exactly explained by psychoanalysis, the cosmos by science, and society by sociology and history. Literature, shaken in its self-belief as the mouthpiece of 'high' culture, retreated to a narrower base and grew wary of proclaiming the greatness of art in ways likely to alienate a growing element in the equation, the power of the book-buying public.

By the end of the century, the literary culture of France was no longer monolithic. The readership for poetry was minuscule, cinema and television drew larger audiences than the theatre, and experimental fiction attracted more attention from the intelligentsia than from the public. The fall of the old 'high' literature and the rise of the new culture may be measured by the standing of *bande dessinée* and film, which will be considered in the next chapter, and by the growth of writings once categorized as the 'sub-genres' of the 'paraliterature' of popular culture. Each has a history, and a survey of the evolution of children's literature, cookery books, the historical novel, the romantic novelettes aimed at women, fantasy in its various incarnations (which include science fiction), or the literature of war or travel, would reveal similar patterns: founding texts, perfected techniques, major practitioners and rising acceptability. Such a study of popular literature exceeds the bounds of this book, but the process may be adequately observed in four major areas: the central phenomenon of the best-seller; the evolution of written humour which reflects the permanent French irreverence for authority; regional writing, the clearest indication of the decentralization of literature; and crime fiction, which, after 1980, emerged as the most versatile of the non-canonical genres.

The Best-seller

The word 'best-seller', coined in the United States in the late nineteenth-century, did not achieve wide currency in France until the 1960s. But the phenomenon was by then well established. In the history of reading, the major nineteenth-century figures are not Balzac, Stendhal and Flaubert but Pigault-Lebrun, Paul de Kock and *feuilletonistes* like Sue, Dumas, Féval and Ponson du Terrail. By 1900, although a small number of literary novelists like Zola and

Anatole France achieved huge sales, the gap between art and what in 1839 Sainte-Beuve had termed 'industrial literature' had widened dramatically. Sensation, sentiment, violence and escape found a ready market; aesthetic experiment and serious studies of the human condition did not.

As the publishing industry grew more streamlined and its techniques of promotion more sophisticated and insistent, art fell further behind commerce and poetry behind fiction. Books had been a commodity since the 1860s and, as literacy and incomes rose, new publishers joined established names and took aggressive methods of selling their products to new heights. They advertised their wares in newspapers, on hoardings and in bookshop windows, and by 1900 had invented many of the promotional methods familiar to later generations. Cheap reprints, sometimes illustrated, publication in parts, the packaging of new genres (romance, regionalism, crime) in inexpensive 'collections' was standard, and literary magazines (*Lectures pour tous*, 1898–1974, being the most durable) made fiction old and new available in inexpensive forms. Publishers welcomed the new literary prizes (the Prix Goncourt, 1903; the Prix Femina, 1904) which became such a focus of public interest that while Gide's *Nourritures terrestres* (1897) sold only 500 copies in ten years, Marguerite Audoux's *Marie Claire*, winner of the Femina in 1910, sold 100,000 in a matter of weeks. In 1914, the fiction list was dominated by Henry Bordeaux, analyst of bourgeois manners, and, despite the success of Apollinaire's *Alcools* (1913), France's most popular poet was the less ambitious Paul Géraldy (1885–1983), author of a book of accessible love poems, *Toi et moi* (1913).

1918–30

The Great War gave a new lease of life to the military novel devoted now not to 'les gaietés de l'escadron' but to the horrors of mechanized combat. Henri Barbusse's *Le Feu* (Goncourt, 1916) and Roland Dorgelès's *Les Croix de bois* (Femina, 1919) won literary prizes but also became enduring best-sellers. But they were exceptions rather than the rule. For while new prizes were created (the French Academy's Grand Prix du Roman, 1918; the Prix Renaudot, 1925; the Interallié, 1930; and the Prix du Roman Populiste, 1931), few winning authors (Duhamel and Proust were notable exceptions) achieved more than passing fame. Complaints which have continued ever since were registered about the debasing effects of prize-giving on serious literature, which was further threatened by the commercial practices of publishers who followed demand.

Book production doubled during the 1920s, with 'literature' accounting for about a third of the total. Yet in terms of sales, what was described in official statistics as literature hardly reflected the themes and authors remembered by literary historians. Established novelists like Anatole France, Bourget, Barrès and René Bazin continued to enjoy large print-runs and Colette, Gide, Duhamel, Mauriac and Giraudoux, of a newer generation, sold well. But Valéry and Proust did not. The decade's best-selling novelists were Pierre Benoît (1886–1962), Paul Morand (1888–1976) and Maurice Dekobra (1885–1973), exponents of the 'cosmopolitan' mode which offered exoticism, lavish settings, *femmes fatales*, and a certain *louche* sophistication. For love in various forms was profitable. The writing team of Delly, with a hundred novels between 1908 and 1943, set the standard for the *littérature à l'eau de rose* aimed at female readers. More provocative were Victor Marguerite's *La Garçonne* (1922) and Dekobra's *La Madonne des sleepings* (1925), which caused scandals and, with novels by Radiguet, Cocteau and Colette, were held responsible for undermining the morals of youth.

Similar charges were made against detective fiction and the new *romans-cinéma* (or *ciné-romans*) which, like numerous cinema magazines, gave the plot, often with stills, of the latest crop of silent films imported in growing numbers from Hollywood. Novels adapted for the screen, like the successes of the Paris stage reprinted by *L'Illustration*, also found a ready market. Humour was supplied by André Maurois and Clément Vautel, but popular taste had its serious side too, as is clear from the interest in myth and spiritualism, the popularity of thoughtful novels about tubercular heroes and heroines facing death in Alpine sanatoria and the books of travel, adventure and exploration which helped create an audience for Malraux's first novels. But the public had been prepared by factual, cynical, heroic accounts of the war and novels which used their authors' combat experience as a background to other stories, as in Joseph Kessel's *L'Équipage* (1923), an early example of the aviation novel later successfully exploited by Saint-Exupéry.

Faced with postwar hardships, the book-buying public welcomed kinds of writing which transported them beyond their everyday, urban horizons. They continued to buy regional fiction (Maurice Genevoix, Alphonse de Châteaubriant, Giono and Mauriac) and gave an enthusiastic welcome to 'populist' novelists like Pierre Mac Orlan and Eugène Dabit who invested contemporary working-class life with a certain exoticism. The same kind of curiosity extended to the snows of Canada, first revealed by Jack London and Louis Hémon, which reappeared in the novels of Louis-Frédéric Rouquette (1884–1926) and in Maurice Constantin-Weyer's *Un Homme se penche sur son passé*, winner of the 1928 Goncourt. The exotic was also found in non-fictional lives set in other times. Popular collections of biographies of historical figures were launched and Jacques Bainville's *Histoire de France* (1924) and Pierre Gaxotte's *La Révolution française* (1928) reached a large public. On the other hand, although Alain acquired a respectable following, philosophy and ideas were commercial only if tailored for the non-specialist or were controversial, like Léon Daudet's pugnacious *Le Stupide XIXᵉ siècle* (1922) or Julien Benda's provocative *Trahison des clercs* (1926). The growth of interest in Freudian psychology may be measured by the success in 1928 of both Breton's *Nadja* and Kessel's study of repressed female sexuality, *Belle de jour*, but it was a more basic need – for heroes, in the uncertainties of the postwar era – which prepared the way, at the end of the decade, for the 'philosophy of action' expressed in the novels of Malraux and Saint-Exupéry.

The 1930s

The recession which followed the Wall Street Crash of 1929 had less impact on publishing than on other parts of the economy. But the status of books was undermined by new developments. Inexpensive literary magazines claimed the mass readership which was also seduced by radio, which broadcast plays, poetry readings and literary lectures, and by cinema, now increasingly dominated by Hollywood. The popular market continued to be led by fiction, but history, memoirs and biography sold well, as did books claiming to explain the modern world to the ordinary citizen. The biggest non-fiction success of the decade was Alexis Carrel's *L'Homme, cet inconnu* (1935) which offered a recipe for achieving personal harmony in a world seemingly at the mercy of technology. Christian reflections on even older problems were supplied by Henri Daniel-Rops (*Mort où est ta victoire?* 1934) and the novels of Bernanos and Mauriac.

The heroics of popular fiction in the 1920s now mutated and the public, alerted by cinema newsreels and the printed press to continuing economic and political crises, preferred individualism to be linked to some greater good. Writers were expected to commit themselves to a cause which was political in Malraux, pacifist in Giono and the triumph of the human spirit in Saint-Exupéry and Roger Vercel (1894–1957), chronicler of maritime adventures. If regional writers continued to explain country life to urban readers, they also campaigned against the encroachments of modern capitalism. And while Benoît, Morand and Dekobra (now joined by equally 'cosmopolitan' foreign authors like Somerset Maugham and Pearl Buck) still sold by the million, the fascination with foreign lands, hitherto centred upon Canada and France's colonies, turned into a curiosity about the Anglo-Saxon world. Middle-brow English novelists (A. J. Cronin, John Galsworthy, Charles Morgan) acquired a solid following, but readers proved even more inquisitive about America. Hollywood adaptations of novels were crucial in giving a French voice to Steinbeck, Erskine Caldwell, Faulkner, Hemingway and Sinclair Lewis. The Anglo-Saxon influence was also palpable in the development of crime fiction where, to the influence of Belgians like Steeman and Simenon, was added that of Agatha Christie and the pulp fiction and gangland movies imported from the United States.

While the rise of translation, a feature of the period, indicates a general widening of horizons, the mass audience remained faithful to its own popular traditions. Dumas *père* was still king of the municipal lending libraries and his spirit was revived by Jean de la Varende (1887–1949) in the adventures of *Nez de cuir, gentilhomme de l'amour* (1937). Women continued to be thrilled by Delly but also surrendered to the romantic novelettes of 'Magali' (Madame Marcel Idiers) and Alphonsine Simonet (1886–1952), author of *John, chauffeur russe* (1931), *Fille de Prince* (1935) and many others in which love conquers all. Humour turned increasingly to satire with Gabriel Chevalier, author of *Clochemerle* (1934), and in the fantasies of Marcel Aymé. Much more cruel views of humanity were provided by Montherlant and Céline, the latter benefiting by the controversy he generated. Better balanced were the first novels (*Faux jour*, 1935; *L'Araigne*, 1938) of the Russian-born Henri Troyat (b. 1911) who, over the next sixty years, produced fiction long and short and numerous biographies mainly of famous Russians, and proved to be the most varied and adaptable of all French best-sellers.

Although best-selling status was achieved by Colette, Malraux, Mauriac, Giono and Montherlant, many of the decade's major authors (and they include Gide, Aragon, Drieu la Rochelle and Julien Green) attracted a much smaller readership: Proust, notably, had more devotees abroad than in France. That their longer-term impact was greater than the number of copies they sold was an indication of the growing gulf between the literary and intellectual elite and the mass of readers who preferred Delly, Simenon, the spy-thrillers of Pierre Nord (b. 1900), or, in 1939 when the film was released, the French translation of Margaret Mitchell's *Gone with the Wind*.

The 1940s

Wartime shortages and the restrictions imposed by the Germans disrupted the publishing industry and the books which appeared were subjected to close scrutiny. Part or all of the previous work of some successful writers (Malraux, Kessel) was banned. Jews like Maurois were silenced as were any, like Benda and Martin du Gard, who were suspected of being crypto-Freemasons. Even so, certain books had an effect not always anticipated by their authors. Roger Frison-Roche's mountaineering novel, *Premier de cordée* (1941), and Saint-Exupéry's heroic *Pilote de guerre* (1942) reminded the defeated French what courage was. Early readers of Camus's *L'Étranger* and *Le Mythe de Sisyphe* (both 1942) interpreted revolt against the absurd as resistance to the German Occupier, and Maxence van der Meersch's *Corps et âmes* (1943), the tale of a doctor who rejects the medical establishment, seemed so much like a riposte to Vichy that copies circulated on the black market. But the demand for literary resistance far outstripped the supply, and openly defiant poetry and fiction (most famously, Vercors's humane *Le Silence de la mer*, 1943) circulated in clandestine forms only.

Those who chose to publish avoided provocation and provided escapism in a variety of registers. Léo Malet relaunched the French *roman policier*, René Barjaval breathed new life into science fiction, Colette published *Gigi*, her last best-seller, and Marcel Aymé continued to graft fantasy on to everyday experience. Regional novelists, like Henri Pourrat, though backed by Vichy, enjoyed wide success by pointing to the unchanging countryside which reminded beleaguered readers that, despite the current troubles, 'la France profonde' was a permanent reality.

The end of the war saw the creation of a number of new and often short-lived imprints, but the paperback revolution was resisted until 1953 when major publishers joined to produce the first 'Livre de Poche', a reprint of Benoît's *Koenigsmark* (1917). Book clubs wooed the popular market and the growing power of Hollywood, through the book-of-the-film, confirmed the status of Hemingway, Steinbeck and Faulkner and made reputations for other newcomers, prominent among whom was Graham Greene (*La Puissance et la gloire*, 1948).

At a time when ideas were controversial, Existentialist texts sold well, as did books by those involved in the highly publicized Kravchenko affair. Poetry, benefiting from its wartime popularity, briefly enthused the public through Jacques Prévert's *Paroles* (1946) before reverting to its status as a minority interest or entering into an alliance with popular song. Those seeking personal guidance found it in Dale Carnegie's relaunched international best-seller, *Comment se faire des amis* (1937), and spiritual questions were treated in new religious studies by Daniel-Rops and in novels by Blaise Cendrars (1887–1961), Gilbert Cesbron (1913–79) and Béatrice Beck (*Léon Morin, prêtre*, 1952). In the early 1950s, non-fiction was boosted by the interest in Thor Heyerdahl's Kon-Tiki expedition (1951) and the conquest of Everest (1953), which helped to promote the mountaineering novels of Frison-Roche. But factual and personal accounts of the war, from J.-L. Bory's *Mon village à l'heure allemande* (1945) and the *Mémoires d'un agent secret de la France libre* (1946), first of the many publications of 'Colonel Rémy' (Gilbert Renault, 1904–84), to de Gaulle's *Mémoires de guerre* (1954–9), also found an eager audience, while the *Journal* (1949) of Anne Frank sparked an immediate response in France, as it did elsewhere. As after 1918, the war created a separate category of fiction which chronicled the heroism, tragedy and horror but also left room for humour, as in Jacques Perret's good-natured account of an escaped prisoner (*Le Caporal épinglé*, 1947) or Jean Dutourd's blistering satire of a small-time wartime profiteer (*Au bon beurre*, 1952). Interest in wars old and new continued into the 1950s with notable successes from Pierre Boulle's tense *Le Pont sur la rivière Kwaï* (1952), to André Schwartz-Bart's *Le Dernier des justes* (1959), which inaugurated the debate on the Holocaust, or Jean Lartéguy's controversial defence of France's fighting men in the Algerian War, *Les Centurions* (1959).

The 1950s

But while fiction dominated the market, the anti-resistentialist 'Hussards' proved too iconoclastic and the *nouveau roman* too challenging for the average reader. One Hussard, Jacques Laurent, writing as Cécile Saint-Laurent, reached a vast readership with his carelessly written but page-turning pot-boilers, and only Butor's *La Modification* (1958) and Duras's *Moderato cantabile* (1958) and *Hiroshima mon amour* (1959), both assisted by widely reviewed screen versions, achieved respectable sales. Even so, the public still supported literature in more traditional forms. With *Moira*, Julien Green managed his only best-seller in 1950, the success of *Les Mémoires d'Hadrien* (1951) established the name of Marguerite Yourcenar, and Simone de Beauvoir, whose *Le Deuxième Sexe* (1949) was still little read, consolidated her earlier success as a novelist with *Les Mandarins* (1954). There was also a demand for the novel of ideas (Emmanuel Roblès, Georges Arnaud and the communist Roger Vailland) and Gilbert Cesbron acquired a large following with his studies of delinquency, the worker-priest initiative and other social and human problems. Established authors like Giono, Troyat and Kessel continued to sell and to them were now added Henri Bosco, who to the success of *Le Mas Théotime* (1945) added *Malicroix* (1948), Bernard Clavel (b. 1923: *Qui m'importe*, 1958) and Hervé Bazin (1911–96) who shot to fame with *Vipère au poing* (1948). The other meteor of the period was Françoise Sagan (b. 1935) whose *Bonjour tristesse* (1954) took France by storm and exported a sophisticated image of a rejuvenated France which had abandoned the old strict moral code.

Strict morality had already come under attack from the provocations of Boris Vian (1920–59) and Roger Peyrefitte (1907–2000) whose first success, *Les Amitiés particulières* (1944), had dealt discreetly with homosexual themes which resurfaced in his *succès de scandale*, *Les Ambassadeurs* (1951) and the many others which followed. Sex treated as a philosophico-literary subject, by Georges Bataille, Pieyre de Mandiargues and Pierre Klossowski, had only a limited circulation. But cheap erotica was made available to a wider public by the collection 'Mirabelle' and sex was used to add spice to many kinds of fiction, notably by Guy des Cars, the specialist in morbid psychology, historical novelists like Laurent and the internationally successful husband-and-wife writing team, Sergeanne Golon (*Angélique, marquise des anges*, 1954). Love in a more sentimental mode was packaged for women by new collections ('Le Roman de Madame') while for men, escapism in the form of violence appeared in numerous crime, espionage and thriller series which published four or more titles monthly. The mainstream public was amused by Giovanni Guareschi's tales of Don Camillo, Pierre Daninos's 'English' humour, and Queneau's *Zazie dans le métro* (1959). The more sophisticated female reader welcomed a new generation of women writers (Christiane Rochefort, Françoise Mallet-Joris, Sagan) while among foreign authors Boris Pasternak's *Le Docteur Jivago* (1957) and Han Suyin's *Multiple amour* (1953) were outstanding publishing successes.

The 1960s

During the prosperous 1960s, the status of the book was further eroded by the rise of youth culture and the impact of television, cinema, the *bande dessinée* and the expanding magazine industry. Non-fiction acquired an increasing share of the market, with Michelin guides reflecting the new mobility of the population and volumes of spiritual reflection (like the Tibetan meditations of Lobsang Rampa) echoing the moral unease of de Gaulle's materialistic France. Self-help books and popular science widened their market share. From abroad came Dr Spock's philosophy of child-rearing and Desmond Morris's behaviourist account of *Le Singe nu* (1967). But history, memoirs and biography also grew in popularity. New volumes of Simone de Beauvoir's autobiography, like Sartre's *Les Mots* (1964) and, to a lesser extent, Malraux's *Anti-mémoires* (1967), found enthusiastic readers, though more commercially successful were Lives of figures from the world of entertainment like Gérard Philipe and Georges Brassens, though even these were outsold by Henri Charrière's *Papillon* (1969), with its racy account of the author's escape from Devil's Island. On a more literary level, Robert Sabatier, in the wake of Pagnol's *Souvenirs d'enfance* (1957–60), published the first of his reminiscences of childhood, *Les Allumettes suédoises* (1969). Only rarely did philosophical or political reflection enter the best-seller lists, one notable exception being J.-J. Servan-Schreiber's *Le Défi américain* (1967) which updated French fears, by now long-established, of American imperialism. Serious poetry lost further ground, though there was still enough interest to guarantee strong sales for Prévert (*Histoires*, 1963) and two anthologies of French verse edited by Pierre Seghers (1961) and Georges Pompidou (1968).

Fiction remained the mainstay of the popular market, which ignored the *Tel Quel* avant-garde and, at most, showed an interest in the literature of ideas only if it took an accessible, which is to say naturalistic, form, as was the case with Michel Tournier's *Vendredi, ou les limbes du Pacifique* (1967). Increasingly influenced by the power of the image universalized by television and cinema, the majority taste was for action, violence and horror, much as it had been in the days of the *roman feuilleton*. For while Mauriac, Kessel, Bazin, Troyat, Clavel, Peyrefitte and Cesbron continued to hold the middle ground, Des Cars, Christie, Simenon and the new stars of crime like Frédéric Dard and Exbrayat achieved a mass readership. The market for espionage stories was cornered by Gérard de Villiers's sadistic, violent but hugely commercial tales of the SAS. While individual titles in the ever-growing number of series and 'collections' sold modestly, prolific authors like Simenon, Dard and Villiers, who produced half a dozen new titles each year, simply outdistanced the competition by quantity and accumulation. Occasionally, however, books caught the imagination of the public: Pierre Boulle's *Planète des singes* (1963) is a case in point. Yet authors were required to work hard for their success in a popular market vulnerable to Anglo-Saxon imports of crime, science fiction and thrillers, notably the novels of Ian Fleming filmed in the James Bond series.

There was still room, however, for less formulaic fiction. Television adaptations (of Eugène le Roy's *Jacquou le croquant*, 1899, for example) took readers back to classic texts and the war theme continued with documentary evocations of the Normandy landings, life during the Occupation and the horror of the camps, but also, through Lartéguy, ventured into more recent conflicts in France's former colonies. The social problems which accompanied prosperity offered new opportunities to authors who chronicled the lives, often from first-hand experience, of those excluded from the benefits of modern capitalism. Christiane Rochefort (*Les Petits Enfants du siècle*, 1961) wrote of life on a housing estate, Albertine Sarrazin of her marginalization through crime and Claire Etcherelli of racial attitudes on the shopfloor in *Élise, ou la vraie vie* (1967). Such themes anticipate the 1970s, as did Violette Leduc's autobiographical *La Bâtarde* (1964) which discussed lesbianism and the struggle against social and moral degradation with a frankness later admired by champions of *écriture féminine*.

The 1970s

The events of 1968 created a mood of political and social contestation which was reflected by the book trade. Giscard d'Estaing found many readers curious enough to buy his *Démocratie française* (1976) as did Georges Marchais, leader of the PCF, for his *Défi démocratique* (1973). However, the dream of the Russian Workers' Paradise was exploded by Solzhenitzyn's *L'Archipel du goulag* (1974) and by a spate of books, usually hostile, by foreign observers and the survivors of Mao's cultural revolution. After 1975, the anti-communist reaction was fuelled by the *nouveaux philosophes* who sought and achieved high media profiles. Around them, authors who denounced the encroachment of the state and the evils of capitalism were also well received, and they included novelists like René-Victor Pilhès whose *L'Imprécateur* (1974) showed national autonomies superseded by multinational companies.

The year 1968 had also given French feminism a new confidence. While its intellectual thrust remained a minority concern, popular expositions of the new thinking, like Benoîte Groult's feminist *Ainsi soit-elle* (1975) or Françoise Parturier's *Lettre ouverte aux hommes* (1976), were eagerly read. The success of Erica Jong's international bestseller *Le Complexe d'Icare* [*Fear of Flying*] (1976) reflected the acceptance of franker discussion of sex by women. The pace was set by Emmanuelle Arsan's *Emmanuelle* series (1972–5), new editions of the writings of Anaïs Nin (1903–77) and novels which took their lead from the American example of Jacqueline Susann. A more thoughtful note was struck by women who wrote of marriage and the family as a prison and argued in favour of more liberal attitudes (Marie Cardinale, *Les Clés sur la porte*, 1972) or rejected the old conformism (Christine Arnothy, *Le Bonheur d'une manière ou d'une autre*, 1978). Studies of depression particular to women (Cardinal's *Les Mots pour le dire*, 1974; Pascal Laîné, *La Dentellière*, 1975) reassured many grateful readers that their problems were not unique. Yet the volume market remained dominated by the tradition of romantic fiction. New collections were launched (one was devoted entirely to Barbara Cartland) and the Canadian 'Harlequin' collection launched at the end of the decade attracted a large readership. Gérard de Villiers, not to be outdone, masterminded 'Cristal', an adult series which featured sexually adventurous heroines, an initiative consistent with the mood of a decade which had taken post-1968 sexual liberation as an invitation to promote pornography in books, magazines and the cinema.

Most of this uninhibited writing was directed at men who, however, were less well served in their traditional interests. Espionage and science fiction were continued rather than renewed and the crime novel, despite stirrings of a *néo-polar*, showed signs of market fatigue. The war theme gained in vigour but turned its attention away from heroic exploits and, by focusing on concentration camps, the Polish ghetto and the fate of deportees, raised painful issues surrounding the Occupation and the Holocaust. Of the many novelists who explored the conflict and its aftermath (Michel Tournier, Christine Arnothy, Max Gallo), Patrick Modiano was, in literary and commercial terms, the most persistently successful. Yet the top-selling novel of the decade was Joseph Joffo's *Un sac de billes* (1973).

Joffo's autobiographical story of the wartime survival of two Jewish boys was assisted by the continuing interest in real experience. Evocations of childhood remained popular (Sabatier continued his series and the last volume of Pagnol's *Souvenirs d'enfance* appeared posthumously in 1977), but many readers, reacting against their insulated, urban existence, were also fascinated by the recollections of ordinary people, especially those who described lives of hardship, like Émilie Carles or Per-Jakès Hélias. A wave of nostalgia revalued not only regionalist autobiography but regionalist fiction too: Jean Carrière's *L'Épervier des Maheux* (1972) sold 1.7 million copies. More generally, biography and memoirs, put to increasingly sophisticated uses by literary authors, widened their hold on the popular market, with strong sales for Roger Borniche *Flic Story* (1973), a revival of the old *littérature judiciaire*, autobiographies of the industrialist Marcel Dassault (1970) and the actress Simone Signoret (1976), and de Gaulle's *Mémoires d'espoir* (1977). The latter also benefited from the perennial curiosity about France's own history which now, influenced by the *Annales* school approach to 'mentalities', centred less on events and personalities than on social history. Emmanuel le Roy Ladurie's meticulously documented account of the persecution of the Cathars, *Montaillou* (1976), best illustrates the way this tendency was packaged for the non-specialist public.

Of course, narrative history did not disappear, nor did the traditional historical novel which was maintained by Maurice Druon's cycle, *Les Rois maudits* (1955–77). But the fascination with daily lives

in other times established a new trend visible in the carefully re-
searched fictions, set in the Middle Ages, of Jeanne Bourin (b. 1922),
whose example would dominate the 1980s. A similar inquisitiveness,
fostered by the media, explains the success of books of reportage
which took up *causes célèbres* at home (like the Gabrielle Russier
affair) and abroad, with the established team of Dominique Lapierre
and Larry Collins, a major force since *Paris brûle-t-il?* (1964), using
the methods of journalism to provide graphic accounts of events in
Israel in 1948 and the separation of India and Pakistan in 1947. This
trend towards real as opposed to invented lives, authentic experience
rather than fabricated stories, marked a retreat from the imagination.
Ordinary people – the victims of war, the socially marginalized, and
smaller heroes generally – had tales to tell that were more immediate
and seemed more true than most of what was supplied by the tired
formulae of fiction.

Though the novel continued to rule the popular market, non-
fiction, often reflecting passing fashions, made significant progress
with books of natural history, works of reference, manuals and practical guides to beauty, diet, drugs, car maintenance and DIY. There
were documented accounts of unidentified flying objects and reflections on death, less in traditional religious terms than through reported out-of-body experiences and pseudo-scientific speculations
about extraterrestrials. Such interests were fuelled by popular journalism which stepped up its challenge to the intellectual elite's ownership of culture. Lists of best-sellers directed the nation to what it
should buy and Bernard Pivot, host of the television book-programme
Apostrophes (1975–90), emerged as an influential arbiter of taste and
much more important in stimulating sales than the literary prizes
which had proliferated since the 1950s. Accused of centralizing,
homogenizing and institutionalizing literary culture, Pivot publicized
books and intellectual debate to levels unknown in the UK or the
USA.

But with or without the guidance of Pivot, the public remained
faithful to less exacting forms of entertainment. The vogue for amusing lists of schoolboy howlers and peculiar advertisements, begun in
the 1960s, gained ground. A higher standard of satirical humour
continued to be provided by Daninos who mocked the absurdities of
advertising, tourism and modern jargon. Foreign fiction (Greene,
John le Carré, James Michener) remained attractive, with Agatha

Christie, who died in 1976, proving as resilient in the crime novel as Enid Blyton was in the children's market. Hollywood, for decades a channel for books-of-the-film, helped launch numerous novels from *2001, l'Odyssée de l'espace* (Arthur C. Clarke), *Le Parrain* (Mario Puzo), and *Love Story* (Erich Segal) in 1970 to *Les Oiseaux se cachent pour mourir* ([*Thorn Birds*] by Colleen McCullough, 1978) and *Kramer contre Kramer* (Avery Corman) in 1979. Readers remained loyal to mainstream writers like Michel Déon, Genevoix, Bazin, Cesbron and Romain Gary who recaptured, maintained or increased their readership. In a decade which came to terms with the anarchic spirit of 1968 and the irresistible progress of youth culture, the most consistent best-selling authors continued to be Bernard Clavel and Henri Troyat.

The 1980s

The election of a socialist government in 1981 produced a crop of manifestos, analyses and commentaries, and books which discussed ideas and current affairs continued to enjoy popular success throughout the decade. J.-F. Revel's *Comment les démocraties finissent* (1983), like Alain Minc's *La Machine égalitaire* (1987), emphasized the threat to the autonomy of nations by the global market and the translation of citizens into customers, while the case against Postmodernism, accused of diluting thought and culture, was stated by Alain Finkelkraut (*La Défaite de la pensée*, 1987). A not-dissimilar cautionary note had already been struck by Raymond Aron's well-received but daunting account of his intellectual odyssey, *Cinquante ans de réflexion politique* (1983). Concerns about the environment found a receptive market, with the Canadian Hubert Reeves, for example, arguing that man's ability to control his environment threatened nature's power to repair the damage. Popular science continued to make an impact. But though Stephen Hawking (*Une Brève histoire du temps*, 1989) quickly entered the best-seller lists, he was more bought than read and the universe was better explained, at least in commercial terms, by the flow of books about extraterrestrials and New Age religions.

The self-help sector of the non-fiction market (health, cookery books, and practical guides of all kinds) expanded, and the curiosity about real lives increased the take-up for biography and memoirs. The continuity with France's classical past was maintained through new lives of Hugo, Chateaubriand or Catherine de' Medicis, though more attention was given to notables of the twentieth century (Marie Curie, Kessel, Jacques Brel) and particularly to current political leaders like Jacques Chirac and François Mitterrand (Catherine Nay, *Le Noir et le rouge, l'histoire d'une ambition*, 1984). But while Jean Lacouture (b. 1921), André Castelot (b. 1911) and Alain Decaux (b. 1925) emerged as the most successful biographers since André Maurois, many public figures, like Giscard d'Estaing or Françoise Sagan, preferred to tell their own stories for a public which was also drawn to the personal experience of ordinary people whose personal courage had enabled them to survive imprisonment, drugs, cancer and other trials.

The market for books aimed at women moved into popular sociology with histories of maternal love and marriage, and surveys of relationships between men and women, mother and child, parents and children. Though such books reflected the new intellectual feminism, works of theory and *écriture féminine* achieved a much smaller circulation. But at a time when more women worked and the rate of divorce and cohabitation rose, many mainstream novels dealt with relationships inside and outside marriage, with some showing hostility to men, as in Benoîte Groult's *Les Trois quarts du temps* (1983). Attitudes softened, however, and over the decade there was a retreat, influenced perhaps by the Aids crisis, from the permissiveness fashionable since the 1970s.

By the late 1980s, 30,000 titles appeared annually of which some two-thirds were reissues. Of the 13,000 new titles, serious literature represented a diminishing proportion, its status weakened by forms of publicity which grew more insistent. Romance, crime and thrillers were loyalty-branded by the Collection in which they appeared, while *Apostrophes*, Hollywood movies and aggressive publishing strategies exerted a powerful effect on purchase choices. The 'Big Six' literary prizes could increase sales of winning titles by between 20,000 and 400,000 copies, and some commentators suspected that major publishing houses were able to manipulate the decisions of the juries. Novels written by people in the public eye began with a clear commercial advantage and authors alert to current trends were not slow to exploit the market potential of the increasingly Americanized youth culture which was encouraged by Jack Lang, Minister of Culture, who now declared publicly that *bande dessinée* was art. This mood was caught exactly in Philippe Djian's *37.2 le matin* (1986), a 'road' novel with acknowledged debts to Richard Brautigan and Jack Kerouac. But not all readers approved, and renewed fears of American cultural colonization gave Fernand Braudel, posthumously, his only best-seller, *L'Identité de la France* (1986).

Fiction, now available in supermarkets as well as in bookshops, reflected a related issue, the consumerist phenomenon which, analysed by François des Closets (*Toujours plus*, 1982), was satirized by Catherine Rihoit's novel *Le Triomphe de l'amour* (1982) and mocked comprehensively by the new-style Sollers in a series of novels from *Femmes* (1983) onwards which attacked the crassness of a materialistic age. Yet money was also a source of fascination and it explains the success of Paul-Loup Sulitzer's 'financial western' unambiguously entitled *Money* (1980) or Loup Durand's *Daddy* (1987). Other reactions included a reminder of older values by regionalist writers while Dominique Lapierre's *La Cité de la joie* (1985) showed that the poverty of Calcutta was not incompatible with its people's zest for life. The *néo-polar* also contributed to the hostility towards the multinationals and big business generally, a fertile area for crime and mayhem.

Meanwhile, readers remained loyal to Déon, Bazin and Sagan, but also helped authors like Patrick Manchette, Jean Vautrin and Sébastien Japrisot to graduate from the crime novel to mainstream fiction. They also responded positively to international best-sellers, like Umberto Eco's *Le Nom de la rose* (1982), and warmed to the grotesque world of the American John Irving. From South America came Gabriel Garcia Marquez and Isabel Allende, Milos Kundera from Eastern Europe, and francophone countries supplied, among many others, Anne Hébert (Quebec), the Lebanese Amin Maalouf (*Samarcande*, 1988) and Tahar Ben Jalloun, the first North African to win the Goncourt (with *La Nuit sacrée*, 1987).

The two major preoccupations of the current literary novel also found an echo in best-selling fiction: history and autobiography. Traditional historical novels, set in times ranging from ancient Egypt through the eighteenth century to the Second World War, continued to appeal. But the success of Jeanne Bourin's 'everyday life' approach prompted authors to complete the biography of background characters (Victor Hugo's mother, for example) or depart from tradition by showing not the influence of an invented character on events but the effect of events on a servant, sailor or some other invented figure. This approach lent itself to the family saga, the modern version of the *roman fleuve*, which was undertaken by well-established novelists, Troyat for example (though his major success was the small-scale *Viou*, 1980), Clavel, with epic sweeps through Franche-Comté and Canada, and Claude Michelet whose trilogy, *Promesses du ciel et de la terre* (1985–8), followed the fortunes of a French family in South America in the 1870s.

The saga dealt, often melodramatically, with death, disaster, family feuds and the clash of generations. But it came in a variety of forms. Félicien Marceau's dynastic novel, *Les Passions partagées* (1987), indulged a certain heavy-handed humour at the genre's expense, though Eric Orsenna's *L'Exposition coloniale* (1988) was more overtly comic. But Louis Gardel's *Fort Saganne* (1980), which reverted to the colonial territory once occupied by Pierre Benoît, found its point of departure in family documents inherited by the author, an approach adopted by Michelle Clément-Mainard who used the life of her great-grandfather as the basis for *La Fourche à loup* (1985). The personal involvement of the author was also at the heart of the Jewish saga of Marek Halter (*La Mémoire d'Abraham*, 1984) and of prize-winning novels by Annie Ernaux (*La Place*, 1984) and Duras (*L'Amant*, 1984). Popular novelists used their own or their family's history as material for their fictions, a trend which confirmed the secondary role of imagination, to which real lives were increasingly preferred. If Sabatier continued to evoke his youth, novels based on personal experience (life in Franco's Spain, for example) now clearly excited public curiosity.

The 1990s

Domestic issues publicized by the media helped sustain the market for political biography, attacks on materialism and the exposé of financial malpractice and government scandals. The debate about the environment produced many contributors, who included Michel Serres (*Le Contrat naturel*, 1990) while Dominique Lapierre's *Plus grand que l'amour* (1990) surveyed the worldwide effort to combat the Aids crisis which was personalized for many readers by the highly publicized novels of Hervé Guibert. The vogue for psychoanalysis and sociology had peaked but demand remained buoyant for self-improvement books reflecting the growth of the leisure society. Cookery books honoured Saint Calorie, Laurence Pernoud's *J'attends un enfant,* first published in the 1960s, continued to outsell most novels, and doubts about the education system encouraged a proliferation of study guides. The new anxieties also reinforced the market for medical handbooks, occultism and esoterica, and traditional religious publications showed signs of a recovery.

Clavel, Troyat and Bazin seemed to have a permanent niche in the fiction lists which they shared with other hardy perennials (Modiano, Sagan, François Nourissier) and newer novelists who had made their names in the 1980s, like Françoise Chandernagor and Régine Deforges. The saga still sold well (Jean Rouaud, *Les Champs d'honneur*, 1990) and writers regarded as 'literary' occasionally reached a wider public, as did J.-M.-G. le Clézio with *Étoile errante* (1992) and Albert Cohen with the paperback edition of *Belle du Seigneur* (1998). But foreign fiction also prospered. Literary authors like Eco (*Le Pendule de Foucault*, 1990), Paul Coelho, Julian Barnes and William Boyd fared well, but less so than American horror (Mary Higgins Clark, Stephen King) and the new English crime queens, Ruth Rendell and P. D. James. History, historical biography and historical novels gained in popularity, and fictions which echoed the Occupation and the Holocaust increased their audience. The strength of the theme of childhood and youth may be measured by the 6 million copies sold of Pagnol's *La Gloire de mon père* which had been filmed (1989), but also in the ascendant were (auto)biographical novels showing the 'trials of life': personal accounts of a fight against illness, injustice or deprivation.

The line between autobiography and mainstream fiction continued to be blurred to the detriment of the latter. Outside formulaic popular fiction, heroes and heroines had been undermined since the time of the *nouveau roman*, which made the novel synonymous with alienation and impotence. It had disempowered the individual who became an element in a world over which he or she had no control. Popular culture had never accepted this diagnosis and the appetite for individualism and heroes was increasingly satisfied by biographies of figures from the past who had conquered all and, increasingly, from the present, where the memoirs or novels of media personalities and the stars of cinema, sport and even crime showed how real people had lived their lives and achieved success, the goal of a material age. It was this mood which boosted the 'trials of life' genre and enabled the crime novels of Didier Daeninckx or Daniel Pennac, not lacking in assertive heroes, to move into the mainstream.

Well-established popular genres (science fiction, the *roman policier*, and even the Harlequin/Duo romances) became less profitable. The downturn was also reflected in other areas of publishing. The explosion of leisure alternatives was partly to blame, but the reading public was ageing and young people were lured away from print by more market-friendly sources of entertainment and information. To cinema, television, *bande dessinée* and the vast range of carefully targeted magazines were soon added video games, the word-processor, the internet and the Playstation. The generation of TV 'zappers' mutated into 'cyber-surfers' who, though they generated spin-off opportunities for publishers, failed to restock the traditional popular reading market.

Even so, successive governments have continued to support books, while highly publicized annual literary prizes, radio reviews and television (*Ex-Libris* and Pivot's revamped show, *Bouillon de culture*) maintained the book as the heart of French literary culture. But France's 5,000 publishers are forced to make financial rather than aesthetic decisions. As in other Western countries, they prefer to invest in authors who have famous names rather than the unknown, first-time writer. At the turn of a new century, it is clear that 'high' culture has not benefited from what Ortega y Gasset termed 'the revolt of the masses'. In 1909, 800 new novels claiming some literary merit were published annually. In 1997, the figure was 400 and of these, three-quarters disappeared within three months without finding a public.

Conclusion

The twentieth century presided over the democratization of the book to the point where its days, according to gloomier observers, are numbered. But at the start of a new century, the habit of reading remains strong. Yet the best-seller phenomenon has clearly challenged the academic view that French fiction in the twentieth century moved resolutely forward from Gide and Proust to Sartre and Camus and thence to Beckett and Duras. In the forty years after its creation in 1953, the Livre de Poche imprint sold 700 million copies. Its best-selling author was Hervé Bazin, with both Zola and Christiane Rochefort reaching several million copies each. According to listings compiled since the mid-1960s, Bernard Clavel and Henri Troyat were the overall highest-selling novelists, but each decade has produced its own outright champion. In the 1940s, it was Jacques Laurent, with

Caroline chérie (1947), in the 1950s Vercors's *Le Silence de la mer* (first published in 1943), and in the 1960s *Noëlle aux quatre vents* (1966), Jacques Tournier's novel of romantic escapism. The greatest commercial success of the 1970s was Joseph Joffo's *Un sac de billes* (1973) and, in the 1980s Régine Deforges's trilogy, *La Bicyclette bleue* (1982–5). But the information on which such results are based is partial. Statistical lists are a tool of the book trade and they define 'best seller' for an essentially middle-brow public having some claim to 'literary' taste. They do not include the far higher sales achieved by pulp fiction, by Gérard de Villiers, the century's overall best-seller, and other publishing machines like Georges Simenon and Frédéric Dard.

The centre of gravity of the nation's taste was permanently situated below the major literary movements of the century. Since the war, Existentialism, the *nouveau roman*, Structuralist experiment, *écriture féminine* and other avant-gardes were a matter for the cultivated, Paris-based elite. That is not to say, however, that popular fiction was ever insignificant. Cocteau and Cendrars admired Judex, Albert Cohen read Paul Morand with enthusiasm, and Sartre was introduced to literature not by Chateaubriand but through the yarns of Paul d'Ivoi and Arthur Bernède. The cinema of the 1930s and 1940s created a vogue for American novelists who played a significant role in the renewal of French fiction after 1945, while the *roman policier*, which attracted literary authors as different as Bernanos and Robbe-Grillet, changed in the 1990s into a versatile literary genre capable of sustaining a wide range of moods and objectives. It is also clear that readers who grazed on popular literature graduated to the higher slopes or, put conversely, high culture and ideas benefited from a trickle-down effect by stimulating the intellectual curiosity of the Livre de Poche-educated citizen.

But in the last third of the century, popular literature, given a new cultural validity by literary theorists and promoted by market forces, acquired a new, autonomous status. The argument that bad books were to be tolerated because they brought readers to good books was undermined by a blurring of the distinction between 'bad' and 'good'. 'High' literature ceased to be the best of what was thought and written and was redefined as the product of a particular pedagogic system and a social elite which set a high value on 'le beau parler': few nations placed such faith in literature as a defining ingredient of national identity. The utilitarian justification of 'good' books (that they exposed the subjectivity of readers to vicarious experience and taught them to express what they felt) was extended to 'bad' books which, far from being mere escapism, also extended personal experience and prompted self-examination: a Harlequin romance too, in its own terms, could be inspirational. The great myths of the private and collective psyche in which all have an interest will continue to be processed, albeit at different levels and by different methods which will certainly include electronic diffusion and perhaps interactive CD fiction. Popular literature, from d'Artagnan to San Antonio, has been highly successful in embodying human values, hopes and fears and will doubtless rise to meet new challenges.

French Humorous Writing

The ancient theory of the four humours was the first systematic classification of human beings according to physiological and mental characteristics. Part of the medical arsenal until the eighteenth century, the humours, singly or in combination, were in regular use by 1600 by moral philosophers, satirists and particularly playwrights to define 'characters'. A mixture of the melancholic and the mercurial was believed to account for the paradoxical man whose misanthropy was leavened by idiosyncrasy: the crusty but kindly father, for example, or the boastful but cowardly soldier. His oddness was perceived as constitutional and his eccentricity made him a naturally comic figure. This unconscious 'humorist' proved to be less interesting to the French, who drew on a wider range of *caractères*, than to the English, from Jonson to Smollett. When, in the later eighteenth century, Sterne judged him less amusing than the man who wittingly assumes his oddity, the paradoxical temperament was turned into a conscious attitude and the divorce between 'a humour' and 'a sense of humour' – the deliberate aping of the 'humorist' – was complete.

This brand of wilfully adopted humour took firmest root in England, which was regarded as a land of eccentrics by the French who, by tradition, were more attuned to wit. Wit and humour, though obviously related, are also quite separate. The first is intellectual and addresses reality in ironic and critical terms. The second has an affective dimension, values the ludic and the ludicrous for their own sake,

and exploits the absurdity of everyday reality for no systematic purpose. *Esprit* is directed outward, against others and the world; humour is often a form of ironic self-disparagement which implicates
the humorist in the follies and absurdities to which he draws attention. The French, more controlled in their reactions and permanently
marked by the sardonic tradition of La Rochefoucauld and Chamfort,
have never surrendered to feyness and nonsense as readily as the
English who, by the same token, have not laughed as heartily at
the more acerbic French fondness for ridicule, satire and the barbed
aphorism. To the French mind, Anglo-Saxon humour can seem
cruel and cold, a complaint echoed exactly by generations of English
readers of French wit.

The beginnings to 1914

The word *humour* entered the language in about 1725 when it defined remarks or acts which gave rise unwittingly to laughter. In
1762 the dictionary of the French Academy omitted *humour* but
included the *humouriste*, who was a physician skilled in the theory of
humours or, alternatively, an eccentric. Mme de Staël (*De la littérature*,
1800) was among the first in France to define humour as a conscious
attitude which she associated primarily with England: the 'gaîté des
propos' of Fielding and Sterne was heightened by 'la gravité de leur
auteur'. Romantic writers also linked 'humour' with England but
saw it as a form of temperamental oddity variously exemplified by
Shakespeare (Hamlet and Jacques), Sterne, Lamb and Byron. Littré's
Dictionnaire (1863–72) still considered it an English concept and Taine
repeated the now generally accepted view of humour as 'la plaisanterie
d'un homme qui, en plaisantant, garde une mine grave'. In 1878,
the French Academy admitted *humouristique* but did not lexicalize
humour until 1932, though it was in regular use in the 1880s. By
then, the phenomenon of laughter had been analysed by psychologists and philosophers, notably in *Le Rire* (1899) by Henri Bergson
(1859–1941) ('le mécanique plaqué au vivant') and the first anthology of French humour (as opposed to wit) had appeared in 1911.

There is humour in French literature from Villon to Marot,
from Rabelais to Molière and from Voltaire and Diderot to Musset
and beyond. Montaigne has been called the most complete French
humorist, a title sometimes also granted to Stendhal, France's major

exponent of gentle self-directed irony. But the French comic tradition proper, in fiction, theatre and verse, relies more heavily on wit, satire and farce than on humour, which had journalistic rather than literary origins. It is first identifiable around 1830 in the caricatural glimpses of the July Monarchy published in illustrated periodicals which exploited new technologies to replace the expensive engravings of the eighteenth century by cheaper line drawings. By the 1850s, Honoré Daumier (1808–79), Gustave Doré (1832–83) and others had created a taste for visual humour which continued to grow with the rise of mass-circulation newspapers. The satirical and political cartoon played a role in the Revolution of 1848, the débâcle of 1870, the Boulangiste crisis, the Dreyfus Affair and the scandals of the Third Republic. But cartoonists also laughed at human foibles, the oddness of life, women, bourgeois pretension and social manners generally. The popularity of André Gill (1840–85), Cham, Abel Faivre, Forain, Caran d'Ache and Steinlen is attested by the significant place they occupied in their century both in general-interest newspapers and magazines designed to amuse, from *La Caricature* and *Le Charivari* in the 1830s via *Le Journal amusant* in the 1860s to *Le Rire* (founded 1894) which quickly reached a circulation of 150,000. By 1918, the cartoon had become fully industrialized and thereafter evolved as a caustic commentary on events, fashion and the idiosyncrasies of everyday life.

Written humour appeared, also in the periodical press, at the same time as the first cartoonists. In 1830, Henri Monnier (1805–77) published the first of his *Scènes populaires* which launched the obtuse and pretentious Joseph Prudhomme who would wear the amiable face of bourgeois stupidity for posterity. Monnier also popularized the meaningless aphorism ('Ôtez l'homme à la société, vous l'isolez') and a number of Monsieur Prudhomme's pompous observations passed directly into the language ('C'est mon opinion et je la partage'). His success was a reflection of anti-bourgeois attitudes but also of the renewed interest in verbal humour.

Puns and word play had been fashionable in the seventeenth century (Molière mocked the vogue in *La Critique de l'École des femmes*) but fell from favour until they were revived in the salons of the Consulate. *Contrepéteries*, anagrams, palindromes, the rebus and other kinds of verbal acrobatics continued to appeal throughout the century to readers of all social levels. Hugo was a fanatic word player but 'mots pour rire' appeared regularly in cheap comic papers. They loomed large in the journalist Commerson's *Petite encyclopédie bouffonne* (1853) and the point of many humorous poems and stories was the punning punchline.

Much early humour was rooted in the comedy of observation. Sketch-writers developed a keen eye for the oddness of everyday life and reported conversations overheard, slips of the tongue, the collapse of stout parties, as well as unintentionally funny remarks and advertisements. A collection of such *Singularités*, published by 'G. P. Philomneste' in 1841, drew attention to the comedy of the ordinary which crossed class boundaries and appealed to both the growing popular readership and to sophisticated authors, like Flaubert, whose *Dictionnaire des idées reçues* was based on the principle.

A related phenomenon was the rise of parody. Of course, pastiche was not new. But just as Scarron and Marivaux had burlesqued Virgil to make a literary point, so the Romantics used parody to pour scorn on classical dramaturgy. They in turn were lampooned (Hugo's *Les Burgraves* was pastiched half a dozen times) and thereafter any high-profile form of writing, from literary manifestos to popular plays and fiction, was likely to be traduced in the press. Hugo was a frequent target, but Ponsard was parodied by Joseph Méry in *Le Globe* and Musset by Raoul Ponçon. From the 1860s André Gill's weekly, *La Parodie*, rewrote everyone from Dumas to Vallès. Popular fiction was a favourite target for sketch-writers and in the 1880s, *Le Chat noir* serialized *La Revanche du guillotiné* which it attributed it to Ponchon (*sic*) du Terrail.

The humorous journalism of the 1830s soon began to develop new and more substantial forms. Out of Monnier's *scènes populaires* grew the *tribunal comique*, a speciality of Jules Moineaux (1825–95), father of Courteline, which also attracted writers of the calibre of Maupassant. More generally, the sketch and the dialogue, which played on language and exploited things seen and heard, quickly turned into the *conte amusant*. The original targets remained concierges, cab-drivers and dim-witted clerks, but during the Second Empire the range was extended by the *vie parisienne* atmosphere of the Boulevards: debts, duels, women, marriage and adultery were the new subjects, as was the ribaldry with which they were often treated. The discovery of Mark Twain promoted the structured anecdote and extended humour beyond words to include situations. Most *conteurs* are now forgotten – Aurélien Scholl (1833–1902) or the versatile Eugène Chavette – but among them were considerable talents like the right-wing polemical journalist Henri Rochefort (1831–1913), Villiers de l'Isle-Adam (better remembered for his *contes cruels*) and the genial Tristan Bernard (1866–1947) who had published several volumes of sketches and humorous tales by 1900.

On the other hand, longer fiction was slower to free itself from the satirical tradition. In the 1830s, the novels of Alphonse Karr (1808–90) or Paul de Kock were strong on caricatured types and light social comment. And although the *Jérôme Paturot* stories of Louis Reybaud (1799–1863) are the most inventively amusing novels of the 1840s, they were primarily satires of the political and financial establishment. *Les Émotions de Polydore Marasquin* (1857) by Balzac's sometime secretary, Léon Gozlan (1803–66) continued to mock bourgeois attitudes in a tale of an adventurer who becomes king of the apes. But Edmond About reflected a new taste for sustained absurdity. *Le Cas de M. Guérin* (1862) tells the story of a man who becomes pregnant, while in *Le Nez d'un notaire* (also 1862), the metamorphoses of M. L'Ambert's refashioned nose add a surreal dimension to About's puncturing of middle-class pomposity. This model was comprehensively realized by Alphonse Daudet (1840–97) in the farcical adventures of the boastful but cowardly Tartarin who appeared in *Tartarin de Tarascon* (1872) and three continuations (1885, 1886 and 1890). While Tartarin was immensely popular with readers, Daudet's non-committed humour proved less so with writers, although Jean Aicard (1848–1921) had some success with the equally flamboyant *Maurin des Maures* (1907). This was in part because Daudet had captured the exuberant humour of the Midi, which was not easily imitated, though it seems most likely that the pull of satire was too strong. What might be called, with some stretching of the word, the 'comic novel' of the *fin de siècle* might highlight absurdity but it normally had a strong point to make, as in Léon Daudet's attack on the medical profession, *Les Morticoles* (1894) or the caustic exposures of university and army life by Abel Hermant (1862–1950). Less satirical and more amusing was *L'Invalide à la tête de bois* (1887) by Eugène Mouton (1823–1902), the story of Sergeant Dubois of whose head, blown off in action, all that remains is an eye and one front tooth.

The humour of military life had been part of the stock-in-trade of newspaper humorists, popular song-writers and music hall artists since the middle of the century. In the 1860s, Jules Noirac's *Le 101e régiment*, a hugely popular collection of farcical sketches about dim soldiers and their officers, was frequently imitated. The stupid Colonel Ramollot was launched by Charles-Théodore Leroy (d. 1894) in *La Caricature* in 1884 before finding his way into volume form, while Christophe's comic-book soldier *Le Sapeur Camembert* (1880) also reflected the popularity of *les gaietés de l'escadron*, a kind of writing associated particularly with Georges Courteline, who invented the phrase in 1887. In addition to his sketches of army life (*Le Train de 8h 47*, 1888), he also satirized the world of bureaucracy (*Messieurs les ronds-de-cuir*, 1893) and staged *Boubouroche* (1893), whose hero is that quintessentially continental figure of fun, the cuckold. Courteline's humour, expressed in one-act plays, tales and *saynètes*, could be black and fantastic, but he has dated badly, partly because his consciously literary style has gone out of fashion but also because by distancing himself from the follies he described, he can seem unsympathetic. Yet he remains a leading figure in the heyday of French humour which lasted from 1880 to the First World War.

Belle-Époque humour was rooted in the often mock-serious literary clubs of Montmartre and the Latin Quarter. Many produced short-lived periodicals which published sober ideas but also comic prose and poetry. The most celebrated was *Le Chat noir* (1881–98) whose fame was consolidated by a magazine which, at its zenith, sold 20,000 copies weekly. It published humorous verse, tall stories, parodies, ingenious plays on words, absurd *pensées* and sketches on traditional themes: military life, café society, middle-class pomposity and intellectual pretension. 'Mac Nab' (1856–89) was known for keeping a straight face when reciting his *poésie mobile* and many performed their work, sometimes, like Jules Jouy, from the piano. A number of contributors, such as Maurice Donnay and Alfred Capus, cut their literary teeth on humour before moving on to the theatre. Strongly influenced by Twain (whose translator, Gabriel de Lautrec, was a club member), the *Chat noir* exploited the taste for the absurd which had no point save to entertain. It mocked the age of technology by describing new inventions (such as the French boomerang which does not come back) in industrial quantities. This particular joke never wore thin and during the Great War Gabriel de Pawlowski, a respected sociologist, devised many such inventions and 'useful' tips in *Le Rire rouge* which was aimed at soldiers in the trenches.

But the humorous journalism of the *fin de siècle* also revived a tendency observable earlier in the century. The Romantic imagination was predisposed to the macabre and disfigurement; infirmity and death were subjects for black humour before Poe and Baudelaire exploited it for more literary ends. Henri Monnier was again the immediate ancestor of a gruesome humour more clearly pursued in the tales (*Rien . . . quelque chose*, 1836), verse and aphorisms of Xavier Forneret (1809–84) who signed himself 'L'Homme noir', slept in a coffin and was later hailed by Breton as a visionary and a precursor of Surrealism. This vein of cruel humour was extensively mined, among others, by André Gill, who left a volume of morbid poems, and Eugène Chavette, whose *Petits Drames de la vertu* (1882) helped spread the taste for ghoulish laughter.

The poet Charles Cros (1842–88) was best known in his day for his connection with the *Chat noir*. He wrote nonsense doggerel, some of it close to the spirit of Lewis Carroll, and comic monologues for the actor Coquelin Cadet. Sometimes bitter, often sardonic but unfailingly inventive, Cros was one of the major humorists of the century. The most comprehensively talented, however, was Alphonse Allais (1854–1905) who wrote for the ephemeral magazines of the Latin Quarter before becoming a pillar of *Le Chat noir* and, finally, editor of *Le Sourire*. Allais, the 'lugubrious Viking', wrote sketches, poems, pastiche, over 700 tales and, between 1891 and 1902, published 11 volumes of collected pieces. A master of whimsy and the illogical, he played with words, devised mock aphorisms ('L'argent aide à supporter la pauvreté'), parodied the 'readers' questions' column, described strange inventions, and pioneered new sources of humour. Devotees of Stephen Leacock, Bierce and the Grossmiths will find him familiar territory while his fantasies and absurdist vision anticipate Boris Vian. Yet if Allais represents the high point of nineteenth-century humour, he was to have few direct disciples.

Humour since 1900

Until the Great War, comic writing continued the tradition of the 1890s, though its touch grew more serious. Colette's Claudine novels (1900–3) ignored the great issues of the day and concentrated on the actions and attitudes of their pert heroine. But the comic novel quickly reverted to its satirical vocation. Anatole France's earlier chronicles of the mild-mannered antiquarian, Monsieur Bergeret, had included elements of whimsy in their exposure of bourgeois ineffectualness. But in *L'Île des pingouins* (1908), an allegorical transposition of the Dreyfus Affair, or *Les Dieux ont soif* (1912), on the nature of revolution, the satire is much more pointed and disabused.

Humour and the press

During the Belle Époque, written humour was mainly the preserve of journalism. Allais's immediate successor, the prolific Pierre Cami (1884–1958), contributed sketches, dialogues and amusing paragraphs to *Le Journal* between 1911 and 1934 and began his long-running column, 'La Semaine camique', in *L'Illustration* in 1933. He published many collections of absurd, fantastic tales and *saynètes* and numerous novels, of which *Les Exploits galants du baron de Crac* (1926) is the best sustained. Pierre Dac (1896–1975) in the short-lived *L'Os à moelle* (founded 1938) specialized in illogicality, nonsense and *histoires de fous*, and devised innumerable mock-advertisements and other *trompe l'oeil* images of reality. Meanwhile, *Le Canard enchâiné* (founded 1915) made humour the tool of political commitment, an approach which still distinguishes it from more abrasive satirical periodicals like *Charlie-Hebdo* (1970–81; relaunched 1992). In various forms, from the ubiquitous cartoon to the amusing column, the absurdity of life, politics and personalities continue to be at the heart of French humour.

Parody

On the other hand, parody, a feature of pre-1914 humour, has declined. The tradition was maintained by Proust whose *Pastiches et mélanges* (1919) was intended as a friendly gesture to the authors he admired. The team of Paul Reboux (1877–1963) and Charles Muller (1879–1914) parodied authors classical and modern in three volumes of *À la manière de . . .* (1908–13), with a view to restoring the tradition of French *clarté* by ridiculing looseness of expression. But less didactic forms of literary pastiche continued to draw support until the Great War. Fernand Fleuret (1883–1945) imitated the satirical poets of the Renaissance (*Le Carquois du sieur Louvigné du Dézert*, 1912) and the early poetry of Max Jacob included a strong element of burlesque. In *La Négresse blonde* (1909), Georges Fourest (1867–

1945) parodied both classical French theatre and recent poets like Verlaine, Laforgue and Mallarmé. Prose writers like Pierre Louÿs (1870–1925) and Anatole France wrote fictions 'in the style' of the ancient world and in French 'period' modes, though here the line between the historical novel and parody is not easy to draw. After the war, parody moved into newspapers and magazines and since 1945 there have been few attempts at either pastiche (essentially a stylistic impersonation) or parody (usually meant as a form of mockery). After 1960, pastiche survived mainly as part of the self-reflexive initiatives of avant-garde fiction. But it also acquired a political charge in the early 1960s with André Ribaud's 'journal' (written in the style of Saint-Simon) of the 'court' of de Gaulle which appeared in *Le Canard enchaîné*. Jean-Michel Royer's *À la manière d'eux . . .* (1977–8) revived the tradition in less satirical, pointed terms by presenting leading figures of the day via the pens of great authors. Parody was given a more aggressive profile in Boris Vian's versions of hard-boiled detective fiction in the late 1940s and his satirical attacks on 'Jean-Sol Partre' and 'l'être et le néon'. But the old art of literary vilification was revived in the *Parodies* (1977) of Patrick Rambaud, author also of a *Roland Barthes sans peine* (1978) and *Virginie Q* (1988) attributed to 'Marguerite Duraille' (i.e. Duras). Yet it is clear that the tradition of literary burlesque has been significantly weakened.

The status of humour

The decline of parody reflects a general retreat from the convivial playfulness of Allais and the habitués of the *Chat noir*. Humour has, of course, remained an integral part of the French comic imagination of the twentieth century, and classic English humorists like Jerome K. Jerome have had a small but appreciative following in France. But for the most part humour has been annexed for other purposes. Critics and reviewers have been reluctant to value it as a form of entertainment and to comic writing apply a vocabulary which establishes classifications by performance and intention, usually awarding higher marks to the latter than to the former. *Cocasse, saugrenu, bouffon, espiègle*, and *loufoque* define and judge a writer's inventiveness. A text which is *onirique, délirant* or, best of all, *noir*, is normally judged superior since it is deemed to engage, beneath its 'ludic' tone, with fundamental truths and urgent issues. The author who is *tendre* and *souriant* is, by these criteria, merely fanciful, a lightweight, uncritical observer. André Breton saluted the anarchism of the sardonic tradition in his *Anthologie de l'humour noir* (1939), but few major literary figures were tempted by comedy, though Proust had a sense of humour, Sartre's *Les Mots* has an uncharacteristic wryness to it and Camus complained that not enough had been made of the humour of his writings. But French humour has been consistently intellectualized in the long line of 'schools' and 'movements' which may be traced from Jarry and 'la pataphysique' ('la science des solutions imaginaires'), through Surrealism and the Absurd, to Vian, the 'Hussards', situationism and Oulipo, which have in common an anarchic playfulness which is, however, invariably overtaken by a preoccupation with ideas: the rejection of dominant, usually bourgeois positions and the search for rational principles and truths.

Spoken and visual humour

French humour has survived better outside the tradition of literary intellectualism. Talleyrand once remarked that if there was a man wittier than Voltaire, it was 'Monsieur Tout-le-monde'. In the first third of the century, music hall and the *café concert* maintained the momentum of popular humour before being overtaken by radio and then television, which provided a home for sketches, comic monologues and the *humour parlé* which remains, for many French people, the clearest expression of *humour*. Robert Lamoureux (b. 1920) pioneered the stand-up routine based on observation and verbal agility which only occasionally transferred to the printed page: the commentaries of Fernand Reynaud and Raymond Davos in the 1960s and 1970s were given extra point by being performed. The *chansonnier* tradition, no respecter of reputations, has also continued to laugh at private hopes and fears and has sometimes encapsulated public moods exactly: the black humour of *Tout va bien, Madame la Marquise* (1936) is still remembered for its defiant mockery of 1930s gloom. To these non-literary forms must be added the strong French tradition of visual humour, from the newspaper cartoons published before the war by Dubout, Sennep and many others, and, after it, by Siné, Sempé, Faizant and, in more extended form, Claire Bretécher. Humour also found a home in comics for children, from *Les Pieds nickelés* to the 'Smurfs' of *Spirou* and the US-inspired *Mickey*, whence it graduated to the more sophisticated *bande dessinée*, of which the adventures of Lucky Luke and Astérix are consistent examples.

Cinema

From its inception, this same popular audience created a demand for broad humour in the cinema: the first international screen comic, Max Linder, was French. If the French, with the rest of the world, laughed at Chaplin and Keaton in the silent era, they were also amused by comic actors of their own, from Fernandel and Noël-Noël in the 1930s to Louis de Funès in the 1950s and 1960s. Cinema has provided comedy of every kind, from slapstick to farce and from black to blue, but has always found a place for the gentler forms of humour. It is immediately accessible in the funny-sad films made by Marcel Pagnol in the 1930s, though the most systematic cinema humorist was Jacques Tati. Between 1949 and 1973, he won a world audience with François, the enthusiastic postman, and his eagerly apologetic Monsieur Hulot, who walks as if into a stiff breeze. Though Tati's visual humour, echoed at a more basic level by Pierre Étaix (*Le Soupirant*, 1962; *Yoyo*, 1965), had no successors, the *nouvelle vague* did not break faith with humour which informs Truffaut's 'Doinel' cycle and the comedy of manners of Chabrol and Rohmer. In the 1960s, Robert Dhéry (*La Belle américaine*, 1961) and the production-line output of Gérard Oury aimed at gross effects, but in the 1970s, cinema preferred more sophisticated comic forms, from the sex farce (*La Cage aux folles*, 1978; dir. Édouard Molinaro) to the cruel, sardonic comedy of derision of Bernard Blier. Since 1980 there has been a return to the film which deals in more affectionate terms with ordinary human lives, a gentler style captured by Coluche (pseud. of Michel Colucci, 1944–86) in Claude Berri's *Le Maître d'école* (1981) or by Coline Serreau's *Romuald et Juliette* (1989). The classic model of the *caractère* or *humouriste* survives in Bertrand Tavernier's *Un coup de torchon* (1981) or Claude Zidi's *Les Ripoux* (1989) which both feature a cynical but essentially benign hero at odds with systems and the establishment. A no less venerable style of knockabout farce resurfaces in *Les Visiteurs* (1994; dir. Jean-Marie Poiré). On the other hand, Patrice Leconte's *Ridicule* (1996) is a sophisticated exploration of the uses of *esprit* which is carefully distinguished from *humour*.

Theatre and poetry

In literary terms, humour has fared less well in the comic theatre which, for the most part, has remained faithful to the more established forms of farce, situation, character and satire. In the 1920s,

Jules Romains's *Donogoo, Knock* and the plays featuring Monsieur le Trouhadec were as playful as they were acute. After the war, Ionesco and the 'New Playwrights' expressed the absurdist vision in inventions which at times seem as close to Henri Monnier as to the philosophy of alienation. In similar vein, the early plays of René de Obaldia (b. 1918) explored the logical extensions of absurd propositions, though after 1970 his humour was turned more against the modern world. Similarly, poetry has confined itself by and large to the great themes, though more relaxed verse, some of it aimed at children, began appearing in the 1930s. Strongly indebted to Lewis Carroll and English nonsense, the Belgian Maurice Carême (1899–1978) and Robert Desnos (*Chantefables et chantefleurs*, 1944–52) attracted readers with their fantasy and play with words and logic. Echoes of these tendencies are observable in the immediate postwar period in the verse of Raymond Queneau, Jacques Prévert and Jean Tardieu. The mood survived in the Oulipo poets, but since the 1960s humorous poetry has been conspicuous by its absence.

Comic fiction

On the other hand, humorous fiction has maintained a strong hold on public taste. After the Great War, new names joined the ranks occupied by Tristan Bernard, Max Jacob (*Le Cabinet noir*, 1922), Fourest (*Contes pour les satyres*, 1923), Henri Duvernois (1875–1937: *Le Journal d'un pauvre homme*, 1930), and other survivors of the Belle Époque. André Maurois (1885–1967) impersonated 'English' humour to perfection in *Les Silences du colonel Bramble* (1918) and *Les Discours du docteur O'Grady* (1922), both based on his experiences as an interpreter in the Great War. Clément Vautel (1875–1974) achieved a wide readership with the good *abbé* Pellegrin, hero of *Mon curé chez les riches* (1920) and a half-dozen other novels which are representative of a strong middle-brow demand for light, intelligent, mildly satirical novels which set recognizable social and human types in farcical situations. Often this meant pitting defenders of the Republic against the Church and conservative right-wing opinion over some trifling legal or administrative matter. The political wrangling surrounding the location of a public urinal, described with mock-Balzacian realism by Gabriel Chevalier (1895–1969) in *Clochemerle* (1934), was the best of these and its success prompted three further titles, the last appearing in 1967. The amusing school story, so popular in England, was a relative rarity, however, though Pagnol turned an ironic eye on his *lycée* days in *Pirouettes* (1932). The following year, Marcel Aymé (1902–67) published his ribald chronicle of country life, *La Jument verte* and, by 1934, had confirmed his reputation as a novelist and *conteur* at home with the fantasy of ordinary life. Aymé was the most Swiftian of the century's comic writers and specialized in the disturbing intrusion of the bizarre into everyday reality: the author who is confronted by his characters, or the man who can walk through walls (*Le Passe-muraille*, 1943). His early feyness acquired a sombre edge during the war when he also moved into cinema and theatre and turned an increasingly jaundiced eye on social and political issues, using devastating irony as a weapon, as in *Uranus* (1947), his novel of the *épuration*, or the essay, *Le Confort intellectuel* (1949), a very sharp critique of the left-wing intelligentsia.

Humour was also part of the arsenal of novelists born at the time of the Great War. Yvan Audouard (b. 1915) acquired a reputation as 'the French Jerome K. Jerome' and in the 1950s, the 'Naïf' sequence of Paul Guth (1910–97) was a revival of the well-tried formula which sent a wide-eyed innocent into a wicked world. Carmen Tessier's tales of the empty-headed Marie-Chantal were enormously popular and Queneau also acquired a large following with a very different kind of girl in *Zazie dans le métro*. One major development in the 1950s was the revival of the tale of military life which, in the inter-war period when many harrowing accounts of the Great War appeared, had already turned into the autobiographical novel of wartime experiences, as in *Les Sabres de bois* (1929) in which Jacques Deval (1899–1972) looked back on his service as an auxiliary with amused detachment. Jacques Perret (1901–92) recalled his time as a prisoner in Germany with Parisian gusto in *Le Caporal épinglé* (1947) while Yves Gibeau (1916–94) had a no less keen eye for the absurdities of war in his controversial *Allons z'enfants* (1952). The same year, Jean Dutourd (b. 1920) published *Au bon beurre*, a wickedly amusing satire of a *régimiste* grocer who profited from the shortages of the war years. But the most consistent representation of the absurdity of war and the German Occupation was provided by the 'Beylisme' of the Hussards, of which Antoine Blondin's Aymé-esque, picaresque *École buissonnière* (1949) may serve as an example.

This kind of bitter war comedy was fading by the mid-1950s when humour ventured into less sensitive areas. After *Le Grand Meaulnes*

(1913), childhood as a literary theme had received serious treatment from writers who identified it with vulnerability, initiation and lost innocence. In the 1950s, the humorous evocation of children, for which the standard had been set in 1912 by Pergaud's *La Guerre des boutons*, entered into a new alliance with autobiography. Pagnol's *Souvenirs d'enfance* became instant classics and his lead was followed by other writers whose childhoods had also been filled with eccentrics and strange adventures, but none more successfully than Robert Sabatier (*Les Allumettes suédoises*).

During the 1960s, comic fiction appeared in the black, often surreal, but almost invariably satirical forms to which it has subsequently remained faithful. Maurice Pons (b. 1928) linked humour to imaginative fantasy while in *Le Beaujolais nouveau est arrivé* (1975), the best of his non-Parisian novels, René Fallet (1927–83) defended the provinces by attacking the contradictions of life in the capital. Post-industrial society is the target of René-Victor Pilhès (b. 1934) who, beginning with *L'Imprécateur* (1974), denounced its inhuman face. With a mixture of murder, farce and irony, he set about multinational companies, ideology and the power of the media (*La Médiatrice*, 1989) and high finance (*La Position de Philidor*, 1992). Such insertions of comedy into crime fiction, encouraged by the 'Série noire' and a central feature of Frédéric Dard's San Antonio series, have multiplied, and are visible in the street-wise humour of Jean-Claude Izzo or the fey inventions of Daniel Pennac who, in *La Fée Carabine* (1987), imagines a training programme which teaches little old ladies to shoot the muggers who attack them. Political life from the 1930s to the 1950s has been rewritten with sharp but good-natured humour by Erik Orsenna (b. 1947). A former speech-writer to President Mitterrand, he chronicled his experience of 'court' life in *Grand Amour* (1988).

Non-fiction

More significant in publishing terms, however, was the postwar revival of humorous non-fiction. With *Deux siècles d'histoire de la France par la caricature* (1961), Jean Duché (b. 1915) provided the nearest French equivalent to *1066 and All That*. Since then, demand has remained strong for tongue-in-cheek manuals and mock guides to management, gardening, childcare and other subjects suitable for deflation. Even more strongly represented have been books devoted to the oddities of language. The most consistent observer of usage was Pierre Daninos (b. 1913), who began as a wartime novelist before finding success with *Les Carnets du major Thompson* (1954), a complete impersonation of 'English' humour. *Un certain Monsieur Blot* (1960) defined the 'average' Frenchman and a score of novels and essays captured the contradictions of public attitudes, the inconsistency of private lives and, above all, the unreliability of language. Less systematic, and with lower ambitions, were the many *sottisiers* which collected schoolboy howlers, misprints and unwittingly funny advertisements. A speciality of Jean-Charles (b. 1922), the *bêtisier* was a popular version of a serious concern for language expressed in more analytical terms by René Étiemble, the enemy of *franglais*, or Robert Escarpit (b. 1918), an academic no less committed to defending clarity of expression. But it is always open season on the abuse of language and the popularity of word-lists and catalogues of solecisms derives essentially from their humour. Jean Duché's *Aventures de Madame la Langue française* (1985) was one of the more thoughtful surveys of usage. But the jesting word-book has proved particularly durable and has ranged from reprints of the *pensées* of 'classic' humorists, collections of Eurospeak, and tilts at modern jargon (such as *L'Hexagonal tel qu'on le parle*, 1970, by Robert Beauvais, b. 1911), to dictionaries of all kinds, from the *Dictionnaire du snobisme* (1959) by Philippe Jullian, to Jean Rivoire's *Dictionnaire des insolences* (1990).

Conclusion

Twentieth-century French literature was dominated by philosophical concerns and attempts to produce solutions to the problems which, in different forms, always face individuals and societies. Yet the dominant mode of intellectualism was regularly challenged by writers with an awareness of the ridiculous as a free-standing phenomenon. This counter-attitude has been recognized, in characteristic French fashion, by the award of prizes. The Prix Courteline (1934) rewarded comic writing which was further encouraged, after the war, by the Prix de l'Humour. The sardonic and the satirical, always more highly regarded, were recognized by the Prix de l'Humour Noir (1964) and the Prix Xavier Forneret (1970). Among winners of the latter have been René de Obaldia and Daniel Apruz (1937–96), author of a dozen novels whose pessimism is relieved by irony and burlesque. It is particularly this quality of disabused, cruel defiance which best characterizes French humorous writing. Authors of serious fiction from Flaubert and Maupassant to Jules Romains, from Céline and Albert Cohen to Vian, Pinget and Pennac, have possessed a comic imagination and have drawn on established comic modes. But their stock-in-trade is not whimsy or eccentricity or the treachery of words, nor has their purpose been to entertain and amuse. This has been left to the popular novelists, Boulevard playwrights, the makers of escapist cinema, compilers of *perles* and, in its most widely diffused form, by the exponents of *humour parlé*.

Regional Literature

Until Paris began to assert itself as the cultural capital of France after 1600, literature produced in France's regions was judged by merit, not geography. This has remained true of writings in languages other than French, for Bretons, Occitans and others have continued to work within separate, non-competing cultures. But in the seventeenth century, regional writing in French was demoted. The centralization of monarchy and the identification of language and taste with 'court and town' created a hierarchy of standards: the king gave the lead to the court, the court to the town and the town to the provinces. Literature which did not respect the hierarchy was not literature at all.

The centralizing drive survived both the *ancien régime* and the Revolution of 1789 and remained the defining principle of the French state. Yet the standardization it required continued to be resisted in both political and cultural terms. The centripetal growth of the state was contradicted by the relativism launched by the Renaissance, which also initiated a reaction against the domination of values by sophisticated courts and urban living. An alternative to the regimented man-made future was found in the past, in the myth of the Golden Age which was traced to Virgil, Theocritus and beyond. Revived in the pastoral novels of d'Urfé and Mlle de Scudéry in the seventeenth century, it was redefined by the philosophical and sentimental idealization of nature in the eighteenth. Rousseau's opposition to progress was rooted in his hostility to towns. Novelists, poets and moralists identified virtue with the countryside and 'noble' agricultural toil.

Marooned in Paris, Restif de la Bretonne evoked his Burgundian past in *La Vie de mon père* (1779) and the first *époques* of his autobiography, *Monsieur Nicolas* (1796–7) which combined a measure of documentary observation with the proposition that the country purifies while the city corrupts. But Restif also displayed the feel of place and that sense of loss which are the basic weapons of all regional writing.

But such voices were rare and Paris remained the cultural focus. During the Revolution, the First Empire and the Restoration, the capital continued to absorb provincial talents and 'French' culture had become irretrievably Parisian by 1830. Regional voices struggled to be heard. Jean Reboul (1796–1864), a melancholy Provençal baker, Joséphin Soulary (1815–91), the Lyons sonneteer, or the Breton Auguste Brizieux (1806–58) are the best remembered of the early regional lyricists. The Romantic poets had more feeling for nature in general than for specific localities, and while painters moved away from classical subjects and 'noble' abstractions towards representations of urban and especially rural life, they did so with considerable idealization. But the development of cultural regionalism took place – and continued to evolve – against a growing political resistance to centralism.

The politics of regionalism

Before 1850, political thinkers as different as Lamennais, Toqueville and Proudhon argued for forms of decentralization as a way of mediating between the individual and the increasingly impersonal state. Some called for a return to the old regions: 22 such proposals were made between 1850 and the Great War. The idea that France should be converted into a federation of regions gained ground and contributed significantly to 'le Réveil des Provinces' in the 1890s. The Ligue Nationale de Décentralisation (1895) attracted not only Charles Maurras but also Maurice Barrès whose *enracinement* promoted the idea that the locality and the *race* which had its roots there were the only true source of moral and intellectual values. Efforts to found a new regionalist party led to the creation of the Fédération Régionaliste Française (1900) which was associated with the political Right, not least because its journal, *Action régionaliste*, seemed to invite identification with the extreme nationalist movement, *Action française*.

Between the wars

The impact of industry and technology on the immemorially stable countryside accelerated after 1918. The view that progress was enshrined in the principles of the Revolution and the spread of mechanization was resisted by regionalists who promoted an anti-modern belief in an ethnic culture rooted in the soil. It was a thesis which challenged the political assumptions of both Left and Right. Capitalism, cosmopolitan intellectualism and the internationalism of the workers' movement were foreign to the deeper-rooted 'national' culture of France which was ultimately an amalgam of the 'eternal' values of its provinces. But while regionalism drew support between the wars as an alternative to centralism and defined a new nationalism shorn of expansionist ambitions, no action was taken to make it a reality. Separatist movements (in Brittany, Flanders and Occitanie) gained ground, but they were committed less to political goals than to the defence of local languages and cultures. Because regionalism had no other object than reconciliation and social peace, and because its enemies (capitalism and centralism) were not identified with any specific party, it attracted widespread support precisely because it existed outside the current ideological, social and political conflicts.

The Second World War

This ability to reconcile differences and contradictions appealed to all participants in the war. For the Germans, the 'Frenchness' of the regions was compatible with the long-term racial goals of the Reich. On the other hand, Resistance leaders regularly adopted regional code-names to signal their solidarity with bedrock France, which was stronger than any passing threat. Pétain also endorsed regionalism for similar reasons: the Vichy slogan, 'Travail, famille, patrie', echoed the dignity of manual labour, patriarchalism and loyalty to the *pays* which were associated with 'eternal' France. Concessions were made (local radios were allowed broadcasts in regional languages) and the Chantiers de la Jeunesse educated city children in country ways. But despite Vichy's support for the folklorization of France, evident in its encouragement of festive celebrations, it intensified the concentration of power and economic activity and, after 1944, local groupings were quickly reabsorbed into national administrative and political structures. Although regionalism was contaminated by its links with Vichy, it quickly resumed its old role as the symbol of national unity:

it was as hostile to American imperialism as it was to Soviet communism. Its cause was supported by the analysis of the imbalance between the provinces and Paris made in *Paris et le désert français* (1947) by Jean-François Gravier, who warned that to neglect the countryside was a recipe for disaster. Grants were made for the relocation of businesses to the provinces, urban development was subjected to stringent controls and a concerted effort was made to improve the infrastructure outside the capital. Regional disparities were temporarily disguised by such initiatives and the economic boom which followed the postwar recovery.

1945–70

Through the colonial crises of the 1950s, 'la France profonde' provided metropolitan France with a set of sturdy, if conservative 'French' values which provided arguments against the break-up of the empire. But by the 1960s, the professionalization of agriculture had produced a more articulate and politically aware generation of regional activists. Regional development was increased, agriculture was restructured and tourist initiatives were subsidized. But culture was not neglected. In 1951, the *loi* Deixonne reversed a long-standing policy by allowing regional languages to be actively promoted in areas where they were spoken. As a 'public' art, theatre was seen as an essential ingredient of postwar moral reconstruction, and the company formed by Copeau in Burgundy (1924–9) served as a model for the new, proliferating Centres Dramatiques Nationaux which led an explosion of provincial theatre in the 1960s. De Gaulle, eager to rebuild France's cultural prestige, created a Ministry of Culture under Malraux who, committed to a policy of decentralization, opened the first purpose-built Maisons de la Culture in the provinces to provide a locus for performance arts, exhibitions and local activities. After 1968, the Malraux formula was attacked for defining culture as middle-class, Parisian and statist, and pluralism was adopted by the 'action culturelle' movement which opposed centralized dirigisme.

Since 1970

The long-standing, conservative call for decentralization and local freedoms had acquired a sharper political edge by 1968. In *Comment peut-on être Breton?* (1965), Morvan Lebesque defended provincial 'difference' against the standardization of the modern world. Robert

Lafont (*La Révolution régionaliste*, 1967) made the case for federal socialism as an antidote to internal colonialism and regional alienation. Such arguments reverberated powerfully in the 1970s. A new awareness of ecological issues invited government action. The 'retour à la terre' movement was an attempt to slow the alarming rural exodus: the active agricultural population had fallen from 60 per cent to 7 per cent in a century. A separatist revival exploited recent history: if Algeria had been given its independence, why not Occitanie or Brittany? In the restless 1970s, political regionalism emerged as form of opposition to economic exploitation and state oppression.

It was ironical that this should happen at a time when Paris was transferring essential powers to Europe. But such was the strength of feeling that, after the socialist victory in 1981, President Mitterrand gave a high priority to devolution. In 1983, new laws at last gave the regions a measure of control over economic planning and cultural affairs, while the policies of the Culture Minister, Jack Lang, boosted the arts outside the capital. Decisions made in Paris or Brussels (agricultural policy, regional aid, the construction of motorways) were still contested and the impact of competition on farmers was noisily resisted. Yet the provinces prospered and by the end of the century cities like Toulouse, Nantes and Lyons were bustling centres of the cultural revival.

Literature to 1914

Regional scholarship, promoted by the numerous provincial Academies founded since the 1640s, was maintained after 1800 by the spread of associations for the study of local history, geology, botany and folklore. Although these learned societies dominated by amateurs remained largely outside the academic system, they benefited from the success of the 'Félibrige', a movement founded in 1854 to promote Provençal as a living language and bring about a revival in the region's literature. Its leaders, Frédéric Mistral (1830–1914) and Théodore Aubanel (1829–86) acquired national reputations, and their example encouraged similar initiatives elsewhere, notably in Brittany where the bardic revival was strengthened by links with Wales and Ireland. But they were hampered by government policy which aimed at making 'le français de Paris' the language of literacy: a common tongue was deemed the minimum requirement for citizens of a modern state. Regional languages, *patois* and dialects were regarded as obstacles to progress and were actively discouraged, especially after Jules Ferry's educational reforms (1881–3). Primary school-teachers, however, were urged to interest their pupils in their locality as a means of creating an awareness of French diversity within the national *héritage*. Bolstering local pride was part of a wider policy which aimed at turning 'peasants into Frenchmen', and extracts from regional writers continued to feature prominently in school text-books until the 1960s.

Poetry

The provincial imagination, however, was much less well served, its main outlet being the numerous collections of transcribed folk-tales. There were no lasting initiatives in regional theatre and regional poets rewrote endless variations in superannuated alexandrines of Lamartine's 'Le Lac' or Hugo's 'Tristesse d'Olympio': in 1900, when Paris had absorbed Parnassian poetry and was digesting the Symbol-ists, the provinces were still locked in the Romantic mode. Evoca-tions of sea, landscape, customs and peasant life, which did not always graduate beyond the pages of local publications, provided (usually melancholy) glimpses of the Landes (Jean Rameau, 1859–1942), Saintonge (Léonce Depont, 1862–1913), Normandy (Eugène le Mouël, 1859–1934; Lucie Delarue-Mardrus, 1880–1945), the Berry (Maurice Rollinat, 1846–1903) and the Rouergue (François Fabié, 1846–1928). There were experimenters (Georges Normandy used the new *vers libéré*) and significant figures: the Provençal Louis-Xavier de Ricard (1843–1911) was one of the founders of the Parnassian movement. But only Francis Jammes (1868–1938), the most admired of the 'Naturist' poets, acquired a national reputation.

From the *roman de province* to the *roman rustique*

On the other hand, novels set in the provinces acquired a hold on the general reading public. For Balzac (the Loire), Stendhal (Franche-Comté), Flaubert (Normandy) or Zola (the Beauce), a town or region was simply a decor for more important business. Less literary but more popular authors painted provincial life from a condescending Parisian perspective, offering a diet of small-town passions and comic or cunning peasants. However, George Sand (1804–76) marked a new departure by linking characters, situations and themes to specific locations. Her rose-tinted *romans champêtres* (1844–53) set in the Berry projected a more positive image of rural life from the inside while giving a specific steer to the concerns of social Romanticism: *Le Meunier d'Angibault* (1845) ends with a scheme for a utopian rural community. Her idealization of the pastoral made 'scenes of country living' fashionable. In numerous novels from *Le Chévrier* (1867), the amorous idyll of Eran the Cévennes goatherd, to *L'Abbé Roitelet* (1890), Ferdinand Fabre (1827–95), a mixture of Hardy and Trollope, promoted the values of rural life and the Catholic faith but also gave a place to *patois* words and saws. Léon Cladel (1835–92) celebrated peasant life in the Quercy region in *Le Bouscassié* (1869), described village rivalries (*Ompdrailles*, 1879) and wrote of country vagrants (*N'a qu'un oeil*, 1882). Provence was milked for its charm by Paul Arène (1843–96) whose *Jean-des-figues* (1868), the first of many engaging novels, appeared in the same year as *Lettres de mon moulin* by Alphonse Daudet (1840–97), creator of Tartarin de Tarascon, the epitome of southern bombast. Like Arène, Jean Aicard (1848–1921) was a poet, though he is best remembered for his accounts of peasant life (*Le Roi de Camargue*, 1892) and the larger-than-life Maurin des Maures. Regional fictions like such as Daudet's *Contes du lundi* (1873) or the Alsace-based novels of Erckmann-Chatrian, gave a human face to the disastrous Franco-Prussian War of 1870–1. But they also helped restore national pride by offering dramatic reminders of the permanent values of 'old France'. Rarely striking an openly *revanchiste* note, novelists after 1870 chronicled the permanence of the French spirit. This kind of reassurance was to be had in the rustic novels of Émile Pouvillon (*Jean de Jeanne*, 1886) and Jean de Noarrieu, and in the tales of small-town and country life of André Theuriet (1833–1907).

After 1900

By 1900, the 'Réveil des Provinces' had given a fresh impetus to regional literature. Between 1870 and 1920, the folklore movement rose to new heights. Anthologies of popular tales were published and festivals celebrating song, dance and costumes reconstructed France's older past. As performance arts, these were more significant than attempts to set up 'popular' theatres which, because they relied on local authors and amateur actors, tended to be short-lived. But there was a surge of regionalist fiction which dominated the new literary prizes between 1907 and 1914. By 1910, authors with regional credentials had mounted a serious challenge to the prevailing novel of bourgeois manners and were more likely to be published in Paris than ever before. Poetry, on the other hand, continued to ally itself with folklore, a link which would remain strong until 1945. But by not responding to mainstream developments, regional poets failed to find an audience and survived mainly in lyrico-sentimental evocations published by local magazines and provincial newspapers.

Regionalist writers

Although it was vigorously promoted, the refurbished image of France's regions was ambiguous. Was it an affirmation of genuine literary decentralization and intended for local consumption? Or the product of the opportunism of a new generation of writers with an eye to the rewards and fame which only Paris could confer? Many provincial hopefuls were middle-class by birth or had escaped their peasant origins through the new Republican education. They often began as poets with fiercely local loyalties and, bearing a sheaf of poems, made an assault on the capital which found them naïve and unsophisticated. Those who stayed quickly abandoned verse for the success attached to fiction. Others returned home and also wrote novels, taking passionate sides against the town, which both fascinated and corrupted, and for the naturalness of the country and its superior moral health. Peasants who wrote directly of their own experience were rare. Émile Guillaumin (1873–1951), a *valet de ferme* turned *valet de plume*, complained about popular novelists who toured the countryside recording picturesque sayings for inclusion in novels which gave a false view of country living. In contrast, Guillaumin's own *La Vie d'un simple* (1903) impressed readers with its unadorned authenticity. No less heartfelt and written with deceptive simplicity was *Marie-Claire* (1910), a thinly veiled account of the experiences of Marguerite Audoux (1863–1937), orphaned at an early age and left to make her way first as a farm-worker in the Nivernais and later as a seamstress in Paris. Charles-Louis Philippe (1874–1909), son of a clog-maker, made his name with *Bubu de Montparnasse* (1901), an exposé of the world of prostitution, but found firmer values in studies of the ordinary people of his native Bourbonnais: *La Mère et l'enfant* (1900) evokes his mother and *Charles Blanchard* (1913) his father in a mood which anticipates the more self-conscious populism of the interwar years.

The defence of the countryside

Many such authors set out to counter the bucolic image of rural life. They used lightly fictionalized autobiography, observation and experience to educate urban readers in the realities of country life. But there were also more ideological approaches. *Jacquou le croquant* (1899), by the self-taught Eugène le Roy (1836–1907), earthy in its realistic detail, was more outspoken politically: here the mood is anti-feudal and the class struggle has a rural face. Middle-class provincial novelists, on the other hand, with just as much local patriotism, adopted a more aesthetic view of the countryside and deplored the disappearance of customs of which they often had only second-hand experience. René Bazin (1853–1932), a militant Catholic, spoke as a liberal conservative in *La Terre qui meurt* (1889) which drew attention to rural depopulation and the abandonment of old ways by both landowners and peasants. His novels lamented the passing of religious values, showed the wretched fate of Bretons forced to emigrate to Paris (*Donatienne*, 1903) and warned of the dangers of peasant trade unions (*Le Blé qui lève*, 1909) which were, however, championed in Guillaumin's defence of technical progress, *Le Syndicat de Baugignoux* (1912).

New themes

By 1914 the *roman rural* had begun to shed its bucolic image. New voices were heard. Some were faint, but others reached a wide audience, like the Nantais Marc Elder, or Jules Renard (1864–1910), the unsentimental chronicler of Burgundian manners (*Histoires naturelles*, 1896; *Mes frères farouches*, 1908). Short stories of provincial life were published in large numbers and the near-monopoly of the Goncourt and Femina by provincial authors guaranteed them large sales after *De Goupil à Margot* (1910) by Louis Pergaud (1882–1915), author of *La Guerre des boutons* (1912), a classic evocation of childhood in Franche-Comté. With *Nono* (1910) and *Le Vieux Garain* (1913), Gaston Roupnel (1871–1946), later a respected historian of the French countryside, gave an important place to local lore and country ways. But the countryside was not simply documented. It played host to psychological studies by fashionable authors like Henri Bordeaux, 'le Paul Bourget savoyard', author of fifty or so novels of provincial life where neither religion nor ties of blood are able to hold marriage and the family together. But it was also made socially controversial. More embattled and less quaint notes were struck across the spectrum, from the working-class Guillaumin to the aristocratic Alphonse de Châteaubriant (1877–1951) whose *Monsieur des Lourdines* (1911) chronicled the decline of a noble estate. Within a generation, regional novelists had asserted themselves. Yet even as they shrugged off their sentimentalized image, the story they had to tell was being hijacked by Zola's socialism (*La Terre*, 1887), Maurras's 'provincial republics', Barrès's *enracinement*, the mistrust of intellectualism and the kind of mysticism associated with Péguy and the Catholic revival. The Great War would reorder regionalist perspectives.

1918–45

The comfortable traditions of nineteenth-century pastoral, though well supported at the popular end of the market, were harder to sustain after 1918. The war had brought men from all parts of France to the trenches. There, in addition to confirming their sense of *patrie*, they acquired a new awareness of their regional identity: the *poilu* was a Frenchman but he was also a Breton or an Auvergnat. In the 1920s, regional writers, many of them returning veterans, better-educated and increasingly political, gave new colours to regional writing.

'Nature naturelle'

Some chose to ignore the modern world (newspapers, tourism, trains and motor-cars) and sought to express the mysterious, beautiful and sometimes harsh face of nature. The real protagonists of the sombre, poetic evocations of the Vaudois by Charles-Ferdinand Ramuz (1878–1947) are not the grim people who do battle with the elements but the epidemics, storms and avalanches which constantly test them to exhaustion and death. Beginning with *Rémi des Rauches* (1922) and *Raboliot* (1925), Maurice Genevoix exploited the Val de Loire to unveil the mysterious and sometimes cruel ties which bind man, the land and animals into a single existence. The Provence of Jean Giono is not a picturesque backdrop to charming tales of peasant life but a primitive place, the home of a living force which both wounds and heals. *Le Crime des justes* (1928) by André Chamson (1899–1980) showed the workings of 'natural' justice in an isolated mountain community which deals with guilt in its own ancient, even pagan terms. A more relaxed note was struck by Jules Reboul whose *Babet le sage et ses amis* (1923) gave an exuberant view of life in the Ardèche, while after *Joffroi* (1933) Marcel Pagnol lightened a number of Giono's dark tales for the cinema. While the novel dominated the expression of the older spiritual mystique, poetry, of a rhymed and traditional cut which travelled badly to the city, was used to celebrate the joys and sorrows of country life. The self-taught Philéas Lebesgue (1869–1958) built on his prewar celebrations of Picardy; Francis André (1897–1976: *Poèmes paysans*, 1928) emerged as the best of the 'proletarian' poets; while the Burgundian Marie Noël, from *Les Chansons et les heures* (1921) to *Chants d'arrière-saison* (1961), touchingly described her daily round and her simple faith.

Political awareness

But if such writers settled for expressing the poetry and drama of hill and plain, others knew that soil meant toil, and toil raised the issue of social justice. After the Great War, the prevalent mood was one of resistance to the urban. When, in his dreadful *Une Fille d'Euskadi* (1925), Eugène Poueydebat denounced signs advertising 'thé basquais', 'Bar basque' and 'concerts basques' and complained that the Basque country was being turned into a folklore reservation for tourists, his stance was at once anti-Jacobin, anti-capitalist, anti-urban and right-wing traditionalist, a peculiar mix given consistency only by its opposition to the modern. The engaging hero of Chamson's *Roux le bandit* (1924) takes a stand as a conscientious objector on religious grounds and manages to embrace equally contradictory political loyalties: he has the pacifism and anti-militarism of the Left and the piety and individualism of the Right. In subsequent novels, like *Les Hommes de la route* (1927) or *Héritages* (1932), Chamson stood up against the destruction of the countryside by creeping industrialization. It was a theme no less fervently embraced by middle-class writers like Bordeaux (*Le Barrage*, 1927) and the aristocratic Alphonse de Châteaubriant. Aostin, hero of *La Brière* (1923), defends his native heath against the developers, though he ultimately succumbs to the pitiless inevitabilities of mysterious nature.

The 'proletarian' tendency

More systematic was the attempt made in 1930 (*Le Nouvel Âge littéraire*) by Henry Poulaille to create a 'proletarian' literature, a broad category which included the novel of working-class Parisian life (construed as 'regionalist' of a sort and exemplified by Dabit's *Hôtel du Nord*, 1929), and 'provincial' fiction set among the poor, such as the socialist-inspired *La Maison du peuple* (1927), set in Brittany, Louis Guilloux's first novel. But Poulaille also championed Ramuz, Audoux and Charles-Louis Philippe and included rural concerns in *Les Damnés de la terre* (1935), his autobiographical account of the fortunes of the Magneux family between 1900 and 1920. Guillaumin (like Lebesgue, a high-profile promoter of regional literature), now a journalist and activist, encouraged the new generation to good effect. In the 1920s, regional fiction featured consistently among the winners of the major literary prizes, though in the 1930s they were overtaken by the stars of the *roman exotique* which offered readers not-unrelated intimations of the picturesque.

Chronicles of rural life

The taste for the reflective country chronicle was catered for by Joseph Pesquidoux (b. 1869), author of a *Livre de raison* (1925), but the novel of rural life, promoted in new 'Collections' (notably Gallimard's Livre du Pays) put living flesh on the bones of the many guide-books which introduced 'unknown France' to city-dwellers. Ernest Perochon (1885–1942) set *Nêne* (1920) in the Vendée and showed the strength of religious bigotry which drives the heroine to suicide. With *Gaspard des montagnes* (1922–31), a rural epic in four volumes, Henri Pourrat (1887–1959) distinguished country archetypes from the artificial types created for the 'literary tourism' market. Even more steely was Lucien Gachon (1894–1984), a kind of peasant Mauriac, who, in *Maria* (1925), wrote of the avarice and materialism of the generation which found itself caught between two cultures: the old rustic civilization had not yet lapsed but the modern world had yet to reach the outback.

The stance of interwar regional literature was predominantly male, though Isabelle Sandy made her mark as a novelist with *Andorra* (1923) and Lucie Delarue-Mardrus maintained her reputation as a poet of Normandy (*À maman*, 1920) and novelist of provincial adolescence (*L'Enfant au coq*, 1934). Writers from peasant, working-class and artisanal backgrounds who retained a local identity formed a minority and most 'regional' writers were middle-class, and stood above what they described. Representative of the first was Henri Bachelin (1879–1941) who adopted the rustic persona he had left his native Morvan to avoid. Among the latter were the comic novels and satires of Marcel Aymé and Gabriel Chevalier, though the preferred modes were 'psychological' studies, family sagas and the novel of well-to-do provincial manners associated with Henri Bordeaux, Gaston Chérau and Armand Lunel (1892–1977) whose *Nicolo Peccavi* (1926) showed the impact of the Dreyfus Affair on the Jews of Carpentras.

A regionalist 'genre'?

Between the wars, regional fiction became a genre, though it took many forms within this broad category. It is defined less by setting than by its spirit. The *roman de province*, set in towns or in a *bourgeois* milieu, dealt with more or less interchangeable temperaments, themes and situations in terms readily recognized by mainstream urban culture. More exotic and less clubbable were writers like Giono or Genevoix who cannot be separated from their locality. They showed human beings confronted by Nature, unprotected by the trappings of civilization: money is less important here than property, intellect runs a poor second to cunning and written laws trail behind older imperatives of 'natural' justice. The 'regional' novel is more exactly defined by the labels which authors often applied to their work, from the *roman de pays*, the *roman paysan* or *rustique* or *rural*, and the *roman du terroir*, to the *roman de mer* or *de village* or *de montagne*. Settings are highly localized – topography, flora and fauna receive detailed attention and linguistic asides inject a unique sense of place – and the life it projects is alien to the town-dweller's experience. Paradoxically, the sense of region is generally flimsy, for the milieu is frequently a closed micro-society – a farm, village or valley – which regards the inhabitants of neighbouring cantons as suspect, even 'foreign'. 'Regional' fiction was in this sense parochial, for it confronted man not with his region but with his locality.

Its parochial nature

In literary terms, it proved impervious to foreign influences and avant-garde experiment and was committed to nineteenth-century realism. Impregnated with a sense of place, it carried a philosophical, social or religious message and promoted (and often personified) the land. It documented local customs and traditions and used literary French studded with local terms, syntax and anthropomorphic images. It was rarely attempted by the young and infrequently by women. It repeated staple plots: the biography of one man from birth to death in the same locality; the tale of a man or woman who leaves country for town, and returns chastened and wiser; the history of a family over several generations; the story of a couple who are prevented from marrying by local prejudice, of parents who struggle to educate a talented child, of a local group's opposition to the building of a dam or road. The time is the present or the recent past. Historical novels were rare but invariably re-enacted a local event: *Les Lurons de Sabolas* (1932), by Henri Béraud (1885–1958), which evokes the industrialization of the Lyons silk trade in the 1830s, may serve as an example. The structure is linear, often following the cycle of the year punctuated by rural rites, and the documentary intention looms larger than in less heartfelt and more melodramatic fictions aimed at the city-dweller. In the cast of characters, patriarchs and matriarchs are given 'respect', the *curé* may be wise or intolerant, the mature male stands four-square for the 'old' ways and youth is tempted by the lure of the city. Women, faithful to the land and less tainted by the town, have a pivotal role. The symbolically named heroine of Charles Silvestre's *Aimée Vaillant* (1924) struggles to keep the family farm going, but as unmarried mothers or 'fallen women' (extra-marital sex and prostitution haunt many of these Manichaean novels) women must earn their redemption.

The defence of the countryside

The formulaic nature of regional fiction, together with its stance as a holding operation against change, ensured that despite its popularity with readers, its literary prestige remained low: 'regional' was not merely a description but a judgement. Authors continued to pursue the same themes and draw attention to rural poverty, depopulation and the rich cultural heritage of the regions: Ludovic Massé (*Le Mas des Oubells*, 1932; *La Flamme sauvage*, 1934) was one of many in the 1930s who protested against the decline of the countryside. For France was changing. The mechanization, dechristianization and politicization of rural life, together with improvements in education and communication, all made the temptations of the town more accessible. At the same time, urban curiosity about country life intensified and the commercial viability of regional writers reached its peak. Cinema played its part by adapting successful titles for the screen and it had the advantage of showing in pictures what writers had described in words.

Conclusion

By 1940 the literary map of France had few uncharted territories: Paul Arène, Jean Giono, Marcel Pagnol (Provence); Châteaubriant and Perochon (the Vendée); René Bazin and Genevoix (the Sologne); Joseph Delbousquet (the Landes); Joseph de Pesqueydoux (the Pyrenees); Eugène le Roy (Périgord); Émile Guillaumin (the Allier); C.-F. Ramuz (the Vaudois); Henri Bordeaux (the Savoie); Henri Pourrat and Alexandre Vialatte (1901–71) (the Auvergne); Lucien Gachon (the Bourbonnais); Marie Susini (1916–93) (Corsica) . . . In their various registers, they looked back rather than forward and collectively made a powerful case for a protectionist attitude to country values.

Since 1940

Though France's rural heritage was exploited by Vichy, paper shortages and other difficulties slowed the flow of regional writing during the war. Henri Pourrat's well-documented history of the peasantry *L'Homme à la bêche* and his novel *Vent de mars* (both 1941) expressed *Pétainisme* exactly, but less docile traditions survived too. Thus Gachon's *La Première Année* (1943) maintained his long-standing hostility to the idealization of the countryside and Joseph Cressot (1882–1964) continued the sentimental tradition of childhood reminiscences with the bitter *Le Pain aux lièvres* (1943).

Despite sharing the 'national' values promoted by Vichy, few regionalist writers were active collaborators. But after the Liberation, strong action was taken against those who were. While Pourrat escaped the purge largely because of his connections with the clergy, Châteaubriant, founder of the anti-Semitic, pro-German periodical, *La Gerbe*, was forced to flee, and Giono, who had contributed to it, was briefly imprisoned. Henri Béraud, who had written for right-wing journals, was sentenced to death, though this judgement was commuted to a ten-year prison sentence.

Postwar revival

But the damage done to regional writing was temporary, for 'la France profonde' was embedded in the national consciousness as a permanent reminder of survival and identity. Films as different as Rouquier's documentary *Farrebique* (1946) and Tati's *Jour de fête* (1948) restored the traditional image of the countryside at a time when farming was being mechanized and modernized as part of the post-war reconstruction drive. On the organizational level, the decentralization of theatre improved the cultural image of the provinces. Slowly at first, then with growing insistence, the new Centres Dramatiques Nationaux highlighted the decline of local economies and its effect on the population in a spirit which, in the 1960s and 1970s, recalled the defence of peasant interests in the novels of the 1920s. The Nouvelle Compagnie d'Avignon, reconnecting with the Félibrige, now a century old, vigorously promoted Occitan culture and traditions. In the same way, the oral and written literature of the provinces became an object of study. The interest in 'mentalities' of the *Annales* school of history, pursued by academic researchers, reassessed France's provincial and rural past and, on occasions, caught the imagination of the public: *Montaillou* (1976), Le Roy Ladurie's case-study of a thirteenth-century Cathar village, was an international success. Arnold Van Gennept (1873–1959: *Manuel du folklore français contemporain*, 1937–58) gave folklore a scientific basis and his lead was followed by Pourrat's *Trésor des contes* (1948–62, 13 vols) of the Auvergne and Paul Delarue's seven-volume *Contes merveilleux des provinces de France* (1953–6). Tape recordings preserved not only the text but also accents and delivery, and stimulated interest in both the mechanics of oral transmission and the role of stories in constructing the collective psyche and the multi-cultural nature of the French tradition.

Poetry

In the 1930s, regional verse was conservative in both substance and form, the artisanal preserve of local magazines and the slim volume. During the war, the École de Rochefort, established in the Loire Valley in 1941, brought together poets who abandoned intellectualism, Surrealist excess and 'obscurity' in poetry. They reverted to the traditions of lyricism and regular prosody and made poetry accessible to a wartime audience. More provincial and non-urban than strictly regionalist, their concern was not to valorize specific localities or

defend rural causes but to celebrate 'la mystique végétale'. Even so, a
sense of place was distilled by distinctive poetic voices. The spirit and
landscapes of Provence were celebrated by Louis Brauquier (1900–
76) and Georges-Emmanuel Clancier (b. 1914) remained marked by
the sights, sounds and values of the Limousin. Brittany was a constant point of reference for Armand Robin, although the most resonant of the Breton poets was Eugène Guillevic who contrasted the
eternal sea and granite with the instability of the moment (e.g. *Carnac*,
1961). The spirit of the Rochefort School was a major force in French
poetry until 1961 and a stimulant to postwar regionalist poetry.

Fiction revalued

In the new climate, rural fiction was quickly rehabilitated. The
miserabilist melodrama of the 1930s resurfaced, as in J. Puech's *Le
Pain de misère* (1946), the tale of a simple-minded country girl who
passes through urban vice and finds peace in her poor but warmly
human village in the mountains. But the 'poetic' strain was also
revived. Henri Bosco struck a chord with *Le Mas Théotime* (1945), a
tale of brooding symbolism set in Provence, and *Malicroix* (1948)
created a magical world the centre of which is the ancestral home.
Peasant writers acquired a local readership, as did Michel Maurette
(1898–1973) for *La Crue* (1949), but a wider audience took to the grim
Bretons of Henry Queffelec (1910–92): many of his thirty novels
(*Un recteur de l'Île de Sein*, 1944; *Un homme d'Ouessant*, 1953) confront
man with the harshness of nature. The metaphysical strain, which
showed that the human and the natural are two distinct orders,
never regained its former hold, however. But neither did it quite lose
its appeal. It resurfaced with Jean Carrière (b. 1928), whose *L'Épervier
de Maheux* (1972) described the slow decline of a Protestant family in
the Cévennes; in the poetic fictions, set in the Jura, of Jean-Pierre
Monnier (b. 1921); through the atavistic, semi-pagan call of the land
(*La Grande Muraille*, 1969) which Claude Michelet (b. 1938) promoted
against the townsman's view of the country as an expensive luxury
(*Rocheflamme*, 1973); and behind the mysterious workings of fate in
the Provençal countryside evoked by Suzanne Prou (1920–95).

Social fictions

The 1950s were a relatively quiet time for regionalist writing, though
the profile of the provinces was significantly raised by Hervé Bazin.

But in the following decade, resistance to the city again brought out regionalist loyalties. The reaction was prompted by economics (the age of the 'peasant' was passing as agriculture was handed to a new generation of professionally qualified farmers), the cultural 'Parisianization' of the provinces (Malraux's Maisons de la Culture were perceived as a new form of centralist imperialism) and the academic invasion of the countryside by the human sciences. One response was a return to the 'social' novel in the tradition of Van der Meersch (Roubaix), Marc Bernard (1900–83; Nîmes), Béraud (Lyons), or Guilloux (Saint-Brieuc). Representative of this trend was Bernard Clavel (b. 1921) who evoked the history of the Jura but also modern problems among his semi-urbanized Lyonnais: delinquency is the theme of *Malataverne* (1960). Yet regionalist fiction failed to recapture its old committed zeal and novelists, turning their eyes to the past, resuscitated battles which had long been won. Avoiding sensitive contemporary problems, they courted an enthusiastic public with family sagas, the story of a farm and its inhabitants, conflicts between village and château and the human cost of the rural exodus. In so doing, they delivered regionalism as a form of popular entertainment.

Memoirs

The major appeal of the memoir was the cultivation of nostalgia. Its commitment to the specifics of time and place gave it the attraction of the picturesque wedded to documentary realism. It also provided reminders of the epic struggle against the elements from which city dwellers were insulated. The pull of this home-grown exoticism helps to explain the lively trade in the non-fictional memoirs of ex-farmers and former primary schoolteachers who remembered the joys of country living before the coming of electricity and the motor car. Jean Robinet (b. 1913) wrote engagingly of his life in *L'Autodidacte* (1955), while Camille-Robert Désert's taped memories of peasant life in turn-of-the-century Normandy, *La Rue d'enfer* (1966), was part of the vogue for the 'témoignage d'une époque disparue' exploited more artfully in Pagnol's *Souvenirs d'enfance*. Legitimized as the less scientific face of oral history projects, new 'regional' collections put out by major publishers found a buoyant market. *Toinon, le cri d'un enfant auvergnat* (1980) by Antoine Sylvère (1888–1963), an account of a peasant childhood, popularized social history. Marcel Scipion

(b. 1922: *Le Clos du roi*, 1978; *L'Arbre du mensonge*, 1980) recalled life as it was in the hills of Provence in the 1920s and Michel Ragon (b. 1924) revisited his happy childhood in the Charente in *L'Accent de ma mère* (1980). The most imaginative of these documentary recreations of time past was perhaps Roger Boussonot's *Vie et mort de Jean Chalosse, moutonnier des Landes* (1976) which combined an evocation of the shepherd's life with a strong plot and gave a particular force to the familiar anti-urban stance. Such books sold well because they recreated a world without electricity or pensions, an era, not so distant, when death was more freely acknowledged and widowhood was not a tragedy but a catastrophe. *Le Cheval d'orgueil* (1977), the most successful of the backward glances of Pierre Jakez Hélias (1914–95), resurrected the lifestyle of the Bretons of his youth. Yet such recollections were also capable of a harder edge. Their popularity coincided with the ecological concerns and the 'retour à la terre' movement of the 1970s, and a more embattled, and specifically political note was occasionally struck. Émilie Carles (1900–79) took her story from her childhood in the Savoie through her life as a primary schoolteacher to the 1970s when she led a campaign against the construction of a motorway through her haven of peace. *Une soupe aux herbes sauvages* (1973) combined the old picturesque with the militant defence of regional interests threatened by the heavy hand of Euro-politics. The success of this kind of social history stimulated public curiosity for 'authentic' documents and by 1980 publications devoted to local history, customs and folklore, together with reprints of ancient guide-books and travelogues outnumbered regional novels on sale in provincial bookshops.

The professionalization of regional writing

Since 1945 new agricultural structures, regional development and the growth of communications have changed French country life beyond return. Regional writers, once hopeful poets with their way to make, have tended to be older, come from a professional background (journalists, retired teachers, businessmen-farmers) and stand less close to their subject, which they view from a more self-consciously comparatist standpoint. Their memories, especially when ghosted by skilled hands, have at times seemed pre-packaged for the same market which required 'authentic' tourism and folk-museums.

But Henri Pourrat said as much in the 1920s when he observed that village life, unchanged for forty centuries, had been transformed in just forty years. But in 1846 George Sand also recalled that in her youth village life was peacefully medieval and warned that the industrial revolution was about to destroy the old ways for ever: the railways (like Émilie Carles's motorway) would ruin both landscape and the ancient ways. In 1779 Restif warned that the insidious encroachment of city manners was about to sweep away the old rustic order for ever. . . .

Its conservatism

Regional writing, perpetually under threat, owes its persistence in part to its literary conservatism. The commitment to documentary and psychological realism is a strong element of the resistance to the avant-garde which characterizes all forms of popular writing. It is perennially out of step because it looks constantly backward. It preserves both the elegiac and the spiritual in its acknowledgement of the irresistible, but impoverishing march of the modern. It reverts to the epic strain by asserting the power of nature and the impermanence of man-made societies. Regional voices contest change and progress and, by stressing a vestigial, pagan religiosity, rewrite the history of the Fall. Twentieth-century literature redefined destiny in collective terms, as the unstoppable advance of history, and the hidden workings which rule our subconscious. Regional writing, on the other hand, keeps alive an older notion of fate as a mysterious force which has more to do with the gods than with Marx, Freud or the gene: the characters of Giono or Queffelec are the prey of impulsions which do not come from within but from the power of the sea, the higher law of magic and the laughter of the wind.

Current trends

However, the onward march of modernization has long since demystified the countryside and turned its mysterious ways into forms of melodrama which, though dated, remain viable. There has also been a return to the humorous observation of village life, associated notably with Jean Anglade (b. 1915), a respected historian of the Auvergne, who since *Le Chien du Seigneur* (1952) has written genial, sometimes tart stories of village life: *Un souper de neige* (2000) shows a village divided into two bickering halves by a white line drawn by administrative *diktat*. But regionalist writing, long dominated by men, has also been opened up by women. The prolific Marie Mauron (1896–1986) produced 130 novels, memoirs and local histories, some written in Provençal, but all committed to preserving an endangered way of life. The ten or so novels of Marie Susini (1916–93) were set in a carefully observed Corsica, rather as Sylvie Germain (*Jours de colère*, 1989) or Françoise Bouillot (*La Boue*, 1989) used the Morvan and Normandy as backdrops to *romans paysans* clearly aimed at a specifically urban audience. Few women writers, however, followed the example of Madeleine Perrein (b. 1935) who introduced feminist issues into novels situated in the Landes (*Les Cotonniers de Bassalane*, 1984). More generally, regional writing has been a net beneficiary of political action and new directions in literature. The decentralization of culture has not only boosted non-Parisian theatre but created conditions in which poetry thrives in literary clubs and little magazines, and artisanal publishing methods offer local writers a chance of seeing their work in print. The image of the regions has been boosted by the rise of autobiography and from their use as settings for a new generation of crime fiction, though it is doubtful if writers like Jean-Claude Izzo (Marseilles) or Pierre Magnan (Provence) could in any way be classed as 'regionalist'.

Conclusion

Ultimately, the reasons for the survival of regional literature are more sociological than literary. The dubious proposition that life was once more 'real' has a special attraction for the French, who at moments still think of themselves as 'landless peasants'. Regional writing combines a search for roots with a form of literary tourism generated by a nostalgia for a past which many readers have never experienced. Pressures exerted by the globalization and Americanization of culture pose a new threat, though the success of new collections of modestly priced *livres du terroir* in the 1990s suggest that regional writing continues to reflect suspicion of the modern world and disaffection with city life. Older loyalties are far from dead and regional writers continue to tug at the guilt of the urban dispossessed.

The *Roman Policier*

While murder, theft and violence have always been essential ingredients of literature, narratives which take crime as their subject are, in historical terms, a recent development. Until about 1850, the public's fascination with lawlessness was catered for by the *littérature judiciaire*, sensational accounts of horrid murders, robberies and executions provided first by collections of *causes célèbres* and, after the advent of cheap newspapers after 1836, by press reports of crime. But while the *roman feuilleton* throve on murders and prisons, crime fiction became possible only with the spread of rationalism, the secularization of thought and the urbanization of society which produced a police force.

Deductive reasoning, a by-product of the Enlightenment, remained the province of philosophy and science until the middle of the nineteenth century. It had few echoes in the novel nor was it a feature of police work. Criminals were brought to justice not through investigation but by having their dark deeds exposed by events dictated by God's justice, that is, through their own recklessness or the testimony of eyewitnesses. By 1789, the process of divine retribution had been reinforced by an extensive network of spies but not by deduction from evidence. Even after the Restoration, François-Eugène Vidocq (1775–1857), creator of the 'Brigade de la Sûreté', did not investigate 'clues' but relied on informers to secure convictions.

The *roman noir* had given violence a Gothic prominence and, in its wake, the Romantics acquired a fascination for criminals and prisons, though only Balzac's *Une Ténébreuse affaire* (1842) comes close to being a mystery story. By the 1830s, however, deduction was entering the nation's thought processes through lessons learned from the woodcraft of Fenimore Cooper's Indians which enabled d'Artagnan to reconstruct events from the evidence of torn turf and broken twigs. Yet Dumas, like Sue – the kings of the crime-ridden *roman feuilleton* – still operated within a moral universe which ensured that law-breakers were caught not as a result of deduction and detection but through the workings of Providence, Fate and Destiny.

1850–90

By 1850, inference from observation, inherited from the Enlightenment by the new positivism, had become part of police methodology, as is clear from the memoirs (1862) of Louis Canler (1797–1865), a former policeman. But its entry into crime fiction was a consequence of profound social changes. The dramatic spread of urbanization not only created readers but also the conditions in which organized crime flourished: the 'cour des miracles' of Hugo's *Notre-Dame de Paris* (1831) is already recognizable as a criminal underworld. Yet the crucial change in emphasis from the reporting of crime in newspapers to the solving of mysteries in stories came from abroad, from the founding 'sealed chamber' story, *The Murders in the Rue Morgue* (1841) by Edgar Allan Poe. It appeared in French in 1846, long before Baudelaire's superior translations, in several pirated versions which, however, diluted the solving of the crime by adding sensational details of its execution in the manner of the more factual *littérature judiciaire*. Thus in France, puzzle-solving, which would be the strength of classic English crime fiction, was from the outset overlaid by a more dramatic account of the crime and its aftermath. Émile Gaboriau (1823–73), the major French pioneer, mixed detection with drama in this way in *L'Affaire Lerouge* (1866), where his amateur detective, *le père* Tabaret, aims to 'raisonner juste' and proceed 'du connu à l'inconnu'. These methods, also adopted by another Gaboriau hero, Monsieur Lecoq, were imitated, notably in *La Vieillesse de Monsieur Lecoq* (1878) by Fortuné de Boisgobey (1821–91), author also of *Le Coup de pouce* (1875) which features another sleuthing priest.

However, until 1870, popular taste was equally satisfied by the sensational novels of Paul Féval and Ponson du Terrail, who continued to give more prominence to the crime than to its solution. After 1870 taste shifted to the melodramatic *roman judiciaire* of Pierre Zaccone (1817–95) and Eugène Chavette (1827–1902) who specialized in stories showing the righting of judicial errors. In social terms, they reflected the conservative tone of the *après*-Commune: by showing villainy invariably unmasked by authority, they created a new respect for law and the police from which the individualistic investigator was excluded. Though there were attempts to follow Poe's lead – such as Jules Lermina's chronicles of his detective, Maurice Parent – the deductive novel made little headway. It was only one option for crime fiction, which itself occupied one corner of the spectrum of genres offered by the thriving *roman feuilleton*.

1890–1920

French enthusiasm for the exploits of Sherlock Holmes, first translated in the 1890s, coincided with the growth of anthropometrics, graphology (which featured prominently in the Dreyfus case) and other scientific methods which caught the imagination of a public increasingly fascinated by science. The unmasker of villains acquired a new status, though he was not yet a *détective*, a word first used in French in 1871 and still defined by the *Petit Larousse* in 1912 as 'an English policeman'. Marie-François Goron (1847–1933), an ex-police officer, maintained the tradition of *littérature judiciaire* with recollections of his cases, but the new righter-of-wrongs was not a professional investigator but an amateur with a robust approach to crime and criminals, a sturdy individualist who enjoyed an ambiguous relationship with the police. By 1900 he was a hero; but so was his opponent. Arsène Lupin, gentleman burglar and raffish hero of Maurice Leblanc (1864–1941), made the first of many appearances in 1904 and the last in 1935: Sartre called him 'le Cyrano de la pègre'. Joseph Rouletabille, created by Gaston Leroux (1868–1927), was a reporter who, between 1905 and 1939, solved a startling series of crimes usually at the expense of slower-witted policemen. But Leroux also launched a counter-prototype, Chéri-Bibi, a criminal who lived outside the law and satisfied a taste for anarchism noticeable also in early science fiction where crazed inventors and mad scientists sought world domination.

Problem-solving was still not crucial to the evolution of the French crime fiction which focused attention on the crime and the criminal. In Leroux's *Le Fantôme de l'Opéra* (1909), it is not Erik's downfall which fascinates but his reign of terror; the appeal of Arsène Lupin lay in his anarchic attitude to authority; while the infallible Rouletabille exhibits qualities of intellectual superiority and outsiderly individualism within a framework of Cartesian logic, a stance which readily appealed to the French mind. The same anti-hero-worship explains the phenomenal success of Fantômas, the embodiment of evil and master of disguise, whose duels with Inspector Juves are reported by the Watsonesque journalist, Jérôme Fandor. Fantômas was the creation of Marcel Allain (1886–1969) and Pierre Souvestre (1874–1914). Starting as a filler for magazines like *L'Auto* and *Le Vélo*, Fantômas featured in 20 titles before 1914, by which time Louis Feuillade's screen versions (1913–14) had turned 'the man with no face' into a craze. The novels were dictated not written, and now seem preposterously melodramatic. But Fantômas caught the imagination of the nation, and he was admired by Apollinaire, the Surrealists, Cocteau and Blaise Cendrars, who called the Fantômas cycle 'a modern

Aeneid'. There was a similar vogue for Judex, an anti-Fantômas, created by Arthur Bernède (1871–1937), who was also successfully translated to the screen.

Meanwhile, the Holmesian model was adapted to suit French taste. The first French investigative detectives used fingerprinting, ballistics and forensic analysis. But they were much more drawn to the new interest in psychology, so that the exploration of the 'criminal mind' was added to the older question of how and by whom the crime had been committed. But if the techniques used to solve mysteries became more sophisticated, the ephemeral nature and hasty composition of sensational *feuilletons* and cheap 'Collections' robbed the genre of any claim to be 'literature'.

1920–40

Between 1918 and 1939, ten or so separate 'collections' of crime fiction were launched, each issuing three or four titles every month. They reached a large audience and helped fill the gap left by the rapidly declining *roman feuilleton*. The most successful were 'L'Empreinte' and the long-running 'Le Masque'. The latter, begun by Albert Pigasse in 1927, gave a high profile to English puzzle-solving and the American 'pulp' model of the *Black Mask* school. By 1988, it had published 1,350 titles, with an average print-run of 25,000 and total sales of 130 million copies of which, significantly, Agatha Christie alone accounted for 50 million. Gallimard's first crime collection, 'Chefs d'Oeuvre du Roman d'Aventures', similarly promoted Anglo-Saxon crime fiction for which twenty 'golden rules' were enunciated in 1928 by Van Dine in *The American Magazine*: the true crime story has a murder, clues, one detective, and should provide enough information for the alert reader to find the solution. Most French writers, like Pierre Véry (1900–60: *L'Assassinat du père Noël*, 1930) and the Belgian Stanislas-André Steeman (1908–70), wrote in this 'Anglo-Saxon' mould which echoed both the genteel style of British sleuthing and the violence of gangsterism and Prohibition as popularized by Hollywood.

Even so, French crime fiction between the wars showed signs of reasserting its Frenchness. Geo London maintained the *littérature judiciaire* tradition with *Les Grands Procès de l'année*, a yearly collection of luridly told real crimes. Dictionaries like *L'Argot du milieu* (1935) by Jean Lacassagne and Pierre Duvoux foreshadowed the fascination with the language of the underworld which would later be used as indispensable local colour. An added impetus to the home-grown product came from cinema. Film-makers like Duvivier and Carné exploited the mood of the marginal heroes of 'Montmartre' writers like Francis Carco and Pierre Mac Orlan. Tough, American violence might be commercial but French taste still welcomed the older interest in the analysis of motive, psychological states and a level of ambiguity which blurred the Manichaean distinction between good (victim/justice) and evil (criminal/lawlessness) on which crime fiction turned. This more sophisticated approach was adopted by Claude Aveline (pseud. of Eugène Avtsine, 1901–92), a protégé of Anatole France and author of literary novels much admired by Gide. Aveline raised the profile of the genre in an intermittent 'suite policière' (1932–70) of five detective novels which pit Inspector Belot against a brilliant criminal mind in an intellectualized duel. Aveline believed that there were no bad genres, only bad writers, and he was one of many to exploit the genre for more literary ends: *Le Prisonnier* (1936) deals with the motives of an introspective murderer who is already an outsider of the kind Camus would describe in *L'Étranger*.

The most enduring crime writer to emerge from the interwar years was Georges Simenon (1903–89), Belgian by birth, who became a full-time writer in 1924. By 1930 he had written 190 pot-boilers (exotic adventures, rakish romances and westerns) under seventeen pen names. Between then and 1973, when he gave up fiction in favour of autobiography, he had written a further 220 novels – mostly psychological studies in a variety of stock 'crime' formats – under his own name. Of these 85 featured his most famous creation, Inspector Jules Maigret. He described his work as 'semi-literary', by which he meant not simply the avoidance of 'fine' prose but also an awareness of the limitations of the genre in which he worked. Whereas a 'literary' novel is free to go where it chooses, crime fiction imposes a death, perhaps a detective, suspects and a guilty party.

Maigret made an inauspicious start in *Détective* magazine in 1930. Unimpressed by Anglo-Saxon models, Simenon set him to investigate crimes committed by men and women who are unhappy and afraid: his aim was to uncover 'l'homme nu' rather than to thrill or offer social comment. In this sense, his books are timeless, though they have dated: Maigret's slow psychological profiling of his suspect have long since been incompatible with the team effort or scientific

methods of modern police-work. But Simenon's pace and facility for
dialogue endeared him to film-makers (50 titles had been adapted by
1960) and subsequently to television, where Maigret smoked his
pipe in many languages. He counted Gide, Fellini and Dashiell
Hammett among his admirers and maintained his huge following
for forty years. In 1961 a Simenon novel was published somewhere
in the world every three days, and in 1972 a Unesco survey identified him as the world's most translated author after Lenin. But
Simenon was not merely a publishing phenomenon. His industrial
output and variable quality may have kept him firmly in the second
rank of literature, but he has been called, with some justification, the
'poet of the sordid'.

1940–60

During the war, when American and English fiction was unavailable,
established or new *collections policières* (e.g. 'Le Labyrinthe' or Steeman's
'Le Jury', founded in Belgium in 1940) resorted to home-grown
products which, like the cinema of the period, clung mainly to models
of the 1930s. In 1941 the poet and surrealist Léo Malet (1909–92)
was recruited to supply American-style thrillers under Anglo-Saxon
pseudonyms. As 'Frank Harding', he created Johnny Métal (an anagram of Malet), a hard-drinking New York reporter. In 1943, *120 rue
de la gare* introduced the pipe-smoking, Chandleresque and enduring
Nestor Burma, 'l'homme qui met le mystère KO'. Malet subordinated puzzle-solving to tales of love and death spiced with stocking-
top eroticism, violence, literary asides and tough dialogue. Between
1941 and 1972, he published 55 crime novels, including an unfinished cycle entitled *Les Nouveaux Mystères de Paris* (1954–9) and, after
being rediscovered in the 1970s, emerged as one of the very best
practitioners of the *roman noir*.

After 1945, though British crime writers as different as Agatha
Christie and Peter Cheyney maintained a strong following, American
'hard-boiled' fiction overtook English detection. The new style was
heavily promoted by the 'Série noire' founded in 1945 for Gallimard
by ex-Surrealist Marcel Duhamel. Duhamel warned readers not to
expect Holmesian problem-solving or optimism but anti-conformism,
violence, tough eroticism and actions expressed 'dans une langue
fort peu académique mais où domine, toujours, rose ou noir,
l'humour'. The 'Série noire' published around four titles a month, all

by English and especially American authors, such as Horace McCoy, Chandler and Spillane, who appeared in specially commissioned tough-talking translations. The first French author, Serge-Marie Arcouet, was not admitted (first as 'Terry Stewart', and later as 'Serge Laforest') until 1948, the second appeared in 1950 and the third in 1953.

If the 'Série noire' defined crime fiction as predominantly American, other collections ('Un mystère', 1949–66, and 'Fleuve noir', (1949, with its subsidiary series 'Spécial police' and 'Espionnage'), were more welcoming to French novelists who grafted American 'noir' on to French stock. While murder retained its central role, the circumstances of the crime, its investigation, a certain lyrical realism in the description of the underworld and an interest in sensational psychological motives now became the distinctive French features of the *roman noir* as practised by M.-B. Endrèbe, Louis C. Thomas or Marcel Lanteaume. The 43 novels of Boileau-Narcéjac (pseud. of Pierre Boileau, 1906–89, and Thomas Narcéjac, 1908–98) aimed at 'poetic cruelty', as in *Celle qui n'était plus* (1953; filmed by Clouzot as *Les Diaboliques* in 1955) which sought, at a cruder level than Artaud had recommended, to disconcert and even terrorize the reader. They show from the inside victims of crime who, as they uncover the truth, slide into hallucination and madness. In 1929, Régis Messac's *Le 'Detective Novel' et l'influence de la pensée scientifique* had defined the genre as a story centred on the slowly unfolding methodical explanation of a mysterious event by the rational analysis of precisely formulated circumstances. A generation later, in *L'Esthétique du roman policier* (1947), Narcéjac expressed the newer view that the *roman policier* used rational analysis to create the fears which it was intended to allay.

This it did through cross-fertilization with transatlantic models. Just as the American underworld turned into the distinctive, *argot*-filled 'milieu', so French individualism took readily to the non-aligned 'private eye' who defended right and honour in the no-man's land between criminals and a corrupt police force. Even policemen tended to be mavericks with a habit of bending laws too feeble or flawed to protect society. There were 'crimes passionnels' and 'psychological' murders. But as a breed, criminals had long ceased to be convicts, dashing anarchists or world dominators. They now lived like wealthy businessmen, surrounded by henchmen, and their crimes were embezzlement and robbery on a grand scale. And pursuer and pursued dispensed escalating levels of violence.

In many ways, the collections were more significant than the authors they published, for each house imposed a different style, though all made atmosphere and psychology more important than guns. This new *roman noir*, which appeared at the same time as the vogue for Existentialism, was devoured by the public but was also taken seriously by intellectuals who saw it as part of the literature of revolt and the investigator as a kind of outsider. Since the time of Balzac, occasional attempts to upgrade the genre had been made by Barbey d'Aurevilly, Zola (*Thérèse Raquin* is already *noir*), Gide, Mauriac and Bernanos. Now, the emergence of a distinctive variety of French crime novel helped bridge the gap between the populism which it represented and the 'literature' of the avant-garde. Boris Vian (1920–59), writing as 'Vernon Sullivan', had taken American violence and sex to parodic lengths in *J'irai cracher sur vos tombes* (1947), which was banned, while Robbe-Grillet (*Les Gommes*, 1953) and Marguerite Duras (*Moderato cantabile*, 1959) pressed murder into the service of the New Realism.

But if American influence on the collections dominated, distinctive French voices gave it a specific political slant. If Chandler, say, is conservative in his attitudes and Spillane overtly illiberal, the worlds of Malet and Jean Amila (b. 1910) were built on anarchic, highly individualistic and generally left-wing values. Typical of the new assimilated style was Auguste Lebreton (pseud. of Auguste Montfort, b. 1913) who published *Du rififi chez les hommes* in the 'Série noire' in 1953. With *Razzia sur la chnouf* and *Le Rouge est mis* (both 1954), he was established as the specialist of the gangland novel and one of the most inventive users of underworld jargon. His main rival was Albert Simonin (1905–80) whom Malet called 'le Chateaubriand de l'argot'. *Touchez pas au grisbi* (1953), *Le Cave se rebiffe* (1954) and *Du mouron pour les petits oiseaux* (1960) were strong on nostalgia for prewar Paris and described, in rich *argot*, the usually doomed efforts of loners to survive the world of the gang. On the other hand, Charles Exbrayat-Durivaux (b. 1906) made little use of violence, gangsters or detectives (save for Imogène, his intrepid, puritanical spinster-sleuth) but concentrated on the crimes of ordinary people. Editor for a time of 'Le Club des masques', 'Exbrayat' wrote 162 titles between 1957 and 1983 with total sales of 20 millions.

Yet the market-leader, the 'Série noire', maintained its policy of publishing mainly Anglo-Saxon authors. Between 1955 and 1960, only 25 per cent of its output was home-produced. French authors fared better with 'Un mystère' and had signed a third of its 769 titles by 1966. 'Spécial police', an offshoot of the 'Fleuve noir' was also more welcoming to home-grown talent, notably Michel Audiard, Serge Laforest and the phenomenal Frédéric Dard (1921–2000) who, with *Réglez-lui son compte* (1947), launched the career of the tough-talking, misogynistic, high-living Commissaire San Antonio. Subsequently, Dard published psychological thrillers under his own name, but after 1954 signed that of his hero on an average of four San Antonio stories a year. By the 1970s, they were being printed in runs of 650,000 copies, with 'classic' titles reprinted in editions of 200,000, making a total of 5 million copies sold annually. In 1983 it was estimated that sales had passed 100 million. A San Antonio novel (the two-hundredth, *Le Dragon de Cracovie*, appeared in 1998) is not read for the repetitive plots but for Dard's brittle cynicism and above all the inexhaustible flow of puns and wordplay which led Cocteau, for one, to see in him a reincarnation of Rabelais. Yet by carrying the taste for 'alternative' (and quite untranslatable) language favoured by the *roman noir* to its extreme, Dard illustrates the insularity of French crime fiction. In this sense, he is the opposite of Simenon, whose limpid prose style and gift for creating psychological tension brought him, alone of all crime writers working in French, a world reputation.

1960–80

During the 1950s, cinema had helped stimulate the taste for crime stories. By 1960, leading crime writers were diversifying into cinema, which offered better rewards. The resulting drop in quality and quantity was exacerbated by the arrival of television, which provided an alternative source of entertainment, and by the James Bond phenomenon which stimulated interest in science fiction and espionage. Starting as a 'Fleuve noir' author in the 1950s, Paul Kenny had by 1990 written some 200 adventures of Francis Coplan (Agent FX 18) which, at the height of his popularity around 1970, were selling 3.5 million copies a year worldwide. Gérard de Villiers (b. 1929), another publishing phenomenon, not only wrote a hundred or so violent, erotic and exotic 'SAS' spy novels, beginning in 1965, but also presented spin-off collections ('L'Exécuteur', 'Brigade mondaine') which illustrate the industrial character of popular culture. Such authors also illustrate the distinction between the *roman policier* proper, which opens with a crime and solves a mystery, and the thriller, which consists of a series of deaths on a rising scale of violence. While the first offered social, political and psychological possibilities, the second traded in basic sensationalism, The public read both but reserved a special affection for the growing Frenchness of the *roman policier*.

Despite these challenges, the 'Série noire' was by 1960 issuing five titles a month and, in 1970, six, plus three reprints of the collection's 'classic' backlist. During this period, only 15 per cent of 'Série noire' novels were home-produced, the remainder being translations of British and especially American originals. While a substantial percentage of 'Série noire' titles were written by foreign women (Agatha Christie remained unavoidable), the first French woman author to be published in the collection was Janine Oriano (b. 1935) with *B comme Baptiste* in 1971. By the end of the 1960s, French crime writing was in decline: repetitive, predictable and over-reliant on stereotyped characters (private eyes and Corsican gangsters) and situations (banks, heists, drugs and blackmail). Yet what readers called the *polar* (a contraction of *policier*) and intellectuals the *roman noir* continued to evolve.

If the 1950s had seen the naturalization of the tough American thriller, the late 1960s turned against organized crime, detection and the puzzle and moved towards fictions with a less formulaic appeal. Guy des Cars (pseud. of Guy-Augustin-Marie-Jean de Pérusse des Cars, 1911–93) returned to the *cause célèbre* format in 60 hugely successful novels, beginning in 1941, which by the 1960s were published in print-runs of up to 700,000. When reissued in paperback form, they sold a further 32 million copies. Des Cars wrote of melodramatic passions among a cast of characters who included sadists, transsexuals and nymphomaniacs. Titles like *L'Impure*, *La Lépreuse* and *La Corruptrice* indicate his interest in the 'pathological' psychology of his heroines. Other writers, especially after May 1968, turned their attention to 'marginal' figures, both in the psychological and in the social sense. Simonin's *Hotu* trilogy (1968–71) explored the underworld from the 1920s onward, but other survivors from the 1950s like Francis Ryck (b. 1920) and Raf Vallet (pseud. of Jean Laborde), who had both tried their hands at the comedy thriller, commented directly on the modern world. Jean Amila attacked modern business in *Les Fous de Hong Kong* (1969) and introduced a post-1968 hippie policeman in *Contest-Flic* (1972). With *Les Morfalons* (1968), Pierre Siniac (b. 1928) concentrated on the 'other face' of society while Jean Vautrin (pseud. of Jean Herman, b. 1933) set a number of novels (e.g. *Bloody Mary*, 1979) in the landscape of high-rise deprivation, projected as an image of the times, where disaffected urban youths lived violent lives described with humour and cruelty. The early *polars* of Sébastien Japrisot (pseud. of Jean-Baptiste Rossi, 1931–2003) subverted the crime genre: in *Piège pour Cendrillon* (1962), the roles of victim, murderer, witness and investigator are deliberately confused. With *L'Été meurtrier* (1977), without abandoning the reader-bait of crime, he found a new audience for thoughtful, broader-based tales of lawless individuals.

Despite the continuing popularity of Agatha Christie and the appearance in French of new Anglo-Saxon 'crime queens' (Ruth Rendell, P. D. James, Patricia Highsmith), the French crime novel developed its own momentum. Rarely genteel, often politically conscious and cynical, the French investigator was after 1970 more often than not an ambiguous anti-hero, rarely a private eye and more inclined to be a maverick policeman who, disenchanted with the delays of the law, gets results by methods as dubious as those adopted by his opponent who was now cast as a public enemy. For criminals had changed again and now wore the face of new public fears. They were involved in the international drug trade, ran gambling empires, manipulated politicians and floated shady business deals. But at the lower end of the social scale, they expressed the mindless violence of street-gangs and drug-crazed delinquents who seemed beyond the reach of the law.

The best of the new authors, Patrick Manchette (1942–95), was an academic who translated American thrillers before writing his first *polar* in 1971, believing the genre ideally suited to exploring the contradictions of post–1968 society. *Nada* (1972), in which the US ambassador is kidnapped and held hostage, is fast-moving and violent, strong on socio-political comment and laced with the black humour which had long been obligatory in the *roman noir*. He experimented with form (*L'Affaire N'Gustro*, 1971, has multiple narrators) and included references to jazz, recent history and a wide range of social and cultural issues from a left-wing perspective. His characters act with cold violence which he intended as a comment on the dehumanizing effects of the consumer society. His main rival, ADG (pseud. of Alain Fournier, b. 1947), took the *néo-polar* into the provinces and abroad. Though no less pugnacious as a social critic, he was more right-wing in his attitudes: *Joujoux sur le caillou* (1987) takes his Tours-based lawyer hero, Delcroix, to New Caledonia and provides a hostile view of anti-colonialist attitudes.

In 1973 the 'Série noire' issued a record 93 titles. The following year, the number dropped to 43 and the launch of the new 'Super noire' did not live up to expectations. There were rumours that the collection would close in the face of a declining market which had been seduced by television, cinema, the *bande dessinée* and other popular genres. Thus in 1977, while the 'Fleuve noir' maintained its monthly output of seven *polars*, it also issued six volumes of espionage and eight of science fiction. Its addition of two special series, 'Frédéric Dard' and 'San Antonio', was an indication of the popularity of a single author rather than of crime fiction generally. New imports, such as Robin Cook, were introduced but the decline continued. In 1978, the 'Série noire' published 37 titles in both collections, of which only five were by French authors. In 1979 the 'Super noire' ceased to exist.

Since 1980

During the 1970s, mainstream publishers began adding crime authors, like Jean Vautrin, Patrick Magnan (b. 1922) and Alain Denouzon (b. 1945) to their general fiction lists, and authors were reaching for new levels of sadism and eroticism in line with current taste. But by the end of the decade, the fortunes of crime revived, partly as the result of the undermining by theorists like Barthes of the concept of 'literature'. The crime novelist was a 'witness to his age' like any other writer and deserved respect. Léo Malet was rediscovered, festivals and exhibitions renewed interest in the genre, and quality newspapers began reviewing crime fiction on a regular basis.

The old collections were given eye-catching covers and new ones appeared. 'Engrenage' (1979) opened its doors to French authors and particularly women (Caroline Camara, Cécile Arbona), and 'Sanguine' specifically excluded the Anglo-Saxons. To the mainstays of the post–1968 revival – Manchette, ADG, Siniac, etc. – were now added Hervé Prudon (b. 1950), Frédéric H. Fajardie (b. 1949) and the team of Jean-Pierre Bastid (b. 1937) and Michel Martens (b. 1940). By 1981 major publishers were investing in crime fiction, which also found its way into general paperback collections like Gallimard's 'Folio' series. The future of the *polar*, now called the *néo-polar* to mark its new energy, was assured. New writers with distinctive literary qualities emerged. Daniel Pennac (b. 1944) began as a 'Série noire' author: *Au bonheur des ogres* (1985) was the first of the Malaussène cycle which quickly graduated to the mainstream. Didier Daeninckx (b. 1949) published six Inspecteur Cadin titles in the 'Série noire' before moving away from its format to reflect upon the plight of urban, marginalized individuals and groups oppressed by author-ity, vested interests and the media (e.g. *Zapping*, 1992).

Pennac and Daeninckx are among a number of writers who have used the *polar* as a launching pad for more ambitious and more consciously literary kinds of fiction anchored in social and human reality. Crime, a common denominator, is the antidote to the anti-heroic abstractions of the literary novel and a peg on which to hang social and political comment. Their success illustrates the adaptability of a genre which was hitherto considered limited by the central role of crime and inescapably anchored in the contemporary world and, outside the English country house mystery, rooted in mean, urban streets and the capital's criminal underworld. But in the last decade of the century, it further demonstrated its versatility by moving to other times and out of Paris.

In the early 1980s, Umberto Eco and Ellis Peters created an inter-national taste for the medieval detective. It was not long before the historical novel joined forces with the *roman policier*. In 1983 a new collection, 'Grands Détectives', relaunched Robert van Gulik's Judge Ti ('le Sherlock Holmes de la dynastie Tang') while 'Labyrinthes' (founded 1997), an offshoot of 'Le Masque', promoted sleuths who operate in many different eras. Olivier Seigneur's observant detective hero solves mysteries in Louis XIV's Paris, Dominique Muller sets a doctor, Florent Bonnevy, on the trail of the criminals of the Regency, and Hubert Prolongeau turns Diderot and d'Alembert into a sleuth-ing duo. Written primarily for entertainment, the new *polar historique* rarely has the political or intellectual bite of established writers like Jean Amila, who attacked the incompetent generals of the Great War (*Le Boucher des hurlus*), or Daeninckx who, in *Meurtres pour mémoire*

(1984), reflected on the consequences of police action against Algerian demonstrators in Paris in 1961.

A separate alliance linked the genre to the restive tradition of regional writing. From the 1970s onward, ADG, Manchette, René Belletto (b. 1945) and Pierre Magnan (b. 1922: *Le Sang des Atrides*, 1977) had taken crime to the provinces. In the 1990s the decentralized *polar* made rapid progress, spreading to Brittany (Hervé Jaouen or Jean-Bernard Pouy, director of a new collection, 'Le Poulpe'), the Vosges (Pierre Pelot), the Pas-de-Calais (Michel Quint) and the Ardèche (Jean-Paul Demure: *Fin de chasse*, 1999). An *école marseillaise* sprang up around Jean-Claude Izzo (1945–2000) whose 'Série noire' trilogy (*Total Khéops, Chourmo, Solea*), featuring ex-policeman Fabio Montale, left-wing rebel and *fin gourmet*, sold 500,000 copies. A similar group appeared in Toulouse, where Pascal Dessaint set *Du bruit sous le silence* (1999) in the world of local rugby. If forsaking Paris meant abandoning many of the genre's staple *noir* clichés, the regional *polar* also resisted the temptation to resuscitate the genteel countryside of Agatha Christie. It gave the *crime passionnel* and provincial lawlessness a local slant. To city criminality in Marseilles were added local government conspiracies, smuggled calvados, rural anarchists, illegal land deals and agri-business scams of all kinds. Written by authors resident in their region and, increasingly, published locally, the non-Parisian *polar* has found a niche in the buoyant crime market, which produced 900 new titles in 1999.

Yet the genre is still not fully acculturated. In 1992, Patrick Raynal, the new director of the 'Série noire', restored a fifties flavour to the jacket of the collection. Four titles continued to appear monthly and new talents emerged, but the list remained heavily biased towards Anglo-Saxon names. A new collection, 'La Noire', offered a more sophisticated fare provided by writers like Manchette whose financial and critical success had distanced them from popular collections. In 1995, the 'Série noire', for its fiftieth anniversary, reprinted a selection of titles which had contributed to its growth. Only a third were French.

Conclusion

The history of French crime fiction, a resolutely male province of popular culture, has been a long battle to define itself against competition from the Anglo-Saxon world. Lacking a founding figure of stature (the Americans had Poe and the 'hard-boiled' school, while the British could look to Sherlock Holmes and the 'Queens' of detection), it was never sufficiently confident in its human concern with crime (why the deed was done) to shake off its public's fascination with the glamour of gangland, the thrills of suspense and the intellectual pleasure of deduction. In its struggle to acquire a specific identity, the French *polar* – prone to philosophizing, anchored in linguistic specificities and dominated by the requirements of the all-important collections – has never escaped a certain insularity. In publishing terms, Simenon, Dard and Des Cars have been phenomenally successful. In artistic terms, the list would begin with Simenon, Malet, Simonin and Manchette. But only Simenon has the international stature accorded routinely to any number of American and British practitioners of the genre.

Yet, whether it is served up in crude or subtle forms, crime fiction provides an example of the way a popular entertainment may acquire cultural respectability. By the 1990s, in its *noir* form, it was used to expose the corruption of society and package the anxieties of a *fin de siècle* grown disillusioned with government, big business and the seemingly losing battle against lawlessness. But crime fiction remains an ineradicable part of popular culture, and the versatile *roman policier, roman noir, polar, néo-polar*, together with its historical and regional sub-sets, continues to occupy a high place in the literary affections of France.

9

Beyond Words

Literary historians have long acknowledged the profound effects of the shift from the oral to the written transmission of culture. In France the process was under way by the eleventh century. By the sixteenth, a clear distinction had been drawn between the culture of the unlettered and the values of the educated elite. The printing revolution confirmed the supremacy of the written word by generating prescriptive practices (the standardization of language and its generic forms of expression) and thus defined culture in terms of the technology it had created. Writers signed books and became authors; multiple copies mechanically reproduced created a reading public. The civilizing benefits of the printed word were rarely questioned until the 1960s, when doubts were cast, by Structuralists notably but also by studies of the oral tradition of France's regions, on the way information is communicated, processed and valued. The debate was most clearly articulated in North America, where Marshall McLuhan and Quentin Fiore (*The Medium is the Message*, 1967) argued that societies are shaped less by what is communicated than by the ways in which it is communicated. The alphabet teaches us to make words from letters and, by extension, sense from disparate data: the permutations are infinite and encourage private thoughts and actions. The 'electric informational media', on the other hand, aim pre-formed sense at us for our consumption, invite us to choose from a narrow set of options and thus unite and involve us in general rather than individual responses. Such ideas were echoed by Baudrillard's 'hyperreality' and Bourdieu's 'cultural capital'. A new cultural shift was in the making, as momentous as the switch from oral to written had been. The proliferating image was already an indispensable supplement to the printed word in almost all aspects of social life, from advertising, to photo-journalism and all-pervasive television. To say that a picture is worth a thousand words meant endorsing a move from the written to a visual culture. While clinging to the old humanist belief in the book, France has been more prepared than most other Western countries to welcome the change and grant a literary patent to graphic forms of expression which elsewhere are regarded with suspicion. Of these, the visualised narrative in particular has acquired both public support and official approval. *Bande dessinée* is commonly acknowledged to be *le neuvième art*, as cinema is *le septième*.

The *Roman-photo*: Graphic Fiction

The links between pictures and story-telling developed slowly. From the time of the Renaissance, narrative texts published in the *Bibliothèque bleue* were illustrated by crude woodcuts, and from the middle of the seventeenth century plays and novels were routinely accompanied by engravings which captured a significant moment of the action. Often restricted to a frontispiece for reasons of cost, or included as a deterrent to pirate publishers, they were intended less as an aesthetic extension of the book than as a visual indication of its content and an inducement to buy. Enlightenment publishers continued to use book-illustrators in this way. But while the *estampe* acquired greater variety (to allegory and realism were added the fantastic and the obscene), it remained static, a moment without continuity. At the end of the eighteenth century, however, Restif de la Bretonne imagined the possibility of devising 'une histoire en tableaux', that is, 'un ouvrage suivi en figures, liées et résultant les unes des autres'. But such a project was beyond his means and his idea was not taken up. Illustrated books remained written texts intermittently visualised.

The child-centred concept of education made fashionable by Rousseau's *Émile* (1762) gave illustrations a pedagogic function. Reading manuals taught the alphabet by linking letters to simple line-drawings ('B comme Berger'): in Flaubert's 'Un coeur simple', Félicité's charges use a geography book which contains engravings of cannibals, Bedouins and whale-hunts. One exception to the subordinate role of the visual was the publication in 1867 by Henri Tournier of a picture version of a popular children's book, *Les Mésaventures de Jean-Paul Choppart* (1834) by Louis Desnoyers (1802–68). In a sense it is the first graphic novel. But the lead given by Tournier, publisher of a number of illustrated journals, was not followed. Images of growing sophistication were added to literary novels, but the graphic remained a supplement, and served, after 1840, as a bait to lure the *roman feuilleton* public. But by the 1850s, the image was beginning its upward march in newspapers and through photography which, though Baudelaire regarded it as a mere aid to the arts and sciences, was attracting attention.

Attempts to produce exact images by optical methods have a long history which goes back to Leonardo's *camera obscura*, the magic lantern of the seventeenth century, the *ombres chinoises* of the eighteenth, and to attempts in the early nineteenth century to fix reality by the controlled exposure of chemically treated plates. The new art of photography was tepidly enrolled into the service of fiction. In the 1850s, there was a minor vogue for sets of stereoscopic photographs which, viewed in order, told a story. By the 1890s, fables and short tales recounted through photographs were popular and in the early 1900s Colette posed for the camera for a simplified version of the adventures of her heroine Claudine. By then, images had been made to move, and during the Great War cinema generated a taste for *romans-cinéma* (or *ciné-romans*). These did not dispense with a written text, however, but simply added stills to the 'novelized' story of popular films. They were an offshoot of the moving-picture industry rather than a new departure in the history of narrative. Nor was the novel which was merely illustrated to be called 'graphic fiction', for the *roman-photo*, in its strict form, tells a story in photographs and makes, at most, a sparing use of the written word. In this sense, silent cinema had already taken this ultimate step and for film-makers like René Clair the advent of talking films was a retrograde development. But the *roman en images* had its supporters. A novel in 165 woodcuts, *Mon livre d'heures* (trans. of *Mein Stundenbuch*, 1919), was one of several such experiments by a Belgian book-illustrator based in Paris, Frans Masereel (1889–1972). He struck no spark even in the picture-conscious Surrealists, so that Breton's *Nadja*, despite the interest of its images, remained within the tradition of the illustrated book.

The image proliferated, however, in advertising, magazines and the *photo-reportage* of postwar journalism. But it was not until after 1945 that the *roman-photo* established itself, first in Italy. A number of publishers found a market for stories told in photographs, but none was so successful as Cino del Duca, who launched the weekly *Grand Hotel* in 1947. The magazine took its name and spirit from one of Garbo's greatest films and at first told stories not in photographs but in tinted drawings. The same year, the magazine transferred to Paris as *Nous deux* and continued to be drawn until about 1950 when photographs became standard. Del Duca had anticipated this development and *Festival* (1949) became the first French magazine to use the techniques of the *roman-photo*. The impact was remarkable and during the 1950s many new titles sprang up to meet the demand, which was at its highest between 1960 and 1985.

As a genre, the *roman-photo* is defined by its large circulation and escapist character. At first it was aimed largely at women and its ethos was cast in the sentimental mould of Delly: sweet, defenceless girls won by virile heroes. All the stories ended happily and happiness meant marriage and financial security. Plots and situations were stereotyped, feelings were predominant and the moral values orthodox: middle-class lifestyles packaged for the lower classes. Characters were tested by Love (rivalry, betrayal, disappointment) but honesty, courage and resignation were rewarded. *Romans-photo* were published in free-standing volume form, but the magazine remained the major vehicle of diffusion.

During the 1960s, the genre was adapted to cater for the new permissiveness. The *roman-photo* was ideally suited to the fashionable eroticism of the time which included explicit elements of sadism. To counter the reservations expressed by the moral and educational establishment, the number of magazines including graphic fiction was reduced by law in 1971, a minimum length was laid down and 40 per cent of pages were required to carry printed text in the form of articles. The market leaders were the various titles founded by del Duca, such as *Intimité* (1947) ('le magazine pour une vie meilleure') and *Télé-Poche* (1966), a TV and general-interest weekly. Good-quality *romans-photo* were published in the Belgian *Femmes d'aujourd'hui* (1933) which had a French edition in the 1950s and carried graphic fiction after 1960: the best were reissued in *Confidences*, founded by Paul Winkler in 1937. In the early 1970s, *Femmes d'aujourd'hui* transposed classic novels (such as Jane Austen's *Orgueil et Préjugé*) into graphic form and *Modes de Paris* continued the tradition of the *roman-cinéma*. Children's magazines like *Podium* also told stories in photographs, and used amateurs to pose for its productions. Some large-circulation *romans-photo* employed professional actors and even, on occasion, celebrities. By 1970 the genre had moved into the youth market and the well-heeled atmosphere of châteaux and wealth had given way to the glamour of the world of pop music and teenage *angst*. Since then, its major focus has continued to be the pursuit of romantic happiness and its home remains the magazine (*Nous deux, Intimité, Lancio*). It has kept a loyal, predominantly female readership which prefers its sentimental reveries to the wider range of stories told by the *bande dessinée*, and its 'real' photographs to the more versatile drawing.

Technically, the *roman-photo* has remained unadventurous. Photographs are used to illustrate written dialogue and the first- or third-person narrative commentary. Half-shots and close-ups predominate, so that action and incident are subordinated to the inner thoughts of the characters who may stare out of the page from time to time to engage the reader's sympathies. The subjective camera is rarely used, though flashbacks and other devices borrowed from the grammar of cinema have long been standard. About two-thirds of the images are used to show backgrounds and set the scene: glimpses of châteaux, estates and richly decorated interiors are part of the attraction. Only a third carry the situation and characters forward. Key photographs are signalled by the angle of the shot, lighting, size and position on the page. The *roman-photo* manages to be both theatrical and static, and events unfold predictably in settings which have more glamour than reality.

In 1979 serially published *romans-photo* were read by one in three French people, and over a third of readers were men. Their mass appeal, however, was achieved by remaining within narrative and linguistic strategies imposed by the cultural horizons of the socio-economic group at which they were targeted. While the detective novel or fantastic fiction proved culturally clubbable and evolved, the *roman-photo* failed to achieve respectability. And yet, in the 1970s Alain Resnais saw how the genre might be exploited in more sophisticated terms. The Editions de Minuit took note and ventured into the field of what is called the *littérature d'expression graphique*. For

Chausse-Trappes (1981) by Edward Lachman and Elieba Levine, Alain Robbe-Grillet wrote a preface which argued that each photograph was a 'pure' narrative instant in a way unmatched even by cinema, and that photographic images start a creative 'discontinuity' which explodes the 'realist illusion'. The challenge was taken up by the Belgians Marie-Françoise Plissart and Benoît Peeters, whose *Droits de regards* (1983) was published with an enthusiastic preamble by Jacques Derrida. They use artfully lit, carefully composed photographs and a range of rather self-conscious techniques (for example, the wide shot which dwarfs the individual against an industrial landscape), and the tale they tell is abstract and intellectually demanding. Thus the tension of *Le Mauvais Oeil* (1986) derives not from the opaque narrative but from the conflict between the 'fallacious' images which we see and 'the misleading certainties' of the written text. These examples of the *roman-photo* are clearly related to the spirit of 1950s New Realism and this may help to explain why, despite attempts to intellectualize it, there is no evidence of the cultural accreditation of the genre which, in any case, hardly reflects the spirit of the audio-visual age.

La Bande Dessinée

Many ancestors have been found for the *bande dessinée*. Medieval churches illustrated the faith in stone, glass and paint. The Bayeux tapestry, medieval and Renaissance 'phylacteries' (banners inscribed with the speech of holy personages), the illustrated *Bibliothèque bleue* and, from the late eighteenth century to the middle of the nineteenth, the 'images d'Épinal' presented Holy Writ, events, and stories to an unlettered public. But the *bande dessinée* (the noun *illustré* was accepted in 1959 and the abbreviation *BD* was lexicalized only in 1981) was a twentieth-century creation and, with cinema and jazz, one of the few new forms of artistic expression to emerge after 1900. Long an entertainment for children, it widened its range in the 1960s and thereafter came to include the intellectual concerns, fantasies and preoccupations of adults through themes often inspired by popular literature (crime and futuristic fiction in particular) and graphic techniques influenced by cinema and modern painting. At the end of the century, over a third of the population were regular readers of *bandes dessinées*, which accounted for 15 per cent of the output of the French publishing industry.

Origins

While the July Monarchy saw an expansion in comic illustration, which had reached new heights of caricature since the French Revolution, Charles Philipon moved beyond the free-standing cartoon with, on occasion, a series of drawings on a single theme or incident. But Rodolphe Toepffer (1799–1846) is generally considered to be the ancestor of the illustrated strip narrative which he conceived as a sequence of rudimentary images printed above a handwritten text. He called his illustrated stories for children, published in Geneva in the 1830s, *littérature en estampes* and judged it closer to the novel than any other written form. In the 1840s, the cartoonist Cham (Amédée de Noé) and the photographer Nadar published satirical strips which told stories in pictures, a form also explored by Gustave Doré (*Désagréments d'un voyage d'agrément*, 1851). But the major French pioneer was Christophe (pseud. of Georges Colomb, 1856–1945) who, for the children's paper, *Le Petit Français illustré*, wrote and drew *La Famille Fenouillard* (1889), *Le Sapeur Camembert* (1890), *Vie et mésaventures du savant Cosinus* (1893), *Les Malices de Plick et Plock* (1893), and *Le Baron de Cramoisy* (1899), each a series of humorous sketches showing the absurdities of the title characters. He regarded images as a language more accessible to children than words and, before the advent of moving pictures, established the essential visual 'grammar' of cinema and television, from the angled point of view to back lighting. Yet he kept pictures and words (dialogue and a large measure of ironic authorial comment) separate.

To 1914

Illustrated children's comic papers, now printed in colour, proliferated during the 1890s, and after 1900 they produced the genre's first major icons. Bécassine, the simple-minded but rarely confounded Breton maid drawn by Joseph Pinchon from stories by Jacqueline Rivière and, after 1913, by Caumery (pseud. of Maurice Languereau), made her first appearance in *La Semaine de Suzette* (1905) and survived until 1950. The text appeared below the illustrations which were essentially static snapshots of narrative moments. Bécassine was aimed at middle-class children. The taste of the working class was catered for by Louis Forton, who launched his legendary anarchic trio, *Les Pieds nickelés*, in *L'Épatant* in 1908. Forton injected movement into his strips, varying depth of field, linking frames dynamically and, on the American model, adding occasional snatches of dialogue and sound effects in a *bulle* (bubble) inside the picture.

Between the wars

In the USA, the newspaper strip, influenced in its visual techniques by Hollywood, catered for a wide public, from fantasy characters for children (Krazy Kat, 1910; Popeye, 1919; Mickey Mouse, 1928) to super-heroes (Tim Tyler, 1928; Tarzan 1929) and the 'family strip' (*Bringing up Father*, 1913; *Little Annie*, 1929). In France, comic papers continued to be aimed at children. Even so, *Zig et Puce* (and Alfred, their penguin) achieved wider fame and became as well known as Mistinguett or Lindberg. Created by Alain Saint-Ogan in 1925, the strip placed all text within the picture in *bulles*, for the first time, an important development which banished direct authorial comment and added immediacy to the action. A similarly uncluttered visual style with its boldly caricatured human types was adopted in Belgium by Hergé (pseud. of Georges Remi, 1907–83). Hergé departed from the standard format of the series of the separate adventures of recurring characters in favour of the extended narrative. Tintin, his roving reporter with boy-scout values, and his dog Milou, first appeared (*Tintin au pays des Soviets*) in a Brussels Catholic paper, *Le Petit Vingtième*, in 1929 before being published in album form in 1932. By *Le Lotus bleu* (1934), Hergé had developed a crisper pictorial line, visual techniques borrowed from cinema and a greater realism of setting. During the war, he added colour and in 1950 set up the Studio Hergé on lines well established in the USA, where characters were the property not of their creators but of publishing 'syndicates' which employed writers and artists to reproduce an established formula. Hergé remained responsible for the scenario and storyboard but delegated draughtsmanship to assistants, some of whom would make separate careers and form the Belgian 'École de Bruxelles'.

In the 1930s the *bande dessinée* faced two major obstacles: its identification with children and competition from the USA. *Le Journal de Mickey*, featuring Disney's characters, began appearing in 1934 and its success spawned titles like *Jumbo* (1934), *Hurrah!*

(1935) and *Robinson* (1936), which imported or imitated transatlantic super-heroes: detectives (Dick Tracy, Brick Bradford), intergalactic warriors (Buck Rogers, Flash Gordon), and the flying, masked avengers (Superman and Batman) of Action Comics. Long-established *illustrés* like *L'Épatant* or *Cri-Cri* closed or bowed to American art-style, characters and story-lines. With few exceptions, such as Daix's *Professor Nimbus* (1934) or *Futuropolis* (1937) by Pellos, who later resurrected *Les Pieds nickelés* (1948–81), the home-grown product looked dowdy in comparison.

1940–58

During the war, the Germans, aware of the importance of visual propaganda, encouraged pro-Nazi and *Pétainiste* strips. American comics were banned by Vichy in 1942, though some titles (*Mickey, Robinson,* etc.) moved to the Free Zone. After the Liberation, despite the return of American weeklies (*Donald, Tarzan*), Marijac's *Coq hardi,* with a circulation of 150,000, established its French credentials with tales of the Resistance, while Calvo's *La Bête est morte* (1944) restaged the war 'chez les animaux'. *Vaillant* offered high-quality imitations of American science-fiction comics, notably Raymond Poïvet's *Les Pionniers de l'Espérance,* which ran between 1944 and 1973. French *bande dessinée* was dominated by Marijac (Jacques Dumas), a writer-illustrator, who launched numerous magazines and heroes, as did organizations of various kinds. *Vaillant* was a Communist Party weekly aimed at communist youth, as were its successors, *Le Journal de Pif* (1965) and *Pif-gadget* (1969), while *Coeurs vaillants* and *Âmes vaillaintes* were intended for Catholic schoolchildren.

The 'Belgian' school

But in addition to US imports, French production also faced a challenge from Belgium. *Spirou,* founded there in 1938, arrived in France in 1947 and helped spread a 'Belgian' style: simple images, clear outlines and strong colours. Offering a mixture of humour, thrilling adventure and crime, it found an enthusiastic junior audience for its greatest successes, *Buck Danny* and, above all, *Lucky Luke,* the 'lonesome cowboy' created by Morris (Maurice de Bevère) in 1946 and scripted, after 1948, by René Goscinny. Centred on *Spirou,* the 'École de Charleroi' of André Franquin, Jiji (Joseph Gillain), Goscinny, Peyo (Pierre Culliford) and others, continued to develop new series: the accident-prone *Gaston Lagaffe* (1957; by André Franquin, b. 1924), for example, and Peyo's internationally successful *Les Schtroumpfs* (1958), little blue men who use one verb, 'schtroumpfer' for every occasion. More sober in style and treatment was the 'École de Bruxelles' grouped around the weekly *Tintin magazine* (1946; launched in France in 1948). In addition to serializations of Hergé's hero, it launched *Blake et Mortimer* (1946; by Edgar Jacobs), the ancient hero *Alix l'intrépide* (1948; by Jacques Martin) and continued to develop new series into the 1980s.

By the late 1940s, *bandes dessinées* were appearing in a variety of forms. In daily strips, comic-books and full pages in Sunday supplements, they normally comprised a series of self-contained episodes based on one or more central characters, though the serial adventure was popular too. By the late 1940s, the 'complete' story was being published in cheaply produced, large-format, black and white 'books' fronted by a coloured cover. During the 1950s, these were temporarily overtaken by the 'pocket' volume before emerging in the standard format of 64 large pages in colour.

The American way

In 1949, legislation, enacted to protect French youth against the dangers of the *bande dessinée*, also protected the publishing industry against foreign (mainly American) imports. Similar concerns about the effects on young people of the new generation of comics, devoted now to horror, war, and subversive, zany humour typified by *Mad Magazine* (1952), surfaced in the USA, where a Comics Code resembling the Hays Code (1930) for the cinema was introduced in 1955. Its effect was to inhibit invention until the 1960s when Marvel Comics devised a new stable of heroes (*The Thing*, *The Incredible Hulk*) and saw its world sales soar from 14 million in 1960 to 40 million in 1970. By that date, the American comic had widened its range dramatically. If the ghoulish, 'eery' yarn and the gentle humour of *Peanuts* (1950–2000) by Schulz mark the extreme limits of the form, the middle ground was occupied by futuristic adventures, cowboys, classic heroes (like Superman) and 'funnies'. But it had also acquired an association with the underground movement. A new generation of writers and illustrators refused to work for the Syndicates, developed bolder graphic techniques and tackled taboo subjects, particularly sex and drugs.

Pilote

These developments did not pass unremarked in France. The weekly *Pilote*, founded in 1959 by René Goscinny, Albert Uderzo and Jean-Michel Charlier, marked a shift from a youth to an adult audience. These, together with Gotlib (Marcel Gotlieb), Moebius (Jean Giraud), Michel Greg and others, originated numerous series – westerns (*Le Lieutenant Blueberry*, 1963), humour (*Le Concombre masqué*, 1964), fantasy (*Philémon*, 1965), science fiction (*Valérian*, 1967) – of which *Astérix* (1959) was by far the most successful. The ancient Gauls of Goscinny and Uderzo, valorized by imaginative artwork, invention, deliberate anachronisms and linguistic humour, proved to have extraordinary staying-power. In 1989 the Parc Astérix was opened as a French reply to EuroDisney and by 1993, 250 million albums had been sold worldwide against sales of 200 million for Tintin. Though its appeal was universal, the essential good humour of *Astérix* remained in touch with childhood. This cannot be said of *Hara-Kiri* (1960), 'journal bête et méchant', or the erotic series commissioned by its publisher Losfeld. Of these, *Barbarella* (1962) by Jean-Claude Forest (1930–1998), achieved a world audience through Vadim's film version (1968). Reflecting both the Pop Art movement and the anarchism of the American underground, racy series like *Jodelle* (1966–7) or *Epoxy* (1968) regularly ran foul of the censor.

The rising status of BD

Even so, *bande dessinée* was becoming intellectually respectable. In 1956, Alain Resnais included it as a treasure of France in a short film on the Bibliothèque Nationale. In 1962 he had a hand in the creation of a Centre d'Études des Bandes Dessinées. Its history, meaning and art were studied in specialist magazines (*Giff-Wiff*, 1962–7; *Phénix*, 1966–7; *Les Cahiers de la bande dessinée*, 1969–90), a Centre d'Études des Littératures d'Expression Graphique was set up in 1964, and a major exhibition was staged in 1967 at the Musée des Arts Décoratifs. Thereafter, conventions and festivals (notably at Angoulême since 1974) would confirm the status of *bande dessinée* on the French cultural scene. It had already been dragooned into education by 1966 with the publication of *Pomme d'Api*, first of a range of magazines using strip cartoons to amuse and instruct the young.

1968 and after

Even so, in the late 1960s, only titles specifically designed for children, like *Tintin* or *Spirou*, were commercially viable. By offering free gifts, *Pif-gadget* sold a million copies per issue but also launched new heroes, some of whom (like Hugo Pratt's *Corto Maltese*, 1970, defender of Irish resistance and other libertarian movements) carried the ideological message of its publisher, the Communist Party. On the other hand, the freedom of expression which followed the events of May 1968 encouraged the growth of erotic and, in the case of Elvifrance's pocket-sized volumes (1969–92), often frankly pornographic, series. Also aimed at adults were 'fanzines' inspired by France's late interest in the now fading American underground movement. *Actuel* (1970) published American materials such as *Fritz the Cat*, but home-grown series also appeared in *Le Citron hallucinogène* (1973), *Le Crapaud baveux* (1976) and *Viper* (1981). Designed for a wider audience, *Charlie mensuel* (1969) and *Charlie-Hebdo* (1970), in the wake of *Hara-Kiri* (banned in 1965), supplied savagely irreverent, satirical comment on political and topical affairs. A more imaginative departure was made by Gotlib, Nikita Mandryka and Claire Bretécher (b. 1940, then a rare female presence in the male world of *bande dessinée*) who left *Pilote*, judged too conservative, and began the satirical, provocative *L'Écho des savanes* (1972) which reflected the new generation's fascination with subversive humour, sex and psychoanalysis. Among numerous magazines which followed its lead were *Métal hurlant* (1975) directed by Druillet, Moebius and others, which focused on science fiction, and *Fluide glacial* begun in 1975 by Gotlib and Jacques Diamant who used parody and the comedy of derision.

By the end of the decade, a new and more violently expressive style (fragmented whole-page images, time-shifts within exploded frames) had been established by series such as Philippe Druillet's *Lone Sloane* (1972) which reacted against the static vignette of classic *bande dessinée*. Bold narrative strategies dispensed with the *bulle* and developed new visual dynamics, as in Moebius's *Arzach* (1975). But *bande dessinée* also developed a subversive agenda on which figured drugs, civil rights, and a general opposition to establishment values, especially in the matter of sexual freedom. But as *bande dessinée* grew more popular, it also grew more fashionable and faced the problems of success.

Since 1980

By the late 1970s, the serious press, forced to take note of the impact of a significant new form of mass communication, began to review albums and report on the growing number of *bande dessinée* festivals. The strip was rediscovered by advertisers, and designers of consumer and other products were influenced by its stylistic innovations. Best-selling titles were bought up by large publishers who rationalized production by targeting age-groups and creating new genre-based collections (westerns, crime, eroticism, science fiction), thus demoting the serial and therefore the magazines which had encouraged new talent and new ideas. *Charlie-Hebdo* was banned in 1982 and resurfaced only in 1992, the humour of established titles like *Fluide glacial* became blunter and more aggressive and, in general, *bande dessinée* exchanged innovation and ideas for a return to the super-hero, the classic adventure and an older graphic realism: westerns, science fiction (Moebius), crime thrillers (Jacques Tardi), political fictions (Enki Belal), special agents and spies (*XIII*, 1984), by the Belgian team of Vance and Van Hamme), and fantasy of all kinds. In the early 1980s controls were relaxed: a ruling modified the law of 1949, which henceforth was restricted to albums specifically aimed at the youth market. The result was a rapid growth in erotic *bande dessinée*. On the other hand, history was represented by Tardi's evocation of the Great War or François Bourgeon's series, *Les Passagers du vent* (1978–84), which sold 300,000 copies per title. Graphic adaptations of literary classics (from Tardi's *120 rue de la gare* (1987–8), based on Léo Malet's novel, to the visualisation of Sade (or even, in 1999, Proust) drew the form back towards mainstream culture.

Educational BD

The educational potential of *bande dessinée* continued to be exploited in the 1970s, when 600,000 copies of the 8-volume *Histoire de France en bande dessinée* (1976) were sold in seven years. There followed cartoon versions of the Bible, the Koran, the lives of great artists, introductions to Darwin, Freud and Marx, and surveys of topics ranging from nuclear energy to the workings of the Japanese economy. Academics studied its history, aesthetics and sociological role. In 1983 the French government formally recognized the status of *bande dessinée* and provided financial aid and practical encouragement for its development and diffusion. It also helped fund the Centre National de la

Bande Dessinée et de l'Image which was inaugurated at Angoulême in 1990.

The decline of the 1980s

During the 1980s American and Japanese cartoons shown by French television, and the growth of interactive electronic games represented strong competition. Although the 15.5 million copies of 600 titles that were sold in 1989 represented 3 per cent of French book production, the market for *bande dessinée* had shrunk by one-sixth since 1980. To win back readers, publishers issued limited, de luxe, signed, subscriber's and 'collector's' editions, republished classic titles, experimented with smaller formats and gave away plastic novelties. Delcourt introduced the interactive *bande dessinée* in 1987. But as the interval between magazine pre-publication and the appearance of the album grew shorter, the public, preferring to wait for the 'complete story', wearied of most of the magazines which had appeared during the 1970s. Only *L'Écho des savanes*, *Fluide glacial* and *À suivre* survived the century and even *Tintin* closed in 1989 and *Pif* in 1993. Yet in the 1990s, smaller, specialist imprints maintained a market for the album and provided outlets for both established authors like Tardi (*Jeux pour mourir*, 1992) and Bilal (whose *Froid Équateur*, 1992, sold over 150,000 copies) and new writers: Lewis Trondheim (*Blacktown*), Nicolas de Crécy and O'Groj. New talent was nurtured by smaller, dedicated imprints, but the major publishers maintained the classic series, using new writers and artists to perpetuate established characters, sometimes encouraging experiment, such as *La Débauche* (2000), a collaboration between Tardi and the novelist Daniel Pennac. By 2000, when 1,563 titles were published, *bande dessinée* had recaptured its market.

BD and women

Its rejuvenation was marked by a strong influx of women into the profession. Most *coloristes* were now female and modern concerns – war, politics, Aids, abortion, the modern couple – were treated by women authors for a readership which was 20 per cent female. The *pin-up* and the heroine in distress gave way to the *executive woman*, an assertive role model pioneered by Claire Bretécher (creator of Cellulite and Agrippine) and Florence Cestac (b. 1949: *Le Démon du midi*, 1996). In *On les aura* (2000), Catherine Beaunez deals with women in politics while Anne Ploy (*Transgénèse*, 2000) uses science fiction to project a view of women in 2029. Old genres (the *politique-fiction* or the *érotico-fantastique*) have been colonized and new forms created, like the *bédécrite* (*Les Quatre fleuves*, 2000, by Fred Vargas, b. 1958), an extension of the drawn *roman-photo*. Women writer/artists continue to cater for children but they have also welcomed the internationalization of the genre. *Persepolis*, by Marjane Satrapi, an Iranian refugee, shows the Islamic Revolution through the eyes of a 10-year-old girl. Joly Guth (*Croqueurs de sable, Iris magicienne*) is one of many influenced by the Japanese 'manga' featured in *Dragon Ball Z*, which sold 60,000 copies a month. The doyenne of the 'Shojo Manga' ('la bande dessinée pour filles'), which features romance, sexually ambivalent male characters and feminine heroines, remains the Japanese Tuu Watase whose series, *Fushigi Yugi: Un jeu étrange* (18 albums since 1992) explores the world of a wide-eyed but independent Japanese teenager.

Conclusion

Once an entertainment for children 'de 7 à 77 ans', the cartoon strip developed into a major vehicle of mass communication. It continues to be used to publicize causes large and small and is now an essential part of the armoury of education and advertising. It is universally understood, not simply because a picture is worth a thousand words but because it developed a simple visual grammar which fully vindicated the remark made by Hetzel in 1864: 'Le dessin est un langage.' That language is international: the light bulb for 'idea', a heart for love, multiple exclamation marks, and a range of onomatopoeic indicators. It borrowed narrative modes, optical effects and editing styles from cinema, but in return it contributed significantly to the growth of the cartoon film, to which it gave heroes and graphic techniques. But its claim to be 'literature' remains controversial.

Its technical sophistication is the product of a range of skills. A scenario becomes a storyboard which is 'visualised' (to concretize a situation and maximize the impact) by an artist, a *lettriste*, an *encreur* and a *coloriste*. Established characters (Superman, Tintin, etc.), controlled by the copyright-holder, are the product of studio teams charged with exploiting a commercial recipe. The caustic *bande dessinée* containing a socio-political critique, which humorists offer to adolescents and adults (but not children), is usually the work of one person. But in both cases, the simplicity of the graphic language of *bande dessinée* is best suited to the narrow range of subject matter associated with popular literature: humour, violence, sentiment and sensation. Imaginative fantasy, its strongest suit, remains yoked to activity and movement, and in this it marks little advance on melodrama or the nineteenth-century *roman feuilleton*. *Bande dessinée* works within a self-imposed formula as rigid as the rules of classicism: it excludes all save the most basic emotions, its values are Manichaean and it sets out not to persuade but to overwhelm the reader.

After the Second World War it acquired enemies, a clear indication of its growing power. Psychologists warned that cartoon images dehumanize, moralists deplored its effect on youth, religion and attitudes in general, and governments banned anti-social themes (drugs, sex) and sympathetic attitudes to crime and criminals. *Zig et Puce* was found guilty of perpetuating racial types, as was Hergé (*Tintin au Congo*), who was further attacked for anti-communism (*Tintin au pays des Soviets*) and anti-capitalism (*Tintin en Amérique*). The rise of youth culture in the 1960s created an adult, and primarily male, market for taboo subjects – escapist fantasy, gore, eroticism and grotesque humour – and established iconoclastic expectations which are still part of the appeal of *bande dessinée*. Yet despite its cardboard heroes, formulaic adventures, shallow psychology and the absence of objective reflection on complex issues, *bande dessinée* played a central role in the shift from written culture to the graphic forms of expression through which the poster, advertising, cinema and the electronic media transmit information. Weaker in content than in style, *bande dessinée* also reflects the importance of design and presentation in a consumer society which, however, is still susceptible to myth: like the Lady of the Camelias, Tintin, Astérix and Barbarella have ascended to super-celebrity. Its major strength, however, lies in its liberating effect on the imagination. Few *bande dessinée* heroes survive translation to the screen. Human impersonations seem dull and earth-bound, constrained by the bonds of reality of which their cartoon originals are magically free.

The Cinema

Fiction, theatre and poetry have always built on the achievements of the past. Cinema, though it draws on all three and on the plastic arts too, had no tradition and made its own way. But from its inception, it offered access to freer flights of graphic representation and more fluid kinds of drama. Its pioneers rose to the challenge very quickly. Cinema rapidly outgrew its image as a fairground entertainment and within a decade had become *le septième art*.

Its status as art has been championed nowhere more enthusiastically than in France, which has generated more theories of film than any other nation. The battles over the coming of sound, for example, or over the *nouvelle vague*, were public and passionate, and almost as much ink has been spilt in attempts to define 'pure cinema' as in efforts to characterize 'pure poetry'. For the avant-garde, cinema means cutting all links with fiction and theatre and 'writing with light' by means of a *caméra-stylo* to exploit its essential material, the image. For mainstream film-makers the medium is the ultimate form of drama, able to move through space and time and reach audiences with an immediacy denied to all other forms of literary expression. But both sides agree that cinema democratizes art: by 1930, it was said that more people had seen the films of Chaplin in fifteen years than had seen plays by Molière in three hundred. But even its stoutest defenders concede that cinema is as much an industry as an art, and have wondered whether it is possible for any personal vision to survive the strains of a collective enterprise. The *auteuriste* theory, practised by Abel Gance in the silent era, by Pagnol and Renoir in the 1930s and most fully stated by Truffaut in the 1950s, argues that any valid film or body of film must be dominated by a single point of view or else must be classed as a commercial product indistinguishable from cheese or motor-cars. Many successful films have been no worthier in artistic terms than the best-selling fiction they so frequently resemble. Even serious film-makers are rarely as free as novelists or poets to project a personal vision because financial pressures require that nothing too 'new' or 'experimental' or 'difficult' be attempted. If cinema is art for the masses, it is art made commercially safe.

1895–1918

Though cinema had no aesthetic past, it had a scientific prehistory. Newton's Disc reconstituted the rainbow because the retina is able to retain images for a split second before being stimulated by fresh light signals. This peculiarity of the human eye, called the 'persistence of vision', was well known by 1800, and by 1820 Roget, Faraday and others demonstrated that, when observed through an aperture in a spinning disc, motion could be accelerated, slowed and even stopped. In the following decades the principle of intermittent vision was used to animate drawings of horses galloping and clowns juggling. But the zoetrope, or 'wheel of life', remained little more than a toy. However, with improvements in photography and the development of sensitive emulsions (which reduced exposure time), the goal of 'living pictures' came within sight. Edward Muybridge's sequence of a trotting horse, projected in Paris in 1881 by means of Émile Reynaud's praxinoscope (1876), produced an exact but brief image of reality. The race to perfect a camera and a means of projecting the exposed images, became urgent, and nowhere more so than in France. In 1882 Étienne Marey developed a 'camera gun' while in Leeds in Yorkshire the expatriate Augustin le Prince (1841–?89) perfected both camera and projector in 1889 while in America Edison was still working on his system. In the event, the best technical response was provided by the Lumière brothers who, in December 1895, exhibited short sequences of moving pictures in a Paris café.

The first paying customers of the *cinématographe* were amused by *L'Arroseur arrosé* and alarmed by *L'Arrivée d'un train dans la gare de la Ciotat*. But they quickly adapted to the novel idea that life could be captured and made into spectacle. Louis Lumière (1864–1948) made or sponsored some 2,000 short films in three years and pioneered visual and narrative techniques which would become standard. His interest in film-making, however, was practical – the films he made were intended to advertise the equipment he manufactured – and he withdrew from production in 1898. Georges Méliès (1861–1938), a professional entertainer, was the first to see the commercial possibilities of cinema as spectacle. He used a studio to reconstruct news stories (such as *L'Affaire Dreyfus*, 1899), exploited trick photography and was first in the field with the narrative film, of which *Voyage dans la lune* (1902) is the best remembered. By the turn of the century, he was showing films in fairgrounds where the public readily paid a few *sous* to see the new 'merveille cinématographique'. In 1902, Charles Pathé (1863–1957) bought the Lumière patents, developed a new camera and built a production company which, he said, 'industrialized' cinema. Léon Gaumont (1863–1943) made fewer films than Pathé's company (300 during the decade 1897–1906) but was

Pathé's most effective competitor. He was particularly interested in his *phonoscènes*, filmed performances by well-known artists screened to the playback of synchronized sound recordings of songs they had made famous. These ancestors of the pop video were among many attempts to create sound cinema.

Enough of these pioneering films have survived for it to be clear that the distinction between the commercial and the artistic was well established early in the history of cinema. For the general public there were short comedies, fantasy films and a spate of melodramas, the more successful of which were turned into series: *Nick Carter, roi des détectives* made the first of many appearances in 1908 and before and during the Great War the action serials of Louis Feuillade (1873–1925: *Fantômas, Judex, Les Vampires*) attracted a huge public. Émile Cohl (1857–1938) experimented with all kinds of animation films. The Film d'Art company (1908) specialized in abbreviated versions of the classical French dramatic repertory and a start was made by theorists who sought to define the nature of cinema and its proper function. By 1905, purpose-built cinemas had sprung up all over France and, to satisfy the new demand, film-makers moved into more ambitious productions with more sophisticated equipment. By 1908, the French cinema industry was firmly rooted: there were chains of cinemas, an effective distribution system, a growing market, dynamic production, and 1912 marked the arrival of the first regular film critics. By 1914, 90 per cent of films shown anywhere in the world were French; the first major international star, Max Linder, was French; and until 1918, 60 per cent of films made worldwide were shot with French cameras.

Serious film-makers were aware that commercial cinema threatened the artistic possibilities of the new medium by turning it into a popular entertainment or anchoring it to 'théâtre filmé'. The awareness of its potential coincided with profound changes in intellectual perspectives. The reaction against nineteenth-century positivism suggested that assumptions about the external world – the world which the camera recorded – stood in need of revision. Darwinism, the principle of relativity and the experience of war suggested that life is not stable and that reality changes. Marx and the Russian Revolution of 1917 undermined bourgeois confidence and signalled the arrival of a new social order. Meanwhile, the psychoanalytical movement gave a new impetus to the film-maker who wished to explore the springs of human motivation and conduct: Freud's work on dreams opened new horizons which beckoned to a medium totally committed to the visual. Young film-makers like Abel Gance and, later, the Surrealists, believed that cinema could be an instrument of change which, through the power of the image, could break the mould of received ideas. It was an early affirmation of a very French point of view which considers cinema less as a form of entertainment than as a means of shaping the general consciousness and thereby of influencing attitudes and events. The intellectualization of cinema in France is a recurrent feature of its history and is one major way in which French cinema differs from its Anglo-Saxon counterpart.

The silent twenties

The cinema debate scarcely touched the public, which forgot its troubles two or three times a week as it consumed films which, after the mobilization of film-makers and the requisition of their equipment after 1914, were more likely now to have been made in Hollywood. Throughout the 1920s, American imports increased their hold on the French market. Audiences which had thrilled to serials such as *The Perils of Pauline* also warmed to Chaplin, Douglas Fairbanks, Lon Chaney and Lilian Gish. French commercial film-makers, alive to the demands of the market, made historical dramas, sentimental love stories and bustling comedies which in content and technique drew on Hollywood models. Yet it was equally a period of serious film-making and theorizing: it was now that the term *cinéaste* was coined. André Antoine, bringing his Théâtre Libre principles to cinema, used natural locations and non-professional actors, and accustomed audiences to watch real life as opposed to studio reconstructions (*La Terre*, 1918/19). Around him, Henri Pouctal (1856–1922) also anticipated neo-realist techniques in another Zola adaptation, *Le Travail* (1919), the first *film-fleuve*, part of which was shot in the Le Creusot ironworks. The Surrealists revelled in the visual anarchy which the medium afforded from *La Souriante Madame Beudet* (1923) to *La Coquille et le clergyman* (1928), both directed by Germaine Dulac (1882–1942), and from *Paris qui dort* (1923; dir. René Clair) to *Un Chien andalou* (1928; dir. Buñuel/Dali). The avant-garde was mediated for the general public by Marcel l'Herbier (1890–1979) and Jean Epstein (1897–1953), and the new techniques were exploited in the historical epics of Raymond Bernard (1891–1977) and the prolific Jacques

Feyder (1888–1948), then regarded as one of the finest European directors. But of the innovators Abel Gance was historically the most influential.

Before 1920, the camera had remained largely static, allowing spectators to see events unfold as they do in real life. To heighten the visual impact, Gance disrupted the sequence with a succession of detailed images. For *La Roue* (1922), he did not film a moving train in long-shot but filled the screen, in close-up, with a 'rapid montage' of wheels, steam and rails which created a sensation of the train's speed in a way that does not occur in nature. For his epic six-hour *Napoléon* (1927), he mounted his cameras on toboggans and horses and swung them in great scything movements from piano wires and, for the climax, projected three films on to three screens to produce the first wide-vision effect. The techniques developed by Gance and other innovators completed the work of the early pioneers so that the whole range of visual resources available to the film-director was more or less complete by 1930. Subsequently, a number of technical advances (colour, wide-screen, animation and so forth) were added, but the basic grammar of film was established long before the coming of sound.

But if many 1920s films were technically sophisticated, their content and mood were frequently backward-looking. Chained to predominantly nineteenth-century literary models, they offered widows, orphans and innocent lovers under attack from black-hearted villains and wicked capitalists. They encouraged heroes to strike poses as they fought for clear-cut causes and rescued languishing heroines. To a modern eye, even *Napoléon* or Carl Dreyer's *Jeanne d'Arc* (1929) have moments of third-class melodrama. The most grandiose of silent film-makers were builders of medieval cathedrals filled, unfortunately, with outdated pieties.

But even as silent film was reaching its peak, it was overtaken by events. The film industry was revolutionized by the discovery of an effective method of recording image and sound simultaneously. Some, like René Clair (1898–1981), saw that *le parlant* undermined the true vocation of cinema: making films speak meant denying the poetry of the visual by injecting a note of banal realism. For Marcel Pagnol (1895–1974), on the other hand, silent cinema had been a variant of mime. By adding words, cinema became the vehicle of total drama. Clair and like-minded defenders of 'pure cinema' countered with the charge that their opponents seemed bent on turning *le septième art* into so much 'canned theatre'. In the event, the debate was settled by the public which delivered its verdict in favour of *le film cent-pour-cent parlant*. By 1931, 25 per cent of French cinemas were equipped to project the new sound pictures.

The 1930s

The French cinema industry was in no state to withstand the Wall Street Crash of 1929. France's prewar hold on the world market had crumbled in the face of competition from Hollywood: in 1928, 85 per cent of films screened worldwide were American. The age of French technical domination had passed – film stock was no longer manu-factured in France and had to be imported – and the new patents were American. The standard sound-recording system (Western Elec-tric) was leased to French film-makers at prohibitive rates. The Amer-icans had no reason to be generous. The French government's imposition of a quota system for foreign-made films was viewed as unfriendly and its decision not to allow American companies to ex-port all their French profits meant that large sums of money lay idle in French banks. In 1930, American film companies like Paramount set up studios in France designed to exploit the French and European markets. In the Paramount studios at Joinville, Hollywood techniques led to the mass-production of films in multiple languages. One of the first films directed there (by Alexander Korda, specially imported from Hollywood) was Pagnol's *Marius* (1931) which was made, using the same sets, in French with French actors, in Italian with an Italian cast, in Swedish, German and so forth. It was not unusual for there to be a dozen different language versions of the same film which, with reduced production costs, could be released to different mar-kets. The practice was discontinued after 1932 when dubbing was introduced.

The Hollywood challenge meant serious competition for the major French film companies. Gaumont went bankrupt in 1934 and Pathé-Nathan in 1936. Paramount withdrew in 1933 for economic reasons but the German Tobis-Klangfilm expanded its operations in France and was responsible for financing about 10 per cent of the 1,200 French films made in the 1930s. At first, the 'artisanal' French cin-ema coped uneasily with the new financial constraints. Paramount made *Topaze* (with Louis Jouvet) in 1932 but Pagnol, its author, was contractually excluded from the production. On his deathbed, Jean Vigo (1905–34) learned that his producer had added an irrelevant but very popular song to the soundtrack of *L'Atalante* (1934). When the backers of *La Nuit du carrefour* (1932) withdrew their financial support, Jean Renoir was obliged to make a film of the material he had shot, even though essential scenes had not been filmed. Even the great names of the decade's cinema had first to be businessmen and diplomats if they wished to function as artists.

Financial constraints were not, however, the only difficulties to be overcome. The first systematic censorship laws had been introduced in 1917 to protect morale in time of war. In 1928 new measures were introduced which sought to protect morality. Sex and violence attracted the wrath of the censors who, to defend 'the social good', were highly sensitive to anti-clerical comment and political extremism. Vigo's *Zéro de conduite* (1932) caused a riot when it was shown in 1933, was banned as an anarchic tract and did not receive a certificate until 1945. On the other hand, makers of newsreels were left largely to censor themselves. There were cinemas in Paris which showed nothing else and cinema-goers everywhere watched filmed news once or twice a week. Some directors (Renoir particularly) attempted to give their feature films a propaganda value, but French public opinion was most effectively formed and informed by the newsreels which outweighed even the written press.

Most films made in France in the 1930s, as in all other periods, were entertainments designed for the mass market: adaptations of popular plays and classic novels, family dramas, sentimental love stories, musicals and farces: there was in particular a thriving line in comic films about military life, collectively known as *les gaietés de l'escadron*. After Cocteau's *Le Sang d'un poète* (1930) and Buñuel's *L'Âge d'or* (1930), Surrealist film faded, but not before bequeathing bold graphic techniques. However, it was a fruitful time for serious film-makers, who turned the cinema eye increasingly to social subjects. René Clair quickly came to terms with sound and *Le Million* (1930), a comedy about a man who chases a winning lottery ticket all over Paris, remains one of the classic choreographed musicals, while *À nous la liberté* (1931) was a stylized satire of the dehumanizing effects of capitalism. Jean Renoir (1894–1979), the most comprehensively gifted of all French directors, satirized the bourgeoisie in *Boudu sauvé des eaux* (1931), and addressed the problems facing immigrant workers in *Toni* (1934), before turning to political cinema (1935–7), and his exposé of shallow bourgeois values in *La Règle du jeu* (1939).

Paradoxically, film production revived after the collapse of the major studios around 1934. Small companies were set up, sometimes to produce a particular film, and directors found new backers. In the run-up to the Popular Front, cooperatives were formed: Renoir's socialist fable, *Le Crime de Monsieur Lange* (1935), was financed in this way. The following year, Julien Duvivier made *La Belle Équipe*, which shows the failure of a group of friends to set up a collective enterprise. A preview suggested that audiences found it too pessimistic and, after this early example of audience consultation, Duvivier shot a happy ending which the public preferred. These two films reflected current attitudes to the Front Populaire but also confirmed the rise of 'artisanal cinema'. From around 1935 to the defeat of 1940, French cinema, freed from the grip of the monolithic companies, rediscovered its freshness and, in reflecting the political and social tensions of the times, regained the role accorded to it by its earliest supporters, that of popular educator.

After 1936, alongside the sophisticated Boulevard cinema of Sacha Guitry, the middle-brow features of Marc Allégret (1900–73), the glories of empire celebrated by Léon Poirier (1884–1968) or the dramas of Jacques Feyder (*La Kermessse héroique*, 1935), cinema turned to more sombre themes. There was a vogue for moody working-class settings against which characters played out metaphysical dramas heavily dominated by fate. 'Poetic realism', anticipated by Vigo, produced a succession of films which showed an ordinary man defeated by life and love. In Duvivier's *Pépé le moko* (1938), Jean Gabin (1904–76) played a small-time criminal who finally dies when he loses the woman he loves. For Renoir, Gabin made *La Bête humaine* (1939) where he is undone by heredity. But it was his work for Marcel Carné (1906–96), whose visualisations of scripts by Jacques Prévert are a high point of French cinema, that show him at his doomed best. *Quai des brumes* (1938) and *Le Jour se lève* (1939) show that love is impossible and that all roads to freedom are closed. In these and other films, Gabin became the incarnation of many of the hopes and fears of French people on the eve of war: strong but vulnerable, he is not quite guilty, yet not quite innocent either. But he was also the leading example of a new phenomenon: the cinema star. From the theatre emerged the irascible Raimu (Jules Muraire, 1890–1946), the sinister Jules Berry (1883–1951), the brilliantly versatile Fernandel (pseud. of Fernand Contandin, 1903–71), the sardonic Louis Jouvet and, among the women, Arletty (1900–92) whose feisty screen persona offered a new image of French womanhood.

At a time of economic depression, political uncertainty, the decline of religion and other social changes, stardom became a new aristocracy which offered new role models. Women emulated Arletty and men Gabin, their imagination fuelled by the large number of popular cinema magazines which revealed the private lives of the stars and spoke of a world of luxury very distant from the everyday reality of most French people. If 1930s cinema influenced audiences, it did so less in terms of social and political messages than on the level of individual behaviour and in the idea of personal happiness. Tragic lovers, heroic gangsters, anti-heroes of every sort made claims for the indulgence of the individual within a framework of established values which in reality frowned on the *fille mère*, criminals and immorality in all walks of life. From the anti-bourgeois satire of René Clair and Jean Vigo, via films which focused on the Popular Front, to Renoir's anti-war tract, *La Grande Illusion* (1937) and the defence of innocence which Pagnol and Carné showed under attack from irresistible forces, the cinema of the interwar period, thoughtful and technically adventurous, was a Golden Age. Classical musicians (Arthur Honegger, Georges Auric, Darius Milhaud) contributed film scores and the professional scriptwriter came into his own: Charles Spaak, Henri Jeanson and Jacques Prévert, Carné's partner for ten years.

The war years

When France fell in June 1940, film production, torpid during the *drôle de guerre*, ceased momentarily, only to start up again in very changed circumstances. In November, the Comité d'Organisation de l'Industrie Cinématographique was set up to coordinate production under German control. Of the 220 feature films made during the Occupation, 85 per cent were produced, with the approval of the censors, by German companies, notably Continentale (October 1940). The Germans placed a high value on cinema as propaganda but the public resisted Nazi-inspired films which included an overtly anti-Jewish version of Maupassant's *Bel-Ami* and the aggressive *Le Juif Suss*. American films were screened in the Free Zone until they were banned in 1942. With few exceptions, like the notorious *Forces occultes* (1943), which denounced Jews and international Freemasonry, French film-makers confined themselves to 'safe' subjects and made historical, fantastic, romantic and crime dramas which, with a high proportion of literary adaptations, remained within the mood and ethos of the 1930s of which French wartime cinema was a continuation.

In the absence of *cinéastes* (Clair, Duvivier, Renoir) and actors (Gabin, Michèle Morgan) who had left the country, established directors like Carné, Jean Delannoy (b. 1908), Claude Autant-Lara (b. 1903), Cocteau, Christian-Jacque (1904–94), Jacques Becker (1906–60) and Jean Grémillon (1901–59) were joined by others who were at the start of their careers, like Robert Bresson (1901–99) and Henri-Georges Clouzot (1907–77). Most wartime films were escapist, but some carried an indirect message of resistance. It was heard in the heart that continues to beat at the end of *Les Visiteurs du soir* (Carné; 1942), in the affirmation of the unshakeable continuity of things (Cocteau's *L'Éternel Retour,* 1942), and through reminders of France's great past in adaptations of classic novels or evocations of her history, among which Carné's *Les Enfants du paradis* (1945) stands out. Occasionally, however, a sourer note was struck. Clouzot's *Le Corbeau* (1943) described reactions to an outbreak of anonymous letters in a small provincial town. The subject exploited the fears and the denunciations which were a part of French life under the Occupation and Clouzot was accused of undermining French morale.

The Vichy government took a keen interest in cinema and introduced significant measures to organize and promote the industry: a system of exhibition licences, the creation of the annual Grand Prix du Film d'Art Français, the establishment of the Institut des Hautes Études Cinématographiques (IDHEC, 1943) and subsidies for the work of the Cinémathèque Française which had been set up by Georges Franju and Henri Langlois in 1936 and would play a crucial role in the 1950s. These initiatives, together with the encouragement given to newsreel and documentary producers, remained in force after the Liberation in 1944 and helped guide the fortunes of the postwar cinema in France.

Postwar cinema

After the war, the exiles returned gradually to find French cinema unadventurously clinging to its conventions. In Italy, neo-realists like Rossellini and De Sica made high-quality, low-budget films and in London the Ealing comedies revived the fortunes of the British cinema. In contrast, the French showed more taste than energy. There were outstanding films, like *La Bataille du rail* (1946; dir. René Clement, 1913–95) which dealt with the sabotage of the railway system during the war, *Les Vacances de Monsieur Hulot* (1953; dir. Jacques Tati, 1907–82) which returned to the visual comedy of silent cinema, or Clouzot's tense, semi-philosophical *Le Salaire de la peur* (1953). But in the main, too many French films of the 1940s and 1950s were *exercices de style* which rarely tested the resources of cinema. Max Ophuls's stagy *La Ronde* (1950), Carné's updated version of Zola's novel *Thérèse Raquin* (1953), or Jacques Becker's *Casque d'or* (1952) were solidly constructed and meticulously crafted productions. But most directors preferred studio work, avoided location shooting and built on their past achievements. They continued to think in terms of bankable stars because securing the services of Gabin, Michèle Morgan, Danielle Darrieux or Gérard Philipe was often crucial in attracting backers. In this climate, experiment was hardly the order of the day. Clément, Clouzot, Autant-Lara, even Cocteau, seemed ultra-professional masters of an impeccable but increasingly sterile art.

If cinema developed at all at this time it was in the field of the documentary. Georges Rouquier's *Farrebique* (1946) followed a year in the life of a farm in the Massif Central and combined authenticity with great sensitivity. But outside the documentary, which built on lessons learnt from wartime newsreel production, the public remained happy with a form of cinema that was highly professional but unadventurous. Politically, film-makers remained prudent, rarely commenting on the ideological issues which divided France in the late 1940s or the war in Indo-China, and they passed over the social and human problems facing the new generation. They preferred adaptations of the classics, *film noir* (*Dédée d'Anvers*, 1948; dir. Yves Allégret, b. 1907), historical films (*Fanfan la tulipe*, 1952; dir. Christian-Jacque), crime thrillers (Becker's *Touchez pas au grisbi*, 1954), psychological tales of varying credibility, farcical comedies (with Fernandel, Bourvil and Noël-Noël) and the unavoidable love story. Feature films remained faithful to well-worn narrative traditions and continued to explore pathological states in the time-honoured way. Occasional voices expressed dissent. In 1948 Alexandre Astruc revived the concept of the *caméra-stylo*. What he meant was illustrated in Cocteau's *Orphée* (1950) and the 'subjective camera' of his own *Le Rideau cramoisi* (1950).

Cinema addicts, however, could vary the diet by watching classic films in the national chain of cinema clubs or, in Paris, in the Cinémathèque Française, directed by Langlois, who had obsessively collected everything he could. It was there that François Truffaut (1932–84), Eric Rohmer (b. 1920), Jacques Rivette (b. 1928), Alain Resnais (b. 1922) and Jean-Luc Godard (b. 1930) acquired a vast knowledge of the tradition of French and world cinema. They revered Orson Welles, Howard Hawks and Hitchcock, and greatly admired Rossellini and Renoir. In comparison, current productions seemed over-stylized and conservative and they found a home for their trenchant views in *Les Cahiers du cinéma*, a review founded in 1951 by one of France's greatest film critics, André Bazin (1918–58). There they developed a new concept of film and denounced the prevailing *cinéma de qualité*, which they disparaged as *le cinéma de papa*. They reacted against the stagnation which stifled individual flair and championed *la politique des auteurs* which held that only films dominated by a single point of view – that of the *auteur* – could ever be considered as art.

There was nothing new in such claims, of course, and history provided many examples of 'cinema artists' of this sort. In the 1930s, Pagnol made his complete independence the essential condition of his work for the cinema. By 1933 he had his own studios at Marseilles, chose his casts, wrote and directed his own scripts, supervised the treatment of exposed film in his own laboratories, masterminded publicity campaigns and monitored the progress of his productions in his own chain of cinemas in the Midi and North Africa. While such total control was possible in the special conditions of 1934, the climate had changed by 1953 when he withdrew from film-making: competition from Hollywood was intense, the financial stakes were higher and the growth of technicians' unions created new working practices. Moreover, cinema now had to face competition from television: attendances started falling in 1957.

The 'Young Turks' of the *Cahiers du cinéma* persisted in their denunciation of bourgeois cinema. Their target was not the frankly commercial cinema journeymen like Gilles Grangier (1911–95) but the hidebound style of *cinéastes* like Autant-Lara, Clément and Becker

whom they, with hindsight, underestimated, as they did Jean
Aurenche (1904–92) and Pierre Bost (1901–75), the most accomplished screen-writers of the period. Finally losing patience, they
began making their own films. Under-financed and oozing theory,
they made documentary and narrative shorts with a new generation
of lightweight cameras, faster film (which made location shooting
easier), portable sound-recording equipment and much ingenuity. It
was on such films that they cut their directorial teeth and paved the
way for a 'New Wave' of feature films which were to transform
French cinema and influence film-makers everywhere in the world.

The New Wave and after

The films of the *nouvelle vague* had the energy and freshness of youth
and many achieved the feat of being both artistically and commercially successful. In the five years after 1958, about a hundred iden-
tifiably 'New Wave' films were made, though not all were of the
quality of Truffaut's *Les Quatre cent coups* (1959) and *Tirez sur le pianiste*
(1960); Godard's *À bout de souffle* (1960) and *Bande à part* (1964); *Les
Amants* (1958; dir. Louis Malle, 1932–95); the sardonic *Les Cousins*
(1959; dir. Claude Chabrol, b. 1930) or *Cléo de 5 à 7* (1961), directed
by Agnès Varda (b. 1928). Avoiding the constraints and artifices of
the studio, the 'New' directors preferred location filming, using *cinéma-
vérité* techniques learned from their probationary experiments. They
relied on a heavy fictional symbolism which was very different from
the poetic realism of the 1930s and turned against literary classics in
favour of adaptations of contemporary, often American crime novels.
Working with small budgets meant dispensing with established stars
and they proceeded to recruit new faces, like Jean-Paul Belmondo
and Jeanne Moreau. The result was a resolutely *auteuriste* cinema
infused with 'the single point of view', adventurous in its techniques
and the antithesis of the mannered art which it replaced. There was
room too for experimental films developed in association with New
Realist novelists: *Hiroshima, mon amour* (1959; Duras/Resnais) and
L'Année dernière à Marienbad (1961; Robbe-Grillet/Resnais).

But if the New Wave created a personal cinema, it avoided commitment. While the militant documentaries of Chris Marker (b. 1921)
raised political issues (colonialism, capitalism), the fiction film alluded
only sparingly to the Algerian War, and the problems of juvenile
delinquency and criminality were given an anecdotal, melodramatic

or 'psychological' treatment. Nevertheless, these years were extremely productive and rank with the best creative energies released in the late 1930s.

After about 1963, however, the New Wave suffered the fate of turning into a New Orthodoxy. Its techniques became increasingly routine and the new stars, too, acquired their own public. Truffaut began his retreat into a world of private concerns and showed that men remain little boys and that 'women are magical'. Godard became increasingly hypnotized by the visual and became as mannered in his own way as *le cinéma de papa* had been. Both, however, acquired world reputations, Truffaut for his tolerantly observed humanism and Godard for his uncompromising style and the high-profile political stance asserted first in *Le Petit Soldat* (1963), then in the futuristic satire *Alphaville* (1965), and in *Weekend* (1967), which openly mocked the complacency of de Gaulle's France. The buoyant economy and a measure of government subsidy (through the *avance sur recettes* formula established in 1959) meant that financing new productions was easier than it had been for many years. One effect was to widen the gap between films made for popular consumption and films which satisfied more demanding tastes.

The perennial taste for comedy was supplied by Jean-Pierre Mocky (b. 1929), Philippe de Broca (b. 1935) and the prolific Gérard Oury (b. 1924), while that other French staple, the *drame policier*, was stylishly represented by Jean-Pierre Melville (1917–73). But there was room too for experiment. The novelists Alain Robbe-Grillet, Jean Cayrol and, towards the end of the 1960s, Marguerite Duras, explored the possibilities of cinema as a freer means of expression and won the support of intellectual audiences. Between these extremes, veterans like Jacques Tati, Georges Franju and René Clair retained a loyal following and New Wave directors turned out a steady stream of middle-brow films: the sentimental melodrama of Claude Lelouch (b. 1937: *Un homme et une femme*, 1967) for example, or Malle's *Le Voleur* (1966) or the sugary musicals of Jacques Demy (1931–90: *Les Parapluies de Cherbourg*, 1964; *Les Demoiselles de Rochefort*, 1967). On the other hand, two names transcend their times: Robert Bresson (1901–99), the major French exponent of religious and spiritual themes, and Luis Buñuel (1900–83), scourge of the bourgeoisie.

Yet as the 1960s advanced, film-directors had to work harder to maintain their position in the face of competition from television.

The million sets of 1959 had become 3.4 million in 1963, 8.3 million in 1968, and cinema attendances had fallen by 30 per cent in a decade. There was talk of a 'crisis' in French cinema, not only in economic but aesthetic terms. That the New Wave had revolutionized French cinema was not denied. But the revolution was now seen to have been the creation of a style, not a renewal of themes and subjects. While 'Angry' British film-makers were drawing attention to serious social problems, French audiences were given the traditional fare of literary adaptations, thrillers, love tangles and melodramatic psychology glossily packaged but more reflective of cinema's view of the world than of reality. Within ten years, the *nouvelle vague* had turned into the kind of stylized, bourgeois cinema which its initiators had once so fiercely denigrated.

1968–80

The furore surrounding the dismissal in February 1968 of Henri Langlois, director of the Cinémathèque Française, meant that the cinema industry was mobilized against the government long before the events of May. When the troubles began, film-making cooperatives were formed, committed documentaries were made and short *ciné-tracts* were shown, the visual equivalent of graffiti and wall-slogans. For a moment, it seemed as though a politically committed cinema was in the making. Godard's *Le Gai Savoir* (1968) and a number of his films which followed, argued a strong Marxist-Leninist line expressed through uncompromising and demanding collages of newsreel, polemic and obscure characterization. Marguerite Duras made *Détruire, dit-elle* (1969), which offered a highly personal view of 'impossible' liberation. Costa-Gavras's *Z* (1969) was a commercially successful political thriller with contemporary overtones. But the most effective politicized film was not fiction at all but a sombre documentary on the German Occupation at Clermont-Ferrand. Marcel Ophuls's *Le Chagrin et la pitié* (1971), a compilation of interviews and archive footage, breathed new life into a subject which, since 1945, had been treated in terms of suspense or comedy. Subsequently, films about the Resistance and the Occupation (like Malle's *Lacombe Lucien*, 1974) reopened old wounds and, thirty years after the event, spearheaded public discussion of a sensitive period of French history.

Yet within months of the promised 'politicization' of the cinema, established directors returned to their preoccupation with traditional subjects and elegance of expression. Truffaut's *L'Enfant sauvage* (1969), a reconstruction of the attempt to educate a wild boy (which might easily have turned into an allegory for modern France), was a sympathetic and faithful piece of realism. Thereafter, he continued his soft-centred studies of contemporary life and his 'Antoine Doinel' cycle which was not so much a social or political history of France between 1960 and 1979 as a picaresque sequence of semi-autobiographical episodes. Truffaut confirmed his reputation as one of the most original, if middle-brow, cinema artists. Claude Chabrol continued to turn out sophisticated studies of middle-class passion and adultery, while Rohmer's elegant 'moral tales' were conversation pieces which revived the tradition of psychological *analyse* of Marivaux and Musset. In other words, established directors continued to tackle problems of the bourgeois soul, and their professionalism constituted a consolidation of the deep-rooted *cinéma de qualité* which audiences clearly still wanted.

But they also wanted pornography, which flooded the market after the relaxation of the censorship laws in 1974. A system of film classification was reintroduced in 1976 and tax disincentives were introduced to counter exploitative film-makers. But demand remained high (in 1978 almost half the films made in France were classed as 'pornographic') and the explicit treatment of sexual subjects moved into serious and mainstream cinema which became markedly voyeuristic. Comic farces became naughtier and the black humour of the anticonformist Café-Théâtre movement was reflected in the films of Bertrand Blier (b. 1939), whose target was bourgeois hypocrisy. Over the decade, the crime thriller throve in the hands of the prolific Georges Lautner (b. 1926), but finally lost its fascination with gangsters, grew markedly more violent, focused on the disillusioned policeman and reflected the problems – drugs, delinquency, lawlessness – posed by the disaffected urban young. Relationships, which had begun to outdistance romantic love in the 1960s, were explored in a variety of settings and reflected the new anxieties of a decade which failed to deliver the open society which had seemed within reach in 1968. Cinema had ceased to be innovative and experiment was left to Raoul Ruiz (*L'Hypothèse du tableau volé*, 1978) and literary figures like Robbe-Grillet and Duras, the major exponent of low-budget *cinéma pauvre*.

Duras trailed her camera with apparent randomness until her audience 'saw' what they were looking at. Her exaggerated use of the 'voice-off' was intended to dislocate sound and image and create new impressionistic reverberations: what we hear in *India Song* (1975) does not seem connected with what we see. By the late 1970s, finally despairing of avoiding the 'tyranny of the director' (that is, the imposition of the film-maker's eye on the mind of the spectator), she inserted passages of blank, exposed film to a spoken text in the hope that her audience would create their own image in their imagination (their *cinéma intérieur*). It was an experiment which proved the superiority of radio drama over cinema, and has had no imitators.

In the tougher economic climate which followed the oil crisis of 1973, problems of finance led to an expansion in co-production and the involvement of television companies, while the Centre National Cinématographique, an important source of state funding since the 1940s, gave support to experiment and promising newcomers. New Wave veterans continued to produce stylish films and to their established stars (Catherine Deneuve, Jean-Louis Trintignant, Yves Montand, Alain Delon, Jean-Paul Belmondo, Jeanne Moreau) added new faces and new talents: Nathalie Baye, Gérard Depardieu, Isabelle Huppert. But striking debuts were also made by a new generation of film-makers. Maurice Pialat (b. 1925) made the first of his examinations of contemporary social issues which included cancer (*La Gueule ouverte*, 1974) and family and school life (*Passe ton bac d'abord*, 1979). Claude Sautet (1924–2000) began his observation of bourgeois manners, and Claude Miller (b. 1942) turned an observant eye on the world of children and adolescents. With Blier, Bernard Tavernier (b. 1941) and Claude Berri (b. 1934), they would occupy the centre ground during the final decades of the century.

In the 1970s, French cinema was home to *auteuriste* film (for the most part well-crafted realism illustrating psychological or social concerns) and embodied essentially conservative values at a time when France was heading towards the election of the first socialist government since 1936. Commercial cinema had become a product designed for the industry's perception of the paying public. Technical innovation was a casualty and the gap between experimental and commercial cinema (which the 'New Wave' had successfully bridged) became wider than ever. Godard's series of films about making films, Rivette's epic semi-documentaries (*Out one*, 1971) and Duras's abstract enigmas received critical praise but not wide popular support.

The 1980s

By 1980, cinema was faced with the problem of dwindling audiences and its absorption into television and video. The traditional French film was threatened by the popularity of big-budget American movies and both *auteuriste* style and traditional genres were undermined by a new New Wave which found its ethos and techniques not in the Cinémathèque but through the television commercial. Films became increasingly a product launched by forceful marketing methods and publicity campaigns, and quality was redefined in commercial terms. The role of the star was consolidated as a major factor in film finance and commercial viability was increasingly defined by 'modern' subject and flamboyant treatment. Because television cornered the market in films for family viewing, cinema moved into areas unsuitable for transmission into homes: violence, sex and big-budget productions (some of which were partly financed by television networks, an increasingly important source of support). After 1981, the new socialist government, aware of cinema's role as a shop-window for French culture, increased state funding to encourage new film-makers.

By 1984, a middle way had emerged between the old *auteuriste* cinema and the big-budget movie, which had yet to materialize but would triple production costs over the decade. The *cinéma du look* was inaugurated by Jean-Jacques Beineix (b. 1947) with *Diva* (1982), which packaged violence, punk aesthetics and designer images for the youth market. Its adventurous photography, eye-catching decors and high-impact visual style reappeared in *Subway* (1985; dir. Luc Besson, b. 1959), a rapidly cut spectacle which used the Paris Métro as a fantastic setting for *amour fou* and marginalized youth and gave glamour a higher priority than social and moral comment. A similar preoccupation with the themes of pulp fiction, if less lavishly filmed, was visible in the brooding thriller, *Mauvais Sang* (1986) which established its director, Léos Carax (b. 1960), as a cult figure whose long-awaited designer film, *Les Amants du Pont-Neuf* (1991) would fail to live up to expectations.

But if such films celebrated the new youth culture, there was, paradoxically, a revival of the historical film which, against the obsession with the new, expressed a nostalgia for France's cultural and rural traditions. Daniel Vigne's *Le Retour de Martin Guerre* (1982) returned to the Middle Ages, Andrzej Wajda's *Danton* (1982) to 1794 and Tavernier's *Un Dimanche à la campagne* (1984) to 1912. The 'retro' vogue also reflected the continuing fascination with the Second World War: *Le Dernier Métro* (1980; dir. Truffaut), *Coup de foudre* (1983; dir. Diane Kurys), *Au Revoir les enfants* (1987; dir. Malle). But it was the international success of Berri's 1986 versions of Pagnol's *Jean de Florette* and *Manon des sources* which marked the launch of the 'heritage' film. Unlike the conventional historical film, which deals with personalities or issues of the past, the 'period' film emerged as a form of cultural tourism which glamorized social history through fine photography and the meticulous recreation of everyday life: here was another answer to the big-production values of the American super-movie. Further literary adaptations followed, notably Jean-Paul Rappeneau's version of Rostand's *Cyrano de Bergerac* (1990), but heritage cinema diversified into other areas, such as the film biography (Bruno Nuytten's *Camille Claudel*, 1989), and laid the basis for its expansion in the 1990s.

Around these major developments, the impact of the New Wave generation continued to weaken. Truffaut's *Vivement dimanche!* (1983), a homage to the *film noir*, ended the career of one of France's most careful cinema artists. Godard returned to narrative film of sorts (*Sauve qui peut la vie*, 1980; *Passion*, 1982), while of the other major figures of the 1970s, Malle was working in Hollywood, Rohmer continued his gentle and amused explorations of love, and Chabrol re-established himself to some extent with the lovingly recreated semi-documentary of Breton life, *Le Cheval d'orgueil* (1980) and further attacks on bourgeois complacency. *Mon oncle d'Amérique* (1980) which intercuts a lecture about human motivation with an episodic story, was an unexpected success for Alain Resnais. The example of such *auteurs* ensured that, to the end of the century, directors were responsible for their own scenarios, generally in collaboration with scriptwriters of whom the most consistent were Francis Véber and the supremely professional Jean-Claude Carrière (b. 1931) who had learned his trade with Buñuel.

Of the perennially popular genres, comedy in various registers maintained its hold on the box-office (five of the largest-grossing French films of the decade were comedies) and the *film policier* was diversified. Bob Swaim's *La Balance* (1982) or Pialat's *Police* (1985) owed less to the tradition of Melville and Chabrol than to the aggressive and violent American 'police precinct' movie. It was treated experimentally by Godard (*Détective*, 1985), with humour, as in Claude

Zidi's *Les Ripoux* (1984), and was the genre on which new directors most frequently cut their teeth. The staple love tangles, empty bourgeois lives, and shallow psychological dramas were given a cosmetic make-over. But the decline of cinema audiences generally and of France's share of the domestic market (which fell further after 1986 when the public was increasingly seduced by Hollywood) did little to dispel pessimistic analyses of current trends.

To maintain its position, the industry fought hard to persuade the government to set quotas for the number of films shown on television and won important concessions in 1986. Broadly speaking, the cinema resisted both the challenge of television and of imported foreign films and attendances remained high compared with the general decline in most other countries: in 1986, there were 5,000 cinemas in France, four times as many as in the UK. The public's loyalty to cinema in general and to French cinema in particular has been variously explained. The French retain an affection for a form of entertainment in which France has a large historical stake. Films made in France are perceived as maintaining specifically French cultural traditions as well as defending the language against the encroachments of English. But, more immediately, French cinema-goers were offered a wide diversity of films which recognized the changing taste of the public.

Social and political problems continued to be aired. Tony Gatlif dealt sensitively with the problems of the gypsy community in *Les Princes* (1982); Magali Clément's *La Maison de Jeanne* (1987) was one of a number of films on feminist issues; and Alain Corneau's superproduction *Fort-Saganne* (1984), like Claire Denis's first feature, *Chocolat* (1987), explored the theme of colonialism. But such subjects were increasingly angled for audiences more likely to be young than middle-aged. Bertrand Blier (b. 1939), a sober, inventive craftsman, deflated bourgeois values through the marginalized rebels of *Les Valseuses* (1973) and a series of equally black comedies: *Buffet froid* (1979), *Notre histoire* (1985) and *Tenue de soirée* (1986). The versatile Bertrand Tavernier (b. 1941), perhaps the best representative of the older French tradition, amused (*Un coup de torchon*, 1980) but also raised social issues, as in his comment on war, *La Vie et rien d'autre* (1989). Contemporary social issues were also the field of Pialat and Claude Miller, who contributed significantly to the cinema of childhood and adolescence with *L'Effrontée* (1985) and *La Petite Voleuse* (1988).

Aimed more specifically at the youth market were films that told of rites of passage, psychological disorders (Jean Becker's *L'Été meurtrier*, 1983) and, especially, picaresque road- and chase-movies featuring 'free spirits': disaffected, marginalized, streetwise adolescents who lived for the moment (Varda's *Sans toit ni loi*, 1985). Drugs, alcohol, sex and violence, the elements of the new romanticism, were exploited by Beineix (*37.2 le matin*, 1986) and Besson (*Nikita*, 1990) with a flamboyance of imagery and a disregard for intellectual positions which, at the end of the decade, defined a new style of film-making. Strong on movement and atmosphere, but often lacking a centre, this was a cinema of glossy surfaces which concerned itself with neither the psychology of its characters nor the significance of its plot, nor any discernible values outside consumerism and escalating levels of thrills and shocks. Not all newcomers embraced the new flamboyance. Étienne Chatiliez moved easily from the quirky television commercial to his first feature, *La Vie est un long fleuve tranquille* (1988), an inventive satire of class differences. Eric Rochant's *Un monde sans pitié* (1989) avoided visual extravagance and offered a more considered view of French youth which, to some, seemed to mark a return to the early phase of the New Wave.

But suggestion that a new New Wave was in the offing met with a varied response. Older film-makers like Louis Malle clung to the *auteuriste* mode which aimed at viewing the human condition through some political or moral engagement in the tradition of French 'cinema of the mind'. For them, the fast editing, brilliant visual effects, action, violence and eroticism of younger directors owe more to the slick techniques of the television advertisement and to comic-strip story-telling than to the traditions of cinema. Yet *bande dessinée* had become a literary tradition and Besson argued, as McLuhan had done, that style is content and that his films were intended for the senses, not the intellect. This 'cinema of sensation' employs a new grammar of film with which young audiences were familiar. To a generation raised more on images than on the written word, this view of cinema as surrender-to-the-visual had a ready appeal (and in a different form revisited the debate surrounding *le parlant* in 1930). Yet the French cinema industry in the late 1980s seemed set on an exploitative course. Film was perceived as a high-profile product which followed market forces.

The 1990s

The tensions between the conservative and progressive trends of French society were reflected in the evolution of cinema in the 1990s. The heritage film increased its share of the audience with sumptuous literary adaptations of Balzac, Flaubert and Dumas. Among 'modern classics' brought to the screen were Marcel Aymé's *Uranus* (1990; dir. Berri), Pagnol's *Souvenirs d'enfance* (1990; dir. Yves Robert) and Giono's *Le Hussard sur le toit* (1995; dir. Rappeneau). Berri's version of Zola's *Germinal* (1993) was launched in a blaze of publicity designed to win back audiences from Spielberg's blockbuster *Jurassic Park*. In their wake, period films continued to return to the Second World War (Berri's *Lucie Aubrac*, 1997) but also reverted to colonial times (Régis Wargnier's *Indochine*, 1991) and to comic exploitations of the eighteenth century (*Ridicule*, 1996; dir. Patrice Leconte) or the Middle Ages: Jean-Marie Poiré's *Les Visiteurs* (1993), was one of the top-grossing successes of the decade.

But while heritage films continued to appeal to the backward-looking, nostalgic mood of the times, audiences were no less curious about the present. Questions posed by the rise of the multi-cultural society were high on the agenda. The issue had been flagged in the 1980s by films which focused on the problems of identity and insertion of the second generation of North African immigrants in France. Relationships formed between *beur* and white working-class youths were treated optimistically in *Le Thé au harem d'Archi Ahmed* (1985; dir. Mehdi Charef, b. 1952) and in good-humoured rites of passage movies like Djamel Bensalah's *Le Ciel, les oiseaux . . . et ta mère!* (1990). But the more committed approach adopted in the 1980s by Farida Belghoul (b. 1958) was now taken up by film-makers who, on low budgets and with more than a nod towards black American cinema, illustrated the realities of France's multi-ethnic society. Malik Chibane (*Hexagone*, 1994; *Douce France*, 1996) reflected the problems of young unemployed *beurs* (and *beurettes*) in a culture of crime, drugs and alienation. Around the middle of the decade, '*beur* cinema' merged into the *cinéma de banlieue* which dealt frankly and often with brutal realism with the class and racial problems of the suburbs. Matthieu Kassowitz's *La Haine* (1995), a vigorous example of the new-style *cinéma vérité*, showed the problems of disaffection and anarchic youth culture in unflinching terms. It was also representative of the rejection of the *look* and the rediscovery of the Hollywood tradition.

For the most part, however, social issues were treated in less challenging forms. The Aids crisis received a melodramatic treatment in François Margolin's *Mensonge* (1992) and Cyrille Collard's stylish but controversial *Les Nuits fauves* (1992). Young love and tangled relationships maintained the perennial attraction of psychological *analyse* in the manner of Rohmer and Sautet, who made his last film, *Nelly et Monsieur Arnaud*, in 1995. Free spirits continued to set the claims of liberated youth against the conformity required by society (*IP5*, 1992; dir. Beineix) and the *cinéma des jeunes* prospered in brittle comedies (*Mon père, ce héros*, 1991; dir. Gérard Lauzier), the 'buddy' movie (*Les Apprentis*, 1995; dir. Pierre Salvatori) and the fantasy of the team of Caro and Jeunet. A certain philosophical vein was explored on a variety of levels, in Rivette's meditation on creativity, *La Belle Noiseuse* (1991) or *Les Trois Couleurs* (1993–4), Krzysztof Kieslowski's trilogy on the theme of destiny.

Middle-class *angst* and mores continued to be mocked by Chabrol (*La Cérémonie*, 1995) but the attack on bourgeois values diversified into new areas. In *Gazon maudit* (1995), Jeanne Balasko (b. 1952) gave a new twist to the satire of monogamy by showing a husband cuckolded by a lesbian while both Rohmer and Costa-Gavras highlighted the *embourgeoisement* of the Left. In the same vein, *La Crise* (1992) by Coline Serreau (b. 1947) offered a sharply critical portrait of a champagne socialist. Alternatives to the religion of success were offered in Jean-Charles Tacchella's *L'Homme de ma vie* (1992) and Robert Guédiguian's unpretentious film about small loves, *Marius et Jeannette* (1996). Meanwhile, the *cinéma policier* moved away from the detection of crime to the psychology and aftermath of criminal acts in youth-centred road movies and films which told of bourgeois mayhem. Comedy continued both to offer farce for popular consumption and to provide sophisticated black comedies, through Blier and Leconte (*Le Mari de la coiffeuse*, 1990; *Le Parfum d'Yvonne*, 1994). But the older style of film-making retained an audience with Lelouch's freewheeling *Hasards et coincidences* (1999) and the versatile Tavernier who examined the policing of the *banlieue* in *L627* (1992) and the underfunding of the *école maternelle* in *Ça commence aujourd'hui* (1999).

One feature of the decade was the final acceptance of women directors who, with the exception of Germaine Dulac, Marie Epstein (1899–1995) and latterly Agnès Varda, had rarely proceeded beyond secondary roles in the industry. While they often privileged the woman's point of view in subject matter and narrative focus, Coline Serreau, Claire Denis, Jeanne Balasko and Diane Kurys (b. 1948) avoided feminist themes and set their sights on popular and mainstream cinema with films ranging in style and matter from race, culture shocks and manners to, most consistently, comedy. The annual festival of Women's Cinema at Créteil provides an important showcase for *cinéastes* who, however, have a stronger presence in the *art et essai* circuit than in commercial cinema. But if French cinema gained by their presence, it also suffered a drain of talent. Besson left to make a career in America, which also beckoned to the new French stars (Daniel Auteuil, Emmanuelle Béart, Sophie Marceau, Juliette Binoche) who, with Sandrine Bonnaire, Baye and the exceptionally versatile Depardieu, provided cinema with a depth of talent. Some, aware that stardom was increasingly dependent on a Hollywood reputation, succumbed. Their departure was one symptom of the malaise which afflicted the industry.

While France remained Europe's leading film-producer and, after the USA, the world's second largest film-exporter, American dominance threatened to engulf the home industry and substitute entertainment for the more thoughtful traditions of French film-making. France's share of domestic screenings fell and in 1993 the international trade organization (GATT) proposed to bring cinema into the free market and end national support for audio-visual industries. By arguing that cinema was a 'cultural exception', France succeeded in resisting the move. Yet while film-makers accepted the distinction between the French 'cultural' and US 'commercial' views of cinema, audiences were less concerned. They continued to prefer the Hollywood product and by 1996, sensitively crafted introspection had declined and the number of farces, costume dramas and glimpses of rural life rose.

But the problem of finance remained intractable. Since 60 per cent of films screened on television were required, by law, to be European, television companies became the industry's largest customer and, inevitably, dictated terms which threatened the tradition of 'quality'. Continuing state funding enabled new film-makers to operate artistically and to that extent insulated them against the realities of the market. Godard may have made film a vehicle for philosophical ideas, but younger audiences felt he had also given a new face to boredom. In 2000, films like Cédric Kahn's *L'Ennui* and Marion

Vernoux's *Rien à faire*, which showed people coping as badly with life as their titles suggest, or Laurent Cantet's *Ressources humaines*, an account of the renegotiation of a labour contract which was hailed as a return to working-class cinema, failed to enthuse a public more attuned to American hits like *The Sixth Sense* or *Saving Private Ryan*. French television companies, now major backers, were not always happy with the product they financed. The pressures are illustrated most acutely by Arte, the Franco-German channel established in 1990, which found that French films drew much smaller audiences than the game shows and light entertainment offered by German television. At the start of the new century, there is a fatalistic recognition of American power, to which actors and directors have surrendered, and a case is made for an international cinema which embodies 'European' values but which speaks English. Despite national pride, the preservation of the French language runs second to the key to survival: access to world distribution.

Yet even this may be enough, for French 'exceptionalism' is under attack from the global information revolution which breaches cultural boundaries. Having learned to live with the television and video revolutions, the industry faces an even sterner challenge from the electronic revolution, from the video game and DVD. Though the first is not an art form on the level of cinema or literature, many of its pleasures are the same. The second, which bypasses the established distribution system, represents a threat not merely to French film-making but to the movie-going industry in general. And yet, as Jean-Pierre Jeunet's *Le Fabuleux Destin d'Amélie Poulain* (2001) demonstrates, there is still an international market for the inventive, elegantly packaged flair of French cinema.

Conclusion

French cinema has aroused fierce public and aesthetic quarrels and has always been more self-consciously an art than in any other country. Yet it has been a victim of style, better able to arouse emotional responses in its audiences than to pursue ideas. Though it has reached wider audiences, it has, in this respect at least, proved to be more limited than the novel or the theatre which have always reacted more substantially to current events and discussed intellectual matters more directly. One picture is worth a thousand words, but not all arguments are reducible to images. If this is indeed the case, it is not because French film-makers have avoided serious issues but rather because cinema is an industry eternally constrained by finance, which is the enemy of risk, controversy and originality. Apart from the mid-1930s and the period of the *nouvelle vague*, writers and directors have had to accept commercial subjects and safe narrative formulae. It is hardly surprising, therefore, if the content of films has trailed behind the techniques of expression. In the 1920s, silent films remained faithful to nineteenth-century sentiment and melodrama. At its height, the 'New Wave' looked back to postwar American *film noir* and the recent 'heritage' film is overtly nostalgic.

For if French cinema found a way of overcoming the collective nature of film art by inventing the *auteur*, it never quite broke with literature. The script adapted from a novel is still often preferred to the original scenario, partly no doubt because literature arrived first and acquired prior rights over areas which are also the proper concern of the film-maker. On the other hand, film both democratized art and exerted a powerful influence on literature and its techniques. Despite the challenge of the electronic revolution, *le septième art* retains its high status as the major French popular art form. For nearly a century, moving pictures have given pleasure and shaped attitudes at home and projected a clear image of French culture abroad.

Bibliography

Since a comprehensive bibliography of the writers, genres and themes of the whole of French literature is impractical, the following brief listing is intended as a general orientation for further reading. It is divided into two parts: general histories, overviews and dictionaries; and surveys and dictionaries of individual centuries and themes. The emphasis has been placed on recent scholarship. All the volumes contain detailed bibliographies.

General

Abraham, Paul and Desné, Roland (eds), *Manuel d'histoire littéraire de la France*, 6 vols (Paris: Messidor/Éditions sociales, 1987).

Beaumarchais, Jean-Pierre, Couty Daniel and Rey, Alain (eds), *Dictionnaire des littératures de langue française*, 3 vols (Paris: Bordas, 1984); 2nd edn, 4 vols (1987).

Birkett, Jennifer and Kearns, James, *A Guide to French Literature from Early Modern to Postmodern* (Basingstoke: Macmillan, 1997).

Charvet, P. E. (ed.), *A Literary History of France*, 6 vols (London: Ernest Benn, 1967–74):

John Fox, *The Middle Ages* (1974).

I. D. McFarlane, *Renaissance France* (1974).

P. J. Yarrow, *The Seventeenth Century, 1600–1715* (1967).

Robert Niklaus, *The Eighteenth Century, 1715–1789* (1970).

P. E. Charvet, *The Nineteenth Century, 1789–1870* (1967).

P. E. Charvet, *The Nineteenth and Twentieth Centuries, 1870–1940* (1967).

Cruickshank, John (ed.), *French Literature and its Background*, 6 vols (Oxford: Oxford University Press, 1968–70).

Favre, Robert (ed.), *La Littérature française: histoire et perspectives* (Lyons: Presses universitaires de Lyon, 1990).

France, Peter (ed.), *The New Oxford Companion to Literature in French* (Oxford: Clarendon Press, 1995).

Godenne, René, *La Nouvelle française* (Paris: Presses universitaires de France, 1974).

Harvey, Sir Paul and Heseltine, J. E. (eds), *The Oxford Companion to French Literature* (Oxford: Clarendon Press, 1959).

Hollier, Denis (ed.), *A New History of French Literature* (Cambridge, Mass., and London: Harvard University Press, 1989).

Krichbaum, Jörg et al., *Les-sites-français.fr: les 1000 meilleures adresses Internet en français* (Paris: Omnibus ('La Bibliothèque du Web), 2001).

Lough, John, *Writer and Public in France from the Middle Ages to the Present Day* (Oxford: Clarendon Press, 1978).

Majault, Joseph, Nivat, Jean-Maurice, Géronimi, Charles and Wintzen, René, *Littérature de notre temps* (Paris: Casterman, 1966; 4th edn, 1972).

Martin, Henri-Jean, Chartier, Roger and Vivet, J.-P., *Histoire de l'édition française*, 4 vols (Paris: Promodis, 1983–6).

Pichois, Claude (ed.), *Littérature française*, 9 vols (Paris: Éditions Arthaud, 1974–84).

Reid, Joyce M. H., *The Concise Oxford Dictionary of French Literature* (Oxford: Oxford University Press, 1976).

Rohou, Jean (ed.), *Histoire de la littérature française du moyen âge à nos jours*, 6 vols (Paris: Nathan, 1983–98).

Sabatier, Robert, *Histoire de la poésie française*, 9 vols (Paris: Albin Michel, 1975–88).

Worth-Stylianou, Valerie (ed.), *Cassell Guide to Literature in French* (London: Cassell, 1996).

Centuries and Themes

Adam, Antoine, *Histoire de la littérature française du XVIIe siècle*, 5 vols (Paris: Domat, 1948–56).

Alessandrini, M., Duveau, M., Glasser, J.-C. and Vidal, M., *Encyclopédie des bandes dessinées* (Paris: Albin Michel, 1979; new edition, 1986).

Albistur, M. and Armogathe, D., *Histoire du féminisme français* (Paris: Des Femmes, 1977).

Atack, Margaret, *Literature and the French Resistance: Cultural Politics and Narrative Forms, 1940–1950* (Manchester: Manchester University Press, 1989).

Austin, Guy, *Contemporary French Cinema: An Introduction* (Manchester: Manchester University Press, 1996).

Bercot, Martine and Guyaux, André (eds), *Dictionnaire des lettres françaises: Le XXe siècle* (Paris: Livre de Poche, 1998).

Billard, Pierre, *L'Âge classique du cinéma français: du cinéma parlant à la nouvelle vague* (Paris: Flammarion, 1995).

Birkett, Jennifer, *The Sins of the Fathers: Decadence in France, 1870–1914* (London: Quartet Books, 1986).

Bishop, Michael, *The Contemporary Poetry of France: Eight Studies* (Amsterdam: Rodopi, 1985).

Bossuat, Robert, Hesenohr, Geneviève and Zink, Michel (eds), *Dictionnaire des lettres françaises: Le Moyen Âge* (Paris: Librairie Générale française, 1992).

Boutet, Dominique and Strubel, Armand, *La Littérature française du moyen âge* (Paris: Presses universitaires de France, 1978).

Bradby, David, *Modern French Drama, 1940–90*, rev. edn (Cambridge: Cambridge University Press, 1991).

Brereton, Geoffrey, *French Comic Drama from the Sixteenth to the Eighteenth Century* (London: Methuen, 1977).

Britton, Celia, *The Nouveau Roman: Fiction, Theory, Politics* (Basingstoke: Macmillan, 1992).

Cave, Terence, *The Cornucopean Text: Problems of Writing in the French Renaissance* (Oxford: Clarendon Press, 1979).

Chamard, Henri, *Histoire de la Pléïade*, 4 vols (Paris: Didier, 1939–40).

Charlton, D. G., *The French Romantics* (Cambridge: Cambridge University Press, 1984).

Coulet, Henri, *Le Roman jusqu'à la Révolution*, 2 vols (Paris: Armand Colin, 1967–8).

Cruickshank, John, *Variations on Catastrophe: Some French Responses to the Great War* (Oxford: Clarendon Press, 1982).

Darnton, Robert, *Édition et sédition: l'univers de la littérature clandestine au XVIIIe siècle* (Paris: Gallimard, 1991).

Darnton, Robert, *The Business of Enlightenment: A Publishing History of the Encyclopédie* (Cambridge, Mass.: Harvard University Press, 1979).

Davis, Natalie Zemon, *Society and Culture in Early Modern France* (Cambridge: Polity Press, 1987).

Déjeux, Jean, *Dictionnaire des auteurs maghrébins de langue française* (Paris: Kathala, 1984).

Descombes, Vincent, *Le Même et l'Autre: Quarante-cinq ans de philosophie française, 1933–1978* (Paris: Éditions de Minuit, 1979).

Duby, Georges and Perrot, Michelle (eds), *Histoire des femmes en Occident*, 5 vols (Paris: Plon, 1991–2).

Duchen, Claire, *Feminism in France from May '68 to Mitterrand* (London: Routledge & Kegan Paul, 1986).

Fallaize, Elizabeth, *French Women's Writing: Recent Fiction* (Basingstoke: Macmillan, 1993).

Fèbvre, Lucien and Martin, Henri-Jean, *L'Apparition du livre* (Paris: Albin Michel, 1958).

Frodon, Jean-Michel, *L'Âge moderne du cinéma français: de la nouvelle vague à nos jours* (Paris: Flammarion, 1995).

Gossip, Christopher J., *An Introduction to French Classical Tragedy* (Basingstoke: Macmillan, 1981).

Goulemot, Jean-Marie and Launay, Michel, *Le Siècle des Lumières* (Paris: Seuil, 1968).

Guichemerre, Roger, *La Tragi-comédie* (Paris: Presses universitaires de France, 1981).

Hargreaves, Alec G., *The Colonial Experience in French Fiction* (Basingstoke: Macmillan, 1981).

Hayward, Susan, *French National Cinema* (London and New York: Routledge, 1993).

Howarth, W. D., *A Study of French Romantic Drama* (London: Harrap, 1975).

Hughes, Alex and Reader, Keith (eds), *Encyclopedia of Contemporary French Culture* (London: Routledge, 1998).

Jack, Belinda, *Francophone Literatures: An Introductory Survey* (Oxford: Oxford University Press, 1996).

Jefferson, Ann, *The Nouveau Roman and the Poetics of Fiction* (Cambridge: Cambridge University Press, 1980).

Jondorf, Gillian, *French Renaissance Tragedy: The Dramatic Word* (Cambridge: Cambridge University Press, 1990).

Judt, Tony, *Blum, Camus, Aron and the French Twentieth Century* (Chicago: Chicago University Press, 1998).

Julliard, Jacques and Winock, Michel (eds), *Dictionnaire des intellectuels français* (Paris: Seuil, 1996).

Jules-Rosette, Benetta, *Black Paris: The African Writers' Landscape* (Urbana and Chicago: University of Illinois Press, 1998).

Kelly, Michael (ed.), *French Culture and Society: The Essentials* (London: Edward Arnold, 2001).

Knowles, Dorothy, *French Drama of the Interwar Years* (London: Harrap, 1967).

Larthomas, Pierre, *Le Théâtre en France au XVIIIe siècle* (Paris: Presses universitaires de France, 1989).

Lathuillère, Roger, *La Préciosité, étude historique et linguistique* (Geneva: Droz, 1966).

Lazard, Madeleine, *La Comédie humaniste au XVIe siècle et ses personnages* (Paris: Presses universitaires de France, 1978).

Lejeune, Philippe, *Le Pacte autobiographique* (Paris: Seuil, 1975).

Lemire, Maurice (ed.), *Dictionnaire des oeuvres littéraires du Québec*, 2nd edn (Montréal: FIDES, 1980–7).

Lever, Maurice, *Le Roman français au XVIIe siècle* (Paris: Presses universitaires de France, 1981).

Lits, Marc, *Le Roman policier: Introduction à la théorie et à l'histoire d'un genre littéraire* (Paris: Éditions du CEFAL, 1993).

Lough, John, *Paris Theatre Audiences in the Seventeenth and Eighteenth Centuries* (Oxford: Oxford University Press, 1957).

Luthi, Jean-Jacques, Viatte, Auguste, and Zananiri, Gaston, *Dictionnaire général de la francophonie* (Paris: Letouzey et Ané, 1986).

Martin, Henri-Jean, *Livre, pouvoirs et société à Paris au XVIIe siècle (1598–1701)*, 2 vols (Geneva: Droz, 1962).

Mason, Haydn, *French Writers and their Society, 1715–1800* (Basingstoke: Macmillan, 1982).

May, Georges, *Le Dilemme du roman au XVIIIe siècle* (New Haven, CT: Yale University Press, 1963).

Mesnard, J. (ed.), *Précis de littérature française du XVIIe siècle* (Paris: Presses universitaires de France, 1990).

Moliterni, Claude, Mellot, Philippe, and Denni, Michel, *Les Aventures de la bande dessinée* (Paris: Gallimard, 1996).

Mourgues, Odette de, *Metaphysical, Baroque and Précieux Poetry* (Oxford: Clarendon Press, 1953).

Muir, Lynette, *Literature and Society in Medieval France* (Basingstoke: Macmillan, 1985).

Mylne, Vivienne, *The Eighteenth-Century French Novel: Techniques of Illusion*, 2nd edn (Cambridge: Cambridge University Press, 1981).

Offord, Malcolm, Chapman, Rosemary, Hitchcott, Nicki, Haigh, Sam, and Ibnlfassi, Laila, *Francophone Literatures: A Literary and Linguistic Companion* (London: Routledge, 2001).

Passek, J.-L. (ed.), *Dictionnaire du cinéma français* (Paris: Larousse, 1987).

Pauphilet, Albert, Pichard, Louis, and Barroux, Robert (eds), *Dictionnaire des lettres françaises: le XVIIe siècle* (Paris: Fayard, 1996).

Phillips, Henry, *The Theatre and its Critics in Seventeenth-Century France* (Oxford: Oxford University Press, 1980).

Prendergast, Christopher, *The Order of Mimesis: Balzac, Stendhal, Nerval, Flaubert* (Cambridge: Cambridge University Press, 1986).

Robinson, Christopher, *Scandal in the Ink: Male and Female Homosexuality in Twentieth-Century French Literature* (London: Cassell, 1995).

—— , *French Literature in the Twentieth Century* (Newton Abbot: David & Charles, 1980).

Sadoul, Jacques, *93 ans de bande dessinée* (Paris: Éditions J'ai Lu, 1989).

Sheringham, Michael, *French Autobiography. Devices and Desires: Rousseau to Perec* (Oxford: Clarendon Press, 1993).

Silverman, Max, *Facing Postmodernity: Contemporary French Thought on Culture and Society* (London, Routledge, 1999).

Tétu, Michel, *La francophonie: histoire, problématique et perspectives* (Paris: Hachette, 1987).

Thiesse, Annie-Marie, *Écrire la France: Le Mouvement littéraire régionaliste entre la Belle Époque et la Libération* (Paris: Presses universitaires de France, 1991).

Todd, Christopher, *A Century of Best-sellers (1890–1990)* (Lewiston, Queenston and Lampeter: Edwin Mellen, 1994).

Tonnet-Lacroix, Éliane, *La Littérature française de l'entre-deux-guerres* (Paris: Nathan, 1993).

Versini, Laurent, *Le Roman epistolaire* (Paris: Presses Universitaires de France, 1979; 2nd edn 1998).

Winock, Michel, *Le Siècle des intellectuels* (Paris: Seuil, 1997).

Zink, Michel, *Introduction à la littérature française du moyen âge* (Paris: Livre de Poche, 1993).

Index